Joschka Fischer and the Making of the Berlin Republic

Other books by Paul Hockenos

Free to Hate: The Rise of the Right in Post-Communist Eastern Europe

Homeland Calling: Exile Patriotism and the Balkan Wars

Joschka Fischer and the Making of the Berlin Republic

An Alternative History of Postwar Germany

Paul Hockenos

OXFORD
UNIVERSITY PRESS
2008

OXFORD
UNIVERSITY PRESS

Oxford University Press, Inc., publishes works that further
Oxford University's objective of excellence
in research, scholarship, and education.

Oxford New York
Auckland Cape Town Dar es Salaam Hong Kong Karachi
Kuala Lumpur Madrid Melbourne Mexico City Nairobi
New Delhi Shanghai Taipei Toronto

With offices in
Argentina Austria Brazil Chile Czech Republic France Greece
Guatemala Hungary Italy Japan Poland Portugal Singapore
South Korea Switzerland Thailand Turkey Ukraine Vietnam

Published by Oxford University Press, Inc.
198 Madison Avenue, New York, New York 10016

www.oup.com

Library of Congress Cataloging-in-Publication Data
Hockenos, Paul, 1963–
Joschka Fischer and the making of the Berlin Republic : an alternative
history of postwar Germany / Paul Hockenos.
p. cm.
ISBN: 978-0-19-518183-8
1. Fischer, Joschka. 2. Politicians—Germany—Biography.
3. Germany—History—1945–4. Political culture—Germany—
History—20th century. I. Title.
DD290.33.F57H63 2007
943.088'2092—dc22 2007012081

9 8 7 6 5 4 3 2 1
Printed in the United States of America on acid-free paper

To Jenni

Preface

This book is a result of my living in Germany and writing about German and European affairs for nearly twenty years. It was pretty much by chance that, in the fall of 1983 on a college year abroad, I landed in West Germany's southwesternmost corner, in the little university city of Freiburg. This was at the height of the Federal Republic's "Hot Autumn," the time of country-wide protests against the stationing of intermediate-range nuclear missiles in West Germany. I gladly tagged along to the demonstrations that October, one of over a million protesters insisting that NATO halt deployment of its U.S.-made "Euromissiles." Although the *Pershing II* and *Cruise* missiles arrived shortly thereafter and I eventually returned to upstate New York, issues associated with Cold War Europe and the two Germanys lured me back to the continent. I would come and go from Germany after that, including some longer stints away during the nineties as a foreign correspondent in Hungary and a civilian member of the international postwar missions in the Balkans. But at some point Berlin became my permanent home. It wasn't a conscious decision—or one that I ever seriously reconsidered.

For years I had considered writing something longer about Germany's protest movements, the Greens, and the nature of Germany's liberal metamorphosis. I wanted to relate the Germany that I knew to non-German readers, and to show how it got that way. But I also wanted to convey the content and evolution of some of the public debates in Germany, debates that fall outside the parameters of narrower political discourses elsewhere. These are often rich discussions—part of a sophisticated *Streitkultur*—that, I felt, could possibly inject fresh critical thinking into debates beyond Europe's borders, not only in the United States. A political biography of Joschka Fischer struck me as the means to accomplish both of these aims.

Although no one German scholar has endeavored to write an entire history of postwar Germany "from below," there exists a wealth of excellent German sources, the most significant for this project I identify in the chapters' end notes. (There is, thus, no biblography.) I feel compelled, however, to mention a number of key sources here. Among the existing German biographies of Fischer, Sibylle Krause-Burger's *Joschka Fischer* was important for my early chapters. Those written by Matthias Geis and Bernd Ulrich, Christian Y. Schmidt, and Michael Schwelien, were also very helpful at different points. Also, never far from my reach were the standard works of contemporary German history, including those of Manfred Görtemaker, Christoph Kleßmann, Konrad Jarausch, among others, as well as one of the newer postwar histories, Edgar Wolfrum's fine *Die geglückte Demokratie*. It is imperative to pay tribute to the foremost scholar of the Federal Republic's protest movements, the Hamburg historian Wolfgang Kraushaar. His voluminous studies and edited collections have contributed uniquely to documenting and understanding postwar Germany's social movements. Nevertheless, it is encouraging that a new generation of scholars, too young to have participated in the student movement, as did Kraushaar and others, is beginning to examine the period from fresh standpoints.

A note on sourcing: all direct quotes in the text that come from secondary sources are cited in the notes. Those that are not footnoted come from interviews conducted by me between 2004 and 2007.

In expressing my gratitude to those who aided this project, I start with the German Marshall Fund of the United States, whose fellowship made this book possible in the first place. The book was part of a process and an important stage was a Bosch Public Policy Fellowship at the American Academy in Berlin in 2000. The manuscript passed through the hands of more than one editor and I am thankful to each in a different way. They include Dedi Felman, Elisheva Urbas, and David McBride. I would also like to express my sincere thanks to the following people, who commented on parts of the manuscript and offered valuable advice: Bill Martin, Jenni Winterhagen, Matthew Hockenos, Anne and Warren Hockenos, Robert Van Meter, Sascha Müller-Kraenner, Detlev Claussen, Uli Cremer, Jim Ogier, Eric Chauvistre, Thomas Pampuch, Christoph Becker-Schaum, and

Hajo Funke. Needless to say, some of these critics objected to certain points or accents, and thus cannot be held responsible for the work's content or flaws. As always I am in debt to Cecelia Cancellaro of Idea Architects, whose deep love of books makes her the fine agent that she is. Werner Kraemer was selfless in providing technical assistance. I also thank my many colleagues at *Die Tageszeitung* and especially those in its archives—above all, Randy Kaufmann. I also acknowledge the resources and patient staffs of the Staatsbibliothek Berlin, the APO-Archiv at the Free University, the Berlin Institute for Transatlantic Security, the Archiv Grünes Gedächtnis, the Informationsdienst für kritische Medienpraxis, and the Lucy Scribner Library at Skidmore College.

Contents

Joschka Fischer and the Making of the Berlin Republic

Introduction

On a blustery morning in March 1983, a spirited procession of several hundred people made its way through the streets of Bonn, West Germany's postwar capital. The troupe was en route to the country's parliament, the Bundestag. It ambled good-naturedly through the old university town to the beat of African drums played from an open, horse-drawn carriage. The event had all the trappings of a demonstration. Marchers young and old brandished signs reading: "Minimum Pension: 1500 Marks!", "My Census Data Belongs to Me!", and "Peace Now in Israel-Palestine!" One woman pushed ahead of her a human-size "planet earth" beach ball, a symbol of the global nature of their concerns.

Although this extroverted assemblage was, in part, a protest march, it was also much more. The entourage was peopled by the Federal Republic's newest political party, the Greens, which was making its debut in the Bundestag that day. The party was an amalgam of protest movement activists—from the women's, the environmental, the antinuclear energy, and the peace movements, among others—as well as the detritus of half a dozen radical left splinter groups. The purpose of the celebratory march was to demonstrate that the Greens were bringing the causes of West Germany's civic movements from the streets into the country's legislature. The little ecology party would be the voice of the grassroots campaigns and pose tenacious opposition on their behalf. Although not the first Greens party in Europe, it would become its most prominent—and a model for environmentally minded parties across the continent and beyond.

Front and center of the procession was a joyful Petra Kelly in red riding britches and a purple plush jacket. The thirty-five-year-old Kelly was the most well-known of the Greens, a German-born, U.S.-educated peace activist with a worldwide following. In her arms, she cradled a large bouquet of spring flowers, emblematic of the Greens' claim to represent the hitherto unrepresented interests of the earth's flora and fauna. Film footage from the day documents the counterculture of the new party: long hair, full beards, and loose-fitting, colorful clothing everywhere. Occasionally, the cameras pause on a youthful-looking marcher in a sweater and collared shirt. He's by himself, on the periphery of the procession. It is the thirty-four-year-old Joschka Fischer, a name known mostly in and around the left-wing scene in Frankfurt. He was one of twenty-eight Greens who would take up a seat that day in the country's highest lawmaking body. Not long ago, Fischer had been a street-fighting anarchist who deemed the Federal Republic so flawed that it had to be subverted—its parliamentary democracy replaced with a socialist alternative.

Fast forward twenty years, almost to the month. It is February 2003, at the annual security conference in Munich, an affair attended by the crème-de la-crème of the free world's diplomats, military brass, and defense experts. Among them are U.S. defense secretary Donald Rumsfeld and the conference's host, Germany's Foreign Minister Joschka Fischer. With a U.S. invasion of Iraq virtually certain, Rumsfeld appealed for international support for the Bush administration's course. Washington's arguments were largely known: diplomacy had been exhausted, and U.S. intelligence showed Saddam Hussein's regime possessing weapons of mass destruction as well as aiding Al Qaeda terrorists. Rumsfeld reiterated that the world's democracies had to take decisive action in the near future.

Shortly thereafter Fischer stepped up to the podium, dressed in a dark blue suit, gold-rimmed bifocals perched on his nose. For well over a year, since the successful invasion of Afghanistan in late 2001, the Berlin leadership—and the overwhelming majority of Germans—had expressed clear differences with the Bush administration over the next phase of the war on terror. Despite Germany's willing participation in the overthrow of Afghanistan's radical Taliban, relations between the two states—the closest of transatlantic allies for fifty years—had never been worse. But no one was prepared for what would happen next.

The fifty-four-year-old Fischer was responding point by point, in German, to the U.S. case for war. "Why now against Iraq? Is this really the priority?" he asked emphatically, in a tone considerably more impassioned than the conference's participants were used to hearing. And then, with the world's cameras rolling, Fischer pushed the envelope further. He broke into English for three short sentences. Staring straight at Rumsfeld, index finger in the air, he continued: "Sorry, I *am not* convinced," referring to Rumsfeld's arguments for military action against Iraq. And then, slapping the podium for emphasis, his voice rising, he added, "You have to make your case. Sorry, you haven't convinced me!" Fischer's broadside landed with a resounding thud. This wasn't diplomacy as usually practiced at the Munich conference, particularly not between Germany and its postwar mentor, also the world's undisputed superpower. Seated motionless in front of the elevated podium, Rumsfeld absorbed Fischer's rebukes with an icy glare. The other participants watched in disbelief, some certainly wondering whether the transatlantic partnership would recover from this latest barrage. The blunt talk in Munich trumpeted more clearly than ever before that a much-changed Germany was engaged on the world stage and that a new generation of Germans was now in power, one with a markedly different relationship to the United States.

Separated by two decades that included the Cold War's abrupt end and German reunification, these symbolic moments—the Greens' entry into the West German parliament and Germany's public upbraiding of the United States over Iraq—denoted ruptures in the history of postwar Germany; they were points at which something qualitatively new about Germany, arguably even about Germanness, announced its presence. The two episodes are also prominent markers on the political journey of Germany's disenchanted postwar generations, which their partisans hailed as "the long march through the institutions," and which, I argue, contributed decisively to Germany's remarkable transformation from an occupied, post-Nazi state into a healthy, democratic country. This book is more than the story of Joschka Fischer, a left-wing radical who became the united Germany's foreign minister. It is the "alternative history" of post-1945 Germany, told through the diverse postwar protest movements, grassroots campaigns, civic initiatives, and later through the Greens themselves. In different ways, these initially unwelcome forces pushed the postwar republic to deepen, widen, and entrench democracy; they insisted that modern Germany become an active, pluralist civil society the likes of which Germany had never known before. Whether they intended it or not, they helped reinvent a German identity that incorporated the lessons of the past but also included many positive references.

This narrative is only one strand, though a crucial one, in the greater historical narrative of Germany's reconfiguration into a liberal state, a state that is not only stable and constructive but also in some ways exemplary.

Germany's political culture and peaceful disposition have many midwives, not least the founding fathers of the Bonn Republic, such as its first chancellor, Konrad Adenauer, and World War II's western Allies, above all the United States. Among them, the multilateral institutions of the West must be included, such as the European Union and NATO, within whose frameworks Germany's rehabilitation was possible. Yet, too often underrepresented in contemporary histories are the roles played by the protest movements and their parliamentary heirs, which helped fill the Federal Republic's democratic structures and western alliances with democratic, western content. In 1998 a coalition of Social Democrats and Greens came to power in the new Berlin Republic, capping more nearly five decades of political activism outside of and then within the state's institutions. I argue that, in their different incarnations, these protagonists contributed enormously to reshaping Germany, to making it more self-critical, worldly, and eventually more environmentally conscious. As evidenced at the 2003 Munich conference and personified by Joschka Fischer, these processes also laid the groundwork for a new post-Cold War relationship to the United States. Paradoxically, it was often the spirit of American democracy in action—the United States' democratic experiments in West Germany, like West Berlin's Free University, or American models, such as the civil rights movement—that inspired Germany's rebellious-minded progeny to challenge the Federal Republic's (and the United States' own) commitment to the principles that it professed.

The arrival of the Greens and their entry into the offices of power heralded the political coming of age of the republic's first postwar generation—one, which though intensely critical of its state, was a product through and through of the Federal Republic. As one of this generation, Fischer is a unique and penetrating lens through which to view Germany's metamorphosis, the "German success story" as historians today call it. He was born in the postwar years, around the time the Federal Republic came to life and just as the Cold War broke over Europe. The republic was a traumatized, makeshift statelet that languished in the shadow of Nazism and other inherited deficits, including weak republican traditions, a population imbued with nationalism, and, not least, a precarious position on the front line of the East–West conflict. Fischer was among those young Germans who grew up in the archconservative 1950s and were politicized during the tumultuous 1960s and 1970s. Yet he was more than a witness to the zeitgeist; he swam in these waters and later he navigated them, even altering their direction. Fischer is Germany's most prominent representative of the "sixty-eight generation," as Germans label the partisans of the late 1960s student movement. Although the young radicals called themselves Marxists and touted revolution, ultimately through revolt and experimentation they were exploring democracy and asking what it meant to be German after the Holocaust. To be sure, their search for meaning set them on a path that included many detours and deadends.

The category of "sixty-eight generation" should be understood broadly. It includes fellow travelers, like the 1945-born Social Democrat Gerhard Schröder, who would become Germany's chancellor; he and others like him shared the general sensibilities of those who actually manned the barricades during the student movement. The agitators of the late sixties also had extraparliamentary predecessors, like the 1950s anti-rearmament campaigns; others came later, younger generations who joined the long march along the way, cutting their teeth in the powerful "new social movements" of the late seventies and early eighties. Fischer was, at times, a key figure in these processes. Yet so were other persons as disparate as Petra Kelly, theologian Martin Niemöller, novelist Heinrich Böll, artist Joseph Beuys, and student leader Rudi Dutschke, to name just a few. And then there were the untold thousands who performed the less flashy tasks that fall outside of history's spotlight—the grunt work that makes mass movements, grassroots projects, and upstart parties effective. They too deserve a prominent place in an alternative history of Germany.

The implications of this political odyssey go well beyond Germany—and remain relevant today. Many of the German protest movements had counterparts elsewhere in the world, as did the trek of the sixties generation into the establishment. College students Bill and Hillary Clinton, for example, were among the Americans demonstrating against the war in Vietnam. Moreover, the experiences of the German Greens encouraged environmental parties across the world and contributed to an ecological consciousness that is today global. The founders of the German Greens set out to practice "a whole new approach to politics," one closer to the people, mindful of the planet's limited resources, and skeptical about the lure and blandishments of power. As elsewhere, many of their ideals were challenged and greatly diluted through the processes of representative democracy.

This is a biography and a study of the Federal Republic, the country that I live in by choice. The idea for it came about as the result of the wall of misunderstanding that I as a political journalist have run up against in writing about contemporary Germany. Whether it be distant editorial offices or visitors to Berlin, the clichés about Germany—inflexible, conformist, guilt ridden, bellicose—remain surprisingly persistent. Even among those who grasp that Germany today is a liberal society with a vibrant democracy, too few realize how decisive these "from below" processes were in making Germany that way. My purpose is to dig below the surface of contemporary Germany, to explore some of the understudied sources that contributed to its transformation. It is impossible to understand Germany today, the Berlin Republic, without knowing the story of the forces that challenged the system from the streets and then became part of it. By the time the ex-rebels and grassroots activists joined the establishment, however, it was very different from the one that they had initially set out to change. This was, not least, a result of their own efforts. Their entry into the structures of power signaled not that this journey was over, but only that another phase had begun.

Part I

Adenauer's Germany

1

Postwar

"The principal Allied objective is to prevent Germany from ever again becoming a threat to the world of peace."
—U.S. Joint Chief of Staff, JCS 1067 April 1945

"Democracy will not take root in Germany because...it is a foreign ideology."
—Bishop Otto Dibelius, May 1945

When Joschka Fischer entered the world in April 1948, the Federal Republic of Germany didn't exist. In fact, at the time no German state did—nor had one since Nazi Germany's unconditional surrender in May 1945. The territory that would become the western republic in just over a year's time was still divided into occupation zones, controlled by French, British, and U.S. forces, and under the law of their military administrations. Three years after the defeat of the Third Reich, the inhabitants of the western zones and, in eastern Germany, the Soviet-occupied zone, were still struggling to pick up the pieces of their shattered lives and rebuild their war-ravaged towns and cities. The terms of survival for many Germans remained precarious, but if they had survived until then, they had made it through the worst.

Hitler's insistence that Germans contest the war to its bitter end—rather than surrender to the Allies—ensured that postwar Germany paid the highest price for the catastrophic world war that it started. Germany was left a devastated, gasping land, its urban landscape bombed to ruins, its once mighty industry prostrate, and its population shell-shocked and impoverished. During the war, Allied bombers and artillery had destroyed half of the housing in Germany's urban centers. Its great cities—Berlin, Dresden, Cologne, Frankfurt, Hamburg, Stuttgart, and Leipzig—had been reduced to rubble. The disruption of transportation routes and energy grids left many people dangerously undernourished and supine to nature's mercy. The record cold winter of 1946–47, followed by a scorching summer, took its toll on the most vulnerable: children and the elderly. The famous "rubble films," like Roberto Rossellini's 1947 classic *Germany Year Zero,* depict the daily hardship that families endured just to survive in the ruins. Tuberculosis, rickets, and dysentery were rampant, medicines and doctors nearly impossible to procure. By spring 1948, conditions had improved for many, especially those fortunate enough to land in the American sectors. But everywhere food was rationed; the black market was the only place to barter for a few extra potatoes or chunks of coal.

Complicating any hope of improvement in living standards were the waves of displaced persons flooding into the occupied zones. Ethnic Germans, the so-called *Volksdeutsche,* constituted most of this chaotic mass of human flotsam. They had been expelled from their homes in central and eastern Europe as the payback—crude and simple—for their (or their compatriots') collaboration with the Hitler regime. The ethnic Germans in Poland, Czechoslovakia, Hungary, Yugoslavia, and elsewhere were stripped of their property and either evacuated by train or forced to trek by foot to the German border. By the end of 1946, the western zones alone had taken in 5 million expellees from the east, among them Joschka Fischer's parents and his two sisters. Another 3 million deportees would follow them, in addition to other refugees, tens of thousands of eastern European Jews, and released POWs returning from Soviet labor camps.[1]

Amid the deprivation and hardship of postwar Germany, the repatriated ethnic Germans found themselves at the very bottom of the heap. The number-one issue everywhere was living space, which automatically pitted the newcomers against the indigenous population. The refugees were herded into makeshift camps or shuttled to local sport halls, schools, former army barracks, cellars, and barns. At a later date local authorities transferred them into private houses, the law compelling reluctant homeowners to take in refugees until they could be resettled again elsewhere. There was no disguising the fact that the refugees were unwanted and unwelcome.

Among the dispossessed millions, the Fischer family consisted of father Jozsef, thirty-seven years old; mother Elisabeth, just thirty; and the two little girls, ages three and seven. Like most of the deported Hungarian

Germans, the Fischers wound up in Germany's southwestern corner.* Southern Germany alone took in 3 million displaced people, nearly a quarter of its total population.

By the time the Fischers arrived, over 800,000 indigenous residents were already homeless in the American zone and competing for scarce resources with the first influx of refugees, those who had evacuated their homes just ahead of the Red Army's advance.[2] Neither local authorities nor the occupation military had prepared for the tidal waves of refugees. A U.S. Army-operated transport deposited the Fischers and their bundled possessions at a refugee station in the low-lying hills of northern Württemberg, along the River Jagst, where they waited out the biting cold winter of 1946–47.

An unvarnished 1948 U.S. military report described the plight of refugees like the Fischers in Germany's southwest:

> The influx from the east has created in Germany a propertyless class whose numbers, embittered by dispossession and by the misery of months spent in the transit camps and emergency accommodation, are obliged to exist in standards which they cannot willingly accept and which are noticeably lower than those of the native western Germans. . . . The misery of the immigrants brings out all of the latent impulses of the German character to persecute the underdog.[3]

The Fischers had fallen a long, long way indeed, into destitution that they, at the time, could see no way out of.

The Budakeszi Years

The world in which Jozsef and Elisabeth Fischer had grown up couldn't have been more different from that in which they would raise their children.

In Hungary, the Fischers were affluent Danube Swabians, descendants of ethnic Germans who had migrated eastward in the eighteenth century. These forefathers settled across the greater Danube basin in Austro Hungarian–ruled Hungary, Romania, and northern Yugoslavia. As Danube Swabians living in Budakeszi, a village just outside Budapest, the Fischers

* The 300,000 Hungarian German expellees who arrived in the occupation zones constituted a far smaller group than the expelled ethnic Germans from postwar Poland (5.5 million) and the Czech lands (2 million).

spoke German at home and Hungarian in public—not the least out of the ordinary in the ethnically mixed communities that dotted interwar Hungary. Yet, the Fischers numbered among a tiny portion of Hungarian Swabians who, by 1940, could still write proper German. In fact, Hungary's Danube Swabians had been blending into the Magyar majority for over a century, each successive generation becoming more Hungarian and less German. To most of them, being ethnic German meant being fastidious, hardworking, and law abiding. Politically, the minority of half a million, about 6 or 7 percent of the population, was virtually irrelevant in post-World War I Hungary. That changed only in the late 1930s, to its misfortune, when the Hitler regime insisted that Hungary's ethnic Germans receive privileged status in the Axis-allied state. The war trapped the minority between German and Hungarian nationalism, and set the stage for its demise.

When Joschka's father, Jozsef, was born in 1909, Budakeszi lay snugly in the bosom of the Austro-Hungarian empire. Descended from a long line of entrepreneurs, he owned a butcher shop as had his father, grandfather, and great grandfather before him. Jozsef's other siblings were just as industrious and business-minded. His sister ran a granary and one brother operated a small hotel. Another brother was a notary. The Fischers were respected folk in Budakeszi, among Germans and Hungarians alike.[4]

Elisabeth's family, also Danube Germans, was considerably less well off. Her father had fallen in World War I, in the service of the Habsburg monarchy. Her stepfather was a regular in the Honved, the Hungarian armed forces. As a girl, practicing Roman Catholicism as piously as she would her entire life, she had studied in the local convent school and at one point aspired to be a nun. Elisabeth met her future husband while working in the tobacco kiosk situated near the Fischers' butcher shop.

Jozsef and Elisabeth married in May 1936, at a time when they probably still believed that their future life together would be as it had been for the Danube Swabians before them. A black-and-white photograph of the newlyweds shows a handsome man with thick, dark brows, a tight-lipped smile, and serious demeanor. He has a boutonniere pinned to his lapel and holds a pair of white gloves. His pretty bride's floor-length veil is pushed back to reveal curly brown hair as she cradles a bouquet of wild flowers. Her almond-shaped eyes and full, expressive mouth lead one to think that Jozsef's proposal might not have been her only offer. The couple looks oblivious to the world's affairs, to Hitler's ascent, and to Hungary's own lurch toward dictatorship. After the ceremony, the newlyweds moved into the roomy Fischer residence anticipating a quiet life of family, hard work, holidays, and church.

Three years later, Jozsef and Elisabeth had their first child, Georgina, and in 1943 Irma Maria Franziska joined her older sister and a raft of cousins in the spacious house. The Fischer family hired one woman to help with the housework and another to mind the children. Their handmade cork shoes were custom-ordered from Vienna.[5] For the most part, ethnic Germans like the Fischers led the good life in Hungary—and they knew it.

Today, the picturesque little town on the western slopes of the Buda hills is practically a suburb of Budapest. Although only a smattering of its residents speak German, Budakeszi (Wudigess in German) proudly displays its multiethnic heritage. The baroque church and over two hundred former Swabian homes are protected monuments, their resplendent pastel facades and thickly thatched roofs evoking the days when Habsburg dukes and princes ruled the land. Joschka Fischer, descendant of Budakeszi butchers, is an honorary citizen of the town. A handful of cousins and distant relatives still live there, not far from the Fischer family's grand house on the former Hauptstrasse—property expropriated by the state after the war. In honor of the vanished Swabians, the town has a two-room museum that exhibits folk costumes, a hand-operated printing press, and other artifacts dug out of cellars and attics. The walls are lined with photographs of the *Vereine*, the clubs and societies around which the German community organized itself. In one, a photo of the Budakeszi Kossuth Soccer Club, a youthful Jozsef Fischer is lying horizontally in front of the rest of the team, propped up nonchalantly on an elbow.

During Nazi rule, some ethnic German communities in central Europe, like those in Poland and the Czech lands, eagerly put their services at the disposal of the German fatherland. They greeted Hitler's army as a liberator and signed up en masse for the Wehrmacht and positions in the occupation administrations. Some served in the brutal Waffen SS units on the eastern front. The Danube Swabians of Hungary had their own National Socialist organization, the newly founded Volksbund der Deutschen in Ungarn, and contributed recruits to the SS, too.

But the circumstances in Hungary differed from those in Poland and the Czech lands, where the Nazis annexed some regions and set up occupation administrations in others. Hungary was an Axis power until March 1944, the ethnic German fascists of the Volksbund standing in a wary partnership with Hungary's homegrown extremists. Many of Hungary's Germans, like the Fischers, felt a deeper loyalty to Hungary than they did to Germany, much less to Nazi Germany. Joschka Fischer, in one of the few stories he tells about his father, remembers him crying after Hungary's national soccer team lost the 1954 World Cup final to West Germany, 2–3. The West

Germans' against-all-odds victory offered a flickering moment of national pride for most Germans in the new postwar state. The "miracle at Bern," the cup championship played in Switzerland, was the first time since the war that many West Germans felt a positive, collective sense of "we." But it was a "we" that didn't include Danube Swabian Jozsef Fischer. His homeland was Hungary and his home sheltered Budakeszi, as he remembered it.

Another indication of their feelings toward the Nazis, Hungary's ethnic Germans enlisted in the Hungarian army in far larger numbers than they did for the Waffen SS. And in the 1939 election, the last before military dictatorship, a phenomenal 74 percent of Budakeszi voted for the nationalist Hungarian party, while only 17 percent voted for an electoral alliance that included the Berlin-loyal Volksbund.[6] How the thirty-year-old Jozsef Fischer and his young wife Elisabeth voted, if they voted at all, is not known. The Roman Catholic youth organizations—the circles Elisabeth moved in—openly butted heads with the fascist Volksbund. Many of the established Germans typically regarded politics as unhealthy, something that could jeopardize relations with the Hungarian state and thus to be kept at arm's length.

When the war came, Jozsef and his brothers enlisted in the Hungarian forces. When Jozsef's unit, part of the Hungarian Second Army, was ordered to the eastern front in 1942, his father pulled every string he could to keep him in Hungary, working in a slaughterhouse rather than fighting the Russians through the winter. His unit shipped out to Russia and eventually fought at Stalingrad, without Jozsef. Just a handful of the men from Jozsef's unit returned from the infamous battle.[7]

The actual nature of the Fischers' politics didn't matter to the Hungarian authorities once the war was over. The interim leadership in postwar Hungary (not, at this early stage, dominated by communists) had a variety of reasons, most blatantly self-serving, to brand their German-speaking minority "Nazis" and "traitors." One was revenge, which the victorious Allies as much as sanctioned in the 1945 Potsdam Agreement, authorizing the "transfer to Germany of German populations, or elements thereof" from Poland, Czechoslovakia, and Hungary. In addition to an element of spite, the planners of postwar Europe reasoned that a central Europe depleted of troublesome German minorities would be a more stable, peaceful place in the future. (Much later in the century similar such "population transfers" in the former Yugoslavia—unauthorized by international treaty—would be called by the less innocuous term "ethnic cleansing.")[8]

Potsdam appeared to legitimize the "collective guilt" of ethnic Germans living east of occupied Germany's new eastern border, providing Hungarian officials with a made-to-order pretext to rid the country of its German minority. In the name of an ethnically homogeneous Hungary, Magyar nationalists had long striven to deplete the German minority in their country. Proponents of a sweeping land reform also wanted the Germans out; such reforms would be enormously difficult as long as the Germans held on to their farms. And postwar Hungary desperately needed housing and land for the hundreds of thousands of ethnic Hungarians streaming out of Slovakia, Romania, and Ukraine.

In February 1946 the Fischers found their name on a list posted by the Hungarian authorities in the town hall.[9] It informed them that they were to leave on the first organized transport. Hungarian authorities permitted each adult to bring 120 pounds of clothing, linens, and food.[10] A month later, the family boarded horsedrawn wagons that took them and other German families to the nearest train station, four miles away. There they boarded a cattle train in which they laid out their bedding on the floor. Eyewitnesses from the time say that the frightened families spoke in hushed tones, petrified that the Red Army soldiers occupying postwar Hungary would pull them off the train, pillage their meager belongings, or take away the young girls.[11] Perhaps, they feared, they too could be sent to Russia and pressed into forced labor as other Hungarian Germans had been in the war's immediate aftermath. When, on the second day of their trip, they crossed from Soviet-occupied eastern Austria into American-controlled territory, the passengers sighed with collective relief. The sight of U.S. GIs meant safety and aid.

Thus, before Joschka Fischer opened his eyes to the world, several factors—none of which he or his parents had any control over—had already determined how his world would look. The first was his nationality, ethnic German. Although the Fischers had neither collaborated with the Nazis nor even identified with Germany as a country, their ethnicity alone was the criterion that turned them into one of the many millions of German families forced to repatriate to Germany proper. Another factor was the actions of the United States. America had obviously played a decisive role in liberating Europe from Nazi rule. But President Harry S. Truman's signing of the Potsdam Agreement effectively robbed the Fischers of their ancestral home. The Allies even gave Hungary logistic assistance to carry out the expulsions. That said, the Fischers' repatriation, as grim as its circumstances, delivered them from Soviet communism, a fate that caused many of their Budakeszi relatives to emigrate voluntarily. The terms of peace, also in the Potsdam Agreement, prescribed the denazification, demilitarization, and decartelization of postwar Germany (the famous "three Ds"), which established the preconditons for a democratic state in the west. And, as it happened, the refugee family would start its life over in western Germany in the American zone of occupation.

A New Consensus

The Fischers got their first break when occupation authorities moved them to nearby Langenburg, a sleepy medieval town surrounded by forests and steep valleys in a Protestant region of southwestern Germany. Jozsef took over a small butcher shop on the main street and the family started to put down roots. On April 12, 1948, just as the Cold War set in across Europe, Joseph Martin, later known by all as Joschka, was born in the neighboring Gerabronn hospital.

In the month of Joschka Fischer's birth, the U.S. Congress approved the European Recovery Program, commonly known as the Marshall Plan, which between 1948 and 1951 poured $13 billion into western Europe's economies, the largest share going to western Germany. Several months later, the western occupation powers took a giant step toward forging a separate state out of their conterminous sectors. A currency reform in the British, American, and French zones replaced the nearly worthless Reichsmark with the Deutsche Mark, the currency that would become synonymous with West Germany itself. In response, the Soviets coined the East Mark in their zone. Although the deep divisions between the wartime Allies were impossible to paper over, Germany's partition into eastern and western states wasn't, at the time, a foregone conclusion. But, in late June 1948, Soviet troops cut off all roads into Berlin, which was controlled together by the four occupying powers. The blockade of the western sectors prompted a spectacular fifteen-month, U.S.-led airlift to supply the former capital. The Berlin airlift demonstrated the United States' commitment to the city and established it as the West's forward-most outpost in soon-to-be communist Europe. If there had been any doubt before the Berlin blockade, there wasn't after it: the Cold War was on. The partition of Germany—and Berlin with it—was fact.

In May 1949 the Federal Republic came to life when its legal cornerstone, the Basic Law, went into force in the west and became the law of the land for 50 million people. Later that same year, another infant state, the Soviet-style

German Democratic Republic, with a population of 16 million, emerged in the east and cemented Germany's division. The Federal Republic, though a common product of German democrats and the western Allies, was propelled into existence by the exigencies of the East-West rivalry and it assumed statehood with a host of existential questions looming over it. Its success—or even survival—was at the time in no way guaranteed. For one, it was the West's eastern bulwark in the superpower confrontation, which, while to its advantage in many ways, was an inexpedient geopolitical position from which to build a democracy from the ruins of a totalitarian dictatorship. The Federal Republic was the first line of defense (or offense) against a powerful Soviet adversary. Unarmed and prohibited from fielding an army, West Germany was reliant on the western powers for its protection, should push really come to shove.

There was also the issue of eventual unification with "the other Germany," a hope and presumably a real possibility that almost all Germans embraced at the time. It was, for example, the Federal Republic's founding fathers who insisted that the Basic Law was a "temporary solution"—and not a full-fledged constitution—in order to avoid shutting the door on unification with eastern Germany. In the future, they hoped, in a different political context, the two sides could reconcile and unify as one state. There were at the time serious doubts about whether the German populace would go along with Germany's division. Allied administrators worried that nationalist-minded Germans might take to the streets or perhaps try to take up arms. Another possibility was that they would opt for a neutral position, at arm's length from both superpowers, and adopt a political system straddling western democracy and Soviet communism. Worse yet, as a consequence of neutrality, perhaps western Germany would go communist and fall into the Soviet camp.

Even barring the worst-case scenarios, there were other problems. Were a people who had identified so thoroughly with an ideology such as National Socialism capable of learning democracy? Might not their illiberal conditioning undermine the efforts of the western authorities and their German counterparts to nurture democratic institutions and practices in the postwar state? German society had been so comprehensively militarized, a process that extended back to Prussian times, that it had penetrated deep into the collective psyche.[12] The Germans had few democratic traditions that they could call upon. The March revolution of 1848 was a long time ago, while the Weimar Republic's interwar democracy proved so frail that it gave way to fascism. The Federal

Republic was a parliamentary democracy in form and structure, one with pacifism inscribed in its law. But the question remained whether the Germans could fill these structures with republican content. If the Allies' initial efforts to denazify the Germans were any measure, the prospects were modest at best. Most Germans resented rather than took to heart the processes of denazification and "re-education." In 1948, for example, 55 percent of Germans in the western zones felt that "National Socialism was a good idea that had been badly implemented."[13] To most, the wartime allies were viewed as occupation armies, not as their liberators from Nazi rule.

Joschka Fischer and his peers were thoroughly products of the Federal Republic, and during its lifetime they would define—and redefine—themselves in relation to the postwar state. The name of one man, Konrad Adenauer, is inextricably bound up with the early decades of the republic, and it was the Adenauer era that served as the backdrop for the first postwar generation's childhood, adolescence, and even some of their early adult years. The tenure of West Germany's first chancellor spanned fourteen years, and his party, the conservative Christian Democratic Union (CDU), would continue to lead governing coalitions for another six years after his departure in 1963. Joschka Fischer would be twenty-one and living in a communal house in Frankfurt before West Germany's foremost opposition party, the Social Democrats (SPD), managed to wrench the chancellorship away from the conservatives in 1969.

The first elections in September 1949 brought a center-right coalition to power in Bonn, the new state's provincial capital along the Rhine River. Only by the narrowest of margins could the Christian Democrats cobble together a coalition and send their most serious rivals, the Social Democrats, into opposition. The government was led by the gaunt, long-faced Adenauer, a seventy-three-year-old Roman Catholic and Cologne's mayor during the Weimar Republic. When the Nazis removed him from office in 1933, the Rhineland native withdrew from public life during the twelve years of Hitler's rule. From the very start of his resumed political career in postwar Germany, Adenauer set a course that aimed to stabilize the country and win it sovereignty, step by step. He would do so firmly within the parameters established by the western Allies, above all the United States, which would earn him the reputation as "Chancellor of the Allies." Over its forty-one-year life, the so-called Bonn Republic never strayed from Adenauer's main coordinates: parliamentary democracy, a social market economy, and unflagging loyalty to the Atlantic alliance.

By the time that Adenauer, also known as "the Old Fox," reluctantly stepped down at the ripe age of eighty-seven, his imprint on the republic had become indelible.

For Adenauer, West Germany's resolute commitment to the West—called the *Westbindung*—and to the United States, in particular, offered the only viable answer to the fledgling state's most pressing concerns. There would be no German *Sonderweg* (special path) this time, a reference to the anti-Western, anti-liberal orientations of past Germanys. West Germany, Adenauer concluded, had to rely on the Atlantic and European West to defend it from the Soviet Union. In return, he pledged loyalty and an unflinching anticommunist stance, both at home and against the Soviet imperium. With West Germany's controversial rearmament under NATO's auspices in 1955—the grounds for some of the republic's earliest extra-parliamentary protests—the Old Fox made the Federal Republic an irreplaceable fixture in the West's security architecture. It also upped the stakes for both Germanys, which had suddenly become the *armed* frontline in an aggravated East–West conflict. This played straight into the hands of West Germany's conservatives by making anticommunism all the more relevant and potent. In decades to come, this same rationale ("Soviet aggression") would be used to deploy nuclear weapons on German territory and to upgrade them—the source of further protests. The conservatives' fierce anticommunism proved valuable in other ways, too: it was the CDU's most effective and frequently employed instrument to discredit left-wing opposition. "All forms of Marxism lead to Moscow," read one 1953 CDU campaign poster, which might as well have had added "including social democracy." Not least, by playing up the threat and evil of communism, German conservatives managed to relativize some of the ignominy of the Hitler regime by endowing the Nazis' crusade against communism with positive justification.

Adenauer deduced that West Germany's quickest route to self-governance was through the confidence of the Allies. The republic that had risen from the ashes of the Nazi dictatorship was on trial: for example, initially all legislation had to be co-signed by the western Allies. Adenauer's game plan was to demonstrate beyond a shadow of a doubt that the Federal Republic was in the western camp to stay. He did, and it paid off handsomely. In May 1955 the Federal Republic became a sovereign state when the Allied High Commission revoked the Occupation Statute. That same month West Germany joined NATO as a full-fledged member. Two years later it became a founding signatory of the European Economic Community, the precursor to the European Union. Adenauer's fervent multilateralism, which meant enmeshing West Germany in a network of international commitments, would be the guiding light of German foreign policy for decades to come.

Another pillar of Adenauer's Germany, and a trademark of the Bonn Republic, was an export-driven social market economy. Aided by Marshall Plan monies and U.S. loans, West Germany's policies, masterminded by the economics minister Ludwig Erhard, prompted an economic recovery that turned the country into one of the world's industrial powerhouses. Throughout the fifties the Federal Republic logged an astounding growth rate of 8 percent a year. By 1960 Germany's gross national product was second in the world only to that of the United States. The country's *Wirtschaftswunder*, or "economic miracle," created a burgeoning middle class through massive job creation and climbing wages. From its beginnings, the West German state set out to avoid the political fragmentation, religious strife, and class divisions that had rent asunder the Weimar Republic. An economically content populace was one that acclimated all the more swiftly to the new system and fledgling state. West Germany's boom also enabled the country to absorb and integrate the millions of postwar refugees like the Fischers.

Adenauer's party, the CDU, and its Bavarian sister party, the Christian Social Union (CSU), were instrumental in forging the conservative consensus that emerged in the 1950s. The CDU was an amalgam of religious and right-wing parties from the Weimar democracy that endorsed general Christian values and appealed to all German Christians. Yet its leadership was dominated by Roman Catholics rather than Protestants, and it inclined to particularly conservative stands on issues related to public morality, gender, and family.* For this reason, among others, Jozsef and Elisabeth Fischer belonged to the Christian Democrats' natural constituency and voted CDU reflexively.

But the conservative party also reached out to other constituencies, like Germans with strong nationalist leanings, including former Nazi party members. The past, believed Adenauer and his cronies (a good number with Nazi histories themselves), was the past and it was time to open a new chapter in

* While Protestants outnumbered Catholics by nearly two to one in prewar Germany, in West Germany there was a rough parity between the two religions and thus cause for some Protestants' feelings of marginalization in the CDU and the Federal Republic in general. This disenchantment prompted many Protestants to steer clear of the CDU and join the first protest campaigns against rearmament when they began in the early 1950s.

German history.* Also, increasingly through the decade, the Christian Democrats lured millions of expellee voters under its wing. The expellees (16 percent of the republic's 1950 population)[14] and their organizations stood on the far right of the political spectrum as a motivated and influential voting bloc. The Fischers, for example, belonged to the Danube Swabians' Hungarian-German Homeland Society, which was established in nearby Stuttgart in 1949. The expellee groups' overriding interest was to get back the property confiscated from them in the war's aftermath. They wanted their houses *and* their *Heimat* (homeland) returned to them, and thus refused to accept the postwar borders drawn up by the Allies. Although the possibility of Germany's ever retrieving the eastern territories that the vanquished Reich lost to Poland and the Soviet Union in 1945 was virtually zero, the CDU and CSU unabashedly pandered to these wishes—and received votes in return. And, not least, while the CDU won the support of much of the up-and-coming new middle class with its economic policies, the party's embrace of market capitalism made it the party of big business and the affluent, too.

Political opposition during Adenauer's reign fell mostly to the Social Democrats, a proudly socialist party with a long and storied history in Germany. The German Socialist Workers Party was founded in the 1860s, a party for the proletariat that vowed to change Germany through the ballot box. Taking up their fight again after being outlawed during the Nazi years, the SPD and its leader, Kurt Schumacher, until his death in 1952, battled the Old Fox every step of the way by waging stiff opposition to Adenauer's agenda. Paradoxically, the democratic socialists initially couched their class-based rhetoric in nationalism. The market economy and Adenauer's uncompromising *Westbindung*, they argued, torpedoed any chance of a reconciliation with East Germany and thus undermined the possibility of German unification. Although Adenauer, in word, always remained committed to a unified German state, by anchoring the Federal Republic so firmly in the West, at the express wish of the Allies, he annulled the preconditions for a compromise that might have led to unification in the near or middle-term future. Unlike the Social Democrats, he strictly ruled out a neutral Germany between the East and West blocs. If the two Germanys were to be unified, then it would be on the West's terms.

---

* Of the twenty-six persons that Adenauer considered for cabinet positions in 1949, twenty-five of them had in some way been active in the Nazi apparatus. The most notorious of these was Hans Globke, Adenauer's chief aide through the 1950s, who had been one of the architects of the anti-Jewish Nuremberg laws in 1937.

Adenauer's strong hand and fatherly manner, which accounted for his popularity in some circles, became an easy target for his critics' ridicule. His opponents saw in him an autocratic patriarch who opened the door to just enough democracy to keep himself and his party in power. Under Adenauer, the chancellorship became the republic's hub of power, earning his style of governance the unflattering label of "chancellor democracy." The first West German chancellor seemed merely to tolerate political opposition and a free, critical media rather than approve whole-heartedly of them. But he obviously understood the postwar mentality well. He won over voters, one historian quipped, by "accustoming Germans to the idea that authority and democracy aren't mutually exclusive."[15]

Very *Kleinbürgerlich*

Remarkably, Joschka Fischer and his surviving sister Georgina remember their years in Langenburg affectionately, not as a time of privation or want. One prized family photograph shows Joschka on his first day of school in 1954, grinning ear-to-ear with his decorated *Schultüte*, an oversized cardboard cone stuffed with sweets and school supplies that all German children receive from their parents on their first school day. Proud as punch in long pants and carrying a new backpack, he looks as happy as a little boy could look. The siblings' nostalgia for a period that included so much human agony, and for the Fischers such a precipitous fall in status, surely speaks favorably of the parenting skills of matriarch Elisabeth. She, not Jozsef, was the dominant presence during Joschka's childhood and adolescence. In general, women bore the brunt of the hardship in this postwar purgatory—circumstances that set the backdrop for filmmaker Rainer Werner Fassbinder's seminal 1950s trilogy *The Marriage of Maria Braun*, *Veronika Voss*, and *Lola*. Like others, Elisabeth Fischer rose to the occasion, although, unlike Fassbinder's antiheroines, she did so by following the straight and narrow.

As for his father, Joschka never really knew Jozsef. Mr. Fischer left the house at five in the morning and returned late in the evening, sometimes after the children had been put to bed. Joschka remembers him as a quiet, withdrawn fellow. On Sundays he was usually found in the kitchen, smoking and listening to classical music on the radio or reading dime-store novels. Growing up in the fifties in Germany with a distant or weak father figure—or none at all, as did 1.25 million German children,[16] including Gerhard Schröder, Germany's 1998–2005 chancellor—was nothing out of the ordinary. In fact, in postwar Germany it was practically the rule.

Elisabeth ran a strict, fastidious household, "very *kleinbürgerlich*," as Joschka put it many years later. "The kitchen table was always so immaculate you could have performed an emergency operation on it," he remembers.[17] Her domain may have been the traditional *Kinder, Küche, und Kirche* (children, kitchen, and church), but it was also much more. She anchored the family after the trauma of expulsion and financial ruin had broken Jozsef.

In the face of adversity, the demure bride had developed into a strong-willed woman, sometimes hot-tempered, always vivacious, and unshakably pious. Former friends remember her charisma, light-hearted banter, and easy way with words. Apparently, she could talk and talk, never tiring of recalling the life they had left behind in Budakeszi. When Joschka Fischer visited Hungary for the first time many years later, he located the old house on his own and immediately recognized other landmarks from the stories told and retold by his parents. Yet, in spite of this fixation with the past, the Fischer elders rarely mentioned the war or their experiences during the 1940s. They never, for example, admitted to the children that they had been expelled from the country. They told them they had left of their own volition "for a better life" in Germany.

Elisabeth's character, as well as her bourgeois regimen, had a profound impact on her youngest. "Without her unique disposition," concludes Sibylle Krause-Burger, one of Fischer's German biographers, "Joschka would never have developed into this exotic figure that he is in the political life of the Federal Republic. Joschka inherited his mother's talent to impress other people, to lead and to persuade. On the other hand, her overbearing love, attention, and authority prematurely drove Joschka out of his parents' house and set him on his own very unusual path."[18]

As youngsters, the Fischer children didn't stray far from their mother's apron, especially not Joschka, the apple of his mother's eye as the youngest child and only son. Joschka was pampered by Elisabeth and his sisters. They loved to tell stories about his sassy behavior and plucky one-liners. One tale recounts his birth in the Gerabronn hospital, when he flailed his stubby legs so hard that he nearly kicked himself off the delivery table. "With this one you're going to have your work cut out for you," the midwife allegedly warned Mrs. Fischer. At two-and-a-half, Joschka tore his hand away from Sister Emma, a local nun, crying out, "Joschka can walk alone!"[19]

These anecdotes and others were repeated time and again to Joschka, shaping his perception of himself as someone special, gifted, and rebellious. "A man who has been the indisputable favorite of his mother keeps for life the feeling of a conqueror, that confidence of success that often includes real success," wrote Sigmund Freud.[20] "A little macho-in-the-making from the very first second," Fischer later admitted.[21] His proud mother wanted nothing more than for Joschka to become a priest or a civil servant, or maybe mayor of the village. In the past, Germany's social mobility was so restricted that such positions were the very most that the son of a butcher could aspire to. But the lost war had shattered those barriers just as it had the infrastructure of Germany's cities, in a way incomparable to anywhere else in Europe. Elisabeth, for her part, unwittingly encouraged those character traits that years later would draw Joschka to the bohemian world of radical politics. To the day she died in 1991, however, she never approved of the path her son chose.

One of Fischer's enduring memories from the Langenburg years is that of U.S. soldiers, black Americans among them, who would throw the kids sweets from their jeeps. Officially, fraternization with the defeated Germans was prohibited by the occupation authorities. But this ban quickly fell by the wayside. The military zones were, according to one cultural historian, "zones of social and cultural contact between occupiers and occupied."[22] They not only constituted many Germans' introduction to American culture and lifestyles but were their first regular, direct contact with black people of any nationality. In this way, the occupation zones were also "informal sites of racial reeducation," a corrective to the Nazis' racial policies.[23] "They were our friends," remembers Fischer. His first words of English: "Do you have chocolate? Do you have chewing gum?" By then, even most adults had stopped viewing the GIs as occupiers, while the U.S. troops had gradually ceased to consider Germans as the defeated enemy. By the mid-fifties, the angst and despair of the immediate postwar years were receding into the past, with life picking up for the West Germans.

The Fischers left Langenburg in early 1956, at the peak of the *Wirtschaftswunder*. Even West Germany's astonishing economic recovery couldn't save Jozsef's flagging butcher shop. Most probably, the double stigma of being refugees and Catholics in an overwhelmingly Protestant region doomed Jozsef's business from the start. Unlike in Germany today, in the 1950s an unspoken code still divided society between Catholic and Protestant. The Fischer family, somewhat in control of their lives in 1956, would make certain that its next port of call would be among Roman Catholics like themselves.

2

Silent Fifties

"If you looked at the blueprints, it was Nazi idiom they were still building in, and if you look at the names of the architects, it was the Nazi architects who were still working."
—The character Keetenheuve in Wolfgang Koeppen's 1953 novel *The Hothouse*

The Fischer family—Joschka now six years old—resettled about fifty miles to the southwest in a Catholic hamlet outside Stuttgart called Öffingen. There, the five Fischers rented three rooms in a small house owned by a Hungarian émigré. In 2005 his German widow still lived in the unassuming white stucco building and remembered the Fischers fondly, especially the devout, hard-working Elisabeth. The prewar size of the village of about 2,000 had grown by half again with the influx of postwar refugees. The newcomers lived in one part of the village, the locals in another. "Our parents always told us not to go there, where the refugees were. It was off-limits," explains Irene Fritz, who, at the age of ten, had a special interest in classmate Joschka.

The Fischers' cramped quarters didn't even have their own bathing facilities, which obliged the family to make a group excursion to the public baths once a week. All the kids slept in one room. Jozsef found work on a construction site and then later in the Stuttgart slaughterhouse. After the move from Langenburg, never again would Jozsef Fischer own his own shop.

Joschka's childhood companions remember him as a bright and outgoing boy, a bit of a show-off, who wore thick, black plastic glasses. They thought he was pampered—obviously mommy's favorite. One of his closest friends from elementary school, Felix Rombold, says they frequently played games like cowboys and Indians with boys from neighboring villages. Joschka was always "the general" of the village's troops, and it stuck for a while as a nickname. "He always wanted to be number one," says another former classmate. But like other kids from "dregs-swilling" refugee families, as they were called, he ranked one notch below most of his village peers, and thus had something to prove.

Joschka Fischer's memories of Öffingen are not nostalgic. When talking about the scene of his turbulent adolescence, words such as *eng* (cramped), *stickig* (stuffy), and *schrecklich* (horrible) inevitably crop up. At the village's St. Basil chapel, Elisabeth enrolled Joschka as an altar boy. Every Sunday was dominated by the ordeal of mass in the morning and long, boring afternoons with the family. As a youth, Joschka was a model student, following in the steps of his sisters. But as the 1950s waned, an ornery streak began to surface. He mouthed off in class, earning him the reputation of a wise guy as well as frequent raps on the knuckles. "Everybody knew that he was very intelligent except his teachers," says Rombold, who would later become a high school teacher himself. The village school's headmaster in particular seemed to have it in for Fischer. "I don't know what it was but those two definitely did not like one another," Rombold recalls.

The red brick Gottlieb Daimler Gymnasium in nearby Fellbach was the setting for Fischer's first real clash with institutions that had been imposed upon him. Even his low opinion of Öffingen pales compared to his loathing, still vivid forty years later, for his "thin-lipped and sadistic" teachers and their pedantic ways. "In my entire school experience there were only three teachers that I remember with any affection," explained Fischer to one interviewer. "For them I would have done anything. Everything else was repulsive. I always had the feeling that I had to defend myself, that I had to box my way through in order to go my own way."[1]

Neither Jozsef nor Elisabeth could comprehend Joschka's growing disaffection. Their family was, after all, finally enjoying some of the fruits of the economic miracle. Like other families, they could begin to purchase electronic kitchen appliances, new clothes for their children, and once they had saved up, a television set. Their offspring were enrolled in the elite *Gymnasium* and would find decent jobs upon graduation. West Germany's booming economy promised them that.

Yet it was exactly this provincial *Kleinbürgerlichkeit* that was getting under Joschka's skin. Ede Fischer (her maiden name), who would become Joschka's first wife and was also born in 1948, grew up a stone's throw away, in Bad Cannstadt near Stuttgart. She too chafed under her family's prudish and restrictive house rules. New refrigerators seemed to be all anyone talked about, she explains:

> For me and for many of my friends then our parents' houses didn't provide any stimulation at all. Any kind of discussion, whether about personal or political topics, was nipped in the bud. There was absolutely no room for personal development or curiosity or discovery. The kind of life that our family members lived was so unbelievably depressive and hopeless. Everything revolved around social status, consumer products, the money value of things, et cetera.

Prosperity for Everyone

Although young people like Ede and Joschka couldn't know it at the time, they weren't suffering alone. The young republic's educational system had sidestepped the far-ranging democratic overhaul that the western allies had originally envisioned. The Adenauer era was a period of reconstruction and recovery—not root-and-branch reform.*

The war-damaged schools had been rebuilt, but brick and mortar were far easier to come by than trained, politically untainted instructors. Teachers from the Nazi era were reinstated, posing before their skeptical students as new-sprung democrats. In the neighboring state of Hesse, for example, between 55 and 75 percent of the active teachers were compromised by National Socialism; in the Hessian city of Würzburg, a full 90 percent had plied their trade under the Nazis.[2] The classes, schoolbooks, and pedagogical methods all remained imbued with the ethos of the past.

In the classroom, West Germany's teachers dealt with the world war and the twelve years of Nazi rule by ignoring them, as best they could. The first line of defense was to skirt the prickliest topics, such as the Holocaust or

* Contemporary German historians have been reevaluating the fifties and argue that the era was not as static or grim as many of the children of the day perceived it. Historian Axel Schildt's *Modernisierung im Wiederaufbau: Die westdeutsche Gesellschaft der 50er Jahre* (Bonn: Dietz Verlag, 1998) and the six-part 2005 TV documentary *Unsere 50er Jahre: Wie wir wurden, was wir sind* present a more dynamic picture of the 1950s. Some observers point out that the former 1960s radicals have a personal stake in portraying the time in as reactionary a light as possible in order to justify the radical politics of the late sixties. Some of the fifties' progeny themselves, like sociologist Detlev Claussen, a contemporary of Fischer's, disagree adamantly: "They [revisionist historians] try to make it look better than it was but it really was that bad! It was a terrible, terrible time to grow up."

the Nazis' rise to power in Weimar Germany. If something couldn't be circumvented, then it was justified: in light of the Nazis' total control and ubiquitous police network, ordinary Germans, like teachers, had had no alternative but to cooperate with the regime. As for the death camps, the dictatorship's most heinous crimes were supposedly carried out behind the backs of ordinary citizens. Some teachers claimed that Hitler's greatest crime was to overstretch Germany's resources and lose the war. The few critical, anti-Nazi films that some instructors showed their pupils about the wartime years, such as Alain Resnais' chilling *Night and Fog* and Erwin Leiser's *Mein Kampf*, tended to portray Nazism as a faceless, disembodied evil. The conclusion that students like Joschka Fischer and his classmates could reasonably arrive at was that Hitler and his little clique were the guilty ones, not average Germans. The fact was that most educators were incapable of conducting an honest discussion about the roots of German fascism and anti-Semitism, much less of beginning the process of confronting German guilt.

Adenauer's prescription for the republic was head down and full-speed-ahead with the economy and western integration. Once the new government took office, the trials and vetting lapsed. By 1950 the western allies' denazification program had petered out. In his inaugural speech, the new chancellor referred to denazification as "our misfortune" and called for the rehabilitation of Nazi-era civil servants and soldiers, as well as for new programs to aid war veterans and returning prisoners of war. As his party would into the 1980s, he openly courted the millions of ethnic German expellees by offering them the (false) hope that one day Germany could regain its lost territories in the east. Although Adenauer did conclude restitution deals for Jewish victims of the Nazi regime and reparations for Israel, in public he never uttered a word about the Holocaust or the concentration camps.[3] Rather, it was left to the opposition's leader, the Social Democrat Kurt Schumacher, whom the Nazis had imprisoned and tortured, to remind Germans of their historical responsibility:

> It is not only the duty of international socialists . . . but of all German patriots to acknowledge the fate of Germany's and Europe's Jews and to offer the assistance that is necessary [for the survivors]. Hitler's barbarism, which included the extermination of six million Jewish people, disgraced the German people. We are going to have to bear the burden of this disgrace for some time to come.

Many compromised former Nazis soon resumed their posts in the new state. In the civil service in 1951, 150,000 dismissed workers got back their jobs. Between 1950 and 1953, 60 percent of the newly named department heads had been Nazi party members.[4] More than in any other field, the justice system's personnel were reinstated virtually wholesale, top judges as well. The government's ministries were also stocked with persons who had headed or worked in the Third Reich's ministries. In the foreign ministry, thirty-nine of forty-nine senior officials were former Nazi party members.[5] Adenauer's rationale was that the country needed skilled professionals to run the state, as well as its hospitals, schools, and industry. Where was it going to find them if not among those who had run the Nazi state? This dilemma is one every post-totalitarian society faces. In exchange for their rehabilitation, the former collaborators had to conform to the new rules and accept the democratic system. And this, for the most part, they did. But this didn't change their thinking over night: in 1951, for example, only 8 percent of western Germans accepted the Oder-Niesse line (the border between East Germany and Poland) as the German border.[6]

In many ways, the ethos of the old order—of Nazi Germany as well as other Germanys before it—permeated this supposedly new Germany. Corporal punishment in schools, for example, was still routine, and at universities students could be expelled for interrupting a lecture. The Federal Republic still had "coupling laws" on the books that forbade single men and women under twenty-one to spend the night together—or even to spend time together unchaperoned. Parents who allowed their children to stray could face legal penalties. In contrast to the GDR's school curricula, in which the churches had no say, in the West German schools there weren't sexual-education programs until the 1960s. The legal head of a household was automatically the male, who could decide, for example, whether his wife would hold a job or not. Even if allowed to work outside the home, the wife was also fully responsible for the housework, a woman's priority and "natural domain." Holdover labor laws from the Nazi era allowed employers to fire women in order to make way for men, such as those returning from the work camps and prisons.*

The republic seemed to dwell in a gray zone between the past and an undefined, uncertain future. The most popular films of the day, for example, were "*Heimat* films," which portrayed a kitschy Germany of blond,

* In 1959 West Germany's highest court granted women full equal rights with men.

long-braided girls and innocent, hunky men in lederhosen. Films with titles like *The Ranger of the Silver Forest, Green Is the Meadow,* and *Black Forest Girl* were 1950s blockbusters, breaking all records for attendance. The films implicitly contrasted an unproblematic, traditional world with the bleak, bombed-out reality of postwar Germany. These films' ostensibly innocuous topics, however, were anything but unpolitical, as German historian Edgar Wolfrum argues. They accurately reflected the collective consciousness of the time, capturing many Germans' yearnings for an uncomplicated happiness and homey quietude. The *Heimat* films, maintains Wolfrum, projected the "daydreams" of a people struggling to adjust in a hectic industrial and post-totalitarian society. Their subtexts addressed the concerns of postwar Germans, such as the lost territories in the east and the elusive certainty and authority that had been promised to them by the Nazis.[7]

One of the earliest cultural products to take the young republic to task was novelist Wolfgang Koeppen's 1953-published *The Hothouse,* a searing indictment of political life in West Germany during the "silent fifties," as historians have since dubbed the decade. Although *The Hothouse* is considered *the* Adenauer-era novel, it achieved this status only much later.* At the time it was published, the book was pretty much ignored; neither the general public nor the political class were interested in such probing analysis. The novel is set in Bonn, the old university city in the Catholic Rhineland, which, at Adenauer's behest, became the Federal Republic's capital. The protagonist, Keetenheuve, is an opposition Social Democrat in the Bundestag who, after exile during the war, returns to Germany to participate in its democratic rebirth. But his idealism gives way to disillusionment when he witnesses the falseness of the republic in which onetime Nazis recast themselves as democrats. The ease with which they seamlessly shift from one system to the other disgusts him, as does the Nazi jargon that they unwittingly employ—because they know no other. The author portrays a political elite constrained and corrupted by a past that it refuses to confront. Keetenheuve's detached, brooding tone expresses his resignation and isolation. This Germany has no place for him, he concludes, and takes his own life.

---

* *The Hothouse* is the second in Koeppen's postwar trilogy, which includes *Pigeons on the Grass* and *Death in Rome.* Koeppen received West Germany's prestigious Büchner Prize for literature in 1962, an indication of the changing environment in West Germany in the early sixties.

Throughout the decade, Konrad Adenauer and his Christian Democrats consolidated power and steadily broadened the party's voter base. In the 1953 elections, the CDU improved upon its 1949 results (31 percent) by capturing 45 percent of the vote. In 1955 the republic entered NATO, the West's military alliance, and was granted conditional sovereignty by the western allies, a momentous achievement for the country and for Adenauer. In the next national elections, in 1957, the CDU won an absolute majority for the first time, which enabled it to rule without a coalition partner. Opinion polls showed West Germans increasingly accepting of the republic, representative democracy, and Germany's division.[8]

It was a stunning accomplishment: in less than ten years, all of the Old Fox's priorities had been turned into policy—the *Westbindung,* rearmament, economic recovery, the expellees' integration, sovereignty, membership in the key international organizations, and stable parliamentary democracy. With the motto "*Wohlstand für Alle*" (prosperity for everyone), the *Wirtschaftswunder* created a broad, new middle class and generated revenue for an expansive social-welfare program. The West Germans had put nose to grindstone and were relishing the dramatically improved living standards that they—along with a little help from their friends—had created. The Adenauer era, however, was entering its final throes by the end of the decade, even though conservatives would lead ruling coalitions in Bonn until 1969, the final six years without Adenauer.

By the late 1950s, more intellectuals were challenging some of the silent fifties' unspoken assumptions. The 1959 publication of Günter Grass's novel *The Tin Drum,* Heinrich Böll's novella *Billiards at Half-Past Nine,* and Uwe Johnson's *Speculations about Jakob* broke new ground in the republic with unapologetic examinations of Germans' complicity with fascism. In one famous scene in Grass's *The Tin Drum,* Germans have to peel onions in order to cry for the Nazis' victims. Wolfgang Staudte's film, *Roses for the Public Prosecutor,* used comedy to underscore the rehabilitation of the infamous *Blutrichter,* the Nazis' judicial arm, in supposedly democratic Germany. The publication of *The Diary of Anne Frank,* along with the film and play, provided Germans with emotional access to the Nazis' victims, in contrast to the abstract horror of concentration camp films like *Night and Fog.*[9] These works and others put faces on the fascist regime's collaborators and its victims, rekindling a discussion about the "brown past" that had been largely dormant since the late 1940s.

Billiards at Half-Past Nine established Heinrich Böll as one of West Germany's most trenchant domestic critics. The panoramic novella about three generations in a family of architects was the first of his fictional works to address the moral crisis of Germans' relationship to their personal and political past. Böll himself came from the Catholic Rhineland, from Cologne as Konrad Adenauer had, but Böll's beliefs led him to pen blistering indictments of the Catholic Church, German militarism, and his countrymen's high regard for obedience and authority. Böll, born in 1917, was raised in a well-to-do pacifist family that lost everything during the economic crises of the Weimar years. In 1939 he was conscripted into the Wehrmacht and fought in infantry units on both the eastern and western fronts. He was a corporal when taken prisoner by the Americans in 1945. Böll began his writing career shortly thereafter, as well as his engagement in the Federal Republic as an outspoken public intellectual, initially in the 1947-founded Gruppe 47, a circle of writers committed to promoting postwar authors and awareness about the Nazi years. In 1972 he won the Nobel Prize for Literature. Like Günter Grass, another Gruppe 47 member, Böll campaigned vigorously for the Social Democrats into the late seventies.

The Federal Republic's judicial treatment of the Nazi years also picked up at the tail end of the 1950s. Initially it was pressure from abroad that prompted the Bonn government in 1958 to open the Ludwigsburg Center for the Investigation of National Socialist Crimes. But the center's establishment created its own momentum and it started preliminary proceedings in hundreds, and then thousands of cases. Televised parts of Adolf Eichmann's 1961 trial in Jerusalem had opened the eyes of many young Germans, including Joschka and Ede Fischer, to the horror of the Holocaust. It was Eichmann who masterminded the transportation of millions of Jews to the death camps and, in his own defense, claimed that he was only following orders. Several years later, in late 1963, the first of the "Auschwitz trials" began in nearby Frankfurt against former SS commanders who had run the notorious camp in occupied Poland. Twenty-four persons were charged with the murder, or complicity in the murder, of Jewish prisoners.

Ulrich Enzensberger, younger brother of writer Hans Magnus Enzensberger, was just beginning his university studies at the time of the Frankfurt trials. He remembers watching on television how the accused grinned and smirked contemptuously in the courtroom. Their behavior, he felt, accurately reflected public opinion at the time—namely, that the perpetrators were considered upstanding Germans and not criminals who should be held to account:

> These men, in the prime of their lives, had in no way been condemned by their fellow citizens. [One defendant] Wilhelm Borger, who had designed a well-known torture device that was named after him, was working as a full-time salesman. Another, the terrible [Auschwitz commander] Oswald Kaduk, was fondly known as "Papa Kaduk" at the West Berlin hospital where he was employed as a health care worker. In Göttingen the pharmacy owned by [defendant] Victor Capesius* was flourishing. I didn't dare ask my father the question "did you know about it?" It would have been like opening the bedroom door at an inopportune moment. They were ashamed, and would have said "no"—and then quickly covered themselves up.... In the 50s, during the Cold War, people excused the atrocities that the Germans carried out in the east with the alibi of anticommunism. But that alibi was wearing thin [by the early sixties]. Yet the majority of Germans still felt innocent. They believed their own alibis.[10]

The Frankfurt trials were the first time that Auschwitz, the largest of the Nazi's extermination camps, appeared on Joschka Fischer's radar. The extensive media coverage of the trials showed that the accused men were normal-looking Germans, not foaming-at-the-mouth killers. How was it, young Germans were prompted to ask, that such seemingly average citizens—academics, civil servants, businessmen, and craftsmen—could be capable of crimes of such stunning cruelty, and then after the war melt back into society as harmless *Kleinbürger.* And why was it that neither his parents nor his teachers were asking these questions? In fact, the war criminals in the dock looked no less "normal" than did their neighbors and teachers.

The end of Adenauer's marathon reign was already in sight when the "Spiegel Affair" in 1962 gave the eighty-six-year-old chancellor a final shove. His disdain for investigative journalism manifested itself when, in a cloak-and-dagger midnight raid, the government had the offices of *Der Spiegel* (The Mirror), West Germany's leading newsweekly, searched and several editors arrested for publishing alleged military secrets. The scandal

---

* Dr. Victor Capesius worked together with Dr. Joseph Mengele performing scientific experiments on human beings at the Auschwitz concentration camp.

attracted international attention and brought West German citizens onto the streets to protest their leader's abuse of power. This public outrage itself was an expression of a budding democratic consciousness in the Federal Republic—and testimony that extra-parliamentary means could and would be used when the organs of governance failed. Less than a year later, Adenauer's rivals in his own party forced the republic's founding father to step down.

No Direction Home

In tenth grade, Joschka Fischer's grades fell off sharply. For the first time his report card was punctuated with Ds and even Fs. The year was 1965. His grades were so poor that he flunked the year and was demoted from the exclusive *Gymnasium* to the village's *Mittelschule.* By the age of seventeen, he no longer aspired to be part of the institutions that hemmed him in—his family, school, the church. Something had begun to tick in Fischer, something that he couldn't quite articulate. Outside sheltered Öffingen, beyond the manure piles and mud-caked tractors, something had also begun to tick in the Federal Republic.

With the possibilities of escape from Öffingen limited for a young teenager, Fischer took up bicycle racing, making use of the long country roads to put distance between himself and everyone in the village. His troubles in school had caused relations with his parents to take a turn for the worse. Elisabeth and Jozsef were prepared to sacrifice everything to have their children graduate from the *Gymnasium*, a prerequisite in Germany—then as now—for a white-collar profession. They didn't understand what more their son could want. Joschka tuned them out and threw all of his energy into cycling.

His choice of sport was no coincidence; it reflected the developing contours of Fischer's character. Long-distance bicycle touring is a fitting hobby for a loner. Competitive cycling also demands enormous discipline, a quality he seemed to possess when the occasion demanded it. Another requirement is a many-geared, thin-tire racing bicycle, an exceedingly costly item for anyone in a village such as Öffingen in the 1960s. Ever supportive, Elisabeth took on part-time work as a cleaning lady to buy her boy a racing bike. Joschka and three teammates from Club Stuttgardia took home gold medals in the 1965 Baden Württemberg state championships.

His long, solitary afternoons on the road gave the budding young man plenty of time to reflect on *Gott und die Welt*, as Germans say—namely, life's greater imponderables. He had begun reading on his own: newspapers, world history, and America's Beat-generation authors like Jack Kerouac and Allen Ginsberg. Over the airwaves, on the U.S. military's Armed Forces Network radio, a new kind of music was penetrating the village's thick cultural walls: first Bill Haley and Elvis, then the Beatles, the Rolling Stones, and the Byrds.

But more than anything else, it was Bob Dylan's songs that captured the imagination of Fischer and other teenagers like him. "I flipped out on Bob Dylan," admits Fischer. When discussing his past, Fischer never fails to emphasize the resonance that Dylan's lyrics had with him. When asked once who had a more profound influence on the young Joschka Fischer—Bob Dylan or Karl Marx—he snapped: "Clearly Bob Dylan. His music has always been a highly emotional thing for me. . . . I wanted to be free. I wanted to leave, go my own way, on the road to the promised idea of freedom."[11]

In Dylan's music, Fischer heard for the first time the rallying cry of left-wing U.S. political activists confronting the establishment. The bard's righteous denunciations of racism and the arms race, as well as the falseness of society's appointed authorities, struck a chord in Fischer. Songs such as "Maggie's Farm" spoke of the spiritual freedom of dropping out and drifting: "Well, I try my best / To be just like I am, / But everybody wants you / To be just like them / They sing while you slave and I just get bored. / I ain't gonna work on Maggie's farm no more." Freewheelin' across Württemberg's vast farm country, he tried to imagine the creative bohemia of Greenwich Village coffeehouses. Dylan's America seemed millions of miles from Öffingen. But the times were definitely a-changin'—in the United States, in France and England, and in West Germany, too.

Fischer was part of a new postwar generation that took the material perks of the *Wirtschaftswunder* for granted and demanded more than shiny new refrigerators and toasters "made in Germany." It began asking questions about the nature of the Federal Republic's democracy, about its aging elite's relationship to the Nazi past, and its stubborn lack of interest in addressing the legacy of National Socialism. Wasn't, they asked, Adenauer's authoritarian style, his disregard for parliament, and his contempt for the opposition a poor start for a people so in need of democratic experience? And didn't the government—even now that Adenauer was gone—treat advocates of leftist political ideologies, such as communism, as the state's main enemy instead of those associated with National Socialism? Didn't it seem that the government, in alliance with the Catholic Church, was trying to force a narrow-minded morality and antiquated lifestyle onto German society? And wasn't the creation of this too-comfortable consumer society the perfect means to depoliticize citizens and render them impassive?[12] Some intellectuals, like Heinrich Böll and the Heidelberg philosopher Karl Jaspers, had been posing these kinds of uncomfortable questions for some time. But now there were people taking those questions seriously.

After a short, unsuccessful stint as a photographer's apprentice, in April 1966 Fischer, just eighteen, hit the road. He packed a bag and stuck out his thumb: any direction would have sufficed. But he chose north, to England, where the Beatles and the Rolling Stones were making music. His first attempt to break out and see the world didn't get very far. Fischer's money ran out, and returning via the northern port city of Hamburg, the minor was picked up late one night by the police. An uncomprehending Elisabeth had to travel to Hamburg to bring her wayward son back to the village.

But Fischer's curiosity had been stirred and now there was no holding him back. Fischer worked part time in the local social services office, saved as much as he could, and set out again, this time to the east, where spirituality and hashish were luring free spirits like himself. Spending the nights in train stations and under bridges, he first returned to England and then hitched southward, through France, Spain, Italy, Yugoslavia, Greece, and Turkey. He had made it as far as Kuwait when word from his family finally reached him. They had been trying for weeks to inform him that Irma Maria, the middle sibling, lay gravely ill with kidney disease.

Fischer sped home to discover that his twenty-three-year-old sister, the village beauty, was dying. The two siblings were obviously very close. His relatives who live in Hungary today saved a small stack of black-and-white glossies that Joschka, fancying himself a fashion photographer, shot of Irma Maria in their backyard in Öffingen. Irma Maria, with a jet-black Beatles-style bob and tight-fitting jeans, is Joschka's female doppelganger. On film, he captures her in one Bridget Bardot or Marilyn Monroe pose after another. Her death must have shaken him deeply, although he never alludes to it.

Shortly after his arrival home to be with Irma Maria during her final days, the market where his father worked called to notify the family that Jozsef had had a serious accident. When Joschka arrived at the hospital, nurses informed him that his father was dead, the result of a heart attack. "He was fifty-six but his corpse looked like that of a seventy-year-old," says Fischer.[13]

He packed up his father's bloodied, fat-spattered work clothes and his butcher's bag full of the tools of his trade, and walked out of the hospital's doors. "That was all he left. He worked himself to death," says Fischer, reflecting on the tragedy. "I said to myself: a life like that, always slaving away, never earning anything. No, no way, that's not for me. That's not how I'm going to live and die."[14] Elisabeth, the family pillar, took the news stoically. Five days later, in the same hospital, Irma Maria passed away.

Face-to-face with mortality for the first time in his life, Joschka Fischer made a renewed effort to fit in and settle down. Living together with his mother, he flirted with the idea of resuming his apprenticeship or even taking another shot at *Gymnasium*. But these vague plans never materialized.

Instead his gaze shifted to the nearest metropolis, Stuttgart, just an hour on the bus from Öffingen. It turned out that the regional capital of 500,000, still in the process of rebuilding its baroque palaces and museums, wasn't as lifeless as the young Fischer had thought. As in other West German cities, a hodgepodge of actors from avant-garde intellectuals to outspoken church figures were testing the republic's narrow parameters—and had been for years. Unbeknownst to provincial folks like the Fischers, by the mid-sixties a diffuse and increasingly vibrant grassroots opposition to the country's political establishment was coalescing after a decade of scattered protests. Critical to the mix, a new generation of young Germans, roughly Fischer's age and a bit older, was coming into its own.

Without Me

A number of protest movements appeared and then faded away during the new state's first decade. From the very beginning though the young Federal Republic had a conflicted relationship with this kind of extra-parliamentary activity. On the one hand, political action taken up outside the given democratic institutions was viewed with intense skepticism. The Basic Law was designed to create a stable democracy, one that could not, as the Weimar Republic had, collapse from within or otherwise be overthrown by political extremists. In this spirit, radical political parties—of the left and the right—could be banned in the Federal Republic, and indeed had been. In 1956, for example, the West German communist party was outlawed. An antidote to the Weimar state's centralized powers, the post-war republic was federalist, with its eleven regional states (*Länder*) granted broad competencies. There was also an explicit ban on direct forms of democracy, such as popular referenda and plebiscites, in order to hinder populists from circumventing the institutions of governance.

Ultimately, the state's German founding fathers distrusted the postwar inclinations of the German people as much as the Western Allies did. The Federal Republic was explicitly created as a *wehrhafte Demokratie* (defensive democracy), one with structures designed to "protect the Germans from themselves."[15] In the early 1950s the Germans were viewed by many observers as unreformed or latent Nazis whose political behavior had to be monitored closely and held in check. The Federal Republic was an occupied country until 1955, its sovereignty partially restricted even after that, as was the Bundestag's autonomy to make laws and the government's to carry out policy. The political activity that the Allies condoned was to happen within the institutions that they had helped establish, such as the Bundestag, according to a principle of compromise and consensus. "Extra-parliamentary movements," noted one scholar, "far from being associated with notions of grassroots democracy and with a stirring of political spirit beyond the relatively narrow confines of political parties, were, on the contrary, seen as clear indications of a democracy in decline."[16]

On the other hand, the rise of the Nazis through the Weimar Republic's democratic structures and the, at best, passive (at worst, complicit) response of so many Germans spoke to the need for principled opposition to state policies—when they go astray and parliamentary opposition fails to pose sufficient resistance. Germany, with its authoritarian traditions, did not have a rich history of this kind of civic opposition. Political activism undertaken by citizens against official policies and outside of the formal institutions was largely anathema to Germany. In the new republic, the state, its administration, and the citizenry were no longer supposed to constitute an organic totality, as had been the case in the past. The state was supposed to be receptive to the wishes of the citizenry without being open to populism. But Germany's new citizens had yet to create an active civil society. The initial response of many to the Nazi debacle was to withdraw from the social realm and avoid anything that smacked of the political.

Most West Germans warmed up to the democracy designed for them, sweetened as it was by economic recovery and guided by Adenauer's firm hand. Democratic engagement meant going to the ballot box every few years to vote, which West Germans did, in impressive numbers. If an individual wanted to be more involved in politics, he could join one of the political parties. Politics was the business of the parties, their professional politicians, and the various government institutions. This suited both a population that was accustomed to being led, and the political parties, which naturally wanted political engagement channeled through their structures.

Contrary to these inclinations, and spurred by the legacy of the Nazis, civic protest did break out in the Federal Republic's early years—over rearmament, the single most divisive issue of the 1950s.* The newly born Federal Republic was a country without an army; indeed, its constitution prohibited it from having one. Moreover, the Allies intended "demilitarization" to go beyond disarmament, to begin a sociocultural process of "extinguishing militarization as a mindset," as historian Konrad Jarausch argues.[17] German history, it was asserted, had bred a national fixation with militarism per se, "a deep-seated respect of the military, a pride in its victories, and a wide-spread belief in the necessity of wars."[18] Jarausch argues that the trauma of the war and the magnitude of Germany's defeat convinced many Germans that demilitarization was necessary. Germany's turn away from "blood and iron," thought many, was nonnegotiable and, in the early fifties, just getting started.

But it wasn't long after the republic's creation that Adenauer began floating the idea of making some kind of military contribution to the western defense effort—in return for greater sovereignty. Adenauer's motives weren't militaristic (he had never fired a gun himself); rather, he saw armament as a means to cement the country in the western camp as well as to put the Federal Republic on a more level playing field with its allies. With the Cold War raging, the United States, so recently the proponent of a thorough-going demilitarization of West Germany, was the first to broach the possibility of Bonn's supplying the Atlantic Alliance with conventional forces. It was inconceivable that the Federal Republic field its own army so soon after the war, but West German units under international command

* In addition to the peace and disarmament campaigns, smaller and shorter-lived protests, including strikes, flared up in the early Federal Republic over issues as diverse as the mistreatment of (West) German communists, housing shortages and price rises, unpaid wages, the (British) confiscation of German factories, the lost eastern territories, and the conditions of fellow Germans in the GDR. During three weeks in 1952, half a million workers and other employees demonstrated against the *Betriebsverfassungsgesetz*, a new law that restricted the participation of workers in the decision-making structures of their firms. See Wolfgang Kraushaar, *Die Protest-Chronik 1949–1959: Eine illustrierte Geschichte von Bewegung, Widerstand und Utopie*, Volume 1, (Hamburg: Rogner & Bernhard, 1996).

was another story, particularly after the communist North Korea's invasion of South Korea in June 1950, which ratcheted up East–West tensions. While the plan to create a West German army this early was vetoed by the wary French, it also encountered impassioned opposition at home.

Although uncoordinated and without strategy, the Ohne Mich (Without Me) movement in the early 1950s attracted sympathy from unexpectedly broad swaths of West Germans, including young people, anti-western nationalists, pacifists and antimilitarists, communists, and trade unionists, as well as many Protestant laypeople and clergy. Its symbolic leader was the outspoken Lutheran pastor Martin Niemöller, who had commanded a submarine in World War I and then done time in Hitler's camps for his resistance to the Nazi regime. The spontaneous protests that erupted in a dozen West German cities in 1950 reflected the extent of the shock and trauma that the war had caused. A sign of the emotional popular aversion to militarism was one opinion poll that showed over 70 percent of Germans[19] (and 90 percent of students[20]) in the American zones opposed to rearmament. But the diffuse protests fizzled quickly. There was too little in common to hold together the protesters who opposed Bonn's military plans for very different reasons.

From the beginning, the country's biggest opposition party, the Social Democrats (SPD), was ambivalent about the early peace protests. The Without Me campaign and other early incarnations of the peace movement attracted strong interest from the SPD rank-and-file and some of its leaders. But, in addition to a reflexive suspicion of initiatives beyond its control, the party was willing to accept partial rearmament under certain conditions. Its reservations about arming the Federal Republic weren't based primarily on ethical or pacifist grounds but rather on the axiom that a West Germany anchored so solidly in the western alliance—and with weapons pointing at the other Germany—lessened the likelihood of reconciliation between the two states and, eventually, German unification. Yet, despite its qualms about the protests, the SPD lent them its reserved support; after all, it didn't want to ignore such a potent source of anti-government sentiment.

At the urging of Washington and London, France reluctantly dropped its opposition to a West German fighting force in 1954. Yet Bonn's scheduled entry into NATO and the formal sanctioning of domestic rearmament still unnerved a great many Germans. At no time during the first half of the 1950s did the creation of a German army have majority support.[21] The peace protests received a second wind in 1954–55 in response to the Bundestag's votes on rearmament and NATO membership. In a belated and futile act, the Social Democrats and the trade unions, joined by church leaders, issued the German Manifesto in Frankfurt's Paulskirche, calling for mass mobilization to stop the treaty. More than a million people demonstrated against the so-called Paris Treaties during the short-lived Paulskirche movement.[22] But the treaties were done deals and West Germany joined NATO's ranks as planned. When the SPD withdrew its organizational support, the protests dissipated almost at once.

A final, equally unsuccessful phase of the 1950s peace movement began two years later, when Bonn announced that NATO forces had nuclear weapons stationed in the country.[23] Throwing fuel on the fire, Adenauer began to lobby openly for equipping West Germany's own military, the Bundeswehr, with nuclear weaponry. A new initiative called Kampf dem Atomtod (Campaign against Nuclear Death), modeled after the recently formed Campaign for Nuclear Disarmament in Britain, was broader based than the Paulskirche movement. In addition to the Social Democrats and West Germany's biggest trade union, which were behind it, the campaign brought together leading scientists and other intellectuals (among them writer Heinrich Böll), student groups, liberal politicians, women's groups, and even a former CDU cabinet minister, Gustav Heinemann. West German communists, with their party banned, latched on to the new campaign, which enabled the government to brand the entire endeavor a Soviet-inspired ploy. The Nuclear Death campaign called upon "all Germans" to voice their opposition to the life-or-death issue. The existential message had considerable resonance despite the Bonn government's attacks on the movement. Surveys showed that between 64 and 72 percent of West Germans opposed arming the Bundeswehr with nuclear weapons.[24] Rallies, demonstrations, petitions, and even threatened strikes were organized through the campaign's regional structures, thereby utilizing new space outside the traditional realm of the political parties. A high point in the campaign, an April 1958 demonstration in the northern city of Hamburg, rallied 150,000 people.[25] However, once the plans became a fait accompli, the Social Democrats began to backtrack on disarmament, leaving the movement stranded again. But this time the lesson was not lost on independent-minded activists, including many freshly disillusioned Social Democrats: an extra-parliamentary movement could not rely on parliamentary parties to do its work.

The Federal Republic's first sustained civic movement came in the form of the Easter March rallies, which gave many young Germans such as Joschka Fischer from Öffingen and Ede Fischer from Bad Cannstadt a taste of street politics for the first time. Another idea borrowed from British peace activists, the first nationwide Easter Sunday rallies in 1960 attracted 50,000 people who marched "against nuclear weapons of every kind in every nation." In Stuttgart only a few dozen activists showed up for the first event. But the low-key protests gathered momentum and sophistication during the course of the decade, peaking in 1967 with 800 events across the country and over 300,000 participants.[26]

The Easter March campaign differed from its predecessors in that it shunned the involvement of political parties and other organizations, stressing instead an "individual's power" to speak his mind. Year after year the movement's scope expanded to issues such as the recognition of postwar Germany's borders, the country's media monopolies, and even university reform. In Stuttgart, by the mid-sixties, the movement sponsored annual marches on August 6, commemorating the day the first atomic bomb fell on Hiroshima in 1945, as well as cultural events, sit-ins, media campaigns, and panel discussions. The Easter March movement, noted one chronicler, transformed itself from an ethical and pacifist movement into a "critical social campaign for the democratization of society."[27]

In neighboring East Germany, the conditions for civic action and extra-parliamentary protest were fundamentally different. The single-party state rejected liberal notions of free speech and assembly, as well as social and political pluralism. There were, in the early 1950s GDR, a good deal of "street politics," but orchestrated from above rather than inspired from below. Mass rallies and demonstrations were carefully choreographed by the various state-allied, communist organizations.

The East German state's reflexes were tested—and its relationship to independent protest crassly underscored—in the fourth year of its existence, in mid-June 1953, when protests broke out in East Berlin and spread throughout the country. The demonstrations, which turned into a full-scale revolt, were initiated by disgruntled workers on the construction sites of East Berlin's Stalinallee, the gigantic, Soviet-style boulevard in-the-making that was to be the showpiece of the workers' and farmers' state. Frustration with a new increase in production norms boiled over as the disaffected work brigade marched through East Berlin's streets, the ranks swelling with other workers and ordinary citizens. After just an hour, a crowd of 5,000 people was venting general dissatisfaction with the regime, some even calling for free elections and the withdrawal of Soviet troops. The protests continued into the next day with more than 100,000 people on the streets in East Berlin and smaller demonstrations in more than 250 other cities across the country.

Shops and parked cars were burned, government buildings were attacked. The unrest had turned into a revolt against the communist regime, and the leadership—with the aid of the Soviets—responded with full force. Tanks descended on the city on June 17, which crushed the resistance together with the East German *Volkspolizei*. When it was over, 267 people had been killed; 1,067 others were seriously injured; 4,000 people were arrested; and 200 had been shot after a year of show trials.[28]

The hard-learned lesson of June 17, 1953, was that the state would not tolerate independent, system-critical activism. Never again (until the wall fell in 1989) would the East German authorities allow civic protest to spin out of control. All independent-minded movements would be subverted or repressed before things got that far. The regime's heavy-handed response (duplicated by other East bloc leaderships in Hungary in 1956, in Prague in 1968, and many times in Poland) illustrated that there would be no reforming the Soviet-style states from below.

The New Social Democrats

The tectonic shifts occurring within the SPD itself were decisive to the events that would shape the Federal Republic in the sixties and beyond. The Social Democrats' sluggish results in election after election forced the party to rethink its program and strategy. Its socialist jargon sounded ever more out of step in modernizing West Germany, as did its commitment to neutrality against the backdrop of the Cold War. Either it had to adapt, agreed its leadership, or remain in opposition forever.

In an extraordinary 1959 congress, in a little spa town outside of Bonn called Bad Godesberg, the party broke with a century of tradition. It dropped its explicit working-class orientation in favor of that of an all-inclusive "people's party," one that appealed to West Germany's burgeoning middle class as well as other voters. Bad Godesberg became synonymous with the party's historic shift to the center when it made its peace with capitalism and other tenets of liberalism. The SPD jettisoned the Marxist-sounding rhetoric of class struggle, planned economies, and nationalized industry. A year later, the party scrapped its longstanding insistence on neutrality for the Federal Republic and accepted the *Westbindung*, as well as the nuclear defense policy, as fact and necessity. Not only were the Social Democrats trying to win votes; they also recognized that if they were ever to come to power, it would be in a coalition. Neither the Christian Democrats nor the liberal Free Democrats—the only two alternatives—would consider the possibility with an unreconstructed SPD.

The new face of the SPD was West Berlin's energetic and popular mayor, Willy Brandt. The handsome, lanky Brandt, with his pronounced Slavic cheekbones and high forehead, was probably the only mayor in all of Europe with international stature. During the hottest years of the Cold War, West Berlin wasn't just any city: it was a dramatic symbol of the West's determination to confront Soviet communism. This symbolism became even more potent when, when on August 13, 1961, the East German authorities erected a cinder-block and barbed-wire partition through the city's center—the first incarnation of the Berlin Wall. With the world's eyes trained on the divided city in summer 1961, Willy Brandt held the Federal Republic's flag high—and indeed that of the entire West. Addressing the outraged crowds in the now-sealed off western side of the city, he personified the West's defiant commitment to a free West Berlin, even if, in the end, President John F. Kennedy wasn't prepared to risk another world war to turn back the Soviet tanks at the border. When Kennedy came to Berlin two years later, TV cameras from around the globe showed the Berlin mayor in an open limousine touring the western parts of the city with the American president. Later that day, Kennedy gave his famous "*Ich bin ein Berliner*" speech with Brandt, who was often compared to Kennedy, standing solemnly beside him.

Brandt was born in 1913, in the former Hansiatic city of Lübeck, an illegitimate child of a working-class mother. His Christian name was Herbert Frahm, "Willy Brandt" an alias that he took later in the anti-Nazi underground. As a youngster, he grew up in the milieu of the German labor movement. As it was in those days, one's parents' class and politics determined which youth groups, summer camps, and sports clubs one belonged to—and the party that whole families voted for. When the Nazis came to power, Brandt fled to Scandinavia, where he worked as a journalist and trade union activist. He covered the Spanish civil war from the Republican side and infiltrated Nazi Germany briefly in 1936. When the Nazis attacked Norway, he donned a Norwegian uniform and was taken prisoner. With his wife, Rut, he returned to Berlin after the war—both of them in Norwegian uniforms, on the side of the occupation powers. Like other émigrés, Brandt came back to Germany to aid in its democratic reconstruction. In 1947 he began his political career with the SPD, first in Hanover and then in Berlin, where he was the western zones' German liaison to the Allied high command.[29]

Because of his anti-Nazi past, Brandt was an extremely divisive figure in West Germany. His biography made him a prime target of German nationalists. Right-wing circles labeled Brandt a coward and *Vaterlandsverräter* (a traitor to the homeland). A sign of the times, in the 1950s and even into the 1960s, many Germans still considered former antifascist exiles like Brandt and actress Marlene Dietrich, to name just two, to be "unfaithful Germans." But Brandt's many admirers found in him a simple, warm, and direct man, a politician who was passionate about politics and about life. He could joke with ordinary people, play the mandolin, and enjoy his drink. Unlike some of his Social Democrat colleagues, he never sympathized with orthodox communism or believed that the SPD could find common ground with East Germany's hardline rulers. With his unique credentials as both anti-Nazi exile and staunch cold warrior, he was the ideal candidate to represent the newly repositioned Social Democrats.

The Godesberg course and Brandt's ascendance paid off for the party, albeit more gradually than anticipated. In the 1961 federal elections, with Brandt as the SPD's lead candidate, the party gained ground and the Christian Democrats lost their absolute majority, although they remained in power. Four years later, the SPD captured even more of the vote, although still not enough to dislodge the conservatives, whose leader and now chancellor was no longer Adenauer but the economist Ludwig Erhard, the father of the economic miracle. The SPD's makeover won it votes from the republic's center but stranded others who remained convinced that socialism was a worthy ideal. Younger voters sensed that the party had acted out of unvarnished opportunism—accepting the conservative status quo rather than be damned to eternal opposition. Easter March activists and their like were already disillusioned with the Social Democrats' equivocation on armament, nuclear weapons, and grassroots activism. A relatively new, explicitly left-wing magazine, *Konkret*, addressed many of the issues of this "homeless left"—those postwar German leftists whose sympathies lay somewhere between that of the (banned) West German communist party and the post-Godesberg SPD.

Club Voltaire

In Stuttgart, activists such as Peter Grohmann, a typesetter with a working-class background, helped nurse the Easter March into a full-fledged movement. An SPD member since his youth, Grohmann paid for his involvement in the marches with expulsion from the party. A disciplinary committee held that Grohmann was working together with East bloc agents. To the best of his knowledge, this was a lie. But years later Grohmann discovered that the tribunal had been right; the Stuttgart Easter March had been infiltrated by East German spies, his co-worker a paid agent. GDR plants and pro-Moscow fronts did infiltrate the peace campaigns in the Federal Republic and would continue to do so through the 1980s.[30] But at no time were these movements controlled by foreign agents, as was charged.

Grohmann and friends from the Easter March circle agreed that Stuttgart needed a permanent location for meetings, as well as for performances and other informal events—a space for counterculture, although they didn't put it that way. The informal search committee included Stuttgarters like the Spanish Civil War veteran Fritz Lamm and the left-wing trade unionist Willi Hoss.[31] "Stuttgart then was so very *spiessig*," says Grohmann, using a hard-to-translate German word that captures the provincial worst of "petty bourgeois." "We wanted to break open the closed discourse, provide a place where people with fresh ideas could meet and talk." They launched Club Voltaire in 1964, turning an old shopfront in the red-light district into a coffee house with regular events. Grohmann, today a cabaret actor in his seventies and still an everywhere-at-once activist in Stuttgart, digs up a fistful of dog-eared Club Voltaire handbills from an old box in his cellar. Faded but legible on coarse dull paper, the schedules are mimeographed and hand-illustrated. They advertise an impressive assortment of jazz concerts, literary evenings, a French *nouvelle vague* film series, open discussions, and art exhibitions.

Club Voltaire had been around for a couple of years when Grohmann first remembers a brash teenager in a rumpled trench coat stopping by. Grohmann was hard at work whitewashing the place one afternoon. "I came from a working-class background," says Grohmann, "so I thought walls have to be white, the place has to look orderly, you know. But this young guy and his girl looked at the job I was doing with real contempt. The guy, it was Joschka Fischer, took the lit cigarette out of his mouth and stuck it in the paint, stirring it around until the paint turned a bit gray. 'There,' he said, 'that's better,' and the two walked away." The encounter made an unpleasant impression on Grohmann—not the last time that Fischer's cockiness would put people off.

It was at Club Voltaire that Fischer crossed paths with his first wife-to-be, Edeltraud Fischer, the young woman from the cigarette story. Only seventeen at the time, Ede was a petite girl with close-cropped dark hair and catlike eyes. The daughter of a local police officer, she sought refuge in Club Voltaire from her overbearing family. For her, the club was an oasis. "It was where all the nonconformists met up, all the leftists, peace activists, the Stuttgart art students," remembers Ede. Among them were people like Fritz Lamm and Willi Hoss, who befriended Ede and Joschka. "You didn't even need any money to sit in Club Voltaire and listen to the music or whatever," says Ede. "Drinks were real cheap. There was nothing like it anywhere else. It was, well, *alive*." Her first sense of Joschka was of a big-mouthed know-it-all, obviously a shared opinion at Club Voltaire. He, however, was smitten from the start.

The two got to chatting one day on the central Schlossplatz, in front of Stuttgart's handsomely restored New Palace, the hangout for disaffected teenagers and street musicians. She one-upped Joschka with tales of shop-lifting sprees and plans for worldly travels. She told him that she was leaving soon for France. He could join her, if he wanted.

With just twenty deutschmarks, one sleeping bag, and a few sandwiches between them, Joschka and Edeltraud hit the road, Paris bound. Only during their first hitched ride did they ascertain that they shared the same last name—or so the story goes. Apparently, they split their sides laughing. It boded well for the adventure. The kindred souls spent nights under bridges and then, as winter turned harsh, on top of the Paris Metro's ventilation grates to keep from freezing. They shoplifted to fill their stomachs, concealing food items in the linings of their long coats, thus sharpening their skills in a trade that would later, as book thieves, provide their main source of income. From Paris they moved to Amsterdam, where they hung out with the anarchist Provos on their houseboats, and then south again to Marseille, earning enough to eat by creating sidewalk art for well-heeled tourists. The former altar boy drew colorful Biblical scenes while Ede's efforts were more abstract. They were a good combo, and before they knew it, they were in love.

In early 1967, their wanderlust temporarily exhausted, the pair returned to a Germany that looked all the more parochial. The two Fischers, both under twenty-one, were ineligible to marry without parental permission, another of Germany's anachronistic rules. Ede wasn't even on speaking terms with her father, and Elisabeth Fischer wouldn't hear of it. But the two were stubbornly determined—not only was it what they wanted but it was an act of rebellion, too. So they hitchhiked to Gretna Green, Scotland, where minors could marry. They returned in April 1967 as Mr. and Mrs. Fischer.

As unlikely as it may seem, in Gretna Green a German photographer snapped a photo of the newlyweds, which, bizarrely, was picked up by the wire services and published in West Germany's biggest tabloid daily, *Bild-Zeitung*. The paper ran the picture and a caption as a short human-interest story. In it, Joschka, serious, slim, and wearing a short jeans jacket over a turtleneck, stands holding the bride's hand. Ede, looking very pretty on her wedding day, appears equally serious in a double-breasted pant suit, her dark hair styled in a pixie cut. Attire aside, neither looks any more rebellious than did Elisabeth and Jozsef thirty years earlier. The caption, "Fischer Wedding in Gretna Green," reads: "Since the parents of Edeltraud Fischer (18) from Stuttgart-Stammheim and Joschka Fischer (19) from Fellbach were against a wedding, the two hitchhiked to the 'Marriage Paradise' Gretna Green. There they wed."

Part II

The Red Decade

3

Anti-Authoritarian Revolt

> "In order to change society you have to change yourself, and in order to change yourself you have to change society."
> —Fritz Teufel, co-founder, Kommune I

> "Today's fascism isn't manifest in one party or one person but rather it lies in the everyday socialization of people that turns them into authoritarian personalities. It is part of the way we are raised. It is intrinsic to the logic of our institutions."
> —Student leader Rudi Dutschke, 1968

On December 1, 1966, the Federal Republic took a historic step into uncharted territory, one with enormous implications for the country. For the first time in the postwar era, the Social Democrats—after seventeen years in opposition—joined the Christian Democrats in the government, in a "grand coalition." The last time that the SPD had shared power was during the Weimar Republic, and there were many who had begun to wonder whether the storied party would ever claw its way out of the opposition, the conservative clinch on the country simply too strong to break. But with the economic miracle running out of steam and West Germany experiencing its first taste of recession, many inside as well as outside of the political establishment had grown exasperated with Ludwig Erhard, a more able economist than chancellor. The Free Democrats withdrew from the ruling coalition and the government fell. The Christians Democrats were still the largest party, but the new situation opened the way for the Social Democrats to become the conservatives' junior partner. In a breathtaking development, the new foreign minister and vice-chancellor turned out to be none other than the former antifascist exile, Willy Brandt.

Yet the creation of the grand coalition outraged the SPD's critics on the left. Now there was effectively no opposition in the Bundestag to the government's will, they charged. The pact was all the more unpalatable to them for the conservative's choice for chancellor: Kurt Georg Kiesinger, who had been more than a mere fellow traveler under Hitler. Kiesinger joined the Nazi party in 1933 and made his career in the propaganda section of the Reich's foreign ministry. He left the party only when it was disbanded by the Allies in 1945. And only marginally less reprehensible was the new defense minister, Franz Josef Strauss, the ham-fisted anticommunist and key player in the 1962 Spiegel Affair, the scandal that precipitated Adenauer's downfall. Writer Günter Grass, a staunch Social Democrat and confidant of Brandt, called the new leadership "a miserable marriage."[1] In a prophetic letter to Brandt, Grass predicted that West Germany's youth "would turn away from the state and its constitution and . . . gravitate to the [far] left and the [far] right."[2] Across the territory of the Federal Republic, SPD dissidents and other leftists launched impromptu demonstrations. At a rally in West Berlin, a student activist by the name of Rudi Dutschke, perched on the top of a truck with megaphone in hand, quoted the interwar communist Rosa Luxemburg, who had called the SPD a "stinking corpse."[3] Opposition in the Federal Republic, concluded many, was now going to have to come from outside of the Bundestag.

Vietnam Is Auschwitz

The repertoire of Club Voltaire in Stuttgart and the evolution of the Easter Marches reflected stirrings of restiveness and awakened curiosity across West Germany. In larger metropolises, such as Frankfurt, West Berlin, Hamburg, and Munich, there were also Club Voltaires or like-minded Republican Clubs, as there were in Tübingen, Freiburg, and many other smaller cities and towns.*

In particular, it was in and around West Germany's universities that a new political consciousness was germinating. This mid-sixties generation

---

* By the late sixties, there were forty-six Republican Clubs as well as an unknown number of Voltaire Clubs in the Federal Republic. See Michael Schmidtke, *Der Aufbruch der jungen Intelligenz: Die 68er in der Bundesrepublik und den USA* (Frankfurt: Campus Verlag, 2003), 130.

of students and junior faculty were avidly reading and discussing the sharp-edged critiques of intellectuals such as philosopher Karl Jaspers, Grass, and Böll, as well as playwright Rolf Hochhuth, writers Hans Magnus Enzensberger, and Alfred Andersch, and the psychologist couple Alexander and Margarete Mitscherlich, among many others. The topics, as well as the modes of expression, were novel to the universities, which in the past had been reliable bastions of conservatism in Germany.

West Berlin and its Free University were shaping up as the hotbed of this dissidence. Ironically, this U.S.-financed institution (the "free" alternative to the "not free" university in the eastern zone*) was attracting a disproportionate number of left-leaning young men for the reason that German males in West Berlin, where the Occupation Treaty remained in force, were ineligible for military conscription. To avoid the draft, men of conscription age, many nonstudents among them, simply moved to West Berlin. (West German authorities tried to stem the flow by patrolling the rail connections and highways between western Germany and West Berlin, apprehending and returning on-the-run draftees.) Another factor was that the young Free University was an experiment in democracy itself, with the student body envisioned to have an active voice in university affairs. This model was understandably attractive to young, independent-minded Germans.[4]

Yet, by the mid-1960s the student body's role was still minimal and impatient students were upping the pressure on the administration to abide by its mandate. They maintained that the structures and curricula of even the comparatively progressive Free University were autocratic, to say nothing of the stuck-in-their-ways universities elsewhere in western Germany. In a way, the students were taking the Americans at their word

---

* The Freie Universität Berlin was founded in December 1948 when a group of students were, on political grounds, turned away from Berlin's main university (later to be renamed Humboldt University) in the city's Soviet sector. The Free University was subsequently financed and built by the (West) Berlin city administration and the American occupation authorities, and it received considerable funding from the U.S.-based Ford Foundation. In June 1963, President John F. Kennedy visited the Free University to underscore the United States commitment to the institution and West Berlin in general. He told the students: "This school in not interested in turning out merely corporation lawyers and skilled accountants. What it is interested in—and this must be true of every university—it must be interested in turning out citizens of the world, men who comprehend the difficult, sensitive tasks that lie before us as free men and women, and men who are willing to commit their energies to the advancement of a free society" (see web.fu-berlin.de/presse/publikationen/img/jfkennedy/pdf [accessed July 20, 2006]).

and picking up democratization where the occupiers had left off, which was what the western Allies had intended.[5] German universities didn't have a tradition of critical discourse on contemporary issues—neither among faculty nor students. So, in study groups, open discussions, and "teach-ins," they were meeting outside the classroom to debate issues that weren't addressed in the classroom: the war in Vietnam, nuclear weapons in the Federal Republic, the plight of the Third World.

The backward state of West Germany's universities, claimed students, reflected the condition of the republic at large. In May 1965, for example, at the Free University, student activists organized a public discussion titled "Restoration or New Beginning? The Federal Republic at 20." But the university's president canceled the event on the grounds that the keynote speaker, a West Berlin author, had in the past "libeled" the university. The Free University administration, like its counterparts in western Germany, wanted to "keep politics out of the university," a response, in part, to the Nazis' crass politicization of education at all levels, as well as to the time-honored disengagement of higher education in Germany from the political world. The students countered that it was the "unpolitical universities" of the Weimar years that had capitulated so feebly to National Socialism. The banned talk, the students insisted, was a free-speech issue, much like the one that prompted the Berkeley Free Speech Movement in the United States two years previously.[6] As far as they were concerned, the president's high-handed response illustrated that the university, like the entire Federal Republic, was democratic on paper but not in practice.

The West German students were acutely aware of the political ferment on campuses in the United States, Italy, Great Britain, and elsewhere. Topic number one was the war in Vietnam. Under President Lyndon Johnson, U.S. military involvement in Vietnam had escalated dramatically in the mid-1960s. In light of China's communist takeover in 1949, the American leadership was convinced that it had to react forcefully to stop the march of communism across Asia. Consecutive American administrations had based their geostrategic security policies on the "domino theory"—namely, that the fall of one country in a given region to communism would set off a chain reaction. The next domino most likely to fall, Washington had concluded, was Vietnam. In 1963, the year of John F. Kennedy's assassination, there were 16,300 U.S. troops stationed there. By 1965 that number had shot up to 184,000 and then a year later to 385,000.[7] The massive U.S. air campaigns against the communist Vietcong were ravaging the country and killing thousands of civilians, but without substantial impact on Ho Chi Min's guerrilla army.

In the United States the first of the spectacular Marches on Washington to End the War in Vietnam in April 1965 attracted about 25,000 people.[8] On American campuses, politicized students were borrowing liberally from the civil rights movement, as well as working together with it, holding sit-ins and staging other acts of civil disobedience to protest mounting U.S. involvement in Southeast Asia. Student-led movements in Great Britain, Italy, and (a bit later than elsewhere) in France were also beginning to mobilize against the war. In West Germany, growing ranks of students marched side by side with activists from the Easter Marches in antiwar protests, as well as organizing their own campus events. While the Bonn government politely declined the Johnson administration's request for direct West German military support for the war, the chancellor at the time, Ludwig Erhard, underlined that Washington's policies in Vietnam had his country's full moral support as part of their larger, common battle against communism.[9] Remarkably, the U.S. government—in the name of anticommunism—was prepared to condone West German military engagement outside its borders long before the West Germans themselves were.

As much as the budding West German student movement shared with its international peers, it had an array of "German questions" that were entirely its own. Self-organized study groups had begun exploring different facets of the Nazi legacy and questioning their implications for the Federal Republic. One focus of their research was the wartime backgrounds of university administrations and faculty. They discovered that a shocking proportion of their academic mentors had collaborated with the Hitler regime, some in high positions. Either explain yourselves publicly, they charged, or resign. A petition started at the Free University demanded that the state purge its justice system of judges and state attorneys who had handed down death sentences during Nazi rule. It gathered 2,000 signatures. Other such do-it-yourself initiatives constituted solid *Geschichtsbewältigung* "from below"—namely, the processing of the past, undertaken by student, church, and other actors because of officialdom's failure to do so. Most of the university administrations responded evasively to the initiatives instead of embracing them; at worst, some even branded the students "Nazis" themselves for their activism.

While the German students of the late sixties weren't responsible for restarting debate about the Nazi legacy in the Federal Republic, as is sometimes claimed in retrospect, they were the first larger audience that was prepared to listen to the critical intellectuals who had—and to act upon the conclusions that they drew from that discourse. The students' engagement with the Nazi past affected the way they looked at just about everything. They arrived at the conclusion that they, as Germans, weren't absolved of responsibility for the world war and the Holocaust simply by dint of being born postwar. One of their key sources was Karl Jaspers's 1946 essay, *The Question of German Guilt,* which was finally being read widely and discussed in West Germany. In it he spoke of Germans "confronting the guilt" of the Nazi era together—and publicly—as a means of national catharsis. Likewise, twenty years later German philosopher Theodor W. Adorno, in a famous radio address "Education after Auschwitz," spoke of reorganizing the entire education system and child-raising around the principle of preventing another Holocaust. "That Auschwitz be never again," he wrote, "this is the very first demand of education."

The children of the postwar era didn't feel that they enjoyed a "grace of late birth," as others would maintain. For them, to abstractly reject genocide and war was too facile, as it was to condemn the Hitler dictatorship in general terms—just about everyone could do that. Rather, they concluded that it was their moral and political obligation to take on the responsibility that their parents and older siblings had abdicated—and to engage in the world accordingly. The West German students, unlike their global counterparts, felt that they had a unique debt to repay to civilization, which, among other imperatives, meant restructuring German society in such a way that "Auschwitz" (which only during the 1960s became a metaphor pars pro toto for the Holocaust) could never happen again. Much later, Joschka Fischer said that through the various twists and turns in his own political journey the two political constants were "Never again Auschwitz" and "Never again war," a declaration that many of his generation could echo.

While Vietnam, for example, was a key issue for student movements everywhere, in the Federal Republic it had unique significance. On TV everyone could see the horrors of the raging war between the U.S.-backed South Vietnamese government and the communist Vietcong—women and children burned to death by napalm, carpet bombing, massacres of civilians. Student activists from Bavaria to Berkeley were of one mind that this was barbaric and wrong. But many West German students jumped quickly to World War II analogies, which obviously were close at hand. They likened the U.S. bombing of Vietnam to the 1940 German invasion of Poland, the use of napalm to the gas chambers. The *Massenmord* (mass murder) in Vietnam was compared to the *Völkermord* (genocide) during the Nazi reign. Germany's past, they concluded, compelled them to act according to moral imperatives, in active opposition to the government and society at large, if that was necessary. They felt a unique—and urgent—compulsion to oppose the Vietnam War, as well as other injustices, based on the lessons of German history.

Moreover, for the West Germans, Vietnam had special geopolitical implications. Many understood the U.S. war against the Vietcong as a displaced "hot front" of the Cold War. The real frontline of the superpower stand-off ran straight through Germany—indeed, it divided Berlin. The United States and its allies were supposedly fighting to keep global communism at bay, in Southeast Asia as elsewhere in the world—for example, in cold-war Europe, where West Berlin was its most vulnerable strategic point, as well as the West's showcase in the East bloc for free-market prosperity. In other words, the Germans interpreted the war in Vietnam as being waged *on their behalf*—and their government in Bonn was actively supporting it, as it supported (so the students claimed) everything Washington did. This was the reality of Adenauer's *Westbindung*, which the ruling grand coalition accepted no more critically than had its predecessors.

Another feature of the West German students' perspective was its deep skepticism about its own government's democratic legitimacy and intentions. There is no better example than the bitter standoff between the West German left and the republic's leaders over the *Notstandsgesetze*, the proposed emergency powers laws. The constitutional amendment would empower the state to take "extraordinary measures" in the case of war or natural catastrophe, including the option of mobilizing the military. In fact, all of West Germany's neighboring democracies, as well as the United States and Canada, were vested with similar powers to declare a state of emergency. But in the case of postwar West Germany these powers still rested with the western Allies. By 1960 the Allies were prepared to hand them over to Bonn once the Federal Republic passed legislation defining the laws. But what might have been "normal" elsewhere in democratic Europe or across the Atlantic was not so in West Germany. So tenuous was the state's credibility with its critics that they saw the emergency laws as the empowerment of the republic's leaders to circumvent democracy by declaring it necessary to do so. After all, this is exactly what Adolf Hitler did in 1933 when, as chancellor, he was granted extraordinary emergency powers that he promptly used to usher in the Nazi dictatorship.

Also, by the mid-1960s, West German students had already begun sampling a theoretical discourse that would inspire their activism and give it direction. A movement called the New Left had recently emerged with input from both sides of the Atlantic. Its proponents, among them the founding editors of London's *New Left Review*, embraced an undogmatic democratic socialism that distinguished itself from the reductive, class-based "old left" of the various communist and socialist parties. Proudly eclectic, it drew from existentialism and psychoanalysis, as well as the full Marxist tradition—in particular Marx's early writings. In contrast to orthodox Marxism, the New Left emphasized the importance of individual emancipation and the transformation of the sociocultural realm. If society was going to be transformed—and the New Left firmly believed that this was its purpose—then social change was contingent on more than altering the mode of production; it had to transform the way people lived, behaved, thought—and even loved. Once consciousness was changed, human subjects would automatically remake the world around them into one that suited their real needs and desires.

A handful of the most important New Left progenitors came from Germany, including the exile philosopher Herbert Marcuse, who was teaching at the University of California, San Diego. One staple of the New Left canon was Marcuse's 1964 *One Dimensional Man*, in which West German students, like their American counterparts, found a fitting description of their apolitical, mass-media-fed culture. Dog-eared copies of *One Dimensional Man* (published originally in English, in the United States) were passed around West German campuses before the translation came out in German. Marcuse argued that through technology a dominant form of thinking is created, one that suspends critical judgment and conforms to the status quo. Social control today, he claimed, functioned without the ugly repressive apparatus required in the past to suppress original, critical thought. Although Marcuse's critique was of contemporary society, the project had its origins in the attempt by Marcuse and other exile thinkers to explain how fascism took root and won acceptance in 1930s Germany.

Another extremely influential work in the same vein was *The Authoritarian Personality*, a study conducted by Marcuse's exile colleagues at the New School for Social Research in New York City during the late 1940s. The survey found that many characteristics of an "authoritarian personality" could be found even in mainstream America—such as a high propensity to conformism, to uncritical political loyalty, to distrust of otherness, and an inclination to persecute the weak. The study's authors, among them philosopher Adorno, didn't however conclude that the United States was thus a fascist society, even if illiberal convictions were more prevalent than one might have suspected. Likewise, Marcuse drew parallels between the Nazi past and the present, but didn't equate the two. To many German students, however, these conditions seemed to describe quite accurately not only the proclivities that inspired Germans to collaborate with the Nazis but also the disposition of a good proportion of their fellow countrymen. It appeared to them that the state form had changed, but not with it the essential mode of thinking in contemporary Germany.

As early as 1966 Marcuse had returned to Germany from California expressly to brainstorm with West German students and encourage their mobilizing against the Vietnam War. In the white-haired Herbert Marcuse, already the sage of the American college-based organization Students for a Democratic Society (SDS), West German students also found an ally and mentor. Importantly, neither Marcuse nor other New Left thinkers stopped at a critique of society; they endorsed the possibility of changing it in order to create a better society. Social groups other than the working class, including student bodies, could initiate social transformation. During his visit, in Frankfurt, Marcuse met with one of the campus groups, the Socialist German Student Union (Sozialistische Deutsche Studentenbund), also known as SDS.*

The German SDS considered itself part of the New Left movement and had recently established a profile on West German campuses through its antiwar organizing and lively discussions and forums. Some students had learned about SDS before arriving at the university through a touring exhibition it had sponsored examining the Nazi justice system. The SDS even had a charismatic frontman in Rudi Dutschke, a twenty-seven-year-old sociology student who was becoming known beyond the circles of the West Berlin SDS.

Founded in the postwar years, the SDS had always been close to the Social Democrats, although never strictly their youth organization. It defined itself as socialist and Marxist but thoroughly democratic, rejecting out of hand, for example, the East bloc's bureaucratic socialism as a model. During the 1950s the budding socialists and radical democrats of the SDS sniped at the SPD's "functionaries" for failing to capitalize on the disarmament and peace movements, and for steadily abandoning the very ideals that inspired them. Rather than reinvigorating social democracy with fresh ideas, the party had cast off its socialist heritage altogether, so the students claimed. The Godesberg reforms were a pill too bitter for

* In spite of their many affinities and links to one another, it was only chance that the American and German organizations bore the same initials.

the SDS. Tensions grew until in 1961 the Social Democrats declared membership in the party and in SDS to be mutually exclusive, and cut off funding for the wayward students. Rather than crumble after being cast out, the SDS turned adversity to its advantage by underscoring its independence from the SPD.[10] It fortified its freethinking socialism with new "anti-authoritarian" impulses and direct forms of protest. Much of the SDS's energy in the mid-sixties went toward democratic reform of the universities where "bad work conditions, miserable lectures, brain-dead seminars and absurd exam requirements" were the rule, as one manifesto put it.[11] Organizing against the war in Vietnam, the emergency law, and the rise of far-right parties, the SDS gained a foothold in many of West Germany's university towns.

Yet, prior to June 2, 1967, it was just one of a host of student organizations active at the universities. The Social Democrats, the Christian Democrats, the Liberals, the churches, Third World students, the right-wing fraternities, and many other groups all had organizations, too. The SDS wasn't by any means the biggest or the most significant at the time.

The Shooting of Benno Ohnesorg

So pivotal are the events of June 2, 1967, to West Germany that some chroniclers divide the history of the postwar Federal Republic into two parts: before and after the shooting death of student Benno Ohnesorg at the hands of a Berlin police officer.[12] Even though a politicization of the universities was already well underway by spring 1967, Ohnesorg's murder has come to mark the onset of *die Studentenbewegung*, the student movement, in the Federal Republic, in which many non-students like Joschka and Ede Fischer participated. In fact, the killing prompted an escalation of extra-parliamentary dissidence by providing stark confirmation of the worst that many leftists had come to suspect about their flawed republic. Nineteen-year-old Joschka Fischer was just one of his generation thrust on a path of political radicalism after Ohnesorg's shooting. According to his own account, he became a "professional revolutionary" that day. The death of Ohnesorg, a theology major and political novice, triggered a furious outcry and swelled the protest movement—also called the "anti-authoritarian revolt"—with new supporters. Although the rebellion would fail to alter the Bonn Republic's formal structures, as its partisans had intended, it set processes in motion that would transform the nature of German society and West Germany's democracy along with it.

The results of investigations, documentaries, trial proceedings, and testimonies make it possible to reconstruct with considerable accuracy the events of June 2, 1967, and the reaction that energized the West German student movement.[13] The day began with Mohammad Reza Pahlavi, the Shah of Iran, and his glamorous wife, Empress Farah Diba, landing at West Berlin's Tempelhof airport, where the West German government rolled out the red carpet for Iran's controversial leader. On the runway, the Shah, in his medal-studded white uniform, was greeted by the Federal Republic's smiling justice minister, the outspoken pacifist Gustav Heinemann, and, notably, the grand coalition's new foreign minister, Willy Brandt. In joining the coalition six months previous, the Social Democrats had become part of the republic's foreign policy consensus, which included bending to the Americans on Vietnam and consorting with Third World dictators.

The repressive rule of the Shah's western-backed regime had come to the attention of West German students through their Third World colleagues. One in particular was the Teheran-born Bahman Nirumand, a young philosophy lecturer who had studied at a number of West German universities. He returned to Iran to teach, but fled back to West Germany in 1965 to escape arrest and shortly thereafter penned a book widely read at the time, *Persia, Model of a Developing Country or the Dictatorship of the Free World*. At first, says Nirumand, the SDS showed little enthusiasm for organizing against the visit, claiming that it was too busy with Vietnam. But eventually SDS joined the anti-Shah events—although the planned demonstration wasn't originally a priority for the student group. Once the Iranian embassy caught wind of the preparations, it responded promptly, irate about a teach-in that exile Nirumand was to lead at the Free University on the evening before the couple's arrival.

Mocking police methods, the student activists tacked up posters that resembled a "wanted man" handbill. "MURDER," it read: "Wanted, Shah Mohamed Reza Pahlevi, for the murder and torture of journalist Karimpour Schirazi, 71 oppositional officers, and hundreds of communists, civilians and students." It cited the regime's corruption and the vast discrepancy between the royal family's enormous wealth and the Iranian workers' slave wages. The handbill is signed "The International Liberation Front." While the Iranian embassy failed to stop the anti-Shah organizing, it kicked up a storm in the media. "We couldn't have had better advertising," remembers Nirumand.

At the informal teach-in, another concept picked up from American students, over 2,000 people packed the university's biggest lecture hall to hear about Iran, hundreds sitting cross-legged on the floor, others lined up against the walls and spilling out into the corridors. Like prom night photos in a high school yearbook, black-and-white film footage of the event captures the German students at a moment of innocence, unaware that they are on the eve of profound change. They look wide-eyed and fresh-faced, not a scruffy character among them. The men have short-cropped hair, collared shirts, and sport jackets or V-neck sweaters, much like the Berkeley students in *The Graduate.* The female students appear just as conventional, their neat pageboys and modest sweater sets no more hip than their mothers' hairdos or clothing.

West Berlin's mayor had beefed-up security in anticipation of the protests, a sign of the growing tensions between the city's officials and student activists in the politically charged city. The authorities couldn't do much against the communist regime that surrounded West Berlin, but leftist agitators in their own house could be dealt with. Under a Social Democrat-led city hall, the police had already resorted to tougher methods to deal with increasingly testy protests, a new phenomenon in the republic. A number of student-led demonstrations had already ended in confrontations with the West Berlin police—but no one had been seriously injured, much less killed. The newspapers *Bild-Zeitung, BZ, Berliner Morgenpost,* and *Die Welt,* owned by the media magnate Axel Cäsar Springer, had contributed to the volatile atmosphere by running stories about "student rabble-rousers," "communist hooligans," and "Soviet stooges." The Springer press applied Adenauer's anticommunism with vigor, no less intensely in the age of the grand coalition.

Just before noon on June 2, the Shah arrived at the city hall in the Schöneberg district, where about 3,000 people had gathered. In addition to curious on-lookers, a shadowy group of counterdemonstrators—pro-Shah Iranians—also appeared on Kennedy Square. Most of them, according to Nirumand, were Iranian secret service flown in from Iran by the embassy and transported there on Berlin city buses. The student protesters wielded banners reading: "Down with the Military Dictatorship," "Don't Arm the Shah for his War against the Persian People" and "Free Political Prisoners." Many wore Shah and empress masks for the event—paper bags painted with ghoulish images of the royal couple, their eyes cut out for peepholes. In hindsight, former SDS leader Bernd Rabehl describes the atmosphere as "irreverent and festive." The heterogeneity of the incipient protest movement was on display, too. One flier circulating that morning had been authored by Ulrike Meinhof, editor of the left-wing monthly *Konkret*.[14] She described the demonstration as a stand against the "inhumane conditions for human existence" which apply "in Germany, Vietnam, Greece, Persia, and other parts of the world."[15]

It wasn't long before the taunting between the pro- and anti-Shah demonstrators turned nasty. The pro-Shah Iranians, overwhelmingly well-built men in dark suits and ties, pushed aside the flimsy police barricades and went after the students with broom handles, wading into the crowd and swinging wildly. In documentary footage not a single one of the thousand-plus West Berlin police detail is to be seen until, after a one-sided half-hour of skirmishing, two officers arrive on horseback. When more police finally show up, they moved against the anti-Shah protesters, not the Iranian monarchists.

Later that evening, the protesters reconvened outside Berlin's Deutsche Oper, where the royal couple and its German hosts were to attend a performance of Mozart's *Die Zauberflöte*. Again, the pro-Shah faction provoked scuffles with the anti-Shah demonstrators and, again, the police stood by. The protestors responded with a barrage of eggs, tomatoes, paint-filled balloons, and "a few stones,"[16] aimed first at the pro-Shah group and then at the Berlin police. The police launched tear-gas canisters into the crowd and pulled protesters out of the scrum, dragging them to their green-and-white wagons. But shortly after the opera began at 7:30 most of the anti-Shah protesters had begun to disperse. Through megaphones, organizers called them to return in two hours when the performance was over. It was, inexplicably, only then that the police started to clear the square by force. Film footage shows the West Berlin police jumping over their own barricades into clusters of demonstrators, swinging nightsticks and then scattering them with water cannons and more tear gas. Once the police took the square, the episode seemed to be over. "We were on our way home," remembers Christian Semler, a student activist at the time. It was then that a shot rang out from nearby Krumme Street.

According to eyewitnesses, police had trapped a group of protesters in a residential courtyard. Then, for reasons that remain opaque even many years later, plainclothes officer Karl-Heinz Kurras drew his service pistol and fired a single shot that entered the back of Benno Ohnesorg's head, fatally wounding the young man. In a trial that later acquitted Kurras, he claimed that he was being beaten by demonstrators when two men pulled knives on him. This is when he fired a warning shot and then, in the confusion, another. He says he never saw Ohnesorg. None of the eighty-three other people in the vicinity of the killing, including fellow police officers, saw anyone with a knife. Kurras was uninjured. No one else heard a warning shot. The twenty-six-year-old Ohnesorg was a first-timer among the student activists, there with his pregnant wife. He was rushed to a hospital, where he died.

News of the killing spread like wildfire. The context of Ohnesorg's death and the students' interpretation of it would color the politics of the West German student movement and inspire more militant factions in the 1970s. (One of the latter groups, for example, would be called the June 2 Movement.) For the first time, the fragmented and diverse extra-parliamentary opposition that had emerged during the 1960s was united: Ohnesorg's "execution" was hard evidence of the state's repressive and authoritarian—according to some—even "fascistoid" nature. "The post-fascist system in the Federal Republic has become a pre-fascist system," declared an SDS press release the following day. "Premeditated murder!" screamed a student-produced leaflet. It warned of a new wave of police terror to come: "The murderers and their executive organs will no longer shy away from committing more murders."[17] Some students honestly expected a full-scale bloodbath to follow, explains Christian Semler. Ohnesorg's killing was part of a strategy, they believed, to create the conditions for the government to declare a state of emergency and then to crack down on anti-government activities. This was the purpose of the emergency powers law. To them, this cold-blooded killing of a peaceful demonstrator summed up the reality of West Germany's Potemkin democracy.

The students rushed to a judgment that many, including Joschka and Ede Fischer, would adhere to even after the student movement's demise. Benno Ohnesorg's death constituted a "qualitative leap" in the thinking of student activists, explains Christian Semler years later. At the time, Semler, born in 1938, was one of the older student activists and a proponent of a more orthodox Marxism. He was on the SDS board and had spoken that day in front of the protesters. Young activists, says Semler, including himself, saw the Federal Republic working arm-in-arm with a brutal dictator like the Shah while the West German police collaborated with his henchmen against students practicing free assembly. "This [Ohnesorg's slaying] was a great shock to us, something deeply disturbing," explains Semler:

> Most students had never personally experienced this kind of violence before and then suddenly something happened that they

> thought could never happen. That's why they didn't need much empirical experience with police brutality to arrive at the most extreme conclusions. With one stroke, this killing encapsulated all of the excesses of the state and confirmed our darkest theories about the country's rightward drift, old fascists clinging to power and the authoritarian state. We were all under the impression that the state could at any moment slide back into an authoritarian mode. All it needed was the slightest push.

Although the students were in error branding the Federal Republic some sort of proto-fascist state, they claim in hindsight that they had not unreasonable grounds for fearing the reemergence of a repressive, nationalist regime. It seemed like the lines of continuity between the Third Reich and the Federal Republic were staring them in the face. The Federal Republic was, after all, the legal successor to both the Weimar Republic and Nazi Germany. In word, its leadership remained wedded to a Germany with its 1937 borders, which included parts of contemporary Poland, Czechoslovakia, and the Soviet Union. The conservatives openly promised the return of these lands to the powerful expellee organizations. And the western students didn't need East German propagandists to underscore that the chancellor had been a Nazi functionary, as had Adenauer's 1953–63 chief of staff, Hans Globke, to name just the most prominent ex-Nazis. But with Ohnesorg's killing, the focus shifted from the continuity of former Nazi personnel in the institutions to the authoritarian continuity of the two systems themselves. With this rethinking, the focus of the students switched from hands-on *Geschichtsbewältigung*, their valuable work "processing the past," to the contemporary implications of their diagnosis on modern-day Germany and a strategy to combat it.[18]

Another factor in the mix that contributed to the student radicals' picture of the republic was a deep-seated wariness of capitalism that extended beyond the circles of university leftists. The collapse of the Weimar Republic and the collusion of Germany's biggest industrialists with the Hitler regime had led many on the left to hold late industrial capitalism—and, for some, by association liberalism—as waystations on the road to an authoritarian state, maybe even a new kind of fascism.[19] This, roughly, was Max Horkheimer's thesis in his 1940 paper "The Authoritarian State," a seminal text for the students. (Horkheimer also included Soviet "state socialism" in his definition of the modern, post-ideological authoritarian state.) "Those who do not wish to speak about capitalism should also be silent about fascism" was a

Horkheimer line that the student movement turned into a slogan, despite Horkheimer's persistent efforts to pry it away from them.

This link between capitalism and fascism, however, had less sophisticated origins as well. Orthodox communists, for example, defined fascism as the "highest stage of monopoly capitalism," which made it easy work for East Berlin, the self-proclaimed "antifascist state," to tar the Bonn Republic as "crypto fascist." Even though very few of the student idealists ascribed to GDR communism, its relentless propaganda had an insidious impact. After all, the East German leadership together with the Soviets had indeed carried out a more thorough denazification in some areas, like the civil service and education, than had the West.

The fact was that at the time the student radicals threw around concepts like "latent fascism" and "fascistization" very loosely. In part, this overreaction was also a consequence of the patchy research that had been conducted on National Socialism, the Nazi years, and fascism in general. German historians, a conservative group to begin with, had themselves compromised in different ways with Nazism. Thus the students of the sixties had limited historical material to draw upon. Even though few directly equated the rise of Nazism in the 1930s with developments in the Federal Republic, many made the mistake of applying the category of "fascism" far too broadly and thereby blurring the specific conditions that contributed to National Socialism's rise in Weimar Germany.

After Ohnesorg's death, the enraged student activists concluded that the West German authorities—including the Social Democrats—tolerated political demonstrations only when they accomplished nothing at all, like the docile Easter Marches. In their eyes, the state was clamping down on its most potent opposition. Unlike Weimar's ineffectual anti-Nazi opposition, they weren't going to be steamrolled so easily. West Berlin's mayor stoked these fears by laying the blame for the clashes and Ohnesorg's killing squarely on the anti-Shah demonstrators. He praised the police, repeated rumors about a killed officer, and declared a moratorium on demonstrations in West Berlin. The Springer newspapers chimed in: "Whoever sows terror, harvests tragedy."[20] According to the June 3 *Bild-Zeitung,* "A young man died in Berlin, victim of the riots instigated by political hooligans who call themselves demonstrators. Riots aren't enough anymore. They want to see blood. They wave the red flag and they mean it. This is where democratic tolerance stops." From that day on, the Springer press was an object of the students' wrath and no less central to their movement than Vietnam.

Despite the ban, in West Berlin and across western Germany, the events of June 2 prompted emotional demonstrations and then vigils on the day of Ohnesorg's funeral. "A lot of people came together for the first time, individuals who were outsiders, bohemians, politically critical, but who didn't know about one another," explains Joscha Schmierer, a student in Heidelberg in 1967. "The mass vigils in early June showed them that there were lots of others who were like-minded," he says. "These demonstrations were so important because they became conscious that they were part of something bigger, a movement." When the floodgates burst open after June 2, the SDS was the obvious option left of the SPD. With the Communist Party banned and, in the eyes of most, discredited, there wasn't much else. The Heidelberg SDS, says Schmierer, had about twenty members before June 1967, and after it more than 500, including Schmierer himself. "The SDS didn't have more than a few hundred members nationwide," explains Semler. "And then all at once there was such a deluge that we couldn't cope. Our offices were overrun. So we just opened SDS up and decentralized everything. We let people in different cities and towns organize themselves into autonomous project groups and then we'd all meet at regular congresses to thrash things out. More or less by chance it turned out to be an incredible experiment in participatory democracy."

Interlude in Stuttgart

In Stuttgart, Ohnesorg's death was memorialized by a silent march. Joschka and Ede Fischer joined about 800 others who snaked their way through the city with lit candles. The June 6 *Stuttgarter Zeitung* deemed the vigil of such unimportance as to relegate it to a page 15 blurb. Another local paper, the *Stuttgarter Nachrichten*, noted that its participants were protesting the alleged brutality of the Berlin police and not that of the Stuttgart force. Older onlookers, the newspaper reported, mocked the procession. The shot fired at Benno Ohnesorg further drove in the wedge between the generations that would endure for two decades.

In Stuttgart, too, the small SDS gained in prominence. Two of the new faces in and around the SDS and active in its sister organization for high school students were Joschka and Ede. Older student activists Christian Semler, Rudi Dutschke, Joscha Schmierer, Bernd Rabehl, Tilman Fichter, and Hans-Jürgen Krahl, all born during the war and not after it, became the leaders of the 1967–69 student revolt. Joschka and Ede were born at the tail end of the years that would constitute "the 1968 generation"—those roughly between twenty and thirty years old during the student movement. Too young to be a leader, Joschka Fischer admits he was just one in the crowd. A remarkable photograph taken in 1967 or perhaps early 1968—probably in Frankfurt—captures Fischer's role at the time: still baby-faced, he sits high on a ladder, a construction worker's hard helmet balanced on his head, watching wide-eyed as a lively demonstration of some sort carries on beneath him.

"Fischer was a very typical [SDS] recruit," explains Gerd Koenen, author of several books on the German left and himself a June 1967 convert to SDS. "Like me, and others as well, he was experiencing a kind of existential radicalization that didn't yet have its own language or theory. Suddenly one was in the middle of it all, of a world-wide revolution it seemed, but we didn't have any practical idea about what we really wanted. That's why we stuffed ourselves full of these rash [left-wing] theories and this new, quickly learned jargon."

The tragedy of Ohnesorg, the movement's instant martyr, gave the Fischers' vague anti-establishment inclinations legitimacy and direction. And it provided answers to questions that had been gnawing at them since they returned from Gretna Green. Where did they fit into this troubled society? Were conformism or dropping out the only options? Perhaps, concluded the teenage newlyweds, there was something happening in the Federal Republic that might be worth sticking around for. Their first abode as a married couple was a two-room attic apartment outside Stuttgart that Elisabeth had found for them and helped furnish, despite her continuing disapproval of the marriage and their lifestyle. The "beatnik couple," as she called them, was an embarrassment to her.* But she didn't abandon them. Joschka worked from time to time delivering mail and continued to sketch, selling his artwork on the street. He and Ede had also begun a lucrative trade in stolen books, booty that they "picked up" from second-hand shops outside of Stuttgart and sold in front of the university and at Club Voltaire. June 2 had anulled any thoughts of going back to the *Gymnasium* to earn his *Abitur* diploma or resuming the photography apprenticeship.

---

* At the time, the Fischers considered themselves *Gammler* and part of the loose *Gammler* movement. The *Gammler* emulated hobos: they didn't work, dressed like tramps, slept under the stars, and, in general, shunned society's norms.

Rather than return to the *Gymnasium*, a humbling prospect, Fischer went straight to college. Although, without an *Arbitur*, he couldn't enroll formally in Stuttgart's technical university, he could sit in on courses. The arrangement seemed ideal; he could learn what he wanted without taking exams, writing papers, or dealing with pedantic instructors. Although Joschka Fischer had jettisoned the petty bourgeois norms of his parents and his village, he hadn't rubbed out a formidable ambitious streak. "When the dictate to study came from outside, he found it unbearable. But when he made the thing his own, he could manage without difficulty," noted one biographer.[21] In fact, he discovered that he was an autodidact, and not only could he manage at the university, he could excel.

Joschka and Ede Fischer were soon to rub up against the republic's rough-edged police forces themselves. When the South Vietnamese ambassador visited Stuttgart in summer 1967, the Fischers were part of a small demonstration that had been organized by their group. The young people met in front of the U.S. consulate and then marched to the New Palace where the ambassador was being received. Their posters and banners read: "Solidarity with the Vietnamese Revolution," "Johnson Out!" and "Stop the Bombing of Vietnam." In the Fischers' account of the run-in, the protest was innocuous enough. The young people just wanted to let Stuttgart's city council know what they thought about their choice of guests. But the Stuttgart police had their own thoughts about the unauthorized demonstration on city property, technically a criminal offense. Joschka Fischer would later recall:

> Suddenly the police were there, and we ran into the palace courtyard. We sat down but they came right at us anyway. Every one of us was roughed up, dragged and kicked. We were taken into police custody. [The police] claimed that I punched one of them. I said, "Excuse me, I was the one punched." [I thought,] how could this happen? In the end we were charged with violating a so-called no-demonstration zone, which was the first time I had ever even heard of such a thing. And then resisting arrest too, which was a bald-faced lie, as well as disorderly conduct.[22]

The righteous teenagers refused to cooperate with the local institutions of justice. The judge struck Joschka as an old Nazi type, a point that he remarked upon aloud. The Fischers declined to sit in the assigned dock and ignored the judge's order to do so. Joschka received a sentence of six days' imprisonment for obstructing justice and six weeks without bail for trespassing. (The latter sentence was eventually suspended when the federal government decreed a general amnesty for such minor offenses in 1970, which affected thousands of student activists.) But Fischer served six days in Stuttgart's Stammheim prison.

From time to time the Fischers took their new means of livelihood on the road to markets more lucrative than Stuttgart. A couple of hours north, Frankfurt beckoned, an urban metropolis with 20,000 students, or, as the Fischers saw them, potential customers. But Frankfurt also piqued the Fischers' curiosity because of its reputation as the theoretical epicenter of the student movement.

Fischer realized that in order to participate as an equal in the student movement, he had to have his left-wing political theory down cold. This among the theory-obsessed student rebels was a precondition for being taken seriously. At the Stuttgart university, Fischer could read Kant, Fichte, and Hegel—the great philosophers associated with German idealism. On his own he began to grapple with the leftist thinkers who weren't covered in university seminars: Lenin, Jean-Paul Sartre, Karl Kraus, Georg Lukacs, and C. Wright Mills. He read Marx "up and down," he says, and learned that he could hold his own with the matriculated students, at least those in Stuttgart. And in Frankfurt, at the prestigious Johann Wolfgang Goethe University, there was a group of German social philosophers returned from wartime exile who combined Hegel and the young Marx, Nietzsche, and Freud, into an original form of social critique—and who took the student activists there seriously. The renowned Institute for Social Research was home to philosophers Theodor Adorno, Max Horkheimer, and Jürgen Habermas, among others.

The Frankfurt School theorists had sharp differences with the students' radicalism—and the students with the institute's arm's length from the nitty-gritty of activism. But Adorno and Horkheimer, as well as some of their younger colleagues like Jürgen Habermas, deemed healthy the young politicos' refusal to accept the explanations—or silence—of their parents' generation, as well as their proactive concept of political participation despite its revolutionary pretensions. The topics that occupied the institute were closely related to the questions the young Germans were asking. How was it that such an ostensibly cultivated *Volk* as the Germans could succumb so pliantly to Hitler's allure? Was there a type of character, an "authoritarian personality," that was predisposed to seek out and follow authoritarian leaders? How was Auschwitz possible, and how could Germans ever come to terms with a past so morally corrupt, with traditions that led to gas chambers? They asked whether the Germans—and West Germany as a state—had a special moral responsibility to redress the Nazi legacy and how democracy fit into all of this. These weren't questions that average Germans wanted to pose, but they consumed Frankfurt's students.

On one of their book runs to Frankfurt, the Fischers met Detlev Claussen, a philosophy student of Joschka's age from northern Germany. He had come to Frankfurt expressly to study with Adorno and had joined SDS upon his arrival. Claussen lived on tucked-away Beethovenplatz in the Kolbheim dormitory, a neon-lit, cement-block structure that would become part of Frankfurt folklore. Kolbheim was a unique postwar project initiated by what today might appear to be unlikely bedfellows: the American military administration, the Institute for Social Research, and Frankfurt's Social Democrat-led city council. In fact, all three actors, in their different ways, pursued a common goal—namely, the turning of postwar Germany into a peaceful, liberal-minded country. The dorm was conceived as an exercise in democratic living, an antidote to the legacy of right-wing fraternities in Germany's universities. It had a student-run administration, co-ed halls, and foreign students from as far away as Israel and Africa.

The inhabitants of the Kolbheim, however, took the experiment much further than either the Americans or the city council had ever intended, turning the dorm into the hub of Frankfurt's left-wing scene. It became the site of SDS meetings on Friday evenings, but only *after* the meetings did the earnest young dialecticians open the basement bar, the Kolb Cellar, for dancing and drinks. Then the scent of hand-rolled cigarettes, hash joints, and spilled beer wafted into the cinder-block stairwell. Some of its residents, like Claussen, edited or wrote for *Diskus*, an anti-establishment student monthly of exceptionally high quality. Forty years later old issues of *Diskus* read like a Who's Who of Germany's leading social scientists, whose roots were in this milieu.

One evening Detlev Claussen bumped into the Fischers in the communal kitchen, the scene of all-night political discussions and furious debates over the dormitory's democratic organization. Claussen remembers that he was immediately fascinated by Joschka Fischer "because he was so different." "I thought, this guy isn't really educated or well read but he has excellent taste in books, and was excellent at stealing them as well—a real professional," says Claussen, today chairperson of the University of Hanover's sociology department. "He had a wonderful collection of Heinrich Mann, first editions that he had 'picked up' somewhere. I saw that he was interested in books and not just in stealing them, yet he had a kind of rough, proletarian attitude unlike your average student. I'd never met a person like this before." Claussen had the strong impression that the Fischers found Kolbheim an exotic and intriguing world.

First Steps of the Long March

Throughout the winter of 1967 and spring of 1968, events in West Germany raced forward. The student leaders had every reason to feel heady as their movement picked up momentum and its size swelled. On campus after campus, departments and whole buildings were taken over by students. Their expectations soared. In West Germany the anti-Vietnam demonstrations received a huge boost after the North Vietnamese launched the Tet Offensive in early 1968. To their delight, the German students observed that the thousands on the streets were no longer just students. People like Joschka and Ede Fischer had joined it. The protest movement was becoming the vehicle of an entire generation, thought the student leaders, not just an educated elite. For the students, the self-appointed vanguard, this was evidence that their movement could eventually branch out into the mainstream and win over large swathes of society, including the working class.

Moreover, the West Germans saw other students and young people elsewhere rising up against their establishments: in Belgium, Italy, England, France, Spain, and Turkey, but also on the other side of the Iron Curtain in Czechoslovakia, Poland, and in Tito's socialist Yugoslavia, too. Even farther afield, in addition to North America, there were campaigns led by discontented young people in Australia, Brazil, Japan, and Uruguay. This was vitally important to the German students as it bolstered their conviction that they were in the right, that their parents were the ones sleepwalking in the past. They were on the cutting edge of an international movement that was making history. This internationalism was also an explicit rebuke to the inward-looking, racial nationalism that had reigned in Nazi Germany and before it. In fact, it was a radical rejection of nationalism as such, of all nationalisms.

Even before the Ohnesorg shooting, Rudi Dutschke, a five-foot-five student from outside of Berlin, was a leading figure in SDS. Since the incident, however, he had become the student movement's public face. The youngest son in a pious Lutheran family, Dutschke was a conscientious objector who had fled the stifling conditions of East German communism. A year after his arrival in West Berlin in 1960, on August 13, 1961, the East German authorities erected a barbed-wire and cinder-block barrier that divided the city in two. The construction of the Berlin wall cut Dutschke off from his family and turned West Berlin into his new home. A sports journalist by training, Dutschke enrolled at the Free University and threw himself into his new field, sociology. Together with his close friend Bernd Rabehl, another East German exile, Dutschke began to collaborate with a small circle of agitprop artists whose group Subversive Aktion was experimenting with cultural products to shock and provoke the lethargic masses. Subversive Aktion, founded in Munich in 1962, saw itself acting in the tradition of the Situationist International and the post-World War I, avant-garde Dada movement, which linked art to politics in order to expose the senseless barbarism of that war.[23] But before long Dutschke and Rabehl grew impatient with the sporadic "happenings" initiated by the anarcho-artists. Where did it lead, they asked? In January 1965 the two friends joined the Berlin SDS, bringing with them some of the spirit of Subversive Aktion and a visceral contempt for Soviet communism.

Despite his rejection of the East German system, Dutschke had not given up on Marxism and the possibility of a classless society. Free-market capitalism, he was convinced, was no answer to mankind's quandary, even if much of western Europe's working class was content with steadily rising wages and a comfortable standard of living. The left couldn't abandon the working class, but neither could it wait forever for it to wake up. As Herbert Marcuse and the New Left thinkers argued, other actors, like students, could also bring about social change—and in doing so could rouse the workers to action. Dutschke's vision was forward-looking, full of utopian hope: "We can change things," he'd say. "We're not the hopeless idiots of history who are incapable of taking their fate into their own hands. . . . We can shape the world around us, into a world that you've never seen before, a world that will know no more wars, won't have starvation, and I mean the whole world. This is our historical possibility."[24]

This kind of revolution *was* possible in the West, maintained Dutschke, but it was a process, not a one-off putsch engineered by an elite vanguard. Dutschke's "long march through the institutions" of bourgeois society implied a permanent revolution in consciousness, as he put it: "the subversive utilization of the contradictions and possibilities inside and outside of the whole state-society apparatus in order to destroy it through this long process."[25] By exposing the contradictions of the system, fringe groups like students could enlighten broader swaths of the population. Revolutions *were* happening elsewhere in the world, such as in the Third World, where capitalism crassly divided society into antagonistic classes and western imperialism extracted profits while leaving behind only misery. There—in Vietnam, Cuba, and Bolivia—existed the revolutionary spark absent in the West. The strategy of western revolutionaries, argued Dutschke, had to be to form a "second front" alongside of that in the developing world. By infiltrating the schools, the universities, and the media—institutions that transmitted social consciousness—West Germany's rebels could democratize and thereby subvert the foundations of the authoritarian state. In practical terms, alternative "critical" and "counter" institutions would replace them, and ultimately the masses had to join this emancipatory struggle. Direct democracy would succeed the establishment's distant representative democracy. The "long march through the institutions" became synonymous with Rudi Dutschke's name as well as the strategy of the West German left long after the student movement's demise. Though it would later come to mean making peace with the system and attempting to reform it from within, Dutschke originally meant something else: entering the institutions in order to undermine them and transform them completely.

Rudi Dutschke's ability to draw from and synthesize diverse theoretical traditions, from the Bible to Malcolm X, as well as his magnetic personality, was among the qualities that made him an icon of the student movement. He was a strident optimist with an ascetic lifestyle, and he seemed to have time for everybody. Invariably dressed in a black, yellow, and red striped sweater and thick wooden clogs that added a few inches of height, he lived and breathed politics. His friend and SDS ally Bernd Rabehl likens Dutschke's speaking style to a cross between sixteenth-century Protestant reformer Martin Luther and a Chicago blues singer. "Rudi was religious and had a strong faith in his owns words, which came through when he spoke. He interacted with his audiences as intuitively as a talented musician does. On paper his speeches look convoluted and dense, I myself often can't make out what he means, but in person the effect was completely different." One German journalist recorded how awestruck he was when he first heard Rudi Dutschke speak in 1966: "Every time Dutschke steps up to the speaker's podium the SDS delegates go silent. . . . His theses fall like cracks of a whip. Beneath his dark brow, his gaze is menacing and his diminutive frame seems to shake with passion."[26]

By 1967 Dutschke had already made his mark on the SDS. His early years in communist East Germany had inoculated him against a more doctrinaire Marxism Leninism, including the kind espoused by "traditionalists" in SDS. This "antiauthoritarian" *Geist* appealed to many young activists from West Germany, like the Fischers, who were staging a revolt against the authority of their parents, teachers, and the crusty culture of the Federal Republic—as well as worldwide capitalism. SDS's "anti-authoritarian wing," led by Dutschke, espoused a largely undefined, open-ended democratic socialism. As much noise as the students made about socialism and revolution, their insistence on the democratization of German society "from the bottom up" infused all of their demands. Their term of choice was "direct democracy," which meant engaged, hands-on participation in all aspects of social organization. Whether factory worker or student, human beings should permanently be enriching themselves, expanding their consciousness, through diverse, self-organized forms of activity.

Dutschke endorsed the use of tactical civil disobedience, which the students called "direct action." Carefully planned illegal actions ranging from unauthorized demonstrations and sit-ins to throwing paint-filled eggs could serve tactical purposes. Civil disobedience could "provoke and enlighten" by exposing the undemocratic nature of the status quo. Direct action could stir things up, capture media attention, and begin to shake a consumption-numbed population out of its stupor. "The rules of this pathetic democracy are not our rules!" claimed Dutschke after Ohnesorg's death. "The starting point of the politicization of the student body must be the calculated breaking of these established rules."[27]

In the Third World, the German students concurred, the situation was different. There, Marxist revolutionaries had to resort to arms to achieve their aims. The reigning imperialist order, which itself relied on violence in order to rule, wasn't going to be overthrown without a fight, a theme integral to the anti-colonialist writer Frantz Fanon's *The Wretched of the Earth*, among the required reading. By its very nature, colonialism produced terror, poverty, repression, and torture—all forms of violence. Even more energetically and more quickly than student protests elsewhere, the West Germans actively supported the Vietcong and linked the revolutionary Third World struggles directly to their own. "One, two, three many Vietnams!" they cried and collected money to arm Ho Chi Minh's troops. But what was right for the Third World wasn't necessarily right for the first. "Let me be perfectly clear," Dutschke said in a 1968 television interview, "If I were in Latin America, I would fight with a weapon in my hand. I'm not in Latin America, I'm in the Federal Republic. We're fighting so that we don't have to resort to arms. But that's not up to us."[28]

The debates over direct action and violence as political tools wracked the student-led movement from its inception. The so-called *Gewaltfrage*, the question of violence, was answered in different ways at different times. Dutschke's rule of thumb was: violence against things, yes; violence against people, no. In spite of this, no one ever saw Rudi Dutschke himself throw so much as an egg at anything or anyone. The debate was full of such contradictions. Many of the same people who touted some form of guerrilla warfare had never held a weapon and, not so long before, had called themselves pacifists. Pacifism was the initial reaction of most young Germans to Germany's military traditions; "demilitarization" was one of the original goals of the Allies, of many of the country's founding democrats, and of the early peace campaigns, too. "Direct action, pacifism, abhorrence of weapons, verbal support for armed struggles—this was all in our heads at the same time," Klaus Theweleit, a SDS member from Freiburg, would explain much later. "In the thought systems of Dutschke and the student movement, pacifism and violence weren't mutually contradictory. [There was the idea of the] urban guerrilla and, simultaneously, no one should get hurt."[29] The debate over direct action and the use of violence raged on without consensus. Eggs? Stones? Molotov cocktails? There was no prima facie rule as to where to draw the line. But during the sixties—in contrast to the seventies—the *Gewaltfrage* remained largely theoretical. The vast majority of demonstrations used protest forms no more "violent" than trespassing or pushing through police lines.

The student partisans' relationship to the United States was equally rife with contradictions, the Vietnam protests being a case in point. At demonstrations, sit-ins, go-ins, and teach-ins, the Germans borrowed heavily from the protest forms and chants of their American counterparts from Greenwich Village to Haight-Ashbury. The U.S. civil rights movement and the Berkeley Free Speech Movement were key precedents for the German students, as they readily acknowledged. Like America's blacks, the West Germans were protesting the discrepancy between their rights on paper and reality in practice.[30] The German students, a remarkable number of whom had been high school exchange students in the United States, blasted Janis Joplin from giant speakers and read all they could find about the Black Panthers, even setting up Black Panther support groups across the country. They introduced American slang into the German language. As the 1960s turned into the 1970s they grew their hair long, donned jeans and cowboy boots, and became almost indistinguishable from American hippies.

The United States was simultaneously the land of Martin Luther King and the headquarters of global imperialism, "the belly of the beast" as Che Guevara put it. At the very same demonstrations that adopted American protest forms, some German protesters chanted "USA-SA-SS!" equating the United States with the Nazi regime. "Amis Go Home!" demonstrators shouted in West Berlin, a city in which most of the inhabitants felt they owed their freedom to the United States. Ironically, West Berlin's Free University was the unofficial center of the student rebellion, just as the American-inspired Kolbheim dorm in Frankfurt was the SDS meeting place. One of the prime targets of "violence against things" was American installations of any kind, including the Amerika Haus libraries and reading rooms that blanketed West Germany, part of the United States' early democratization measures. It was there that young West Germans growing up in the 1950s, like the Fischers, borrowed the very books that gave them the purchase to question the postwar status quo. Freiburg's Klaus Theweleit explains that although at the time in the late sixties he condoned the stoning of the local Amerika Haus on ideological grounds, he never participated himself because he regularly took out books and records from its collection. He also knew the people who worked there, and liked them.[31]

The enigma of the United States couldn't have appeared greater to anyone more than Joschka Fischer. The unlikely paths of his central European family and those of U.S. GIs had crossed more than once. The United States had helped liberate Germany (and Hungary, too) from fascism; it had both signed the agreement that legitimized the Danube Germans' expulsion from Hungary and simultaneously delivered the Fischers from a life under Soviet-style communism. U.S. soldiers tossed little Joschka treats from their jeeps in U.S.-occupied Württemberg. His family was solidly pro-American and even at one point in the 1950s deliberated moving to Chicago. Fifteen-year-old Fischer had cried and lit a candle for the murdered John F. Kennedy in November 1963. The spirit of freedom that Fischer found so attractive in the words of Jack Kerouac and Allen Ginsberg, Bob Dylan, and Woody Guthrie was exactly what was missing in postwar Germany. The Vietnam War, he admitted later, caused a "radical break" in his picture of the United States. "The liberators became the oppressors," he explained:

> Vietnam was an anti-colonial liberation war, which the U.S. was in because it believed in the domino theory. . . . From then on, for me, America had two faces: the one that led a war as colonial oppressor in

> Vietnam, and another that protested against this war and resisted it. For me and others like me it was never a question of being against the U.S. as a country, but rather we understood ourselves as part of a protest movement that was very strong *in* the states.[32]

In the Fischers' case, the extent of this shift in perspective manifest itself in one of the *Aktionen* thought up by their Stuttgart-based political group, a high school affiliate of SDS. A story that still makes the rounds in Stuttgart today, the teenage activists had set their sights on stealing the American flag off the façade of the U.S. consulate building on Urbanstrasse in downtown Stuttgart. The youngsters erected a human pyramid in front of the building, with Joschka climbing to the top to snatch the stars and stripes off the flagpole before the security guards could catch them.

Although the German students were deadly serious about their politics, neither for the Fischers nor for any of the young activists was their rebellion exclusively about Vietnam and ex-Nazis in the civil service. "A magical year," Fischer calls it in retrospect, a breathtaking time of abandon and personal experimentation.[33] In hindsight, most German commentators label the 1967–69 student movement a "cultural revolution," when the social and cultural norms of the young republic were challenged and reshaped. In effect, the students were trying to recast Germanness by negating its traditional affirmations and replacing them with their opposites—and then seeing what would happen. So corrupt was Germanness after Auschwitz, they concluded, so void of positive content, it had to be discarded completely. Everywhere that it could, the 1960s generation countered the German petty bourgeois ethic with its antithesis, as they interpreted it: prudery with free love, nationalism with internationalism, the nuclear family with communes, provincialism with Third World solidarity, obedience to the law with civil disobedience, tradition with wide-open experimentation, servility with in-your-face activism. One of the students' flippant riffs was: "Whoever sleeps with the same partner twice belongs to the establishment." Nothing was too sacred to be re-examined and, if so desired, tossed into history's dustbin.

One of the most colorful exponents of this assault on convention was West Berlin's legendary Kommune I, a combination hippie commune and agit-prop collective. The commune's goal was to create a "*Homo subversivus*" that both rejected West Germany's consumerist culture and "bourgeois individualism" *and* replaced it with something else. Its founders weren't prepared to wait for a socialist revolution. The Kommune's aim was to create spaces, at first just a single house, in which people lived according to different principles. "We not only set out to make familial bonds, traditional mores, and exclusive sexual relations redundant through the application of a hedonistic pleasure principle," explains one of Kommune I's founders, Ulrich Enzensberger, in his memoir of the project *Die Jahre der Kommune I: Berlin 1967–1969*,[34] "but we wanted to pose a real-life alternative to social relations in the Federal Republic."

Gretchen Klotz-Dutschke, Rudi's long-braided American wife originally from Chicago, was there with Rudi Dutschke and others at the very beginning, when the commune was just an idea. In preparation, she explains, the original founders went about it all in a very German way. First, they read everything they could and then sequestered themselves in an old country house to discuss it for days on end:

> We dug out the commune experiences of the 1920s and stumbled upon Wilhelm Reich's work and Russian experiments from the time of the [1917 October] revolution. In order to better analyze our own personal needs we read Marcuse's *Eros and Civilization*. The foundations of the anti-authoritarian movement were laid there. [We felt that] the liberation of one's sexual needs should be possible in unconventional ways. This would happen hand-in-hand with the liberation of society from capitalism which would open the way for the free development of the person independently of [bourgeois society's] repressive sexual morality and work ethic. New forms of communal living had to emerge to undermine the nuclear family. Children, for example, would be raised in communal groups.[35]

In the end neither Rudi nor Gretchen Dutschke participated in the eccentric indulgence that went on at Kommune I. Orgies, nudist photo shoots, and LSD trips weren't their style. In practice, they were much too straight. Nor were the agit-prop stunts of the commune pranksters what Rudi understood as serious political work. But there was a dose of the Kommune I's countercultural ethos and hedonistic spirit everywhere across West Germany where young people were questioning their society's mores by violating them. When it came to replacing them with new norms, however, there were no formulas to pick out of Marx and Engels. The great leftist thinkers could point them in a general direction, but young Germans would have to get there by themselves.

From Protest to Attack

By late 1967 the SDS had set into motion Dutschke's idea to stage an international "Vietnam Congress" in West Berlin that would bring together antiwar activists from across Europe and beyond. The plan was to coordinate the international left's response to the U.S. war in Vietnam. Imperialism is a global system, so the argument ran, and had to be countered with a global strategy. The decision to hold the congress in West Berlin in February 1968 was itself audacious. "The choice of West Berlin was a provocation," explains Tilman Fichter, a leading voice in the Berlin SDS and co-author of a history of the student organization. "Every demonstration in West Berlin resonated as if blasted through international loudspeakers. It was such a critical geostrategic point for American foreign policy and clear that when the United States was criticized here all of the American press, all of the TV stations, etc. would report on it," says Fichter. The general climate was such that the SDSers didn't see any paradox in the fact that they were using the only island of liberal democracy (defended as such by U.S. tanks and, ultimately, nuclear weapons) in the entire communist bloc where they could exercise their rights of free speech and assembly in order to call for western democracy's overthrow—and expect help from the West's free media to do so.

Dutschke's master plan was to get activist leaders from across the globe to shift from protest to attack, from a defensive to an offensive stance. For this to happen, the various national movements had to unite and, more critically, to support the Vietcong with more than just words. The Vietnam Congress in Berlin represented not just an escalation but a decisive shift in strategy and direction—one that would have far-reaching consequences for the German left.

Fifteen thousand people converged in bone-chilling West Berlin in February 1968. For many who participated it is remembered as the high point of that magical year. In the conference's venue, the technical university's biggest auditorium, a gigantic red banner draped one wall dwarfing the speaker's platform beneath it. In huge letters, the banner's message read: "Victory to the Vietnamese Revolution! It is the duty of every revolutionary to make revolution." Even though philosopher Marcuse was there, surrounded like a prophet by the crème de la crème of the international movements, it was Dutschke's keynote speech, translated simultaneously into a dozen languages, that captivated the audience.

He spoke out passionately about "changing the movement's course." The major impediment to radical social change, he underscored, was the intransigence of the working class and the trade unions. "The revolutionizing of the revolutionaries is the necessary precondition for revolutionizing the masses!" he roared, concluding his speech with "Long live the world revolution!" On the final day, in the dead of winter, the demonstrators marched through subzero West Berlin chanting "Ho Ho Ho Chi Min!"

Stop Dutschke Now

Meanwhile, 300 miles to the south, the Fischers scheduled their move from Stuttgart to Frankfurt for Easter weekend 1968. For months Joschka had been getting on everyone's nerves, carping about sleepy Stuttgart and saying that the place to be was Frankfurt, "where it's really happening." The couple was certainly looking forward to the move and anticipating the nationwide Easter March that was likely to attract record numbers and provide fireworks galore. They had no way of knowing just how many or why.

Also traveling north that week was twenty-four-year-old Josef Bachmann, who was making a longer trip from Munich to West Berlin on the overnight train.[36] A jobless worker from Bavaria, Bachmann shared none of the left-wing zeal of the Fischers or the student radicals. He had with him the latest *Der Spiegel* and *Bild-Zeitung*, as well as a single clipping from the ultra-right *Deutsche Nationalzeitung*. The headline of the clipped article read: "Stop Dutschke Now! Or else there'll be civil war. Hunt Nazis–Coddle Communists?" The piece included five black-and-white photographs of Dutschke's head, each from a different angle to resemble a "wanted man" handbill. Bachmann was traveling with just one piece of luggage, a gym bag that contained two pistols wrapped in laundry and about a hundred rounds of ammunition. He could afford to travel light, as he had come to West Berlin for one reason: to kill Rudi Dutschke.

On the afternoon of Holy Thursday, Bachmann went to find Dutschke at SDS's 140 Kurfürstendamm office. Rudi Dutschke emerged from the house with his clunky bicycle and beat-up leather briefcase—two of his trademarks—on his way to pick up medicine for his infant son, Hosea Che. Bachmann approached the bicyclist and asked if he was indeed Rudi Dutschke. Upon receiving an affirmative response, according to his own account, Bachmann called him a "dirty communist pig," pulled out a revolver from his shoulder holster, and shot Dutschke point-blank in the face. Dutschke fell to the ground, and Bachmann fired two more shots. Blood streaming from his head, Dutschke managed to stand up and stagger toward the SDS office before falling to the ground, unconscious. He was rushed to a hospital in critical condition.

"We all thought Rudi was dead. We didn't think he'd make it," says Tilman Fichter, who arrived shortly after the shooting. "But at some point that night we received a call from the hospital saying that he might live. Apparently the West Berlin senate and the federal government leaned on the hospital to call us again and say that Rudi's condition had actually stabilized. They wanted us to announce this because they were really scared that things would spin out of control. Of course we didn't because we didn't believe them."

Concerned and angry crowds began to gather at the SDS office and at the technical university nearby. For them, there was no doubt about the identity of Dutschke's "murderer." It wasn't Josef Bachmann but the Springer consortium's newspapers whose campaign against Dutschke had incited this far-right nobody. Bachmann simply took their imperatives literally.[37] The assassination attempt against Rudi Dutschke sparked the deepest domestic crisis of the postwar republic since the Spiegel Affair.

That night 1,500 people marched through West Berlin to the fifteen-story Springer media building, which was positioned along the wall near Checkpoint Charlie, for maximum propaganda effect. As they passed the Amerika Haus, a hail of stones rained on the building. "Spring-er, Mör-der!" they screamed, and over and over again "Ru-di Dutsch-ke!" One of the protesters was Michael Baumann, later a member of the terrorist June 2 Movement. He wasn't a student at all, but rather a disaffected working-class guy, the kind that the student-led movement had begun to attract in ever larger numbers. It was the Dutschke shooting, he writes in his classic urban guerrilla memoir *How it All Began*, that pushed him over the edge: "At this demonstration, my whole life passed before me. All of the hits that I had taken, every injustice I had suffered. Outrage over the assassination attempt on Rudi was so great that night that something took place everywhere [protests across West Germany]. . . . I felt like those bullets had been shot at me. By then it was clear: now we hit back, no excuses anymore."[38]

In front of the Springer building, a thick cordon of police met the enraged crowd. Another salvo of stones broke the windows on the building's lower floors. The protesters, Baumann among them, surged into the

Springer compound's parking lot, overturning a dozen of the delivery trucks and setting them ablaze with Molotov cocktails. (It was later ascertained that the Molotov cocktails had been made and distributed by an undercover West German secret service officer. This was neither the first nor the last time that police plants would supply arms to movement activists and encourage their use.[39]) "A lot happened on this evening," remembers Baumann. "As I stood before the flames, it was clear to me that you can really accomplish something this way... In this instance, the other side stepped way too far over the line, and we had the appropriate response. The atmosphere was so tense, everyone knew there was no kidding around anymore. They were going to liquidate you sooner or later, so it didn't matter what you did."

Elsewhere too, in Essen, Frankfurt, Hamburg, Hanover, and Munich—in total in twenty-seven cities—tens of thousands of protesters blocked the Good Friday deliveries of the Springer newspapers and besieged their offices.[40] "Yesterday [Martin Luther] King, today Dutschke, tomorrow us!" they chanted, convinced that Bachmann's bullet was meant for the entire extra-parliamentary opposition. The Fischers, still in Stuttgart, joined hundreds of others to block one of the biggest Springer printing houses in nearby Esslingen. "It was spontaneous," says Peter Grohmann of Stuttgart's Club Voltaire, about the Esslingen blockade. "It was as if everyone knew exactly what to do. We jumped into cars and headed straight there. We cut off the printing houses for four days by parking cars at every exit. It was the first time that so many different kinds of people took part in a direct action, workers, intellectuals, high school pupils, the Club Voltaire crowd, the students and others." The atmosphere was considerably more relaxed than in frontline West Berlin. "It was more like a 'happening,' " remembers Ede Fischer, describing the blockade. "It was upbeat. We made a big camp fire and people were playing guitars. But the blockade was very effective—nothing got through."

Their participation in the Esslingen blockade didn't delay the Fischers' move to Frankfurt for the big Easter March and anti-Springer demonstrations there. Across the country, nearly 300,000 people took part in the Easter Sunday peace march, which, with antipathy on both sides at boiling point, didn't transpire peacefully everywhere. The days of churchy peace marches were long passé, as the Fischers were to experience upon their arrival in Frankfurt. They went straight to the Frankfurt Union publishing house where the protestors had already decamped. The Frankfurt mayor, a left-leaning Social Democrat, warned them that it was his duty to protect free speech, not to censor *Bild-Zeitung*. Soon thereafter, a police force much better equipped and considerably less timid than that in Stuttgart broke through the blockade. The trapped protesters sat down Gandhi style, while the police cudgeled them with nightsticks and mounted police charged.

According to Ede Fischer, "This was the first time that we experienced this kind of brutality. And I was really shocked. It wasn't like there were just militant protesters there, everyone was there—trade unionists, women, people from the churches. When the mounted police charged suddenly there was blood everywhere, flowing from peoples' heads and everything. And then if you got it with one of those long night sticks, you thought, well, that was it—this was no joke." Ede "completely flipped out," remembers Joschka Fischer. He vented his disgust with the nonreaction of the demonstration organizers: they had no plan for responding to police brutality. They just took it, quite literally, sitting down.

Marx on the Main

Frankfurt, the republic's financial capital on the Main River, is where the story of Fischer's ascent through the ranks of the West German left really begins. In Frankfurt, he was in the thick of it, from the very minute of his arrival. But the angry and ambitious young man wanted more than just to be present; he wanted to be someone in the movement. He had picked the right place, even though keeping up with the students of Stuttgart's provincial technical university was one thing, holding one's own with the star protégés of Adorno and Horkheimer quite another. He knuckled down, but in those days almost *all* of the serious left-wing students burned the candle at both ends, between their books and political activism. Curiously, the rebels—in their own minds the epitome of anti-German—were known for their grueling German work ethic.

At Frankfurt's Goethe University, by then renamed Karl Marx University by the students, the Fischers sat in on the jam-packed seminars of Theodor Adorno, Jürgen Habermas, Oskar Negt, and the leading voice of the Frankfurt students, Hans-Jürgen Krahl. Philosopher Krahl was Frankfurt's theoretical counterpart to the praxis-oriented Dutschke in West Berlin. He was Adorno's favorite protégé and he spun lectures on epistemology and the dialectic off his cuff. Krahl, always disheveled and in the same soiled two-piece suit, didn't have a residence—even a room—to call his own. He carried a small suitcase with him everywhere and slept on friends' (or barroom) floors—whichever was nearest after long nights of drink and discussion. In addition to his personal effects, he always had with him a messy sheaf of papers, a manuscript undergoing revision after revision.

Initially, neither Joschka nor Ede Fischer felt comfortable in the new environment. "It was totally foreign to us, totally," remembers Ede who was intimidated by the university and didn't hang around the lecture halls for long, even for the dazzling Krahl. Joschka stuck it out. Everyone who knew him from the time says he picked up the material unbelievably fast. Most students would never have guessed that he wasn't a registered student or hadn't graduated from *Gymnasium*. After a while, he began to participate actively in the seminars, and as he gained confidence, he gravitated toward classes with more discussion and less lecture. Through seminar discussions and SDS meetings, Fischer learned how to speak in public, how to make complex points succinctly, and how to drive them home.

Fischer's face became familiar, although he remained small fry in the student movement to its end. In photos from the time, he can be picked out in crowds sitting on the floor at packed SDS congresses or marching anonymously in demonstrations. In one priceless shot he is ostentatiously smoking a thick cigar in a crowded auditorium. Ede is by his side, looking the other way, long loopy earrings dangling from her lobes. His autodidactic gifts notwithstanding, there was no way Fischer could best Frankfurt's brightest when it came to Kant and Hegel. He, however, had another card to play. Fischer exploited his working-class background for all the considerable worth that it had. His father was a butcher, he'd been arrested, beaten up by cops, worked a number of jobs, and hitchhiked through the world, too. He made his living as a book thief. Yet in contrast to Michael (later nicknamed "Bommi") Baumann or the SDS's philistine "leather jacket faction" (nonstudent toughs like Baumann), Fischer came off as thoughtful and tempered. He could now quote from *Das Kapital*, but uniquely, he had proletarian credentials to back it up.

Had the Fischers moved to Frankfurt much later than they did, they would have missed the transient high point of the student movement. In May 1968 revolution was most definitely in the air—and not only in Berkeley and Berlin. Events elsewhere, particularly in neighboring France, were avidly watched by the Germans. In Paris, student rebels took over the Sorbonne and the Quartier Latin. During the legendary Paris May, barricades burned and civil war-like scenes transformed the streets into battlefields where thousands of French police clashed with students throughout the nights. In Dijon, Lyon, Rennes, and Toulouse, too, students took over the universities. In Paris, police eventually stormed the student strongholds, using tear gas and incendiary bombs. The next day the burned-out husks of automobiles littered the contested terrain. In solidarity, trade unions struck for twenty-four hours; a million workers laid down their tools. The French students had succeeded in mobilizing the working class! Ten million Frenchmen took to the streets in mid-May—two-thirds of the workforce—which sent the message to the Germans that they were on the right track, that their rebellion, too, could be a genuine mass movement. At the forefront of the French movement was a pudgy redhead with tousled hair and a boyish face. His name was Dany Cohn-Bendit. The French authorities saw in the twenty-three-year-old such a threat to public order that they banned him from the country. Ironically, the move turned out to be the West German left's gain: Cohn-Bendit's expulsion stranded him in Frankfurt.

The events of the Paris May instilled in West German student activists the confidence that they could actually make the Bonn government back down on the proposed emergency laws, which they understood as critical to halting the state's rightward drift. In May 1968, in a last-ditch effort to deny the government the possibility of assuming these extraordinary executive powers, the SDS and other student organizations joined forces with the peace movement, as well as with prominent intellectuals, artists, and churchmen, to stage a mass demonstration in Bonn. Sixty thousand people took part in the protest, but not the major trade unions. The SDS's appeal to mount a nationwide "political strike" as a final stand against the law's passage came to nothing. The Bundestag—with the combined votes of the Christian Democrats and the Social Democrats—passed the bitterly contested laws with ease. Despite its unprecedented breadth and strength, the extra-parliamentary opposition had failed to block the single measure it deemed most dangerous for the republic.

The student-led movement didn't dissolve then and there, but entered a drawn-out process of decline that ended with SDS's disbanding in early 1970. The failure to stop the emergency law prompted a flurry of accusations, critical self-reflection, and the pronounced radicalization of some student movement currents. "Democracy in Germany is finished," said Krahl. "Through concerted political activism we have to form a broad, militant base of resistance against these developments, which could well lead to war and concentration camps. Our struggle against the authoritarian state of today can prevent the fascism of tomorrow."[41]*

Heidelberg's SDS, led by Joscha Schmierer, opined, "The organization of the students at their own workplace [the university] with the goal of revolutionizing academia runs the danger of revolutionizing the philosophy department and nothing more."[42] *Konkret* magazine's Ulrike Meinhof argued for an overtly offensive strategy to "disempower the dictatorships of state and society."[43] Sentiments like these gained currency as the sixties gave way to the seventies.

But summer 1968 wasn't the apex or end of anything for twenty-year-old Joschka Fischer. It had all just begun. The Frankfurt SDS was the perfect springboard for him, and he grabbed the opportunity. "Things were so fluid, moving so fast," remembers Christian Semler, "it was possible for someone from outside, like Fischer, to come to Frankfurt and make it in a way that at just about any other time would have been nearly impossible. You get involved with SDS, learn the lingo, take part in some meetings and demonstrations. If you were clever, persistent, and well, were good-looking, too, you could climb very quickly. Before long you could be addressing full auditoriums, completely convinced of your own historical importance." As a measure of just how fast he was rising, by the first 1970 issue of *Neue Kritik*, the SDS's theoretical journal, Fischer's name appears in the editorial box alongside Detlev Claussen's and others.

Another feather in Fischer's cap was his participation in a five-person SDS delegation to a Palestine Liberation Organization (PLO) solidarity congress in Algeria. In the final weeks of 1969, although the depleted student movement was sputtering to a stop, invitations to conferences and international student congresses continued to pour into the Frankfurt office, the SDS's national headquarters. The congress in Algiers was nothing special, and as it happened, there was an open spot on the delegation. None of the more senior members could go. Fischer, in the right place at the right time, volunteered.

The student movement's relationship to the Middle East and the Israel–Palestine question in particular had undergone a peculiar transformation since the Six Day War, which, coincidentally, broke out on June 5, 1967,

* Ironically, the law, passed in 1968, was never used by the state authorities and faded completely from the left's agenda. Ultimately, the measures passed in response to the Red Army Faction's terror campaign in the 1970s curtailed civil liberties far more than did the infamous but ultimately innocuous emergency powers law.

the same week that Ohnesorg was murdered. Until then most of the West German left and the student activists were "pro-Israel" and even pro-Zionist, a reaction defined by the shame of the Holocaust and the socialist ethic of the kibbutz movement. Israel's creation and legitimacy as a state was based on the centuries-long legacy of anti-Semitic persecution that the Jewish people had endured in Europe and that culminated in the Holocaust. The state of Israel was a safe haven for Jews, one that Germans above all were compelled to back, with federal monies as well as moral solidarity. SDS, for example, organized student exchanges with Israel. Palestine and its people were not yet issues. In West Germany, anti-Semitism as such persisted above all in conservative-nationalist circles. The extra-parliamentary opposition's condemnation of this kind of Nazi-era holdover came naturally.

The left's views shifted abruptly, however, when the Six Day War broke out between Israel and its Arab neighbors, ending in Israel's occupation of the Palestinian territories. With the war, the New Left "discovered" the Palestinians and opened their eyes to the fact that Israel's staunchest allies just happened to be Washington, Bonn, and the right-wing Springer media group. Among the New Left, Israel was thereafter construed as the United States' "imperialist bridgehead" in the Middle East, the same way that West Germany was Washington's "front-position lackey" in central Europe. The Palestinians' liberation struggle fit squarely into the students' Third World paradigms and critiques of colonialism. In addition, Frantz Fanon's *The Wretched of the Earth,* with a sympathetic forward by French philosopher and New Left thinker Jean-Paul Sartre, justified (Sartre even extolled) armed uprising in the anti-imperialist liberation movements of oppressed Third World peoples. The Palestinians were heralded as valiant freedom fighters. Add to the equation that Israel was bankrolled by the United States and, in some circles, the strong arguments about the necessity of a Jewish state in the aftermath of the Holocaust fell by the wayside.

Photographs that surfaced years later show Joschka Fischer at the Algiers conference, translation headset on his head. In a dark turtleneck sweater and jacket, Fischer stares thoughtfully into the camera. In another snapshot he can be made out standing and applauding at the congress's conclusion when the delegates passed a resolution calling for the "ultimate victory of the Palestinian people." Much later, Fischer said that the SDS delegation was appalled by Yasir Arafat's militant appearance and that they attended the conference only intermittently, bored by the repetitive and long-winded speeches.[44] Whenever they could, they escaped from the hall to explore the streets of Algiers, drink mint tea in the cafes, and chat with ordinary people in the land of Fanon and Camus. But uncritical pro-PLO sympathies were prevalent in the student movement as well as the greater German left. The rebel students' insensitivity to Jewish issues and unmediated pro-Arab leanings were among its glaring blind spots—and the Algeria trip would come back to haunt Fischer decades later.

Cultural Revolution, After All

By the time of Fischer's Algeria trip, the West German student movement had begun its retreat into subcultural niches. The SDS itself was little more than a loose union of groups in West Germany's university towns. In the aftermath of May 1968, Dutschke's anti-authoritarian wing lost its way, the more doctrinaire SDS factions gaining ground. With the "anti-Marcuse turn," many saw Leninist party structures as the means to guide the working class to a real revolution, October style. SDS's underrepresented women rose up and demanded equal treatment in the male-dominated German left. Armed with a bag of tomatoes, they pelted Hans Jürgen Krahl at an SDS congress, the last of which was held in September 1969. Dutschke was convalescing in London, barred from political activity in West Germany. His absence from the movement was a greater blow than the students had, at first, realized. According to Rabehl:

> The SDS activists, wary of strong leaders and their importance, underestimated the role that personalities like Rudi Dutschke do indeed play in political movements. Dutschke had a number of unique qualities, one of which was the ability to unite different factions under his name. Dutschke had personified the unity of a movement that really wasn't unified at all. All of the different currents and parties could identify with Rudi, from SDS and Kommune I to the Marxist Leninists and the communist party. No one else could do that, not me, not Krahl, not Semler.

Other developments expedited the student movement's fragmentation and demise. In November 1969 West Germans voted the Christian Democrats out of power for the first time in the postwar period. The new chancellor-elect was Social Democrat Willy Brandt, who exhorted his fellow West Germans to "dare more democracy." The grip of the Adenauer generation on the Federal Republic had finally been broken—although not by the student movement. The new Social Democrat–Liberal coalition promised renewal, reform, and chances for all West Germans. Thousands of SDS sympathizers gravitated back to the SPD, in effect conceding that a socially conscious liberalism was preferable to airy notions of revolution. For some student partisans, so great was the letdown of their intense, flash-in-the-pan rebellion that they packed their bags for abroad, taking off to South America or Italy or France, to places where, presumably, people knew better than Germans how to wage a proper revolution. But elsewhere, too, the student-led movements were in retreat. In France, the student uprising was quashed by police, never again to reach the heights of the Paris May. In the United States, the American SDS was also in shambles, the antiwar movement spent. The Soviet crushing of the Prague Spring movement in August 1968 and then the crackdown in Poland extinguished any rational hope that "socialism with a human face" could emerge in the Eastern bloc.

The rebels of 1968 walked away from the student movement convinced that their insurgency had failed: it couldn't mobilize the working class, stop the emergency law or the Vietnam War, or even put so much as a dent in the ruling structures of the Federal Republic. They had vastly overestimated their reach into the mainstream of society and their potential to effect broad political change from the streets. They failed utterly to grasp how far away they really were from "the proletariat." Notably, in their self-critique at the time, they neglected to include among their errors the movement's relative indifference to Jewish questions, as well as the elitist nature of its self-assumed vanguard role and relationship to ultra-leftist ideologies in general. The men of the student movement still had some lessons to learn about the meaning of *egalite* and anti-authoritarianism in practice. Also, even though very few favored the communism of the Soviet bloc, too few had fully come to grips with the fact that "real existing socialism" was a blind alley, an unreformable totalitarian ideology that deserved none of their sympathy. Arguably, by 1970, after the crackdowns in East Germany, Hungary, Poland, and Czechoslovakia, this should have been obvious.

On the other hand, nor did the disillusioned student radicals take credit for giving the country a "democratic push," which, paradoxically, helped transform it into a more stable, genuinely liberal republic. "The success of the '68 generation," writes German political scientist Claus Leggewie, "lies in that its primary goals [such as socialist revolution] were, fortunately, never realized." But rather, he argues, it "upended the system" by recasting its political-cultural foundations and anchoring civic culture in the Federal Republic.[45] The tremors caused by the sixty-eighters and their mishmash of unorthodox Marxism, visceral anti-authoritarianism, and participatory democracy would jar loose the stodgier attributes of Germanness, even if some of those characteristics would remain embedded in the republic's political institutions for some time to come. An irony that neither the left nor the right could appreciate at the time, this jolt would prod the Bonn Republic in the direction of the western mainstream and set it on a more modern path. Unwittingly, for example, the anti-authoritarian revolt set processes in motion that contributed to turning the *Westbindung* into a transatlantic alliance of shared political values rather than merely an expedient strategic pact. German historian Konrad Jarausch argues that the late sixties, broadly, constituted a decisive step in the republic's "learning process." He speaks of the "democratization of democracy,"[46] which included "a westernization, inner democratization, and social mobilization that further increased the Federal Republic's [political] distance from the GDR."[47]

The crestfallen students couldn't possibly know that their "cultural revolution," as it turned out to be, would alter the relationship of many Germans—particularly entire generations of younger ones—to traditional notions of authority, governance, child rearing, and sexuality, among other norms. "Questions were raised that most citizens didn't trust themselves to ask," notes social movement historian Wolfgang Kraushaar in hindsight.[48] The student activists would have been pleased to learn that even decades later German conservatives, including in 2005 the German pope, Benedict XVI, would blame them for eroding the foundations of a society based on Christian morality, the work ethic, and respect for law.[49] This, after all, is what they set out to do.

In addition, the very notion of "the political" was broadened beyond the traditional realm of parliaments and parties. Self-initiative, civic courage, and collective responsibility would gradually become respected values of the Federal Republic, among the left and the right alike. And, argues Kraushaar, the student rebellion did have an impact on the republic's structures—only it took longer to see the results than the impatient sixty-eighters had anticipated: "The [late sixties] extra-parliamentary opposition set off a real storming of the institutions—of the schools, the universities, the organs of justice, the civil service, the penal system, psychiatry, the political parties, and the parliament."[50] This "long march through the institutions" would end up transforming the republic by changing it from within. It wouldn't create an entirely new society as Dutschke had envisioned ("a world that you've never seen before"), but one considerably more open, pluralistic, and participatory than the society that had given rise to it.

One of the most insightful voices at the time, Frankfurt philosopher Jürgen Habermas, took stock of the student movement on the eve of its expiration. The student movements in the United States and West Germany, he said, illustrated the "new and serious possibility for the transformation of deep-seated social structures."[51] The German students' original goal had been to "politicize the public sphere" and to break through the ossified mindsets and routines of West German society. To an extent, he said, they had done just that by provoking critical thought and forcing West German society to examine its own assumptions. But the students, he criticized, had vastly overestimated their power and reach. He admonished the student-led movement for its wildly unrealistic expectations and its failure to recognize that it lacked the most basic conditions for "storming the Bastille." In order to move forward, they had to calibrate their strategies to reality, which included promoting reform from within the state's structures—in and through the Bundestag, the media, the courts, and the universities. These were wise words, loaded with foresight. But Habermas's message was one that some left-leaning young Germans, including Joschka Fischer, weren't quite ready to hear.

4

Radical Left

In the wake of the imploded student movement, its partisans scattered like leaves across the left side of West Germany's political spectrum. Those who gave up on revolution found homes in Willy Brandt's Social Democrats, as well as in the new women's movement or the multitude of community-based citizens' initiatives that opted to work *alongside* the system, if not necessarily *within* it (see chapter 5). But there were also those who refused to acknowledge the Federal Republic's reformability and stuck to a picture of the authoritarian state. Among them, many dozens of radical leftist splinter groups—Maoist, Trotskyite, anarchist—emerged from the wreckage of the student movement, including the Frankfurt Spontis and a bewildering array of Marxist Leninist parties. There were yet others, a tiny handful with few active members, who embraced military strategies, such as the urban guerrillas of the Red Army Faction (RAF). And, lastly, for those who saw something redeemable in East German communism, the Deutsche Kommunistische Partei (DKP) was a political home, the German Communist Party legal again in the Federal Republic for the first time since 1956.*

* The 1970s West German left consisted of basically five categories: (1) Social Democrats; (2) the new social movements, such as the women's and the antinuclear energy movements; (3) the radical left—post-student movement Marxist parties and anarchists, including Spontis; (4) armed factions, such as the RAF and the June 2 Movement; and (5) the West German communist party, the DKP. There could be overlap: a SPD or DKP member, for example, could have been active in one of the social movements, as indeed many were. Also, it should be noted that many of the participants of the new social movements, particularly in their early phases, didn't consider themselves "left wing" at all.

Though ultimately just a fraction of the greater German left, the sheer number of those who went the way of radicalism in the 1970s was astonishing. In West Germany, many more took this path than did in France or other countries, including the United States, where it happened too.[1] "This broad, ideological left-wing trend was less the source than it was the *product* of the student movement," argues chronicler Gerd Koenen in his critical book on "the red decade."[2] A May 1969 survey reflected the zeitgeist: 30 percent of West Germany's high school and university students claimed to sympathize with Marxism or communism. "The early seventies were, in terms of the intellectual climate, even more left than the late sixties, and the young brothers and sisters of the 68ers who followed in their footsteps often more radical," contends Koenen.[3] Rather than refine some of the more overblown contentions of the sixty-eighters or extract the liberating, civic impulses from the movement—as others did—these radical left strains refused to rethink some of the students' most egregious misanalyses. They rejected the "half-hearted reforms" and "technocratic adjustments" of Willy Brandt and his Social Democrats, and labeled the new grassroots social campaigns "petty bourgeois." In some of these circles, in the name of anti-imperialism, the pro-Arab sentiment of the late 60s morphed into unvarnished anti-Semitism; the critique of U.S. policy in Vietnam and elsewhere turned into blanket anti-Americanism. And, in the late seventies, the tactics of the armed factions shook the Federal Republic's democracy, posing the state—and the German left itself—with its greatest challenge since the country's inception.

As heterogeneous as the radical left was, there was broad agreement among its different incarnations that the student rebellion had "failed" because it couldn't mobilize the working class. The student uprising had left the republic's formal structures intact and its right-wing assumptions in place, even though the conservatives were no longer in power. This in itself—a change in leadership that in fact changed nothing—was further proof of bourgeois democracy's bankruptcy. The way forward, they generally concurred, was new forms of political agitation in the name of "class struggle." A spate of wild strikes in late 1969 in Germany's industrial Ruhrgebiet fired their imaginations. In Italy and in France, militant workers had risen up in defiance of their union bosses. The potential existed in Germany, too, they believed, if only they could tap it.

A bizarre menagerie of Marxist parties and initiatives replaced the loosely organized SDS, some with classic Leninist structures. Former SDS leader Christian Semler called to life the Kommunistische Partei Deutschlands/

Aufbauorganisation, the self-proclaimed avant-garde of the German workers movement and Maoist nemesis of both superpowers. The SDSers Joscha Schmierer in Heidelberg and Gerd Koenen in Frankfurt threw in their lot with the Kommunistische Bund Westdeutschland, which idealized communist Albania, China, and Pol Pot's Cambodia. There were also anarchist groupings such as Joschka Fischer and his Frankfurt troupe, the "Spontis."*

The Spontis never belonged to the party builders or dogmatic Maoists. But there were many common threads within the 1970s radical left that distinguished it from the SPD left and other reform-minded groups. A Marxist critique of late industrial capitalism, for example, was the starting point. The aim now was to mobilize the proletariat—one way or another—and make a "real" revolution, namely a socialist one, possible.

We Want Everything

The remnants of the Frankfurt SDS's anti-authoritarian wing set out to explore routes to socialism that skirted the perils of "reformism" (read "social democracy"), on the one hand, and Stalinism, on the other. Reflexively, the anti-authoritarian veterans leaned toward anarchist ideas. They scrapped Hegel and Adorno in favor of Italian and Russian anarcho-syndicalists, as well as the writings of hands-on communists like Rosa Luxemburg, Georgi Plekhanov, and Antonio Gramsci. But like the more orthodox Marxists, they too started their inquiries with the quandary of Marx's historical agent, the worker. Why was the working class so docile? What had to be done to awaken "class consciousness," to snap the workers from their slumber?

A fresh but by no means unfamiliar face on the Frankfurt scene was Dany Cohn-Bendit, whose celebrity status in France followed him to Germany. Everybody had seen the news photos, his face contorted in rage as police dragged him from the Paris barricades. He was "Dany le Rouge," an anarchist in deed as well as in temperament. Cohn-Bendit's background

---

* There were anarchist groupings of different sizes in most of the cities or towns in which the student movement had been active. Some were called Spontis, as in Frankfurt, others "libertarians," while others had no proper name at all but were organized around a periodical—such as *Der lange Marsch* in Munich. Most of these usually quite small groups sprang from the anti-authoritarian wing of the SDS and defined themselves in opposition to the top-down Marxist parties. Only in Frankfurt did anarchists define the entire scene the way the Spontis did.

and that of Joschka Fischer couldn't have contrasted more starkly. Born in southern France in April 1945, shortly after France's liberation, he was the son of left-wing Jewish intellectuals who had fled Berlin when the Nazis came to power. In Paris, the home of his parents (father German, mother French) was a meeting place for other political exiles. Regular houseguests included émigré philosophers Hannah Arendt and Walter Benjamin. Dany attended his first demonstration at the age of eleven, protesting the 1956 Soviet invasion of Hungary. An anti-Stalinist and antifascist ethic was instilled in him early. After boarding school in Germany he returned to France to study sociology at Nanterre University outside of Paris. But the French students were rising up too and Cohn-Bendit, a natural agitator, was soon at their front—as well as expelled from the university and, not long after that, from the country, too.[4]

By late 1969 an informal section called the Factory Project Group had formed on the fringes of the Frankfurt SDS, with the aim of first investigating, then infiltrating local trade unions. The first phase, seemingly obligatory, concentrated on the theoretical and historical precedents for a strategy. Cohn-Bendit was one of the section's initiators, which would, with SDS's demise shortly thereafter, become Revolutionärer Kampf (RK), or Revolutionary Struggle. Cohn-Bendit remembers urging Fischer to join:

> I knew Joschka from around "the scene." We'd met many times in a café called Libresso and we'd talked about a lot of the issues around the student movements in Germany and France. He was really taken with the undogmatic French groups, the *spontanéistes*, and with what was happening in Italy at the time. I was fascinated by the way he had picked up Hegel and Marx and everything on his own. And then in the Factory Project Group we were talking about doing some theoretical training before we entered the factories. So I suggested that we ask Joschka to lead one of these sessions.

This, their first instance of political cooperation, marked the beginning of an intimate friendship and a tight working relationship. In contrast to Cohn-Bendit, literally world famous, Fischer was a personality only within Revolutionary Struggle's circles and would remain so for some time. Joschka Fischer would have to work very hard for the notoriety that Dany of the Paris May enjoyed; but being by his side was already a step in the right direction. Before long Fischer and Cohn-Bendit were a force to be reckoned with within the Frankfurt left: close personally, of one mind politically, and nearly impossible to get around. By the time the

Factory Project Group was renamed Revolutionary Struggle, one of the four study groups was being led by *Gymnasium* dropout Fischer. Who better than a lettered prole to bridge the gap between radical theory and revolutionary praxis? Especially when the goal was to get beyond the theory as quickly as possible—and to get into the factories. It was in Revolutionary Struggle that Fischer made his first move to the top of a political organization.

The post-student movement shift within the West German left was auspicious for Fischer. The trend away from the university, toward the streets and the factories, suited him perfectly. "He was the big man of action, born enemy of intellectuals," remembers Richard Herding, who ran an alternative news agency called Information Service for Neglected News. One time, says Herding, he curiously peeked over Fischer's shoulder at a teach-in to read a program paper. "Papers, papers, that's the intellectuals," Fischer mocked him sharply, "always reading, reading." On another occasion, in preparation to defend the Frankfurt squatters' territory, Fischer and others had the job of lining up industrial-size garbage bins as a barricade against police raids. When one fellow activist questioned aloud the best way to tackle the job, concerned that it be determined in the most democratic way possible, Fischer expressed his contempt for the inquiry with unmistakable body language and turned on his heels to grab a huge garbage bin and drag it into the street. "Don't talk about it, do it, that was his message," explains Herding, who also acknowledges that Fischer was an articulate orator when the situation required it. "Most of the so-called revolutionaries just shouted slogans. Fischer really thought about how to make it happen," says Herding. "For Fischer it was always about strategy, the acts themselves and their consequences. Theory and analysis were means to an end, not ends in themselves."

Fischer and Cohn-Bendit constituted such a formidable tandem for the very reason that their backgrounds, styles, and needs were so different. Cohn-Bendit was a flamboyant personality and congenial talker who had attracted journalists and TV cameras like moths to a lamp since his eighteenth birthday. At the meetings of Revolutionary Struggle and later in larger forums, Cohn-Bendit often led the discussions. To the outside world, the paunchy, garrulous redhead from France was the face and voice of the Frankfurt left. Fischer, however, was the man on the inside, the tactician, and later the muscle. After Cohn-Bendit had rambled on, Fischer would pick his words apart, make sense of them, and turn them into strategy. These divisions of labor, even as they changed forms, were such that the two never competed for turf.

Revolutionary Struggle's political model was the Italian "factory-floor guerrillas" of Lotta Continua, who had led tens of thousands of Italian workers and students in street fighting and factory takeovers. On the run from Italy's police, some of *militanti* had landed in Frankfurt. The Italians' slogan *Vogliamo Tutto!* (We want everything!) was adopted as the title of the newspaper *Wir Wollen Alles,* which in addition to Frankfurt served anarchist groupings in Munich, Erlangen, Hamburg, Bochum, Hanover, Kassel, Cologne, Saarbrücken, and Nuremberg. The anarchists' code, summed up in one word, was *spontaneity*—in private life and at the workplace. They called themselves "Spontis," the name itself mocking Lenin's condemnation of impromptu political action. Revolution, they believed, could only happen from the bottom up, waged by radicalized masses. The Spontis rejected the role of class-conscious vanguard, instead practicing what they called "first person politics"; this meant that they would engage only in causes that they personally had a stake in, not on behalf of others. Revolutionary Struggle wasn't a political party and didn't aspire to be. Its targets were the "bought-off union bosses" and, ultimately, capitalism's structures. But in order to get there and to inspire the alienated proletariat, first they had to understand what made the West German wage laborer tick. Their strategy was to integrate themselves into the rank and file, and then sow dissent on the shop floor.

In Frankfurt, in fall 1970, one morning before dawn, two dozen saboteurs bundled into their second-hand wrecks and headed to Rüsselsheim, a town forty minutes outside the city limits. Home of the sprawling Opel automobile factory, it was the workplace of some 35,000 members of the industrial proletariat. At the time, it couldn't have been easier to find assembly-line work in West Germany's overheated economy. The Revolutionary Struggle group applied for jobs with made-up stories about their backgrounds and, once in the factory, remained undercover. For every cadre inside the auto works, there were two outside, producing the newspaper and distributing leaflets.*

---

* In retrospect, the cast of Revolutionary Struggle who did time on the Opel assembly line or agitated outside its doors is impressive. *Wir Wollen Alles* editor Thomas Schmid, for example, would become the editor-in-chief of the conservative weekly *Frankfurter Allgemeine Zeitung am Sonntag;* Johnny Klinke, the owner of the well-known Tigerpalast Theater in Frankfurt; Thomas Hartmann, co-founder and for many years editor of the alternative daily *Die Tageszeitung.* Matthias Beltz, who worked at Opel for five years, was a celebrated nightclub performer until his death in 2003. Barbara Köster would found and run the Frankfurt School for Women. Georg Dick and Tom Koenigs later took top jobs in the German foreign ministry, and Cohn-Bendit, a European parliamentarian, would lead the Europe-wide Green Party. Michaela Wunderle became a journalist.

In their first Opel pamphlet, the infiltrators announced to their new colleagues: "Naturally we're communists. We want this factory *not to* run! This is the only way to turn our program into reality: namely, a society that's really ours, without exploitation, without shit work, without everything that is constructed simply in order to best exploit us. That means: WE WANT EVERYTHING!" Despite such an immodest introduction, they went about their work cautiously at first. One of their first observations was that surprisingly few of their co-workers spoke German. Most of the low-skilled jobs were in the hands of Greek, Italian, Portuguese, and Yugoslav *Gastarbeiter*, or guest workers. Their ideas and mores were a world apart from those of the western, big-city former students, and most of them initially planned to return to their homelands, with as much money in their pockets as they could save. Never before had the workers, the German and foreign employees alike, earned as much as they were then at Opel, the case for almost all of West Germany's autoworkers at the time.

Initially, it was the former students with upper-class backgrounds who showed keener interest in taking on factory work and impersonating the proletariat than did those from working-class families. The Fischers knew the misery of morning shifts all too well from their parents. "For me it was exciting, a whole new world," remembers Thomas Hartmann, who spent a year making axles and exhaust pipes at the Opel plant. Fischer, though, had to be dragged out of bed every morning and stuffed into one of the car's back seats. Ede Fischer flat-out refused to do it. Cohn-Bendit, because of his visibility, couldn't work undercover and instead took a job in an anti-authoritarian nursery school, one of many started up across the country in the post-student movement years. Ede joined Dany there.

One fact that confronted Revolutionary Struggle's women on the factory floor was that of Opel's thousands of full-time employees, only 800 women were directly involved in production. Moreover, most of them were southern Europeans and subject to male-dominated family relations that rendered them, for political purposes, elusive. "We asked ourselves, 'Where is the young, female German proletariat?' " remembers Michaela Wunderle, a long-time Revolutionary Struggle activist in Frankfurt. She went to work in Neckermann, a major department store, where more of the staff was female. After six months, though, the management suspected her (correctly) of pasting up Revolutionary Struggle propaganda in the employees' bathroom and fired her on the spot, to Wunderle's great relief. "I found this kind of work terrible and decided then and there to go back and finish my studies. For me, there wasn't anything admirable or attractive about the proletariat's existence. I was healed of that illusion once and for all."

A year after the first Revolutionary Struggle agitators infiltrated the Opel works, the seeds they had sown seemed to be germinating. Fischer had been on the job nearly six months. At a 10,000-man general assembly, organized by the Opel workers' union, the undercover activists planned to call for a wild strike in defiance of the union. As scripted, communist-led Spanish and Italian workers joined the German radicals and rushed the speaker's stage. Fischer and others grabbed for the microphone, which the factory unionists promptly switched off. A brawl ensued, chairs were thrown, and tables were smashed to pieces.

This was the spontaneous, radicalizing moment that the anarcho-Spontis had worked toward. It was happening! The momentum of the events was supposed to radicalize the workers and prompt them to take over the means of production. "All hell broke loose," Barbara Köster remembers. "The Italians occupied the podium and there was a free-for-all for the microphone. Then, at this moment, we made a crucial mistake. Because we were Spontis we had tried to radicalize the movement but then, we thought, now the workers have to take charge. It was their thing then to launch a strike and start a demonstration. But the whole imbroglio fizzled out in no time. All I can remember is confusion."[5]

Fischer and other "outed" provocateurs lost their jobs at once. There was some positive fallout, however, and a feather for Revolutionary Struggle's cap: a "one mark for everybody" raise was eventually approved, a small bonus for the workers. But Revolutionary Struggle was no closer to subverting the factory. For Fischer, his firing had a silver lining: he no longer had to get up at 5 a.m. and break his back on the Opel assembly line.

The infiltration of the Opel factory dragged on for almost two more years. Wunderle wasn't the only student whose sampling of working-class culture sent her scurrying back to the books. Even the hardier ex-students who could hack the grind eventually lost hope. An early 1973 Revolutionary Struggle protocol describes the grim mood at the end: "Now we've been at Opel for so long, doing factory work and busting our asses. And? Why—what for—where to—to accomplish what? It's simply bull-headed to rail on against the number of hours worked when most workers would gladly take on even more.... Those workers who absolutely must have a color TV, the new car or bedroom, simply will not take a stand against overtime."[6]

That same year, strikes did finally break out in West Germany. Auto workers in Dortmund and at the Opel plant in Bochum took to the picket lines. But the machines at Opel Rüsselsheim hummed on without pause. By then, Revolutionary Struggle was prepared to throw in the towel anyway. The strikes at the other factories just rubbed salt in the wounds.

Co-op Counterculture

Photos show Joschka Fischer in late 1969 still looking like the wiry, near-sighted schoolboy he was when he left Stuttgart. But by the onset of the 1970s, "alternative culture" was blooming in West Germany—and Fischer with it. Long hair, psychedelic drugs, West German rock bands, and the hippie attire usually associated with the sixties, in fact, took off in West Germany only in the seventies. The essentials of a left-wing wardrobe included patched bell-bottom trousers, black T-shirts, a faded jeans jacket, and either an olive-green U.S. army parka or a scuffed-up leather jacket. Big, thick heads of hair and unkempt beards of varying shapes, lengths, and hues were everywhere. One 1973 snapshot shows Fischer looking the part, with a mop of dark wavy hair concealing his prominent ears, the requisite jeans jacket, and a zippered seaman's sweater. He sports an untrimmed beard and balances a self-rolled cigarette on his lower lip. He has filled out some, his torso no longer washboard flat. The clunky eyeglasses are gone. Radical, cool, streetwise, and aloof, this was the Fischer that his seventies' comrades from Frankfurt knew.

Likewise, university dormitories were as passé as sixties blazers. With the splintering of the student movement came smaller, politically defined groups living together outside the walls of the university. Left-wing groups everywhere in West Germany set up what they called *Wohngemeinschaften*, awkwardly translated as communal apartments or perhaps better as "co-ops." Co-op members didn't room together simply to save a few deutsche marks, although that played a part, but rather to live communally and work together for common political ideals. These many-roomed apartments were explicitly political projects, with anywhere from three to a dozen or more co-op members living together. In the co-ops, the personal was expressly political. *Everything* was political. There was no issue so private that it couldn't be laid out, usually on a big wooden table in the kitchen, and dissected according to that particular co-op's evolving political criteria. These included gender roles, romance, friendship, possessions, parents, child rearing, personal habits, hygiene, and sex. Not least, the topic that probably inspired the most debate—and ill will—was that of a democratic, egalitarian, nonsexist way of distributing household chores, in particular the washing of dishes. Another bitterly contested topic was whether, for reasons of hygiene and general consideration, men should be required to sit while urinating in the co-op bathrooms.

Every bit as political as the infiltration of the factories, "the first co-ops in Frankfurt constituted an attempt to find a model for a 'new kind of man,' one suited for the post-1945 world," explains Georg Dick, a former Frankfurt Sponti. "The co-ops were the smallest unit of something much bigger, a community based on principles such as solidarity and group responsibility. With these alternative forms of collective living we tried to break through this sense of isolation, this atomization that defined the [West German] fifties and sixties, in which the individual confronted everything alone, responsibility, family, school, and even history."

Activists from the time inevitably smirk and nod when they recall their experiences in the co-ops. The general spirit was "everything together in one pot," from possessions to income. None of the doors, including to the bathroom, had locks. Evening meals, inevitably huge pots of spaghetti and red sauce, were planned, cooked, and eaten together. Weekend brunches lasted for hours. By early afternoon the kitchens were brimming with coffee cups, tea pots, granola dishes, candles, and ashtrays. The site of parties moved from co-op to co-op, the big plastic tubs of cold pasta salad, drenched in mayonnaise, moving with them. Legend has it that in the earliest experiments there was just one bedroom with mattresses spread out across the floor, heaps of blankets, and sheets strewn around the room. Who woke up where or slept on which mattress changed daily. The communal bedroom, or "mattress barracks," was an idea that came and went very quickly, say inhabitants of the first co-ops. No matter, it was a favorite and enduring image of the tabloid press.

In early 1970 the Fischers moved into a Revolutionary Struggle co-op on Rossert Street, the first of four communal apartments that Joschka would co-habit and the last time that he would live together with Ede, even though they remained a couple for years after that. The Rossert Street house had high ceilings, varnished wood floors, and spacious rooms. Apartments in such big, old houses were easy to find and cheap in Frankfurt's abandoned West End. Modern Germans with proper salaries didn't want to live in places like these with leaky faucets, coal heating, and crumbling bathrooms.

It was in the co-ops that the men of the West German left were first taught some sobering lessons about women, in particular about recently emancipated German women and their distaste for German men with oversize egos. With the flowering of the women's movement, the women of the left insisted that the men practice what they preached about gender equality. To Fischer, as to many of his male peers, it initially came as a shock: "I grew up a little prince, the much longed-for son after two daughters, raised by a woman whose picture of the world was that a proper man would be attended to first by his mother and then his wife. I was taught that boys don't do dishes. I mean, I had two sisters for that."[7]

Within Revolutionary Struggle, a women's faction formed to address an array of issues. The young women of the West German left had already stood up and demanded to be heard during the student movement. But they found things in Revolutionary Struggle hardly better. It was the men who formulated the political line, decided on strategy, and led the study groups. In the co-ops, too, men dominated the supposedly democratic decision-making. When the women spoke out at meetings, it was not uncommon for men to begin talking to one another, sorting things out among themselves. Women were chastised as being "too emotional" and "hysterical." Fischer and Cohn-Bendit counted among the Frankfurt scene's biggest machos. Michaela Wunderle speaks highly of Fischer, a bright, capable autodidact. But she admits that he had a bossy way about him that rubbed a lot of people, especially women, the wrong way: "He had a surly manner and tone. As a woman, one got the feeling that they [Fischer, Cohn-Bendit, and others] just didn't take you seriously. You could criticize them all you wanted to but it didn't make a bit of difference. I'm describing a pretty harsh and undemocratic state of affairs here, I know. There were always fierce battles and long discussions over the issues but in the end, for them, it was all about driving a certain agenda forward, regardless. This Fischer definitely did."

These experiences prompted some of the Sponti women, among them Barbara Köster, to set up the first all-women co-op. They wanted to try living without domineering men constantly around them and they chose for the experiment 64 Bornheimer Landstrasse, a red brick building on a corner in Frankfurt's North End. The Sponti men, with little choice, had to strike out on their own, too, and ended up across the hall, sharing "the 64" with the women. Today, when Frankfurt tourist buses lumber by the renovated apartment house with a trendy bar on the first floor, the guide doesn't mention the first-ever all-women co-op. He says with a wink, "In the seventies, this was the co-op where Joschka and Dany lived." The tourists snicker and cameras click before the bus moves on. The Fischer-Cohn Bendit co-op became the most famous in Frankfurt—perhaps even the most illustrious of the Federal Republic. At the time, however, most of Frankfurt's citizenry didn't find anything cute about it at all.

"Things were wild in the co-ops then," remembers Michaela Wunderle. "But the 64 Bornheimer, that was *really* wild." The co-op in which Fischer, Cohn-Bendit, and several other men lived was one of five in the house. There was a constant flow of fellow politicos from abroad who would stay for indefinite amounts of time. Among others, the American New Left icons Abbie Hoffman and Jerry Rubin passed through "the 64." Television crews, interested primarily in Cohn-Bendit, came and went with regularity. So did the police, usually responding to neighborhood complaints about loud music. Lovers, comrades, guests from abroad, revelers from the night before—there was always a place in the "open" co-ops like 64 Bornheimer. One resident returned late one night to find German rock star Rio Reiser in his bed. Another, in the all-women co-op across the hall, identified Red Army Faction member Margrit Schiller between her sheets.

Into the Underground

At the time of Revolutionary Struggle's infiltration of Opel, other post-student movement groups were making their own preparations for revolution, including Ulrike Meinhof and Andreas Baader, the future founders of the Red Army Faction. The twenty-seven-year-old Baader had been languishing in a West Berlin prison cell, serving a four-year sentence for arson. In April 1968, together with political cohort Gudrun Ensslin, he had set fire to two department stores in downtown Frankfurt, a vaguely defined political act to protest consumerism and U.S. involvement in Vietnam. The nighttime fires resulted in their capture just days later. By early 1970, Ensslin was out on parole, eager to spring Baader and take up where they had left off.

On May 14, 1970, West Berlin prison guards transported Baader across West Berlin to the Institute for Social Issues in the Dahlem district, the leafy suburban home of the Free University, as well as of the U.S. military's command center. There, Baader, under guarded supervision, was scheduled to meet former *Konkret* editor Meinhof, ostensibly to discuss a co-authored book on socially marginalized youth. Baader's armed escorts led him into the institute's library where Meinhof awaited him, then unclasped his handcuffs. For the morning, the library was closed to the public, with the building's entrance manned only by the institute's sixty-two-year-old porter. The security for the visit was quite light, hardly indicative of the iron-fisted state that Baader, Ensslin, and Meinhof claimed they lived in.

The trio's backgrounds were as typically postwar as the Fischers'. Andreas Baader was the 1943-born son of a Wehrmacht soldier who never returned from the front. He was a bright but unruly student who dropped out of high school in Bavaria after run-ins with his teachers. Living in West Berlin, he was a known motorcycle thief and barroom brawler. Ensslin, twenty-seven years old, was a thoughtful pastor's daughter from southern Germany who had spent a high school year in Warren, Pennsylvania, before enrolling at the Free University to study German literature. She had a baby boy from another relationship. Baader and Ensslin met during the student movement and soon became known in the left-wing scenes in West Berlin and Frankfurt. Much like the SDS's Leather Jackets, the duo scorned the *weltfremd* intellectualizing rampant among the students and called for "harder measures" to fight the West German "police state."[8] Meinhof came from a well-known Protestant family, one which had defied the Nazis. She was educated in a Catholic day school. At university the gifted psychology student became involved in SDS during the late fifties and was active in the peace movement. She was an ardent pacifist before she became an urban guerrilla. Meinhof penned article after article on disarmament and the arms race in student newspapers until she joined the monthly *Konkret*, where she became a columnist and then in 1961, at the age of twenty-seven, chief editor of the republic's foremost leftist magazine.

Heads together in the library and chain-smoking, Baader and Meinhof whispered intensely to one another. The plumes of tobacco smoke prompted one of the guards to open a window just a crack. About an hour later, the institute porter, Georg Linke, impatiently seated two young women in another room. Although he had told them the day before that the library would be closed to the public for the morning, they just wouldn't take "no" for an answer. Then without warning a man, wearing a full-face ski mask and brandishing a revolver in one hand and a gas pistol in the other, burst through the institute's front door. A masked woman, wielding a Beretta with a silencer, followed on his heels. As Linke tried to block the intruders' way, the man fired at him. The breakout plan did not include the use of live ammunition, but in the tumult the man, a hired gun, panicked, wounding Linke in the arm and the stomach. The shot was the first of the West German militants' urban guerrilla war, the innocent Linke its first victim.[9]

The two women in the adjacent room, now also armed, rushed into the library, fired into the air, and shouted *Überfall!* (raid!). One of the prison guards jumped the masked woman, who was Gudrun Ensslin, starting a confused skirmish. Baader, Meinhof, and then the others raced to the opened window and jumped. They sprinted to a waiting silver Alfa Romeo and fled, accompanied by the screech of tires. The romantic and intoxicating flair of Germany's home-grown terrorists wouldn't be lost on a generation of imitators, nor on German movie makers, authors, and artists.

The militant clique that had gathered around Baader, Ensslin, and Meinhof had not, by the spring of 1970, named itself the Red Army Faction (RAF) nor had it openly committed itself to armed resistance. But the Dahlem break-out was the first armed strike of the so-called Baader Meinhof Group, and the act marked its entry into "the underground," the no-return world of guerrilla struggle. In different formations and fortified by consecutive "generations" of cadre, the RAF would wreak havoc in West Germany throughout the 1970s and would force the entire left, Joschka Fischer included, to take a stand on its maximalist positions.

Street Fighting Men

Strolling through the genteel neighborhoods of Frankfurt's West End today, one is hard-pressed to picture the backdrop of the "house wars" of the 1970s, which turned the then-decrepit quarter into the primary theater of confrontation between the Frankfurt police force and anarchist squatters. Today, the stately brick and sandstone villas are the pricey residences of bankers, gallery owners, lawyers, and professors. Branches of flowering bushes reach out through the high, wrought-iron gates and ancient chestnut trees line the streets. The only traces of the guest workers who lived in the derelict structures forty years ago are the upscale Italian restaurants offering dining on the alfresco patios that spill onto the sidewalks.

Even though the boarded-up West End estates lay in the immediate vicinity of the Kolbheim dorm and the Institute for Social Research, it wasn't until the early 1970s that students and other disenfranchised types took notice of the opportunity they presented for rent-free housing and communal ventures. By 1971 Frankfurt activists like Ede Fischer and

Michaela Wunderle had wrenched off the padlocks and pried open the doors to the dark, foreboding structures and picked out the former master bedroom or high-ceilinged living room that most suited their fancy. With a mattress on the floor and a couple of rolls of toilet paper, it became their new home; whole co-ops re-formed and moved in. The squatter movement in Frankfurt had begun.*

The disrepair of historic neighborhoods like those in the West End was a hot issue in Frankfurt, and not just for penniless students and politicos. The city on the River Main, like many other postwar West German cities, still suffered an acute housing shortage: the student population and burgeoning numbers of foreign guestworker families exacerbated the crunch and made the vacant buildings all the more conspicuous. The city's policy was to entice Frankfurt investors to buy the condemned houses, tear them down, and erect in their place office buildings. Once they had been sold, the turn-of-the-century villas could remain empty for years before the wrecking ball razed them. This drew the ire of many ordinary citizens—people concerned about the housing shortage, as well as the quality of life in their neighborhoods and the historic preservation of old Frankfurt. The first squatters wandered into a political minefield without knowing it.

Wrapped up as they were with the Opel factory, the squatters' movement in Frankfurt began with Fischer and the others still on the assembly line. But when civic disgruntlement turned into scattered protests, Revolutionary Struggle's members opened their eyes to a grassroots movement in the making, one that they sanguinely interpreted as lashing out at the contradictions of late industrial capitalism. Here was a constituency they didn't have to mobilize from scratch. The so-called *Häuserkampf*—literally "the war of the houses"—broke out around the time that Fischer's call for the workers at Opel to strike miscarried so badly. By fall 1971 so many old houses had been occupied in the West End that Frankfurt's mayor announced that the properties would soon be raided by the police.

By the cover of night, about a dozen people, Ede Fischer and a handful of law students among them, had moved into the three-story, turreted, red-brick villa on Grüneburgweg. The owner was an Iranian banker with close

* The squatter movement took off first in Frankfurt and then elsewhere, including in smaller cities on a smaller scale. In the late 1970s and early 80s, West Berlin was the bastion of the squatter movement. An offshoot of the squats were *Jugendzentrum* (youth clubs), small buildings or rooms that young people in nearly every small town occupied (or were given by the local authorities) in which they could meet, shoot pool, hold concerts, and the like.

ties to city hall and, supposedly, to the Shah himself, whom the former student insurgents hadn't forgiven for Benno Ohnesorg's murder. It was no surprise, then, that the police showed up the next day as promised, half of them in full riot gear. By the look of their new white Plexiglas helmets, the police were better equipped to quash civil disobedience than they had been in the sixties—even if nothing compared to what would come later.

In fact, it was the police who were in for the surprise. The squatters and their allies were waiting for them, prepared not to yield an inch. Linked defiantly arm in arm, about 100 defenders, including Cohn-Bendit and the Fischers, stopped the police at 113 Grüneburgweg's iron-gated entrance, refusing to let them pass. When the police regrouped and charged, the squatters held their ground as best they could. This time, unlike during the 1968 Easter protests against the Springer consortium, they actually returned blows rather than suffer them Gandhi style. Blood flowed and bones snapped under the crack of nightsticks. The clash escalated, with hand-to-hand combat between the police and the squat's guardians pouring out into the road. Photographs of the day show plumes of white smoke billowing from the front yard after the police had broken through the front line. A long-haired Fischer is clearly identifiable in one shot, looking a bit bewildered about what to do next. "It was so incredibly brutal," remembers Wunderle. "We hadn't experienced anything like that until then." From the villa's balconies, as solid as parapets, bottles and stones rained down on the police. Furious as their injured colleagues fell around them, police reinforcements fired tear gas in through the windows, rammed the front door, and stormed the building, laying into anybody within reach.

The police drove the tenacious squatters from the property and the residence was taken back by the city. But the Battle for Grüneburgweg would go down as lore and would open a new chapter in the confrontation between the city authorities and its opponents in Frankfurt—one that was beginning elsewhere in the Federal Republic, too. More than twenty police officers and scores of the squatters' defenders sustained injuries. Two dozen activists (notably, half of them women) were cuffed and carted off. Frankfurt's mayor, irate over the debacle, rescinded his order to clamp down on the houses, citing the safety of both his officers and the demonstrators.

The local media were so appalled by the police's actions that it even sided with the squatters, as did many Frankfurt burghers. "It was amazing," says Wunderle, "the enormous solidarity that we experienced from mainstream people. We weren't used to that at all. Their anger was directed at the investors and the police, not at us!" At a demonstration to protest police brutality and the city's housing policies a few days later, 3,000 people showed up, a turnout unlike anything the Revolutionary Struggle could ever amass on its own. Frankfurt's radical left now had a new political locus.

The Grüneburgweg clash was a caesura in more ways than one. It sent the blunt message to the Frankfurt left that brute force had to be met with counterforce. Violence, the language of the state, was the only language that it understood—and would respect. There would be no more gratuitous beatings taken by the Frankfurt left, not if Joschka Fischer and the Revolutionary Struggle had a say about it. The Battle for Grüneburgweg ushered in a new phase of militancy in Frankfurt, a hallmark of the West German seventies. In other cities, similar experiences sent radical leftists the same message. The new dictum was: if they were hit, they would hit back. The *Gewaltfrage*—the question of when, how much, and what kind of violence the left should employ—was on the table again across West Germany, but this time without the level heads of Rudi Dutschke and Herbert Marcuse around. Dutschke's rule of thumb—violence against people, no; violence against things, yes—no longer applied.

With the Grüneburgweg events, the Revolutionary Struggle shifted its focus away from the proletariat and toward the defense of the squats. For Fischer, so recently liberated from the assembly line, the organization of this militancy would become his domain. It is how Joschka Fischer would emerge from the shadow of his world-famous French friend and become a big shot on the Frankfurt scene. It would also, thirty years later, jeopardize his position as foreign minister of the united Germany.

In Frankfurt's West End, one house after another was squatted, with Revolutionary Struggle and the Lotta Continua exiles leading the way. The squats functioned as territory "liberated from the state." On the corner of Bockenheimer Road and Schumann Street, a block of squatted buildings positioned like a miniature fortress became the militant left's new headquarters. The squats were essentially urban communes, along the same lines as the co-ops only bigger, although there could be several co-ops in a house, each with different politics and rules. Although the working class was clearly missing, the Frankfurt squats fit the spirit of Italian anarchism and SDS anti-authoritarianism better than the mindless factory work at Opel. Rain-streaked banners made from bedsheets and red-and-black anarchist flags sagged from the open windows and steepled turrets of the villas. Speakers propped up on the balconies blared Pink Floyd, the Rolling Stones, and Germany's own Ton, Steine, Scherben (Clay, Stones, Shards) all day long. The latter's 1971-recorded squatter anthem (in fact, written about West Berlin's first squats) contained the refrain: "But the people in the squats cry: You're not getting us out! This is our house!" The graffiti sprayed across the facades spoke for itself: "Private Property is Theft!" and the anarchist classic: "Destroy that what destroys you!"

It's hard to say exactly when the Spontis as such emerged, or when just about the entire Frankfurt scene "turned Sponti," but as the 1970s began to unfurl and the alphabet soup of left-wing splinter groups expanded even further elsewhere, the diverse Frankfurt left coalesced into the Sponti scene. The "Sponti turn" in Frankfurt entailed an anarchistic re-evaluation of things that many radical left groups had extolled not so long before. The assembly line was no longer heroic and the proletariat life no longer glamorous. On the contrary, hard work, or more specifically "wage labor," as Marx defined it, was something to be avoided if at all possible. The first principle of the "spontaneous anarchists" was that the personal is political. In the co-ops, squatted houses, and other countercultural niches, the Spontis lived by their own political ethic, in defiance of the political culture sanctioned by the state and West Germany's compliant majority. Much like West Berlin's Kommune I founders, the Spontis' aim was to create a practical utopia in the here and now, not to sacrifice the present for a more perfect socialist order in the future.

At no time did the Spontis ever have a party platform, party membership cards, membership lists, an official central organ, or even an organization name. As former Sponti Georg Dick tells it, being a Sponti meant, first of all, *not* belonging to a dogmatic political organization:

> In Frankfurt, to be Sponti meant not to be a Trotskyist, Maoist or communist party member. It was an attitude and lifestyle more than a set political program. The goal was to realize your own individual potential within the larger community. The individual was the center of the revolution. One's personal development was an important part of a bigger political project. What held the Spontis together were the spaces that we created and co-habited, like the co-ops, the teach-ins, the squats, our newspapers, the Sponti assemblies.

Dick was a late arrival to the Frankfurt Sponti scene but quickly became part of the Cohn-Bendit-Fischer inner circle. With his scruffy strawberry-blond beard and rag-bag attire, he was a character who, like Fischer, came to the world of radical politics and communes in a roundabout way. The son of a sculptor, he dropped out of school early and trained as a car mechanic. Before long, he was too much for his parents to handle and was put in a reform school for troubled youth. When called up to register for the Bundeswehr, he fled the country, signing on to a Norwegian merchant ship as a sailor. When he returned to his hometown of Aachen a few years later, the student movement was in full swing. In the little college town, he and accomplices aided American GIs trying to desert by arranging passage for them to Holland or Denmark. The anarchist bent in Frankfurt attracted him to the university there and to the Spontis.

The loose Sponti community was essentially a forum for a hodgepodge of groups, projects, and initiatives in Frankfurt, including Revolutionary Struggle and the squats. Neighborhood outreach, social work with underprivileged kids, women's counseling, anti-authoritarian nursery schools—these counted as "politics in the first person," issues that directly affected the activists themselves. The Sponti ethos was creative, impulsive, irreverent, flamboyant, action-oriented. Living and working together as part of the anti-establishment left was something to be celebrated—it was fun and fresh, not a grind. The Sponti women swapped their dour black sweaters and army-green fatigues for colorful flea-market castoffs. Ede Fischer's brash outfits were considered the cutting edge of Sponti chic.

Cohn-Bendit with his off-the-cuff chutzpah and Paris May resumé personified the Spontis like no one else. Fischer threw his whole person into the Sponti movement. It was in the Sponti assemblies, their weekly forums, where Fischer made a name for himself as an orator and strategist. "You had to sell your ideas in the assemblies and the teach-ins," says Dick. "There was a bit of the spirit of the French Revolution there—the open public assembly, people gathered to govern themselves. There were a set of unwritten rules and Fischer mastered them quickly."

Cohn-Bendit and Fischer would become the head honchos in a movement that supposedly shunned authority figures. According to Ulrike Heider, a former Sponti woman, "These guys couldn't give orders and supposedly everybody could have a say before anything was decided. But even after everything had been thoroughly hashed out it was still in their power to make something else happen. When the co-ops of Cohn-Bendit and Fischer were of one mind, everything went the way they wanted it to."[10]

The blossoming of the Spontis and the Frankfurt left's reappraisal of its relationship to violence in the aftermath of the Battle for Grüneburgweg happened against the background of mounting political violence of another kind in the Federal Republic. Andreas Baader, Ulrike Meinhof, and Gudrun Ensslin were back in the country after a guerrilla training stint at a PLO camp in Jordan. Other West German groups committed to armed struggle, like Bommi Baumann's June 2 Movement and Frankfurt's own Revolutionary Cells, were active around the same time. Half a dozen Red Army Faction (RAF) members were behind bars and would soon go on trial. Post offices across the country had posters tacked up, showing grainy black-and-white photos of the republic's most wanted.

In early May 1972, the RAF launched a terror spree that horrified the Federal Republic. In Frankfurt, Munich, Karlsruhe, Heidelberg, and Hamburg, bombs exploded at U.S. military bases and at one of the Springer publishing houses. The RAF took credit for the attacks in its signature communiqués, starkly hand-typed on single sheets of typing paper. "West Germany is no longer a safe area for the U.S.'s extermination strategies in Vietnam," it declared after two pipe bombs went off in the officers' casino in Frankfurt, so close to the squats that Fischer heard the detonation from the Bornheimer Road co-op. One U.S. officer was killed, thirteen injured. In the austere lexicon of the guerrillas, "You must know that your crimes against the Vietnamese people have made you new, bitter enemies and that there won't be any place in the world where you can be safe from revolutionary guerrilla units."[11]

Hundreds of people crammed into the Frankfurt university's fabled lecture hall IV (the former location of Adorno's standing-room-only lectures) for a teach-in sponsored by the RAF support group, Red Aid. The crowd went silent when a reel-to-reel tape recorder was switched on. The high-pitched, singsong voice of Ulrike Meinhof cast an eerie spell over the hall. She called upon "all left-wing comrades" to jettison their "fear and hopelessness" and to "stop hiding behind the masses." She implored them to abandon their futile pacifism and to arm themselves in an international struggle against imperialism. "Dare to fight, dare to win!" she challenged them. Together with the RAF, they would turn "all American installations into the target of their attacks."[12]

The left-wing scene in Frankfurt, as everywhere in the Federal Republic, was abuzz with talk about the RAF attacks—reactions ranging from "secret pleasure" to "pure fear."[13] The circles in which West Germany's urban guerrillas moved, and that from which they drew recruits and logistic assistance, were concentric with those of the Spontis and the militant squatters in Frankfurt, West Berlin, Hamburg, and elsewhere. The likes of Baader and Ensslin, figures known in the Frankfurt left, could count on some of the squats for short-term refuge. Holger Meins, a prominent RAF member, had lived in a Frankfurt co-op with fellow SDSers in the sixties. Members of pro-RAF solidarity groups, such as Red Aid, included types like Ede Fischer and were integral to the Sponti community. Some activists drifted back and forth among the underground, the squats, and the solidarity groups.

Ultimately, there was nothing new about the RAF's themes: Vietnam, western imperialism, German–U.S.–Israeli collaboration, the crimes of the Nazi regime, and the falseness of bourgeois democracy. They were the same as raised by the student movement, but now shorn of any ambiguities, as well as the sixty-eighters' democratic, antiauthoritarian impulses. The armed factions reduced the student movement's concerns to their crassest possible expression. At the moment they adopted overt military strategies, their political development was stopped cold; their actions were essentially no more political than those of ordinary soldiers. Indeed, they claimed to be at war with the "fascist state."

Yet in the Frankfurt scene as elsewhere, the RAF commanded a certain amount of sympathy, even respect. They were referred to as "our comrades in the underground." The RAF's ultra-leftism was a cruder version of how much of the West German radical left saw the world: the Bonn state was an agent of global imperialism working as one with the United States and Israel. In its propaganda, the anti-Zionism of the New Left became crude anti-Semitism. As for the rationale for armed struggle, the RAF was just striking back, claimed many, even if, like the Fischers, they harbored grave reservations about murder as a political tool, guerrilla warfare as a political strategy, and the collateral damage of dead innocents. In the August 1973 edition of *We Want Everything,* one anonymous writer, probably a member of Red Aid, wrote: "The RAF is exercising its right to defend itself. That's a legitimate right! Everyone has the right to defend himself or herself against the daily violence of the state, against the violence inherent in our society. . . . A revolutionary has to adjust to the demands of the situation, not to the laws of his executioner."[14] There were already casualties among their own—Benno Ohnesorg and Rudi Dutschke, to name just two—not to mention the underclasses in the Third World, who paid in blood and sweat for the western world's prosperity. Scores of West German leftists would soon languish in prison. The ostensibly inhumane conditions of their incarceration were issues for the entire left, from writer Heinrich Böll and French philosopher Jean-Paul Sartre to Joschka and Ede Fischer.

Yet there was plenty that separated the Spontis from the armed underground. In the audience when the Meinhof tape was played, Cohn-Bendit blurted out, "Only the masses can make a revolution!"[15] If a bit melodramatic, his outburst nonetheless captured a key difference between Baader-Meinhof and Frankfurt's anarchos: the latter believed that the masses had to be radicalized (the buzzword was *Massenmilitanz*), that socialist revolution had to come from below. An avant-garde of German revolutionaries couldn't possibly "bring the struggle of the Third World to the metropolises of the West," as the RAF claimed to do. The Spontis also recoiled from the rigid hierarchy and vulgar Marxism. The RAF's ideological proximity to Eastern bloc communism—not to mention active cooperation with the East German regime as filmmaker Volker Schlöndorff portrays in *The Legend of Rita*[16]—won them no converts in the Frankfurt scene. What disturbed the Spontis wasn't simply the violence itself but also the apolitical way that the urban guerrillas employed it. "We didn't invent bourgeois violence, we were confronted with it," wrote one anonymous Revolutionary Struggle member in *Diskus*. "[But] the violence that we employ must be linked with positive moments: like the experience of solidarity and the opening of new modes of communication [with the masses.]"[17] In retrospect, the grave error of Fischer, Cohn-Bendit, and so many of the left at the time was to not undertake everything in their powers to distance the greater leftist community from RAF-style terrorism even sooner than they did.

To the Brink and Back

A year after Frankfurt's moratorium on raids, the city announced that all buildings illegally occupied could and eventually would be raided. For the Spontis, the squats had become more than a symbolic cause: they housed their own little left-wing world. Like any other territory, theirs had to be defended. The defense of the squats took on qualities of medieval sieges. In anticipation of police raids, the squatters nailed boards over their ground-floor windows and barricaded the properties. Outside the houses, mini-Maginot Lines of garbage dumpsters, junked cars, and other debris piled high demarked the front. The combatants clad themselves with padded leather jackets, helmets of all shapes and sizes, groin cups, and even gas masks. The uniform was complete with a bandana tied around the lower half of one's face, Butch Cassidy style.

Their arsenals included paving stones stocked on the upper floors, as well as discarded TV sets and even bathtubs, which could be unloaded onto the shoulders of charging police columns. The squatters' protectors were linked by a telephone chain; should the police launch a raid, one squatter would alert the next and so forth. In theory, the troops, like Minutemen, could be assembled to fight at a moment's notice. When the ragtag commandos showed up at demonstrations or house raids, the melees provided the city with uniquely gruesome spectacles. Within the Frankfurt left, the core of Revolutionary Struggle rose to the front of the Sponti movement through the house wars. It is difficult, or perhaps even impossible, to pinpoint exactly when or how Joschka Fischer emerged as one of its unofficial commandants. The loose contingent responsible for these matters called itself the Putz Group. In German, *auf den Putz hauen* is slang for having a wild, rowdy time. Perhaps "to raise hell" fits the meaning best. But the militancy of the Putz group wasn't empty hooliganism or violence for its own sake; it was understood as a response to the brutality and incursions of the police.

The Sponti scene and the new aura of militancy were attracting street-hardened types along the lines of the SDS Leather Jackets, but even tougher, including some with criminal records. The so-called Staffelberg kids, for example, were a group of troubled youth whom Frankfurt activists had "liberated" from the Staffelberg reform school near Frankfurt. They floated around the squats and, left unsupervised, set up drug dens in cellars and stole from people whose belongings were in the unlocked rooms. Another recruit was Hans-Joachim Klein, an auto mechanic by profession whose long face with its thick jaw was well known in the scene. A rough-cut plebe with a chip on his shoulder, Klein was a bruiser who relished being in the middle of the action. A key member of the Putz, he drifted between Revolutionary Struggle and other organizations like Red Aid and the circles around the terrorist Revolutionary Cells.*

* Frankfurt activists watched stunned and speechless as, in December 1975, television pictures of a wounded Klein, held up on either side by Austrian police officers, appeared on their television sets. Led by the internationally wanted terrorist Carlos, a six-person German–Palestinian commando attacked the OPEC ministers' conference in Vienna, killing three people and taking thirty-three hostages. The terrorist team, including Klein, escaped with the hostages and flew to Algeria, where they found safe haven. Klein spent twenty-six years in hiding, mostly in France, before handing himself over to German authorities in 2001.

What made Fischer so special in this milieu was that thuggish elements like Hans-Joachim Klein respected him. They could communicate with fellow-prole Fischer in a way that they never could with the cerebral student revolutionaries. Joschka could understand Hegel and talk on Cohn-Bendit's level—and with guys like Klein, too. Within the scene, Fischer became known as the "minister of defense." One story told about the Sponti years was that of the rape of a Sponti woman in one of the squats. The squatters quickly apprehended the rapist but agreed that calling in the police wasn't "the Sponti thing to do." Rather, Fischer and the Putz guys doled out the punishment, supposedly a beating that the perpetrator wouldn't forget.

Fischer got himself into tip-top shape for the purpose. He had long been a regular at the left's weekly soccer games in Ostpark (his position was right wing). In addition, he started working out everyday, for the first time since his days on the Stuttgart bike team. On Sundays, Fischer and the Putz, as many as forty men and women, drove out to the Tanus forest to train. Drills included stone throwing, one-on-one street fighting, and hostage freeing. Later, around 1974, claims German journalist Christian Y. Schmidt in his highly uncomplimentary biography of Fischer, the Putz added Molitov cocktail throwing to its repertoire.[18] Former Sponti Klein remembers the Tanus training: "We had the complete gear that the cops had, except for guns."[19] Sometimes the simulated fighting was so rough that comrades wound up in the hospital.[20] The women and those men "too soft" for it stopped coming, leaving Fischer with a loyal clique of men around him.

By 1974 most of the RAF's "first generation" were either behind bars or dead. Meinhof, Baader, and Ensslin were incarcerated in the maximum security blocks of the Stuttgart Stammheim prison. The West German left followed every twist and turn in the RAF members' trials. On the outside, a new generation of urban fighters and their nationwide solidarity groups took their instructions from the inmates, usually smuggled out by the lawyers or paroled comrades. Their designated mission was, first, to free their imprisoned leaders and only then to resume liberating the Third World. The RAF's lawyers stood between the state and the imprisoned militants and their supporters, trying to bridge the widening gap between them.

The only defense attorney not appointed by the court was the West Berlin lawyer Otto Schily, who by then had a reputation for representing left-wing causes. Yet Schily himself was atypical of the West German left, and indeed he vigorously distanced itself from the radicalism of the students and the militancy of the RAF. Born in 1932, Schily came from a well-off family that lived by the principles of anthroposophy, the naturalistic spiritual beliefs associated with Rudolf Steiner and Waldorf schooling. Studying in West Berlin, he befriended Rudi Dutschke, attended SDS meetings, and demonstrated against the Vietnam War. Yet Schily's professional activism on behalf of the left was motivated by a deep commitment to civil liberties and the rule of law. Unlike the students, many of whom were a good decade his junior, he believed in the rights inscribed in the Basic Law and the possibility of turning the Federal Republic into a healthy democracy. Never in public without a jacket, white shirt, and tie, Schily was proud to be "bourgeois." With his pageboy haircut and stiff-as-a-board demeanor, he cut an odd figure in the courtroom alongside the defendants in their zipped-down leather jackets and sunglasses. But the militants, especially his client Gudrun Ensslin, trusted him implicitly.

The RAF prisoners, along with just about the entire West German left, charged that the severe conditions of their imprisonment, particularly solitary confinement, amounted to torture. In the lingo of the day, the radical left claimed that the "state terror" practiced against the "politicals" was the equivalent of the methods of the Nazi police, the Gestapo. The Frankfurt Spontis, Red Aid, and many other groups associated with the radical left across the country orchestrated campaigns to have the conditions of confinement modified. The death of the RAF's Holger Meins after a two-month hunger strike confirmed suspicions that the state intended to liquidate the prisoners, one way or another. "Solitary Confinement is Murder!" screamed *We Want Everything* in October 1974, with a full front-page photo of the deceased Meins. Holger Meins's death triggered violent demonstrations in Frankfurt, West Berlin, and across West Germany.

But it was all going to get much nastier in the Federal Republic before things began to get better. On the morning of May 9, 1976, the corpse of forty-one-year-old Ulrike Meinhof was found hanging in her cell, suspended by a noose fabricated from torn towel strips. The radical left's reaction was that Meinhof had been murdered by the state, her suicide crudely faked.*

* Although this belief was widespread at the time in leftist circles, it was not true. Commissions and special investigations that followed amassed overwhelming evidence that Meinhof committed suicide. The myth that she was murdered was propagated by the RAF leadership itself for strategic reasons. Within RAF circles, those who truly believed that Meinhof had been murdered were looked down upon as naïve and gullible. See Aust, *Baader Meinhof*, 390; Peters, *Tödlicher Irrtum*, 450.

In Frankfurt an angry demonstration gave way to rioting. Flaming Molotov cocktails were hurled by the protesters, and cars and streetcars were burned. Although the use of "Mollies" at demonstrations was par for the course in Frankfurt, on this impassioned evening something happened that had never happened before. A group of protesters with three or four Molotov cocktails took aim at a passing police car. At least one of the projectiles sailed through the cruiser's open window and exploded, turning the vehicle into a furnace. Those nearby could see that at least one police officer was badly burned—or dead. The demonstrators, scared and shocked at their own brutality, dispersed at once.

The following day local newspapers reported that twenty-three-year-old Frankfurt police officer Jürgen Weber sustained burns over 60 percent of his body and lay in critical condition, his survival uncertain. The city, livid over the fiasco and Weber's injuries, formed a special commission to investigate and announced a $20,000 reward for information leading to the perpetrators' capture. Several weeks later, in early June, the Frankfurt police raided a dozen co-ops, among them Fischer's, detaining twelve men and two women on suspicion of attempted murder, first-degree assault, and membership in criminal organizations. Photos of the suspected "terrorists" flashed across television screens that evening. One of them, with scraggly beard and glasses, was the unemployed, twenty-eight-year-old Joseph Fischer.

Fischer's first incarceration since his teenage years lasted only one night. The Frankfurt Spontis took to the streets to force the city to come up with evidence to support the detentions. The authorities were indeed bluffing: there was no concrete evidence against Fischer or the others.*

The violence at the Meinhof demonstration and his own scrape with the law shook Fischer to his innermost core, prompting a crisis that would alter the course of his life. Following the May 1976 demonstration, more bombs had gone off, with more casualties. The war raging between the armed factions and the Federal Republic showed no sign of tapering off but, rather, every sign of escalating further, as indeed it would. Until then, the left's solidarity with the underground constituted a form of passive collaboration in which many activists were complicit. Perhaps, during that night behind bars, Fischer finally came close enough himself to imagine the rest of his life wasted in a florescent-lit cell, like the RAF comrades. Or perhaps the accumulated horror of the May 10 events

* Police officer Weber survived the attack. The case was, as of 2007, still open.

and the underground's pointless war with the state shocked his conscience to the extent that, at long last, he came to his senses and a voice within shrieked "Stop!"

Whatever the precise source of his epiphany, it was now clear to Fischer that this tryst with violence had gone way too far. The left had to slam on the brakes at once and pull back from the abyss it was careening toward. On the evening of his release, Fischer met with Cohn-Bendit and other Sponti leaders. They agreed that they not only had to renounce violence but also that they had to go further, to try to steer the entire West German militant left away from this reckless path. But coming clean in public and confronting the radical left with its folly was a high-stakes proposition: comrades who dared to express misgivings about the underground—reservations that many harbored privately—could pay for it with a brick through their window or much worse. Among the Sponti bigwigs, there was disagreement about who should be the bull to charge forward. "Some wanted me to do it," recounts Cohn-Bendit, "but I insisted that it had to be someone from the militant left, like Joschka. The radicals wouldn't listen to me as they would to him."

The next day, Fischer stepped up to an outdoor podium on Frankfurt's Römer Hill to address a crowd of 10,000 that had assembled for a conference on political repression. The Römerberg address was one of the most important, and most impassioned, that he would ever deliver. In order to get the militant left to listen—and take him seriously—he had to speak to them in their language, from the vantage point of the left. "Comrades," he began at the podium, elevated above a sea of demonstrators waving banners and placards, "what I have to say concerns what has happened here in Frankfurt over the last three weeks. . . . Ulrike," he said, using Meinhof's first name as the radical left did, "has been liquidated, in the true sense of the word." The Frankfurt left, he went on, expressed its repulsion and vented its rage at the "state's terror" through demonstrations and ferocious street battles. But as justified as this was, the use of militant direct action had hit a brick wall, Fischer told them. The Frankfurt left threatened to fall into the same trap that the urban guerrillas had, which would drive them even further into isolation, even further from the masses. Violence had become "an end in itself rather than a means to an end," Fischer preached with the conviction of the recently converted. "The more isolated we are, the easier it is for the cops to label us 'terrorists' and slap criminal charges on us. [At the Meinhof demo] we acted in the tradition of the house and street-car wars* without noticing that, politically, we're dangling in the air. This nearly broke us! But the Sponti movement is strong enough to learn from it!"[21]

The difference between the underground and the Spontis, Fischer continued, was that the Spontis integrated political praxis into their daily lives—as in the squats and the co-ops. There was a vivid, positive moment there, while for the RAF and the others there was nothing between "hopelessness" and "lashing out blindly." The guerrillas dwelled in a grim world of pure opposition and perpetual war, like soldiers. This, pleaded Fischer, can only lead in one direction, "to a fight to the death and with it self-destruction." Fischer, for the first time, publicly criticized the terrorist groups in unmistakable terms and urged them once and for all to lay down their weapons: "For the very reason that our solidarity belongs with our comrades in the underground and because we feel so closely linked with them, we call upon them to end this death trip at once, to return from their 'armed self-isolation.' We call upon them to put down the bombs and to pick up stones again."[22]

The crowd applauded with brio, sensing what was at stake. "Only someone like Fischer, with his street credentials, could have made a speech like that and be listened to by the spectrum of the Frankfurt left," explains Richard Herding, a former Sponti who was there. "It wasn't like some pacifist was telling us we should be peaceful. No one would have listened. But it was Fischer." This is exactly what the RAF feared most—penetrating questions from the ranks of the left, questions to which it had no answers. Fischer's address was a decisive turning point in Frankfurt and was discussed in left-wing circles across the country.

On the heels of these events, a June 1976 hijacking carried out by the Revolutionary Cells (its leader, Wilfried Böse, from Frankfurt) rammed home the points Fischer had made on the Römerberg. The Germans, acting on behalf of imprisoned Palestinian comrades, landed an Air France jumbo jet in Entebbe, Uganda, where on the runway they sorted out the hostages into two groups: Jews and non-Jews. They announced that the Jews would be executed if their conditions weren't met. Before the militants could act, the airliner was stormed by Israeli paramilitaries and the hostages freed. All of the terrorists as well as one passenger and a commando were killed. The episode shook the Frankfurt scene again, forcing many to re-examine the

* One of the Spontis' campaigns in the early 1970s was against a price increase for public transportation.

implications of their black-and-white picture of the Middle East. Even if their sympathy for the Revolutionary Cells was minimal, none of them thought that persons from their circles—from the Frankfurt scene—could, acting in the name of common causes, undertake such Nazi-like actions as to "select" Jews for execution simply for being Jewish.*

In Frankfurt, the street militancy petered out. The Putz was disbanded. The Spontis lay down the Molotov cocktails *and* their stones, too. Fischer withdrew from political activism, demoralized and lost. He drove a taxi to pay the rent and during the long night shifts he tried to make sense of the last decade of his life.

The German Autumn

The Frankfurt Spontis stepped back from the brink just in time—but West Germany's terrorist left still had one last cataclysmic burst of self-destructive fury in it. The grisly events of the German Autumn a year-and-a-half later would leave permanent scars on the West German body politic. The Federal Republic emerged from the German Autumn of 1977 severely shaken, its democratic principles pushed to the breaking point and the country deeply divided as never before between the state and its radical critics. It would also mark the end of the "red decade," which had begun with Benno Ohnesorg's death in June 1967.

On April 28, 1977, Baader, Ensslin, and Jan-Carl Raspe, found guilty on four counts of murder and thirty-four of attempted murder, received sentences of life imprisonment. In response, the sentenced RAF leaders sent out the order to the newly formed commandos in the country to undertake every measure to free them. In Cologne, on September 6, an RAF commando kidnapped Hanns-Martin Schleyer, the president of the German Employers Union—the "boss of the bosses," as the far left called him. The RAF's demands were the immediate release of Baader, Ensslin, and nine others. Their statement of conditions arrived at the police headquarters with a Polaroid photo of Schleyer, his faced bloated and scraped,

* In hindsight, Fischer places greater emphasis on the horror of the Entebbe hijacking opening his eyes to the senselessness of militancy and ultra-leftism than the Molotov cocktail attack at the Meinhof demonstration and its aftermath (see Paul Berman, *Power and the Idealists*, 57–60). The historical record, however, indicates otherwise. Perhaps Fischer stresses the former because he had no role in it—he watched the Entebbe events on television—while he was centrally involved in the Frankfurt excesses in May 1976 and even spent a night in jail.

his eyes hooded in fatigue. Behind him was the RAF emblem—a red star with a machine gun positioned horizontally in it; in front of him was a hand-scrawled sign that read: "9/6/1977, Prisoner of the RAF."

Coming on the heels of the assassination of several other prominent West German figures, including the federal attorney general Siegfried Buback, the Schleyer kidnapping triggered a crisis of major proportions in the Federal Republic. The chancellor, Brandt's successor Helmut Schmidt, also a Social Democrat, went on the air the next evening to steady the nerves of an on-edge nation. "In the long term, terrorism has no chance," he declared. "Not only is the will of the state against it, so is the will of the people." The Schmidt administration was prepared to spare no resources to track down Schleyer's abductors. It was equally committed to not acquiesce to the RAF's demands. The ensuing manhunt was the biggest ever in the republic: 150 officers were on duty at all times at the Special Commission 77 offices in Cologne, aided by teams of specialists, such as psychologists and international terrorism experts. Over 15,000 phone calls were monitored daily from the war room. Across the country, another 3,000 police officers were actively involved in the search for Schleyer.[23] Ultimately, the operation was directed from Bonn, by the chancellor himself.

The tension across the republic grew as the stalemate stretched into its first full week, and then a second, a third and, interminably, a full month. Neither the RAF nor the state blinked. Police checkpoints and spot searches backed up traffic on highways and roads across West Germany. All border crossings were on high alert and train stations crawled with soldiers and police. The Schmidt government assumed emergency powers to tap phones and search "suspicious private residences."

The pressure on West Germany's leftists was enormous. The state authorities suspected the entire movement of harboring the fugitives and assisting them through their networks. So bleak and menacing was this period for the left that it would become known as *die bleierne Zeit*, or "the leaden time." Activists describe the uncanny feeling of being trapped between a frantic, determined state authority, on the one side, with which the overwhelming majority of Germans identified, and the RAF and its hard-core sympathizers, who equated any kind of criticism with disloyalty, on the other side. They say they felt as if they were suspended in lead, unable to move forward or backward.

The Leaden Time is the German title of filmmaker Margarethe von Trotta's 1981 film (known in English as *Marianne and Juliane*), a classic of the politically charged New German Cinema of the seventies and eighties. In it, two sisters, the daughters of a Protestant pastor, go the way of the left in postwar West Germany. Yet, while Juliane works for a liberal feminist magazine, Marianne is part of the political underground. Even though Juliane and her colleagues believe that armed struggle is futile and shun the narrow, ultra-leftist thinking of Marianne and her guerrilla clique, they empathize with them, as fellow leftists who are hunted by the state's repressive security apparatus. Just as Marianne and Juliane are of the same biological family, their respective groups are of the same political family. When the imprisoned Marianne is found dead in her cell, everyone suspects that she was murdered by prison officials. In the penultimate scene, Juliane proves that Marianne couldn't have hanged herself with the noose provided as evidence; in other words, she was murdered by the state. The film illustrates how pervasive the angst and paranoia within the left was at the time, as well as the chasm of perception that divided the left and majority of average Germans.

In Frankfurt, as around the country, co-ops and squats were raided one after another, individuals were called in for questioning, and phone lines were tapped. "[The police] really turned the scene upside down," remembers Ede:

> They were everywhere and it created an incredible hysteria. Any kind of discussion about it [the RAF, the use of violence] in the scene was nearly impossible. People would flip out and break down crying. Fassbinder's film *Germany in Autumn* captures this paranoia very well. The doorbell rings unexpectedly and he thinks it must be a police raid. Imagine, some of us were even picked up [by the police] while we were collecting mushrooms way out in the forest. You felt like you were being watched wherever you were. It was a terrible, terrible time.

Cohn-Bendit appraised those weeks as follows:

> Around this time there was a lot of talk in the left about the Federal Republic having become some kind of all-powerful *Sicherheitsstaat* (security state). And it became a self-fulfilling prophecy: the RAF, through its campaign of terror against the state, turned the Federal Republic into just that, a *Terrorstaat*. In my opinion the state reacted in a very authoritarian way, in violation of fundamental rights, although, admittedly, it was in a very difficult position. Parallel [to pursuing the RAF] it launched a campaign against its sympathizers too. The logic was to "drain the swamp" in

> order to isolate the RAF. This was a completely ludicrous idea. Instead of seeking a dialogue with the left, the state restricted freedom of expression. It would have been a lot to ask of any state to keep a cool head in such a situation, but this one definitely didn't, not at all. It ended up turning the RAF's credo "either you're a friend or an enemy" into its own. There was no middle ground on either side, no space for discourse.

One—and perhaps the only—positive by-product of the hair-raising German Autumn was the initiative undertaken to set up an alternative, undogmatic left-wing daily newspaper in the Federal Republic. The idea had existed for some time, but it was the experience of the German Autumn that made it happen. As Ede Fischer and Cohn-Bendit attest, it was virtually impossible to have a rational discussion about the RAF, either within the left or outside of it. Leftists were completely shut out of the republic's media, which refused to print anything other than full denunciations of the terrorists and their methods. "They demanded that the left clearly distance itself from the RAF, forswear violence, and pledge allegiance to the constitution. We couldn't do that, not in the form they wanted," explains Thomas Hartmann, a former Frankfurt Sponti and the first editor-in-chief of *Die Tageszeitung* (The Daily News). "We realized that we had to have our own media, in order to discuss these topics and others important to us in our own way."

There were already many weekly and monthly alternative publications in cities across the Federal Republic. Almost every larger city had one.* "But we needed something daily and nationwide, more like France's *Liberation*," says Hartmann, who was close to the Paris-based daily. Several congresses followed at which leftists from across West Germany hashed out ideas for their own country-wide publication. The next year, initially twice weekly, *Die Tageszeitung*, known to all as the *taz*, rolled off the presses in West Berlin.

The RAF–Schleyer crisis escalated on October 13, when a commando unit of the Popular Front for the Liberation of Palestine, a South Yemen–based terrorist organization and old friend of the RAF, hijacked a Lufthansa airliner en route from the Canary Islands to Frankfurt, carrying eighty-seven, mostly West German passengers. The skyjackers demanded the

* Much like *Pflasterstrand* in Frankfurt, there was, for example, the *Kölner Volksblatt* in Cologne, the *Karlsruhe Stattzeitung*, and *Das Blatt* and *Der lange Marsch* in Munich, as well as the Information Service for Neglected News, among others.

release of the RAF prisoners, as well as two Palestinian comrades, and $15 million. The Boeing 737 hopscotched from Bahrain to Dubai to Aden in South Yemen before it landed in Mogadishu, Somalia. One of the pilots had already been executed when, on the Mogadishu runway, West German special operations, the GSG-9, stormed the plane, killing three of the four terrorists and freeing the hostages. In Bonn, Chancellor Schmidt wept for joy. But his relief was cut short.

The next morning, guards at the Stammheim prison reported that they had found Baader, Ensslin, and Raspe dead in their cells: the two men had been killed by bullet shots, pistols lying near their bodies. Ensslin hanged herself from a noose fastened to the window grating. Irmgard Möller, the fourth RAF prisoner on the seventh floor, was hospitalized from blood loss that appeared to have come from wounds to her chest inflicted with a fork. Even before a proper investigation could be conducted, West German authorities pronounced the deaths a collective suicide. The left, even louder than with the Meins or Meinhof deaths, screeched "Murder!"

Suspicions that prison officials had killed the RAF leaders and faked the suicides were not confined to the radical left, as von Trotta's *Marianne and Juliane* attests. Others, too, asked how it could have been possible for the inmates to get pistols in the country's highest-security prison. How did the prisoners, all in isolation cells and cut off from the world, know that the hijacking had failed? And how could the four communicate with one another in their sound-proof cells? Why were there no recordings from the bugging devices that had previously monitored the prisoners' every word? There were answers to these questions, as future investigations would bear out,[24] but at the time, with the paranoia and hysteria of the left at its zenith, there was no persuading anybody that the "security state" hadn't "liquidated" their comrades from the underground.

If anybody thought that with the Stammheim deaths the nightmare of the German Autumn was finally over, they were wrong. The next day, in the French town of Mülhausen in Alsace, the corpse of Hanns-Martin Schleyer was found in the trunk of an old Audi, three bullet wounds in the back of his head. The RAF's telephone message to the Stuttgart police was: "After forty-three days we have terminated the wretched and corrupt existence of Hanns-Martin Schleyer. In the context of the pain and our anger about the massacres in Stammheim and Mogadishu his death is meaningless to us."

Never before had the postwar republic been so divided, so fraught with mutual suspicions, so insecure about itself and fearful about the future. Given the hysterical climate of the moment, no one would have predicted that this chasm between the state and its critics would eventually close, and that the beginning of this process had already begun, before the corpses of Cologne, Aden, Mogadishu, Stammheim, and Mülhausen were lowered into the ground.

Part III

From Protest to Parliament

5

Between Harrisburg and Hiroshima

With a mandate to reform and liberalize, the Social Democrats put the Adenauer era and two decades of conservative rule definitively behind the Federal Republic. "We haven't arrived at the end of our democracy, we're just getting started," Willy Brandt announced with pomp to the Bundestag upon his 1969 inauguration.[1] He replaced Adenauer's slogan "No Experiments" with his own: "No Fear of Experiments!"[2] The Brandt government ushered in the new era with a flurry of domestic reforms and obsessive restructuring. New legislation in the domains of voting rights, the environment, labor law, social policy, the tax code, and civil liberties breathed fresh life into the body politic. Funding for education was doubled, which dramatically facilitated the access of lower income groups to higher education. Between 1970 and 1975, federal outlays for social and welfare policies increased by more than a third.[3] Also, in an act of extending the olive branch to the post-student movement left, the new government declared a general amnesty for extra-parliamentary activists who had run afoul of minor laws, such as trespassing.

In foreign affairs, Brandt's heralded *Ostpolitik* at the height of the Cold War brought his administration international kudos and earned him, in 1971, the Nobel Peace Prize. The Federal Republic's reaching out to the Eastern bloc encouraged reforms and diplomatic openings in eastern Europe in exchange for financial and other concessions. Relations with the Federal Republic's difficult communist neighbor, the German Democratic Republic, were put on a new footing that eased travel, communication, and trade between the adjacent German states. Although in word unification remained the Federal Republic's objective, in practice a "two-states" status quo was accepted and neighborly relations became the order of the day. In 1972 Bonn and East Berlin "normalized" their relations; permanent missions were opened in each other's capitals. Not least, the *Ostpolitik* helped bring about a geopolitical thaw in relations between Washington and Moscow, paving the way for détente.

This, many West Germans felt, was where their postwar republic was meant to stand: firmly on the side of peace, as a civil mediator between belligerent powers, working for compromise and rapprochement in multilateral forums. Brandt's initiatives inspired young West Germans and gave them reason to be proud of their country. They streamed into the SPD and membership jumped by a nearly a quarter between 1969 and 1972.[4] By the early 1970s, most West Germans had subordinated nationalist ambitions to the general good of the supranational collective, in the form of the European Community. In stark contrast to a decade before, roughly two-thirds of West Germans considered European integration "more urgent" than German unity; among young people, pro-Europe sentiment was even higher.[5] "Never again war," it seemed, was etched into the conscience of the postwar generations—and through the *Ostpolitik*, as well as the ever-more-united western Europe, it became reflected in the country's *Staatsraison*, too.

Surveys from the mid-1970s depict a decidedly more modern and mature Federal Republic, with a citizenry increasingly self-confident and worldly.[6] Identification with the traditional German values of duty, hard work, social conformity, and sacrifice had dropped off significantly. Instead, West Germans had begun to set more store in personal freedom and individuality. For the first time, the republic's citizenry ranked "post-materialist" issues like the environment high on its list of priorities. The same surveys showed that churches, trade unions, and political parties were less important to West Germans than they had been, especially to the generations born and raised after the war, which included the children of the late 1950s baby boom, who in the mid-1970s were entering young adulthood. So, too, attitudes toward the patriarch-led nuclear family had shifted. Families were smaller, divorces were more prevalent, and sexuality was more open. The birth control pill was not only available to women as it had been since 1961, but also was acceptable for young women to use in a way that it hadn't been before. Women could increasingly be found in professions that had been the sole reserve of men, while the latter now shared household duties and child care. The educational system had been revamped so that young people no longer had to endure what the Fischers and their contemporaries had. West Germans' horizons had expanded to the world beyond their living rooms, and that included more active involvement in the processes of democracy to shape that world.

These modern attitudes and new expectations, however, contributed to a sense of frustration and dissatisfaction that seemed to pervade the republic as the seventies wore on. Brandt resigned as chancellor in 1974 upon revelations that one of his closest aides was an East German spy. The scandal shook the republic to its core. This national calamity came on top of the onset of the worldwide oil crisis in 1973 and the devastating 1972 Munich massacre, when Palestinian terrorists murdered nine Israeli athletes at the Munich summer Olympic games. The Olympics were supposed to show off a new, optimistic, healthy Germany—one that had come so far since the last time Germany had hosted the games, in 1936, under Hitler. The Social Democrat–Liberal coalition under Brandt's successor, Helmut Schmidt, never had the same momentum that propelled Brandt's landmark first term. The "reform euphoria" that accompanied the Social Democrats to power in 1969, and was potent enough to reelect the coalition resoundingly in 1972, dissipated soon after that, giving way to the somber realism that characterized the Schmidt years.

By the mid-1970s, the Social Democrats' "reform from above" stalled before it could deliver many of the far-reaching changes that its enthusiasts had anticipated. Conservatives managed to block or dilute a host of liberalizing measures, including women's increased access to abortion. In 1972 the government had incensed the left by banning communist party members and other radical leftists from the civil service, including as teachers in public schools—evidence that anticommunism wasn't the purview of the Christian Democrats alone. A bitter reality for all West Germans, after nearly two decades of economic boom, unemployment was a factor and would become a permanent part of the republic's landscape. Inflation hit 7 percent. The Schmidt government was on the defensive, floundering as the party's support waned. In 1976 the coalition eked out a narrow election victory. Soon on its heels, the harrowing German Autumn pushed the republic's democracy to its breaking point and left in its wake a country suddenly unsure of itself after so many triumphs.

No longer so cowed by the state and its officialdom, West German citizens responded by taking measures into their own hands even before the Social Democrat reforms had begun to flag. A sure sign of West Germans' evolving familiarity with democracy, thousands of locally organized "citizens' initiatives" arose during the early 1970s to push for change from below when it failed to come from government. In the spirit of a civil society that had never before existed in Germany, grassroots projects that focused on local issues, like airport noise, public transportation costs, housing, landfill sites, highway construction, paths for bicyclists, and urban planning, as well as dying forests and violence against women, among many, many others, had sprouted up across West Germany. "The fixation on institutional politics," noted a 1980s study, "a deeply anchored authoritarian syndrome of the postwar society, had been broken through. The whole political system suddenly seemed open to change, so long as one applied enough pressure and seized the initiative."[7] Historian Manfred Görtemaker gives the 1968 partisans a piece of the credit: "Although the cerebral student movement was quite distant from the rest of the population, its actions and conscious breaking of the rules of the political game showed what possibilities there were when one employed a provocative, media savvy strategy."[8]

But unlike the student movement, or much of the 1970s New Left, the citizens' initiatives emerged in order to effect change on specific issues, usually in a given community or region, not to alter the political system as a whole. These local campaigns were initially non-ideological, consisting of concerned residents whose politics cut across the republic's spectrum. They understood themselves as complementary to local government and, though opposed to certain policies, not as a political alternative to the liberal democratic order. In and around Frankfurt, for example, the most pressing issue was the planned expansion of Frankfurt's international airport, already the biggest in West Germany. The proposed new runway would wipe out a huge chunk of old-growth forest; the primary beneficiary of the airstrip would be the U.S. Air Force, whose headquarters were in Frankfurt. Other local citizens' initiatives had names like the Rhine-Main Initiative against Environmental Destruction, the Single Mothers and Fathers Tea Room, the "Women Help Women" house for battered women, and the Upper Rhine Direct Action Committee against Ecological Damage through Nuclear Power Plants. According to one estimate, by the mid-1970s, between 15,000 and 20,000 citizens' initiatives had formed across the country.[9] By cautious calculation, they included more than three times as many people as had the student movement.[10] By the end of the 1970s there were more than 38,000 civic groups, with more members (2–3 million) than any of the political parties.[11]

Citizens' initiatives as such were nothing new to Joschka Fischer and the Spontis. Since the early 1970s they were active in Frankfurt-based rent boycotts as well as protests against real estate speculation and ticket price hikes for the city's streetcars. These were citizens' initiatives of the early 1970s. Yet the left's program to "radicalize" these campaigns, like the housing issue in Frankfurt, had the effect of scaring off ordinary folk. The radical left scoffed at the notion that German "citizens" could meaningfully transform the republic through grassroots engagement. And, frankly, many of the local initiatives looked rinky-dink to the Spontis. "Come on, let's be honest," Joschka Fischer asked laconically in a 1978 essay, "Who among us is really interested in the water shortages in Vogelsberg [40 miles northeast of Frankfurt], the city highway in Frankfurt, or nuclear power plants anywhere, because he feels personally affected by them?"[12]

At first the citizens' initiatives across the Federal Republic functioned independently of one another. Most were single-issue projects that would dissolve after they'd remedied the problem at hand. But that began to change in the course of the 1970s as the "new social movements" arose out of this diverse array of projects, initiatives, and campaigns. The contours of the powerful new movements—the ecology, antinuclear, women's, and peace movements, among others—were gradually coming into focus as citizens' initiatives banded together and widened their agendas. In the late 1970s and early 1980s, these movements would mobilize hundreds of thousands—even, at their height, millions—of Germans, politicizing many people who fell outside of the German left, as well as the young generation that followed the sixty-eighters.

Fischer in Purgatory

The 1976–77 events that culminated in the German Autumn sent Joschka Fischer into a deep funk. For the first time since Benno Ohnesorg's death in 1967, his certainty about his place in the world was severely shaken. Fischer remained a Sponti but retreated from political activism into the sphere of the private, where he would practice "politics in the first person" for the first person only. Until then, he had moved effortlessly from one front to the next, from the student movement to the Opel factory, from Opel to the house war and the Putz. But all of this happened within the parameters of revolutionary Marxism. He wasn't sure what existed for him beyond it. Fischer's political crisis enveloped his whole person. His soul-searching would last six long years. Where had the left gone so wrong? he asked himself. How could it have taken him so far down a deadend road? And just who was Joschka Fischer if not a professional revolutionary?

Fischer pondered these and other questions as he drove a night taxi in Frankfurt. During the day, Fischer and his faithful hound Dagobert, a friendly reddish brown mutt, often dropped by the Karl Marx Bookshop on Jordan Street near the university, a collective run by Cohn-Bendit, Tom Koenigs, and a handful of other Sponti veterans. Koenigs was the straitlaced son of an investment banker, who upon receiving his substantial inheritance in the late 1960s donated it to the bank accounts of the Vietcong. The hole-in-the-wall bookshop, which still existed as of 2007 under the same name, stocked both the classics and the latest in literature, politics, and philosophy. Books were stacked to the ceiling on brick-and-board shelves. The Sponti guys would sit around for hours, drink espresso, smoke, and talk. Fischer later opened a reputable second-hand book section in the shop's cellar, used books being an area in which he had some expertise.

With his repudiation of violence, Fischer shed the macho image that went with being part of the tougher-than-thou Putz. He traded in his black apparel and scuffed leather jacket for corduroys and sandals. In one 1979 photo he appears relaxed and untroubled in a Norwegian ski sweater, his stringy hair shoulder length, almost feminine. He knocked around the idea of joining a rural commune, dropping out and "getting back to nature" as many others had. He took up the drums and swallowed hallucinogenic mushrooms to escape his inner demons. During the "years of disillusionment," as he calls them, no one was harder on Fischer than Fischer himself. He applied rigorous self-critique to his person and his politics. "He wasn't depressive, that's not Joschka, just empty. He had to work it all through for himself," explains Cohn-Bendit, who was quicker to adjust. Some of Fischer's confessions appeared in *Pflasterstrand*, the flippant bi-monthly of Frankfurt's diverse left-wing scene, edited by Cohn-Bendit and then later Georg Dick. The rambling *Pflasterstrand* essays chart the depths of Fischer's disillusionment and his gradual re-entry into the world of politics.

In one piece Fischer mulls over the New Left's compulsory anti-imperialism. "Yes, yes, good old anti-imperialism, which not so long ago took up about half of my life," he confessed in diary-like style. Every weekend the West German left had hit the streets to display its solidarity with the revolutionary movements in one or the other Third World country. "This trip began with Persia," wrote Fischer, referring to the 1967 demonstrations against the Shah's visit, "and over the years led through the labyrinthine jungle paths of Indochina, saw the uprising of the Red Guards in the Chinese Cultural Revolution, was present at the building of socialism in Cuba, followed Che Guevara and his guerrillas to Bolivia, and experienced the Russians' brotherly march into Prague." All without ever leaving Frankfurt! But the endless demonstrations didn't really have to do with the Third World or its oppressed peoples, he argued. Through these movements on the other sides of the globe, the New Left projected its own utopian hopes for another kind of state and society, one that never existed–and never will. "Our revolution never happened, neither here nor in Vietnam, Persia or China," he wrote bitterly. In contrast to orthodox communists who applauded the "real existing socialism" of the Eastern bloc, the New Left had no tangible conception of what it really wanted. More often than not, these glorious struggles ended in one-party dictatorships, nationalist regimes, and state-run industrial capitalism. What happened when the Iranian people finally overthrew our long-time nemesis, the Shah? Fischer asked. Who would have ever thought it? An Islamic theocracy comes to power! "Looking back," he concluded soberly, "Marx and his proletarian revolution have served over long years as an ersatz religion that gave my life whatever meaning it had."[13]

It was during this period that his relationship with Ede, his wife of ten years, fizzled out for good. Their childless marriage had followed the course of the "red decade" and fell apart, like the West Germany's radical left, around the time of the German Autumn. The relationship hadn't been on solid footing for some time. The couple hadn't lived together since the co-op in Rossert Street; both had had other lovers and they had tried to split up many times. "It had been clear to us for a while that it didn't have a future," explains Ede, who never remarried and lived, as of 2006, in Frankfurt, in a co-op. She still wears dangling jewelry, rolls her own cigarettes, and exudes an unpretentious, bohemian air, much like the person her acquaintances describe from the old days. "We'd break up and then one of us would get so down that the other would come back. It went on like this for years but I knew it was over when he got together with Inge [Pensgens, his second wife]. Then I realized that it was really over." Nevertheless, the final separation crushed her.

The sectarian 1970s may not have gotten the West German left any closer to revolution than did the student-movement 1960s, but during its various battles a thriving "alternative scene," as it was called, established itself in West Germany's urban centers—a counterculture much broader and more diffuse than the squatters, the Spontis, or any other explicitly political group, although its origins are there. In Frankfurt, Cohn-Bendit's *Pflasterstrand* was the linchpin of the city's subculture, and flipping through its pages one gets a sense of the scene's vibrancy. Its early editions look and read like a cross between punk-rock fanzines and *The Village Voice*. The first issue in October 1976 contained articles about the Brokdorf nuclear power plant on the North Sea, a hunger strike by RAF prisoners, health food, and the sterilization of men. Its pages, full of witty montages and illustrated cartoons, promoted a subculture that included cafes, concert halls, cinemas, theatres, women's self-help groups, farmers' markets, and experimental schools. The Karl Marx Bookshop was just one of the alternative businesses that took out ads in *Pflasterstrand*. Others, from the "Anti-Supermarket" to the "Freak-Auto" mechanic shop, enabled scene dwellers to circumvent the bourgeois world if they chose to.

Sourly, some referred to *die Szene* as a left-wing ghetto. Wasn't this the very opposite of a "long march through the institutions"? Marginalized and inward-looking, lefties and freaks inhabited their own little world, cut off from the reality of most ordinary Germans. This alternative world could be more accurately described as the product of a long march *around* the institutions. Conversely, one could argue that these alternative establishments and their patrons were part of a much changed, more pluralistic West Germany, one no longer exclusively populated with the likes of philistines, bankers, and ex-Nazis. The dissidents had infiltrated and participated in transforming German society without acknowledging their own accomplishment. What at that time was freakish and *Szene* would, decades later in somewhat milder form, become part of everyday culture.

The remnants of the New Left were only slowly coming to grips with the fact that the Federal Republic had benefited from a complex learning process. Throughout the seventies, West Germany's radical leftists maintained the fiction that the republic was an authoritarian police state. "Our belief was that the state was becoming more and more fascistic," explains Cohn-Bendit in 2006 in Frankfurt's Café Laumer, the old West End café where philosophers Adorno and Horkheimer once shared afternoon coffee and torte. "We thought at some point it will become an absolute fascist state, like in Orwell's *1984*. And then suddenly we were there, it was [nearly] 1984 and we look around and say, where is it? Wait a minute, something's wrong here."

During long-night shifts driving his taxi, Fischer was put back in touch with "normal Germans," the types who didn't read *Pflasterstrand* or live in co-ops. As he chatted with his fares, he experienced a West German society unlike the one he dropped out of. The values and expectations of the German burgher had undergone a sweeping transformation, in part, at least, a by-product of the jolt they had received from the student movement and its extra-parliamentary heirs.

Uprising in the Kaiserstuhl

The tiny town of Wyhl (population 3,612) in southwestern Baden, along the French border and just north of Switzerland, was where citizens launched the first full-fledged grassroots stand against a planned nuclear reactor in West Germany—and, against all odds—succeeded in blocking it. Until Wyhl appeared on the republic's radar in 1974, the government's decade-old nuclear power program had hummed along with little attention paid to it. The industry and its backers in all three of the republic's main political parties claimed that nuclear power was the cheapest, cleanest energy that humans had ever produced and that, one day, might even make household energy bills obsolete. But as an incipient antinuclear movement grew in the United States and the possible side effects of this new *wunder*-technology came to light, West Germans in the vicinity of nuclear power plants, nuclear-waste processing plants, and reactor construction sites had begun to take notice and to grumble. The West German government, they feared, may have bought into nuclear energy too hastily, without assessing its risks or consulting the people.

The nuclear plant scheduled to be built in Wyhl united the region's wine growers and other farmers, who charged that the steam generated from the plant's cooling towers would block the sunlight to their vines and other crops. Local women questioned the implications of higher than normal levels of radiation on pregnancies. Fifty related citizens' initiatives sprang up in the eight counties around Wyhl,[14] as well as many more in border regions in France and Switzerland.[15] The first demonstrations in 1974 brought together protestors ranging from traditionally Christian Democratic–voting farmers to lefty professors from the nearby city of Freiburg, as well as concerned citizens from around Basel, across the Swiss border, and French Alsace—all residents of the transnational Kaiserstuhl region. In February 1975 demonstrators stormed the construction site and occupied it. Their occupation was illegal—and peaceful. The police raided the site and cleared out the protesters, only to have it reoccupied by the locals a few days later, who set up an encampment of hammered-together wooden huts and tents that would remain there for nearly a year. Eventually, the authorities backed down and scratched their plans for a reactor site in the Kaiserstuhl. Without willing it, the citizens of Wyhl and the transnational residents of the Kaiserstuhl created the template for the West German antinuclear movement.

"At first no one thought that they had a chance," explains Roland Vogt, an early campaigner against nuclear power and arms:

> The citizens' initiatives in the Kaiserstuhl faced down gigantic opponents, the state government of Baden Württemberg and the energy company Baden Works. David slew Goliath but, importantly, without the use of violence or institutional power. It was a genuine popular uprising that undermined institutional power by using classic means of non-violent protest. For the first time "success" and "nonviolence" were linked, an incredible breakthrough for the environmental movement. Suddenly Wyhl was an example and a legend. Elsewhere people near planned or existing nuclear sites said, "This could happen to us to. If this is so dangerous, we should do something about it."

The dramatic occupation of the Wyhl site in Germany's southwestern-most corner caught the eye of a twenty-seven-year-old woman named Petra Kelly, who at the time was working for the European Commission in Brussels. Kelly was born in Bavaria in late 1947, just a few months before Joschka Fischer, and had attended grade school at a Catholic convent. She spent her high school and college years in the United States with her mother and stepfather, a retired U.S. Army officer. Kelly graduated from American University in Washington, D.C., and had volunteered on Bobby Kennedy's and then Hubert Humphrey's 1968 presidential campaign. Kelly was politicized in the United States during the 1960s, but not first and foremost through the protests against the Vietnam War. She was a student activist and, in contrast to peers in the West German student movement, she was a pacifist, a liberal feminist, and a mainstream Democrat. Her heroes included Martin Luther King Jr. and Mahatma Gandhi. She had taken a special interest in nuclear power and the effects of radiation on human beings following the death of her younger sister from cancer at the age of ten. Shortly after her sister died she attended a conference held by the U.S. consumer rights advocate Ralph Nader, who was speaking on the links between radiation and cancer.[16] This was her induction into antinuclear politics.

A mid-1970s photo shows Petra Kelly in front of her Brussels office building, her thumbs hitched into her jeans' pockets, wearing a typically American hooded sweatshirt with the slogan (in German) "Better active today than radioactive tomorrow." This was pure Petra Kelly: a bit of America, a dash of Germany, and a pinch of the united

Europe, all in one. Kelly's combination of frail physical beauty, down-to-earth poise, and emotional devotion to her beliefs endeared her to audiences everywhere. One of her books was titled *Think from the Heart*. She did exactly that. The petite Kelly, with her dirty-blonde 1970s shag cut, was known for her alluring charisma as well as her passionate engagement. "Men and women immediately fell in love with Petra," said one colleague from the Greens who worked with her closely.[17] Her lovers were inevitably her political soulmates—politics and romance inseparable for Kelly.

The first time that Roland Vogt experienced Petra Kelly "live" was at Wyhl. She had come from Brussels to participate in the Easter peace march, a tradition that was being revived. Vogt, the event's organizer, was at the time still in the Jusos, the Social Democrats' youth branch. As a law student during the late 1960s he had shunned the Social Democrats and steered clear of SDS as well. The lesson that he took away from Benno Ohnesorg's death and the attempt on Rudi Dutschke's life was very different from that of the student radicals. The shock that he experienced sent him searching for ways to circumvent violence. He switched his major to political science and immersed himself in the teachings of Protestant pacifists. In 1971, impressed with Brandt's reforms and the *Ostpolitik*, he joined the Jusos. But by the time of the Wyhl occupation he had already become disillusioned with the Schmidt-era SPD.

In Wyhl on this Easter Sunday, under a powder-blue sky, Kelly spoke from a lectern perched on a NATO bridgehead high over the River Rhine. Vogt was spellbound—and in love, too. Roland Vogt would become, for a time, Kelly's lover and political confidant. "It was a fantastic, down-to-earth speech and against this striking backdrop," he remembers. "The Wyhl farmers were awed that this woman they'd never heard of, from far-away, bureaucratic Brussels, would come and speak their language, about their issues." In her American-intoned German, Kelly told the Kaiserstuhl activists that they were not alone, but part of a worldwide movement against nuclear power and arms.

The Easter event in the Kaiserstuhl was one of the very first that linked antinuclear power politics and peace issues—a bond that wasn't, by any means, obvious to the traditionally conservative farmers of the Kaiserstuhl. "The Wyhl activists were very skeptical about the Easter march because the peace movement was considered 'left,' " explains Roland Vogt, who admits that, at the time, the diminished peace movement included many German Communist Party (DKP) members, which was the worry of the Wyhl campaigners.* "But we convinced them that these issues superseded categories of 'right' and 'left,' and that nuclear-generated power and nuclear bombs are different sides of the same coin," Vogt says.

During the course of the 1970s, many local citizens' initiatives reached out and linked up with like-minded groups in neighboring towns and regions. The Wyhl activists, for example, found common cause with those protesting nuclear power plants elsewhere in the Federal Republic. They coordinated their campaigns with one another and across borders as well. These same issues, they learned, were fueling antipathy throughout western Europe and in North America, too. It is impossible to pinpoint a date or event that marked its birth, but by 1976–77 the antinuclear movement was a loose, flexible network of activist groups that spanned the country. Its symbol was a laughing yellow sun and the simple slogan "*Atomkraft? Nein Danke*" (Nuclear power? No thanks).

The burgeoning ecology movement with ever broader demands brought together ostensibly unrelated constituencies such as organic farmers, disillusioned Social Democrats, health food enthusiasts, Christian pacifists, old leftists, outdoorsmen, *Blut-und-Boden* nationalists, and middle-class liberals. Opposition to nuclear power became the common denominator of nearly all of the environmental groups—*the* mobilizing issue in West Germany during the latter half of the 1970s. Indirectly through it, the peace and disarmament movements of the postwar decades were reanimated in a new form. New coalitions were forged and networks thickened. Led by Roland Vogt and the left-wing Social Democrat Jo Leinen, the Federal Union of Environmental Citizens Initiatives (BBU), founded in 1972, was the first umbrella organization for over a thousand environmental citizens' initiatives in southern Germany alone.

The size of the antinuclear movement dwarfed the paltry thousands that the student movement or the radical left could ever coax onto the streets. For the environmentalists, 1977 wasn't first and foremost the year of the German Autumn (although it affected them, too); it was the year that the antinuclear

* The mid-1970s peace movement—a much smaller, narrower version of its 1950s and 1960s predecessors—included organizations, media, and undercover plants financed by the East German government. These elements dominated the depleted peace movement during much of the 1970s, something that independent activists, like those in the anti-conscription campaigns, tried to resist. By broadening the peace movement to include antinuclear energy activists and grassroots types like the Wyhl wine growers, Vogt, Kelly, and other independent activists marginalized those elements.

movement exploded in numbers. In the village of Kalkar, near the well-heeled Rhine metropolis of Düsseldorf, 60,000 people demonstrated against a planned breeder reactor there. Others converged on places whose names became synonymous with the antinuclear movement: Brokdorf, Gorleben, Hanau, Grohnde, and, later, Wackersdorf, among others. The demonstrations against the planned nuclear waste-storage site in Gorleben, in old salt mines that lay between Hamburg and Hanover, attracted over 100,000 protesters.[18] The protests and occupations of the nuclear sites that began in the seventies would continue into the eighties and some even into the nineties. The activists endured freezing winters in the "anti-atomic villages," drenchings by police water canons, and seemingly endless legal battles. They made enormous commitments of time to champion a nuclear-free Germany.

In the late 1970s, radicalism and the debate over employing violence wracked the antinuclear movement much as it did the radical left. "The *Gewaltfrage* wasn't just an issue for the radical left alone," explains Uli Cremer, a member of the Hamburg section of War Resisters International. "The whole left, including the antinuclear movement, debated how best to respond to the repressive force of the police and the surveillance methods of the security services. Out of sheer frustration even mainstream currents in the movement seriously considered and at times condoned the use of violence—against things, though, not people—in response to the actions of the police." One major difference was that in the antinuclear movement, this kind of militancy existed mostly on the fringes, a distinction that West German police regularly overlooked, turning demonstrations into smoky battlefields with state-of-the-art counterterrorism technology purchased for use against the urban-guerrilla factions.

West Germans' concerns about the environment had been stoked by a confluence of contemporary events and new currents of thought. The energy crisis peaked in autumn 1973, shocking West Germans as it did the rest of the industrialized world. The cost of oil quadrupled and in the Federal Republic gasoline prices skyrocketed. West Germany's traditional industries found themselves staring at red numbers. A ban on nonessential driving left streets completely empty on the weekends. One amusing newspaper photo that appeared during the crisis shows a Volkswagen van being pulled along a rural road by two plow horses.[19] But at the time, it was anything but humorous. The notion that the world's resources were finite, and that there was a tangible price to pay for unregulated economic growth, hit home with a bang.

A parallel development—a spate of new books critiquing western notions of progress and growth—exacerbated the pessimism that seemed to pervade the late seventies: fears about the sustainability of the ecosystem, about nuclear war, about humanity's fate in general. A much discussed report was issued by a global think tank Club of Rome, entitled *The Limits of Growth*,* which ominously warned that depleted resources jeopardized the kind of growth that the industrialized world had experienced during much of the twentieth century. Following the lead of American thinkers examining issues around sustainability in a postindustrial world, West German authors from diverse backgrounds questioned the industrial world's blind rush forward in the darkest of terms.

Some of these critiques tapped a romantic, naturalistic vein that cut through West German society, on the right as well as the left. *A Planet is Plundered*, penned by a leading Christian Democrat, Herbert Gruhl, became an unlikely bestseller. Gruhl argued that the destruction of the environment through unchecked economic growth and overpopulation would expedite the decline of the West. Some critics saw in the book a racist call for an ecological dictatorship; others called it a quirky but disturbingly accurate analysis of the challenges facing global society. Gruhl was eventually made persona non grata in the CDU for his freethinking and quit the party.

Also, many Germans were profoundly uneasy about the new forms of technology that had recently come into their lives. There was deep-seated suspicion that the promises of modernity for a better world could lead to a brave, new world à la Huxley. These fears—called hysteria by some, reactionary romanticism by others—were compounded by the heightened security measures, antiterrorism laws, and surveillance practices that the Federal Republic's law-enforcement authorities had put in place to combat terrorism and, as the activists contended, were regularly employed to spy on and infiltrate the new social movements.

The intertwined ecology and antinuclear movements weren't alone. Other nationwide movements had coalesced around issues such as civil

---

* The 1972 report was widely read outside of West Germany, too. It was translated into thirty-seven languages and sold 12 million copies. The report concluded: "If the present growth trends in world population, industrialization, pollution, food production, and resource depletion continue unchanged, the limits to growth on this planet will be reached at some time within the next 100 years. The most probable result will be a rather sudden and uncontrollable decline in both population and industrial capacity." Donella .H. Meadows, Jorgen Randers, and Dennis L. Meadows, *The Limits to Growth* (New York: Universe Books, 1972).

liberties, the Third World, seniors, and gay/lesbian rights. Since it had surfaced from within the student revolt, a vital autonomous women's movement had reached out across class and social barriers. The women's movement also took its cue from across the Atlantic, from American feminists who had been pushing for women's rights since the mid-sixties. Both movements insisted on gender equality, emancipation, and full-fledged representation in society. In the early seventies, the scattered women's groups that existed in bigger towns and cities in the Federal Republic (among them Revolutionary Struggle's women's section) rallied to protest West German laws restricting a woman's access to abortion. The so-called Paragraph 218 Campaign, named after the statute curtailing access to abortion, lacked broad-based support until, in June 1971, the outspoken journalist Alice Schwarzer (later icon of the women's movement) pulled off a publicity stunt that startled the country. In an article in the weekly magazine *Stern*, 374 West German women, all of them public figures, acknowledged having had abortions. The magazine published passport-size photos of several dozen of them on the front cover. The banner headline was: "We've Had Abortions." Their message to the male German establishment was: "We demand the right to abortion for all women."[20] The initiative provoked an uproar, but it obviously struck a nerve with German women from different walks of life. Women across the country joined existing women's groups or started their own, effectively bringing the West German women's movement into being.

The women's groups first coalesced in local niches before they emerged nationwide. Locally, self-organized women's groups initiated projects like centers for abused women and runaway girls, feminist bookstores and publishing houses, counseling centers and support groups. Lesbian groups formed as well. Studies showed that most of these projects' participants were usually young (seventeen to thirty-five years old), well educated, and mostly middle class. Yet political fault lines divided them, too: socialist feminists struck out at mainstream factions, while a new breed of "radical feminist" saw men—all men—as the natural enemy of women. Despite these differences, the women's groups concurred that they had to fight gender-specific discrimination, dismantle patriarchal structures, and unite in a front of common opposition. The new feminist magazines *Emma*, edited by Alice Schwarzer, and *Courage*, as well as regular nationwide congresses and workshops, forged the links of a broad network, much as the ecology movement had done. West Germany's feminists also discovered that some of their principles overlapped with those of the other new movements, like their dissatisfaction with the republic's "two-and-a-half" party democracy* and their commitment to nonviolence. Their link to the peace movement was particularly strong, with the feminists locating an expressly male ethic in the art of warcraft.

Although the urban-based women activists realized that they had to make contact with German women who lived outside of the cities, they weren't, at first, certain how—or whether it was possible at all—to break through the imposing cultural barriers. "There was an enormous gap between women from the urban alternative scenes and those from the citizens' initiatives in smaller towns and the country," says Eva Quistorp, one of the founders of Frauen für Frieden und Ökologie, a Europe-wide network of women peace activists. "When we saw that something was happening beyond the cities in the form of citizens' initiatives and other campaigns, we said, 'Hey, we've got to learn about this.'" Quistorp, a flamboyant and garrulous red-headed woman, remembers the stares she received from rural activists arriving at the Gorleben antinuclear encampment with a copy of *Courage* under her arm. "I could barely bring myself to admit that I had anything to do with this magazine," she says today. "These women, whether in citizen initiatives, rural communes or local cultural circles, simply hadn't experienced emancipation as we had. The farming families were often very conservative. But through common ecological concerns we began to build bridges to these communities."

The sites of the antinuclear encampments became rolling experiments in a participatory democracy and pluralism considerably broader than the urban leftist scenes. At the Wyhl site, for example, in the hutlike Friendship House, the Wyhl Forest Open University offered a wide variety of informal courses and guest lectures to people of different ages and backgrounds. Unconsciously, perhaps, it was an antidote to Germany's elitist educational structures, going even further than the student movement's innovations that, as radical as they were, remained mostly within the universities. "It showed that education isn't simply a matter of intellectuals telling everyone else what to think," says Eva Quistorp. "Other people got a chance to speak, and to write their own history, too. This had an incredibly emancipating effect as people learned to think together. We tried to deconstruct

* Since 1954 only three parties were represented in the Bundestag: the Christian Democrats, the Social Democrats, and the much smaller Free Democrats (the "half party").

the authoritarian character in practice, by embracing *Lebenslust* (a zeal for life) and open discussion as forms of political resistance, of democratic process from below."

As exhilarating as the environmentalists' victory at Wyhl was, other citizens' initiatives elsewhere weren't duplicating its success in equal measure.* Whether against nuclear power plants or planned highways, the grassroots campaigns found themselves limited in what they could achieve. Increasingly, attempts by protesters to defend occupied building sites or block access to nuclear-waste processing plants resulted in bloody trouncings by the local police. Protesters' attempt to storm and occupy the Grohnde power plant southwest of Hanover ended in a particularly brutal melee between demonstrators and hundreds of well-armored special police.

Most activists agreed that resorting to violence themselves wasn't a solution. The German Autumn reinforced that message loud and clear. Some concluded that they had to link extra-parliamentary activism and representative democracy in order to be taken seriously. Without a voice in regional legislatures to lobby for their causes, they were too easily marginalized, shut out of the institutions in which policy was made. The decision to "go electoral" unfolded differently from location to location, but none of the heterogeneous activists envisioned parliament as a substitute for hands-on local projects.

It also became ever more transparent that their most likely electoral ally, the SPD, wasn't going to help them. Chancellor Helmut Schmidt's "rightward drift," as they saw it, only substantiated this conclusion. The Social Democrats did include factions within the party, comprising mostly younger members like Lower Saxony's thirty-something Gerhard Schröder, who sympathized with some of the goals of the antinuclear and peace movements. Often these types would show up at demonstrations and even address the protesters. But Helmut Schmidt counted as one of nuclear power's staunchest proponents and was backed by the trade unions, the SPD's rock-solid base, which saw the eco-radicals threatening German jobs. Moreover, most of the top Social Democrats were no more trustful of grassroots movements in the 1970s than they had been in the 1950s and 1960s. Their rule of thumb was, if the party couldn't control it, it couldn't

* Over the years the antinuclear movement did indeed rack up an impressive armful of victories, however most of them were less spectacular than Wyhl, usually coming aftrer years-long legal battles in the German court system. See Ruud Koopmans, *Democracy from Below: New Social Movements and the Political System in West Germany* (Boulder, CO: Westview Press, 1995), 165–70.

be good. Committed Social Democrats like Petra Kelly, Roland Vogt, and writer Heinrich Böll fought doggedly to change the SPD's stance on nuclear arms and nuclear power. But in the end, says Vogt, "We hit brick walls. We came to the conclusion that the only language the comrades understand is that of power. In other words we understood that we needed to build a rival party with an entirely new political composition and program." All three—Vogt, Kelly, Böll—quit the SPD in the mid-1970s.

Many activists felt that their existential concerns superseded the republic's rigid categories of right and left. Issues like clean air and drinking water, nutrition, and the nuclear threat affected everyone regardless of class or religion. Likewise, women's issues were relevant to all women, not just those in one party or another. The new social movements gradually began to think in larger terms, linking their issues to the broader critiques of modernity. The environmental umbrella group BBU put it this way:

> Protection of the environment today means more than limiting or moderating some of the worst effects of the industrial system. This would only be dealing with the symptoms. . . . We are beginning to understand that the destruction of the environment, economic inequality, social injustice and the growing dependence of the individual on the powers of the state are not avoidable side effects of the system, they are essential features of it. Our interest is not merely the correction of errors and the elimination of unpleasant side effects. Our goal is a more just, freer and more human social order.[21]

The First Greens

Two and a half decades later, Greens party genealogists would trace the origins of their party back to the twenty or so activists of the diminutive Citizens' Initiative Schwarmstedt (very near Hanover) in Lower Saxony.[22] The members of the Schwarmstedt initiative, which was originally formed to oppose the construction of a nuclear waste processing plant, felt that they needed representation in the *Landtag*, the regional legislature, in order to get the state's politicians to address their concerns. In May 1977 the Schwarmstedt group and three other nearby civic initiatives renamed themselves the Umweltschutzpartei (USP; Environmental Protection Party) and announced their intention to run for seats in Lower Saxony's legislature. The USP started modestly with a program that called for a nuclear-free Lower Saxony, the conservation of local wildlife, and the expansion of certain local structures of self-government.

Not far away, in the neighboring town of Hildesheim, another citizens' initiative, freshly renamed the Grüne Liste Umweltschutz (GLU; Green Slate Environmental Protection), was itself preparing to test the state's electoral waters. In contrast to the Schwarmstedt USP, it was led by a former Social Democrat influenced by contemporary "third way" theories that sought to steer a path between "western private capitalism" and "eastern state capitalism." But the cleft between the two parties wasn't so great that they couldn't merge, which they did, taking on the GLU's name and the USP's platform. In June 1978 the GLU garnered a surprising 3.9 percent of the vote in Lower Saxony, just short of the 5 percent needed to enter the *Landtag*. Much of its support came from younger voters, the educated middle class, and from cities with universities like Hanover and Göttingen. Their program, which had expanded since the slate's founding, drew heavily from Herbert Gruhl's book and spoke of an "ecologically oriented society," as well as women's rights and a "rotating system" to limit the terms served by elected politicians.

The GLU wasn't alone in its thinking or intentions. Across West Germany like-minded slates were forming. In the northern port city of Hamburg, the Rainbow Slate came into being while in West Berlin the Alternative Slate was formed. Alike in many respects, the political accents fell differently. In Kiel, Hamburg, and West Berlin animosity flared at once between ecologists and former Marxists. The mixed bag of environmentalists also included national conservatives and spiritually minded naturalists who wanted nothing to do with the left. Yet there was remarkable overlap in the slates' language and agendas. Most of their programs mentioned grassroots democracy, decentralized governance, environmental protection, alternative energy sources, and women's rights and included bits and pieces of the critiques of progress and technology. Not one of these slates captured enough votes in 1978 to win a seat in any of the regional legislatures.*

In Fischer's state of Hesse (capital city Wiesbaden, not Frankfurt), a spectrum of activists and local initiatives called the Greens List Hesse (GLH) to life in summer 1978.[23] Two of its overriding priorities were

* The German Greens were not the first ecology party in Europe. The British Greens were formed in 1973. In French local elections in March 1977, the Pouvoir Vert (Green Power) was elected to municipal councils across France. The Swiss Greens were the first to enter a national parliament, in 1979.

the blocking of a proposed plutonium processing plant in Hanau outside Frankfurt and the expansion of Frankfurt's international airport. Among the slate's founders were the radical feminist Jutta Ditfurth and her partner, the left-socialist Manfred Zieran, who would later be Fischer's archrivals in the Greens. Both were newcomers to Frankfurt but not to the social movements or left-wing politics. Along with the leftists such as Ditfurth and Zieran, however, Hesse's early Greens also included environmentally concerned German nationalists. One of the conservative Green factions in Hesse was led by the renegade ex-Christian Democrat Herbert Gruhl, author of Germany's first ecological bestseller. With agendas to save German forests and restore a vaguely defined lost social harmony, eclectic groups like Gruhl's would also be present when the nationwide Greens party was founded two years later.

The idea of creating a nationwide Greens initiative to promote the social movements had gained momentum since the founding of the regional Greens, Alternative, and Rainbow slates. Intellectuals like artist Joseph Beuys, the quirky "third way" theorist Rudolf Bahro and Heinrich Böll had become involved, as had Rudi Dutschke, the former voice of the student movement. At the time, Dutschke was living with his family in Aarhus, Denmark, where he was lecturing at the university. The head injuries he sustained from the 1968 shooting had initially impaired his faculties so badly that at first he was unable to speak or even remember more than a few dozen words. With daily lessons and flash cards he relearned German word by word at a clinic in Switzerland. His tutors were baffled at how quickly he absorbed theoretical concepts and then moved on to complicated texts. He reread Marx, Marcuse, and Lukacs, and by 1969 was living in London and studying in Cambridge, with the proviso that he not engage in political activities there. Before long, however, the English authorities withdrew his visa, charging that Dutschke was a "security risk." Without income and worried about Rudi's safety, the Dutschke family moved from country to country until settling in Denmark. He had been traveling to West Germany and lecturing since the early seventies, but Gretchen, now mother of two, flatly refused to move back to the country in which her husband had nearly been killed.

During his exile, Dutschke had maintained contact with his good friend, the Czech exile and human rights activist Milan Horacek in Frankfurt. Horacek, a barrel-chested, six-foot-four Czech with thick brown hair and a prodigious beard, had wound up at Frankfurt's university after being jailed and then expelled for subversive political activities in the aftermath of the Prague Spring reform movement in communist Czechoslovakia. In West Germany he published a newspaper for the Czech exile community. The two had been traveling around the Federal Republic in an old Citröen taking the political pulse of a society much changed since Dutschke's heyday. Even after a decade's absence from the West German political scene, the sixty-eight veteran still commanded immense respect in left-wing circles. Many hoped that Dutschke could unite the splintered left. But he found the remnants of the New Left unbearably doctrinaire. Instead of engaging in the sectarian battles, the two political exiles spoke at meetings of human rights groups that were in close contact with the dissident movements in Poland, Czechoslovakia, and East Germany. At the anti-atomic villages across West Germany, the pair met with people from the social movements, including Christian activists and conservatives like Herbert Gruhl. They discussed the possibility of creating a broad-based party to challenge the republic's "two-and-a-half party" establishment.

In March 1979, with the first-ever European Parliament elections imminent, a jumble of the existing Green and Rainbow slates met in Frankfurt to create an electoral initiative to get on the ballot. Among those in attendance were Rudi Dutschke, Petra Kelly, Roland Vogt, Eva Quistorp, Milan Horacek, Joseph Beuys, Heinrich Böll, Rudolf Bahro, and Herbert Gruhl. But the impromptu alliance lacked a name. The Social Democrats were known as the "reds," the Christian Democrats were associated with the color black, the liberal Free Democrats with yellow. So they called themselves the Greens. Their symbol would be the sunflower. In the nick of time, the Greens alliance was registered to contest the summer 1979 direct elections to the brand new European Parliament.

Next to Kelly and Vogt at the top of the Greens' slate was an odd assemblage of mostly conservative, older men, including Gruhl and Baldur Springmann, the latter an organic farmer from Schleswig-Holstein in northern Germany. In fact, the conservatives and their followers outnumbered the alternative types and antinuclear activists. This unlikely group of bedfellows concurred that the alliance's guiding motif would be "the preservation of human life" in a threatening world. They settled on four pillars that would remain central to the Greens for the next three decades: ecology, nonviolence, grassroots democracy, and social justice. "This was our canon," explains Vogt, "our reason for existing. It wasn't like you could take one of them away and have the others still make sense."

With a budget of just $20,000 cobbled together by the founders, the first nationwide Greens candidates crisscrossed the country in a last-minute, whirlwind campaign tour. The German media, including the newly founded left-wing *Die Tageszeitung*, took scant notice of the Greens alliance, even when it captured an astounding 3.2 percent of the West German vote—nearly a million votes. The Greens fared particularly well in southern Germany's university towns and localities where the antinuclear movement was active.[24] Its showing wasn't good enough to win seats in the European Parliament, but it entitled the Greens alliance to nearly $2 million in funding, money none of its founders had anticipated. With a budget beyond the alliance's wildest expectations, the next election in their sights was the Federal Republic's 1980 vote. But first they had to form a proper party.

The Last Sponti

While the Federal Republic's biggest experiments in participatory democracy and protest were blooming in all their resplendent colors, thirty-one-year-old Joschka Fischer was still sulking in the drafty cellar of the Karl Marx, surrounded by stacks of second-hand books. He was watching, but he was not convinced that either the new social movements or the embryonic Greens pointed to a way out of the abyss in which both he and the German left found themselves. His head aswirl with political uncertainties and his relationship with Ede on the rocks, Fischer was soon in love again, this time with someone wholly different. The object of his desire was Inge Pensgens, a vivacious, redheaded math major, a tender seventeen years old when they met. A year later, Fischer's first child, David, was born. Bringing new life into the world and raising a family seemed a soothing antidote to exchanging blows with the Frankfurt police. Four years later, Inge gave birth to David's sister, Lara.

Meanwhile, Fischer, getting restless, attended some of the antinuclear demonstrations as well as the protests at the Frankfurt airport. "This aimlessness, the hanging around, not knowing what to do, it's becoming unbearable," he lamented in *Pflasterstrand*.[25] "The air in the ghetto is suffocating and our reality hasn't changed a bit with this retreat into ourselves." But Fischer was still assessing the arguments of the new movements and the Greens slates, both of which included many close friends. The Sponti men had debated the option of joining Hesse's Greens slate and of actually casting a ballot—most of them for the first time—in the fall

1978 Hessian elections. Their skepticism about Greens politics was still too deep. "In Germany it's easier to save six million trees than six million Jews," quipped the Sponti cabaretist Matthias Beltz.[26] The presence of conservative-populist elements in the ecology movement and their use of Nazi-tainted words like *Volk* unnerved the coffee drinkers at the Karl Marx Bookshop. Fischer dug in his heels. He saw the Greens as a passing fad, a blip on the republic's radar screen. And Fischer still hadn't overcome his misgivings about parliamentary democracy.

Fischer poured out his heart in *Pflasterstrand*: "What in the world do we Spontis have to do with Greens?" he asks. "We've decided to live a different kind of life, to practice a different kind of politics and political resistance. We try to adhere to a kind of radicalism in our daily lives . . . in which we both personally and politically withdraw from the republic's dominant culture." The Spontis are part of the socialist tradition, the Greens aren't, he wrote. "Now, to jump a train going in the opposite direction just because it has more steam, and to think that you'll arrive at the same goal, this exceeds dreaming in the direction of stupidity." Although there was barely anything left of the Spontis of old, Fischer bemoaned, he admitted he had no better ideas. "Politically, in the near future," he conceded, "I don't see a force anywhere that could credibly open up a revolutionary option. Where anything at all is happening [a reference to the Greens], it's reformist, often even conservative. . . . The ecology movement, despite the mass demonstrations, relies more on the institutions of society rather than on direct action." What's the point? he asked, referring to the Greens' mixture of radical protest and electoral participation. Playing the defiant rebel in local legislatures may be irreverent, but politically it's not going to get anyone anywhere, he concluded.[27]

The New Peace Movement

The republic's new scourges, however, weren't waiting for Joschka Fischer to break out of the doldrums. On his very doorstep, the Greens were gearing up to mount a radical democratic challenge to the republic's institutions. Crucial to that challenge, another protest campaign was brewing, the peace movement, which would burst onto the country's stage that same year. The casus belli was the announced NATO deployment of new intermediate-range nuclear missiles in West Germany. In terms of size, the peace movement dwarfed the social movements of the

1970s and it would turbo-charge the gate-crashing ecology party. At its apex in the early 1980s the movement brought millions of West Germans into the streets, making it the largest extra-parliamentary movement in the Federal Republic's history.

In the past, malcontents within the SPD, including the likes of Petra Kelly and Roland Vogt, had voiced their objections to West Germany's stationing of U.S. nuclear weapons on its soil. U.S. nuclear-equipped missiles had been in West Germany since 1955, their presence the target of the Nuclear Death campaign in the late fifties. But over time most Social Democrats had resigned themselves to the fact that the postwar Federal Republic, America's Cold War proxy, was in no position to buck Washington on this most central of geostrategic issues. West Germany's leaders were still on a short leash, and they knew it. During the early seventies most Social Democrats contented themselves with Willy Brandt's peaceful overtures to the Soviet Union and the thawing processes of détente.

Indeed, the superpowers' nuclear sabre rattling had subsided considerably by the 1970s, thanks in part to West Germany's role in the onset of East-West diplomacy. For nearly a decade, Washington and Moscow had negotiated limits to their stockpiles of intercontinental missiles in Europe. In 1972 Soviet leader Leonid Brezhnev and President Richard Nixon signed the first Strategic Arms Limitation Talks Agreement (SALT I), which froze the number of these nuclear-equipped projectiles on both sides of Cold War Europe. The rough parity implied that a war launched by one camp would trigger a response from the other, starting a nuclear exchange that neither side could win. The horror of this prospect, of "mutually assured nuclear destruction," was itself supposed to be the deterrent for starting such a war. This was the logic of the nuclear standoff and the basis for the security of the European continent. Surprisingly, few had questioned it.

In 1977 a new American president, Jimmy Carter, took office, pledging to slash the U.S. defense budget and build on disarmament progress. In the Federal Republic, Chancellor Schmidt, like Brandt, initially basked in the international limelight. For example, in 1975 he helped launch the Convention on Security and Cooperation in Europe, the first pan-European organization that included all thirty-five countries on the continent, including those of the Eastern bloc. The convention constituted a de facto recognition of the 1945-drawn borders and normalized relations with the communist leaderships of central Europe, including East Germany. This, however, was both the peak of détente and the beginning of its end.

It was none other than Social Democrat Schmidt, the heir of Brandt's bold East–West diplomacy, who sounded the nuclear alarm that brought détente and disarmament to a screeching halt. SALT I allowed Washington and Moscow to maintain intermediate nuclear missiles. In line with those provisions, the Soviets built up their conventional ground forces and deployed the SS-20 missiles in the Soviet Union, which enabled Moscow to target West German cities and NATO airfields more accurately than had their SS-4 and SS-5 missiles. Schmidt believed this upended the military equilibrium and put the West at a distinct disadvantage. In a 1977 speech from London that reverberated around the world, Schmidt called upon the United States not to abandon the Federal Republic, and ultimately all of western Europe, to the Warsaw Pact's mercy. NATO allies should rearm, he pleaded, adding to medium-range missile reserves in Europe in order to win bargaining leverage, and thus to coerce the Soviet Union to withdraw the SS-20s. This was the crux of the "double-track" strategy: to pursue a nuclear build-up in order to force Moscow's hand in negotiations. Schmidt's cry was music to the ears of NATO's generals, who had long argued that the United States needed to beef up its nuclear stockpiles to counter the Soviets' advantage in conventional forces. In response, NATO announced the deployment of nearly 600 new mid-range U.S. missiles in Europe, known as Euromissiles. Among them there would be 108 Pershing II and 96 Cruise missiles on West German territory.

Schmidt's famous "angst speech" and the pending new missile systems were the impetus that revived the West German peace movement. It took the NATO decision in December 1979 "to break a 20-year taboo on public debate over the meaning of mutually assured destruction and flexible response" in Germany and to begin a "push for détente from below."[28] Suddenly, it was apparent to Germans on both sides of the front line that, in a nuclear war, their countries would be the first targeted and destroyed. Germany would be the battlefield for the superpowers' nuclear holocaust.

A series of related international events heightened the sense of impending catastrophe. For five days in March 1979 the worst-ever civilian nuclear accident unfolded at the Three Mile Island plant near Harrisburg, Pennsylvania. The source of the partial meltdown was traced back to a combination of technical malfunction and human error. The failure of the cooling system and then the emergency warning signals caused the core of the reactor to overheat and the plant's nuclear pellets to begin to melt. Emergency pumps and safety valves failed as the reactor began to spin out of control. Pennsylvania's governor advised all pregnant women and preschool-age children to leave the area. Had the molten fuel breached the reactor's outer walls, the entire plant could have melted down, releasing enormous amounts of deadly radiation into the atmosphere. Although the worst was avoided at the last moment, many people extracted a lesson from Three Mile Island: nuclear power was not safe.

The Soviet army's invasion of Afghanistan in late 1979 and the election of the tough-talking, hawkish Republican, Ronald Reagan, the next year pushed superpower tensions back up to an all-time high. Reagan's escalation of the arms race and talk of the Soviet Union as the "evil empire" seemed to confirm many Germans' concerns about the recklessness of the world's leaders. One of Reagan's first acts was to restart the production of neutron bombs, a tactical nuclear weapon that supposedly killed people while leaving buildings and other real estate unscathed. (Jimmy Carter had canceled it on ethical grounds.) The possibility of a third world war no longer seemed unimaginable, certainly not to Petra Kelly, Protestant church leaders, East German dissidents, and a broad spectrum of others around the world. The 1980s peace movement reached far beyond the borders of the two Germanys and Europe—it was a global movement that, at its peak, mobilized tens of millions of people on four continents in a score of countries.[29]

In the Federal Republic, the peace movement was still incubating when the activists behind the European Greens voter initiative met in January 1980 to form a political party that could run in West Germany's nationwide elections later that year. The media may have overlooked the environmentalists' solid showing in the 1979 European elections, but the West German left certainly hadn't. The Greens voter alliance swelled with new members, quadrupling its membership from 2800 to 12,000 by December 1979.[30] Significantly, this surge came disproportionately from the ranks of the left, among them members and ex-members of the radical left groupings.

The party's pioneers still envisioned this new political creation to be "above" the republic's confining categories of left and right. One of the few stipulations of party membership, agreed its founders, was that one couldn't be a member of another political party at the same time. According to Eva Quistorp:

> We didn't want to exclude anybody interested in democratic revival but we immediately saw the danger of the Marxist parties instrumentalizing the social movements—and the Greens—for their

> own purposes. As for the conservatives, they didn't scare me [as much as they did others]. I thought we should consider ourselves fortunate to have someone like Gruhl among us because it was crucial that we maintain a dialogue with conservatives and other political parties. Even though they still had outmoded ideas about women in society, for example, I felt that their ideas were undergoing a transformation. Working together with the citizens' initiatives we found that there was space that no longer belonged exclusively either to the right or the left. We wanted the Greens to utilize this space to address the big, future-oriented issues and to try to solve them together. We wanted to move away from the old clichés about either you're right or left, friend or enemy, toward a concept of "democratic citizenry."

The weighty presence of the left in this early phase of the Greens, on the one hand, and the centrality of conservatives, on the other, drew the first battle lines for the kind of knock-down, drag-out political brawl that would become as much a part of the Greens' identity as their sunflower symbol. The conservatives demanded the exclusion of the "reactionary communists." The left, strengthened by the heavily socialist-dominated factions from Hamburg and West Berlin, vehemently objected to the party's commitment to pacifism as well as to the presence of the *volk*ish nationalists. Kelly bent over backwards to keep the Greens as diverse and nonideological as possible. But by the conclusion of the Karlsruhe congress, it took all of the organizers' persuasive powers just to reaffirm the Greens' four cornerstones: ecology, nonviolence, grassroots democracy, and social justice. And so, the Greens entered the world of German politics as the Federal Republic's newest party.

One person absent from the Karlsruhe congress was Rudi Dutschke. On Christmas Eve 1979, Dutschke drowned at home in the bathtub during a seizure that resulted from injuries sustained in the 1968 shooting. A few days previously, the Bavarian *Süddeutsche Zeitung* asked him about his hopes for the coming decade. He talked enthusiastically about the Greens: "I hope that in the eighties we can force a turn away from the increasing social atomization and chemical poisoning of our society. Freedom, peace and security in an enriching social context, namely democracy and socialism, these are my primary hopes. I expect no solutions from the current governments in either the East or the West."[31] Dutschke was buried in West Berlin, near the Free University.

A series of follow-up meetings to the Karlsruhe congress hammered out the Greens' first program. The party also suffered the first losses among its founding fathers and mothers—namely, the conservatives. A key battleground was women's access to abortion, which the conservatives and other Christian activists opposed. Over conservative objections, the delegates also pushed through program drafts that included demands for the abolition of NATO, ending the blacklisting of West German communists, solidarity with the exploited peoples of the Third World, unilateral disarmament, and gay rights. This was much too much for Herbert Gruhl and his ilk, who quit the party in protest. Not long afterward, the other top conservative, Baldur Springmann, resigned in the face of revelations about his Nazi past. The Greens lurched to the left, where they would stay, arguably, for the next twenty-five years. In hindsight, some early Greens say that their single-most important achievement at this juncture was yanking the ecology card from the hand of the right. Others, like Roland Vogt, say that their greatest error was being too lenient with the orthodox left. "These former Marxists," says Vogt, "saw the Greens as nothing more than a vehicle with which to obtain power. But we, the early Greens, we didn't want this kind of institutional power, we wanted to deconstruct it."

The Greens' first program, a rambling twenty-five-page document, is a proud testament to the party's early creativity and political imagination. It is a diagnosis of and prescription for a political establishment that had run out of ideas and seemed impervious to new ones. New ideas were something the Greens had aplenty. The preamble reads:

> The established political parties in Bonn act as if an unlimited expansion in industrial production is possible on this very limited planet Earth. They are forcing us to decide between nuclear war or a country dominated by nuclear power—between Harrisburg and Hiroshima. The worldwide ecological crisis worsens from day to day. Natural resources become ever more scarce. Chemical waste dumps are topics for scandal after scandal. Whole species of animals are exterminated while entire plant varieties grow extinct. Rivers and oceans are turning slowly into sewers, and humans verge on spiritual and intellectual decay in our advanced industrial, consumer society. We are compiling a dismal inheritance for future generations. . . . A complete restructuring of our current near-sighted planning is necessary. We consider it mistaken to believe that our present spendthrift economy can still promote human happiness and the

> fulfilment of life goals. We opposed the blind, one-dimensional policy of ever more and more production.[32]

The Greens' vision went far beyond environmental issues. They foresaw a richer, more vibrant democracy—one more open, less bureaucratic, with transparent and decentralized structures, as well as with citizen participation at every level. There should be more plebiscites and referenda to strengthen direct democracy, as well as term limits for all political offices. (Also, one of the more idealistic demands was that all political posts be unpaid.) The Greens wanted to show up the mainstream parties for the "electoral machines" that they were and relocate governance among the people. They were taking Brandt at his word, "daring to practice democracy" in a way that the great Social Democrat had most probably not intended.

From the get-go, the Greens never set out to be just another party. Petra Kelly called the Greens an "anti-party party," a force of "fundamental opposition" that would represent the social movements in the Bundestag. "Parliament isn't the goal," she said, "but part of a strategy" for radical social change.[33] They would work hand-in-glove with the citizens' initiatives, and at the same time, agitate in legislatures in order to make those bodies more accountable, not to compete for power. "A radical opposition in parliament can achieve something but most important is to work at the grassroots level," said Kelly, who ruled out the compromises necessary to participate in coalitions with other parties. Life-and-death issues like nuclear power, disarmament, and poverty weren't negotiable. "When the Social Democrats shut down all the nuclear power plants, quit the arms race and start building ambulances instead of tanks, then we can begin to talk," she said. Should the Greens lose their connection to the movements from which they sprang, then it wasn't the "fundamentalist anti-war, ecological and pacifist party" that Kelly envisaged—and she would leave it. "The day the Greens start to send ministers to Bonn," she said, "then it's not the Greens that I wanted."[34] Whether Petra Kelly would really have quit her own party when the Greens did send ministers to Germany's capital, we will never know. She didn't live to see the day.

The Greens' march into the republic's governing institutions had already begun by the time of its founding. In October 1979 the Greens Slate Bremen made it into the regional legislature in the northwestern port city (also a federal state), squeaking by with 5.1 percent of the vote. Months later, the party repeated its success in southwestern Baden

Württemberg. With the antinuclear power campaign at its height and the peace movement beginning to unfurl, the West German press was abuzz with talk of the little sunflower party.

But the Greens' first foray into politics on the federal level flopped spectacularly. The October 1980 elections pitted the Schmidt-led Social Democrats against the Christian Democrats and their candidate for chancellor, the ultra-conservative Bavarian Franz Josef Strauss. The possibility that Strauss could become West Germany's most powerful figure struck terror in the hearts of left-of-center voters. For them, the corpulent, jowly Strauss, friend of Latin American dictators and notorious red-baiter, symbolized everything wrong with the West Germany of the 1950s and 1960s. Many Germans otherwise open to the Greens voted Social Democrat or Liberal just to stave off the worst. The Greens eked out a dismal 1.5 percent of the vote—far short of the 5 percent they needed to enter the Bundestag. The Social Democrat–Liberal coalition captured another four-year mandate, the last before a new political era dawned in the Federal Republic.

Initially, the potent force that would propel the Greens onto the center of the republic's stage—the peace movement—was slow to coalesce in the face of the government's plans to station the new nuclear missiles in the country. One of the movement's first manifestations was the 1980 Krefelder Appeal, a petition that demanded that the Federal Republic revoke its request for the missiles. By 1983 the petition had 5 million signatures. Among its initiators was the soft-spoken Bundeswehr general Gert Bastian who would become a central figure in the peace movement, as well as Petra Kelly's devoted partner. The fifty-eight-year-old Bastian was one of a handful of military brass who had publicly voiced concern that the new missiles would undermine the strategic equation of "mutually assured destruction."

Bastian's path to the peace movement could hardly be more different from that of other activists.[35] Born in Munich in 1923, his parents were enthusiastic Hitler supporters. The son joined the Hitler Youth at fourteen and entered the war five years later. He belonged to a tank division and fought on both the eastern and western fronts, earning himself the prestigious Iron Cross. Taken prisoner by the Americans, he waited out the last months of the war in a U.S. prison camp.

After the war, Bastian joined the Bavarian branch of the Christian Democrats, the CSU, and worked as a bookbinder. He married and fathered three children. When the Bundeswehr was formed and conscription began in 1956, he signed up at once. This new German army appealed to Bastian, a man who had slowly and unspectacularly faced up to the ignominy of Nazi Germany. The Bundeswehr was created as a "citizen's army," in which soldiers ("citizens in uniform") were ultimately accountable to a moral imperative higher than the dictates of their superiors. Never again could a soldier or officer claim "following orders" as an excuse for committing war crimes. Bastian sailed through the Bundeswehr's ranks and became a general in 1976. Restraint, however, was no longer his defining characteristic, as he grew increasingly critical of the army's democratic shortcomings. He had quit the CSU years before, impatient with its foot-dragging while the rest of the country was modernizing by leaps and bounds. When he resigned from the Bundeswehr in 1980 and aired his differences publicly in an open letter in a major newspaper, peace activists were ecstatic. A two-star German general on their side! Even if his thoughts on many of their broader issues were vague or nonexistent, landing Bastian was a coup for them.

The initial rumblings of the peace movement in 1979 and 1980 were amplified by the disclosures of the first independent "peace researchers"—activists who made it their business to dig up information on security-related issues and make it public. The first peace research institutes were introduced by the Brandt government in the early 1970s, publicly funded thinks tanks that explored new approaches to peace and security. But later, "critical" peace researchers, often associated with the churches and universities, began looking into the military-industrial complex in West Germany themselves—and posing tough questions. Hamburg's Otfried Nassauer, one of the early critical peace researchers, explains that the sudden public interest in military-security issues was something entirely new in Germany:

> Topics associated with the state's military strategy had never been part of public discourse in Germany, ever. This wasn't the kind of thing that ordinary people were supposed to know anything about or to engage in. But gradually people began to ask questions and since they weren't satisfied with the answers, they started to do research themselves, to look into the background of state projects, to discover risks that were never mentioned. People began to grasp that there were big holes in the state's rationale for some of its most important security policies. We found that there were valid counterarguments that were never raised.

Oddly enough, one of the richest caches of information for the German peace researchers was official sources in the United States, including the records of congressional hearings. The kind of information that was part of the public record in the United States wasn't available in West Germany. Peace researchers like Nassauer would travel to the United States, fill box after box with photocopies of reports, manuals, hearings, and archival material, and ship it back to Germany. Through this channel, the West German public's relative ignorance of the nuclear weapons in their midst vanished abruptly in early 1981 when West German media, first the weekly *Der Stern* and then more explicitly in the *Tageszeitung* and the Protestant *ProTest*, published maps of the Federal Republic, revealing the number and location of its nuclear missile sites and depots. "Neither in West nor East Germany did people at the time have any idea of how militarized their countries were," explains Nassauer. "This was the first time that people realized that there were over one hundred nuclear missile sites in [West] Germany and that some of them were in their backyards. The response was immediate and beyond anything we could ever have predicted."

The *Stern* article and the Krefelder Appeal, coming on top of the re-escalation of Cold War tensions, alarmed West Germans. The American president Ronald Reagan was actually talking about a "tactical" and "limited" nuclear war, one that would most likely be fought in Europe, not in the United States. Opinion polls showed that 70 percent of Americans believed that a nuclear war was unavoidable.[36] Why, West Germans asked, did Washington endorse a "first use" battlefield strategy unless it thought that it could win a nuclear war? Why did their own political leaders resist engaging citizens in an open discussion about the country's nuclear strategy? And why didn't Germans, East *and* West, have anything to say about United States and Soviet policies that concerned their very existence?

In addition to the media, the republic's publishing houses too had been transformed by the late 1970s and contributed greatly to the dissemination of information that the peace researchers were digging up. Since the early seventies, established presses, such as Suhrkamp in Frankfurt and Rowohlt in Hamburg, had been issuing high-quality, low-cost paperbacks on a range of progressive topics, from the Nazi era and social theory to gender, sexuality, and the Third World. From 1975–1983, for example, Rowohlt published 30 paperbacks on topics associated with "war and peace," with runs of 20,000–90,000[37] (considerable numbers for the little Federal Republic and all the more important in the pre-Internet age). The rise of the political *Taschenbuch*, or "pocket book," wasn't so much the doing of the long march as it was of the free market: there was high demand for these products. In other cases, new presses were explicitly left-wing, post-'68 projects, with names like Neue Kritik, Red Star, Syndikat, Konkret Literatur, and Rotbuch. They released title after title on liberation struggles, squatters movements, alternative culture, radical thought, poverty, the military–industrial complex, and many other issues—usually with a sales price of just a couple of dollars.

In fall 1981 a staggering 300,000 people converged on Bonn's tree-lined Hofgarten park to protest the Euromissile deployment, the first of the big Hofgarter rallies.[38] Follow-up demonstrations in Brussels and Amsterdam drew nearly as many. The next year even more packed the Hofgarten to greet President Reagan and other NATO leaders.*

By then, West Germans were getting used to the sight of the peacenik odd couple, Petra Kelly and Gert Bastian, the headline speakers at rally after rally. Kelly sometimes wore an olive-green army-issue helmet decorated with daisies. At the front of marches and sit-ins, the grandfatherly general never left her side. Bastian seemed to grow into the peace movement as Kelly tutored him in the ways of extra-parliamentary opposition. The two had become inseparable, with Bastian acting as her personal assistant and, importantly, emotional crutch. Petra Kelly's sunken eyes and sallow complexion spoke the toll that her frenetic activism was taking on her health. Kelly would drive herself until she dropped, stopping only long enough to convalesce.

No one person expressed the social movements' eschatological visions more vividly than did Petra Kelly, dubbed by one journalist the "Cassandra of the nuclear apocalypse."[39] Tongue-in-cheek, Dany Cohn-Bendit nicknamed her "the Ulrike Meinhof of the eighties." Although somewhat unfair to the ardent pacifist, there was something in her dire tone and do-or-die, now-or-never message that made the analogy fit. As if in a race against time, Kelly shuttled from occupied reactor site to blockaded U.S. military base, from NGO meeting to international congress, warning those who would listen that mankind's very survival was in their hands. At a 1983 rally in Nuremberg, for example, she told the crowd:

> We live in an unpeaceful "time of peace." The NATO upgrade, neutron bombs, Pershing IIs, first-use weapons, cruise missiles and SS-20 rockets—mega-tons of atomic munitions are aimed at us.

* On the other side of the Atlantic, the U.S. peace movement was drawing even bigger crowds. In June 1982 nearly a million people gathered in Central Park to protest the arms race, the largest political rally in American history (Wittner, *Nuclear Abolition*, 176).

> We are the potential victims, counted in mega-deaths. . . . Even if these weapons aren't used, their cost kills the world's poor because it sentences them to death by starvation. . . . We're told that in order to protect peace we have to be prepared to destroy all human life. We stock atomic bunkers with band-aids and canned food although in a [nuclear] crisis we would never even be able to reach them. We have the choice between a sudden death in a nuclear Holocaust and a step-by-step ecological suicide. We have to finally break through this conspiracy of silence. When injustice becomes law, nonviolent resistance becomes duty![40]

Kelly's renown soared. She was not only the leading lady of the Greens and the West German peace movement, she also became internationally recognized, appearing at conferences, demonstrations, and book signings from Sydney to Los Angeles. The peace movement *had* to be international, she exhorted. Nuclear war knew no national borders. "In the nuclear age," she told the *New York Times* in 1981, replying to a question about anti-Americanism in the German peace movement, "you don't have an enemy, you only have neighbors."[41] And indeed, the Germans weren't alone: like-minded peace movements were gathering steam everywhere in Europe and beyond. Even across the so-called Iron Curtain, in East Germany, a small peace and human rights movement had plucked up the courage to question the regime. The U.S. peace movement was growing rapidly; this time the Americans took their cue from the Europeans, not vice-versa.

During its peak the peace movement politicized millions in the republic and provided a snapshot of West Germans' changed sensibilities and values. In contrast to the campaigns of the 1950s, the "new peace movement" was an authentic mass movement, mobilized "from below," not through either the established parties (including the Greens) or the churches, although Christians, trade unionists, and Social Democrats participated in large numbers. The 1980s peace movement was led by a postwar generation that hadn't personally experienced war (many hadn't even experienced the 1960s) but appeared to have internalized the lessons of Germany's recent past. They understood it as their moral imperative for Germans to stand up and oppose both their state and protector-mentor, the United States, on matters of military policy. Quite remarkably, much of the country's younger generations, just four decades after Nazi rule and the Holocaust, seemed to be pacifists with an intensely critical relationship to nationalism and an unflinching inclination to question authority.

A New Left-wing Majority?

Living in Frankfurt, Joschka Fischer couldn't have had a better vantage point to watch the peace movement blossom and the Greens rebound from their 1980 drubbing in the nationwide elections. In March 1981 Frankfurt's local Greens fared well enough in municipal elections to put six members into the city assembly. Among them was Dutschke's traveling companion and also Fischer's friend, Milan Horacek, the Czech dissident who helped found the party, as well as the radical feminist Jutta Ditfurth. Milan Horacek says he will never forget the response when the local Greens made their debut in the Frankfurt city assembly, all of them wearing dark-green WW II–vintage gasmasks strapped to their faces and long white doctors' smocks. In this attire, they marched into the first session wielding a giant hand-written sign that read: "Green Anti-Catastrophe Service: Parliamentary and Extraparliamentary." The other assembly members, almost exclusively men in suits and ties, sat there dumbstruck, recalls Horacek. "They looked completely baffled!" he says. "They had absolutely no idea how to respond."

For some time Horacek had been urging Fischer to stop moping and to throw in his lot with the new party. Several times he had stopped by the bookshop with a membership application form. In jest, Fischer would ball up the application and toss it into the garbage can. Or at other times he would curse Horacek and pretend to sic old Dagobert loose on the hearty Czech. But Horacek says he felt Fischer's resistance ebbing, even though Fischer wouldn't admit it. Fischer's last rational arguments were being eroded and giving way to a new synthesis.

One day in summer 1981, without much ado, Fischer filled in one of Horacek's forms and became a member of the Greens. No single event or discussion prompted it. Rather, Fischer's decision was the culmination of a long process, one that paralleled the metamorphosis of the German left in general. For nearly three years, Dany Cohn-Bendit and Georg Dick had been holding meetings of a "Sponti Voter Initiative for the Greens" in the *Pflasterstrand* offices to discuss the various issues around the Green phenomenon, including the possibility of tactical cooperation with the Social Democrats. For Fischer, the Greens' rapid ascent and the breathtaking mobilizations of the new protest movements obviously added to the attraction. At long last, the masses had awoken—not to overthrow the system but to make it live up to its promises of democracy and pluralism.

Was Fischer's decision the result of a dialectical metamorphosis or, as his critics charge, a calculated, career-oriented machination for a man with few other options? Certainly, he didn't then nor would he ever identify with the ecologists the way he had with the Spontis. It is also true that his options were limited and Fischer, a politics junkie second to none, was raring to climb back into the ring. Also, there is ample evidence that Fischer had long, arguably since his childhood, been strongly attracted to power and sensed intuitively how to pursue it. Yet, that said, his own political evolution was similar to that of many other New Left veterans—in West Germany, but also in France, the United States, and elsewhere—who were alert enough to critique their own misanalyses and change with the times. Would Fischer be a more sincere character were he still today driving a taxi in Frankfurt? There are ex-Spontis in Frankfurt who still work nights as cabbies and believe that the state murdered Ulrike Meinhof. Are they somehow the real purists? Whatever the case, with his entry into the Greens, first as a simple party member, Fischer ended his transit in political limbo.

Yet, it was a full year later that Fischer experienced the epiphany that led him to jump into the political fray and never look back. This happened against the background of two important events. The first was the collapse of the ruling Social Democrat–Liberal coalition in September 1982, which brought about a sea change in West Germany's politics. The Schmidt government had been teetering for some time, under attack from the Social Democrats' own left, on one side, and from their coalition partner, the pro-market Free Democrats, on the other. The main bone of contention was the Federal Republic's costly public expenditures in a time of economic downturn. The straw that broke the coalition's back was a strident Free Democrat memorandum that demanded reversal of the traditional Social Democratic welfare state policies. This was too much for Schmidt, who rejected the ultimatum. The Liberals withdrew from the coalition and then signaled their readiness to join the Christian Democrats in a new ruling majority. The Free Democrats' abrupt shift in allegiance stranded the Social Democrats with neither a majority nor an acceptable coalition partner.

Following the dramatic events in Bonn, the *Landtag* elections in Fischer's own state of Hesse produced a hung legislature, the second at the time in the country. In Hesse, as well as in the electoral city-state of Hamburg, neither major party, the Social Democrats nor the Christian Democrats, had captured enough votes to rule alone. Remarkably, in Hesse, the Greens (with 8 percent of the vote) dislodged the Free

Democrats as the third party in the regional legislature. After the acrimonious drama in Bonn, Hesse's Social Democrats weren't about to form a grand coalition with the Christian Democrats. That left only the little antiparty, which until then had been heaping abuse upon the Social Democrats without mercy.

As early as autumn 1982, neither most Greens nor most Social Democrats could imagine an alliance with the other. There were others though, if exceptions at the time, who could imagine something of the kind. In the wake of the Hesse vote, the Social Democrats' elder statesman Willy Brandt spoke obliquely of a new "majority to the left of the [Christian Democratic] Union" in the republic, perhaps implying the possibility of "red–green" coalitions down the road. Whether Brandt meant this or not, his words hit Fischer like a lightning bolt. His response to Brandt's observation, as recalled by the editor at the New Left journal *Neue Kritik* at the time, Wolfgang Kraushaar:

> After not having shown up for barely a single meeting of the [Sponti] Voter Initiative [for the Greens], there he stood on this Monday evening waiting impatiently outside of the unopened [*Pflasterstrand*] editorial rooms. All at once, at that moment, he thought that he had finally recognized the situation as it really was. From this evening onward he pursued his political objectives as goal-oriented as a military offensive."[42]

On that day, Fischer stepped onto the Greens stage as a committed reformer, a pragmatist who saw—as he believed Brandt did—the future of the German left in ruling coalitions of Greens and Social Democrats. Fischer identified himself from the start with this Realpolitik that would take the Greens—and him with them—to the top of the republic. It would also tame the colorful, inspired creation of West Germany's grassroots activists and split the party down the middle. Fischer's strategy (though never his alone) envisioned the Greens as a results-oriented party that would wheel and deal and broker compromises, as other parties did, in order to turn its objectives into policies and laws.

This was an entirely different raison d'etre for the party than that espoused by Petra Kelly and most of its founders, who had created the Greens as an "antiparty party." At the time, the concept of "fundamental opposition" dominated within the Greens. Fischer's was a minority position. The hard-learned lesson that Fischer took away from the debacle of the far left was that "radical opposition" in and of itself wasn't going to change anything. If the Greens were going to step onto the playing field of parliamentary politics, then they had to aspire to win—and that meant sharing power in coalitions and joining strategic alliances. Fischer wasn't prepared to wage another losing battle. The Federal Republic was a democracy that was now mature enough to be reformed from within, if the West German left was mature enough to participate in it.

The first person Fischer set out to persuade was his political sparring partner and Greens assemblyman in Frankfurt, Milan Horacek. "There is a majority left of the Christian Democrats [in Hesse]," Fischer tells Horacek in a heated discussion at the Karl Marx, which was taped and later published in *Pflasterstrand*. "A majority [the combined seats of the Greens and the SPD] that is capable of making real reform happen. This majority is divided within itself, that I admit, and it's a risky strategy. But why not at least make them an offer [terms for a red-green coalition], that's the duty of an alternative politician."[43]

The big Czech gave no ground. He didn't help create the Greens so that they would "jump into bed" with the established parties at the first chance, especially not *these* Social Democrats in Hesse. If Fischer finds the Social Democrats so congenial, said Horacek, then he should have cast his ballot for them. "The Social Democrats have to see that we can't keep living like we've been living," he explained to Fischer. "That's our demand: we want a completely different approach to life. We want to pose the question of the whole sense of life in a completely different way, deeply and fundamentally. This is our only possibility to avert catastrophe. Cobbling together new majorities won't do it." Fundamental opposition doesn't mean coming up with better recipes within the parameters of established politics, argued Horacek, but rather it aims to question those very parameters. The animated discussion went on for hours without resolution.[44] In Hesse, in autumn 1982, the Greens voted against making the local Social Democrats a coalition offer in exchange for concessions on the airport's new runway and a nearby nuclear reactor along the upper Rhine.

Exit Schmidt, Enter Kohl

The fall of the Social Democrat–Liberal government in Bonn ushered in a new epoch of conservative rule. The Christian Democrat–Liberal coalition, led by the fifty-two-year-old Rhinelander Helmut Kohl, took power in late 1982 and called nationwide elections for early the next year. The conservatives may have been in ascendance, but so were the Greens. Nationwide voter surveys showed them polling enough to make it into the Bundestag. This alarmed no one more than the Social Democrats, who feared losing a generation of voters. The Free Democrats were also panicky as they suddenly saw their revered status of third force in the republic, as kingmaker between the major parties, slipping away.

The story of the so-called Fischer Gang and its "takeover" of the Greens begins during the run-up to the March 1983 Bundestag vote. In hindsight, its victims make it look as calculated and ruthless as mafia boss Michael Corleone's purge of New York City's gangland in *The Godfather.* Actually, the story of the Fischer Gang—or "clan" or "lobby"—began well before 1983, in the Frankfurt co-ops of the 1970s, when Sponti guys Fischer, Cohn-Bendit, Georg Dick, Tom Koenigs, Matthias Beltz, Raoul Kopania, and others met up and forged bonds that would prove both durable and propitious. They had learned a thing or two about political organizing during their reign over the Frankfurt *Szene*. In different strategic functions—as part of Fischer's team, in the party, and at various levels of government—they would provide the scaffolding for Fischer's ascent.

With the Greens' successes in regional elections, the Frankfurt ex-Spontis around *Pflasterstrand* moved to get one of their own on the bandwagon. They quickly banged out a manifesto that outlined their pragmatic vision for the party. It began with a realo maxim: "Parliament isn't the place for an ecology seminar. . ."[45] *Pflasterstrand*, by then under the editorial hand of Georg Dick, published a barrage of articles and editorials trying to convince its dubious readership, the greater Frankfurt scene, that West Germany's democracy was finally ready for them. On at least one occasion, Fischer and Cohn-Bendit were answered at an open discussion with rotten tomatoes and paint-filled balloons. It wasn't all that long ago that they too branded "reform" a synonym for "moral corruption" and "careerism."

But who would run for the "Sponti spot" on the Greens' Hesse slate in the upcoming federal elections? The obvious choice, Cohn-Bendit, deferred—too much donkey work, too many headaches. "But I told [Joschka] that he should run. I'd support his candidature," remembers Cohn-Bendit. Fischer didn't hesitate. At the Hesse Greens' congress, Fischer wound up on the ticket's third slot, ahead of Milan Horacek.

Nationwide, the Greens put together a smorgasbord of candidates that reflected the heterogeneous party and the strong regional differences within it. In Bavaria, Petra Kelly and ex-General Bastian topped the list. In Rhineland Palatinate, it was antinuclear activist Roland Vogt. The heavily ex-Marxist Hamburg section put forward the radical leftist Jürgen Reents. Baden Württemberg's Willi Hoss (one of the founders of Stuttgart's Club Voltaire) was a locksmith and maverick trade unionist, while pensioner Christa Reetz was one of the organizers of the Wyhl protests. West Berlin's candidate, Dirk Schneider, later turned out to be a spy for the Stasi, the East German secret police. The only Greens candidate never seen without a suit and tie was Otto Schily, the civil libertarian-lawyer who had represented Gudrun Ensslin and other Red Army Faction members before the West German courts. (Even Gert Bastian, the other suit-wearing Greens, would at least attend demonstrations without a tie.) As straight-faced as a cigar store Indian, Schily understood it as his personal mission to make the Federal Republic live up to the principles of the *Rechtsstaat*—a democratic state based on the rule of law. Otto Schily would count among the most popular and influential Greens of the 1980s.

The Greens' election campaign was a spectacle to behold. The "Green Caterpillar," a sixty-foot double-decker bus painted as a smiling caterpillar, toured the country full of clowns, performance artists, musicians, and speakers. Sometimes it would roll into towns unannounced in well below freezing weather and set up on the main square, attracting crowds through the performances—no two alike but all of them poking fun at the country's distant political elite. Curious onlookers could enter the bus and sample organic cookies and drinks. At some stops Nobel Prize laureate Heinrich Böll would appear or the former East German dissident and musician Wolf Biermann with his guitar. In larger cities well-known bands like Spliff and Udo Lindenberg played, attracting several thousand fans. One small-town mayor called the police: surely writing poetry on sidewalks in colored chalk broke some kind of law. The Greens' central demands were the shutdown of the country's nuclear power plants and the scrapping of the Euromissiles. "Greens in, missiles out" read their leaflets, when they had leaflets. In an article entitled "The Caterpillars from another Planet," one journalist from Munich's *Süddeutsche Zeitung* wondered aloud whether these Greens even came from the same solar system as their colleagues in the established parties.[46]

On election night in Frankfurt, the Hesse Greens gathered together with the other parties to await the results. The first returns indicated that the Greens hadn't breached the 5 percent hurdle necessary to make it into the Bundestag. Then it looked good. "It went up and down," recalls Fischer. Other guests remember him pacing around the hall as nervously as an expectant father. Then, at 7:39, came the projected result: the Greens had made it into the Bundestag! The activist-politicians were jubilant. Sparkling wine and tears flowed. They received more than 2.1 million votes nationwide, coming largely from the leagues of disgruntled Social Democrats, although not exclusively. Greens voters tended to be young, twenty-five to thirty-five, and included many first time voters under twenty-five. They scored particularly well among educated, urban voters, especially in the country's university towns and localities where environmental campaigns were active.[47]

But the Greens' twenty-eight seats combined with the Social Democrats' total wasn't nearly enough to challenge the Conservative–Liberal coalition that had, as expected, won an easy majority in the Bundestag. This was the formal beginning of the Kohl era. During its sixteen-year tenure, the Greens wouldn't fade away or combust as many predicted; rather, they'd endure and change in ways that no one could have predicted.

6

Autumn of the Euromissiles

The Federal Republic's reactions to the newest party on the national stage ranged from intense skepticism to mild bemusement. Bavaria's premier conservative, Franz Josef Strauss, invoked vintage Adenauer-era anti-communism, labeling the Greens a "Trojan Soviet cavalry."[1] The chancellor-elect, Christian Democrat Helmut Kohl, wagered that the rebel ecologists would find their way back under the wing of the SPD, vanishing completely from the political scene in two years time. This is exactly what the Social Democrats themselves hoped.[2] In the meantime, however, the new party wasn't going to get a free ride from the republic's oldest. Hesse's minister president, the Social Democrat Holger Börner, boasted that in the old days, on the construction site, types like Greens were brought to heel with the flat side of a two-by-four.[3]

Every editorial page in West Germany had an opinion on the Greens. Frankfurt's *Abendpost* opined, "These parliamentary greenies have the reputation of being troublemakers and naysayers who don't comply with the decisions of the majority. The Bundestag is the country's highest lawmaker. All MPs have the duty to respect its authority."[4] The radical leftist *Konkret* also delivered the Greens a punch in the ribs, paraphrasing Lenin to do so: "This party won't last long. . . . Like an ostrich, the Greens stick their heads in the sand and imagine that the landscape has disappeared."[5] Not alone, however, the *Spiegel* was grateful for the fresh breeze that the Greens could blow into stodgy Bonn: "If the handful of talk shows on which the Greens have appeared are any harbinger, they have shown our TV nation that the days of dull-as-dust political discussions are now the past. The Greens say what they think and, at the very least, they provoke on topics that the other parties would otherwise gladly circumvent with platitudes."[6]

The Greens didn't presume themselves to be an ordinary party, and thus they weren't about to make an ordinary entry into the Bundestag. They were gatecrashers, coming uninvited from the streets, barging their way into the halls of the German establishment. On the overcast spring day that the new parliament convened in late March 1983, the elected Greens MPs, their staffers, party loyalists, and a grab bag of several hundred activists gathered in a Bonn neighborhood to march together on the Bundestag. The street procession underscored that, through the Greens, civil society and the grassroots movements across the country would now, for the first time, have a place in the West German parliament.

No one among the entourage was empty-handed. Many brandished homemade placards that distinguished their movement affiliations: Third World solidarity, the anti-census campaign, senior citizens, the initiative against the new Frankfurt runway. TV cameras were everywhere as the troupe ambled cheerfully through Bonn's neighborhoods to the beat of African drums played from an open, horse-drawn carriage. Newly elected MP Roland Vogt carried a potted forsythia bush. Petra Kelly, radiant in a bright purple velvet waistcoat, white blouse, and red riding britches, led the way with Gert Bastian and Otto Schily on either side of her—both de rigueur in suit and tie. Red hair streaming in the wind, activist Eva Quistorp pushed along a giant blue-green "planet earth" beach ball. Others lugged felled pine trees, withered from acid rain.* Every now and then, when the cameramen panned the procession behind Kelly and Bastian, a fresh-faced Joschka Fischer was easy to pick out among his new colleagues. He's by himself on the periphery of the procession, wearing a bemused grin.

Shaking Up the Bundestag

For the first time in thirty years, a new party sat in the Bundestag. Like a neon exclamation mark, the twenty-eight Greens MPs occupied a thin strip of seats that shot up the middle of the decorous assemblage, Social Democrats to the left and Christian Democrats and Liberals to the right. Before they had uttered a word on the floor, the party's mere presence

---

* While Bundestag guards allowed the potted plants into the building, the beach ball globe and the pines had to be abandoned at the door.

fulfilled at least part of Petra Kelly's promise to shake up this "rigid, sterile parliament full of incompetent, elitist men of retirement age."[7] The swath of Greens MPs—colorful clothing, unfurrowed brows, full beards, and flowering bushes—signaled that the shake-up had begun. With an average age of forty-two, the freshman lawmakers laid claim to represent a new generation.*

At the time, only 8.5 percent of the Bundestag's MPs were women, a figure just a shade higher than it had been in 1949.[8] Over a third of the Greens' representatives were women and the Greens women would soon thereafter insist on full male–female parity on all of the Greens' electoral lists. The twenty-eight Greens MPs also constituted nearly a third of the 520 person-body's new, nonincumbent members, another sign of how "old boy" the Bundestag had become. In the past, the traditional parties could get away with such flagrant imbalances because there had been no one to call them on it.

In the Bundestag, before the first session opened, the Social Democrats' seventy-year-old party chairman, Willy Brandt, came over and shook Petra Kelly's hand. After all, he saw the Greens as the Social Democrats' "lost children," even if they now, in present form, represented the first serious left-wing alternative to the SPD since the founding of the Bonn Republic. Other MPs welcomed the Greens with greetings or smiles. But the honeymoon didn't last even a day. When Helmut Kohl rose to take his oath of office that afternoon, the Greens filed out of the hall in protest. They claimed that support for the stationing of new nuclear weapons in Germany implicitly contradicted the chancellor's oath to act in the interests of the German people. The unprecedented gesture understandably outraged the conservatives who, after all, had been democratically elected.

The venom that conservatives spat at the Greens was doubly poisonous when aimed at the party's women. "The conservative men were unbelievably agitated by our being in the Bundestag," remembers Christa Nickels, then a thirty-year-old nurse and mother of two. She says that the Greens women were regularly the object of lewd comments, dirty jokes, and other

---

* A 1983 poll underscored the generational attraction of the Greens: 74 percent of people under nineteen and 58 percent of those twenty to twenty-nine years of age "welcomed the entry of the Greens into the Bundestag," while 67 percent of those fifty to sixty-four and 79 percent older than sixty-five opposed it. See Joyce Marie Mushaben, *From Post-War to Post-Wall Generations: Changing Attitudes towards the National Question and NATO in the Federal Republic of Germany* (Boulder, CO: Westview Press, 1998), 76.

sexist remarks. "They obviously couldn't deal with young, self-confident women," explains Nickels. "They could only imagine women in the roles they were used to having them in, as *Hausfrauen* secretaries, or lovers. They had no respect for us whatsoever. They had to learn that—and they did."

There was no mistaking that West Germany's flagship democratic institution was being opened to scrutiny as it had never been before. In part, the Greens critiqued by means of example, introducing innovations, some of which, while making valid points, often overshot their mark. In order to curb the "corrupting lure of power" and to keep fresh blood circulating in the parliament, for example, the environmental party required that every one of their MPs "rotate" after two years with a predetermined successor who would serve the second half of the four-year term. The MP-in-waiting and the one in office literally shared a single mandate, an innovation that seemed preprogrammed to fuel discord, as indeed it would. Also, the Greens MPs slashed their own monthly salaries from DM 12,000 (about $4,000) to just DM 2,000 (about $650), the difference going to worthy grassroots projects. And in the name of transparency, the party allowed the media to cover all of the parliamentary group's internal meetings from beginning to end. This put the MPs permanently in the public spotlight, a practice that weighed very heavily on some of the newcomers and, indeed, was eventually abandoned. In fact, through a process of trial and error, the Greens discovered that some of the establishment's practices weren't so frivolous after all.

In hindsight, Christa Nickels admits that there were more than a few things that the first batch of Bundestag Greens exaggerated ad absurdum in the name of principle, such as their interminably long meetings:

> [The Bundestag group's meetings] often carried on well into the night. They were impossible to participate in and also care for a family, which I had as did other women. I called the phenomenon of these meetings "the dictatorship of the rear ends" because those who could sit for the longest were those who eventually decided everything. On the one hand, by discussing everything to the last detail and in the public eye we certainly made things more transparent, but it's also the case that this form of *Streitkultur* is extremely intensive and can be very impolite and wounding. By its very nature, it cancels out other values that we wanted to bring in the politics, like gentleness and consideration. For people who weren't used to it, like many such as myself from the Christian-pacifist

> tradition, it was too much. Some just said, "No way, I'm not going to subject myself to this anymore." Many conservatives left the party for this reason, which, in my opinion, was a real loss for the Greens.

One of the faces that didn't shrink from the media glare was Joschka Fischer's. Fischer had been speaking to public audiences in teach-ins and Sponti plenums for over a decade and he appeared to relish the spotlight after his long hiatus. In the Bundestag, Fischer distinguished himself as one of the party's best orators, as well as the Greens' most prominent heckler, ceaselessly taunting the conservatives during their addresses. His irreverent quips and cooler-than-thou manner made him a darling of the media in no time. In response to one journalist's inquiry as to why he declined to provide the Bundestag directory with a curriculum vitae, he shot back: "After I read what the other Greens wrote, like *Gymnasium* diploma on such-and-such a date, college here or there, then this and that, I thought maybe I should write in 'produced my first political leaflet, got my first whack on the head with a billy club, beat up my first cop then and then.' But they never would've printed it. So I thought, they can kiss my ass. I'm not writing anything."[9] (In fact, he listed himself simply as "book seller.")

If Kelly was the party's heart and soul and Schily its elder statesman, then Fischer was its *enfant terrible*. He would show up for press conferences with a four-day beard, in old jeans and green bomber jacket. His attitude pure prole, he played up his radical past for the media's benefit. Within months, Fischer had acquired a profile in the Greens on a par with the star trio of Kelly, Bastian, and Schily. To help him out in the office, he called upon a few old acquaintances: *Pflasterstrand* editor Georg Dick to lead the press office and former co-op flatmate Raoul Kopania to manage the Greens' Bundestag office. Together with student movement-veteran Hubert Kleinert from Marburg, one of Hesse's MPs-in-waiting, the nucleus of the so-called Fischer Gang had a foothold in Bonn.

Inside the Greens' Bundestag group, Fischer was elected its first parliamentary manager—the person responsible for all of the party's parliamentary business, from protocol to vote counting. Unlike other Greens who felt overwhelmed by the Bundestag's complex rules and legalistic jargon, autodidact Fischer learned fast how to navigate within the system and use its structures to the Greens' (and his own) advantage. In both Revolutionary Struggle and Frankfurt's Sponti scene Fischer had been the man on the inside, responsible for the groups' internal workings—above all for strategy and tactics. This, roughly, was the purview of a competent parliamentary manager. The political playing field in Bonn had different rules from those he knew, but he discovered they were accessible. In contrast to Fischer, many Greens believed that they were, as a matter of principle, above the down-and-dirty of parliamentary trench warfare. Engaging in it would rob them of the moral high ground that they were confident they occupied. Instead, they staked out maximalist positions that stood no chance of becoming policy or even influencing it.

Fischer's competency as parliamentary manager impressed many of his new colleagues, even those such as the Hamburg socialist and publishing house owner Jürgen Reents, who knocked heads with Joschka Fischer many times over the years. Nevertheless, Reents appreciated Fischer's political guile:

> He was someone who could not only get his way in the Greens' parliamentary group—although by no means every time—but he could also do so with the other political parties, behind the scenes. And he earned a lot of respect that way. Especially in our first year, there was the question of whether we were going to do a serious, professional job in the Bundestag or simply pass on every press release that we got from the citizens' initiatives and read them out on the floor. We had to prevent the party's work from being dilettantish. Joschka and Otto [Schily] deserve a lot of credit for the Greens not becoming a one-hit wonder, a party that slipped into parliament on the tails of the protest movements and then disappeared again.

Within the parliamentary faction, particularly vicious infighting among the newly elected MPs broke out almost at once in Bonn. Not a single one of the parliamentarians (or their successors-in-waiting) had anticipated the kind of emotional, knock-down, drag-out battles that the MPs waged against one another during the first term. Tears, shouting, walkouts, threats, name-calling, breakdowns, and meltdowns were all part and parcel of the Greens' marathon meetings. Since all of their meetings were televised, the acrimony among the Bundestag Greens was no secret. But Fischer, in an April 1983 interview in *Pflasterstrand*, was the first to call it by name—and doing so provoked more ill will. The different Greens factions, he said, weren't debating political issues as they should be but were waging a "psychological war of everyone against everyone. You have the feeling that the twenty-eight MPs and [the in-waiting] successors are engaged in a dog-eat-dog battle among themselves, each against the other, hour after hour, day after day." Fischer added that he felt like he was trapped in a "permanent unification congress of [West Germany's] various communist sects, Sponti freaks, eco-freaks, and feminists."[10] No wonder he felt this way: this is exactly what the early Greens were.

Indeed, the grounds for the hostile vibes within the party were many, and not quite as illegitimate as Fischer implied. They reflected the diverse origins and internal contradictions of an experimental party that had set its sights very high. It would take the Greens a full decade to smooth out the most debilitating of those contradictions. One source of the early friction was simply the nature of the Greens beast. The Greens were a proud jumble of antinuke activists, various strains of feminists, Third World proponents, peace activists, anticensus campaigners, disaffected Social Democrats, Christian pacifists, and regional environmentalists of many stripes, as well as the flotsam of diverse radical left splinter groups, like the Spontis and the post-SDS Marxist parties. Christa Nickels, for example, a provincial, fast-talking Pax Christi activist from a Catholic Rhineland village on the Dutch border, found herself in the Bundestag seated next to the former Maoist Jürgen Reents from big-city Hamburg. "He had *absolutely* no idea what to do with me," she says, not unkindly. Others, like civil libertarian Schily and ex-general Bastian, didn't fit into any of the movement categories. The elected Greens had divergent agendas, which they insisted reflected the wishes of their particular constituencies. Some of the antinuclear power activists represented single-issue citizens' initiatives. On the other hand, Reents and a group of self-proclaimed "eco-socialists" endorsed a sweeping structural transformation of the Federal Republic's "bourgeois order," with an ecological slant.

In addition, unlike the Social Democrats or the Free Democrats, for example, the Greens had neither track records nor rich traditions to fall back on. Of course, there were the antirearmament campaigns of the 1950s, as well as the Easter March, the student movement, and the new social movements, all of which the Greens implicitly drew from. But these campaigns were all extra-parliamentary. Thus much had to be invented anew, under pressure and on deadline. The Greens had a lot of high-flying ideas, but they hadn't given much thought about how to put them into practice. It was usually clearer what they were against than what they were for. All of this was complicated further by the fact that the new MPs barely knew one another. Under any circumstances, getting a new, untested party up and running would have been a monumental challenge. But the Greens' commitment to grassroots democracy only made the undertaking more ponderous and nerve-racking.

Life in Spaceship Bonn

The general unhappiness within the Bundestag Greens was exacerbated by the culture shock of life in West Germany's postwar capital, Bonn, a Catholic nest on the River Rhine. This was the Germany that the teenage Fischers had run away from. The MPs lived and worked in Bonn's Regierungsviertel, the government district, a cocoon-like residential area of small turn-of-the-century villas that housed all of the buildings used by the parties. It was possible for MPs to remain in it for days and even weeks at a time without interacting with the city of Bonn or its inhabitants. Most resided in dreary three-star hotels, living out of their suitcases and dining in the same restaurants night after night. For the Greens, "Spaceship Bonn" as they called it, reflected the vapid, insular political culture of the Bundestag itself. To their shock, they discovered that West Germany's cultural revolution of the late sixties and seventies had bypassed the German parliament. The 1950s Bonn that author Wolfgang Koeppen had described in *The Hothouse* still, in many ways, lived on in 1980s Bonn.

In the same interview in which Fischer took a potshot at his own party's asocial behavior, he wheeled out the heavy artillery for his Bundestag colleagues from other parties. He called the Bundestag "an uptight pack of old hens" who hadn't loosened up "since 1952 . . . And that's true for the Social Democrats, too." Fischer continued: "The Bundestag is an unbelievable collection of alcoholics who can stink just like schnapps. The longer the session lasts, the stronger it stinks. You can see them in the canteen boozing it up, falling further under the table with every hour. And by the time to vote, well . . . It's an open secret, any journalist will tell you, that especially at the end of long sessions the decision-making capacity [of the MPs] is almost completely impaired by alcohol. The health of the High House [the Bundestag]—and with it the functionality of our democracy—would do well to legalize grass, which is much more healthy."[11]

Fischer's denunciation of the Bundestag's drinking habits in spring 1983 lacked any empathy whatsoever. A year later he wouldn't be so judgmental. The rigors of his job as party manager and the psychological strains of Spaceship Bonn drove Fischer himself to imbibe, red wine his anesthetic of choice. Almost every night until the wee hours he could be found in one of the rathskellers, debating the issues of the day with journalists or holding forth to colleagues on party strategy. By this time, Fischer's second marriage was already faltering. Although he and Inge were together for six years, their marriage lasted barely one. He saw less and less of his children. Instead of returning to Frankfurt at week's end, he often stayed in Bonn, putting in many seven-day work weeks. Fischer's brief fling with family life was over—as was the heyday of the nuclear family in Germany. By the 1980s the family relations of the postwar generations looked quite different from those of their parents: the divorce rate had shot up, as had the prevalence of childless marriages, unwed couples, women living as singles, and single-mother families. With a trend toward smaller families, the German birth rate entered a period of steep decline.

During their early years in the Bundestag, the Greens' foremost accomplishment was not self-destructing. Full-scale implosion was a real danger that some observers felt they only narrowly avoided. Gert Bastian actually left the faction because of its bickering and became an independent MP in the Bundestag. But as a whole, the iconoclast party managed to do more than survive. The Greens waged tenacious opposition to the conservative government, such that it regularly put the much tamer Social Democrats to shame. The Greens also opened up the High House by bringing a range of new issues to its floor. They challenged the traditional parties to address such topics as air pollution, chemical-waste disposal, U.S. chemical and biological weapons in West Germany, environmental destruction in the Third World, German arms exports, political asylum provisions, rape within marriage, everyday sexism, organic farming, toxic pesticides, and ecological damage caused by the autobahn, among others. One Greens bill would have closed all nuclear power plants in West Germany by 1986. It, however, was defeated, as were all of the Greens-sponsored bills during the first couple of years save one, namely a resolution to stop West German imports of endangered sea turtles.

Despite the string of legislative defeats, there were more than a handful of Greens highlights in those early years. In the highly symbolic year 1984 the Greens led the charge against the planned national census, which they claimed would sanction Orwellian spying on the population. The opposition's challenge went all the way to the constitutional court, the highest in the land, where the census in its proposed form was deemed unconstitutional, delivering the first real setback to Chancellor Helmut Kohl. The party's profile was helped enormously when the "Flick scandal" blew open and evidence surfaced that during the 1970s members of all three major parties had accepted private monies in return for political favors. Former Red Army Faction lawyer Otto Schily represented the Greens on the Bundestag committee investigating the scandal, which eventually forced the government's economics minister to resign. On women's issues, the Greens broke much new ground, not least by having the first all-female party directorate—Annemarie Borgmann, Waltraud Schoppe, Antje Vollmer, Christa Nickels, Heidemarie Dann, und Erika Hickel—in the history of the republic.

The Greens also forced another topic onto the Bundestag's agenda, one that during the course of the 1980s provoked a contentious debate in West Germany. Fifteen years after the student movement, Germany's "coming to terms" with the Nazi past remained a central concern of the republic's critics on the left and reflected the political and generational fault lines that still shot through the republic. However, by the 1980s, the context of the discussion over the Federal Republic's identity, its democratic foundations, and the Nazi legacy, was much changed from that of the 1960s. For one, the mainstream German left now accepted the parameters of liberal democracy, as it did the legitimacy of the republic as a democracy. The Greens' mere presence in the Bundestag was testament to this. Yet, even though West German leftists no longer branded the Federal Republic (or the CDU) as "latently fascist," most still felt that the republic's political culture—and German conservatism in particular—was tainted by the vestiges of nationalism and other authoritarian traditions. The development of a healthy, civic democracy in the republic, they argued, was stunted by illiberal values and prejudices that lay deeply embedded in the national consciousness, that Germany's political class had refused to own up to and purge. The postwar *Geschichtsbewältigung,* the processing of the past, had brought the republic a long way, they felt, but most Germans had still not fully internalized the lessons of recent history.

As for the conservatives, the Christian Democrats of the 1980s were no longer those of the Adenauer era, prodded as they, too, had been by the liberalizing tremors of the anti-authoritarian revolt and the 1970s Social Democrat–Liberal coalition, among other factors. There had been a generational shift within the Christian Democrats as well. Many of the older conservative politicians—those who had Nazi pasts—had by now retired. There was no one in the Kohl administration, for example, comparable to former chancellor and Nazi-party careerist Kiesinger or Adenauer's chief of staff, Hans Globke, co-author of Hitler's racist Nuremberg laws. And by accepting the Greens' presence in the Bundestag (however grudgingly), the Christian Democrats acknowledged the new breadth of the republic and, implicitly, the legitimacy of the newcomers' probing, if not of their conclusions. In addition, prolific historical work had been carried out over the last two decades that had brought to light much about the Nazi regime that had before been obfuscated or simply ignored. Moreover, the Bundestag itself had become a forum in which the issues of Germany's relationship to its past could be aired and debated, usually in a rational way.

Despite this tempered rapprochement, West German leftists and many liberal intellectuals still harbored positions decisively more critical of the Federal Republic's relationship to the past than did conservatives. In early summer 1983, Joschka Fischer found himself involved in this tug-of-war over history, identity, and the politics of memory. The episode began with a comparison that Fischer had made between the logic of the arms race and that of the Holocaust: "I find it morally shocking that even after Auschwitz, it isn't taboo, in the logic of modernity, to lay the grounds for mass extermination. But this time not in the name of a racist ideology but in the name of the East-West conflict."[12] Not surprisingly, the remark drew the ire of the Christian Democrats. In the Bundestag, Christian Democrat Heiner Geissler shot back: "Mr. Fischer, let me make you aware of the following: it was the pacifism of the 1930s, whose rationale differs only marginally from the rationale of today's pacifism, that made Auschwitz possible." The reference alluded to the policy of appeasement that the western powers, France and Great Britain among them, took toward Nazi Germany in the 1930s.

Fischer pounced on the conservatives' reactions in order to make a much broader point—one that just about any Greens member could have made—about West German conservatism and the legacy of the Nazi regime. The superpowers' arms race and the formula of mutually assured destruction, he maintained, could only be understood within the context of the world wars and the Holocaust. In World War I, said Fischer, mankind was first confronted with the full destructive potential of modern industry; during World War II, "it wasn't any longer armies that were sent to be gassed but rather whole peoples. The crematoriums and gas chambers in Auschwitz-Birkenau admonish us even today because the deathly spiral that was set into motion then hasn't been broken.... How sick does a civilization have to be to establish as a prerequisite for its own security the imminent, technically feasible threat of the incineration of whole peoples in atomic conflagration—and this supposedly in the name of defense?"[13]

Fischer went further, making an argument that had never been expressed quite so plainly on the floor of the Bundestag. The conservatives' disingenuous treatment of the Nazi legacy distorts West Germany's entire political culture, he argued. German conservatives had long tried to shift the blame for Hitler and the Holocaust away from the German people, either onto other actors—including the Jewish people—or onto a sinister clique around Hitler. They still posed the German people as the foremost victim of Nazi Germany, as well as of the Allied bombings and the post-1945 expulsions in eastern Europe. In doing so, they had effectively circumvented a thorough examination of illiberal elements in their own political traditions and tried to pave the way for a nationalist revival. "You buy into the old German national fairytale that it was other countries that were guilty for everything," continued Fischer, amid ever louder jeering from the conservatives' rows:

> According to the German right, it was always the others—other countries, the Versailles Treaty, the Bolsheviks, the November criminals, high treason, and now pacifism. But it was never the perpetrators themselves, clean and proper Germans in tails and uniforms and, of course, steeped in nationalism. Mr. Minister . . . you should consider this: was it other countries that brought Hitler to power in 1933, or wasn't it really German nationalists, the Hugenbergs and Papens, the Krupps and Flicks, and the rest of them?[14]

By the time Fischer concluded, calling for the government's resignation, he could barely make himself heard over the conservatives' heckling.*

Just one year later, on the fortieth anniversary of Nazi Germany's surrender, West Germany's president, Richard von Weizsäcker, himself a Christian Democrat, appealed to all Germans to take responsibility for the

* The Fischer-Geissler exchange presaged the much broader and publicly acrimonious *Historikerstreit*, or historians' debate, which broke out in the mid-1980s when conservative historians argued that the Nazis' crimes were not unique, but rather stood in a long tradition of totalitarian terror, including Stalin's atrocities. The crux of the revisionist position was that German nationalism and patriotism were no more contaminated than those of other countries with checkered pasts. Germany had suffered enough, they argued, the stigma of the Nazi era could finally be lifted—and Germany returned to the fold of "normal" nations. Leftist and liberal intellectuals, foremost among them the Frankfurt philosopher Jürgen Habermas, responded by charging that this "relativization" of the Holocaust resurrected an old-fashioned German nationalism, one "cleansed" of Nazism and Auschwitz. He argued that the Federal Republic's owning up to these horrors—and their singularity—had finally put (West) Germany on a Western path. See Charles S. Maier, *The Unmasterable Past: History, Holocaust, and German National Identity* (Cambridge, MA: Harvard University Press, 1988).

Nazi past, to remain acutely aware of this dark chapter in German history in order to prevent it, or anything like it, from ever happening again in Europe. Weizsäcker's courageous speech was one of the Bonn Republic's most salient and constituted to a giant step forward in Germany's reckoning with the Nazi past, as well as mending the rents that still divided the republic. "We need and we have the strength to look unblinkered at the truth—without embellishment or distortion," he said. "We remember especially the six million Jews who were murdered in German concentration camps," and the sufferings of all peoples in the war, "above all the countless citizens of the Soviet Union and Poland who lost their lives." Only after mentioning the Nazi's Jewish and foreign victims, as well as communists, homosexuals, and the handicapped, did the German president acknowledge the millions of German refugees and expellees, the leveled cities, and the raped German women.[15] Weizsäcker's words were evidence that German conservatism was changing with the times too, albeit haltingly.

The debates about the past were implicitly debates about the Germans' post-Holocaust identity, and by the 1980s there existed in the Bonn Republic not one but a number of competing sources of identity, no one dominant. As the 1980s historians' debate showed (as did the Christian Democrats' unabated pandering to the expellee lobbies), there remained factions that clung stubbornly to a nationalist identity, despite the discrediting of traditional German nationalism. For its proponents—mostly the republic's right-wing fringe—topics such as unification, recovery of the lost eastern territories, and the country's growing foreigner population were prime concerns. But other identity paradigms had arisen during the postwar decades too—for example, the pride that many West Germans' felt in the Federal Republic's stunning economic recovery, its export prowess, and its status as a world-class economic powerhouse. This had been dubbed "Deutschmark nationalism" after the country's strong currency. Others expressed more pride in what had been called "Model Germany"—the Federal Republic's system of business-labor cooperation, high growth rates, price stability, and a dependable social safety net. Also, since the 1970s, ever more Germans had transferred feelings of pride and loyalty from the traditional nation-state to Europe; a strong European identity and commitment to the European Community is unmistakable in polls and surveys from the time. Lastly, and not exclusively, there was "constitutional patriotism," a term made popular by the philosopher Habermas. Also called "civic nationalism," it defined state loyalty and pride in terms of the liberal principles of the Basic Law, West Germany's constitution. Particularly on the left of center, constitutional patriotism informed part of a new German identity that many could live with comfortably: a secular, civic answer to nationalism, one based on the rule of law and democracy rather than ethnic exclusivity or jingoism. This pride in the constitution was particularly remarkable considering that the Basic Law had originally been written to counteract the inclinations of the German people rather than to articulate their collective aspirations.

The Peace Movement's Hot Autumn

The Greens' shaky start in the Bundestag received a mighty boost in the form of the peace movement, which peaked during the "Hot Autumn" of 1983. Literally millions of West Germans took to the streets to try to stave off deployment of new U.S. nuclear weapons, known as the Euromissiles. A revived peace movement had been gathering steam since the first big demonstrations in 1980–81, in reaction to the announcement of the NATO upgrade. The location of the largest nationwide rallies—and symbol of the anti-missile movement—was Bonn's tree-lined Hofgarten, the university's spacious green, where year after year hundreds of thousands of West German peace activists congregated to petition the government. By summer 1983 one spectacular blockade of military bases or missile sites followed the other. While the Greens actively aided the popular protests against the Pershing II and Cruise missiles, the Euromissile campaign attracted significantly more heterogeneous swaths of the population—young and old, rural and urban, students and professionals, trade unionists and churchgoers—than did the quirky party. A new generation of Social Democrats, politicians including the Saarland's Oskar Lafontaine and Lower Saxony's Gerhard Schröder, claimed to stand shoulder-to-shoulder with movement activists, among them many rank-and-file SPD members. In fact, sensing the direction of the shifting sands, nearly the entire SPD leadership, the very same that called for the new arms in the first place, pulled a U-turn and disavowed Helmut Schmidt's plea for the additional nuclear weapons. Even life-long conservatives began questioning the wisdom of their party's Cold-War dogma.

The new weapons systems still needed the Bundestag's stamp of approval before they could be deployed, as planned, at the end of the year. Although the solid Christian Democrat–Liberal majority was certain to give the go-ahead come November, it seemed that the German people were thinking twice about the Euromissiles. Despite the fact that the pro-missile conservatives had just sailed to a convincing election victory, one opinion poll after another showed West Germans in rapidly increasing numbers opposed to hosting more nuclear weapons. By July 1983 surveys showed between half and three-quarters of all West Germans in favor of further arms-reduction talks and against new weapons systems.[16] (A sliver of hope still existed at the time that the ongoing Soviet–U.S. arms-control talks in Geneva might result in a compromise that would forestall the scheduled deployment. This was the West's "dual-track" approach: the threat of the Euromissiles was supposed to force the Soviets' hand in negotiations.) "There's no two ways about it," wrote *Spiegel*, "no topic in postwar Germany has stirred such emotions and awoken such fears in large parts of the population than the planned arming of the Federal Republic with 108 Pershing II and 96 Cruise missiles, weapons that are supposed to serve to protect our country."[17]

Locally organized peace initiatives had been popping up across the Federal Republic like mushrooms after a fall rain, no town or local parish too remote to stage some kind of symbolic "die-in" or declare their immediate vicinities "nuclear-free zones." Throughout the summer of 1983, U.S. bases, NATO arms depots, and future Euromissile sites were blockaded by protesters linked together in human chains. Others rolled out sleeping bags and pitched tents in front of guarded military installations. The West German police picked up the passive resisters one at a time and threw them in the back of their green and white paddy wagons. Usually, they were out of the lock-up and on the front line again in hours.

From the North Sea to the Bavarian Alps, many ordinary, work-a-day Germans insisted they were exercising their constitutional right to resist the state in the face of immoral, militaristic policies. It was their civic duty, in the light of Germany's unique historical burden, to stand up to the state. "Civil disobedience" was the concept of the hour, its merits and hazards debated in the nation's periodicals with the intensity of a political science seminar. Was this the docile, authority-revering German people who had marched so dutifully to Hitler's drums? It seemed that the motto "Never again Auschwitz, never again war" had become the political ethos of a substantial part of the West German public by the 1980s. The Bonn Republic's postwar journey had bred a nation of pacifists, which, remarkably, wasn't prepared to bend its convictions, even for Washington.

The Kohl government was clearly on edge about the prospect of the mass demonstrations called for October. The stakes were huge: could West

Germany convince that it was still a dependable link in the West's security architecture? Bonn could easily lose face with the western allies should the popular groundswell force the deployment to be delayed—or stopped altogether. The leadership also worried that the protests might turn violent and U.S. military installations or personnel be attacked. In June militant leftists had hurled stones at U.S. Vice President George H.W. Bush's motorcade while he was visiting for a NATO conference. So soon after the terror spree of the 1970s, the threat of more such violence seemed all too real. And, indeed, there were radical strains in the antinuclear and peace movements that weren't pacifist at all. What, they reasoned, was sabotaging a U.S. military base or a nuclear reactor site compared to exposing innocent populations to radiation or nuclear annihilation? Radicals aside, otherwise upstanding burghers were breaking the law in order to obstruct U.S. military operations in West Germany. Had they taken leave of their senses, forgetting that these troops and these missiles were *to protect them* from "communist aggression"? The West German leadership asked itself how much of this nonsense the U.S. military would tolerate before it reacted, perhaps even with live ammunition. Storming a proposed site of a nuclear reactor in the Baden Württemberg countryside was one matter; besieging U.S. army bases was another, entirely.

The Euromissiles were topic number one for the Greens throughout the summer and fall of 1983. As promised, the party acted with "one foot rooted in the movements, the other in the Bundestag." The Greens' offices in Bonn were put at the disposal of peace movement organizers and became a coordination hub for the campaign's countrywide activities. But never, stresses the former peace movement organizer Andreas Zumach, were the movement and the party synonymous. "The Greens were new and because they weren't so ideologically fixated on the bloc logic they were more attractive to many peace activists," he explains. Zumach himself was a disillusioned Social Democrat and member of Action Reconciliation Service for Peace, a postwar pacifist group dedicated to confronting the legacy of the Nazi regime. "The Greens pursued their interests as ruthlessly as did the Christian Democrats and the German Communist Party, both of whom were present in the movement. Although there was a certain natural affinity to the Greens, there was also a wariness that they too wanted to instrumentalize the movement for their own purposes."

For the Greens, stopping the Euromissiles was more than a single-issue campaign that would end either with the missiles' cancellation or their deployment. Unlike the Social Democrats, who would have been satisfied to halt the deployment and return to the status quo, the Greens' challenged the very assumptions of the Cold War. They also claimed to have viable, alternative security concepts to replace those of the military-industrial complex. This function—the formulation and, eventually, the implementation of alternative policies—was beyond the capacity of the peace movement and exactly why many activists had insisted that their grassroots initiatives required a parliamentary arm.

The Greens called their geostrategic program *Friedenspolitik*, or "peace policy." The premise of their argumentation was that a sustainable peace was unthinkable within the context of the Cold War, which should and could be brought to an end. At the core of *Friedenspolitik* was the dissolution of both of the postwar military blocs: the West led by NATO and the East under the Warsaw Pact. The goal was a demilitarized, nuclear weapon-free continent from the Urals to the Atlantic. One of the Greens' central security concepts was Petra Kelly's "Europe of regions," which the party promoted as antidote to a Europe of blocs and nation-states. With a prospect that at the time may have seemed utopian, Kelly, the Brussels bureaucrat, argued for a continent in which national borders were increasingly deemphasized, to the point that one day they would be meaningless. She pointed to the Kaiserstuhl region, where its French, Swiss, and German residents had banded together in common cause to derail the nuclear plant in Wyhl. The first step toward a bloc-free Europe was West Germany's withdrawal from NATO and the onset of unilateral disarmament, *the West first*. The West German government could get the ball rolling by suspending military conscription at once and begin dismantling the Bundeswehr. If the West were to start cutting its continental arsenal, argued the Greens, the cash-strapped Soviet Union would soon thereafter follow suit.

As was the case with most of the Greens' positions, there was no full-blown consensus in the party on the different aspects of *Friedenspolitik*. Among the most controversial was the party's stand vis-à-vis the United States and the Soviet Union. There were German Greens, particularly from the social movements, who had forged enduring ties with their counterparts in the United States and counted the American protest movements of the 1960s and 1970s among their strongest influences. Andreas Zumach's Action Reconciliation Service for Peace, for example, had sent scores of young Germans to the United States to work with the historic American "peace churches"—the Quakers, the Mennonites, and the Brethren—as well as with the progressive United Farm Workers union. Some Greens, like the United States–raised Kelly (and Joschka Fischer too), held Moscow and Washington equally responsible for the Cold War and the runaway arms race. Their demands for halting the Pershing IIs were coupled with calls for the Soviets to dismantle their mid-range nuclear missiles, the SS-20s. Kelly was aware of a sweeping anti-Americanism in the peace movement and actively resisted it. Her position, however, wasn't made any easier by President Ronald Reagan's confrontational approach—for example, his calling the Soviet Union the "evil empire," as if godless communism were the source of everything amiss in the world. Washington's arms build-up both infuriated and scared German activists, no matter how some of them bent over backwards to be "fair and even-handed." It was, after all, a U.S.-led policy on U.S. nuclear weapons stationed on U.S. bases that West Germans were protesting. Even those more favorably inclined toward the United States would have agreed that NATO's missile plans constituted a gratuitous escalation of the nuclear arms race.

The "curse on both your missiles" view, however, was contested by a vocal contingent in the party that reflected the vigorous anti-American sentiment in the German left. It singled out the United States as the main protagonist of the Cold War and the perpetrator of an aggressive, worldwide imperialism. It was easy enough for these critics to point to a host of Reagan administration policies, from its plans for "Star Wars," a space-based missile shield, to its backing of right-wing elements in Nicaragua and El Salvador. And bolstering the claims of its detractors, in October 1983 the U.S. administration deployed troops to the Caribbean island of Grenada, again in the name of anticommunism. To this strain of the German left, Washington's ideological rhetoric was nothing more than a veil to mask its imperialist aims. The Soviet Union, on the other hand—though not put on a pedestal—was often portrayed as a more benevolent, or at least a "less bad" power reacting to Washington's provocations.

Often ferocious disputes broke out within the Greens over these issues and others that were in some way connected to the "U.S. imperialism vs. Soviet Stalinism" debate. One such point of contention was the party's relationship to dissident human rights groups in eastern Europe. For the likes of Kelly, it was a given that these pro-democracy groups were partners and that the Greens should support them. She and her party allies understood the Eastern bloc regimes as dictatorships that trampled on human rights. Others, like Jürgen Reents and the "eco-socialists," claimed that any criticism of the Eastern bloc leaderships played into Washington's hands, providing fodder for the kind of anticommunism that the West relied on to justify its arms expenditures, interventions in Latin America, and stationing of nuclear weapons in western Europe.

"There were standpoints within the Greens that ranged from open to implicit sympathy for the [East German] regime," explains Wolfgang Templin, a former human rights activist in East Germany who met with Green politicians during the 1980s in East Berlin. "Some," he says, "thought: 'well, compared to the glaring contradictions that we have here in the West, the East is the lesser evil.' Yet another bunch just didn't care but simply said, 'that's not our field, it's a secondary priority to the Third World or the pressing issues here in West Germany.' " Joschka Fischer, notes Templin, was in the latter group. Wolfgang Templin and fellow dissidents began meeting with Petra Kelly and others in the early eighties. Like his colleagues, he was enormously impressed by Kelly. "Those like Petra were a minority in the party," he says. "She made it plain that she stood on our side. She saw the situation as we did: as a confrontation between liberal democracy and Soviet totalitarianism."

Paradoxically, while West Germany's major parties hurled invective at the Warsaw Pact leaderships in public, they cooperated with them—and largely ignored the dissident groups. This was the cruel flip side of the Social Democrats' *Ostpolitik*: by recognizing the legitimacy of the Eastern bloc states, the West delegitimized the claims of the pro-democracy dissidents. The SPD's virtual ignoring of Poland's Solidarity movement in 1979–80 was a by-product of official *Ostpolitik*, the price for the normalizing of relations with the Eastern bloc leadership. Kelly, in contrast, was optimistic that political change initiated from below could happen in the Eastern bloc and one day overthrow those regimes. She also understood that, ultimately, her vision for a united, nuclear-free Europe was only possible in a democratic Europe made up of countries with freely elected parliaments and vibrant grassroots movements.

In May 1983, during the European Nuclear Disarmament congress in West Berlin, Petra Kelly, Gert Bastian, Roland Vogt, Milan Horacek, and a handful of others forayed into East Berlin to express their solidarity with the "unofficial," and thus illegal, East German peace movement, whose members were prohibited from attending the congress. The independent peace movement in the GDR comprised small groups scattered around the country, most of which operated under the wing of the Protestant churches and in the face of constant harassment by the state security service. On the central Alexanderplatz, under the mammoth, globe-topped television tower, the Green contingent unfurled a banner of the independent East

German peace group called Swords into Plowshares. One of the Greens' aims was to win the group publicity in the West, which was one of the East German movement's few sources of protection from the state. Also, they wanted to demonstrate to their GDR-friendly colleagues in the Greens and the Western peace movements exactly what kind of regime this was. True to form, the East German Volkspolizei apprehended the entourage in no time and deposited on the other side of the wall. But later that year as a result of the excursion, East German leader Erich Honecker agreed to meet with German Greens officially in East Berlin to discuss disarmament, among other issues, one of which, the Greens made certain, was his government's treatment of independent peace activists. Photos from the meeting show Kelly in a Swords into Plowshares T-shirt pulled over her white turtleneck and glaring at an obviously very uncomfortable Erich Honecker (see figure 15, photo gallery).

If she could circumvent the official channels to meet with the East German head of state, felt Kelly, then she could talk eye-to-eye to the president of the United States—and the Soviet leadership, too. That summer a small Greens delegation crossed the Atlantic to venture into the lion's den, to make their case to the U.S. leadership and the larger public. Kelly wanted to reach out to the American people, in part in order to counter the perception that the German Greens harbored a one-sided antipathy toward the United States. She wanted an opportunity to explain the German peace movement to the American public and its political class as well, including President Reagan. (Although Kelly and the Greens met with many senior U.S. officials and congressmen—to the displeasure of the West German embassy in Washington—the delegation did not receive an audience with President Reagan.) Not least, the German Greens were coordinating plans with U.S. peace groups for simultaneous antimissile demonstrations in Europe and North America, come autumn.

At the time, Petra Kelly was at the height of her celebrity, in Germany and internationally as well. The frail-looking woman with an unearthly pale complexion (one German journalist described her as looking as if she were perpetually freezing) and dark-ringed eyes, had gained world renown. She was a figure that peace movements on both sides of Europe, in North America, Asia, and Australia, too, recognized and respected for her missionary activism on behalf of disarmament, world peace, Tibet, Australian Aborigines, and alternative energy. When she spoke in Washington in July 1983, American peace groups and her alma mater, American University, gave her a hero's welcome. But she charmed adversaries as well. On NBC's

Meet the Press, Kelly dazzled the conservative moderator Robert Novak and a team of veteran U.S. journalists, who shot questions at her like poison-tipped arrows. After the performance the studio crew put down their equipment and applauded Kelly.[18]

As summer turned to fall in 1983 and the November vote on the Euromissiles approached, the Bundestag Greens used every means at their disposal to throw the rationale for the in-transit nuclear arms into question and put the government against the ropes. The centerpiece of the Greens' parliamentary strategy was a proposal to hold a popular referendum on the nuclear upgrade: let the people decide, now that they fully understand the implications of NATO's nuclear doctrine for their towns and families. The referendum bill, which would have required a constitutional amendment, was shot down before it could come to the floor.

The Hot Autumn of the Euromissiles climaxed during an October Action Week when up to 1.5 million people participated in nationally organized demonstrations and thousands of local "peace events" across the country. Most of the mainstream press covered the extra-parliamentary events of the Hot Autumn fairly, often even favorably. West Germany's media landscape had evolved considerably since the postwar decades, not least because the media were one of the first "institutions" to be infiltrated in the long march. That notwithstanding, by far the best place to follow the October events was in the nearly five-year-old *Tageszeitung*, published daily in West Berlin. The *Tageszeitung* had been scrupulously covering the preparations for the Action Week and providing a forum for the debates and discussions within the peace movement. During the peak of the protests, the *Tageszeitung* devoted several pages in every issue to the peace vigils, peace strikes, peace fasts, peace breakfasts, peace caravans, women's peace marches, peace camps, peace blockades, peace declarations, peace sit-ins, and myriad other peace-related activities. Each day of the October *Aktionswoche* was designated for a specific group within the movement—that is, women on one day, trade unions on another, and so on. The day assigned to students, including high school pupils, created something of a stir because it was in the middle of the week, a school day. Teachers who worked in Christian Democrat–run states faced disciplinary measures if they gave the kids the afternoon off. Many did anyway.

Just a glimpse at the run-up to the weekend's nationwide demonstrations gives some idea of the breadth and spirit of the Hot Autumn. In the port city of Bremerhaven, along the River Weser, 40,000 missile foes encircled and blockaded the U.S. army barracks there. On the rain-soaked

Women's Resistance Day, female protesters congregated in front of the Defense Ministry in Bonn under a banner that read: "This country doesn't need new arms, it needs new men." Doctors, nurses, civil servants, judges, lawyers, and architects all staged events during the week. On Anti-Militarism Day, pacifists blocked the entrances of several West German arms manufacturers. Another day, the Ministry for Development in Bonn was surrounded, protesters with red-and-black flags yelling: "Resume aid to Nicaragua! Stop aid to El Salvador and Guatemala!" Smaller groups conducted hunger strikes. Everywhere there were folk songs, homemade banners, huge cauldrons of thick soup, rock bands, and candle-lit vigils—in other words, "nonviolent resistance"—just as Petra Kelly and Roland Vogt understood it.

The protests reached their crescendo on October 22, when over a million Germans demonstrated against the Euromissiles in Bonn, Hamburg, Stuttgart, and West Berlin. In southern Germany, 250,000 people formed a forty-five-mile-long human chain from Neu-Ulm, one of the new missiles' future homes, to Stuttgart, the headquarters of U.S. European command center. In Hamburg, 400,000 people marched together, a record number for the Hansiatic city. Elsewhere in Europe, and in the United States, too, the international peace movement expressed solidarity with its brothers and sisters in Germany by calling demonstrations of their own, some of them nearly as big as those in the Federal Republic's cities.

A whiff of controversy surrounded the final rally in Bonn's Hofgarten that bespoke the differences within the movement beyond the common plank against the Euromissiles. The keynote speaker was seventy-year-old Willy Brandt, who many activists deemed unacceptable in light of the Social Democrats' role in requesting the new weapon systems in the first place. But, argued others, Brandt illustrated that opposition to the new nuclear missiles extended deep into the mainstream of society. Packed buses and special charter trains had been arriving in the capital city since the crack of dawn. By the time Brandt stepped up to the podium, an estimated 500,000 protesters[19] had gathered in and beyond the tree-lined Hofgarten park. "Germany," said the Nobel laureate to the largest crowd that he had ever addressed, "doesn't need more means of mass annihilation, but fewer. Therefore we say 'no' to ever more new nuclear weapons!"[20] Although Brandt rejected the nuclear upgrade, favoring "serious negotiations rather than deployment," he never once mentioned the Pershing II or Cruise missiles by name. Also, there could be no question, he stressed, that West Germany's rightful place was in NATO, firmly under the wing of the western alliance, a remark that elicited whistles and heckling from the crowd. But on this matter Brandt was in step with most West Germans who may have objected to the Euromissiles but didn't question the Federal Republic's place in the U.S.-led camp.

The elder statesman, however, didn't have the last word. Petra Kelly did. She stepped up to the lectern and at once took Brandt to task by retorting that Europe didn't need "fewer" weapons of mass annihilation, but "none at all." The Social Democrats' "no" to Euromissiles and "yes" to NATO is absurd, Kelly insisted. It is a blatant contradiction, she argued, to claim to want the dissolution of the military blocs and then say that until that happens, West Germany should remain in one of them. "We have to take the first, calculated steps in order to overcome the logic of adversarial military blocs." She warned the peace movement about the Social Democrats' overtures: "I hope that the Social Democrats understand the change in their security policy as reparation for their past nuclear errors, and not as a strategy for integrating the independent [peace] movement [into its ranks] in order to betray it once again," she said, referring to the party's co-opting of the 1950s peace campaigns.[21]

The upheaval in the Federal Republic didn't cause the conservative-liberal coalition to blink when it came to approving the Euromissiles. On the days of the November 21–22 Bundestag debate and vote, protesters besieged Bonn, even invading the government district and other "no protests zones." On the Bundestag floor, the debate raged on for two full days, although there was little mystery about the vote's outcome. The Greens draped banners inside the Bundestag and encouraged the peace protesters outside. Joschka Fischer peppered Helmut Kohl's standard cold-war defense of the Euromissiles with acerbic catcalls. But at the end of the day, the vote split pretty much down party lines: 286 Christian Democrats and Free Democrats in favor, 226 Greens and Social Democrats against. The missile hardware was already on its way and would be stationed in West Germany, fully operational by January 1, 1984.

The Hofgarten Generation

Ostensibly, the Hot Autumn petered out in defeat, a blow not just to European security, the missile opponents charged, but also to West German democracy: the political elite, supine to Washington, had imposed its will on that of the popular majority. Actually, the participants in West

Germany's biggest-ever experiment in direct democracy accomplished more than they might have thought at the time. The nationwide protests in West Germany rank as the largest and broadest mass movement in the history of the republic. The postwar peace campaigns, the student movement, and the protests against nuclear power never came close to the peace movement's size and breadth. And the 1980s peace movement had a profound and long-lasting impact on the West German political consciousness, leaving in its wake a deeper, livelier democracy, one intensely suspicious of military options.

"Even though we lost the larger battle over the Euromissiles," explains peace researcher Otfried Nassauer:

> We won an important victory for democratic accountability. The people confronted the military on its own turf. They dared to call the military on a security issue, to stand up to it as informed citizens. Our argument wasn't primarily a moral one, as with the peace movements in the past, but rather geostrategic. We said mutual assured destruction didn't make sense, that it won't work and we had the facts to back it up. By the time the missiles arrived most West Germans and most of the media, too, not to mention most Social Democrats, were of this opinion.

In late 1983, polls showed that 61 percent of CDU voters, 68 percent of Free Democrats, 83 percent of SPD followers, and 95 percent of Greens rejected a nuclear "defense" of German territory.[22] Five years later, in 1988, polls showed that 79 percent of West Germans supported a full denuclearization of Europe.[23]

The Federal Republic exhibited a new sense of self during the peace movement. This Germany wasn't an aggressive force bent on destabilizing Europe, as it had been in the past, but rather a stabilizing actor in the middle of the continent. Many West Germans, it seems, understood their country as one that should be devoted to peace; and during the peace movement, they linked national security policy "with what it meant to be German at the individual level."[24] Critics from diverse ideological camps, argues political scientist Joyce Marie Mushaben, joined forces "to reclaim their right to a bona fide German identity vis-à-vis the superpowers."[25] West Germans were saying that their state should go further than its constitution, which simply restrained the Federal Republic's own military power. Rather, the Bonn Republic should be a proactive force promoting moderation, dialogue, and negotiation in the name of peace. In this vein, the peace movement and *Friedenspolitik* followed in the footsteps of West Germany's signature *Ostpolitik* by posing constructive alternative approaches to European security policy. This understanding of the Federal Republic as a voice for peace and, even, in the best case, a constructive progenitor of new policy ideas, constituted a source of positive identification in a country with so many negatives.

The Federal Republic's relationship to the United States would never be the same after the Hot Autumn. "The new movement," noted one German commentator, "opposed not only the arms race and the policy of deterrence but it mounted a frontal attack against one of the greatest taboos of the postwar period: the Federal Republic's dependence on the United States, its western orientation, and its membership in NATO."[26] The peace movement constituted the first instance in which the West German public, in opposition to its leadership, took a firm stand against an American policy that directly affected the Federal Republic. In the sixties, rebellious-minded students marched against Washington's war in Indochina, which, while considered insolent at the time, was a far cry from challenging the U.S. military *in* West Germany on a decisive matter of Cold War geostrategy. It had been the Federal Republic's postwar duty, even the raison d'etre for its creation, to man the front line of the East–West conflict—not to question it, lest Germans forget that this state of affairs was the result of their world wars. But now they were saying as loudly as they could that they were no longer willing to be pawns in the superpowers' game of nuclear chess.

The republic's traditional political parties couldn't ignore the vox populi. The Social Democrats backtracked on their own nuclear-defense doctrine, and in doing so, also took a step out from beneath America's paternal wing. "More than ever before," writes political scientist Steve Breyman, "it was clear to the Social Democrats that United States and West German interests diverged on many crucial issues. . . . And more than ever before, the party was prepared to represent German interests within NATO councils and against Washington."[27] The Social Democrats' new bearing illustrated that it was entirely possible to break with Washington on a specific issue without upending the western alliance as a whole.

The Christian Democrats were more flustered than they let on. "Never again would any German government, no matter how conservative, pursue another nuclear upgrade," says Otfried Nassauer. Indeed, the Kohl government later turned down NATO offers (pushed vigorously by Washington and London) to modernize West Germany's short-range nuclear missiles. Kohl, noted the weekly *Die Zeit*, had to make "it plain that he could not be counted on as an automatic, uncritical executor of American orders."[28] In line with popular sentiment, the West German defense budget fell off during the course of the 1980s; by 1986 it was lower than it had been in the Schmidt years.[29] Also, the Kohl government renewed its commitment to push ahead with East–West cooperation, even in the face of renewed tension between the superpowers.

The peace movement's broad diversity and the wide-ranging creativity of its protest forms also enabled many ordinary Germans to engage in extra-parliamentary politics in their own way, be it in demonstrations, blockades, petitions, street theater, pamphleteering, or church parish fund-raisers. An entire generation, one too young to remember the 1960s protests, was politicized during these years, through these protest experiences. The numbers of young men applying for conscientious objector status quadrupled between 1979 and 1981, and then tripled again between 1981 and the 1990s.[30] A sign of the broader civic spirit was the clear majority of young adults who expressed a willingness to participate in extra-parliamentary politics. And even among people over fifty, the proportion willing to be in a citizens' initiative shot up from 19 percent in 1981 to 31 percent in 1983.[31] The Hot Autumn may have ended in a whimper, but elements of its ethos seeped into the republic's political consciousness.

In a larger, world-historical context, the German peace movement—as part of a global disarmament movement—has even been credited with expediting the conclusion of the Cold War. Contrary to those narratives that claim that the U.S. arms build-up pushed the Soviet Union to reform and, ultimately, to abandon the Cold War, the preeminent historian of worldwide disarmament movements, Lawrence S. Wittner, gives the peace movements, together with Soviet leader Mikhail Gorbachev, the lion's share of credit for the seismic shifts that would occur in the late 1980s and early 1990s.

According to Wittner, many of the peace movement's key ideas—a nuclear-free Europe, the winding down of the arms race, the withdrawal of U.S. and Soviet troops from central Europe—were picked up upon by the new Soviet leader Mikhail Gorbachev. Wittner sees Gorbachev as a genuine convert to the antinuclear cause, who adopted its message and aims. He argues that with the wind of the disarmament movements at his back, the Soviet leader:

> [began] a dramatic campaign against nuclear weapons and nuclear war that, eventually, convinced [U.S. President] Reagan to make a

> break with the Old Thinking. Thereafter, working together, they routed conservative supporters of nuclear weaponry, opening the way for significant disarmament measures... [Reagan's successor, President George H.W.] Bush entered into a partnership with Gorbachev and the two leaders implemented the farthest-reaching nuclear arms reductions in world history. They dropped plans for nuclear modernization, signed strategic arms reduction treaties, halted nuclear testing, closed nuclear facilities, halted plans for new weapons systems, and even scrapped substantial portions of the nuclear arsenals unilaterally.[32]

Wittner admits that this course of events would have been unlikely without a willing Soviet leader. But, he concludes, "it also seems unlikely that Gorbachev, Bush, or most other world leaders would have followed this scenario without the impetus of the nuclear disarmament movement."[33]

Figure 1: The Fischer family shortly after Joschka's birth in April 1948. The elder sister Georgina is nine years old, the younger Irma Maria Franziska is five. Rights: Fischer family.

Figure 2: In Hamburg, on April 17, 1958, a demonstration against the stationing of nuclear weapons in the Federal Republic. Credit: bpk/Erich Andres.

Figure 3: Fifteen-year-old Joschka Fischer (far left) with friends from the local *Gymnasium*. The following year he flunked out of the elite school and was demoted to *Mittelschule*. Rights: Fischer family.

Figure 4: Joschka Fischer and Ede Fischer on their wedding day in April 1967 in Gretna Green, Scotland. Rights: Joschka Fischer.

Figure 5: 1967, Willy Brandt, foreign minister in the 1966–69 grand coalition, and his wife, Rut, at a ball in the foreign ministry in Bonn. Credit: Federal Government of Germany.

Figure 6: Student movement leader Rudi Dutschke (in striped sweater) and fellow demonstrators besieging a West Berlin court house in November 1967. One of the founders of Kommune I, Fritz Teufel, was being tried for minor offenses on the day of the death of Benno Ohnesorg earlier that year. Credit: bpk/ Klaus Lehnartz.

Figure 7: 1974 Frankfurt rally in solidarity with the Chilean labor movement and against the military regime there. The banner is one of Fischer's anarchist group, Revolutionary Struggle. Credit: bpk/Abisag Tüllmann.

Figure 8: Joschka Fischer, André Glucksmann, Dany Cohn-Bendit (from left to right) at a 1978 discussion in Frankfurt University's legendary lecture hall IV. The topic was new trends in French philosophy. Credit: bpk/Abisag Tüllmann.

die Tageszeitung

Dienstag, 17. 4. 79

taz

ab heute täglich

Erdbeben in Jugoslawien

Neue Verhaftungswelle im Iran

Havemann wird ausgehungert

Redaktionen

Eigentumsvorbehalt

A 4100 AX

Seit Gründung der „BILD"-Zeitung 1952, vor mehr als 25 Jahren, hat es in dieser Republik keine überregionale, parteiunabhängige Tageszeitungsgründung gegeben: Im Gegenteil, viele sind eingegangen. Wer kann da heute noch von Pressefreiheit reden? Wir werden versuchen, ein Blatt gegen jede freiwillige Zensur und Nachrichtensperre zu publizieren. Kein Linienblatt, aber eine linke, radikale, auch satirische Zeitung — täglich! Den unterschiedlichsten Leuten soll darin Platz gegeben werden, gegen traditionellen, distanzierenden Profijournalismus zu schreiben. Ein Versuch, den Gebrauchswert des Mediums Tageszeitung zu verändern — Lesern das Blatt zu Verfügung zu stellen! Eine Hoffnung, die Presselandschaft in Bewegung zu versetzen.

Inhalt

Volksentscheid über Atomenergie

„Natürliche Abgänge"

P.P. Zahl: Sondermaßnahmen aufgehoben

Italienische Winterreise

Geburt nach Stoppuhr

Figure 9: The front page of the first issue of West Germany's left-wing daily *Die Tageszeitung*. Credit: *Die Tageszeitung*.

Figure 10: West German police and border guards destroy the anti-atomic village at the Gorleben site on June 4, 1980. Credit: bpk/Günter Zint.

Figure 11: Early Greens poster, 1980. "Nuclear power isn't safe. Let's use nature's powers! The Greens." Rights: Heinrich Böll Foundation.

Figure 12: A demonstration in Bonn on April 4, 1981, of the nationwide Alliance of Citizens' Initiatives (BBU) against the nuclear energy program of Social Democratic chancellor Helmut Schmidt. The banner in the middle reads: "Soon it's over for Schmidt and Strauss. The Greens." In the background another reads: "Send the Nuclear Power Lobby to Harrisburg [PA]." Credit: Federal Government of Germany.

Figure 13: On October 10, 1981, in route to Bonn's Hofgarten, 300,000 people demonstrated for peace and disarmament. Credit: bpk/Jochen Moll.

Figure 14: On their first day in the Bundestag, Greens MPs Gaby Gottwald (left) and Petra Kelly (right) unfurled a banner that took aim at West German and U.S. policy in Nicaragua. Credit: Darchinger.

Figure 15: In East Berlin, a Greens contingent met with East German leader Erich Honecker on October 23, 1983. The Greens are (from left to right) Antje Vollmer, Lukas Beckmann, Michael Kraemer, Otto Schily, Petra Kelly, Gert Bastian. Honecker holds a "peace treaty" drawn up by the Greens. The poster depicts Germany's leading politicians who point to a sunflower (the Greens' symbol) against the backdrop of industrial wasteland and say: "It's disfiguring our political landscape." Credit: Ullstein Bild/The Granger Collection, New York.

Figure 16: The biggest demonstration ever in the history of East Germany on East Berlin's Alexanderplatz (November 4, 1989). The eastern Germans called for free elections, free media, free speech, and freedom of assembly. The Berlin Wall fell several days later. Credit: bpk/Gerhard Kiesling.

Figure 17: Fischer as Greens politician campaigning in Frankfurt during the 1991 Hesse election campaign. Credit: bpk/Abisag Tüllmann.

Figure 18: A candle-lit vigil of 100,000 people in front of Brandenburg gate in Berlin on 60th anniversary of Nazi seizure of power in January 1993. The words spelled out by the candles read "Never again." Credit: Federal Government of Germany.

Figure 19: The sweet taste of victory. Gerhard Schröder, Joschka Fischer, and Oskar Lafontaine celebrate the signing of the first-ever "red–green" coalition contract at the federal level. Schröder would become chancellor, Fischer foreign minister, and Lafontaine finance minister. Rights: Federal Government of Germany.

7

Going Realo

"In 1968 we began our long march through the institutions. The first of us have arrived, others will follow."
—Bernd Messinger, a Green MP, to the newly elected Hesse legislature in December 1985

The peace movement didn't dissolve all at once. Into the late 1980s, missile foes staged spectacular blockades of NATO installations and organized rallies of tens of thousands in the Bonn Hofgarten and elsewhere. But the missiles' deployment pierced the high-flying idealism and "can do" spirit of the campaign. For a moment, it had seemed to peace activists as if anything were possible, with reason, moral rectitude, and people power united against the forces of nuclear Armageddon. Yet three years of mass demonstrations and untold thousands of antimissile events hadn't slowed the delivery of the new weaponry by even a day.

The Bundestag Greens couldn't help but feel dispirited as well. "In the first days after the November vote, everyone was completely exhausted," remembers Hubert Kleinert, a mustachioed Greens MP from the little college town of Marburg in Hesse.[1] "A lot had been staked on this. Now that it had happened, defeat hung in the air like poison. It wasn't just your typical lethargy that tends to creep in after a setback but one that grasped that the movement euphoria of the early 1980s was definitively over." The implications for a handful of the Bundestag Greens, including Kleinert, Joschka Fischer, and Otto Schily, were staring them in the face: in order to make an impact in the real world, the Greens had to start acting like a serious party. The earliest "realos" believed that the Greens had to pursue a pragmatic realpolitik with the goal of eventually forming coalitions with Social Democrats. "While before the Greens could swim along with the current of the social movements, this was no longer the case," concluded Kleinert at the time. "Now the Greens had to rely on themselves and on their work as a parliamentary party."

Kleinert's conclusion, however, wasn't widely shared in his own party. Most Greens, even in the face of the Euromissile defeat, still saw the role of their party as one of "fundamental opposition." For the fundamentalists, or "fundies," the Greens were, and remained, an "antiparty party," just as Petra Kelly envisioned it, rooted in the extra-parliamentary social movements. These were the lines of confrontation within the Greens that would divide the party for almost a decade–and very nearly destroy it. "It was 'us against them,' realos against fundies, between which next to nothing was possible," wrote the *Tageszeitung* in hindsight. "Delegates turned into voting blocs, discourse into a barroom brawl."[2] The realos and the fundies would fight one another tooth-and-nail for the soul of the Greens until finally, on the cusp of the 1990s, one emerged victorious, the other defeated and exiled.

The Hesse Greens, with their man Joschka Fischer at the fore, were the pioneer realos and no figure rendered the realo case more forcefully than Fischer himself. It was Willy Brandt's ambiguous remark about "a new majority left of the [Christian Democratic] Union" that electrified Fischer, who understood it unambiguously to mean that the future of the republic's left lay in electoral constellations of Social Democrats and Greens. The party, he insisted, had to move away from hollow, symbolic gestures that altered nothing. Social change in the Federal Republic was possible only through a long-term, step-by-step process of reform. One case in point, charged Fischer, was nuclear power. The Greens perpetuated the myth that shutting down the Federal Republic's nuclear reactors should and could happen right away. But, he argued, "no one dares pose the question: where have the Greens shut down or stopped anything?" The Greens, he maintained, have to come up with a workable political strategy to close the country's nuclear plants, just as they must formulate nuts-and-bolts policies to achieve other goals. This way forward didn't preclude vibrant grassroots movements, but the business of representative democracy happens in elected legislatures, not in front of nuclear reactor sites. "The Greens are losing momentum," Fischer warned, "and no one should be surprised that the party's verve and political creativity are being sapped in the process."[3]

This conception of the Greens had vehement opponents in the Bundestag Greens and in the Hesse branch of the party, too. Prominent among them were the radical ecologists Manfred Zieran and Jutta Ditfurth, a Frankfurt activist couple who would become the standard-bearers for the fundies, just as Fischer and Schily would for the realos. In the tall, broad-shouldered Ditfurth, Fischer was matched up against an equal: someone as self-confident, resourceful, and tenacious as himself. An imposing woman with an in-your-face way about her, Ditfurth left no uncertainty about whether she considered one friend or foe—and foes beware. She was born in 1951 as Jutta von Ditfurth, daughter of a widely known and well-to-do West German scientist who had a popular talk show on German television. As with many German students, her studies in sociology, political science, and art history took her to university towns across West Germany, as well as to Scotland and the United States (Detroit). A founding member of the Greens, she came to the party through the women's and antinuclear movements, and she prefaced her essays and talks with fist-shaking quotes from Marx, Rudi Dutschke, or Rosa Luxemburg. Ditfurth belonged to the party's radical left and was proud of it, determined not to water down her politics in exchange for a place at the establishment's table.

For Jutta Ditfurth and the fundies, the Greens were a bug in the body politic, not a tonic to rejuvenate it. They would blast the realos' overtures to the Social Democrats as a "betrayal" of Greens ideals, of the social movements and the party that neither Fischer nor any of his ladder-climbing crew ever really gave a damn about. "Sellouts," "power-hungry opportunists," "chameleons," "cynical ex-Spontis," and "Social Democratic Greens" were just some of the epithets that Ditfurth, Zieran, and others would hurl at Fischer and the troupe. They were returned in kind. Although Petra Kelly tried to stay above the internecine feud, she ultimately came down on the side of the fundies: "When Joschka says 'Euromissiles out by 1987,' well, that's the Social Democrats' position. So, tell me, what is it then we're fighting for? Our demands have to go way beyond that."[4]

Hesse was the realo stronghold and logically the earliest theater of the realo–fundi clash. While Fischer was in Bonn, the gang, led by former Sponti Tom Koenigs, had been at hard work. In spring 1984 the Hesse Greens voted to back a deal that would bring the Social Democrats, who lacked an outright majority, to power in the state legislature in exchange for concessions on Greens issues. The informal pact (in contrast to a proper coalition) entailed that the Greens, with just seven of the 110 *Landtag* seats, would "tolerate" an SPD minority government without actually participating in it. In other words, the Hesse Greens would have no ministers in the cabinet or a direct role in governance, but with their votes the Social Democrats could count on a slim majority and govern accordingly.

This experimental red–green pact in Wiesbaden, Hesse's capital, had more detractors than just Greens fundamentalists. At the time, the bulk of the country's Social Democrats had interpreted Brandt's words less literally than had Fischer. The party's old guard ruled out including the environmentalists in governing coalitions, even at the local level.* The Greens, they charged, were "unfit to govern." Many Social Democrats understood the party as a historical accident, whose demise would only be prolonged by dangling the possibility of red–green coalitions in front of it. Old-school Social Democrats argued that the Greens' "radical" ecological agenda ran roughshod over the interests of their core constituencies—namely, industrial workers and the country's powerful labor unions.

The charge that environmental reforms would cost jobs was one that Social Democrats would make again and again to discredit the Greens and defer environmental reform. Better, thought skeptical Social Democrats, to pinch a few Greens ideas and spice up the traditional SPD fare with a handful of nature-friendly programs. At the end of the day, most Social Democrats still felt more comfortable in coalitions with the Christian Democrats than alongside the unruly Greens.

The red–green coalitions that would, contrary to their skeptics, come to life across western Germany's federal states in the 1980s and 1990s were never partnerships based on mutual affection but, rather, were hard-boiled alliances born of necessity. As much as it pained them, the Social Democrats would have to acknowledge that their ability to rack up outright majorities, as they had for years in their bedrock states, was ebbing. On the federal level, never again would the SPD be the party that Willy Brandt led to victory in 1972 with 46 percent of the vote. Moreover, the option of red–yellow coalitions with the Free Democrats was now considerably less attractive in the wake of the bad blood caused by the liberals unceremoniously jumping ship in 1982 and letting the Schmidt government sink in favor of the Christian Democrats.

There were, however, younger Social Democrats pushing their way through the ranks of the postwar cadre. They could be found at some of the antinuclear and peace demonstrations, not necessarily on the front lines but in attendance nevertheless, their collars open, corduroy jackets unbuttoned

* The SPD leadership, however, did not exercise control over the party's every state and municipal branch, and indeed they turned a blind eye to the first red–green experiments. In Kassel, for example, a medium-size city in Hesse south of Frankfurt, Social Democrats and Greens had quietly cooperated in the city administration since 1981.

for the occasion. Included among them were the thirty-nine-year-old firebrand Oskar Lafontaine from the diminutive western state of Saarland on the French border; Lower Saxony's popular Gerhard Schröder; and Hans Eichel, the mayor of the first red-green city, Kassel. Also products of the generational shift from which the protest movements had sprung, they were more open to Greens ideas, as well as to building majorities together with the eco-party.

A spate of election results in early 1984 seemed to bear out the conjecture that the Greens might be around longer than the doubting Thomases predicted. The Greens captured 8 percent of the vote in the CDU bastion of Baden Württemberg, south of Hesse, and then again as much in nationwide elections for the European Parliament. Noteworthy, in those places where the fundi-led Greens vetoed cooperation with the Social Democrats, the environmental party fared poorly, failing to even clear the 5 percent hurdle. This was evidence that the realo logic was taking hold in state and local constituencies. Yet realos and fundies alike had reason to smile: by the middle of 1985, five years after its creation, the Greens had seats in six of eleven *Landtags*, in 1,400 municipal assemblies, and Greens mayors in two small cities.[5]

In Bonn, however, Fischer's fifteen minutes were drawing to a close. After a year on the job, he had been replaced as party whip by Christa Nickels. ("He certainly wasn't happy about it, but those were our rules," says Nickels, referring to the one-year limit on party posts, as well as the fact that Greens women insisted they assume more key posts.) Also, in early 1985, two years after the Greens marched on the Bundestag, the first rotation of MPs was scheduled, which would make way for the benchwarmers. To its credit, the party had mastered a very steep learning curve and, in doing so, had earned a certain professional gravitas in the High House. But the Greens' inconsistencies and eccentricities kept the party on a breathtaking ride: double-digit triumphs in one regional election would be followed by embarrassing faux pas and dreary numbers in the next. The realo–fundi battle could make the party look like a pack of squabbling school kids. One Greens MP was thrown out by the party for molesting female colleagues. The conservative press shrieked with glee when Petra Kelly and Gert Bastian, alone among the first Bundestag group, refused to rotate their seats. A charge with more than a grain of truth to it, the Greens often acted as if they were somehow "better people" than those who identified with other parties: more selfless, righteous, purer. This posture and the party's sometimes indignant tone grated on many people and became an incentive for journalists to point out examples to the contrary, of which there were many.

Fischer fomented his own little brouhaha by insulting the Bundestag president, Richard Stücklen, on the floor of the parliament. Christian Democrat Stücklen had raised the ire of the Greens by disciplining them at every opportunity, especially when they employed unconventional tactics in the Bundestag. He would regularly cut off Greens MPs in mid-sentence at the speakers' stand. When he expelled MP Jürgen Reents from an ongoing session for implying that the chancellor's motives for a China trip had been influenced by corporate money, Fischer rose to his colleague's defense. Stücklen warned Fischer aloud: if he breached the High House's rules of order again, he would go, too. Absolutely furious, Fischer stood up and spoke words that would go down in Bundestag history: "Excuse me, Mr. President," he said quite calmly, "but you're an asshole!"[6] As promised, Stücklen expelled him, too.

Soon after the Bundestag rotation all eyes were back on Hesse, where the informal red–green pact was teetering. Fundi critics charged that the Hesse Greens had been outfoxed by the Social Democrats, having sold their soul and gotten nothing in return, neither the scrapping of the Frankfurt airport's additional runway nor a commitment to shut down a single nuclear reactor, ever. In terms of concessions, the crumbs that Tom Koenigs and friends accepted from the Social Democrats had been on the table anyway, said the fundies with some justification. The tentative experiment proved short-lived. The Social Democrats' nod to the construction of a plutonium-processing plant in Hanau, outside of Frankfurt, was more than even the thickest-skinned realo could bear. In late 1984 the Hesse Greens withdrew their backing for the minority government, precipitating its collapse.[7]

Minister in Sneakers

Despite the falling out, the Hesse SPD and the statewide Greens were prepared to take one more shot at patching together a legislative majority. This time around no one harbored illusions that anything as flimsy as a Greens-tolerated minority government should be repeated. If Hesse was going to sample the red–green option, then it had to be the real thing, a proper two-party coalition with the Greens installed as junior partner. The coalition contract would be in writing and the Greens, too, would then bear responsibility for the coalition's success—or failure. Even though Hesse was a realo bastion, other considerations made it less obvious as a place to see if a first-ever red–green coalition would fly. For one, Hesse's top Social Democrat was Holger Börner, a party soldier of the old mold, not an up-and-coming buck like Lafontaine or Schröder. Before red–green emerged as a possibility in Hesse, he was quoted as saying that Greens should be disciplined with the flat side of a two-by-four. The rotund, fleshy-faced Börner had long been a staunch advocate of nuclear power and of bigger, faster autobahns, as well as the patron politician of Hesse's industrial unions. But Börner's alternatives were limited, and he was confident that an operator like himself could bring such dilettantes as the Greens to heel, with or without a two-by-four.

The hard-fought coalition negotiations between Hesse's SPD and Greens in the fall of 1985 illustrated the wide gulf between West Germany's two left-wing parties. From the outset of the talks, Börner put some issues off-limits, including Hesse's existing nuclear program. The Greens demanded the portfolios of at least two ministries and the creation of a new ministry for women's issues, as well as "regulatory authority" over Hesse's nuclear industry. In the end, the junior partner settled for far less: the Ministry of Environment and Energy and a newfound office for women's issues. The Greens accepted Hesse's nuclear facilities at Hanau and Biblis in exchange for the promise that no new nuclear-related installations would be commissioned. As consolation, the Greens also received the portfolio of the Office of Forestry, which prompted the *Spiegel* to wisecrack: "The Greens pretend to be pleased that in the future they will deal with overseeing bird species and not the dismantlement of nuclear power plants."[8]

Among the names tossed around for the Greens' single ministerial position, Otto Schily was the clear frontrunner, a logical choice from the side of the Social Democrats who saw in the straight-as-an-arrow lawyer a man with whom they could do business. (Schily proved them right years later by quitting the Greens and joining the Social Democrats.) But Hesse's realos knew that they needed someone more in sync with the party's alternative spirit than the suit-and-tie Schily. Fischer's untucked T-shirts and rebel image fit the bill much better.

Fischer was still in Bonn when the negotiating teams' nominations were made public: for environment minister, Joschka Fischer, age thirty-seven; for the other posts, Karl Kerschgens, forty-six, and Marita Haibach, thirty-one. Fischer would be "the first Green minister on the planet," as he immodestly put it, and the unlikely duo of Holger Börner and Joschka

Fischer the leaders of the republic's first red–green coalition on the state level. Not to be overlooked, both the coalition agreement and the nominations had first to be approved by an extraordinary congress of the Hesse Greens.

The reaction outside of Hesse's realo circles was hardly ecstatic. The state's fundies set in motion plans to block the deal. The Social Democrat leadership in Bonn had renewed its pledge not to, under any circumstances, entertain the possibility of a red–green alliance come the 1987 federal elections. The country's Christian Democrats were of two minds. They were miffed that this new equation left them in the cold, whereas in the past such a Social Democratic setback would have played straight into their hand. At the same time, they were beside themselves with delight about the new ammunition they could add to their arsenal portraying the Social Democrats as left-wing zealots, out-of-step with ordinary Germans.

In no time, Hesse's industrial giants were also ringing alarm bells. The state was home to West Germany's financial center, Frankfurt, as well as its showcase international airport and many of the country's biggest firms, including the chemical conglomerates Hoechst and Merck. In addition to employing hundreds of thousands of workers and contributing millions to state and federal coffers, they also counted among the region's most notorious polluters. In the past they had gotten away with burying toxic waste near community water supplies and dumping pollutants straight into the Main and Rhine Rivers. Thus, the companies' strategy was to cripple Fischer's upstart ministry before it took its first steps. Hoechst, the largest private business in the state with 178,000 workers and an annual turnover of U.S. $20 billion, mused out loud about relocating. West Germany's heavyweight Federation of German Industry warned that Hesse's *Chaos Koalition* threatened the creation of "thousands of new jobs" in the state.[9] And *Bild-Zeitung,* the German left's nemesis from way back, announced—inaccurately—on its front page: "Because of Red–Green, Firms Flee Hesse."[10]

But before anything could happen, Fischer had to get the stamp of approval from his own party. The primary reservation among Hesse's Greens was that Fischer had no experience or competence in environmental affairs. He hadn't even been part of the environmental or antinuclear movements; in fact, not long ago he had publicly ridiculed their aims as parochial dabbling. And there would be little time to cram on the ins and outs of water-purification processes and public waste-disposal systems as he had on Marx and Hegel in Frankfurt. To the fundies it was obvious that

Fischer was a power-obsessed adrenaline jockey who not only knew nothing about green causes but didn't care about them, either. Where was Fischer when they were manning the" atomic villages" in Wyhl, Gorleben, and elsewhere? During the historic Hofgarten demonstrations Fischer was just one in the crowd, nothing more. Nevertheless, when the votes were counted, 70 percent of the assembled Greens approved the coalition contract and the nominations. It was a major victory for the Greens' pragmatists and a milestone for the party and the republic.

Even before he took office, Fischer's first task was to steady the nerves of Hesse's agitated industrialists and fearful *Kleinbürger.* His ministry, he announced to the media, would reach out to engage the state's industry in dialogue; in good Bonn Republic fashion, consensus not confrontation was the order of the day. That said, his ministry would stick to the letter of the law on environmental issues, which is exactly what worried the owners of the toxin-belching factories that earned Frankfurt the epithet "Stinkfurt." In the past, Hesse's Social Democrats had appointed facile, second-tier candidates to run the 1970-created office, which had never, until then, had the status of a full ministry. Fischer also underlined that the red–green coalition pact included a major outstanding bone of contention between the new partners—namely, the continued operation of the nuclear power plant at Biblis and the plutonium-processing facility under construction in Hanau. By agreeing to disagree with the Social Democrats, however, the Greens accepted Hesse's nuclear status quo.

On December 12, 1985, the nation's television cameras were trained on the capitol building in the old spa town of Wiesbaden for the debut of the country's latest Greens act. In his introductory speech, one of the *Landtag*'s new vice-presidents, the Green Bernd Messinger, said with much pomp and what some probably thought was Panglossian hopefulness: "In 1968 we began our long march through the institutions. The first of us have arrived, others will follow."[11] The anticipated high point of the day was Fischer's swearing-in, conducted personally by Holger Börner. As the two men stood face to face, the differences in their ages, styles, and physiques couldn't have been more striking. In a pair of gleaming white high-top Nikes, blue jeans, and a thrift-store herringbone sports jacket, Fischer raised his right hand to take the oath of office. The Nikes were Fischer's message to Greens voters and West Germany's postwar generation: Joschka Fischer wasn't going to be a state minister like any other the republic had known. At that moment, as Fischer repeated the oath after Börner, the cleft in the republic that had broken open so dramatically during the "red decade" became a little narrower. The sneakers, bought just for the occasion, were never worn again and would years later wind up in a Plexiglas case in Bonn's Museum for German History.

The political diary that Fischer kept during the 425-day coalition offers a fascinating insight into the obstacles and illusions that the realo avant-garde encountered in trying to make its ministry and the coalition as a whole work. The team's new home was the tenth floor of an old government building that had been hastily assembled for them with discarded furniture and half-broken telephones from other ministries. Late at night, after an exhausting and frustrating first day, Fischer, alone in the linoleum-floored rooms, made his first diary entry as minister: "Everything is deathly quiet. I try unsuccessfully to make a few telephone calls but either I don't get through or I'm cut off after ten sentences. This can't be! Resigned, I sit in my minister's office and reflect about how power looks from the inside out. At least today, from here, it looks like a joke."[12]

Fischer soon learned that making symbolic history was easier than endowing a toothless ministry with bite enough to make West German industry take notice. Naturally, he had surrounded himself with his trusted helpers, first among them Georg Dick as ministry spokesperson and Tom Koenigs as budget director. The new minister found that he needed all the allies he could muster, considering his array of enemies: Greens fundies in the Hesse *Landtag* voted against him; most of the Bundestag Greens opposed red–green coalitions in principle; the SPD leadership was bent on discrediting the "Hessian model"; Börner and his cabinet ministers aimed to keep the new ministry down and weak; the civil servants in Fischer's own office, skeptical of a Greens boss, were uncooperative; and then, of course, there were the opposition conservatives, the state's hostile industry, and the trade unions, too. Even Hesse's realo women marched into his office one day steaming about the dearth of female appointments he had made and demanding to make all further appointments themselves.

By the hundred-day mark, Fischer was ready to throw in the towel, or so he says. The twelve-hour days, six-day weeks had obliterated any illusion of a private life outside the ministry and taken a toll on his health as well. Most problematic, he discovered that the resources of Hesse's industrial behemoths dwarfed those of his miniscule ministry, which was short on expertise, basic technology, research facilities, and legal staff, not to mention functional telephones. Fischer learned the hard way how immensely easier it is to demand sweeping changes and compile political wish lists than to push through even modest reforms from inside the halls of power.

Nevertheless, the ministry could point to a few accomplishments. "The first was that we existed at all," says Georg Dick looking back at the experiment. Just getting the neglected ministry up and running was an accomplishment that, he says, went unrecognized among Greens purists. Were the nuclear power plants in Hesse less hazardous than a year ago? they demanded to know. And Hesse was still exporting 70,000 tons of chemical waste annually to East Germany, another lump the ministry had to take. But, to the ministry's credit, the firm Hoechst had been forced to halt its pumping of untreated liquid waste into the River Main. For this, Fischer received a pat on the back from an unlikely source—Helmut Kohl's federal health minister in Bonn. "First class, what he's doing there," the lifelong Christian Democrat said. "I've been calling for that for fifteen years without success."[13]

The Greens' Wiesbaden contingent still had some way to go to convince its skeptics that it was on the right track. According to Dick, the most important tools that the ministry had were the laws and regulatory guidelines that already existed, but that had never been enforced. With the law in hand, he says, David could slay Goliath. But it was an uphill battle to convince other Greens of this. "So many of us came from the citizens' initiatives and it had always appeared that it was industry and the political elite that had the law on their side, not the demonstrators," says Dick. "We had to explain this is a chance for us, but it is a slow process. We had to have more than the moral high ground and the right intentions. The law seems so dry and aloof to movement activists but translating it into practice, that's what politics is all about."

In Chernobyl's Path

In late April 1986 Fischer's ministry was thick into the nitty-gritty of toxic-waste disposal and urban sanitation policy. On April 26 he made no entry in his diary. The West German media were busy with the possibility of U.S. air strikes against Libya, a relatively new virus called AIDS, and sinking property prices. It wasn't until two days later that Swedish scientists on the Baltic Sea picked up extraordinarily high levels of radiation in weather patterns coming from the southeast. Before long, the entire world would know that a nuclear reactor at the Chernobyl site in Ukraine had spun out of control and melted down. Air currents could blow radioactive clouds over the rest of Europe at any time. Fischer got the news at 1:12 A.M. on the April 29. It had really happened—exactly what the Greens and antinuclear campaigners had been warning about for years.

Anxious West German citizens were glued to their TV sets and radios, hungry for any scrap of information they could get about the disaster and its implications for them. The Soviet authorities had hushed up the accident from the beginning and remained tight-lipped about the details. Eyewitnesses reported that one reactor was still burning and that inhabitants within thirty miles of the site were being evacuated. As many as 2,000 people could be dead, reported the media.[14] The threat to Germany depended on the weather: a strong westward wind would put the Federal Republic directly in the path of the poisonous clouds.

Frantic, West Germans wanted more facts and demanded to know what precautions to take. But the government seemed as bewildered as its citizens. Bonn played down the incident. "We're 900 miles away from the site of this accident," said the federal interior minister, Friedrich Zimmermann. "It's entirely out of the question that the German people are in any danger."[15] Scientists and other experts contradicted him, one after another on news and call-in shows. The nuclear content of the reactor was the equivalent of 1,500 Hiroshima-type A-bombs, they said. There were reports that radioactivity levels in eastern Poland were 500 times normal. Children should stay indoors, everyone should take iodine pills, vegetable gardens should be covered with plastic tarps.[16]

In the 2005 feature film *The Day Bobby Ewing Died* (news of the meltdown was broadcast on German TV just after the legendary *Dallas* episode), director Lars Jessen tells the story of a frumpy group of antinuke protesters in the village of Brokdorf, the site of an under-construction nuclear reactor just outside of Hamburg along the Elbe River. The full-time activists, who wear baggy, 1980s-style overalls and bulky down vests, live in a communal house, the base from which they agitate against the energy company building the reactor. Huddled together, they stare in wide-eyed horror at the first television reports about the meltdown. "Everyone was really shocked, of course," says Jessen, living in Bremen at the time, "but in [West] Germany there had been lots of discussion and even best-selling 'day after' books about the possibility of something like this and what it would look like. So in a way many people were actually expecting it. The difference was that after Chernobyl these concerns became mainstream."

Several days later, weather patterns pushed the airborne radioactive gases over southern Germany. There still wasn't reliable information on ways to protect one's self against the radiation. No two "authorities" seemed to agree. There were strict warnings that fruits and vegetables grown out-of-doors were absorbing dangerous amounts of radioactivity and must be avoided. Children should drink powdered milk and sleep with bedroom windows shut. Everyone should stay out of the rain. One Greens politician in Munich insisted that all children be evacuated to Portugal.[17] A woman from Bavaria called in to a local talk show, asking whether she had to wash her cat every time it came indoors.[18]

With federal elections in less than a year's time, pundits concurred that all bets were off until the crisis passed. For the Kohl government, Chernobyl was an unmitigated public-relations disaster. For the Greens it was a bonanza and the man of the hour was Hesse's Greens minister. "We got hundreds and hundreds of calls from all over Germany," remembers Dick. "People only believed us. They wanted to hear it from the first Greens environmental ministry, not from Bonn. One couldn't switch the TV channel without seeing Fischer's face." For the first time, the international spotlight fell on Fischer. "He wasn't the most knowledgeable about nuclear issues but he brought the right points home, clearly and forthrightly, unlike the government," says film director Jessen, who calls the Kohl administration's policy at the time one of "unbelievable disinformation."

Across Germany foremost on people's minds was their own and their families' safety. But once the radioactive cloud had passed, the issue became the safety of the Federal Republic's own nineteen nuclear power plants—as well as the five in adjacent East Germany, the forty-one to the west in France, the five in Czechoslovakia, and eight in Belgium.* Citizens demanded to know whether cities near nuclear installations had evacuation plans. Why, it was asked, had the federal government been so cagey about addressing these issues? Five years before, surveys had shown West Germans split down the middle over nuclear energy's viability—that in itself a plaudit for the antinuclear movement. The combined efforts of the citizens' initiatives, the social movements, and the Greens had turned nuclear power into a national issue, one that politicians and citizens debated in the open rather than behind closed doors. But after Chernobyl, public opinion in West Germany swerved dramatically against nuclear power. By June 1986, two months after the meltdown at Chernobyl, polls showed

* At the time there were ninety-one nuclear power plants in the United States and forty-eight in the Soviet Union.

well over 80 percent of West Germans against the building of new atomic power plants, only 18 percent in favor. Seventy-two percent of the populace said that the country's nuclear power plants should be shut down, either immediately or over time.[19]

The Chernobyl disaster also provided the flagging antinuclear movement with a powerful, angry infusion of new activists and supporters. Although there were ongoing protests at Brokdorf, Wackersdorf in Bavaria, and elsewhere, the robust antinuclear power movement of the late seventies had been eclipsed somewhat by the peace movement and, charged some, "co-opted" by the Greens. Now, tens of thousands converged again on tiny rural places like Brokdorf, Wackersdorf, and Gorleben (in the Elbe River Valley, north of Hanover), and they were no longer mainly long-haired *muslis* (tree huggers), punk rockers, and guitar-strumming Protestants. Senior citizens, mothers, housewives, teachers, and children were the ones telling the Kohl government that they were not prepared to accept the risks of nuclear power.*

Chernobyl and its fallout had paradoxical implications for Joschka Fischer and the Greens. On the one hand, it boosted the credibility of the environmental party whose Nostradmus-like warnings no longer smacked of hyperbole. The Greens' ratings skyrocketed. But the doomsday scenario-come-true unexpectedly cast Hesse's Green minister between Scylla and Charybdis. The meltdown in Ukraine suddenly made his nuclear compromise with Holger Börner and the Hesse SPD look mealy-mouthed and even irresponsible. Were the citizens of Hesse safer with their Greens minister than people in conservative-run states with nuclear power plants? The answer was no, and smelling blood the fundies attacked with Chernobyl as testimony. They had always maintained there could be no compromise on life-or-death issues such as nuclear power. A proviso synonymous with the Greens had to be the closure of all of the Federal Republic's nuclear installations and removal of all nuclear arms—at once, not sometime down the road.

---

* In the 1980s militant, black-masked street fighters, called *Autonomen*, appeared on the scene transforming some of the protests into running battles with the West German police. The *Autonomen* resurrected the anarcho-Marxist arguments of the previous decade that justified militancy against the "bourgeois state." West German authorities estimated their numbers to be around 5,000 nationwide. In the months after Chernobyl, ghastly civil war–like scenes unfolded at the Brokdorf and Wackersdorf sites. Helicopters equipped with antiterrorism accessories, including tear gas bombs, were deployed to disperse the protests.

The post-Chernobyl atmosphere boxed Fischer and his realos into a corner. They had argued that the closing down of Hesse's, and all of West Germany's, nuclear power plants at once was neither practical (the energy sources had to be replaced) nor politically viable (the Social Democrats would never go for it). Rather, they insisted, the party had to formulate a plan for replacing nuclear power with renewable energy sources during a phased disengagement from nuclear energy. But the party would have none of it. The realos' pact with the Hesse SPD ("no *new* nuclear facilities") was no longer workable. The crisis had not only caused the red–green coalition to flounder, the entire realo project was on the rocks.

Although the country's Social Democrats were backtracking as fast as they could on just about everything they had ever said about nuclear power, in Hesse, the old warrior Holger Börner stood firm: there would be no rethinking of the state's nuclear policy. With the red–green coalition staring into the abyss, Börner took the final step by signaling that Hesse was forging ahead with plans to upgrade the plutonium plant in Hanau. Minister Fischer drew the line: if the new facility applied for an operating permit, the Greens would walk. It was an ultimatum, and Börner didn't flinch. If the red–green coalition was the casualty, then so be it. The SPD would not bow to ultimatums from the Greens.

Over the course of the fifteen-month alliance, Joschka Fischer and Holger Börner had grown close personally, despite their political differences. Fischer learned from Börner as an apprentice would from a master craftsman; Börner grew fond of Fischer and took him under his wing. Once the damage had been done—the coalition's back broken by the plutonium plant—Fischer strolled over to Börner's office for a final chat. His thoughts that evening could apply to just about any of the red–green coalitions that would emerge in the future. "As Börner spoke and I listened," wrote Fischer in the last entry in his coalition diary, "the old conflict over the Frankfurt airport's runway came to mind. We wouldn't be sitting here today, the minister president and the freak from the Frankfurt scene, had Börner not made such a grave mistake [by refusing to compromise on the new runway]. . . the conflict today between Hesse's Social Democrats and its Greens is, in its essence, much the same. Börner tried to integrate us only because he had to." In the end, "two-by-four Börner" hadn't given a millimeter, concluded Fischer: "Börner had the guts to bring the first red–green coalition to life, but not to give this newborn child a future, an identity more than electoral arithmetic. For that, he lacked the guts, and perhaps the vision too."[20]

Reconstructing Industrial Society

The swan song of Hesse's red–green coalition coincided with the 1987 federal elections, a full four years after the Greens first scraped into the Bundestag. With the realos' star dimming, the fundies dictated the election platform underscoring original Greens positions that included the Federal Republic's withdrawal from NATO, as well as abolition of the army, the border guard, and the intelligence service. The SPD's top candidate, the gravelly voiced Rhinelander Johannes Rau, was the last of the SPD's old titans to head up a national ticket. He directed the party's campaign as much against the "radical" Greens as against the ruling conservatives. But when the votes were counted on the eve of January 25, 1987, it was the Social Democrats who were delivered a sobering reality check. The SPD posted its worst showing in the party's postwar history, while Helmut Kohl and his Christian Democrat–led coalition were re-elected, although with fewer votes than four years earlier. The surprise victor of the evening was the Greens. Not only did they clear the 5 percent hurdle, the party increased its share of the vote by nearly half, capturing a solid 8.3 percent. Instead of twenty-eight MPs, they would have forty-four. The Greens' strongholds were in the north, in the city-states of Hamburg and Bremen, as well as the southwest in Baden Württemberg and Hesse.

For the inauguration of the tenth assembly of the Deutscher Bundestag, the freshly elected Greens showed up promptly, some with briefcases in arm. The new crop of Greens MPs, among them eleven returnees—including Christa Nickels, Otto Schily, Willi Hoss, Petra Kelly, Hubert Kleinert, and Marieluise Beck—was as heterogeneous as ever. But unlike the buoyant march into the Bundestag four years before, it was a somber reunion. The brief campaign truce between fundies and realos had been shattered by the post-election scramble for positions. Kleinert remembers the feeling among the Greens lawmakers: "Even on the first day one could sense that it wasn't going to be easy with this group. It wasn't just the disharmony between realos and fundies... the emotional solidarity was missing, which, despite all the tensions and fights, had been there in the first group."[21]

In Hesse, Fischer, the Hesse Greens, and the SPD, too, retreated into opposition, where they'd spend the next four years. The experimental coalition had not only buckled, it brought down with it what had been a reliable SPD stronghold until then, paving the way for conservative rule in Hesse. Although working in Wiesbaden and living in Frankfurt (with his new bride, the journalist Claudia Bohm) Fischer continued to maintain a national profile, weighing in on the issues of the day in the media, and of course, in his own party's ongoing dramas. The slugfest in the Greens between realos and fundies showed no signs of letting up. On nearly every question, from human-rights violations in Chile to Greens party structures, the antagonists banged heads. It seemed that they could agree on nothing. In fact, the blocs within the party were holding separate congresses and drafting opposing position papers. In the Greens party's hierarchy, the fundies reigned dominant with the combative Jutta Ditfurth at the helm. Her re-election to the leadership re-entrenched the purists in the Greens' highest office. This time the *Spiegel* splashed her picture, not Fischer's, across its cover page.

The more leisurely pace of life as an opposition politician gave Fischer time to ponder what went wrong in the first-ever red–green coalition—and what could go right in the future. The realos conceded that despite a handful of accomplishments, the red–green coalition hadn't made West Germany's nuclear power plants any safer, its drinking water any cleaner, or its cities less smoggy. The combination of ministerial posts, grandiose intentions, ecological disasters, and public hysterics hadn't added up to effective environmental policy. But unlike a decade ago, Fischer wrote in his post-coalition book *The Reconstruction of Industrial Society,* there existed a broad public awareness about environmental issues, as well as a tuned-in media, relevant NGOs, local citizens' initiatives, and even alternative research institutes, like the Darmstadt Institute for Applied Ecology in Hesse. But, he argued, "the creation of pro-environment structures in the economy, society, and the state lag far behind the country's environmental consciousness and democratic mobilization . . . on behalf of ecological issues."[22]

Among other things, *The Reconstruction of Industrial Society* was an explicit response to those who had questioned Fischer's competence (and interest) in environmental matters. Most of the book was high-level, technical discussion of the day's relevant ecological issues. He had indeed crammed on ecology the way he did Marx and Hegel during the student revolt—and mastered it much the same way. Despite his initial ambivalence, he had made the Greens cause his own and presented cutting-edge, policy-feasible options for a nationwide environmental program. Fischer biographers Matthias Geis and Bernd Ulrich argue that Fischer is not an easy man to convince—or to sway from his convictions—but once he has taken the plunge and internalized the merits of a position, he becomes a formidable, articulate proponent of that stance. "When he's certain that he's seen something the way it really is, he does everything in his powers to justify and defend those ideas. His ability to convince himself—and others—is enormous. This is one of the reasons—contrary to those who accuse him of shifty opportunism—that the ordeals of breaking with former positions are so laborious and protracted."[23]

In *The Reconstruction of Industrial Society,* Fischer argued that the republic had to imbed ecology in its very *Staatsraison*. In such a green republic, basic environmental interests—providing citizens with safe and healthful environs—would take priority over profit. His experience in the Hessian government had taught him that the supremacy of ecological values had to be inscribed into law, turned into policy by competent institutions, and implemented by public administrations with the technical and legal capacity to do so. Ultimately, wrote Fischer, this kind of environmental overhaul has to be orchestrated from the very top, at the federal level in Bonn. When in office in Wiesbaden, he had been given a bracing lesson in the limitations of regional administrations. His office had lacked the authority to shut down nuclear power plants and the clout to regulate the chemical conglomerates. The big-ticket items, those that really mattered, like ecological tax reform, environmentally sustainable economic policy, new transportation and energy concepts, and a neighborhood-friendly industrial policy, had to be pushed through by federal ministries. Though it was sacrilege at the time, even for an ultra-realo, Fischer contended that such a program *is* conceivable in a free market economy. It would be a different kind of capitalism than that which gave full rein to resource-guzzling, toxin-spewing industries and their corporate executives, but, nevertheless, the greening of the republic was possible without altering most of its essential features. Here, Fischer parted company not only with Jutta Ditfurth and the fundies but even many of his closest allies.

8

One Two Many Germanys

So preoccupied were the Greens in the late 1980s that they failed to grasp the full significance of the momentous events unfolding next door in central and eastern Europe. The Soviet Union's charismatic new leader, Mikhail Gorbachev, had embarked on sweeping political and economic reforms, called *glasnost* and *perestroika*, that were reverberating across the continent. In Poland, Hungary, and even staid East Germany, outlawed pro-democracy groups were raising their voices against the single-party states. In the eastern German city of Leipzig, the "Monday demonstrations," which had begun in early September 1989 with a few hundred people at the Nikolai Church, had burgeoned into mass protests of thousands and then tens of thousands, and even hundreds of thousands. Elsewhere in the GDR, too, initially under the protective wing of the Protestant Church, ordinary citizens were plucking up the courage to participate in peaceful marches, candle-lit vigils, and hunger strikes. Soon they were demanding free elections, an independent media, respect for the rule of law, and multiparty democracy. On the streets, the unthinkable was happening: a popular, nonviolent uprising against the dictatorship—people power *par excellence*. It was exactly what Petra Kelly and others said could happen, a revolution from below, led by those same outspoken critics and fragmented peace groups that Kelly, among others, had stuck up for in the early 1980s.

One could reasonably have assumed that the Greens would have been celebrating these nearly miraculous events, as well as supporting the democracy-minded dissidents and planning their party's future in a post–Cold War Europe, one that could quite possibly be bloc-free and disarmed. Given the party's connections with many of the opposition factions in eastern Europe, and the shared anti-establishment heritage, perhaps it could even have been the Greens' finest hour. This, however, wasn't how it played out. The trendsetting party that had been a jump ahead of the republic on so many issues stood by discomfited, suddenly looking very much like a quaint ornament of a bygone era.

On the evening of November 9, 1989, East German authorities announced that GDR citizens were free to cross the country's hitherto sealed borders. The monumentality of this proclamation found its most vivid expression at the Berlin Wall, where jubilant crowds scaled the blunt symbol of Germany's and Cold War Europe's division, falling into their countrymen's arms on the other side. That night the political coordinates of postwar Germany changed forever; the very ground from which the Greens sprang, and the only one they knew, was quaking beneath their feet.

When the news of the wall's breach reached the Bundestag in Bonn, it was deep in a session devoted to tax policy. The confused reaction of the Greens MPs foreshadowed the dilemmas that the party would soon face. At first, everyone in the hall stood up, cheered, and applauded, a rare moment of unity in the High House. Then, after words by the Bundestag president, the Christian Democrats were unable to contain their swelling national pride and broke into the third stanza of the "Deutschlandlied," the German national anthem:*

Unity, justice and freedom
For the German Fatherland.
This is what we all must strive for,
Brotherly with heart and hand.
Unity, justice and freedom
Are the foundation for happiness,
Bloom, oh German Fatherland.

Hesitantly at first, the Social Democrats also chimed in. But the Greens were completely flummoxed. Many of them had never even mumbled these lyrics, if they knew them at all.[1] "There wasn't a lot of time to think it over," remembers Hubert Kleinert.[2] Some, like Kleinert, stood up but remained silent. Others stayed seated. Still others walked out in

* The first and second stanzas of the song had been dropped after World War II because of their objectionable, nationalistic lyrics. The first, for example, began with "Deutschland, Deutschland, über alles, über alles in der Welt."

protest. The republic was stepping onto uncharted territory, for which the German left had no map, no compass, and no way back.

The stunning course of events in East Germany and the rest of communist-ruled Europe caught the Greens badly off guard. Although they had long espoused a bloc-free continent, they hadn't in their wildest fantasies imagined that it could materialize practically overnight. And although most Greens earnestly despised the dictatorship of "the other Germany," they certainly didn't want its carcass devoured by the Federal Republic. They hadn't envisioned the end of the Cold War happening as the triumph of West over East. The fall of the Berlin Wall set in motion a chain of events that culminated in German unification in less than a year's time. The Greens opposed unification long after it was a fait accompli, while Chancellor Kohl pounced on the opportunity to write his name into history's books—and win himself another two terms in office.

Human-rights activist Wolfgang Templin had been expelled from the GDR in winter 1988 for oppositional activities. He experienced the dictatorship's toppling from the other side of the wall, in West Berlin, where he moved in Greens party circles. The response appalled him. "The Greens weren't even voyeurs because voyeurs are at least fascinated by their subject and are involved in the act of watching. The Greens didn't seem to care one way or the other," says Templin. "Some felt: 'My God, we had such a nice plan for [West] Germany and we were finally coming to power, and then you guys had to come and ruin everything.' Even the realos didn't really understand what history had put on the agenda. It wasn't just German unification but Europe's unification, in which Germany could play a positive role."

Arguably, the Greens' befuddled response to the events of 1989–90 shouldn't have been so surprising. First, as heterogeneous as the party was, a trenchant, historically conditioned aversion to German nationalism was an article of faith. Phrases like *blühe deutsches Vaterland* just weren't in the Greens party lexicon. If their allergic reaction to national patriotism appeared a degree too severe, it was, they'd respond, a reaction proportionate to the severity of the crimes committed in its name. The German left didn't see Nazism as a perversion or abuse of an otherwise sound national concept but, rather, as nationalism in its most extreme form. They understood it as part of their civilizing mission to sweep the vestiges of this bankrupt ideology from every nook and cranny in the republic. There was consensus among the Greens that whatever course events might take—and in late 1989 and early 1990 matters were very much up in the air—the option of unification, the Adam and Eve of all German questions, simply wasn't on the table. The party accepted Germany's *Zweistaatlichkeit* (division into two states) as permanent and just, even healthy.* In the Bundestag, the Greens had in the past tried to have the federal constitution's explicit reference to unification deleted. As far as the Greens were concerned, talk of German re-unification belonged in the same cauldron with the rantings of the expellee groups, who lobbied vociferously for the return of their former homelands in Poland, Czechoslovakia, and elsewhere.

Germany's division, argued Fischer in a long *Tageszeitung* essay a week after the wall fell, was the price that Germany had to pay for Auschwitz and a precondition for a "pan-European peace order," even in the aftermath of the Cold War. "We are the left and engage in politics as such in a country that created and ran gas chambers and crematoriums at Auschwitz, that was loyal to its *Führer* Adolf Hitler until his own self-destruction," he reminded the readership. It wasn't the German people who rid the country of the century's most sinister criminal, the Allies had to do it for them. "This is the real underlying reason for the German question and Germany's division—and we can't ever forget it. The sovereignty and self-determination of this country are restricted, for good reason. Our nation bears a heavy burden that extends across generations." Germany remained on probation, concluded Fischer: "Forty-five years after Auschwitz, there is no reason to be ashamed about being alarmed by German nationalism. On the contrary, in order to survive it is our democratic duty to do so for another forty-five years."[3]

Paradoxically, most Greens feared the untethering of *Furor Teutonicus* more than did neighboring countries—France and Belgium, for example—that had every reason to fear it.[4] In the United States, polls showed that 76 percent of Americans welcomed the two Germanys' merger, while only 13 percent were against it. A majority of U.S. citizens described Germany as a "peace-loving nation."[5] But German Greens were of another mind. They

* By the late 1970s most West German citizens had reconciled themselves to the existence of two Germanys and the reality that unification might not happen in their lifetime. Polls showed that while 38 percent of the population in 1953 and 1956 felt that unification was "the most important question" for the republic, it had fallen to 1 percent or below by the late 1970s and remained this low through the 1980s; see Joyce Marie Mushaben, *From Post-War to Post-Wall Generations: Changing Attitudes towards the National Question and NATO in the Federal Republic of Germany* (Boulder, CO: Westview Press, 1998), 118. Unlike the majority of West German citizens, however, most Greens actively *opposed* unification.

insisted that nothing good ever came from a *Grossmacht Deutschland* in the heart of Europe. The German left tended to see Germany as a reformed alcoholic: it would take only a whiff of power—the cause of its addiction—for the country to fall back into old and brutal habits. Opening the first German question meant reopening all of them, a Pandora's box of well-known afflictions that twenty-first-century Europe could do without. Also, for most Greens—and most non-Greens as well—the reality of two Germanys was part of their postwar consciousness. Two-thirds of all Germans had been born into a divided Germany and had never known anything else. Likewise, these generations of West Germans were strangers to eastern Germany, to its people, its culture, and even its geography. They knew Tuscany or Paris better than Thuringia or Rostock. In contrast, figures of their parents' generation, even a man of the left like Willy Brandt, experienced unification as a dream come true.

With or without the Greens, events in the two Germanys hurtled forward. Chancellor Kohl's at-the-time bold "ten-point plan," which envisioned a confederation of the two states and unification sometime in the future, was very soon eclipsed by the velocity of history in the making. In the East, movement-linked groups and newly formed democratic parties broke the communists' forty-year grip on power and called free elections. One of those new parties was the Greens Party–East, cobbled together by environmentally conscious activists. At the time, a surprising portion of the most prominent democratic revolutionaries professed to want an indigenous, democratic brand of socialism—not western capitalism or eastern communism—for their side of Germany. This was music to the ears of the West German left, but the tune didn't play for long.

On the streets of Leipzig and Dresden, the easterners' cries changed from "we are *the* people" to "we are *one* nation,"[6] announcing an unmistakable nationalistic turn. The major West German parties set up offices in the East and began campaigning. In March 1990, in the GDR's first-ever (and last-ever) free elections, the East Greens and their independent-minded colleagues from the democracy movement received a bracing lesson about the hitherto unknown political disposition of their fellow citizens. A coalition of the indigenous "movement parties" called Alliance 90, including people such as Wolfgang Templin and Gerd and Ulrike Poppe, received just 2.9 percent of the vote in the eastern states. The Greens Party–East took 2 percent. The explanation, according to Alliance 90 founder Ulrike Poppe: "All at once during the election campaign, it was obvious that no one was listening to us anymore. Until then it had been such an emancipatory process. There was a spirit of awakening and renewal, not only in Berlin and Leipzig, but in the towns and villages too. But then, suddenly there was one giant image that overshadowed everything else: the Federal Republic."[7]

The news for the Social Democrats was bleak, too. Their miserable showing in the GDR vote extinguished any quixotic notion of a social democratic or democratic socialist state emerging from the ruins of communism, an "alternative Germany" alongside the set-in-its-ways Federal Republic. Election day's big winners were the Christian Democrats, whose unabashed nationalism and promises of "prospering landscapes" in the eastern states struck a powerful chord. Also, its conservatism appealed to a population socialized in an authoritarian system, one that was, in its own way, profoundly conservative. The Kohl party's campaign slogan was "No more experiments," a spin on Adenauer's "No experiments." The March 1990 election hammered the final nails into the coffin of the GDR, one failed experiment, as well as the possibility of any future experiments, such as democratic socialism or the Greens' ecological republic.

The election year 1990 thus started on a down note for the Greens, just an inkling of what would prove an *annus terribilis* for the party. The Greens launched their campaign for the autumn 1990 federal vote simultaneously on both sides of the country. Yet the party's earnest initiatives, like their showcase campaign on global warming* (a worldwide first), met with blank stares in eastern cities like Leipzig, Dresden, Cottbus, and Potsdam. After forty years of "real existing socialism," eastern Germany didn't have the urbane, middle-class, movement-bred voter base that fed the Greens in the West. With their economy in a shambles and an uncertain restructuring process ahead, the easterners' concerns were more mundane than the porous ozone layer, rights for homosexuals, and multicultural curricula.

The Greens' relationship with the pro-democracy groups in Alliance 90 (including the East Greens) was equally vexed, a by-product of their very different opposition cultures. (Later, in 1993, the two camps submitted to a shotgun marriage upon the sobering realization that neither had the staying power to survive in the united Germany without the other.) The fact was that work-a-day easterners weren't bonding with the politically correct Greens, and the average westerner felt no rapport with the mixed

---

* The Greens' campaign slogan—"Everyone is talking about Germany, we're talking about the weather"—was considered an extraordinary gaffe that summed up the distance of the party from ordinary Germans, as well as its inability to grasp the epochal implications of reunification.

bag of former East German dissidents. The easterners' churchy ways and acerbic anticommunism looked pre-1968 to the West Greens. The German Greens were an intrinsically West German phenomenon, a product of movements and debates that the East Germans had never had. As for the easterners' take on the Greens, in early 1991, Vera Wollenberger, the leader of the East Greens, offered an opinion on the modern-day representatives of the New Left, saying that they should "get out" and "see the world as it really is—and not as is in Karl Marx's *Das Kapital*."[8] Shortly thereafter Wollenberger quit the Greens to join the Christian Democrats.

Reluctantly, many Greens began to shift their position on unification once it became obvious that there was no turning back. At the time, and to their credit, the Greens warned against the West German establishment's steamrolling the east in the process, riding roughshod over everything that had a uniquely eastern German flavor. The Greens, among others, protested the hasty monetary union that overnight put the five new eastern states on a competitive footing with their western counterparts. As predicted, the unprepared firms disintegrated in the face of western competition, exacerbating a run-away unemployment problem that would endure more than fifteen years later. No matter, it was full speed ahead with unification. People weren't listening to dire warnings from the Cassandra party. It was time for heady celebration, not more prophecies of *Götterdämmerung*.

Yet, a profoundly disturbing phenomenon accompanied the dictatorship's demise in the east, one that seemed to bear out the darkest prophecies of the Germany skeptics. Racist violence wasn't new to western Germans—it had been present throughout the postwar decades, as had a far-right.* In the mid-1980s, "New Right" parties had won some electoral support during the emotional national debate over immigration. Next door, in the GDR, the dissolution of the police state lifted the lid on a problem that the East German leadership had tried its best to keep under wraps. Racist youth groups, skinheads among them, emerged with unsettling vitality from the ruins of the "antifascist state."

Opinion polls showed the population at large harboring little sympathy for Germany's immigrants, the vast majority of whom lived in the west

* The far-right Nationaldemokratische Partei Deutschlands (NPD) was founded in 1964 and entered a number of *Landtag*s in the late 1960s. No far-right party, however, has ever held a seat in the Bundestag. Since the fifties, there had been racist and anti-Semitic violence in West Germany, including the desecration of Jewish cemeteries.

anyway.[9] During the early 1990s, a series of pogrom-like attacks on foreigners in the eastern states appalled the country—and made embarrassing international headlines for the united Germany. In 1991, the first year of unity, the number of attacks on foreign nationals jumped tenfold.[10] In the western states, right-wing thugs firebombed the houses of resident Turkish families, killing eight people, while the far-right Republikaner Partei made inroads in regional legislatures. Could an ugly German nationalism make a comeback in the united state? Maybe *this,* thought some, *was* the new German nationalism. Fifty years after the Holocaust there were Germans trying to create an ethnically pure state again.

Although no one seriously believed that fringe parties like the Republikaner or the NPD could ever come to power in the united Germany, their mere presence in post-Holocaust Germany was cause for reflection, their assaults against immigrants grounds for swift action. The explanations that different quarters offered for the right's appeal and their policy prescriptions for addressing it went to the heart of the competing conceptions of Germanness and the united Germany that coexisted in the Federal Republic.

Conservatives, while not condoning the far right, tended to downplay the phenomenon's explicitly political nature. They regularly attributed the violence to "adolescent frustration," and the far right's appeal in general to social alienation and "disorientation" in a fragmented, postmodern society, one in which the traditional bonds of family and religion had lost their pull. For this predicament, conservatives blamed the 1968 generation, whose cultural revolution had discredited traditional values and sanctioned decadent youth culture, from skinheads to punks to heavy-metal cults. The conservative view also blamed Germany's liberal asylum statute, which enabled many foreign nationals to enter—eventually to stay—in the country on the grounds that they were politically persecuted in their own countries. "The boat," Christian Democrat politicians said, referring to Germany, "was full."[11] From this diagnosis issued political imperatives such as the strengthening of traditional values, restricting the influx of foreigners, and instituting tougher law-and-order measures. Moderate German nationalism like their own, they charged, had no connection to racist violence and the New Right, even though parties like the Republikaner drew largely from the right fringe of the Christian Democrats' voter base.

Those experts and observers closer to the left–liberal weltanschauung explained the same phenomenon differently. They tended to diagnosis far-right ideologies as the legacy of ethnic nationalism and authoritarian thinking, which had long histories in Germany and had found their most extreme expression in the Nazi period. Although West Germany's democratization had done much to erode these illiberal attitudes, it was an ongoing exercise. Left–liberals fretted that a Germany declared "normal" would no longer be so acutely aware of its past and could thus veer from the path of liberal democracy in times of crisis. Racism, anti-Semitism, and national chauvinism in Germany in the 1980s and 1990s persisted because of an inadequate "coming to terms with the past." Moreover, argued such critics, these kinds of ideas were legitimized and bolstered by the conservative parties, which indirectly appealed to racism, xenophobia, and feelings of insecurity—for example, through the charge that there were in fact "too many foreigners" in the German "boat." The Greens and other liberal-minded observers claimed that the political response to right-wing extremism should be campaigns for public tolerance, respectful integration measures, and a serious political commitment to a multicultural society, including regular immigration. "Civic courage" (*Zivilcourage*) had to be a part of Germany's social ethic—that is, a speaking out or taking action against racism, whether in a private or public setting. Above all, the left-of-center demanded that Germany's 1913 citizenship statute, which defined citizenship in terms of German descent and bloodlines, be revamped and naturalization be made more accessible to non-Germans.*

Made in West Germany

As of October 3, 1990, Germans had a new holiday to celebrate: Reunification Day. From then on, the Federal Republic's perimeters extended from the Rhine River bordering France to the Oder River adjacent to Poland, from Lake Constance buttressing the Swiss Alps all the way to the eastern waters of the Baltic Sea, a body of water connecting Germany with Scandinavia, the Baltic nations, and Russia. This new Germany, 82 million strong and situated at Europe's geopolitical nexus, had cast off the postwar Federal Republic's Cold War straitjacket to become a full-fledged sovereign nation-state—no longer, directly or indirectly, the custody of the World War II allies.

---

* In 1991, according to the Federal Ministry of the Interior, of the 5.8 million foreign nationals living in Germany, only 27,000 of them were naturalized citizens.

Nevertheless, there were in late 1990 no self-evident answers to a host of knotty questions that would, ultimately, determine what kind of Germany this new one would be. Opening the first German question (unification) meant that a multitude of others were now wide open, just as skeptics had forewarned. In the rush to unification there hadn't been sufficient time to reflect on many aspects of the content that would fill the republic's new shape. Postwar citizenship in the West had been based on democratic values first and nationality second. Now that Germany was a proper nation-state, for example, would it drop constitutional patriotism in favor of "normal" nationalism? Moreover, seventeen million easterners now had their say in such matters. Could they be so patriotic about a constitution that they hardly knew? Also, there had been precious little discussion about this new Germany's proper role in Europe and in global affairs now that its keepers were departing. Should German political clout and military power expand to become commensurate with its economic might? Would this unfettered, turbo-charged giant straddling the continent spell the Germanization of Europe, or would Germany further consent to a Europeanization of its country? What would be Germany's relationship to its new eastern neighbors, where memories of the not-so-distant past still burned brightly? And, critically, to what extent would this Federal Republic and its post-postwar generations feel compelled to abide by the lessons of their predecessors' pasts? Germany now had a double historical burden: not one but two dictatorships to process. Would one take precedent over the other? The Germans were locked in public debate over moving the new republic's capital from its stoop on the Rhine to Berlin, the former capital of Prussia and the Third Reich. This was a German question in itself. It seemed that the search for German identity hadn't ended with unification, it had just begun.

Certainly, there were conditions that the former Allies, including the Soviet Union, secured in writing before they would leave Germany on its own. The Unification Treaty stipulated that Germany would be a constitutional democracy with its powers decentralized and separated, individual rights anchored in a constitution, and pluralism respected, among other standard trappings of modern republicanism. The entire Federal Republic was prohibited from having nuclear, biological, or chemical weapons (as had been the Bonn Republic), and the German army would forever be limited to no more than 370,000 men. It was definitely not a merger of the old Federal Republic and the GDR. Rather, the latter was subsumed by the former (some even called it an *Anschluss,* or annexation) with few institutional alterations. The east contributed people, territory, and a menagerie of problems to the expanded republic but little that informed its political essence. As for Germany's place in the wider world, much would be determined in practice, in the years to come. The old Federal Republic had relied on the United States for global leadership, France for its orientation in Europe, and the Atlantic Alliance for security. Without prodding, Chancellor Kohl, as ardent an Atlanticist and true-blue European as they came, ensured there would be no German *Sonderweg* (special path) this time around: Germany was part of the West to stay. But this still left a daunting array of uncertainties.

From Frankfurt, Joschka Fischer summed up the feelings of those who were gradually coming to grips with the fact of a united Germany. "So, as pragmatic as we've become these days, I accept Germany's unification because I have to accept it," wrote Fischer in an essay entitled "Hurra Deutschland."But this didn't mean he could suddenly see good coming from it. On the contrary, "I can't shake my distrust of this 'we are one nation' thing. . . . The Germans in this century have delivered us two world wars, two dictatorships, Hitler, Auschwitz. Is all of this simply coincidental, explicable accidents of history?"[12]

But, at the same time, Fischer took a step back to reflect on the events that unified Germany. "Then it hits me," he wrote, "we're talking about the Federal Republic, a forty-year democratic success story, which has become a western European democracy with strong democratic roots in its institutions, culture, and broad social strata." This was a striking admission for a West German leftist. The Federal Republic had more going for it than they'd ever given the Allied-created rump state credit for, including aspects of a new German identity with much "positive" about it. Fischer stopped short of awarding any credit for this *Demokratiewunder* to the postwar social movements or the Greens. And, it remained to be seen, Fischer added less confidently, whether "the Germans can deal with their new power in a democratic and self-disciplined way."[13]

In the run-up to the Bundestag vote in December 1990, the first all-German election, the Greens and Alliance 90 forged an informal electoral coalition, although the Greens would run alone in the western states while Alliance 90 (including the East Greens) would run on the eastern side of the country. During the campaign, surveys showed the Greens polling well. The flickering of a revived peace movement, in response to the first Gulf War, buoyed their spirits.

When the votes were counted on election night, there was just one surprise—and it was a bombshell for the little environmental party. The

Greens took only 4.8 percent in the western states—.2 percent too little to return to the Bundestag for a third time. On the east side, Alliance 90 scraped together 5.8 percent of the vote—enough to put eight of their people into the new 656-member Bundestag. As expected, the Christian Democrats and the Free Democrats reaped the windfall of unification, while the Social Democrats sank to their worst postwar result since 1957. The year 1990 marked the Greens' tenth anniversary in the Federal Republic, but instead of celebrating they found themselves cast out of the Bundestag.

A number of external factors certainly contributed to the 1990 election debacle, foremost among them were unification and all that came with it. Some observers, however, traced the defeat back to the Greens themselves. War still raged between the party's factions. The realos argued that the Greens' "grassroots-democratic" rules paralyzed the party, dictating that it be run like an oversized NGO. The Greens still forbade MPs from serving two terms in a row, although the original two-year rotation requirement had long been dropped. The term limit automatically eliminated the best-known figures from running again, those who had made names for themselves through work in the Bundestag. The Greens' election slate was thus a collection of no-names and new faces. This and other "anti-party" safeguards were there to discourage Greens party politics from relying on charismatic types and media pizzazz, to keep power decentralized, and to undercut the possibility of boss-run fiefdoms. In other words, they were there to prevent someone like Joschka Fischer and the Frankfurt gang from taking over the party.

All the considerable bad news, however, was tempered somewhat for the party's realos by the combustion of the fundies. When the fundi–realo clash did finally end, it wasn't in a cataclysmic Big Bang, as one might have expected. In fact, neither the fundies nor the realos realized that a minor financial scandal would open the way to a rout of the fundies, during which much of the party's far left exited the party. A bookkeeping irregularity combined with a chain of fundi miscues forced the Jutta Ditfurth–led party leadership—the fundies' power base—to resign in toto in 1989.*

Partially, the fundies' disintegration after years of supremacy was a sign of the zeitgeist. Their dogmatism and angry radicalism looked evermore

* Ditfurth and several of her closest allies actually left the party in 1991. Although the fundies were gone, there were still many "left Greens." They accepted an electoral strategy for the party but not the realos' mainstream drift on the issues. From then on, the lines of confrontation within the party were between right and left, not fundies and realos.

anachronistic the further the 1970s retreated into the past and the 1990s inched closer. This Federal Republic was no longer that of Rainer Werner Fassbinder's films and Heinrich Böll's novels. Those in the party who sought an end to the rift had grown larger, as had a willingness to reach out to a younger, more modern SPD. The likes of Christa Nickels and Milan Horacek had long abandoned the antiparty model. In early 1989, in West Berlin, the second red–green coalition at the regional level came to life, yet another reverse to the fortunes of hold-out fundamentalists. In addition, segments of the Greens' left wing defected eastward, to the revamped East German communist party, newly christened the Party for Democratic Socialism, or PDS. Indeed, there was a new party in the republic, one to the left of the Greens.

Even with the fundies vanquished, some observers thought that the end of the 1980s might spell the end of the Greens, the quintessential 1980s party. But if there was to be a comeback, there was no better place to start than in Hesse, where elections were just around the corner. The *Landtag* vote four years after the collapse of the first-ever red–green coalition would reveal whether the ecology party was really out for the count or just bloodied. Taking no chances, the Hesse Greens jettisoned the party ban on organizing campaigns around individuals. Their poster boy, Joschka Fischer, was front and center, and everyone else was supporting cast.

As a member of the opposition in the 1987–91 Hessian *Landtag*, Fischer had shed the role of *enfant terrible*, which he had played in the Bundestag with boyish élan. He was nearing middle age, bulging some around the belt line, and married for a third time. Blonde-beauty Claudia Bohm had been a wide-eyed teen visitor to the Bundestag when they first met. Twenty-two when they exchanged vows in 1987, since then she had earned a university degree in literature and had a job as a TV journalist. One of Fischer's German biographers argues that his self-set challenge during the opposition years in Hesse was to perfect a balance between "Realpolitiker and rebel, minister and scene freak, dropout in a leather jacket but someone who also heeded etiquette, a cult figure for a younger generation representative of the new 'in' topics like the environment and *Friedenspolitik*, and simultaneously a political pro."[14] This multidimensional persona is exactly what made Fischer an attractive figure to Greens voters and beyond. Unlike other Greens, Fischer possessed an uncanny ability to span disparate milieus, something he had done successfully since his teenage years.

In 1991, in Hesse, the Social Democrats and the Greens fought their way back into the Wiesbaden government. This time, however, the context for a red–green coalition was much different from that in 1985–87. For one thing, red–green coalitions were no longer novelties. West Berlin, Lower Saxony, and even the northeastern state of Brandenburg had red–green track records; the North Sea city-state of Bremen was soon to follow.* There were also now the experiences of hundreds and hundreds of red–green alliances in towns and municipalities across the country. Equally important, the Social Democrats' top dog in Hesse wasn't any longer a snarling Holger Börner but a willing, forty-nine-year-old Hans Eichel, who as the mayor of Kassel had governed with Greens for years. This time, the Greens weren't offered a place in the Hesse coalition as "apprentice" junior partners, as they had been in 1985–87. They were afforded the respect and the positions that junior coalition partners normally received.

"The second time [in Hesse] everything was different. We knew what we had to do and how to do it," says Georg Dick, at Fischer's side again. When the ministry renewed its offensive against Hesse's nuclear facilities and chemical giants, it was from an up-and-running office and with rule-book confidently in hand. The minutiae of day-to-day governance, like the relentless legal challenges the ministry waged against its adversaries, may have been less spectacular than the helter-skelter run of 1985–87, but it packed substantially more punch. The Greens also controlled a second ministry, for youth, family, and health. New kindergartens, employment quotas for women, and improved accommodations for asylum-seekers were now on Hesse's agenda, as were Greens-tinged programs, in one form or another, in most of the western states. Almost every state now also had full-fledged environment ministries and offices for women's issues. It was the Christian Democrats, responding to the debacle of Chernobyl, who established the first Federal environment ministry in Bonn in 1986. This type of end run by the other parties was supposed to take the wind out of the Greens' sails, to make them redundant.

I Just Shot Petra Kelly

Petra Kelly, though still the dominant face of the Greens internationally, had in Germany navigated herself into the party's margins. Kelly's free-wheeling politics, America-infused showmanship, and celebrity status

* The Brandenburg and Bremen governments were three-way coalitions that included the SPD, the Free Democrats, and the Greens (Allliance 90 in Brandenburg).

never endeared her to the Greens' fundi left. Because she steadfastly repudiated overtures to the SPD, there was no love lost between her and the realos, either. Loath to engage in the energy-sapping party feuds, Kelly tried to ignore them and pursue her own globetrotting agenda. When the conflicts in Yugoslavia broke out, she was one of the first to agitate for a peaceful solution. But the enormous popular resonance that she enjoyed in the early 1980s had dissipated by the end of the decade, along with the perceptions of impending doom that boosted her to political stardom. In perpetual motion, she continued to push herself beyond her own limits, the breakdowns ever more frequent. In 1990, unable even to secure herself a place on the Greens' ballot, she unhappily bid farewell to the Bundestag. If she had had any doubts about her stock in the party, they were dispelled when she ran for a party post. Of the three candidates, Christiana Weiske received 344 votes, Antje Vollmer 263, Kelly just 39. By removing herself from the battles in the party, she wound up with no allies at all.

The aging Gert Bastian—lover, psychological crutch, domestic keeper of the emotionally volatile and fragile Kelly—was by her side at all times. He had become indispensable, always there during Kelly's manic highs and lows, tending to her every whim, toting her boxes of papers behind her like a Tibetan Sherpa. From two-star general to bag boy, joked malicious observers. None of this was out of the ordinary—others had played this role for Kelly in the past. Friends say that she rebounded from the snubs of the party that she had nursed to life, even though they hurt her deeply. Only forty-five years old, she made plans to run for the European Parliament. In September 1992 she spoke at the World Uranium Hearing in Salzburg, Austria, and then the World Conference of Radiation Victims in Berlin, her last public appearance.

Sixty-nine years old, Bastian, the courteous Old World officer, had of late appeared withdrawn to some, preoccupied and melancholy to others. He had financial problems, an estranged wife and family in Bavaria, and a handful of physical ailments. But none of this was new or particularly acute at the time. He seemed as enamored with Petra Kelly as ever, as intractably part of their symbiotic relationship as she. None of this explained what happened next.

On the evening of October 1, 1992, Petra Kelly and Gert Bastian retired early in their Bonn row house after a taxing day. Bastian awoke a few hours later, typed a newsy letter to his wife, and made a pot of coffee. He began another letter, odds and ends to his lawyer, stopping in mid-word.

He located his service revolver in Petra's sweater drawer and entered the bedroom in which she was sleeping peacefully. Bastian put the barrel to Kelly's temple and pulled the trigger. Then he turned it on himself.

The couple's death and its bizarre circumstances sent shock waves across the country. The nationwide outpouring of grief defied political allegiances. The conservative *Frankfurter Allgemeine Zeitung* called her the Joan of Arc of the nuclear age, "a politician out of empathy—an empathy that spanned the whole world."[15] But the Greens expressed her significance to their common cause most accurately, if too late for Kelly to appreciate: "Without Gert and Petra there would have been no Greens party. From the very beginning they personified the ecological and pacifist ideals of our opposition culture. They reached people far beyond the horizons of the alternative movement and helped prompt a broad social shift in the country's collective consciousness."[16] Today, fifteen years after her death, Kelly has been all but forgotten in Germany. A devout pacifist who was spurned by her party, murdered by her true love, and then ignored by history: a figure more tragic would be hard to invent.

Balkan Tragedy

By late 1992 the conflicts in what had been socialist Yugoslavia were raging at full blast. The wars in Croatia and then in Bosnia Herzegovina had compelled the reluctant political classes of western Europe to improvise ex post facto to stem the worst bloodshed in Europe since World War II. Europe's slow-motion reaction to Yugoslavia's disintegration wasn't a matter of indifference. The images of emaciated prisoners circumscribed by barbed wire and columns of traumatized refugees moved consciences everywhere, and especially in Germany. The likes of ethnic cleansing (the new vernacular) and genocide (the old) were assumed to belong to bygone epochs or far-away continents. Europe's leaders were as ill-prepared as they were trenchantly divided over the proper response—the Greens and Alliance 90 no less so. The Balkan wars threw the German left for another loop. For a start, the Balkans simply weren't on the left's map. Latin America, Southeast Asia, the Middle East, and even Russia had been of greater interest than Tito's Yugoslavia.

Freshly sovereign Germany had become entwined in the Yugoslavia conundrum early on, openly siding with the independent-minded Croats and Slovenes, who understandably recoiled from the bullying tactics of

Serbia's nationalist strongman, Slobodan Milosevic, and then quickly moved to separate themselves from a Serb-dominated Yugoslavia. The German government's highly controversial 1991 decision to recognize Croatian statehood in advance of its European counterparts couldn't have looked worse for Bonn. Germany's dilemma was that any move that it made on its own in the Balkans was bound to be contentious, politically loaded in extremis, since Nazi Germany had, on the one hand, occupied Serbia and, on the other, set up an exceptionally brutal quisling regime in Croatia. For some on the German left—and Germany-skeptics elsewhere—the conservatives' Balkan policy looked like their worst nightmare come true: a resurgent, belligerent greater Germany acting unilaterally in Europe and reconnecting to its World War II allies. This wasn't the case (Bonn's decision was a well-intentioned, poorly timed gaffe), but it was a conclusion that some minds came to.

In this context, Serbia's propaganda made sense to parts of the German left. Here was Serbia, supposedly socialist and proudly Yugoslav, as well as a western ally in the two World Wars, pitted against a separatist nationalist regime in Croatia that had insensitively rehabilitated World War II–era symbols and mistreated its Serb minority, the primary victims of the World War II state. The obscure Bosnian Muslims were largely ignored. Others on the German left, including many pacifists in the Greens, didn't fall for Milosevic's line, but they were simply at a loss to make heads or tails of the killing and they repeated, like a mantra, the need for more negotiations, more economic sanctions, more peace delegations—anything and everything but western military intervention.

The debate over Germany's reaction to the slaughter in Bosnia immediately rammed up against the outstanding German questions. Until the 1990s no thought whatsoever had been given to Germany's deploying armed German troops abroad. Not only did the highest law of the land, the Basic Law, prohibit the Bundeswehr from participating in nondefensive military operations, but also there wasn't a respected voice in all of Germany who thought that the country could or should deploy its armed forces to foreign conflict zones. Even in the wake of unification, with Germany in full possession of its national sovereignty and command of its armed forces, the postwar consensus still held firm: German troops, even under NATO or U.N. command, could not participate in missions that were "out of [NATO's] area"—namely, Europe. No one had even posed the question: Now that Germany was surrounded only by allies and friends, what was the purpose of the Bundeswehr anyway?

But, through the early 1990s, this consensus eroded bit by bit and an impassioned national debate ensued about the role of the Federal Republic and its armed forces in world affairs. In the aftermath of the 1990–91 Gulf War, several Bundeswehr minesweepers trolled the Persian Gulf to help clear mines, while thirty German pilots flying Bundeswehr helicopters aided the U.N. weapons inspectors in Iraq.[17] The Greens accused the government of abating Washington's imperialist agenda, violating the Basic Law, and closing its eyes to Germany's debt to history.[18] The Greens, left-wing Social Democrats, and the PDS cited the same rationale with which they would later veto German involvement in Balkan missions: such operations, even humanitarian in nature, put Germany on a slippery slope to military adventurism.[19] In fact, Germany's major contribution to the first Gulf War was money, to the tune of $6.5 billion.[20] The Germans weren't willing to fight alongside their allies, but they'd generously help pay for the wars. Germany's huge Gulf War bill earned its foreign policy the unflattering label of "checkbook diplomacy." But the real watershed was Bosnia. In 1992, by deploying a destroyer and three reconnaissance aircraft to the Adriatic Sea to monitor U.N. sanctions against Yugoslavia, the republic stepped out onto new territory.[21]

In the Greens, the debate veered unexpectedly, turning inward on the "pacifist party" and plunging it into turmoil once again. This dispute would rock the party to its foundations and send it, as well as the new Germany, into the twenty-first century much-changed. As the atrocities in Bosnia showed no sign of subsiding despite round after round of international mediation, a dissident handful of party members led by Dany Cohn-Bendit stood up to demand that tougher international measures—military force if need be and involving Germany should it be required—be employed to halt the Serbs' onslaught against the Muslim civilian population in Bosnia. Furthermore, Cohn-Bendit told the Greens straight out that it was their moral responsibility to join him in turning official Germany policy around, not in a more pacifist or neutral direction but in staunch defense of the Bosnian Muslims and multicultural society in Bosnia Herzegovina.

Cohn-Bendit, pushing fifty himself, had lost none of his fire. Though a father now and settled comfortably in Frankfurt, he hadn't been inactive since the days of *Pflasterstrand* and the Karl Marx Bookshop. When a red–green coalition took over the Frankfurt city assembly in 1989, Dany Le Rouge moved into city hall as head of the new Office for Multicultural Affairs, in a city in which one in three school kids had foreign-born parents. In fact, all of (western) Germany's major cities included large populations of Turkish, Croatian, Italian, Serbian, Albanian, and Greek inhabitants, among others. Many of the eldest generation had been the first *Gastarbeiter*, or guest workers, who later summoned their families and then settled in West Germany permanently. But, unlike in France and the Netherlands, it was extremely difficult for immigrants to become citizens and thus enjoy the same rights as Germans did, even if they had lived in the country for decades—or were born in Germany to non-German parents. Frankfurt was the most extreme example: 29 percent of its total population, people from 181 different countries, didn't possess citizenship.[22] Germany had become a multicultural, religiously diverse country without owning up to it, and had not created the necessary institutions and policies to deal with its immigrant population.

In Frankfurt and after hours at some of the old haunts, Cohn-Bendit and the gang, including Fischer, Koumpania, Koenigs (also in the Frankfurt administration), Dick, and others, would meet for beers and debate. On the issue of Bosnia, however, Cohn-Bendit and his old friend Joschka Fischer remained on opposite sides. The dogged arguments of Cohn-Bendit and his handful of allies at first changed few minds in the Greens. No one in the party could have imagined that their postwar imperatives "Never again war" (military intervention) and "Never again Auschwitz" (ethnic cleansing and mass murder) would ever conflict with one another, that they would one day be forced to choose one over the other. But this, ultimately, was the dilemma before them in the Balkans.

In a June 1993 op-ed in the *Tageszeitung*, Cohn-Bendit showed zero sympathy for their soul searching: "Shame on us! We, the generation that held our parents' generation in such contempt because of its political cowardice, now we watch on seemingly helpless, powerless and yet still holier-than-thou as the Bosnian Muslims are ethnically cleansed." He reminded his former co-revolutionaries of the way the world watched on when fascist forces crushed the Spanish Republicans (1936), invaded Czechoslovakia (1938), put down the Warsaw Ghetto uprising (1943), and murdered Europe's Jewry at Auschwitz and Treblinka. "Now we're part of this glorious tradition!" he fumed. "Where are the smart asses now who talked so loud about *an entirely different approach to politics*? Where are the internationalists who, in the name of socialism, supported every, and I mean *every*, terrorist or pacifist movement in Salvador, Nicaragua and everywhere else?" And it isn't just the Greens, he underscored, who have bowed to Serbia's nationalist thugs but the entire republic, which is not only too spineless to intervene by force of arms but doesn't, at the very least, even have the decency to take in all of the war refugees fleeing for their lives. "We have failed so miserably because we've wrapped our aloof self-centeredness in a protective cloak of starry-eyed pacifism. Sometimes there's something more important to defend than the illusion of peace, namely the survival of human beings," he concluded acidly.[23]

Cohn-Bendit was never alone. From the beginning, he found some unfamiliar voices on his side. The former East German dissidents in Alliance 90, like Gerd and Ulrike Poppe, Wolfgang Templin, and others knew eastern Europe well and were passionately committed to human rights. Also, they understood the Federal Republic differently from the West's jaded ex-rebels. "There were actually Greens who seriously argued that Hitler could have been stopped by pacifist means," says ex-dissident Gerd Poppe. "This was completely absurd, as it was that the mass murder in Bosnia could be stopped with pacifism. We didn't want Germany to be involved on its own, but as part of the greater international community," says Poppe, at the time one of the eight Alliance 90 MPs in the Bundestag. At a Greens party congress in Bonn, when he tried to present the report of an Alliance 90-led fact-finding mission to wartorn Bosnia, Greens in the crowd booed and jeered Poppe off the stage, branding him a "war monger" and screaming for his resignation.

Swayed by the pro-interventionists but not yet convinced, Fischer struck a middle course. Armed intervention in Bosnia, though not to be ruled out, would at the time, in 1993, only throw fuel on the fire and escalate the fighting, he charged. He also maintained, as did many others, that there could be no German military presence in territories that the Wehrmacht had occupied during World War II, such as the Balkans. Old friends Fischer and Cohn-Bendit went head-to-head on the issue at a televised panel discussion in Frankfurt, which was supposed to address the legacy of the student movement, twenty-five years later. But the topic switched quickly to Bosnia. Tempers flaring, Fischer lit into Cohn-Bendit: "And would you, Dany, be prepared to send *your son* to fight in Bosnia, and maybe even to die there?" The Frenchman retorted: "That'll be his decision, but I ask you, Joschka, if that high-rise across the street was in flames and *your son* was a fireman, would you stop him risking his life to go in and try to save people?"

Greens Comeback

Although the tug-of-war over Bosnia and humanitarian intervention had just begun, the Greens prudently lay the issue aside in order to channel their full energies into making a national comeback. The 1994 Bundestag elections were in sight, and although the party was still at loggerheads on many key issues, it was at least now fully united in its aspiration to return to the national parliament. Should the numbers add up, they could transport the red–green model from the states to the capital, since 1991 officially Berlin (although the government still resided in Bonn and would until 1999). In marked contrast to four years earlier, the entire party accepted the fact that its number-one realo, Hesse's environment minister Joschka Fischer, was the Greens' surest ticket to get to where they wanted to go.

Fischer was now the party's undisputed chief and standard-bearer, even though he didn't hold an official post in the party. "Joschka Fischer Superstar," taunted the *Tageszeitung*, rubbing it in the face of the feminist, anti-authoritarian former antiparty.[24] In order to lead the charge back onto the national stage, Fischer handed over his ministry in Hesse. This time, the Greens didn't flinch from assembling a dream team to flank him, which included popular Greens veterans Antje Vollmer, Christa Nickels and Marieluise Beck; Lower Saxony's Women's Affairs Minister Waltraude Schoppe; Stuttgart's first-hour realo Rezzo Schlauch; and Brandenberg's ex-Education Minister Marianne Birthler. To shore up the party's still potent left, Ludger Volmer, whose past lay in the Third World movement, rounded out the top of the slate.

Certainly, Fischer's nationwide appeal, first among Greens but still not on a par with the republic's prime-time politicos, was one factor that propelled him to the front of the party. He was the only Greens or Alliance 90 campaigner who could pack halls everywhere, including in the otherwise Greens-disinterested eastern towns. At forty-six, slightly graying, bags under his eyes, and nearly as round as the barrel-torsoed chancellor, he'd also become a veteran political operator on a scale with, and often compared to, the republic's heaviest hitters. He was also the one and only Greens figure who the Social Democrats trusted to co-run a red–green coalition at the national level. The SPD was conflicted about the wisdom of a red–green government in Bonn, even if most had become used to coalitions with the Greens in the federal states. The Greens' reputation as intemperate and unpredictable still made them suspect in the minds of many Germans. But Social Democrats were slowly coming to the realization that the red-green option was probably their best bet to return to power. Over Fischer's strenuous objection, the party's 1994 election platform again called for abolition of the Bundeswehr, as well as Germany's exit from NATO. This holdover fundamentalism delighted the conservatives, who could all the more easily fan fears of the red–green bogeyman. Even should red–green become a reality on the federal level, in 1994 there was no one suggesting that any Greens receive the internationally sensitive post of foreign minister, the republic's number-two position. The Greens weren't *that* normal yet.

"Everything I do, I do excessively," Fischer told Herlinde Koelbl, the well-known photographer and author of the classic *Traces of Power,* a chronological collection of yearly photographs and personal interviews with up-and-coming German politicians over the course of the 1990s. In Koelbl's work, subtitled "The Transformation of Man by Power: A Long-term Study," she captures in black and white Fischer's physical metamorphosis over the decade. From year to year his once handsome face grows bloated and puffy, blurring its familiar angles and boyish features. His chin doubles and the vertical lines become longer, ever more deeply etched in his face. Usually in a sports coat, loose tie, and jeans, his girth expands from photo to photo, his prodigious gut bulging far over his waistline by the mid-1990s. Fischer still made it out onto the soccer field, chugging along two steps behind the opponents' defenders, admittedly disgusted with the deterioration of his skills, especially when the Christian Democrats' team pummeled the Greens. In the political ring, however, he was now a bona fide heavyweight and his physical bulk only added to the aura of party patriarch and force to be reckoned with.

Finally in 1994, after four long years outside the Bundestag, the Greens' regimen of relative moderation and enforced camaraderie paid off in the nationwide elections. Even if the Greens' and the Social Democrats' combined total failed to dislodge the conservatives, serving since 1983, the Greens chalked up 7.2 percent of the vote, a stellar result thanks to the party's reliable bastions in western urban centers and Berlin. With the vote, the contours of the Berlin Republic came more sharply into focus. As the breach between right and left in the western part of the country closed a little further, a worrisome new divide was opening between the old (western) and the new (eastern) federal states. The Greens knew that their charms fell flat in the east, but this territory was supposed to be the purview of Alliance 90, the heroes of the 1989 democratic revolution. But the newly merged party showed pitifully in the east, not breaching 5 percent anywhere outside of Berlin's eastern neighborhoods. Of Alliance 90/Greens' forty-eight freshly chosen MPs, only four would come from Alliance 90. As vocal political dissidents in the GDR, the likes of the Poppes, the Templins, and the Wollenbergers had always been an infinitesimal minority, and in the post-communist era their against-the-grain convictions would be equally unpopular. By 1998 neither Alliance 90 nor the Greens would have a single seat in any of the five eastern *Landtags*.

Even more shocking was the easterners' volte-face on the Christian Democrats. Their love affair with Helmut Kohl ended when they found themselves saddled with a defunct economy rather than "prospering landscapes." Surveys showed that the easterners were profoundly unhappy with sky-high unemployment (14 percent in the new states and climbing) and, disturbingly, with parliamentary democracy as well. Fewer bothered to show up at the polls than did civic-minded westerners, a trend that would worsen. Also, the high turnout for the PDS—the revamped version of the discredited former Leninist party—baffled everyone, another flashing signal that all was not well in the new states.

The 1994 election also afforded the Greens a good look in the mirror, at a voter base that had matured and expanded since its creation. While the Greens still polled quite well among new and young voters, their constituency was no longer overwhelmingly the youngest voters. Rather, in a phenomenon dubbed "the graying of the Greens," almost as many of their supporters now fell into older age groups, such as the twenty-four to thirty-four and the thirty-five to forty-nine year brackets.[25] In other words, the generations that brought the Greens to life, those Germans who were socialized during the student protests or the new social movements, were still backing the Greens. One poll showed that in contrast to the disenchanted eastern voters, in 1994 more Greens voters than ever before expressed "satisfaction" with the quality of the Federal Republic's democracy. And, another shift, Greens voters were now also among the most well-off of those of any party—evidence that the protest generations were growing up and becoming successful in their professions. Unexpectedly perhaps, the long march was proving lucrative. The Greens voters were now part of Germany's burgher classes, their values integrated into the republic's political culture. Nevertheless, a conservative elite still clung to their ideas and offices in the very highest corridors of power, in Bonn, unprepared to vacate them without a fight.

Part IV

The Berlin Republic

9

German Questions

In the early 1990s, neither within the Social Democrats nor the Greens had there been talk of a Greens-held foreign ministry, should a red–green coalition in fact come to power. The Greens' priority was the environment ministry, ideally one fortified with broad competencies in other prime areas of Greens concern, including transportation, consumer protection, and energy. The Social Democrats swore to strategic allies that, in the event of a red–green government, the anti-NATO environmentalists wouldn't get close to the precious Auswärtiges Amt (foreign ministry). In official trips to Washington, the Greens' foreign affairs spokesman Helmut Lippelt calmed U.S. policymakers: "I'd go through Congress or to the State Department and say that it is very, very clear to us that we are just a little pacifist party and that we won't have any influence on the coalition's foreign policy. We'll never have the foreign or defense ministry portfolios, I'd say. We won't rock the boat."

The issue arises when examining the metamorphosis of the Greens' foreign policy stands during the 1990s. Fischer's critics argue that he forced the party's hand to disavow its antimilitarist roots in order to prep it for prime time: a nationwide red–green coalition, and himself for the prestigious post of foreign minister. Fischer's centrality in pushing the Greens toward the mainstream on foreign policy is undisputed, and it positioned him for the Berlin Republic's number-two spot. But there's more to the story than ambition run rampant. During the first half of the 1990s, the Greens as a whole grappled poorly with the epochal geopolitical shifts that were transforming the world around them. The Cold War–era party was out of step with the new realities of the post–Cold War world, which demanded a rethinking of once-fixed assumptions and flexible, creative responses to new problems. Instead, too many Greens clung to their pacifist credo despite the slaughter in Bosnia and they remained adamant that their nemeses of old—NATO, the World Bank, Washington, and industrial capitalism—were still their adversaries, despite the fact that the recently liberated countries of central and eastern Europe were clamoring to join the Atlantic alliance, as well as to jumpstart freemarket miracles of their own.

In the reconfigured new world order, a good part of the Greens' "peace policies" appeared timeworn. The bipolar world had been replaced by one with a single superpower, Pax Americana, which presided over economic and military resources dwarfing those of any previous empire in human history. There was no obvious alternative but to somehow cooperate with the United States to address the multifarious challenges of a globalized world. The arms race and the Cold War's nuclear balancing act had lost their ultima ratio, and world leaders were now talking optimistically about the "peace dividends" they would reap from the slashing of military budgets.* The plight of Third World hotspots, such as those in Central and South America and in Africa, faded with the end of the East-West conflict. Now there were festering ethnic conflicts much closer to home, in Central Asia, in the Caucasus, and, of course, in Europe too—in the Balkans. These were "new wars" that didn't conform to the old paradigms. Not least, the West had to respond to the expectations of the central Europeans who insisted on concrete security guarantees vis-à-vis Russia and access to the West's institutions. It seemed that the world had changed but the Greens hadn't.

It wasn't until the publication of Fischer's 1994 tract *The German Risk*, which outlined a foreign policy agenda for the united Germany, that those with their ears to the ground suspected that he coveted the foreign ministry, should the 1998 elections oust the conservatives.[1] *The German Risk* was a vision-in-progress. It began by asking how best to curb Germany's historical inclination to meddlesome great-power politics. But Fischer soon

---

* The Greens lobbied—though unsuccessfully—to have the peace dividends invested in environment-friendly policies. These measures and others stemmed from the international environmental treaties that emerged from the 1992 conference in Rio de Janeiro (also known as the Earth Summit), in which the German Greens played an integral role. The summit resulted in several important advancements in global environmental law, including the United Nations Framework Convention on Climate Change, the Convention on Biological Diversity, and the Declaration on Environment and Development.

veered from the standard left-wing script. Although Germany remained for Fischer a potential source of international mischief, he underscored that the Federal Republic also had "positive traditions and structures" to call upon. In the same breath, he mentioned the student movement, the 1989 democratic uprising in East Germany, and, remarkably, the early Federal Republic's commitment to the *Westbindung*, a stance emblazoned with Adenauer's signature. According to Fischer, the proper place for the united Germany, like the old Federal Republic, was among the western allies, including the United States, not somewhere in a nebulous middle zone between East and West. "It was exactly this radical 'strategy of westernization' (in other words, democratization) [*sic*] that turned the Bonn Republic into an unprecedented success story in German history. Who knows," mused Fischer, "maybe with the passage of time the Bonn Republic will go down as the happiest period in Germany's history."[2]

With a flick of the wrist, Adenauer's *Westbindung*, so reviled by the sixty-eighters and the peace movement, now constituted an inspired break with perilous *Sonderwegs* and great-power nationalisms in favor of representative democracy, a social market economy, multilateralism, and European integration. Using words that in the past any Greens supporter would have been loath to speak, he stressed the necessity of "continuity" in German foreign policy, arguing that the cornerstones of future diplomacy be essentially the same as those of former West Germany. Helmut Kohl himself couldn't have said it better. It seems that it took the break up of communism, the outbreak of fascism in the Balkans, and the emergence of authoritarian nationalist regimes in eastern Europe to make Fischer realize how good West Germans had had it in the little republic that, ultimately, the right *and* the left, the postwar *and* the pre-1945 generations, had forged together.

What worried Fischer most was the possible "re-nationalization" of Germany, the attempt by national conservatives to subvert the republic's liberal legacy by dredging up chauvinistic, prewar traditions, much the same as they had tried to do during the 1980s historians' debate. This he saw as part of a larger trend throughout Europe toward illiberal ideologies and entangled, competitive alliances, like those that reigned in Europe before World War I. During the first half of the 1990s, there was ample evidence to stir such fears: the ethnic wars in former Yugoslavia, the shifting alliances produced by the Balkan wars, an explosion of far-right violence in Germany, and the growing influence of intellectual-led New Right thinkers across Europe. Despite the breakup of communism, the continent's place in the democratic fold appeared anything but incontrovertible.

The definitive answer to both Europe's quandary and Germany's outstanding questions, wrote Fischer, was one and the same, and could be summed up in two words: European integration. Germany and its neighbors—indeed, all of Europe—had to bind themselves as tightly as possible into the structures of the European Union and other multilateral institutions, including NATO. "Since unification, democratic Germany with its [geopolitical] position and [economic] potential is one of the most powerful countries in Europe west of Russia and therefore now has the chance to anchor itself in a democratic, united Europe. In doing so, it will finally and forever put to rest the dangers inherent in its precarious 'middle position' in Europe and the temptation of nationalist aspirations." In other words, "Europe" is the silver bullet to quell the continent's simmering nationalisms, to spread prosperity and stability, and to sow democracy from the Atlantic to the Urals, from the Baltic to the Balkans. Step by step, Europeans must relinquish national sovereignty, handing over state functions to supranational institutions, foremost the European Union. It had to build and expand upon its existing structures, argued Fischer, not only in the economic sphere, but also in foreign, security, agricultural, immigration, and environmental policy as well.[3]

If they had bothered to read *The German Risk*, conservatives like Chancellor Kohl would surely have guffawed at Fischer's belated discovery of the European project and his wide-eyed enthusiasm for a process that Adenauer and his postwar allies had set in motion in the 1950s. Helmut Kohl, a "Europe" devotee second to none, emphatically underscored Germany's role as the motor and deep-pocketed financier of European integration. In contrast, for years it was the Greens who had hammered away at the European Union as an undemocratic, rich man's club. Although they supported European unity in principle, they called the union "Eurocentric," "radically free market," and "Fortress Europe," the latter a reference to restrictive immigration and asylum laws.[4] In the European Parliament, the Greens voted against the milestone Maastricht Treaty, which set an agenda for Europe's political union, including common foreign and security policies, as well as a shared monetary union (the euro) among member states. The Maastricht process, they charged, would turn the European Union into a "militarized superpower."[5] The Greens' overzealous critique tended to obscure their more astute points: the institution's opaque structures and glaring "democracy deficit."

As sensational a deviation from Greens orthodoxy as *The German Risk* was, it didn't in itself prompt a rupture in the Greens' foreign policy stances. Srebrenica did. In early July 1995, Serbian forces captured the Bosnian Muslim-populated city of Srebrenica in eastern Bosnia. Although the enclave was under U.N. protection, a designated "safe area," the Serbs entered the town without resistance. Over the next three days they rounded up Muslim men and boys and proceeded to execute them, burying their corpses in shallow graves. The massacre of an estimated 7,000 people constituted the bloodiest single event of the three-year war, if not in Europe's entire post–World War II history. It happened on the watch of the United Nations and in the wake of countless international efforts to end the war.

The singular magnitude of Srebrenica jolted many Germans from their positions of conflicted ambivalence and forced them to abandon their objections to intervention on behalf of the victims, the Bosnian Muslims. More broadly, it set many Germans to rethinking the roles that Europe, and Germany as part of it, should play in the wider world. Within the Greens this debate was particularly polarizing. In a thirteen-page open letter addressed to his party, Fischer reversed his own position and exhorted the Greens to wake up to the reality that international policy in Bosnia had failed.[6] He argued that the Greens' nonviolent options—tighter sanctions, further negotiations, more humanitarian aid—were paper tigers in the face of full-blown war and the deliberate ethnic politics that fueled it. "Are pacifists prepared to accept the triumph of brutal, naked violence in Bosnia? What should we do when all existing [non-military] means to stop military violence have been exhausted?" The Greens—*above all*, the Greens—Fischer argued, can't stand by and watch as whole populations are ethnically cleansed, and men herded into concentration camps and slaughtered. His arguments differed little from those that Cohn-Bendit shouted in his direction a full two years before. "Doesn't the German left run the massive risk of tainting its soul when, regardless of the justification, ultimately it looks away from this new fascism?" asked Fischer. "What becomes of our nonviolence when it bows to a kind of violence that takes human lives?" Fischer concluded that the international community either had to act with force of arms to protect the U.N. safe zones or allow the Bosnian army to arm and defend its own population. The Greens have to make their choice or become complicit in more bloodshed and the creation of a Greater Serbia.[7]

Fischer's Srebrenica letter ignited a firestorm in the party. "Take a gun and go to Sarajevo yourself!" cried Ludger Volmer, the party's speaker at the time.[8] Kerstin Müller, Claudia Roth, and Jürgen Trittin—all prominent

Greens—took Fischer to task in similar terms. Many Social Democrats as well, including Oskar Lafontaine, pounced on Fischer's proclamation. Negotiations and sanctions didn't amount to "doing nothing."[9] A yes to intervention in Bosnia amounted to a blank check for other German interventions worldwide, they claimed. If "humanitarian intervention" was justified in Bosnia, then why not in Chechnya and Afghanistan, too, where egregious human rights violations were also happening? It was a valid question, but one that got lost during the mudslinging.

Yet other Greens and assorted leftists, also shocked by the brutality of Srebrenica and the United Nations' record in Bosnia, gravitated toward Fischer's new position. In dozens of letters to the editor that appeared in the *Tageszeitung*, which had printed Fischer's letter in full, conflicted peace activists debated the pros and cons of Fischer's arguments. "In my opinion," wrote one reader from Ludwigsburg, "although Fischer's letter will certainly make him a lot of new enemies, I think he argued sensibly and realistically. The question of military intervention in Bosnia isn't about future coalitions," referring to charges of opportunism that dogged Fischer. "It's about people who are being expelled, murdered, tortured or raped—and feel abandoned by the world."[10] Another subscriber from Munich wrote, "Hopefully the majority of the party will realize that in extreme situations the saving of human lives and the protection of human rights will entail the employment of military violence. Nevertheless, we can still remain, in principle, a pacifist party committed to antimilitaristic traditions. But if radical pacifists stick to dogma regardless of the circumstances then ultimately they play right into the hands of the mass murderers."[11]

Until the Srebrenica letter, only a handful of maverick Greens backed armed intervention in Bosnia. MP Helmut Lippelt was one of them. "I had hoped for a shift in the party even earlier but it took Srebrenica to bring Fischer around. Thank God, I told him, you're finally with us." Lippelt admits that neither he nor the other early pro-intervention Greens had the clout to transform the Bosnia debate into a full-scale discussion over German foreign policy. "We couldn't move the party the way Fischer did," says Lippelt, one of the Greens' founding fathers, adding that even with Fischer, it took another four years of tenacious infighting to do so. "He had learned a lot as minister in Hesse, especially the second time around. He had the skills to push things through at congresses, to sway the whole party. We didn't."

In retrospect, the Srebrenica massacre and Fischer's strident letter marked a critical turning point in the party's history. But like the Greens' halting rapprochement with parliamentary democracy, their coming to grips with a new post-unification German foreign policy was arduous and incremental. In late 1995, in the wake of U.S.–led peace talks that ended the war in Bosnia, 60 percent of the party delegates voted against German soldiers participating in the NATO–led stabilization force in Bosnia, the purpose of which was to support civilian peacekeepers. The vote, however, was interpreted as a victory for the party's interventionists: nearly 40 percent of Greens delegates supported the resolution.

While debate in the party raged, Fischer struck out on his own. He journeyed to Israel, Bosnia, the United States, France, Great Britain, and Poland to float some of his evolving geopolitical thoughts with state leaders. In Tel Aviv, he tried to patch the tattered relations between the German Greens and the Israelis. In the past, the Greens' pro-Palestinian leanings had infuriated the Israelis, leading to nasty (and highly embarrassing) exchanges.* In Poland, Fischer assured Warsaw that the Greens wouldn't block its entry into NATO, even though the party opposed NATO's eastward expansion.

This jetsetting and foreign policy freelancing raised eyebrows everywhere and prompted irritated denials from the Greens that MP Joschka Fischer was speaking for the party.[12] In fact, he wasn't even on foreign affairs committees in the Bundestag or working groups in the Greens. "It was easy for Fischer to abandon Greens foreign policy positions because they weren't his," explains Uli Cremer, one of the Greens' international affairs experts who had spent incalculable hours in Green committee meetings hammering out policy options. The former Hessian environmental minister was viewed in Germany as an *Innenpolitiker,* a domestic affairs expert, with only cursory knowledge of—or interest in—foreign affairs. "Why is he doing this?" asked the *Süddeutsche Zeitung* correspondent in Poland upon Fischer's July 1997 visit. "The Poles would like to know too. Does he really want to become foreign minister?"[13]

* There existed both pro-Palestinian and pro-Israeli currents in the party, the former usually with backgrounds in the anti-imperialist, Third World solidarity campaigns of the seventies. The first Greens working trip to the region in 1984 ended in disaster, with the Israeli press blasting the delegates as "Hitler's children," "green-browns" and "potential Nazis." The more Israel-friendly Greens argued that because of Germany's past, even the postwar generations had no place criticizing Israeli policy, regardless of its content.

Reinventing Fischer

Fischer likened the process of revamping the Greens' foreign and security policies to "open heart surgery."[14] He had appointed himself the chief surgeon on an unwilling and conscious patient. But in the midst of the operation, disaster struck in Fischer's personal life. It was also a matter of the heart—but one that surgery couldn't remedy. His wife of nine years, the thirty-one-year-old TV journalist Claudia Bohm, called it quits, abruptly leaving Fischer in late summer 1996. Her grounds were that she wanted children. Joschka already had two and for him, never a natural parent, that was enough. There was no middle ground.

The couple had discussed the issue before, long and hard, but it hadn't prepared Fischer for the emotional shock of the split. "This lightning bolt struck me from out of the blue," remembers Fischer. "I was standing on the brink of the abyss and under the impact of this emotional catastrophe my whole life fell completely apart in no time at all."[15] Fischer's life had hitherto been marked by pivotal breaks: when he fled the provincial life of his Catholic family; then in the aftermath of the Meinhof demonstrations a decade later terminating his foray into radical politics; and more recently when his entry into the Bundestag as a Greens MP ended one phase and began another. His loss of Claudia—entirely her decision—was yet another terminus and it devastated Fischer, now forty-eight and set in his ways. The last time he had been single he was seventeen years old. Then, at least, he had his mother. Now he was alone for the first time in his life.

The crisis compelled him to take a hard look at who he was, at what politics, ambition, and twelve-hour workdays had made of him. He was disgusted with what he saw: a 256-pound lummox whose physical and spiritual existence had become one with the day-in, day-out grind of party politics. He had become, as he put it, "a hamster on a treadmill." Heartbroken, he knew he had a long spell of mourning and soul-searching ahead of him, but he also knew there was no turning back. "The choice was suddenly very easy: either I continue on as I had and go to the dogs completely or change," he writes in his inspirational ode to jogging and healthy eating entitled *My Long Journey to Myself*, his seventh book. His decision was "Now, immediately! I'll make a radical break and change my personal program completely, leave everything behind me: the good living and the schmoozing and the fine wines and all the extra pounds. From now I'll concentrate on myself."[16] At their holiday house in the rolling hills of

Tuscany, where the couple was at the time of the breakup, Fischer tossed his size XXL Hawaiian shirt into a corner and dropped to the floor for push-ups. But under the poundage his arms buckled. From here on out, he swore, only fresh fish, whole grains, fruits, and vegetables would grace his table.

It was back in Bonn, however, one fog-enveloped morning along the Rhine that he laced up a pair of running shoes and set out, long before the first journalists and photographers had risen. He didn't last a quarter of a mile. "Those first steps were pure torture because I was carrying so much fat. I started slowly but after just a few hundred meters I was gasping for air. Wheezing, I dragged myself around the Bundestag and home again."[17] The start, however, was made and each day he set himself a new goal: a tree, a church, or a bridge farther along the riverbank. In jogging, too, he was a realo—convinced that change would be gradual, step-by-step and long-term, but that it would definitely come if he stayed the course.

As pledged, Fischer remade his life. The bars and restaurants of Bonn (no longer the German capital but still the seat of the Bundestag) lost their appeal. Mineral water replaced wine and beer. Baseball cap on backwards, in shorts and hooded sweatshirt, he expanded his daily loop to a couple of kilometers and then five and then ten. "With every additional hundred grams that I shed, the distances became longer and the strides lighter."[18] And with jogging, his new love and excess, Fischer discovered another passion: classical music. With a Discman strapped to his body, operas, concertos, and requiems resounded in his head during the dawn workouts. If he couldn't do a morning run, he lit out at night through Bonn's deserted streets.

Less than a year after his first outing, Fischer had shed eighty-two pounds. He now ran by day as well, to the delight of photographers who gladly documented his latest transformation. Lean in body and face, drenched in sweat and with a grimace of determination, he looked like a new man, the one he had set out to create. In Herlinde Koelbl's black-and-white portraits, his double chins and the flesh that had encased his features melt away. His expressive eyes and generous outcrop of a nose dominate an angular face again. The massive belly is entirely gone. His look is of a man at peace with himself, someone who has won a second lease on life and knows it—but also of a man more cocksure of himself than ever. His goal of slimming down to 176 pounds seemed assured. "Now I had to know," he wrote, "the question had to be answered: could I really get down to 165 pounds. 165 pounds! That was exactly my weight in 1983, when I ended my comfortable bohemian life and entered the Bundestag."[19]

By the kickoff of election year 1998, Fischer was in fact proudly down to his old "fighting weight," as he put it, and well into training for his first marathon.* The image of ascetic monk had replaced that of indulgent connoisseur. In the meantime he had also published another book (on globalization and economics) and was soon to meet his fourth wife, the twentysomething journalist Nicola Leske.

Project Red-Green

By the sixteenth year of Helmut Kohl's "eternal chancellorship," as weary observers put it, Germany was overdue for a change in leadership. Had it not been for East Germany's disintegration and the "unification bonus," the conservative-liberal government, by then already a spent force, would probably have been shown the door in 1990. The coalition had long since run out of fresh ideas for a country desperately in need of them. Germany labored under nearly 11 percent unemployment (an astounding 17 percent in the east) and a flat economy that belied no signs of rebounding. The sixty-eight-year-old Kohl and his Christian Democrats seemed too lethargic and old-school to tackle the challenges of a dynamic, global, digital world.

The fact that the German government still officially resided in Bonn spoke volumes about the Kohl administration's worldview: seven years after naming Berlin as Germany's new capital the government still operated from the sleepy banks of the Rhine. Kohl was a Rhinelander himself and his Germany was that of West Germany, now with the remnants of a failed state tacked on to it. Even though he laid the foundations of the Berlin Republic, the term as such never crossed his lips. The best the conservatives could do in the 1990s was to keep the creaky welfare state afloat through soaring budget deficits and look away from the thickening malaise in the new eastern states (the territory of the former GDR). The Kohl administration had vastly underestimated—or, according to some, purposely fudged—the cost and complexity of integrating the five new states into the Federal Republic. Since 1990 the gross annual transfers from the federal budget to the eastern states was approximately $125 billion a year, three-quarters of which was in aid and subsidies.[20] Estimates for just moving the

* On April 19, 1998, Fischer completed the Hamburg marathon in 3 hours and 41 minutes—4,179th place of the 10,134 runners to go the entire distance.

capital from Bonn to Berlin ranged from $11 to more than $15 billion. These costs were largely picked up by the (western) taxpayers in the form of a "solidarity tax."

The conservatives' lackluster performance made it easy for the Social Democrats to shine—and promise better things without providing details. The party's candidate for chancellor, fifty-four-year-old Gerhard Schröder, cut a figure of vitality in contrast to the Christian Democrats' tired guard. His shirtsleeves rolled up at the elbows, the compact square-jawed man, son of a simple working-class family, cast himself as a can-do modernizer who would push for innovation and reform without losing sight of social responsibility. Schröder urged his party to appeal to the "new center" of society, extolling the way Tony Blair had refashioned New Labour in Great Britain and Clinton had revamped the Democrats in the United States. Very little was said about the kind of reforms that Germany required or the price that would have to be paid for them.

The Social Democrats had more or less accepted that the price they might have to pay for the chancellorship was a ruling partnership with the Greens. The only other reasonable alternative was a grand coalition with the Christian Democrats, which some Social Democrats still favored. Yet the SPD's guiding lights, Schröder and Oscar Lafontaine, knew the Greens and themselves came from the broader sixty-eight generation. During the Hot Autumn of 1983, together with Petra Kelly they had appeared on the streets with millions of other Germans protesting NATO's Euromissiles and, at one time, had even questioned the straitjacket of the Atlantic alliance in the same breath as they did the free market. In Lower Saxony, Schröder as state president had headed a red–green coalition for four years; and the left-winger Lafontaine was one of the first to embrace the Greens as a viable coalition partner in the 1980s. Among most voters as well, the eco-pacifists were by now familiar, their bite in office considerably less ferocious than their bark in opposition. That said, the Social Democrats stopped short of explicitly promoting a red–green republic as their objective. The Greens were partners of necessity for the Social Democrats, just as they had been in the first ever red–green coalition in Hesse, and they would be accommodated at the lowest possible price, which entailed the SPD's remaining coy about a coalition until the ballots were counted.

While the possibility of a red–green coalition didn't unravel Germans the way it had in the past, left-baiting still packed a punch, especially when the Greens invited it. At their pre-campaign congress in the depressed eastern city of Magdeburg, the party endorsed an ecological tax that would triple the price of gasoline by 2008, as well as a sharply reduced speed limit and the legalization of soft drugs. There was general agreement on the leitmotifs that should guide Germany's interaction with the world beyond its borders: universal human rights, multilateralism, German self-containment, European integration, conflict prevention, disarmament, and aid to the developing world. But the party's pacifists, with a single-vote majority among the 500-plus delegates in Magdeburg, ruled out German soldiers' participation in peacekeeping missions, including in Bosnia. A majority also stuck resolutely to NATO's eventual dissolution, as well as a halving of the German army, a complete ban on arms sales, the abolition of the draft, and hefty cuts in the defense budget.

Ever on the lookout for left-of-center "excesses," the day after the Magdeburg congress *Bild-Zeitung* plastered the good news across its front page: "Gas 5 marks, speed limit 100 [kilometers per hour], hashish free, dissolve NATO–GREEN NIGHTMARE!"[21] While the so-called excesses weren't bad policy (for example, the receipts from the "eco-tax" would go toward research for alternative energies while promoting energy conservation and cutting carbon dioxide emissions), they were inopportune politics. The Greens experienced a backlash almost at once; they began to hemorrhage votes in one state contest after another.

Yet for the most part, the Germany that the Greens envisioned in their election platform combined a dash of utopia with many reasonable, nuts-and-bolts policies. In fact, in contrast to some of their rivals, their platform was packed with solid policy ideas and proposals, the by-product of sympathetic think tanks, NGOs, and university institutes that now existed across the country. In the universities, the student renegades of the late 1960s and 1970s were full professors, department chairs, and even deans. The concerns of the social movements had been institutionalized in well-funded "peace research" institutes and environmental think tanks. Their specialists weren't "counterexperts" anymore, simply experts. Their research and analysis fed Greens policy in areas such as the energy sector, for example, where the Greens laid out detailed plans to switch over to renewable energies and meet—even exceed—the carbon dioxide emission benchmarks set by the Kyoto Conference on Climate Change.

Nevertheless, despite its many sound ideas, the Magdeburg platform hung like a millstone around the party's neck, causing the Greens to lurch into a tailspin just as the 1998 election campaign kicked off. The gas tax couldn't have struck a more sour note in down-and-out eastern cities like Magdeburg. Leading Social Democrats warned that there'd be no coalition with this kind of Greens party.[22] The Greens stumbled and then scrambled to right themselves before all was lost. A damage-control "100-day" mini-program omitted the details of the gas tax and emphasized social programs like job creation. No sooner did pragmatists backtrack on nuclear power—proposing a two-year phase-out period—than they had environmental groups at their throats. The detractors put it this way: the Greens' once unique vision for the country had faded to the point that it was now simply the lesser of evils.

The Greens' party politics seemed to go on below the clouds that were buffeting Joschka Fischer into ever higher realms of the republic's stratosphere. In a bright green, double-decker "Joschka bus" that would become his campaign hallmark, the party's undisputed maestro stumped nonstop throughout the blistering summer, filling town squares, farmers' markets, and auditoriums from the Alps to the Baltic Sea. Kids and policemen alike sought his autograph. Joschka Fischer, pop star. Every day, in front of the cameras, he'd set out in shorts, tank top, and sneakers for a brisk eight-, ten-, or even fifteen-kilometer workout. His aides estimated that by the September vote the newly dubbed "marathon man" would have traveled over 9,000 miles, 600 of them on foot. "A tour to the brink of exhaustion," commented the *Spiegel*. "Fischer always goes for broke."[23]

In the Bundestag, the trim and buffed Fischer took on yet another incarnation: statesman. In a gray suit, immaculate white shirt, and silver-blue tie and with gold-rimmed bifocals perched on his nose, the urbane citizen of the world assured establishment doubters that a Fischer foreign policy wouldn't deviate from the sound norms established by its predecessors. In a speech at one of Germany's most esteemed think tanks, Fischer emphasized the "continuities" of German foreign policy. As for the transatlantic partnership, he reminded the seasoned diplomats in attendance that the United States had intervened in Europe three times during the twentieth century (World War I, World War II, Bosnia) to secure peace on the continent for the very reason that Europeans couldn't do it themselves. There would be no spurning of this tried-and-true ally so critical to Germany's democracy. But his most intriguing comment came in the context of the escalating conflict in Kosovo, Serbia's southernmost province, where a new round of Serb-led ethnic cleansing was driving ethnic Albanians from their homes. Fischer warned that Europe couldn't afford to make "the mistakes of Bosnia" again. The international community had to have "an option of last resort" should all peaceful means to resolve the crisis fail.[24]

The more prominent Fischer became, the more those around him noticed that some of his less appealing qualities were growing more and more pronounced. Fischer had always been full of himself, a know-it-all, and somewhat of a bully, as those in the Frankfurt scene or the Bundestag groups could attest. He dominated those around him, be it significant others, colleagues, journalists, even friends. This was a side of him, however, that was largely shielded from public view. It didn't come across on the cameras and, until the election year 1998, wasn't worthy of media attention. But the German journalists with him on the campaign trail began to note it in their publications. "He was always rude, that wasn't new," explains Bettina Gaus, Bonn correspondent of the *Tageszeitung*, and admittedly, not an admirer. In the Greens-friendly paper she noted how he spoke down to waiters in restaurants, ignored acquaintances when he felt like it, and verbally abused her colleagues.[25] "He seemed to enjoy being rude and [in the 1998 campaign] seemed to be testing how far he could go, just how rude he could be and get away with it." "Those people who seem to like Fischer most," commented another journalist, referring to the opinion polls, "are those who don't personally know him."

On September 27, 1998, in Germany's last federal election of the millennium, 50 million voters sealed one epoch and unveiled another. The historic evening belonged to the next chancellor, Gerhard Schröder. His Social Democrats captured a commanding 41 percent of the vote. Together with the Greens' serviceable 6.7 percent, the two parties owned a solid majority of Bundestag seats—a majority to the left of the Christian Democrats, fifteen years after Willy Brandt had heralded it, and in a united Germany. In terms of its implications, commentators likened the vote to the momentous victory of Brandt's Social Democrats in 1969. Yet unlike all hitherto transfers of power, a red–green administration would spell the first time in the republic's history that a change of government would make a clean break with all of the parties in the incumbent coalition.

Arms raised over his head flashing the victory sign, a radiant but duly respectful Gerhard Schröder personified the popular will for a fresh start. "How smoothly it all went," reported the *Spiegel*, "as if everybody in Germany was just waiting for this new force to sweep away Kohl's structures. The Bonn Republic is history."[26] The landmark vote ushered in a new generation, a new administration, and a new seat of government—the leadership of the Berlin Republic would (very soon) reside in the German capital. At SPD headquarters in Bonn, the pent-up frustration of sixteen years in opposition was vented with jubilation, thundering applause for

Schröder, and case after case of Champagne. When SPD supporters began to chant, their words were muffled, nearly inaudible. On stage, Schröder grinned and playfully cupped his hand to his ear. "I can't hear anything up here," he toyed with them. "*Rot–Grün*!" [red–green] they boomed back at him, practically shaking the building's walls.[27]

In the course of the evening, the Greens' leaders trekked over to congratulate the chancellor-to-be. The prospect of hardnosed coalition negotiations ahead didn't spoil the buoyant mood. Neither did the fact that stemming the country's chronic unemployment would require more than sloganeering. Germany's stubborn joblessness fueled Schröder's victory; a staggering 90 percent of all voters said jobs were this election's key issue.[28] Voters passed to Schröder the mandate that Kohl couldn't fulfill, and he goaded them to hold him to his promise: "If we haven't turned around the labor market in four years, then we don't deserve to be re-elected."[29]

The frustrated eastern states did their part to turn out Kohl, emphatically switching their allegiance to the left-of-center. Eastern voters responded to the bread-and-butter rhetoric of social democracy. Yet the SPD wasn't any longer the only party in town that spoke that language. One of the election's biggest surprises was the Party for Democratic Socialism, PDS, which captured nearly 20 percent of the eastern vote, compared to a niggardly 1.1 percent in the west. Most onlookers thought that the PDS, the reformed and not so long ago despised former East German communist party, would vanish over time. But it was staging a vigorous comeback, slipping into the Bundestag and emerging on a par with the SPD and CDU in many regions of the east. To just about everyone's relief, the far-right parties flopped on both sides of the country. This Berlin Republic was one of the very few European states without a far-right party such as France's National Front or Jörg Haider's Austrian Freedom Party in its national parliament.

In contrast to the Greens' Bastille-storming entry into the Bundestag in 1983 or into the Hesse government in 1985, their entry into the federal government was welcomed by many of the German media's op-ed pages (whose editorial offices were now saturated with the children of the protest generations). Günter Hofmann of *Die Zeit* described the red–green victory as capping an era of cultural change. "Not only the Kohl era comes to an end but definitively the [Helmut] Schmidt years too," he wrote. The Greens arose from the new social movements, he reminded readers, "above all to pose an alternative to the ruling SPD, which the Greens accused of being unable to think in utopian categories or broach new questions. An entire generation broke away from the SPD." The way the Greens pushed the other parties to think about ecology and to open up political discourse was a "successful democratic experiment. Now, small but grown up, they sit by the side of the Social Democrats. One can almost speak of a kind of unification."[30]

The coalition talks between the SPD and the Greens produced a cabinet stacked full of protest-movement progeny and an agenda that came as close to a common red–green vision as the two parties would ever come. Greens occupied three ministries: Fischer as foreign minister* (and vice chancellor); the outspoken ex-fundi Jürgen Trittin in the environment ministry; and former *Tageszeitung* staffer, thirty-eight-year-old Andrea Fischer, as health minister. In addition to Schröder and Lafontaine, many of the Social Democrat ministers and deputy ministers had agitated in the Jusos, the party's left-wing youth organization, during the sixties and seventies. In total, five women were appointed to ministerial posts, the most ever, crowning three decades of women's liberation. (Women also took 30 percent of seats in the Bundestag, another statistic for the record books.)[31] The new interior minister, Otto Schily, was a first-hour Greens turned Social Democrat. In other top posts, too, there were familiar faces like Greens party founder Marieluise Beck, Third World campaigner Ludger Volmer, and eco-feminist Christa Nickels. The former East German dissident Gerd Poppe of Alliance 90 headed up a newly created office for human rights.

Although the new red–green government was immediately dubbed "the political project of the '68 generation," it wasn't by any means a homogeneous bloc of ex-sixty-eighters that had stormed to the front of the republic but, rather, a smorgasbord of the postwar protest generations. The youngest MP and later deputy minister, Greens Matthias Berninger, was born in 1971, an impressionable teenager during the peace movement. The sum total was a team that shared a common political culture and assumptions about Germany's past, the nature of the republic's democracy, and what a modern Germany should look like. The long march through the institutions may not have taken the path that Rudi Dutschke envisioned, but its representatives were there, at the helm of the republic, with the opportunity to leave an indelible mark.

---

* There had been talk of the Greens receiving four ministries—namely, both the Third World development ministry and the Transportation, Construction and Urban Development Ministry rather than the Foreign Ministry. Advocates of this option argued that the Greens could accomplish much more of the Greens agenda in these two "lower profile" ministries, both areas central to Greens' concerns, than in the much higher profile Foreign Ministry. But Fischer insisted on the esteemed Auswärtiges Amt for himself.

Any pretence of red–green harmony vanished the moment the doors closed and coalition negotiations began. Even though seasoned in the rough ways of red–green coalitions, the Greens' frontmen Fischer and Trittin found there would be no grace period in the Schröder era, either. Although in word the SPD heralded a fresh approach to immigration, the soon-to-be interior minister Schily squelched hopes for a progressive immigration law. The coalition's security policies sounded suspiciously similar to those of the Christian Democrats. The Greens' stamp, however, did appear elsewhere on the coalition contract, if not quite as boldly as they had wished. The government committed itself to formulating a new citizenship law and three-stage ecological tax. The new partners also pledged to "set into law and make irreversible" Germany's exit from nuclear energy. Here, however, consensus ceased: the Social Democrats envisioned a (very) long phase-out plan that would be crafted in consultation with the utility companies. Since the government would not—the Social Democrats underlined—pay a *Pfennig* of financial compensation to the energy companies, a compromise between the government and the power companies had to be the basis of a deal.

In the realm of foreign policy, the mediators put cautious red–green touches on familiar postures. Front and center was a line taken verbatim from the Greens' 1980 charter: "German foreign policy is peace policy." German arms exports would be linked to human rights criteria, the Organization for Security and Cooperation in Europe (OSCE) strengthened, the Third World prioritized, and conflict-prevention mechanisms developed. The European Union's foreign and security policies were to be given real clout (when the Germans took over the rotating EU presidency in 1999.) In dealing with troublesome regions and ornery dictators, the contract stressed conditionally linked aid over military coercion, creative diplomacy over threats and ultimatums, and multilateralism over everything. Despite all public avowals to the contrary, three words in a brief sentence might arguably have indicated an incremental shift in orientation: "The United States is Germany's most important partner outside of Europe." In the days of the Bonn Republic, the last words would surely have been omitted.

Baptism by Fire

While the red–green coalition talks were in progress, an extraordinary series of parallel events unfolded in Bonn. They would have an enormous impact on the red–green government and, indeed, on the character of the

Berlin Republic. Behind the scenes, frantic diplomacy was being enacted between Germany's defeated but still governing leadership, the German leadership-elect, and the United States, including President Bill Clinton personally. The issue was Germany's involvement in NATO's plans to launch an air campaign against Slobodan Milosevic's Yugoslavia should Belgrade not cease hostilities against the Kosovar Albanians. The situation in Kosovo, the mostly Albanian-populated Serbian province, had been deteriorating steadily since 1996. Belatedly, international diplomacy shot into high gear to find a solution—before the nightmare of Bosnia repeated itself. After seven years of passive nonviolent resistance, an armed ethnic Albanian guerrilla movement had arisen and had begun staging attacks against Serbian police units. Milosevic responded by dispatching paramilitary police and national army units, which stomped through the Kosovar countryside in the summer of 1998, forcing hundreds of thousands of ethnic Albanians to flee their homes. A September U.N. resolution demanded that Serbia stop the offensive and that ethnic Albanians and Serbs begin negotiations. The Serbs ignored it.

President Clinton felt that the international community had to back up its demands with a credible threat of force: NATO air strikes against Serbia, if it came to that, similar to those launched with result against the Bosnian Serbs. Clinton's dilemma was that to employ military force within the bounds of international law (against another sovereign state that hadn't attacked a NATO member), alliance forces required the authorization of the United Nations Security Council, one of whose five permanent members was Russia, China another. It was a certainty that Moscow, having stood by the Serbs in the past, would not acquiesce. Thus, a NATO combat mission without a United Nations mandate would be, technically, illegal. This was one interpretation. Another, preferred by Washington, maintained that intervention could be justified in order to avert a humanitarian catastrophe in Kosovo—in other words, in the spirit of international human rights conventions, also part of international law. Washington was in a tricky legal and moral bind, and it needed its closest allies' full backing to legitimize any bombing. One of those allies was Washington's long-loyal friend in continental Europe, the Federal Republic of Germany.

This was the geopolitical backdrop to the September 1998 German elections in which two unfamiliar, untested left-of-center parties emerged victorious—one of which called itself pacifist and shunned NATO. Twelve days after the vote, even before coalition negotiations had begun, Schröder and Fischer commenced diplomacy with a blitz trip to Washington, D.C., to meet with the president and discuss the crisis. In a half-hour working lunch, the Germans convinced Clinton that although Germany was resolutely on his side, until a new government was formed, preferably in a few weeks time, it would rather sit out a bombing campaign against Serbia. Germany would condone air strikes against Yugoslavia—even without a U.N. mandate—but would not contribute aircraft or military personnel until the new Bundestag could vote on it. Clinton consented.[32]

Fischer and Schröder returned to Germany greatly relieved to have this hot potato out of their laps, if only for the moment. But their relief was premature. Three days later, in Bonn, Chancellor Kohl called them out of coalition talks on an urgent matter. In his office, Kohl informed them that Washington had changed its mind: Clinton wanted the Germans fully on board, including pilots and military hardware at NATO's disposal. The reason given was that a third of NATO's AWACS (airborne warning and control systems) were manned by Bundeswehr officers and Germany's fourteen Tornado aircraft were specially equipped to take out antiaircraft weaponry. NATO was on red alert, poised for its first active deployment in its fifty-year history. "Fifteen minutes," remembered Fischer, "We had fifteen minutes to decide on the question of war or peace."[33]

Their answer was yes. Kohl and his team (still in office) were already on board, although few bought the story about the AWACS and a handful of Tornados. More likely, the whole drama was a ploy to put the red–green novices to an early test, to see if they really stood by their declarations of allegiance. Another rumor was that Kohl's men had tipped off Washington, whispering in the right ears that this course would be a lot easier than a drawn-out debate later in a Bundestag dominated by Social Democrats and Greens. "The effect was to lock in the decision without a full-scale, open debate," says Otfried Nassauer, the former peace movement organizer, since 1991 director of a small peace research institute in Berlin.

Yet Bundestag confirmation of the decision was still needed. If Greens and Social Democrats objected to the Schröder-Fischer "yes," then they could cast their ballots against it. In a historically unprecedented, legally questionable move, Chancellor Kohl reconvened the old Bundestag for a special session on October 16. The debate over the momentous issue was scattered and rushed. In the end, 500 of 580 MPs approved German participation in the NATO action. Even among Greens there was a supportive majority: twenty-nine for, nine against, seven abstentions. (There were also twenty-one Social Democrats as well as the entire PDS faction that voted "no".) With this decision, the Bundestag Greens put their pacifist legacy behind them and voted against the will of the majority, the party's grassroots, as expressed at its party congress a year earlier. A showdown between the party's grassroots and its elected leadership was thus foreordained. The decision not only violated the Greens' nominal pacifism but also their virtually sacred commitment to international law and to the United Nations as the world's highest multilateral body. They had, de facto, sided with Washington and NATO over the United Nations.

The one-sided Bundestag vote illustrated that a new set of criteria guided Germany's geopolitical engagement in the world, even if these criteria hadn't been publicly debated or even clearly articulated by any party or person. A ferocious debate, just as Kohl's team had predicted, was in the offing. Its parameters would distinguish the Berlin Republic from its predecessor. What, for example, were the political goals or national interests that justify Germany's waging war? Is the inviolability of sovereignty (the rights of states) or the protection of human rights (the rights of people) the higher good? What principles guided German foreign policy now that the coordinates of Cold War Europe lay at the bottom of history's dustbin?

Although the way was now cleared for Germany's first "hot war" in half a century, the day would be postponed. In typical Milosevic brinksmanship, Belgrade backed down at the last minute, agreeing to a cease-fire and the deployment of several thousand international monitors in Kosovo. There would be no bombing in 1998. Relieved, the SPD and Greens leaderships prepared to take office, although no one believed that Kosovo had gone away.

In his new post, Germany's top diplomat tread softly his first days in the foreign ministry, keenly aware that he was regarded with considerable misgiving and that ruffling the feathers of Germany's high-brow diplomatic corps was not the foot to begin on. "We were foreign there, for sure, and we felt it," says Georg Dick, Fischer's loyal spokesman from Hesse, who'd been brought to run the planning office. The word in the halls of the ministry itself was that German foreign policy would remain firmly in professional hands—and not fall into those of neophyte left-wing politicians. This was typical of the German Foreign Ministry, which tended to see German foreign policy as something above the hurly-burly of politics, to be interpreted and turned into policy by its elite corps. To ensure this remained the case, Fischer was able to bring just four of his own people with him into the ministry of 8,500 employees. The message was unmistakable: it will be business as usual, regardless of this new bunch. Fischer signaled that he understood; not one of the four appointees came from the Greens' prodigious ranks of peace researchers or foreign policy specialists.

From the outset, Fischer emphasized he wouldn't be playing party politics in his new office: "I'm not a Greens foreign minister but the foreign minister of all Germans. There won't be a Green foreign policy."[34] As it turned out, he wouldn't break his word. On the job, Fischer, true to form, took quickly to the diplomatic jargon and protocol, as well as to his new colleagues and they to him—at first. "He's very open-minded, open to new ideas and intellectual provocations. He asks for our opinion and listens, unlike the last guy," a ranking diplomat said at the time, referring to Fischer's unloved predecessor, Klaus Kinkel. Although by now an old pro at learning and internalizing system logics, this challenge was a quantum leap even for Fischer—one false step or an indelicate remark could set off a diplomatic brouhaha.

As his initial move, Fischer had to shore up the confidence of Germany's most important strategic allies. First, to Warsaw, to underscore Germany's commitment to Poland's membership in the European Union and NATO, as well as Germany's recognition of its special historic debt to that nation. Next to the key western European leaders, in Paris, London, and later Moscow. The mantra he'd repeat was: continuity, human rights, multilateral cooperation, and, of course, Europe, Europe, and more Europe for Germany.[35] A week later, it was off to Washington—officially this time—to meet his new counterpart at the State Department, Madeleine Albright (nee Korbel). The tough-talking madam secretary wanted a reading on this "committed pacifist," as she put it in her autobiography, apparently oblivious to Fischer's nonpacifist past.[36] The American media, also unfamiliar with Fischer, had preconceived reservations, thinking perhaps that they were getting a male version of Petra Kelly. They wondered aloud whether this alliance, so critical to U.S. interests in the past, would remain as cozy as it had been for half a century. Some speculated that maybe the common central European heritage of Fischer and Albright would enable the two to bond. The journalists, however, overlooked the fact that her family (the Korbels) fled Nazi-occupied Prague for London during the war (and later sought asylum in the United States when the communists took over Czechoslovakia), while Fischer's family had collaborated with the Nazi-allied Hungarian army and had been expelled for being ethnic Germans. But this baggage was irrelevant. What Albright wanted was a pledge of support for U.S. policy in Iraq, where at the time Saddam Hussein was impeding United Nations arms inspectors.

Albright's apprehensions about Fischer were quickly dispelled. In fact, they hit it off at once. After dispensing with the ritual pledges of cooperation and eternal German-American friendship, the two emerged later from a tête-à-tête as chummy as old school buddies. Chuckling through a press conference, they jested about Albright's bright green dress (she protested she hadn't chosen it for the occasion) and announced that after their short acquaintance they were on first-name basis: Joschka and Madeleine, the beginning of a diplomatic friendship.

If Fischer had surmised that his profuse deference to western alliance orthodoxy might win him marginal room to tinker with it, he soon learned otherwise. His first foray outside the straight and narrow was blown straight back at him. Fischer, in line with the red–green coalition manifesto, challenged his alliance co-members to rethink NATO's "first-use" nuclear option, a central tenet of Cold War nuclear doctrine.[37] According to NATO strategy, the western alliance required the first-use option because of the Soviets' alleged superiority of conventional ground forces in Europe. The prerogative to launch a "defensive" nuclear strike in response to a nonnuclear Soviet attack on NATO territory was at the heart of deterrence theory. The first-use option had been a key part of the equation that supposedly kept the overall military balance—and thus the peace—on the continent. Fischer argued that since both the Soviet Union and the Cold War had withdrawn into history's recesses, the original justification of NATO's first-use doctrine was presumably superfluous—a holdover that now, arguably, had a destabilizing effect on a world armed to the teeth with nuclear weapons. An array of international peace groups, Europe-wide Greens, and even the Canadian government advocated a general "no first use" pledge by all nuclear powers and, further, the scrapping of first-strike nuclear missiles. The foreign minister had barely uttered the words before the rebukes came fast and furious. NATO's three nuclear powers—France, Great Britain, and the United States—as well as the Social Democrat–run German defense ministry, sprang to defend NATO's first-strike capabilities, clamoring that what wasn't broke shouldn't be fixed. Fischer was forced to climb down; he found himself meekly defending the right of all NATO member countries to discuss new ideas. This idea, however, was never discussed again.

An idea more important and closer to Fischer's own heart was that of a federal Europe. At first in bits and pieces, and then in a much-heralded address at Berlin's Humboldt University, Fischer unveiled an open-ended proposal for a federal Europe, a project even more ambitious and visionary than the ad hoc union of states that the European Union had become.[38] Nearly a decade after the erasure of Europe's synthetic division, he beseeched his colleagues in Paris, London, and Rome to bring European integration to its rightful culmination: a European federation with a bicameral parliament, one president, a constitution, and democratically invested supranational powers. The task ahead of European Union leaders was to turn the institution that had started as a free trade zone with six members—and since grown to a community of fifteen—into a single political union that could one day embrace as many as thirty members, expanding eastward into central Europe, the Baltic states, and southeast toward the Balkans. The first round of eastward expansion was already in the works and the euro would soon become the European Union's common currency, tying together the members' economies more tightly than ever before. But all of this was just the beginning of an even bigger project.

This blueprint wasn't all Fischer's own; some of the Scandinavian countries, perhaps the Netherlands, too, as well as clusters of Europhile elites in nearly every country also ascribed to broadly similar conceptions for Europe's future. But elsewhere—in fact, most everywhere else—the idea of such a strong federal system with authority in economic, foreign, security, and other policies was definitely not en vogue. Although nation-states wouldn't be abolished or their powers completely eviscerated, they would indeed hand over more and more sovereignty to a federal authority. "Fischer's ideas on Europe, which were basically Kohl's from the late 1980s, still had a realistic chance as late as 2000," says the German Marshall Fund's European Union expert Ulrike Guerot. "There was a window there but it required having both France and Germany, the twin engines of postwar European integration, thinking and acting in unison. They had to create that dynamic together in order to bring the others along." The way forward would have been to set a date for enlargement, to replace consensual with majority voting, to strengthen the European Parliament, to draw up a constitution, and to democratize at every level, explains Guerot.

But the French and the profoundly dubious British were not the only naysayers. There were also the Greens' Social Democratic coalition partners. On the one hand, virtually the entire German political class and, according to frequent opinion polls, well over two-thirds of Germans welcomed "more Europe." The Germans had been, and would remain, among the most passionate "Europeans" of the continent. They were used to surrendering authority to supranational bodies—and the Federal Republic had benefited from it, tremendously, over the postwar decades. A united

Germany, for example, was unthinkable without the Federal Republic's unswerving commitment to European integration. But a feature that would come to characterize the new Berlin Republic, particularly Gerhard Schröder's Berlin Republic, was a Germany that gave less selflessly and less uncritically to the European project than had the Bonn Republic.

With very little international experience, Schröder came to power determined to slash Germany's massive net payments to the European Union budget. Germany had long been the union's financier, its biggest net contributor by far. In 1998, for example, Germany paid 16 billion U.S. dollars more into the union's budget than it got back, accounting for nearly 60 percent of the total budget. In the period 1994–96, for the $29 that every French taxpayer contributed, his German counterpart paid in $264.[39] Schröder never claimed to be a Europhile, as both Fischer and Kohl did, and he didn't hesitate to speak forthrightly about "German national interests," as he saw them. "We cannot and will not solve the problems of Europe with a German checkbook," he pronounced.[40] This assertive, unselfconscious tone was new for Germany, which in the postwar past had never dared to speak so brashly about "national interests." Schröder wasn't in principle opposed to "more Europe." He, for example, claimed that he and his generation were European "because we want to be, not because we have to be."[41] But his fighting like a terrier to wrestle back rebates from Great Britain or cut French agricultural subsidies diverted attention and energy from the larger goal. These issues and others set France and Germany against one another, undermining the possibility of driving the political union forward. In fact, paradoxically, Fischer's vision of a United Europe collided with the Berlin Republic. Schröder's assertiveness and unashamed national tone ensured that the idea never made it past square one. Although there were many other reasons for the dooming of a federal Europe, one could argue that it fell victim to the new Germany itself.

Kosovo Again

In no time, Kosovo was back on the front pages. Hopes were quickly dashed that the imposed cease-fire, monitored by the OSCE, might buy the party's time to broker a settlement. The Kosovo Liberation Army, or KLA, resumed sporadic attacks on Serb points. Serb police and army units reinfiltrated the province and struck back in typically bellicose fashion. Hardly a week passed without some combination of kidnappings, raids, murders, bomb explosions, public funerals, and street protests. The Balkans were spinning out of control again.

On January 19, 1999, after skirmishes all week with the KLA in the vicinity, Serb forces entered the village of Racak and killed forty-five Kosovar Albanian civilians, including a twelve-year-old boy and two women. This was for many, including Fischer, the final straw. An atrocity like that at Racak, all too reminiscent of atrocities in Bosnia, was exactly what the West feared most—another Srebrenica. The actors on the ground were virtually identical: Yugoslav army units, local Serb police, roving paramilitary gangs, and an under-armed international mission with an inadequate mandate.

With the cease-fire in tatters, western leaders pulled out all stops to reach a political solution before the entire region burst into flames. Serb and Kosovar-Albanian representatives were summoned to meet with international mediators in Rambouillet, outside of Paris. The setup was along the lines of the 1995 Dayton peace talks, when Washington sequestered Balkan leaders at the Wright-Patterson Air Force Base in Ohio to hammer out an accord for postwar Bosnia. But this meeting, convened by Madeleine Albright, was in Europe, and this time the Europeans were speaking with one voice. Since Germany held both the EU and the G-8 presidencies at the time, that voice was very often Fischer's, a tall order for the newcomer. The Rambouillet talks ended in failure as the Serbs refused the international demand for NATO troops in Kosovo to aid a peacekeeping mission there.

In a last-gasp effort to avert war, Fischer traveled to Belgrade to offer Slobodan Milosevic all the carrots that the Euro-Atlantic alliance had to offer: the lifting of sanctions, Yugoslavia's reentry into international organizations, loans, foreign investment. But Fischer returned from the two-and-a-half hour parley empty-handed. In the wake of the good cop from Europe followed the bad cop from Washington—U.S. top negotiator Richard Holbrooke, not bearing carrots but wielding a stick, namely air strikes if Belgrade didn't acquiesce.

A week later, on March 24, 1999, NATO aircraft took off from bases in northern Italy to bomb Serbia into submission. In the first sortie were four Tornadoes flown by German pilots. Germany was in a shooting war for the first time in fifty-four years—without a U.N. mandate, against a sovereign state that hadn't attacked it or a NATO ally, in a region the Nazis had once wreaked terror upon, and under the leadership of a red–green government. "Germany goes to war, silently. No enthusiasm, naturally not, but also with astonishing little uproar," commented an editor of the weekly *Die Zeit.*[42] "What's so incredible is the simple acceptance of this in the Federal Republic after half a century of nonviolent foreign policy and a societal pacifism that we thought was deeply rooted." Was it blind conformism or "normality in the good sense"? asked *Die Zeit.* But, speculated the same author, if the bombardment dragged on, opposition could mount quickly. "The millions of peace demonstrators from the 1980s are all still there, even if not on the streets at the moment. Has their world really changed as much as Joschka Fischer's?" Had a Christian Democratic government attempted this forbidden step, the streets would have been full—with outraged Greens and Social Democrats.

Within the Greens camp, however, all was not tranquil; tensions were at breaking point from the start. This was a crisis bigger and more threatening than any of the others the party had weathered over two decades. The atmosphere was "extremely chilly," remembers Uschi Eid, a Greens MP at the time from southern Germany. "This was an exceptionally hard time, especially for those MPs who supported the intervention." Eid, fifty-six years old and American-educated, had come to the Greens through the Third World movement. She had called for U.N.–led international intervention—with German participation—in Rwanda in 1994 to stop the genocide there. For her, the use of military force against Milosevic's Yugoslavia was permissible. This, however, wasn't the opinion of a good chunk of her constituency from near Stuttgart, a region that contributed untold thousands to the peace movement, many of whom either belonged to the Greens or voted regularly for them. "My office was flooded with e-mails, letters, faxes, telephone calls," says Eid.

A Greens "antiwar faction" formed within the party, which included Greens Bundestag MPs. The dissidents' objections to the war went beyond the usual issues connected to the German questions. They claimed that the Kosovo intervention was a ploy to create a new justification for NATO—as global policeman—now that its original raison d'etre, the East–West confrontation, was no more. Atlantic alliance leaders, one of whom now was Fischer, had been spoiling for a war against Milosevic and had relied on falsified evidence to launch it. At Racak, they claimed with some, but not overwhelming documentation, the dead were KLA soldiers killed in a shoot-out, not civilians at all. And at Rambouillet international negotiators had intentionally "held the bar too high" for the Serbs, so high that they couldn't possibly sign. Moreover, Schröder and Fischer had knuckled under much too pliantly to the U.S. president's pressure. If Germany had stood up and said no to Clinton, other skeptical NATO countries, like Italy and Greece, would have been emboldened to join it in opposition.

The Greens critics' chief demand beyond an immediate cessation of bombing was the convening of an extraordinary party congress as soon as possible. The real Greens, the grassroots, they claimed, had yet to pass judgment on this war. Around the country, pro-intervention Greens like Eid had plenty of explaining to do. She says that many older constituents, not necessarily Greens voters but people who had directly experienced World War II, expressed trenchant reservations. To them "*nie wieder Krieg*" meant exactly that: war never again. At public panel discussions Greens like herself were practically "put on trial," she says. In the process, they were booed down and cursed as traitors, war-mongers, bomb-droppers. Eid argued that Germany had to decide about the use of force on a case-to-case basis:

> The question we had to ask is whether the use of force is absolutely necessary in this case. Not: I'm against it because I'm a pacifist, because I'm German. Rather, what evidence speaks for the case that mass murder is happening or genocide imminent that could be prevented? That's the question. This was a special case, under specific historical conditions, with no other alternative.

As the *Die Zeit* editorial warned in late March, the longer the air campaign stretched on, the more precarious the already tenuous position of the red–green government became. Initially, military strategists expected Milosevic to capitulate after a few days of bombing, at most a couple of weeks. But a solid month into the air strikes the Serbian leader stood fast and war consumed Kosovo. Hundreds of thousands of ethnic Albanians fled to overflowing refugee camps in neighboring Macedonia and Albania, thus destabilizing those countries. Civilian casualties mounted. Running out of targets, NATO was increasingly hitting Serbian infrastructure and industry. What was the point, critics asked, of bombing Serbia into the Stone Age? What would be left for a democratic post-Milosevic era? And, contrary to its purpose, the war seemed only to bolster Milosevic's popularity in Serbia while creating a living hell for ethnic Albanians in Kosovo. No one dreamed the campaign would last for seventy-eight days.

For no other state leader in the NATO alliance was the situation as high risk as it was for Fischer. He knew that his party would take only so much before it abandoned him. Without Greens support, the coalition would crumble, turning the red–green government into a historical footnote. The whole realo project, in fact, arguably, even the long march through the institutions, rode on Kosovo. If the Greens jumped ship now, their chances of ever returning to power would be nil. The Greens were the alliance's weakest link; it was Fischer's job to keep them on board. "The question isn't how long the Greens can hold out," he said at time, "but whether we as a ruling party are capable of coping with this extreme, wartime situation, engaging with the issues in a way so that the government can remain in office and be effective. That's the challenge. I would have been shocked if this war hadn't provoked a discussion in the party so fierce that it could tear the Greens apart."[43]

The day of reckoning was set for mid-May, when the Greens as a party would vote on the war. The clock was ticking and Fischer knew it. Two-thirds of Germans now felt that air strikes should be halted, negotiations restarted.[44] Washington appeared hamstrung, refusing to bend on its original demand that Milosevic accept the Rambouillet agreement or suffer the consequences. There was no Plan B should the Serbian leader not capitulate. The only alternatives to more and yet more bombing were a ground invasion or calling off the air campaign, basically an admission of defeat. The former option—deploying (German) troops to march on territory the Nazis once occupied—didn't have a wisp of support in Germany. Fischer and Schröder unequivocally ruled it out.

This was the context in which the Fischer plan surfaced in mid-April. All was not as static inside the walls of the German Foreign Ministry as might have appeared from beyond them. In contrast to Washington, the Fischer plan set the divisive Rambouillet document to one side. It would no longer be the basis of a settlement. In this spirit, it pulled the sidelined United Nations, and with it Russia, back on board by proposing that a U.N.–led peacekeeping mission administrate the postwar province, sanctioned by the Security Council and supported by U.N. blue helmet troops. The United Nations would run the interim protectorate until a long-term political solution could be found. This was something more palatable to Milosevic than the Rambouillet stipulations. Critically, having Russia with the West rather than against it would deprive Milosevic of his ostensibly staunchest ally and lend the alliance significantly more leverage to deal with Serbia.

The Fischer peace plan was a bold and shrewd initiative, a classic piece of West German diplomacy—a creative alternative to superpower thinking, broadly multilateral and reaching out to bridge the gap between East and West. Although it initially met with an icy silence from Washington, the peace plan would form the basis of the accord that would end the war.

First, though, Fischer and his allies in the Greens had to quell a growing rebellion much closer to home. The Greens' extraordinary party congress, called for May 13 in the northwestern city of Bielefeld, would be the most important, turbulent, and drama-packed of the little party's twenty-year history. The nearly 800 delegates from across the country would cast their votes on the red–green government's Kosovo policies. Had red–green not been in power—or a Greens not been foreign minister—the outcome of the congress would have mattered little. But this was not the case. Germany's red–green government was a cornerstone of the international alliance against Milosevic. It was imperative that Fischer's party back him, and it was this he was asking for in Bielefeld.

For party pacifists, like Hamburg delegate Ulrich Cremer, the congress's purpose was to get the Greens' elected representatives in the government to adhere to the positions that the Greens as a party had already agreed upon. "Throughout the entire 1990s a majority consensus in the party supported pacifist positions, every time," says Cremer, pointing to the recent congresses. "We expected a Greens foreign minister to implement the party's foreign policy positions. This is why we voted for him. If he doesn't, then there should be consequences." Cremer says that leading up to the congress, the government tried to "blackmail" party delegates by posing a vote against the party leadership as a death knell to the red–green coalition. "There was no reason the coalition would fall apart or have to step down," he argues. "Germany could have simply withdrawn its support for the bombing and demanded a unilateral, unconditional cease-fire. If it did, there would have been a chain reaction. Other countries would surely have followed."

Never had a Greens party congress experienced a security presence such as at Bielefeld. The tables had turned 180 degrees. Hundreds of riot police ringed the congress hall to protect the party leadership from Germany's disgruntled left. Skirmishes with far-left *Autonomen* and Serbian émigrés caused the congress to start late. Inside, the atmosphere was fetid. Long-time fellow veterans of the social movements weren't speaking to one another. Others engaged in shouting matches. As the speeches and the complex process of formulating resolutions began, so did the competing ovations and booing.

On the stage, against a bright green backdrop with the Greens' sunflower symbol and the congress theme "Bringing together human rights and peace," sat the party's national leadership, Fischer among them, wearing a black T-shirt and black sports jacket, his bifocals the only familiar accessory from his foreign minister apparel. Shortly before the congress got under way, a small group of anarchist *Autonomen*, one dreadlocked, completely naked young man among them, burst through the security lines and into the hall. Scuffles broke out as they rushed the elevated podium. In the commotion, one protester let fly a paint-filled balloon in the direction of the stage. The projectile hit Fischer squarely in the head, exploding against his ear and covering the right side of his face and torso with red paint. As the security guards pushed back the assailants, Fischer's colleagues rushed to his aid. Fischer winced with pain as he wiped the paint off his face and jacket with napkins. Although doctors would later diagnosis a broken eardrum, at the time Fischer refused medical help. He had to give what was probably the most critical speech of his life since May 1976, when he pleaded with the West German left to renounce violence. This time he was telling them why they had to support it.

Amid a hail of interspersed invective and applause, Fischer, with the red paint smeared on his jacket and traces still visible on his face, appealed to the delegates to endorse the government course. It had and would continue to do everything in its power to end the war. "No other government has done more than ours to find a diplomatic solution to end the crisis," he pleaded. His arguments were already known to everyone there. He never thought he'd have to choose between the two axioms that had always guided his political activism: "Never again war" and "Never again Auschwitz." But it had come to that. The international community had to use the instruments of war to stop mass murder, to prevent another genocide in Europe. The veins in his neck pulsing wildly as he spoke, Fischer strained his voice to conclude: "I understand all too well your arguments and reservations. They're mine, too. I wage this debate with myself everyday. But I nevertheless ask you to have the strength to accept responsibility, as difficult as that may be. What I ask as foreign minister is that you help me steer this course. Please support me, strengthen me, don't weaken me."[45]

At the end of a very long day, the congress reversed its former positions: 444 for the leadership's resolution, 318 for that of Cremer and the pacifists. Fischer had won time—but not limitless time. Despite the Unites States' initial reservations, the Fischer plan kickstarted another round of diplomatic activity after a long impasse. Over the course of weeks, Russian, U.N.–European, and U.S. envoys, in consultation with Belgrade through Moscow, began to cobble together a resolution to end the conflict and lay the grounds for a postwar international presence in Kosovo. The civilian peacekeeping component would be a U.N. mission, the military force NATO-led but including Russia. Yugoslav troops and paramilitaries would withdraw from Kosovo. All refugees could return. Milosevic, worn down after ten weeks of war, his country debilitated by 15,000 NATO bombs, signed the agreement on June 9. The air strikes were halted the next day.

Germany's red–green government had survived an ordeal that no one would have thought possible when it came to office just seven months before. The geopolitical implications of the Kosovo campaign for German foreign policy outstripped anything undertaken by the Kohl administration over its sixteen years, save unification. "It was the very parties that wrote pacifism and a nonmilitaristic foreign policy on their banners," notes political scientist Hans Jörg Hennecke, "that dared to shake the republic loose from its Bonn origins and pursue a course that would have an even greater imprint on Germany's collective consciousness than their vaunted environmental and social reforms."[46]

The Kosovo intervention established that not only could a united Germany participate in foreign wars in the name of humanitarianism but that its neighbors and allies expected it to do so. At the same time, the general skepticism in Germany about involvement in armed conflicts provided the Berlin Republic with a unique, built-in check against irresponsible military ventures. In no other country was the debate over war and peace in the Balkans as heated as it was in Germany. There would be more to come. The unique role that Germany could play in world trouble spots, as it did in Kosovo, came more sharply into focus. Taking a page from West Germany's *Ostpolitik*, Berlin could act as mediator, as bridge between East and West as well as between Europe and the United States. Germany could also come up with alternative security options. Germany was both a loyal ally and the source of constructive, diplomatic options. Kosovo showed that Germany was in the position to lead when it has sufficient support and allies behind it. According to Egon Bahr, a former adviser to Willy Brandt and one of Ostpolitik's fathers:

> Kosovo illustrated the full parameters in which German foreign policy could operate. We can take the lead in some cases, as the Fischer plan did. On the other hand, in vital questions, like introducing ground troops into Kosovo, we can say "no," which we did. Thus Germany also has a negative, preventive power on important issues. Today's Germany can't ask for more than that: a say in vital questions where we can prevent things, like the misuse of force, and the power to propose good ideas together with our allies. So we're not dangerous, we're useful.

In addition, the episode starkly underscored both Europe's considerable might when it acts as one and, conversely, its inability to resolve conflicts in its own backyard, such as those in the Balkans, without the United States. The continent's leading powers had obviously come a long way since their catastrophic post-Cold War debut in Bosnia when the Balkan actors so deftly manipulated their indecision and differences. During the Kosovo crisis they presented a significantly more united face and in the process recognized common principles that underlay their approaches, in contrast to those of their mighty ally across the Atlantic. But the Kosovo war could never have been waged without Washington's diplomatic resolve and military hardware. Germany's handful of fighter planes were nothing compared to the 300-plus aircraft that the United States flew over Serbia. This recognition generated new momentum on behalf of the Europeans to forge common foreign and security policies. The same week the war ended, the European Union appointed Spaniard Javier Solana as its "special representative" for foreign affairs. By the end of the same year, plans were in motion to establish a deployable 60,000-person rapid-reaction force, an EU contingent to respond to just such crises.

10

The Price of Power

Even though Berlin had been Germany's capital since Unification Day, it wasn't until the federal government and both houses of parliament picked up and moved in the summer of 1999 that the Berlin Republic left behind its 1949–90 predecessor on the Rhine, at least physically.

In the aftermath of unification there had been considerable qualms about whether the seat of government should be moved from Bonn to the new German capital at all. In addition to the high cost, Berlin was loaded with symbolism, so much of it negative. It had been the capital of the Third Reich, of the doomed Weimar Republic, and of militaristic Prussia. Many of the "new" government buildings in Berlin would be the very same as had housed Nazi ministries. The home of the Bundestag, the locus of German democracy, would be the austere, battle-scarred Reichstag building along the Spree River. No German legislature had met there since fire gutted the building in February 1933, the pretext that enabled Hitler to assume emergency powers and dismiss the Weimar parliament.

Some worried that, in terms of political orientation, a shift from the Rhineland to Berlin would denote a departure from the politics of the Bonn Republic. Bonn's very location, on the Federal Republic's westernmost border, had embodied the country's commitment to the West. Perhaps a relocation 370 miles to the northeast would send the wrong message or even alter this emphasis. After all, the new German capital was closer to Warsaw than to Brussels. Moreover, the single-most important historical reference point of the Bonn Republic had been 1945; the Federal Republic had taken its bearings from the catastrophe of the Third Reich. Would a shift to Berlin herald a new "zero hour" that would distance Germany from the Nazi past and the responsibilities that came with it? Another concern: perhaps the specter of the most recent dictatorship, that of East Germany's communist regime, would overshadow that of the Hitler years, pushing them even further into the back of history books.

Yet the arguments in favor of Berlin were surely more persuasive. Berlin was the only city in all of Germany where east and west met—its population of 3.5 million, roughly half *Ossis*, half *Wessis*. Moreover, both the people of the old Federal Republic (65 million) and those of the five eastern states (17 million) saw themselves reflected in Berlin. As the unified Germany's capital and seat of government, Berlin would signal that this new Federal Republic was more than just an institutional extension of the old one; it was hoped that the easterners would feel like respected, constituent citizens and not merely like tolerated guests. And just as Berlin could link Germany's two halves, so it could serve as a bridge between western and eastern Europe. As for symbolism, the metropolis on the Spree was also, of course, the symbolic site of German unification, where the Berlin Wall had divided the nation and where, on November 9, 1989, it had fallen. This throwing off the yoke of dictatorship in a nonviolent revolution was a democratic first in German history. The people taking to the streets, demanding that they govern themselves (*Wir sind das Volk!*) had inspired, and made possible, the united state. Berlin had other positive associations too: the 1948–49 airlift, the June 1953 workers' uprising in East Berlin, Kennedy's defiant 1963 "*Ich bin ein Berliner*" address, and the student movement, among others. Berlin was also a bona fide metropolis that attracted artists and intellectuals; it was a city that exuded creative, cosmopolitan energy that, one hoped, the Berlin Republic itself would reflect.

Those who feared Germany's drifting from its postwar moorings, argued the Berlin lobby, really had nothing to fear: the state had the same name, the same constitution, and the same set of symbols as the Bonn Republic. The Berlin Republic remained an enthusiastic, loyal member of the European Union and NATO. Its geographical location could enable it to reach out to Russia and the central Europeans, just as the Bonn Republic's *Ostpolitik* had. As for the history-laden Reichstag building, it could stand as a monument to safeguarding democracy and its handsome new glass copula, designed by a British architect, gave it a brighter, more open feeling, as well as serving as an emblem for the Berlin Republic.[1]

Remarkably, when the decision came to a vote in the Bundestag in June 1991, Berlin edged out Bonn by only eighteen votes. More western MPs cast ballots for Bonn than for Berlin! It was the unanimous votes of the eastern lawmakers from all parties that pushed Berlin over the top. Some observers surmised that the real reason for the westerners' preference for Bonn was not the weighty German questions at all but, rather, their unwillingness to forsake their summer houses along the Rhine for cold, gray Berlin. Yet many of the questions about the Berlin Republic remained relevant and unanswered, left open to be settled at an unspecified, later date.

A New Republic?

Even before Chancellor Schröder moved into the brand new chancellery on the Spree, a boxlike, concrete monstrosity designed by Kohl's architects, he had appropriated the nebulous concept of the "Berlin Republic" for his administration. He also began to fill it at once, proclaiming in his inaugural speech that the transfer of the government's seat to Berlin was more than just a change of address. He stressed Germany's imperative to modernize, to spur economic recovery through innovation and initiative. More than once, Schröder underscored a new ethic of entrepreneurial drive, individual responsibility, and business savvy—something, he implied, that had been lacking in the latter decades of the Bonn Republic. This spirit didn't mean neglecting social responsibility, he added, but social welfare was only for the most needy.[2]

Schröder maintained that Germany had long been a self-confident and grown-up nation, "a normal *Volk*" "without guilt complexes," one that had learned from the past. The Berlin Republic had an array of positive traditions to build upon, including the emancipatory spirit of 1989, West Berlin's courageous defense of freedom, and even, he said explicitly, that of the new social movements of the 1970s and 1980s. This didn't mean, he said, that he thought, as had Helmut Kohl, that today's Germans enjoyed a "grace of late birth" and were therefore somehow exempt from history's burden. On the contrary. Nor, he hastened to add, would the legacy of the Bonn Republic be shunted aside; it was a forty-year success story and the democratic precondition for reuniting Germany. The Berlin Republic would follow in Bonn's footsteps as a civilian power—one that, when it acted in world affairs, would do so in tandem with allies. It remained the most solid of European citizens, among the staunchest advocates of monetary and political union. In 1999 the euro was scheduled to replace the Deutsch Mark, yet another milestone in the transfer of sovereignty to all-European institutions.

Germany's involvement in the Kosovo conflict, a momentous rupture in tradition, would prove only the first act of the Berlin Republic's entry onto the world stage and the evolution of a new German foreign policy. It was, however, in domestic affairs that the red–green government pledged to make its mark on the country. As it happened, the administration's first twelve months in office were tragic drama often painful to behold. The year of seemingly endless false starts and missteps caused both ruling parties to plummet in public polls and drop a string of crucial regional votes, an ominous trend that began shifting the balance in the upper house of parliament, the Bundesrat, to the conservatives.* The demands of governance put both parties, the SPD and the Greens, to the test. Now they were forced to perform rather than just promise and, predictably, the results exacerbated tensions just beneath the surface in both parties.

The first battleground was economic and social policy, which in the coalition was the domain of the Social Democrats and had been their bread and butter for as long as the party had existed. In the SPD, however, there were conflicting approaches: one represented by Chancellor Schröder, the man of the "new middle," and another by the proudly traditional Social Democrat Oskar Lafontaine, the new finance minister and SPD chairman. They were, respectively, numbers one and two in the party, and their positions in the coalition were supposed to reflect a power-sharing arrangement. There was no love lost between the long-time rivals and the ensuing friction soon burst into the open. Their differences went to the crux of the meaning of social democracy in the twenty-first century. Both men, life-long, dyed-in-the-wool Social Democrats of the postwar generation, were fighting for the soul of their party and, implicitly, over the future of Germany's vaunted social welfare state, the pride of the Bonn Republic.

Lafontaine, also known as "Red Oskar," was the standard-bearer of a left-wing social democracy that had deep roots in Germany. In the rich European tradition of social democracy, Germany isn't just any country; it is the cradle of democratic socialism, the birthplace of August Bebel's and Karl Liebknecht's Sozialistischen Arbeiterpartei Deutschlands nearly 140 years ago. Nor was Oskar Lafontaine just another social democratic politician. He had a Europe-wide following, his writings translated into a dozen languages. Although the party had gone through many transformations

* The Bundesrat, composed of the leaderships of the sixteen federal states, must approve all major federal legislation.

since the days of Bebel and Liebknecht, not least the Godesberg reforms in 1959, it still considered itself the party of Germany's workers and trade unions as well as protector of the lower classes. It stood for the redistribution of wealth from the haves to the have-nots and for maintaining a reliable social safety net. Lafontaine believed that the state could and should use its macroeconomic levers to spur growth.

One of Lafontaine's first moves as finance minister was to draft a tax-reform package that cut rates for families and low-income earners while slapping new levies on big business—in particular, the insurance and energy companies. Child benefits were increased, family medical costs cut. Lafontaine began work to have stricter curbs put on world financial markets. This is what most Social Democrats expected of a SPD-run government. But Lafontaine's initiatives obviously ruffled the feathers of the German business community. Groups of top executives fired off blistering letters of protest to Schröder, charging that his administration was unfriendly to business. Lafontaine was accused of meddling in the affairs of the European Central Bank, even causing the value of the newly introduced euro to flag.[3]

Schröder had never been as left-wing as Lafontaine. He wanted to streamline the social welfare state, deregulate the market, and break with the cradle-to-grave mentality. This was modernization, Schröder style, the bitter pill that the ailing *Sozialstaat* had to swallow in order to compete in a globalized world. As for the chancellor's "new middle," supposedly the prime mover of this rejuvenation, this wasn't the traditional blue-collar SPD clientele at all. Rather, as one political analyst put it, the new middle was envisaged as an "innovative, creative, flexible and experiment-willing stratum who placed a higher value on economic change than risk, who are highly motivated, act independently, and stand on their own to feet rather than feed at the trough of the state."[4] This however sounded more like the target voters of the Free Democrats, Germany's free-market liberals, as well as the language that they spoke. To many observers it wasn't clear whether this new middle existed at all in Germany. Perhaps the chancellor's new middle smoked thick cigars and wore flashy Italian suits—as he had recently taken to doing. But these were symbols that the German left associated with capitalist fat cats.

In cabinet meetings, tense exchanges between Schröder and Lafontaine had become routine, their unusual power-sharing arrangement transparently on the rocks. Some thought that Schröder would be the one to buckle first, since Lafontaine had more backing in the party. But in March 1999, Lafontaine, then fifty-five years old, exasperated with the standoff, conceded defeat and, in an extraordinary move, quit the government, resigned his Bundestag seat, and left the SPD leadership. This course, he concluded, was not what he had devoted his life to.

Schröder and his backers now had an open field to pursue a New Labour-style economic reform course, one that paid considerably less heed to classic social democratic sensibilities. By midterm the first Schröder-designed reforms of the tax code and pension system, as well as a stark austerity package aimed at plugging the state's vast budget deficit, were firmly in place. In line with free market doctrine, Schröder backed cuts in the income and corporate taxes in order to promote private incentive and international competitiveness. Although Schröder had vanquished Lafontaine, there was still plenty of reservation in the party about this direction. In fact, there was more opposition to such pro-market reforms in the SPD than in the conservative and liberal opposition parties—or even in the Greens. Nevertheless, they were a start for Schröder, the self-acclaimed "reform chancellor," and a sign that he had located the coordinates that would guide him, and the Berlin Republic, for the rest of the term and beyond.

The more impressive accomplishments of the first term belonged to the government Greens, even if these victories looked meager next to their lofty visions of not so long ago—or even compared to those in the modest coalition contract. The junior coalition partner emerged as the motor of social and ecological reform while the Social Democrats applied the brakes, slowing down, diluting, or outright blocking progressive legislation in one case after another. Yet even as scaled back as they were, the early measures with Greens tags on them—the new citizenship law, an ecology tax, the nuclear energy phase-out, the legalization of homosexual partnerships, and a renewable energies packet—were arguably the most important of the government's entire tenure.

The new citizenship law, for example, relaxed the stringent naturalization requirements for foreigners living long term in Germany, which finally enabled them to enjoy the full civic rights of citizenship, including the vote. The new criteria literally changed the meaning of what it meant to be German—and embodied a commitment to integration as part of Germany's future. Until this watershed legislation, foreign nationals could reside, work, and pay taxes in Germany for decades without qualifying for citizenship. Even the grandchildren of the early guest workers, many of whom spoke better German than Turkish or Greek, had to jump through hoops to get a German passport, while ethnic German refugees from Russia and eastern Europe (some of whom who could no longer speak German) automatically received citizenship because they were of German descent.[5] The former German law, in stark contrast to France's republican ideal, defined a concept of Germanness that was volkish and ethnocultural.

By excluding foreign nationals from citizenship, the old law had effectively marginalized them in German society and kept the "German nation" ethnically homogenous, at least on paper.[6] But, ultimately, the Federal Republic had been a multicultural society since the 1970s, even if this wasn't reflected in official statistics. In the case of citizenship, and other social legislation as well, the red–green government inscribed into law much that was already, de facto if not de jure, reality in Germany. One in five people in Germany had a recent "migration background," for example. In every major city, newspaper stands carried dailies in a dozen languages. Urban school classes included kids from diverse, mixed backgrounds. These "peoples with migration backgrounds" were already part of Germany before 1999, even if they didn't have full political rights.

Likewise, homosexual partnerships were nothing out of the ordinary in Germany. The so-called gay marriage law gave rights to gay people who had been living together as couples for years. The statute was actually more of a "gay partnership law" since it didn't invest gay couples with the same full rights as married heterosexual couples, as the Greens had fought for. Unlike in the Scandinavian countries, for example, gay couples in Germany still can't be legal parents.

Although compromises like these caused many Greens to grumble, the real trial for the party was the phasing out of nuclear power. A priority second to none, the goal of a nuclear-free Germany was etched into every party manifesto since its first. The Social Democrats had in principle agreed to shutting down Germany's reactors; the sticking point was the duration of the phase-out period. Before the elections, the Greens had consented to a two- to six-year phase out. Environment minister Jürgen Trittin had recently mentioned eight years, the Social Democrats ten.

During coalition negotiations, both parties agreed that rather than shut down nuclear power plants by decree and incur enormous reparation damages, as had happened in Sweden, they would sit down with the energy companies to find a compromise solution. The negotiations, led by the Greens' Trittin, dragged on for nearly twenty months. Environmental and regional antinuclear groups complained that Trittin was allowing the electricity companies to lead him by the nose. Trittin complained that Schröder wasn't backing him. Schröder complained that Trittin was behaving like a bull in a china shop. The electricity companies complained that the whole crazy idea would spell Germany's ruin. In the end, a deal was reached that allowed most reactors to remain online until the end of their "natural lives." No new nuclear facilities would be built in Germany, the reprocessing of spent plutonium in the country was banned, and all nineteen existing plants would be shut down by 2030. A nuclear-free Germany was now in sight—if one could see thirty years into the future.

So, were Champagne corks popping from Wyhl to Gorleben? Not a chance. This was not the outcome that antinuclear activists had braved countless freezing nights at blockades for, or months of manning the atomic villages, or the billy clubbings and water canons of the West German police. Antinuclear activists from across the country—20,000 strong—assembled in Gorleben under the banner "Nuclear Exit? All Lies!"[7] The compromise was denounced as a "capitulation to the nuclear industry."[8] Many antinuclear activists declared their local initiatives, as of then, formally in opposition to the Greens. Longtime party members, even elected officials in municipalities near nuclear installations, quit the party. They pointed out that the first plant to go off-line, a 1968-constructed facility destined for the junkyard anyway, would do so only in 2003, *after* the red–green coalition's first term had expired.

One of the Federal Republic's most Greens-friendly NGOs, the 1975-founded Bund für Umwelt- und Naturschutz (the German branch of Friends of the Earth), issued a blistering press release predicting that Germany could have nuclear power plants in operation thirty-five years hence:

> This so-called "nuclear consensus" [between the government and the power companies] ensures that the electricity firms will continue to "operate undisturbed." There are no binding deadlines for shutting down these plants. A solution to the problem of nuclear waste is even further away because of the long life spans of the reactors. The 19 nuclear plants in the Federal Republic will, according to the federal government's plans, produce more than 5500 tons of radioactive waste before they go off-line.[9]

The red–green government's renewable energies law, on the other hand, was its ecological masterpiece—according to some observers even the coalition's single greatest accomplishment. The package offered a range of tax breaks, subventions, and investment incentives to encourage the technological development and use of wind, solar, hydroelectric, geothermal, and biomass-generated energy. In several categories, the legislation proved even more effective than predicted—and set an international standard. It also had an immediate impact: between 2000 and 2004, Germany's production of electricity by regenerative sources climbed from 6.7 to 9.3 percent. Energy from wind power tripled.[10] During the same period, the country doubled its use of solar power (second worldwide only to Japan), although it remained under 1 percent of total electricity production.[11] The German "model" for promoting alternative energy production was quickly picked up by other countries, including Spain, Sweden, and the Czech Republic. And, icing on the cake, this Greens initiative didn't threaten jobs, it created them. The Federal Republic became the world's number-one exporter of wind-power technology. Friends of the Earth estimated that, in total, the alternative energies sector accounted for 130,000 new jobs by 2005.[12] Somewhat ironically, front and center on its Web site just a couple years later, the Federal Ministry of Economics and Technology—the very SPD-led office that obstructed one Greens initiative after another—proudly displayed a host of German firms offering cutting-edge alternative-energy technology. Among them were the world's largest solar plant and offshore wind stations, as well as documentation of one multimillion-dollar deal after another; one of them, for example, was to provide solar-produced electricity to rural provinces in China.

The other cornerstone of the Greens' "environmental modernization" was a five-phase ecology tax. The incremental levy on fossil fuels was intended to reduce carbon dioxide emissions, promote conservation, and increase energy efficiency. But from the start it ran into fierce resistance from a welter of familiar adversaries including the entire Bundestag opposition, the business lobby, trade unions, electricity companies, and, not least, the SPD. The wrangle over the bill was so down-and-dirty that there were calls for Jürgen Trittin's resignation, which Schröder implied might suit him just fine. Nevertheless, a truncated three-phase eco-tax was passed, the revenues of which went not to alternative energies research, as Greens had envisioned, but toward bolstering the country's strapped social security system, a worthy cause as well. As intended, the country's total consumption of fossil fuels dropped (gasoline by 10 percent) as their price rose and carbon dioxide emissions began to fall off as well, although not by the 21 percent that Germany, according to the Kyoto Protocol, was supposed to reach by 2005. In contrast to alternative energy, Germany wasn't a pioneer in ecology taxes but was catching up to the Scandinavian states, the Netherlands, Austria, and Slovenia.[13]

1968 on Trial

Irrespective of the government's fortunes and the Greens' electoral setbacks, Joschka Fischer's own popularity climbed steadily, overtaking Schröder, among others, as the republic's number-one *Liebling*. This throne he would occupy uncontested for the next five years. While, in the past, Fischer had been the most broadly respected figure among the Greens, this new national stardom was of another order. One survey showed that every fourth German could imagine taking a holiday with Joschka Fischer.[14] His seemed to be the face that Germans wanted to present to the outside world, that they felt best represented them to non-Germans.

Why, one might ask, would Germans make a former rock-throwing *Gymnasium* dropout—and a Greens, of all persuasions—their favorite politician and, arguably, the chosen face of the Berlin Republic? There are a handful of reasons that German commentators offer. One is that the foreign minister is almost always the Federal Republic's most popular political figure. He (it has never been a "she") appears regularly on television, looking self-important, shaking the hands of other world leaders. Rarely are foreign ministers held responsible for the kinds of tough domestic-policy choices that benefit some Germans and hurt others. But there was more to Fischer's profile than that. It seemed that rather than shame his fellow countrymen, Fischer's unorthodox vita flattered them. It spoke for a Germany in which a man like Fischer could make his way, not only from the outer fringes of the republic into its center, but also from the very bottom of the social ladder to the very top—a feat unthinkable in the highly stratified Germany of old. This kind of trajectory was possible only in a modern state, one broadly heterogeneous, its structures permeable, and its powers of integration strong. This pop star of a politician signaled to the world that Germany was different now—more colorful, more liberal, more spontaneous. Fischer was the nation's prodigal son, a young man who had gone astray but had learned from the experience and returned a better man, a classic protagonist from a German *Bildungsroman*, like Goethe's Wilhelm Meister. After all, the Federal Republic was a state based on the premise that it is possible to err—and still repent and become a good citizen.

Fischer was also exceptional in the world of German politics in that he hadn't spent his entire life climbing the rungs of a political party, like the typical "party soldiers" in the Christian Democrats and SPD. In the past Germany had been a country governed by a political class that was either preordained at birth or groomed by a party in order to rule in the name of ordinary people. It was exactly this type of party apparatchik that the Greens of the early 1980s wanted to dislodge from power in order to connect democracy with ordinary people. That said, many Greens politicians, including Fischer, had become much like that—professional politicians—the party's earlier practices of rotating seats and limiting terms having long fallen by the wayside. But even so, they were considerably less cardboard than their counterparts in the other parties.

Because of Fischer's popularity, no scalp would have been more dear to the floundering, scandal-ridden conservatives—and try they did to get it. Shortly after the first term's halfway mark, a noisy debate unfolded in Germany over the left-wing militancy of the 1960s and 1970s and, implicitly, the political judgment of the now-ruling generation. Fischer was its polestar.

First, Fischer was called to testify as a background witness in the trial of one of his less reputable street-fighting comrades, Hans-Joachim Klein, who had recently surfaced from the underground after twenty-five years on the run. Klein was charged with murder in a 1975 terrorist attack in Vienna. Even though markedly aged, sitting in the dock, the one-time Frankfurt Sponti was easily recognizable by his sad, long face and hulking physique. After the nearly three-hour interrogation, the German foreign minister strode over to the impassive Klein, shook his hand, and exchanged a few courteous words with him. This association was embarrassing enough for Fischer, but after his testimony the Frankfurt court charged him with perjury (the charge was later dropped). The prosecutor claimed that Fischer had lied about a former RAF member using the 64 Bornheimer Landstrasse co-op as a hideout. But the floodgates were now wide open, with more questions and fresh accusations coming one after another.

"Can a man who threw stones and beat up police officers represent the Federal Republic and the chancellor to the rest of the world?" asked *Der Spiegel*, echoing the charges of conservatives.[15] At the core of the brouhaha was not just Fischer's radical past but also the legacy of the entire 1968 generation. German conservatives had long felt that the sixty-eighters had gotten off too easily, their lawlessness and hedonism dismissed as youthful eccentricity. The *Gewaltfrage*, the protest movements' strategic use of violence, was on the table again, but this time as a historical issue. Should this generation as a whole be made to confront its own ambiguous history—such as their recourse to violence and activism in "undemocratic" Marxist groups? Did the sixty-eighters have the right to occupy the high moral ground that they lay claim to in the republic? This holier-than-thou generation had taken their parents to task for ignoring history, but was it prepared to confront its own? What about anti-Semitism, the idealization of leftist Third World dictators, and anti-Americanism? Legions of journalists dug frantically to unearth damning evidence of Fischer's exploits as an angry young man. Had he whitewashed his past? Had he thrown a Molotov cocktail in the 1976 Frankfurt attack that nearly killed a police officer?

In January 2001 the monthly magazine *Stern* dropped a bombshell. It published a series of black-and-white photographs showing Fischer, then twenty-five years old, doling out a gratuitous beating to a Frankfurt police officer on the margins of a 1973 demonstration. A dark twist to this episode was that the photos were sold to *Stern* by a little-known journalist named Bettina Röhl. Her name may not have meant much in journalistic circles, but her identity was no secret: Röhl was the daughter of the Red Army Faction's late Ulrike Meinhof. It was at the May 1976 demonstration in Frankfurt that Fischer, protesting Meinhof's alleged murder, was arrested on suspicion of participating in the Molotov cocktail attack.

The photos that Röhl found showed Fischer, head to toe in black leather and wearing a motorcycle helmet, lure the Frankfurt officer into a one-on-one confrontation in a side street, on the periphery of the demonstration. The officer is wearing a white helmet and the full-length green jumpsuit of the riot control squads. In his left hand he holds a large, round Plexiglas shield, in his right a nightstick. Fischer, staring him straight in the eye, is waiting in a crouch, knees bent and arms positioned to defend or extend a blow. Fischer's eyes and nose are visible through the visor. In the next frames, two of Fischer's Putz comrades, also helmeted, appeared from behind nearby parked VWs. They jump the police officer and, in the final frame, one can see the three of them taking the officer down. Fischer's gloved fist is poised high in the air, ready to deliver a punishing blow to the fallen officer.

The spectacular photos were genuinely shocking to those unaware of the nature of the 1970s militancy in West Germany, and they stoked an already furious debate, one that pitted the old nemeses of West Germany's "culture war" against one another again. The 1960s were suddenly to blame for everything, including Germany's sagging birth rate. Out in front as it had been three decades ago, *Bild-Zeitung* led with a picture of the 64 Bornheimer Landstrasse house and the headline, "Here's where Fischer and the RAF terrorist lived."[16] Leading conservatives called for Fischer's resignation. In Frankfurt, journalists combed the old Sponti scene for bits and pieces of evidence that could tie Fischer to more violence. More photos surfaced, this time those of Fischer's 1969 participation in the SDS trip to Algeria for the PLO congress. Could Fischer today really represent Germany in the Middle East? The Maoist past of environment minister Trittin was also dredged up. The focus of the debate on the scene's militancy in the 1970s had the effect of blurring the boundaries between the student movement and the urban guerrillas, in effect, between the legacy of 1968 and that of the German Autumn. If conservatives could succeed in drawing a straight line from Rudi Dutschke and the anti-authoritarian revolt to Meinhof, Baader, and terrorism, then perhaps they might retake ground they had lost in the cultural revolution.

At first Fischer's responses did little to stem the barrage. The media claimed that he provided as little information as possible, causing one writer to scoff: "He tries to explain away the reasons for the use of violence against the backdrop of the times and then adds quickly that, God forbid, he doesn't want to justify anything. And then he goes on justifying. The pattern is well-known: Fischer learned it from his father's generation."[17] A generation of noble idealists? it was asked. Or flesh-and-blood opportunists, just like everyone else? Fischer responded in the same *Stern* issue that ran the damning photos. "Yes, I was militant," he shot back. "That's my biography. That's me, Joschka Fischer. Without my biography today I'd be someone else and I wouldn't like that." He denied ever taking up arms—or even a Molotov cocktail—and underscored that he, Cohn-Bendit, and the Spontis had spoken out against armed struggle in the Federal Republic. As for other kinds of violence, "We squatted houses, and when the police raided them we defended ourselves. We threw stones. We got beat up by the cops but we dished it out too. I've never covered that up."[18]

In the end, the whole episode blew over surprisingly quickly. Turning back the clock on women's rights, lifestyle choices, pop culture, and sexuality was going to be harder than dislodging one politician from office. Anyway, the calls for Fischer's head seemed half-hearted, as if the conservatives never really believed they had the goods to make him resign. Israel's ambassador to Germany stuck up for Fischer, calling him a good friend of the Israeli state. As for the German public's response, most people seemed ready to accept that the leftist militancy of the 1970s was part of their history—an extreme, wrongheaded reaction but one that was by now part of the past. Although the controversy didn't scratch Fischer's popularity ratings, the back-and-forth did take some of the shine off the sanctimonious mantle of the sixty-eighters. The business of "coming to terms with the past," it seemed, was better handled by subsequent generations than by the participants in those pasts themselves.

Attack on America–and Afghanistan

Despite all of the early fuss, under the new German administration U.S.–German relations plodded along uneventfully, with an occasional hiccup. The initial apprehension in Washington that the red–green leadership would deviate from the well-rehearsed drills of the Atlantic partnership seemed, in retrospect, alarmist. The new administration's deference to the United States on Kosovo and amiable relationships with Bill Clinton and Madeleine Albright helped. In terms of personal histories and lifestyles, as well as on many issues, there was undeniably much common ground between the two administrations. The Clintons had marched against the Vietnam War, too, and partook in the 1960s counterculture, even if Bill Clinton, unlike Joschka Fischer, "didn't inhale."

The George W. Bush administration, however, was another story. The left-of-center German government and the new conservative leadership in Washington eyed one another with suspicion from the start. The strident "America first" tone of the Bush team during the 2000 campaign in the United States put Germans and many other Europeans on guard. For their part, Bush and his neo-conservative advisers were wary that embryonic EU defense and security structures could eventually displace NATO as the chief guarantor of security on the continent—and thus limit U.S. influence. In addition, this new Germany was reaching more confidently into foreign policy areas beyond Europe—toward Vladimir Putin's Russia, for instance, as well as in the Middle East and as a pioneer on global environmental issues. The Berlin Republic, it seemed, wasn't content with being "an economic giant and a political dwarf," as the Bonn Republic had been. This wasn't the same Germany that George W. Bush's father knew.

But the mantra of transatlantic brotherly love was dutifully repeated by all and everything seemed cozy enough for the time being. Fischer even forged an unlikely bond with the new secretary of state, Colin Powell, who was a Vietnam vet, former West Germany–based cold warrior, and Gulf War general. The two fifty-something men had been on opposite sides their entire lives. But no matter, the times had indeed a-changed. Fischer learned of Powell's affection for northern Germany's renowned Flensburger beer and schlepped a case with him every time he traveled to the United States. Fischer would wink at Powell and say confidingly, "the new shipment's come in." When the U.S. media asked Powell at a press conference, with Fischer standing next to him, his opinion of Fischer's recently publicized youthful sins and transformation into a respected colleague, the five-star general cracked a disarming smile and, with a twinkle in his eye, responded, "Amazing, isn't it?"[19]

On the afternoon of September 11, 2001, Chancellor Schröder was sitting at his desk in the new Berlin chancellery sorting through files when his secretary burst through the door. "Turn on the television!" she screamed. By the time Schröder tuned in, both of the World Trade Center towers in New York were colossal piles of smoking debris. "*Grosser Gott*," (oh my God) Schröder was said to have muttered under his breath. His first move was to call his foreign minister.

Two hours later, the federal security council, the country's highest security organ, convened in a crisis session. Schröder, Fischer, interior minister Otto Schily, and Rudolf Scharping, the defense minister, understood that for the first time in NATO's history its hallmark Article 5, the mutual defense clause, was almost surely applicable. The famous article states that a foreign attack against one ally is equivalent to an attack against all NATO members—and requires the alliance's full support. That evening Schröder appeared live before the nation, a graven Fischer standing next to him. Schröder then uttered words that would have lasting and unforeseen consequences for U.S.–German relations: "Now is the time for solidarity with the United States. Germany has to stand shoulder to shoulder with the U.S. and show unlimited solidarity." He reinforced his message: "This is a declaration of war against the entire civilized world."[20] In its hour of crisis, Germany was there for its postwar mentor, as it always had been.

Across Germany, the shock and outpouring of sympathy for the victims of the mind-boggling atrocity was sincere and heartfelt. German kids spontaneously conducted candlelight vigils outside their schools. At a memorial under Berlin's Brandenburg Gate, 200,000 people, including just about the entire German political elite, gathered to express their empathy with the country to which they owed so much. "We are all Americans today," said the speakers. Perhaps because two of the terrorist ringleaders had lived for years in Hamburg, the September attacks seemed to hit Germans especially hard.

Nevertheless, at the same time many wondered what exactly Chancellor Schröder meant by "unlimited solidarity." Was he committing Germany to participate in any and all of the military reprisals that were virtually certain to follow in the declared war on terror? Just months before, the deployment of German troops to the postconflict mission in Macedonia caused the red–green coalition to fray again, this time with more Social Democrats joining uneasy Greens in opposition to Germany's expanding worldwide military presence. The deployment of German soldiers outside German borders was no settled issue—far from it—and Schröder's open-ended pledge seemed to be a blank check of sorts, to be filled out by Washington's hawks. The Bundeswehr was a "parliamentary army" and could undertake no substantial military venture without the Bundestag's approval. This kind of pledge wasn't Schröder's alone to make. Fischer traveled to Washington to find out what the Bush administration had on its mind. The list of fifty potential targets presented to him included Iran, Iraq, Afghanistan, Pakistan, Syria, and North Korea, among others, none of whom had directly attacked a NATO ally.

Yet the first consequences of September 11 for Germany were on the domestic front. The counterterrorism campaign was going to be prosecuted first at home before it went on the road. Within a week, the first of two sweeping antiterror bills were turned into law, prescribing the most far-reaching new security-related measures for the country since those adopted during the German Autumn of 1977, when West Germany grappled with an indigenous terrorist problem. At the time, one of the most prominent opponents of the West German government's intrusive policies was lawyer and civil libertarian Otto Schily, who had taken his visceral distrust of authoritarian states with him into the Bundestag for the Greens. In autumn 2001, the author and unflinching proponent of the new antiterror bills was the very same man, now a Social Democrat and law-and-order interior minister. The new legislation actually curbed the personal-data protection rules introduced by the Greens in the 1980s and tightened procedures for handling foreign nationals. In the Bundestag the heartiest applause for Schily's measures came from gleeful Christian Democrats, who even at the height of conservative rule couldn't have passed such measures.

The looming U.S.-led military campaign against a still unidentified enemy set off another impassioned debate in Germany, no less rancorous than that over Kosovo. Opinion polls showed Germans deeply divided over the meaning of "unlimited solidarity." Interestingly, a trend that would persist, the eastern Germans expressed considerable more skepticism about supporting Washington militarily; should it come to that, than did their western countrymen.[21] Since it was now the Greens, the former antiwar party, that was sending German troops into battle, the reform-communist Party for Democratic Socialism (PDS) took over the antiwar cause and made it its own. Germany's foremost intellectuals, including writers Günter Grass, Martin Walser, and Christa Wolf, came out against the war option.

When the United States' first military target emerged as Afghanistan, the stronghold of Al Qaeda, Germany volunteered to take on additional regional security responsibilities in Europe in order to free up U.S. and British troops for combat operations. By assuming command of the international peacekeeping contingent in Macedonia, the government set yet another milestone for the Berlin Republic—Germany as commander of multinational forces abroad. But there was no time to reflect on "firsts." On October 2, NATO officially declared the terrorist attack on the United States an Article 5 case, the perpetrators of the September 11 attacks protected by Afghanistan's Taliban leadership. This compelled Germany to aid the coalition in the campaign against the Kabul regime, as Schröder had already promised he would do.

Washington, in a stunning decision, opted not to prosecute the war through NATO but rather in partnership with Great Britain. On October 7, with a green light from the U.N. Security Council, U.S. and British air forces launched their first attacks on points in Afghanistan. Although the United States and Britain would wage the war on Afghanistan independently of the NATO command structures, Washington requested from Germany the mobilization of 3,900 troops—the majority naval forces, as well as anti-aircraft units, air transport support, and elite German special forces—that could be deployed anywhere within the NATO area, the Arabian peninsula, middle and central Asia, and northern Africa. For this, however, the government required Bundestag approval—as soon as possible.

This time, in contrast to the Kosovo intervention, it was the Social Democrat- and Greens-dominated Bundestag that would put Germany's latest foreign military venture to a vote—and there were ominous signs that the Schröder government didn't have a majority in its own ranks. The coalition was teetering again, talk suddenly in the air about a Social Democrat–Free Democrat or even a grand coalition replacing the red–green government in order to meet Berlin's alliance obligations and wage an effective war on terror.

If Washington's snub—circumventing NATO and treating its continental allies like minions—fazed Schröder, he certainly didn't let on. He told the Bundestag:

> On October 7, as a necessary response to the terror attacks on New York and Washington, the United States began military actions against the infrastructure of the terrorist network of Osama bin Laden and against the Taliban state in Afghanistan. In this situation, active solidarity and dependable behavior is expected from Germany and it will be offered. This solidarity isn't just lip service; it means a response appropriate to Germany's responsibility today in the world. . . . Just 10 years ago none of us would have expected that Germany would take part in international efforts to secure freedom, justice and stability in any other way than with "secondary assistance"—such as infrastructure projects or providing funding. But this stage of German postwar policies is irretrievably past.[22]

Fischer stood resolutely by the chancellor and the wartime coalition, despite the predictable dissension in his party. The Greens should be under no illusion what "saying no to the Americans would mean," he said. It would be "fatal for Germany" and the end of the red–green experiment, warned Fischer, just as he had during the Kosovo crisis. If Germany wants to have a say in this war and its aftermath, if it wants to agitate for diplomatic solutions as it had during Kosovo, then it has to play the game, not pout on the sidelines, he told them.[23] At one point, Fischer exploded, slamming his hands on the table and jumping to his feet when Greens MPs insinuated that the government was using the campaign against terrorism to divert attention from the country's economic woes. Some leading Greens even demanded that Fischer resign on the spot. "I'm not glued to this post . . . *Ich klebe nicht am meinem Stuhl*," he shot back, implying he would resign if his party left him in the lurch, and marched out of the meeting.[24]

Schröder understood the Bundestag vote as a life-or-death matter for the coalition. The full backing of both his party and the Greens was key to maintaining the government's credibility during the crisis. Since the opposition conservatives and liberals would have backed him almost to a man, the chancellor could easily have prevailed in the Bundestag with the help of their ballots. If he did so, however, he knew that he would be beholden to his rivals and most probably too weak to wage a controversial war with full freedom of action. The red–green coalition would never survive it.

Instead Schröder chose to gamble with the highest of stakes: he linked the Afghanistan vote to a confidence vote in the government, the first time such a move had been taken since 1982, when the last Social Democratic chancellor, Helmut Schmidt, precipitated his own fall from power. The confidence vote ensured that the entire parliamentary opposition—the conservatives, the liberals, and the reform communists—would all vote against the government and thus against the war, too. This meant that everything lay in the hands of the Social Democrat and Greens MPs who enjoyed a fragile ten-vote majority in the Bundestag. Should more than five MPs break ranks, the coalition would go up in smoke, then and there; new elections would be called and the Greens headed back to the opposition benches, perhaps forever. The intention of Schröder's strong-arm tactic was to torque up pressure on the dissenting Greens to the highest degree possible. Were they willing to throw everything away over this one issue? It was an all or nothing gamble by Schröder.

Of the eight holdout Greens MPs uncompromisingly opposed to the war, four voted with the government and for the war, four voted against. The chancellor thus commanded the thinnest possible of majorities, just one vote—but it was a majority all the same. His gambit had paid off. Germany was actively involved in another shooting war, this time outside of Europe, a shaky red–green coalition behind its leadership. As during the Kosovo war, Schröder and Fischer knew that they were on the shortest of leashes. But, much more quickly than many had predicted, U.S. and British airpower neutralized the Taliban and allied infantry troops launched a ground invasion, an astounding blitz victory in sight by mid-November.

In part a recognition of the delicate circumstances around German participation, the Petersberg guesthouse high above the Rhine near Bonn was chosen as the location for the postwar talks where the rival Afghan factions were to hammer out a peace accord and the shape of an interim government. Fischer opened the Bonn conference and proud host Schröder closed it, beaming like a new father over the agreement for a broad-based transitional government and soon-to-begin postwar reconstruction. On the heels of the accord, the Germans sponsored the donors' conference in Berlin for rebuilding the country. Foreign ministry officials were full of themselves bubbling over about Germany's importance as an actor for world peace and its enhanced position in Europe. Some even mused that Germany might now be in line for a permanent seat on the U.N. Security Council, a goal that the red–green government would indeed pursue (unsuccessfully) in the coming years.

One of the few cautionary notes came from German Defense Minister Scharping. Talk of a lead military role for Germany in postwar Afghanistan was premature, he warned, pointing to the thinly stretched Bundeswehr forces in three Balkan peacekeeping missions.[25] Germany's limited armed forces with their paltry defense budget (small even by European standards) and outdated Cold War hardware weren't up to playing deputy to the new global sheriff. But this didn't stop it from trying to help. As part of the International Security Assistance Force (ISAF), over 2,400 German troops would soon be on their way to Afghanistan, in addition to 1,800 donated to a U.S.-led contingent patrolling the strategic waters off the Horn of Africa, as well as a smaller antiterrorism unit in Kuwait. In addition, by the end of 2002 Germany would also have Bundeswehr troops in operations abroad of one sort or another in East Timor, Sudan, Macedonia, Kosovo, Bosnia, Georgia, Kuwait, Kenya, the Strait of Gibraltar, Uganda, and in the Mediterranean Sea. When the red–green coalition came to power in 1998, Germany had troops abroad only in Bosnia and Georgia.[26]

This meant that at the onset of the twenty-first century only the United States and Great Britain supplied more soldiers to international missions worldwide than did Germany. Fischer had certainly kept his promise not to pursue a "Greens foreign policy." But it was still unclear just what kind of foreign policy it was—or what Germans themselves expected. As much noise as there had been around the interventions there hadn't been a full public debate over this remarkable metamorphosis in German foreign and security policy. Nothing of the kind had been mentioned by the Greens or the Social Democrats during the 1998 campaign. While before the Afghanistan invasion 60 percent of Germans were against German participation in such a combat mission outside of Europe,[27] after its initially successful conclusion popular support for the German role in Operation Enduring Freedom shot up to two-thirds.[28] (Yet during the air strikes, a clear majority of Germans backed an immediate stop to the bombing, at least temporarily, in order to get humanitarian aid to civilians.[29]) And even after the Taliban's overthrow, most eastern Germans, in contrast to westerners, and most of the political left, in contrast to conservative and liberal voters, remained principally opposed to Bundeswehr missions abroad.[30] It seemed that Germans were deeply divided about their country's new international responsibilities and profile. Only ten years earlier, two-thirds of all Germans felt the model for their foreign policy should be neutral Switzerland. The first Gulf War brought several hundred thousand protesters onto the streets. Although most Germans now accepted some kind of expanded global role for Germany—as long as it happened squarely in a multilateral context—only 14 percent endorsed increasing the national defense budget to meet the costs of these new operations.[31] And, despite the "feel good" vibes in the aftermath of the Afghanistan campaign, by late 2001 Germans' backing for Chancellor Schröder's professed "unlimited solidarity" with the United States had dropped off considerably since 9/11[32]—(this despite continued high pro-American sympathies in general). This mixed picture reflected a country profoundly conflicted about its role in the world, even those accepting of the recent developments in German foreign policy uncertain about exactly what they wanted for Germany.

11

Continental Drift

Even during the most placid stretches of the Bonn Republic, the U.S.–German relationship was never as smooth as it is sometimes portrayed in hindsight. The West German and American leaderships butted heads on a range of issues throughout the Cold War decades, from German participation in the Vietnam War to the treatment of Poland's independent trade unionists in the 1980s.

Although the 1998–2000 overlap of the Clinton administration and Germany's red–green government was relatively harmonious, irritations between the allies occasionally flared into awkward transatlantic tiffs. There was no disguising the two administrations' divergent approaches to global climate policy, world trade, disarmament, and military budgets. Washington's cold-shouldering of Fischer's "no nuclear first use" proposal was just one example. Another classic U.S.–German spat occurred in 1999, when an Arizona court sentenced to death two German citizens, the brothers Karl and Walter LeGrand, for a 1982 stabbing murder in Arizona. Germany's constitution bans the death sentence and opinion polls consistently show a clear majority of Germans opposed to capital punishment. Schröder, Fischer, and Germany's president, Roman Herzog, all weighed in with their counterparts in the United States to stay the German brothers' execution. But to no avail. The LeGrand brothers were executed, one with a lethal injection, the other in a gas chamber.[1] The potent symbolism of the gas chamber only amplified the outcry in Germany, where some angry Bundestag MPs even demanded sanctions against the United States. Germany's justice minister called the executions "barbaric."[2]

But, in general, transatlantic amity was back at a high point in the late 1990s, having rebounded since the debilitating acrimony over Bosnia. The Kosovo intervention and the post-conflict multinational peacekeeping missions in the Balkans had illustrated what the two sides of the Atlantic could do working together. In the spring of 1999, the United States' favored transatlantic body, NATO, reached out to incorporate the central Europeans into the Euro–Atlantic community, a historic achievement on the fiftieth anniversary of the Atlantic Alliance.

But the Germans' unease with the folksy style, moralistic vision, and unilateralist accents of the Bush team was aggravated early in the administration's first term, in large part by its treatment of international arrangements and institutions. Washington's repudiation of the Kyoto Protocol on Climate Change was unequivocal, unlike the Clinton administration's conflicted position. President George W. Bush himself was unconvinced that global warming was a man-made phenomenon in the first place. Moreover, the Republican-controlled Senate had already torpedoed U.S. ratification of the comprehensive nuclear test ban treaty, which would have prohibited nuclear testing everywhere in the world. The treaty had been signed by 177 countries and ratified by 137. In addition to the United States, those states that had signed but hadn't ratified included Colombia, Egypt, Indonesia, Iran, and Israel. On top of these affronts, Washington unexpectedly announced the United States' withdrawal from the 1972 Anti-Ballistic Missile Treaty, an agreement between the United States and Russia that had limited antimissile systems for thirty years. In the wake of 9/11 and the anthrax scare in the United States, Washington then effectively gutted the Biological Weapons Convention. The Bush administration added insult to injury by coupling its shunting of the International Criminal Court with the demand that the Europeans sign waivers to exempt Americans from its jurisdiction. Those who didn't sign would face consequences. The overture struck Europeans as gratuitous bullying. In addition, in mid-January 2002, the existence of a special detention camp at the Guantánamo Bay Naval Base, Cuba, came to light. Washington's contempt for the Geneva Conventions, when they applied to the United States, elicited protests from human rights groups and, in general, consternation from the Europeans.

These issues had been festering when President Bush's combative State of the Union address was beamed around the world in late January 2002, his first major foreign policy speech since the Afghanistan war. In it Bush coined the phrase "the axis of evil" to denounce Iran, Iraq, and North

Korea, and he implied that wars against terrorist-friendly regimes had only just begun. In unusually muscular and urgent language, Bush warned Tehran, Baghdad, and Pyongyang that they could face military retaliation as part of an expanded war on terrorism. Inexplicably, the president declined to make even a courtesy bow to the western allies' engaged solidarity since the attacks on New York City and Washington. Despite the international coalition that had galvanized in the aftermath of September 11, the American president implied that the allies were poised to desert the United States, "indifferent" (as he put it) to the threats at hand. "Some governments will be timid in the face of terror. And make no mistake about it: if they don't act, America will," Bush declared. In the speech, the central planks of what would be called the Bush Doctrine were recognizable: preemptive military action against rogue states; countries supporting anti-American terrorism to be treated as terrorists; allies were welcome but the United States would not hesitate to act alone.[3] The strident, go-it-alone tenor of the address unnerved European politicians across the continent.

By dint of happenstance, the German leadership was the first of the Europeans to pay Washington a visit after President Bush's address. It was an obligation that none of its European allies could envy. In Washington, Schröder, Fischer, and a small handful of German diplomats dined on Florida stone crabs and roast venison together with George Bush, Vice President Dick Cheney, Colin Powell, and security adviser Condoleezza Rice. Strained moments between Bush and Schröder, whom the president called "my old friend Goerard," were nothing new. Cheney talked about his passion for hunting and about the Afghanistan campaign. But little was said during the two-hour meal about the future—and not a word about Iraq, which the Germans suspected might be next on Washington's list. "We've got to do it to them before they do it to us," Bush said over coffee and cigars later.[4] None of the guests ventured to pursue exactly what he meant. But before anything happened, he reassured the visitors, he'd consult with them.[5] Bush was convinced that Germany would follow the United States, as it had in the Balkans and Afghanistan—indeed, as the Federal Republic pretty much always had. The Germans departed as mystified and anxious about Washington's next move as when they had come.

The axis of evil speech brought the frictions in the greater transatlantic alliance percolating to the top. The Europeans' testy responses to the national address reflected an overarching consensus that armed force was one—but just one—of a palette of options that the international community could use to combat terrorism. Chancellor Schröder tried to get this message through to the White House. He said that he agreed wholeheartedly that undemocratic states had to be thwarted from obtaining weapons of mass destruction, but he added, "The obvious question is: what are the right tools and measures to bring this about?"[6] With the Afghanistan war behind them, political diplomacy and multilateral pressure were the order of the day in the Middle East. First on the Germans' list was the Israel–Palestine conflict. Another priority, felt Berlin, should be Iran, which was obviously interested in obtaining nuclear weapons itself. The foreign ministry also believed that the time was right to begin a dialogue with the Islamic world in order to promote modernization. The sources of the Muslim world's hatred and resentment, including poverty, had to be treated, not just the symptoms.

There was also dismay in European diplomatic circles at the lumping together of three countries with such disparate profiles as Iraq, North Korea, and Iran. Iraq, the Germans believed, was being adequately contained. Tighter sanctions and resumed weapons inspections could deter Iraq from directly threatening its neighbors and the West. Moreover, German intelligence couldn't verify Washington's claims of links between Saddam Hussein and Al Qaeda. As for North Korea, with whom the United States had broken off talks, Schröder lauded the South Korean government's policy of engaging the Pyongyang regime.[7] German diplomats didn't feel that further isolating the unpredictable dictatorship would aid the cause. Lastly, Germany and other U.S. allies had been making decent headway promoting moderate, reform-oriented currents in Iran. Even Spain's conservative leadership, a particularly loyal ally of Washington, chimed in saying that the European Union, the rotating presidency of which it then held, would continue to seek maximum cooperation with Iran on trade, the fight against terrorism, and human rights.[8]

Inside the red–green cabinet a week later, according to one account, Fischer first breached the possibility of breaking with the United States should it strike Baghdad.[9] He confided to colleagues gathered in the chancellor's office that he feared the international campaign against terrorism could be transformed into a global war. In a newspaper interview that the *New York Times* covered at length, Fischer buttressed Schröder's messages: "The international coalition against terror can't be a launching pad for action against whomever, whenever—and certainly not unilaterally. All of the European foreign ministers see it this way." Even the mighty United States couldn't create a peaceful world all by itself, he continued. "I don't have any patience for anti-Americanism. But despite all differences in size and weight, alliances can't be reduced to follow-the-leader. Allies aren't satellites."[10] These were strong words from Germany. As for Iraq, Fischer explicitly emphasized the strategic short-sightedness of military action; it would stir ill will in the region and possibly disrupt the delicate Middle East peace process.

Importantly, the nature of Germans' misgivings about Washington's post-Afghanistan orientation—a full year before the Iraq invasion—belies some of the conventional speculation about Germany's motives for opposing the U.S. policy toward Iraq, when it finally did. Much later, there was an oft-repeated charge that the French somehow coaxed the Germans onto an anti-American horse and led them into battle against the United States. According to this narrative, Germany doesn't—and can't possibly—have a mind of its own on foreign policy issues. Rather, on decisive international matters Germany swings like a pendulum between the United States and France depending on the political weather, too frightened of its wartime shadow to set its own priorities. On Iraq, so goes this line, the red–green government signed up with the French out of a mixture of timidity, "EU-firstism," election-year posturing, anti-Semitism, and a common anti-Americanism.[11] The facts, however, contradict this simplistic presentation, as they do other explanations, including those that attribute the transatlantic breakdown to poor public relations, miscommunication, or Schröder's electoral tactics. None of these interpretations view the tumult over Iraq as the upshot of essential differences between the two leaderships on foreign policy principle and approach: Germany and the United States held opposing views on how to address Iraq and the situation in the Middle East in general. Although the rupture didn't have to be as ugly as it was, bruised egos were inevitable the first time Germany told Washington to its face that its most faithful of allies wasn't on its side on such a major international issue.

Moreover, contrary to popular beliefs at the time, the Germans' initial wariness, and then outspoken resistance to the military option in Iraq, was expressed much earlier, more persistently, and for the most part more categorically than France's.[12] At various points in 2002 and even early into 2003, France seriously considered going along with the United States in Iraq, even militarily, if the use of force against Hussein's regime had the sanction of a U.N. mandate. As late as November 2002, France and the United States worked hand in hand drafting the first of the U.N. resolutions that could have authorized force against Baghdad. The so-called Paris-Berlin-Moscow axis emerged only in early 2003; by then, however, Paris had indeed taken over the lead opposition role against the war. But it was the Germans' resolute antiwar stand that laid the ground for France's and Russia's defiance, not vice-versa.

Also, although Germany's foreign policy doctrine was indeed in flux at the time—in fact, crying out for definition—it contained a number of steadfast principles and road markers that had evolved through the postwar decades and took on new forms when the world, and Germany, changed so dramatically in the 1990s and then again in September 2001. German foreign policy was informed by the Nazi past but no longer cowed by it—and incorporated positive legacies from more recent German history. This orientation prioritized economic power and the mechanisms of soft and civilian power to effect change, including conditionally linked aid, innovative diplomacy, democracy and governance programs, as well as an ardent commitment to multilateralism, human rights, and a belief in the transformative power of engagement. These were principles similar to those that the various incarnations of the European Union had implemented with result to bring democratic governments and economic prosperity to the western side of the continent. In a way it was a "realo" rather than a "fundi" approach to fostering stability and initiating change: long-term, pragmatic, compromise-oriented. The Germans tended to see poverty, globalization's impact, and resentment over Washington's heavily pro-Israel policies as the root causes that bred antiwestern sentiment in the Middle East and, ultimately, terrorism. With the Kosovo intervention, September 11, and the Afghanistan war coming one on top of the other, Germany hadn't yet undertaken a thoroughgoing public discussion or political debate about its international interests and priorities in this new context. When it began in earnest in 2002, it wasn't coordinated with France or anyone else.

Limited Solidarity

The year 2002, however, *was* an election year in Germany—and foreign policy would feature prominently in the summer campaign, although no one could have known that as early as February. At the time, the entire German political spectrum, including leading Christian Democrats, expressed deep reservations about prematurely attacking Iraq. The year began with the red–green government up against a wall and the conservatives' ascendant again. Opinion polls showed the Christian Democrats ahead of the Social Democrats for the first time since the former's disasterous finance scandal; this gap would only widen over the course of the spring and early summer. In spring 2002 the

SPD was clobbered in state elections in the east, the Greens faring no better, as the *Ossis* reversed their sympathies again, payback for the government's failure to revitalize the economy as promised to them so explicitly.

Morale in the Schröder administration had sunk to rock bottom, no one truly confident that it could stem still-climbing unemployment. The government's economic reforms had neither spurred growth nor had their rationale won over the hearts and minds of tried-and-true Social Democrats. With the statewide electoral defeats, the upper house, the Bundesrat, fell into the hands of the conservatives, a devastating blow for the red–green government. This meant that the Berlin government could pass major legislation only with the Christian Democrats' say-so. It was as if the red–green government had gained an additional, unwanted coalition partner—one much bigger and more important than the Greens. Now all legislation had to be negotiated first with the conservatives before it was put to a vote. Whether on television or in the halls of the chancellery, the normally indefatigable and supremely confident Schröder came across as dejected, just as clueless as the rest of his floundering party. Even his friend Joschka Fischer admitted that he couldn't get through to him.

Over the spring months the saber-rattling in Washington grew louder even though the Bush administration consistently denied that it had plans to attack Iraq. In another affront to European sensibilities, the Bush administration proposed upping the U.S. defense budget by $48 billion, an increase that was alone bigger than Great Britain's entire military expenditures (which were the highest in Europe). International efforts to head off a military confrontation shifted into high gear. Baghdad still refused to readmit U.N. weapons inspectors into Iraq. The Schröder government, as most European leaderships, remained polite but adamant: much could still be done to pacify Saddam Hussein's regime.

In late May 2002 President Bush embarked on a European tour aimed at regreasing the axles of Euro-Atlantic relations. Addressing the Bundestag in Berlin, he made the effort to compliment the European allies' contributions to the war on terror and swore that there were no "war plans on the table." Schröder and Fischer welcomed the conciliatory speech as "historic," "an important step forward," and a "completely new tone."[13] Over apple strudel and Berlin's modest culinary specialty, sausage drenched in curry ketchup, Bush reassured Schröder that Washington would consult—not inform—Germany should the use of armed force against Iraq become a serious option. President Bush left the German capital believing that he and the Germans were of one mind.

But in Berlin for nineteen hours the U.S. president got a firsthand taste of the mounting public hostility, not just toward his Iraq policies but also toward a raft of U.S. positions. As if bottled up for too long, the animosity came gushing out. In welcoming the American president to the Bundestag, its venerable and usually soft-spoken president, the former East German dissident Wolfgang Thierse, warned Bush that force should only be the means of last resort and chided him for Washington's stand against the international court.[14] The Greens authored a sharply worded open letter criticizing the administration's "unilateralist tendencies," such as its positions on global climate change and capital punishment. The growing number of executions in the United States did no service to the cause of human rights elsewhere in the world, the Greens sniped.[15]

In Germany a revitalized peace movement—calling itself the "axis of peace"—had coalesced, the biggest since the 1990–91 protests against the Persian Gulf war and one made up of eastern and western Germans. Finally, it seemed, the nation had found a theme that united it. "There were protests in Germany against attacking Afghanistan too but the war came too fast," explains Annelie Buntenbach, one of the four Greens MPs who voted against German participation in the Afghanistan war. "Then there was the insinuation that sympathy with the 9/11 victims somehow automatically implied supporting U.S. policy, even if was an overreaction or outright wrong, as some of us felt. But by 2002 this was less credible. Many thought that Afghanistan was the end, an exceptional case, but this huge military budget and Bush's rhetoric, this crusade mentality, made many realize that the war on terror could go on and on, to Iraq, then to Iran or wherever. By 2002 there was space and time in Germany for real political dialogue and the feeling that demonstrating could make a difference."

The street protests exhibited both the potent antimilitarist convictions in Germany and an unremitting anti-Americanism linked to a traditional leftist critique of imperialism. Although the two currents often overlapped, they weren't identical. The diverse sentiments behind chants like "No blood for oil" and "War is terror" spanned groups that ranged from liberal Protestants to nostalgic East German communists to the Berlin-based Americans Against War initiative, a group of antimilitarist expats. But the Bush administration's excesses brought out the worst in German anti-Americanism, virtually identical to that which flourished during the 1980s peace movement and the first Gulf War protests. Yet there was something novel in its most recent incarnation—the consent of the newest Germans, the easterners. The official anti-America line propagated by their deceased and discredited system had left a permanent mark on the collective consciousness of many former East Germans. The difference between the two variants of anti-Americanism lay not so much in form as in origin, one the product of a left-wing political subculture, the other of a communist state ideology. Unlike the westerners, so conversant in American culture, the easterners hadn't been liberated by U.S. troops, weaned on Bob Dylan, or educated in American high schools. When *Wessis* were learning English as their second language, *Ossis* were tackling the Cyrillic alphabet in their Russian language classes. The easterners didn't know the United States as the westerners did; and much of what they thought they did know had come through East German propaganda. There were thus few were positive reference points for them, only negatives—and most of those clichés.

Interestingly, the same opinion polls that showed over 90 percent of Germans opposed to Bundeswehr participation in a U.S.-led war in Iraq—even with a U.N. mandate—also revealed that most Germans still valued U.S. leadership and the transatlantic partnership.[16] This also echoed the West German 1980s, when most people wanted the Euromissiles to go but the Federal Republic to remain in NATO and closely allied to the United States. But the new surveys clearly documented increasing frustration with the Bush administration and an intensely critical view of Washington's management of global affairs. In one survey, more than half of those questioned felt the U.S. president was incompetent or even dangerous. Only 19 percent felt Bush was doing a good job.[17] (At roughly the same time, Gallup surveys in the United States showed between 75 and a record-high 84 percent of Americans supporting Bush).[18] On security-related issues there was an ever widening gap: while nine years earlier 62 percent of Germans considered the United States a force for peace and stability in the world, only 48 percent did in May 2002.[19] Yet 68 percent considered themselves "pro-American." The western states were significantly more pro-American (70 percent) than their eastern counterparts (59 percent).[20]

There has been much speculation over when and how Gerhard Schröder decided to turn Iraq policy into a campaign issue. German journalists with friends in high places say it was in late July 2002, upon urging from Fischer—something the foreign minister never denied. Fischer simply didn't see the United States and Europe coming to terms over Iraq. "We have to position ourselves before we get positioned," he allegedly told the chancellor.[21] And, to boot, the opinion polls were as clear as day: Germans didn't want this war. Still, many questions were wide open. The red–green administration would oppose war—but how? In what terms would it make its case? In the past, the Bonn Republic—or even Kohl's post-1990 Germany—would have, at most, meekly abstained. The leadership would have explained that, as Germans, such an undertaking, in light of their past, would be out of the question and then, after an all-party expression of solidarity, go on to offer airspace, logistic assistance, postwar reconstruction funding, and anything else that might be helpful. But not this time—unlimited solidarity in this form had expired in the Berlin Republic.

On a scorching August day on Hanover's Opernplatz, Chancellor Schröder unveiled his antiwar stance to the German public. In a gray suit and the red tie that Social Democrats proudly wore, he addressed 5,000 loyalists in Lower Saxony's capital city, his home turf. The SPD, he exhorted, stands for social justice, a free civil society, equality, and in that "great tradition of SPD peace policy."[22] When Schröder came to the topic of foreign affairs and Iraq, he didn't mince words:

> This much my government has proven, that in times of crisis it is in the position, with determination and a level-head, to stay a reasonable course. . . . We're also prepared to show solidarity but under my leadership this country won't participate in adventures. . . . And concerning the discussion about military intervention in Iraq, I warn against speculating about war and military actions, and I say to those who are planning something, they should not only know how they're going to go in but how they're going to get out. That's why I say: pressure on Saddam Hussein—yes, but playing around with war and military intervention—this I warn against. With me, that's not going to happen.[23]

Now it was official. Germany—the first major country to do so—would neither send troops nor write checks for an attack on Iraq. The crowd on Opernplatz in Hanover burst into applause. The SPD found itself, quite suddenly, back in the race.

"The German people had opposed the United States before in these terms," explains the former U.S. ambassador to Germany, John Kornblum, who lives and works in Berlin. "In the '80s with the nuclear missiles and in 1991 with the Gulf War—there were hundreds of thousands on the streets, but never had a German chancellor actually joined them." The Iraq issue remained front and center in the campaign throughout the record-hot summer. At times Schröder sounded disturbingly populist, with anti-American overtones, a tactic that made some in his own party cringe. "The existential issues concerning the German nation will be decided in Berlin and nowhere else," Schröder would say.[24] At other times he attacked Bush in personal terms reinforcing a clichéd image of the American president as a trigger-happy cowboy out for Iraq's oil. But to attribute the red–green government's opposition to the Iraq war to electioneering alone, as the Bush administration did, downplays the seriousness of the Germans' nuanced stand.

The disagreement between the best of transatlantic allies rapidly escalated into the nastiest crisis in fifty years. In late August, Vice President Cheney, before the Veterans of Foreign War in Nashville, Tennessee, upped the ante, calling for "regime change" by force in Iraq and denounced the readmission of U.N. weapons inspection teams as "worthless." "Simply stated, there is no doubt that Saddam Hussein now has weapons of mass destruction. There is no doubt he is amassing them to use against our friends, against our allies, and against us."[25] Seen from Europe, the loaded rhetoric was tantamount to a declaration that Washington had already committed itself to war against Iraq, regardless of its allies' positions or Hussein's actions in the future.

So perfectly did it play into the chancellor's hands, Cheney's speech could have been drafted by the Committee for the Reelection of Gerhard Schröder. Schröder fired back at once, threatening to withdraw German units from Kuwait if Washington went ahead and attacked Baghdad without a U.N. mandate. A few days later he went even further—now breaking taboo with abandon—declaring that Germany wouldn't back military action against Iraq *even in the event* of a U.N. mandate.[26] No other country had taken such an in-your-face tact. Germany was way out on a limb—and all by itself. This was wholly without precedent: Germany, on its own, upstaging its postwar protector and mentor and then, ostensibly, contradicting the multilateral ethic at the heart of the Federal Republic's *Staatsraison*. But by early September, just three weeks from election day, the poll numbers of the SPD and the Greens had drawn even with those of the CDU and the liberals for the first time.

The Greens' 2002 election campaign was also an extraordinary come-from-behind rally. Despite its impressive list of first-term accomplishments, over the past four years the environmental party had hemorrhaged votes in sixteen consecutive regional elections. In the eastern states, the party didn't occupy a single seat in any of the five *Landtags*. Moreover, younger people across the country were turning up their noses at the frumpy environmental party. Apparently, its graying ex-rebels and bulging-at-the-beltline left-liberals reminded the kids of their parents and social studies teachers. "The Greens no longer have an imaginative vision," explained Hans-Christian Ströbele, a Greens party founder and left-wing Berlin lawyer. Ströbele remained a vehement critic of Fischer and the party's mainstream drift. (Ströbele's campaign slogan—catchy in the German: *Ströbele wählen heisst Fischer quälen*—was "Torment Fischer, vote for Ströbele.") "Politically engaged young people want to change the world, not hear about the day-to-day business of governance. The Greens have lost their credibility."

The Marathon Man set out to prove otherwise. Fischer was the headline act of the Greens' campaign again, traversing the country in his double-decker "Joschka bus," his team scheduling his ten-kilometer workouts as if they were press conferences. Fischer flaunted the grueling six-week campaign tour—and the runs—as if to show that there was nobody steelier than he. He also knew that he was fighting for his political life. Fischer suspected that the race would come down to a handful of votes and should red–green not prevail, his political career in Germany was most likely finished. His stump line: "If you want *me* to remain foreign minister, then vote for the Greens."[27] Never had a Greens campaign been so disciplined or focused on a single person, so far from its grassroots antiparty origins.

At the "Joschka rallies" the contrast between the Greens' former constituency and the new swath of Greens voters couldn't have been more stark. Fischer and Jürgen Trittin, the Greens environment minister, were regularly heckled by peace, antiglobalization, and antinuclear power activists, and even pelted with tomatoes. Those politely applauding didn't look like the Greens' clientele once looked. They were well-dressed seniors, autograph-hungry teeny-boppers, guys from the local sports clubs, yuppies, and, of course, more than a smattering of parents and social studies teachers.

In contrast to Schröder and his SPD, Fischer and the Greens had real fodder for the campaign—tangible results from the first term that the Social Democrats lacked. While Schröder rarely mentioned the word *reform*, the leitmotif of the SPD's 1998 campaign, the Greens could brag about ending the era of nuclear power, promoting gay rights, an eco-tax, and more than a dozen other major environmental laws, as well as the linking of ecology and economics in Germany's booming alternative energy sector. A new government ministry for consumer protection, nutrition, and agriculture was headed by the Greens' up-and-coming star Renate Künast, a forty-two-year-old woman considered by many to be Fischer's successor in the party. This list of accomplishments may have bitterly disappointed hardcore activists and Greens leftists, but the average burgher seemed to find them sensible and worthy.

On the campaign trail, Fischer played the antiwar card, too—just as opportunistically as Schröder but more shrewdly. Fischer was also scrambling to find a hot issue, one he could sell to the Greens' dispirited core constituency. After four years in office, he, as foreign minister, had nothing to offer in the area of *Friedenspolitik* (peace policy). The coalition couldn't even boast that Germany's arms sales had been cut. In fact they had gone up.[28] Yet, unlike Schröder, Fischer steered clear of national-tinged populism, sticking to nuts-and-bolts arguments about the ramifications of dislodging Saddam Hussein by force. When journalists at the *Tageszeitung* grilled him on the ostensible hypocrisy of consenting to the invasion of Afghanistan but not war against Iraq, he responded:

> Intervention in Afghanistan was the response to a type of international terrorism that posed a new threat to international peace. This terrorism possessed a destructive capacity that in the past only states had. You can't negotiate with it. But, in addition to this terrorism, it is at least equally as important to resolve regional conflicts so that the people involved in them won't establish links with terrorist organizations. This is the lesson of September 11: not to permit these forgotten regional conflicts to fester.[29]

But Iraq is another story, he continued:

> With Iraq, we're dealing with the future of the entire Near East. The real question is whether a war against Iraq is the proper means to bring about a new order there. Or whether the point of departure should be brokering a peace between Israel and the Palestinians, and then with that as a basis going on to address other regional problems. Also, we should be moving forward in the spirit of cooperation rather than confrontation: in order to defuse hatred in the Near and Middle East, to integrate it into the world economy and open a way for Islam into modernity.[30]

Washington's Iraq policy was one external windfall that unexpectedly breathed new life into the red–green campaign. The other was literally heaven-sent. In mid-August it began to rain across Europe, the storms inundating southern Germany. Flood waters poured over the banks of the Danube and the Elbe bursting through dams and swamping whole towns and cities, including Dresden. Schröder, a can-do, hands-on type, always at his best with his sleeves rolled up, reacted immediately, approving a huge aid packet for the hardest-hit regions. He swapped his Italian suits for an anorak and rubber boots in order to oversee the evacuations and aid-distribution efforts in person. On TV screens he looked engaged, concerned, in control.

The Greens portrayed the catastrophe as an environmental issue. "We feel vindicated," said Greens spokespeople on nonstop newscasts and talk shows, reminiscent, for those memories that stretched back that far, of the Greens' profile during the 1986 Chernobyl crisis. The Greens noted that they had long warned about the consequences of global warming and urban overdevelopment. Unlike in the United States, there was a consensus in the country and across the political spectrum that the floods were associated with climate change. The Greens—and a tad disingenuously the Social Democrats, too—pointed out that the Christian Democrats voted against fourteen of sixteen of the new Greens-inspired environmental laws. Schröder's discovery of environmental politics suggested that perhaps, belatedly, he was warming up to the merits of a "red–green project."

In the campaign's final, frenzied week, the back-and-forth between Washington and Berlin grew even shriller, the wild exchanges often surreal. Germany's justice minister, Herta Däubler-Gmelin, poured fuel on the fire with a misguided analogy between Bush's manipulation of popular anxiety to wage the war on terror and Hitler's demagogy. The White House, understandably, was incensed. Condoleezza Rice, National Security Advisor at the time, called German–U.S. relations "poisoned."[31] President Bush refused to accept a telephone apology from Chancellor Schröder.

Red-Green II

When the polls closed on the evening of September 22, 2002, the parties and their supporters crowded around television sets for the preliminary results. The forecasted cliff-hanger lived up to all expectations. At first, the conservatives led. The Christian Democrats' top candidate, Bavarian Edmund Stoiber, announced to ecstatic supporters in Munich that they had won the election. "Edmund, Edmund!" they chanted. At 9:30 p.m., in Berlin's Temopdrom, a sprawling tented concert hall, the Greens were milling around nervously. As long as they had hired a band and splurged for a party, the Social Democrats decided to celebrate with the outcome still up in the air. As more votes were tabulated the SPD drew closer to the CDU, the Greens ahead of the Free Democrats. Minutes before midnight, Queen's "We are the Champions" blasted from speakers in the conservative's party center. Half an hour later the music faded in Munich as the SPD's Willy Brandt House in Berlin erupted in pandemonium. The Social Democrats and Christian Democrats had drawn even, but the Greens had gained a stunning 1.9 percentage points above and beyond their 1998 result, increasing their share of the vote to 8.6 percent, its highest nationwide poll ever in the closest Bundestag election since the first, in 1949.

The Greens' surge was enough to put the red–green coalition over the top by the slimmest of margins, just four seats in the 603-member Bundestag. In a photo finish, the Greens' votes had won it for the SPD. The next day the Berlin daily *Der Tagesspiegel* ran a cartoon with a caricature of a gasping Fischer in running gear crossing a finish line with a contented, child-size Gerhard Schröder relaxing in his arms. Schröder is saying: "I knew we'd make it." Political analysts attributed at least 2 percent of the Greens' result to "the Joschka factor" and his determined campaign tour.

The Greens' showing reversed its years-long slide and proved that it could reach out beyond its traditional voters, that it wasn't a "one-generation party." But if the Greens imagined that their heavy lifting might earn them a little more respect—or even ministerial posts—in the new coalition, they would soon learn otherwise. Neither would the junior partner wind up with more ministries nor would the Social Democrats relent on ending military conscription or consent to further raises in the fossil fuels tax. The second term would be devoted to the structural economic reforms that Schröder had once promised—as well as dramatic budget cutting that he hadn't. The Greens would take a back seat during most of it.

The possibilities for mending fences with Washington in the immediate aftermath of the election were dim. U.S. President Bush declined to call Schröder to congratulate him on the victory, as protocol normally required. The White House answered curtly that it was prepared to work with all "democratically elected governments." Rice refused to meet with Fischer the next time he traveled to Washington—making good her promise to "ignore Germany"—and later took at pot shot at Fischer, saying that his "background and career do not suit the profile of a statesman."[32] Although relations between Germany and the United States would eventually thaw—well after the Iraq invasion—Bush would never forgive Schröder for, as he saw it, betraying him. U.S. Secretary of State Colin Powell and his German counterpart did, however, chat after the vote, a sign that lines of communication were still open and that beneath the political storm the mechanics of the transatlantic partnership were largely intact.

The transatlantic estrangement, however, had yet to run its full course. Schröder, though, with his categorical opposition to the use of force in Iraq, had prematurely taken Berlin out of the diplomatic game. Germany was now sidelined, to Fischer's dismay. Germany's no vote had been cast. If Cheney's hawkish address was a gift to Schröder's campaign, Schröder's rigid position was a gift back to the Washington hardliners and unilateralists, a boon to their campaign for war against Iraq.[33] France, although skeptical of U.S.-style regime change in Iraq, sensed that Germany's course was a strategic blind alley. Paris understood that if it wanted Washington to play by the international rules, it had to do so as well. As a permanent Security Council member, France not only had a voice in the debate but also a veto in the council. It thus had to agree to the possibility of the use of force against Iraq should Hussein not meet the United Nations' conditions. Otherwise, the United States would simply circumvent the United Nations and go it alone.

French and American negotiators labored together throughout the fall of 2002 in drafting resolution 1441, which mandated the return of U.N. weapons inspectors to Iraq. It was only in late January 2003 that the French, finally convinced that the United States was intent on vanquishing Saddam Hussein no matter what, reversed course and grabbed the lead role against Washington. With France front and center, isolated and ignored Germany (as of 2003 a voting but nonpermanent member on the Security Council) became a player again, this time as member of an alliance. What most infuriated the United States was that France and Germany, joined by Belgium, didn't just disagree with Washington, they actively rallied resistance against it. This time around the red–green administration had no electoral motives.

The most spectacular episode in the rift came in February 2003 at the annual security conference in Munich, when Fischer stepped up to the podium and responded to U.S. Secretary of Defense Donald Rumsfeld's case for war. He began by responding point by point, in German, to the U.S. case for war. "Why now against Iraq? Is this really the priority?" he asked. And then, with the world's cameras rolling, Fischer pushed the envelope further. He broke into English. Staring straight at Rumsfeld, index finger in the air, he continued: "Sorry, I *am not* convinced." And then, slapping the podium for emphasis, his voice rising added, "You have to make your case. Sorry, you haven't convinced me!" The German news shows showed the footage over and over. The seventy-year-old Rumsfeld silently fumed, looking like a reprimanded schoolboy. The last word clearly hadn't been spoken.

Between September 2002 and March 2003 there was a drawn out tug-of-war over the two Iraq-related Security Council resolutions. Yet, before the U.S. air campaign commenced against Iraq, the list of collateral damage produced by the transatlantic dispute would grow even longer, and include inner-European unity. In a remarkable turn of events—orchestrated in part by neo-conservatives in Washington—the central Europeans (the so-called Vilnius 10), virtually on the eve of their entry into the European Union, opted to throw their backing behind the United States rather than the Franco–German alliance. Rumsfeld had already tried playing off the Europeans against one another, distinguishing between a pro-American "New Europe" and an anti-American "Old Europe" led by Germany and France.[34] Paris and Berlin assumed that a common "European position" would automatically crystallize behind their leads (public opinion everywhere in Europe opposed the war). But they erred egregiously. The positions of the central Europeans, and those of Spain, Italy, and Britain as well, laid bare foreign-policy differences within Europe toward the United States and the Middle East. With these grave disagreements over Iraq, the goal of a common European foreign and security policy took the first of two crushing blows that would dash hopes for a strong EU foreign policy in the near future. The second would come in 2005, delivered by the French themselves, when they rejected the EU constitution treaty in a popular referendum.

Out like a Lamb

At the end of every month, a seven-digit number flashes across German television screens, indisputably the republic's most closely watched statistic. The monthly unemployment figures from the Federal Labor Office in Nuremberg are the unvarnished indicators of the government's progress in combating joblessness and a vital benchmark for its economic policy as a whole. That number had crept higher and higher since 2000. It had long passed the psychologically critical 4 million mark and was inching relentlessly closer to 5 million. Nationwide, unemployment had pushed up to over 10 percent in 2003 (the highest in five years) and the jobless number in the depressed eastern states more than twice as high as that in the west. Gaping budget deficits, which violated EU standards, were forcing almost all Germans to tighten their belts. In the chancellor's office and the halls of the Willy Brandt House the word *crisis* was by now on everyone's lips.

"Agenda 2010" was the name that Schröder and his Social Democratic allies gave their program to fix to the ailing German economy—and that would be synonymous with his second term in office. Unveiled in spring 2003, the Agenda 2010 package presented sweeping reforms for Germany's economy. Schröder, making his case to the German people, pledged to push ahead with ambitious structural reforms that would modernize Germany's economy, make it competitive worldwide, and get Germans back to work. The health and welfare contributions that employers paid out for every hired worker were among the highest in Europe. So wage costs would be lowered by slashing non-wage labor costs. The job market would be deregulated so that employers could hire (and fire) more easily. Slashed unemployment benefits would supposedly boost the incentive for people to take lower-paying work. The *Sozialstaat* had to be pared down, outlays for the long-term jobless reduced along with other benefits.

"I don't want people to be able to read the social status of others by the condition of their teeth," Schröder told the Bundestag in a nationally televised speech. But, he warned, referring to the pressures of globalization, "either we modernize as a social market or we are going to get modernized by unbridled market forces."[35] Schröder was staking everything on Agenda 2010. The surge of that seven-digit number had to be stemmed; the urgency of the reforms was palpable to everyone. Schröder's post-election honeymoon proved breathtakingly short, the windfall from the Iraq war evaporating almost at once. The Social Democrats were pounded again and again in state-wide elections.

Before he could begin to enact Agenda 2010's prescriptions, Schröder needed the backing of his own party, which was anything but guaranteed. The Social Democrats were divided, their century-old party adrift. The in-progress tax reforms and other pro-market measures had alienated many steadfast Social Democrats, the likes of whom would have felt more at home in an Oskar Lafontaine–led SPD. This was not "social justice," as they understood it, a concept at the heart of every campaign that the German Social Democrats had ever run. The welfare system reforms were creating a new underclass in Germany—of elderly, socially disadvantaged families, and immigrants. The last thing they wanted was the German job market turned into something like America's low-wage economy with its "McJobs" and uninsured millions.

Yet when push came to shove, the SPD majority fell in line behind their chancellor, approving Agenda 2010 and launching a battery of reforms that would further transform the Federal Republic. Although the social welfare state wasn't being dismantled lock, stock, and barrel, as some critics charged, the remedies amounted to more than tinkering at its edges. Among the most disputed measures were the labor market reforms, which reduced benefits of those unemployed for more than two years to the same allowance received by long-term welfare recipients. This implied a painful fall in living standards for those without jobs in Germany.

But experts inside and outside of the government agreed: if the reforms bore fruit—in terms of new jobs—even just a little at first, the leadership could quickly win back the trust it had lost. It was, as Schröder acknowledged, a race against time—and the political clock was ticking. Negative fallout from the reform offensive came fast and furiously. The exodus from the SPD accelerated; members were abandoning the party at a pace faster than even the previous year, when it lost a not insignificant 6 percent of its membership.[36] In July, an unknown unemployed train worker, Andreas Ehrhardt, called for weekly rallies in the eastern city of Magdeburg to protest the cuts in social benefits. The first week 600 people showed up, 6,000 the second week and 12,000 by the third. By mid-August there were weekly "Monday rallies" in 200 cities and towns across Germany, strongest though in the east. At the front of the demonstrations were the reform communists of the PDS and the antiglobalization group Attac. One familiar face in the crowd was former finance minister, Oskar Lafontaine, who quit the SPD leadership because of its rightward drift. Lafontaine openly accused Schröder of betraying the party's socialist origins. He and other Social Democrat discontents, it was rumored, were contemplating the formation of a new party to challenge the SPD from the left.

Popular disaffection was nowhere thicker than in the eastern states, where the reforms hit hardest. In many pockets of eastern Germany unemployment soared over 30 percent, the unofficial jobless rate even higher. In state elections in southeastern Thuringia, the Social Democrats scraped together just 14 percent of the vote, a full 12 percentage points behind the PDS. But even worse was to come. In Saxony, another eastern state, the SPD scored under 10 percent—yet another record low, while a neo-Nazi party managed to clear the 5-percent hurdle and land in the regional parliament. Until the Saxony vote, one of the red–green government's claims was to have marginalized the far right, which, in the past, had intermittently captured seats in regional legislatures on both sides of the country. The east was proving fertile ground for populists, of both the left- and the right-wing varieties.

This government seemed to be having no more success than Chancellor Kohl and his conservatives had had in winning over and integrating the 16 million easterners into the Federal Republic. Certainly they weren't coming anywhere close to reproducing Adenauer's feat of integrating 15 million expellees and refugees into the postwar Federal Republic. Apparently, a full fifteen years after unification, a shocking portion of the easterners still felt alien in their adopted republic. Only every second easterner believed that the Federal Republic's form of democracy was right for the country (compared to over 70 percent in the West.)[37] While the easterners resented their western counterparts' prosperity, the westerners in turn resented the billions of euros that came out of their pay checks to subsidize the east. At public appearances in eastern cities, Schröder was regularly booed and even forced to duck airborne eggs. As chancellor, Kohl had endured the same abuse after the honeymoon of unification ended. Schröder's message to easterners, westerners, the trade unions, the SPD left, and everyone else was unwavering: "I cannot do otherwise," he'd say, paraphrasing the Protestant reformer Martin Luther.

Fischer Is History

Fischer and the Greens, on the other hand, were sailing through the second term. Most—although not all—Greens MPs backed the Agenda 2010 reforms, but unlike the Social Democrats, they were not in the public's eyes directly associated with the economic fallout. In regional elections, the Greens chalked up gains again. In the 2004 European Parliament vote they doubled their numbers. According to polls, most Germans thought environmental protection was the government's greatest strength.

Fischer, it seemed, could do no wrong. Germany tittered with delight when the country's most beloved pol brought his new romantic interest, the dark-hued twenty-eight-year-old Minu Barati, to the annual Press Ball in Berlin.* In a sexy, low-cut black gown, the Germany-born Persian beauty was the center of attention at the star-studded gala. Though Fischer didn't crack a smile often these days, he must have grinned at the *Bild-Zeitung*'s gushing front page the next day. "What makes Joschka so sexy?" its banner headline read.[38] "*Bild* explains the sexy secret of Germany's adored Green

* Joschka Fischer and Nicola Leske married in 1999 and divorced in 2003.

politician." The same article—in the newspaper that had blasted the student rebels as Moscow stooges and had Joschka and Ede Fischer beaten black and blue in 1968—claimed that two-thirds of German women wanted to have a baby with Joschka Fischer. Had *Bild-Zeitung* really changed its stripes? More likely, Fischermania was just too lucrative to pass up.

Yet, away from the public eye, Fischer's élan had long worn thin. Journalists grumbled constantly about his narcissism and abusive behavior. He'd regularly snap at and even berate correspondents and blame them for his lapsed exercise regimen (and expanding waistline) as well as their stupid questions. Similar noises had been coming from within the foreign ministry, from the same colleagues who had initially praised Fischer's intellectual verve and openness when the trim Marathon Man first entered the office. It seemed that heavyweight Fischer no longer considered himself merely Germany's foreign minister but also a kind of master geostrategist whose unique intellect was better employed devising grand solutions to deal with globalization, the Middle East, the energy crisis, and China-India relations than the routine chores of German foreign policy. In fact, in his spare hours late at night or on overnight plane trips while his diplomats slept, Fischer was penning a new book that addressed these epic questions.[39] He accepted ever less advice from the career diplomats, countering their suggestions with rejoinders such as "What's your name?" The department heads would exit his office fuming, having been lectured to or dressed down like interns. The atmosphere in the foreign ministry, said insiders, had *never* been worse.

The gathering storm was predicated by a uniquely German inner-office tiff in the Auswärtiges Amt. It had come to Fischer's attention that deceased foreign-service officers with Nazi pasts were receiving fawning obituaries in the ministry's in-house publication. The foreign office was one of the few German institutions that had circumvented a coming to terms with its past during the postwar decades. Hundreds of former Nazi party activists—and even former SS members—had been recruited after the war, many going on to distinguished careers in the foreign service. The row was provoked when the ministry's internal newsletter published an obituary glorifying a recently deceased diplomat who had spent twenty years in prison for his crimes as a senior prosecutor in Nazi-occupied Czechoslovakia. The obituary disingenuously stated that the man had spent ten years in an internment camp and then lauded him for his "services to the country."[40] When a retired staff member alerted Fischer to the gaffe, he reacted at once, ruling that in the future all such obituaries would mention only the posts that the person had held.

Ostensibly the issue was thus closed, a faux pas from times past belatedly scratched from the republic's books. But no. Fischer's move infuriated a surprising number of the ministry's older personnel as well as conservative politicians. They claimed that the ruling sullied the reputations and service records of ministry staff who did indeed have Nazi pasts but later performed distinguished work in the foreign service. The acting German ambassador to Switzerland published an open letter in *Bild-Zeitung* claiming that Fischer's order effectively branded all wartime-generation diplomats as war criminals.[41] In early 2005 more than seventy senior diplomats signed an open letter to Fischer that read, in part: "The withholding of this honor because of the single criteria of membership in an organization of the Third Reich is blatantly high-handed and reflects the Manichistic historical schema of those who in 1968 believed that you can't trust anyone over thirty."[42] Nevertheless, Fischer stuck to his guns—with support from much of the diplomatic service. But the affair added to the ill will simmering in the ministry.

The resentment that had been building on many fronts exploded into the open when a full-blown scandal engulfed Fischer and the foreign office. The imbroglio revolved around an initiative that Fischer and his deputy, the Greens Ludger Volmer, took in early 2000, making good on one of the Greens' campaign promises—namely, to relax German visa requirements for foreign visitors. The policy move had its roots both in Greens party history as well as that of the divided Germany (when GDR citizens were denied travel rights). The little party had long propagated a less insular, less provincial Germany, one more open to foreign cultures and influences. The Greens buzzword was *multiculturalism*—different cultures coexisting together in one vibrant, inclusive society. The new citizenship law, for example, which had converted more than a million foreigners into full-fledged Germans, was a step in this direction. An immigration law was in the works. But another barrier to such a worldly, open Germany was the strict visa requirements for entering the country—applicable especially to people from poorer countries. The Greens didn't want the European Union to be, as they put it, "Fortress Europe."

In early 2000, to very little fanfare, Volmer announced new visa rules for entering Germany. Although Fischer's signature was on the directive, it was not insignificant that Volmer presented it. Volmer, a Third World specialist, had been a leading figure in the antimilitarist wing of the party and among Greens pacifists he was seen as their man in the foreign ministry. The new visa policy, known as the Volmer Directive, was thus a crumb that Fischer and Volmer could throw to left-wing Greens. Here, finally, was *something* Greens-tinted about the new German foreign policy.

Although the directive raised hackles inside the administration, it went into effect largely unnoticed by the German press or opposition. But in some countries, the impact on travel to Germany was immediate. In Ukraine, Russia, and Belarus, the number of approved visa applications doubled in less than a year. On the form one only had to write "sightseeing on the Rhine River" or "visitation of the Cologne cathedral" and name a hotel in order to have it stamped. If all this meant was that Germany had more paying tourists, there wouldn't have been a problem.

The problem was that the new laws enabled shady German middlemen and eastern European mafiosos to bring women and girls into Germany (and then into other EU countries via Germany) for the purpose of exploiting their labor, predominantly in the sex business. At informal labor markets in Cologne and elsewhere, Ukrainian "tourists" offered to work for four dollars an hour. The queue at the Ukrainian embassy in Kiev resembled a giant rugby scrum, which was in fact ruled by criminal gangs. The cries of the swamped German embassies in Kiev and elsewhere back to Berlin went unheeded. It took the foreign ministry four years to revoke the simplified visa rules.

The full facts surrounding the Volmer Directive surfaced not during the peak of abuse but only afterward, in an opposition inquiry into the 2000–04 visa policy. Only then did the media, the Bundestag conservatives, the ministry's miffed diplomats, and the other plentiful enemies that Fischer had accumulated over the years finally have what they needed to attack him, which they did like famished wolves. Never would the affair have escalated so wildly had Fischer—and to a certain extent the Greens—not grown overconfident and haughty. The word *hubris* could be found in more than one scathing op-ed.

Fischer was accused of incompetence, inattention to detail, and being an accomplice to organized crime. It was pointed out anew that he was really just a taxi driver. *Der Spiegel* devoted several hard-hitting articles in one issue to Fischer's high-handed behavior in the ministry and the gripes and accusations of the career diplomats.[43] Now it was "pay back time," quipped the weekly. Fischer was even reminded of the vulgar seven-letter word that he, in 1984, called the Bundestag president; it was indelicately suggested that this now applied to him. Fischer appeared uncharacteristically confused, unable to parry the charges.

The Greens came in for a political flaying as well. For much too long they had held their noses high, posing as "the better Germans," valiant crusaders against forces of greed and self-interest. Their moralistic tone could indeed grate like finger nails across a blackboard. At the heart of the crisis, argued critics, was the Greens' naïve, rosy vision of a world with no borders and no security threats, in which all foreign nationals were good and only Germans were evil. A blunder of this magnitude, charged conservatives in the press, was bound to happen with such wide-eyed dilettantes in power. They put security, German jobs, innocent women, and the esteemed foreign ministry's reputation at risk. As exaggerated as these charges were, the debacle stung the Greens: a badly implemented Greens idea had indeed facilitated the trafficking of women, something that Greens considered a modern form of slavery.

The affair put Fischer on the ropes like never before and, clearly rattled, he seemed suddenly bereft of his legendary political instinct. He faltered in front of the press and at first blamed his colleagues in the ministry for the lapses. His popularity ratings sank for the first time. Calls for his resignation grew, and many speculated that stepping down was the only way out. The chancellor's office, initially unconcerned, went into crisis management mode. As much as Schröder bullied and belittled the Greens inside the coalition, he knew that Fischer and his party had secured the administration's reelection—and would be necessary again, in 2006. An independent parliamentary commission was set up to investigate.

It took the parliamentary inquiry and the barrage of criticism (one journalist called it a "schadenfreude orgy") to snap Fischer out of his untimely funk. During the twelve-hour marathon grilling, Fischer found his old form, jousting with adversaries as he had when he was a freshman lawmaker in the 1980s. When one of the investigators, a Christian Democrat, mocked Fischer saying that his response to one question wanted to make him cry, Fischer shot back deadpan: "Well, I'm sorry I don't have a tissue for you. I hate to see crocodiles cry."[44] He admitted mistakes and pointed out that not a single statistic showed an increase in crime or trafficking during the period in question. His mea culpa took the wind out of his detractors' sails, leaving them with little to pin on him save "mistakes made." The affair ended harmlessly but with Fischer yanked back down to earth and the Greens no longer riding quite so high.

It wasn't the visa fiasco that precipitated the fall of the red–green coalition and, ultimately, ended the political project of the protest generations. Rather, the Social Democrats' numbing string of losses on the state level and withering popularity across the country had boxed Chancellor Schröder into a corner. The Agenda 2010 reforms had failed to brake the rise in unemployment or stimulate growth. One state after another had fallen into conservative hands. The coalition was hamstrung, unable to move forward.

The May 2005 vote in North Rhine-Westphalia was make-or-break for Schröder and the SPD. Germany's most populous state and industrial heartland, the "Red Ruhr," had been in Social Democrat hands for thirty-nine years. But when the votes were counted, the SPD faced a crushing defeat, punishment pure and simple for the job crisis and unpopular reforms. In a brazen and wholly unexpected move, Schröder announced new nationwide elections for fall 2005, a full year ahead of schedule. The alternative, as he saw it, was a paralyzed government with no mandate for further reforms or power to enact other meaningful legislation.

The long faces in the Greens' party headquarters said everything about the implications of early elections for the eco-party. The day after Schröder's surprise announcement, the *Tageszeitung* front-page headline summed up its implications: "Fischer is History."[45] Every poll showed the reelection of the red–green coalition a long shot of staggering odds. Although the Greens' numbers had fallen off only slightly, it appeared nearly impossible that the SPD would be able match its 2002 results. Germany was headed for either four years of conservative rule or, as it turned out, a grand coalition between the Social Democrats and the Christian Democrats.

One last time Fischer climbed into the Joschka bus and campaigned as if every vote might turn the election. By his side was Minu Baruti (who at the end of October in Rome would become Fischer's fifth wife) and her three-year old daughter. On election night the Greens polled an admirable 8.1 percent, but it was nowhere near enough to compensate for the Social Democrats' losses. Whatever the composition of the next German government, it wasn't going to include Joschka Fischer, the Greens, or Gerhard Schröder. The political project of the protest generations had come to a premature and anticlimactic end.

Conclusion

> "There are difficult fatherlands. One of those is Germany. But it's our fatherland."
> —German President Gustav Heinemann, 1969

> "The only thing fixed about Germany seems to have been the continual dispute about what being German might mean."
> —Historian Konrad Jarausch, 2005

In the summer of 2006, the world glimpsed a Germany it didn't think it knew. Seven cities in the Federal Republic hosted the World Cup, the single-most anticipated sporting event for most of the world, held every four years. Thirty-two soccer teams from around the globe, thousands of journalists, and over 3 million fans descended on the country. As it happened, however, Germany was more than just playing turf for the games; its latest incarnation, the Berlin Republic, was itself on display to the world.

Germany's twenty-first century demeanor surprised many observers. The country opened its arms to the far-flung visitors, embracing them in a spirit of transnational fraternity. The jovial, feel-good atmosphere of Germany's "summer fairytale" seemed so very "un-German." The foreign media delighted in the easy-going German fans, their faces painted black, red, and gold. They sported silly wigs, Day-Glo necklaces, and outlandish cloth top hats, also in the national colors. In a country that had for decades shunned open expressions of nationalism, there were suddenly German flags everywhere, the streets and stadiums awash in them. Yet there was nothing belligerent or jingoistic about this new patriotism. In fact, the Germans seemed to be playfully mocking themselves—and, implicitly, the self-important claims of nationalism as such. Visiting commentators gushed that Germany had reinvented itself without their knowing, as if the transformation had happened overnight.

Although it was proclaimed that Germany had now finally entered the company of "normal" nations, this lighthearted nationalism was, in fact, anything but normal. Few other nationalisms would jest with symbols as sacrosanct as the national flag or any other emblem of the patria. While today's average German seems to feel comfortable identifying with Germany, in a way that many postwar countrymen weren't, it is a patriotism shorn of arrogance and bluster. This German nationalism has been informed and in a way neutralized by the past, but not freed from it. In Germany today the lessons of history are embedded in national identity, to the extent that being "proud to be German" implies pride in the fact that it isn't the ethnocentric nationalism of old. The German soccer fans were exhibiting, as the Federal Republic long had, a unique capacity to absorb critique and exercise self-criticism. This national thing, the Germans seemed to be saying, is important to us, but only "so important"—and we're proud of that, too.

Nearly two decades after unification, this new German patriotism illustrates that neither conservatives' efforts to "renationalize" the unified Germany nor the left's "constitutional patriotism" has carried the day. Conservative intellectuals had hoped that the country's return to nation-statehood would open the way for a revival of German nationalism and, implicitly, a welcome end to the preoccupation with the Nazi past and the limitations it implies. This didn't happen. Nor did the kind of postnational, civic patriotism or "European identity" embraced by many West Germans at the end of the 1980s take hold. More Germans than ever say they are "proud to be German," a sentiment previously as politically incorrect as flag waving.*

The world wars, the Nazis' rise to power, and the Holocaust remain conscious reference points in Germany today—with implications for public policy. They are, however, buttressed and often overshadowed by an array of positive affirmations picked up along the way during the postwar decades. One survey taken in 2005, for example, asked Germans, "What best defines Germany?" The highest number answered its tolerance for "freedom of expression," followed by postwar reconstruction, the constitution, the quality of schools, and the country's peaceful reunification.

---

* Nevertheless, this pride is comparatively restrained. A 2006 University of Chicago study showed Germans at the bottom of a list measuring "pride" in their country. The United States was first, Austria fourth. ("Deutsche nicht stolz auf ihr Land," *Bild-Zeitung*, March 2, 2006.)

(At the list's bottom were German wine and the postwar loss of the eastern territories.) The persons who best exemplify Germany? Albert Einstein (a Jew), Johann Wolfgang von Goethe, and Konrad Adenauer, in that order. As for the living figure who best "represents" Germany: the former Social Democratic chancellor Helmut Schmidt came in first, Joschka Fischer second, and Helmut Kohl a distant third.[1]

"Since unification," writes German historian Edgar Wolfrum, "the Germans find themselves in a process of re-creating the nation, or indeed creating it anew, yet it is a concept of nation for which history and memory still take a leading role. One more time, or perhaps still, the Germans are 'in transit.'"[2] The red–green government's stands on Germany's relationship to its history illuminate the complex political geography of this new terrain. In a tricky and at times contradictory balancing act, Joschka Fischer and Gerhard Schröder walked a fine line between acting as representatives of the generation that had accepted the guilt of Germany's past and being the spokesmen of postwar-born Germans (two-thirds of the population) who felt they had conscientiously incorporated the lessons of the past into their worldviews. In the foreign ministry, for example, Fischer clamped down on glowing obituaries written about Nazi-compromised diplomats. This little tempest was very "Bonn Republic," evidence that its concerns hadn't been abandoned with unification and the shift to Berlin. Much different was the clash over German participation in the 1999 NATO bombing campaign of Milosevic's Serbia. A sign of a new approach to the politics of memory and history, Fischer invoked the Holocaust and Germany's world wars to *justify* the deployment of German forces against Yugoslavia. This was the same rationale that for decades had served to *restrain* Germany militarily. Welcome to the Berlin Republic.

In striking contrast to his predecessor Helmut Kohl, Gerhard Schröder demonstrated that he was not prisoner to history's dictates, even though he accepted their general wisdom. In European Union budgetary negotiations, the chancellor defended "German interests" in a way that Kohl never would—or could—have done. The equating of German national interests to European Union interests, so axiomatic to the Bonn Republic, no longer held in Berlin. Another example, Germany's compensation for Nazi slave labor was something previous administrations had dragged their feet on, while the Schröder government struck a deal with camp survivors. Although, to its credit, the Berlin government (together with German industry) settled with the plaintiffs, the total compensation, $5.2 billion, was half of that the victims had demanded. Berlin had struck a tough deal, after hard-nosed negotiations. On another front, France acknowledged the new Germany when, in 2004, Paris invited Chancellor Schröder to commemorate the sixtieth anniversary of D-Day, an honor never extended to other German chancellors. In foreign affairs, Berlin's active involvement in the Middle East, formerly a no-go area for Germany, demonstrated the many possibilities open to the Federal Republic in the twenty-first century. As it happened, Joschka Fischer's unique relationship to both the Palestinian and Israeli leaderships enabled Germany to intervene diplomatically in the region, with positive result. Germany is one of the main architects of the Middle East "road map," the 2003 peace plan that envisions a two-state solution to the Israeli-Palestinian conflict.

Red–Green Republic?

Even before the red–green government took office, this was a Germany that reflected the 1960s cultural revolution, the long march, and the spirit of civic empowerment that energized the extra-parliamentary campaigns. The array of "from below" movements helped to deepen and broaden democracy in the postwar state, a narrative that Germans in neighboring East Germany could only join in 1989. A new ethic of political participation and civic responsibility took root, a concept of popular sovereignty that put the citizen before the state. In the guise of the Greens, the extra-parliamentarians took their causes into the Bundestag and went on to govern in coalitions across western Germany. Although, initially, they had to kick down the door to get in, these institutions ultimately proved more permeable—and malleable—than they had imagined. While the compromises the Greens made narrowed the scope of their project, the process enabled their ideas to penetrate deep into German society and, in many instances, to win a degree of consensus. All of the republic's parties, including the Christian Democrats, have borrowed liberally from the Greens in areas such as ecology, women's rights, and consumer protection. Were it not for the women's movement, it is hard to imagine a woman, such as Germany's conservative chancellor Angela Merkel, elected in 2005, making it to the top of the republic.

As diverse as they were, most of the grassroots movements were in some way reacting to the constraints, as well as the consequences, of tradition. In the cultural realm, many old traditions were replaced by new ones. Much of the "alternative culture" of the 1970s, for example, has blended into today's mainstream—to the extent that younger Germans accept it as if it had never been another way. Just one example: Few of today's students who live in shared apartments trace the idea back to the early seventies' co-ops, although aspects of "co-op culture" are present in the communal living and decision-making processes of today's *Wohngemeinschaften*, the same term that the sixty-eighters used for "co-op." Although unintended, alternative culture meshed better with "consumer culture" than any of its progenitors could ever have imagined. Organic foods, all-natural products, regenerative energies, socially conscious investment funds, and eco-tourism are highly profitable businesses. This said, many of the original countercultural experiments were also rethought over time and discarded, the traditional ways—or at least variations of them—looking less harmful in hindsight. The sixty-eight-inspired "anti-authoritarian child rearing," for example, turned out not necessarily to lead to more creative, free-thinking children but rather, all too often, to entirely self-centered and unmanageable kids.

Germany today is a vastly richer, more heterogeneous society than it ever had been, a reality that makes contemporary Germanness so much harder to pin down. This is only partly a consequence of the long march. Nevertheless, its elected representatives, the red–green government, managed to codify into law much of the social diversity that distinguishes today's Germany from past selves. By recasting the legal requirements of citizenship, it overhauled the ethnically exclusive concept of Germanness that had been on the books for a century. In the same spirit, the 2004-passed immigration statute, the first ever in postwar Germany, belied the myth that immigration was somehow anathama to Germany and a threat to Germanness. Similarly, antidiscrimination legislation pushed by the Greens,* as well as the gay marriage law and prostitution's decriminalization, acknowledge that Germany is a society that includes and respects its gays and lesbians, peoples of all races and religions, handicapped persons, the elderly, and sex workers, too. This Germany no longer belongs to straight white Christian men and their nuclear families.

Certainly, the seven years of red–green administration etched an ecological stripe into the republic that will be difficult, though not impossible, to rub out. The renewable energies legislation turned Germany into a pioneer in the multibillion-dollar industry, testament that climate-compatible

* This legislation was drafted by the Greens and finally, in watered down form, passed by the newly elected grand coalition in 2006.

strategies don't necessarily impede modernization and the pursuit of profit. The Berlin Republic also set Europe-wide standards with rigorous quality standards for agribusiness, as well as the toughest worldwide controls on foodstuffs made from genetically modified crops. The Greens-led Ministry for Consumer Protection, Food and Agriculture gave organic farming an enormous boost, over the fierce protests of the powerful farm lobby. These measures, in addition to the eco-tax, the nuclear-power phaseout, and laws governing climate protection, flood waters, consumer safety, and nature conservation, make Germany among the greenest—although not necessarily *the* greenest—in Europe and the world. Its environment friendly policies, for example, put it roughly on a par with the Scandinavian countries. These kinds of environmental programs are models for the post-communist countries of central and eastern Europe, which are struggling with the legacy of ecology-blind state-planned economies, on the one hand, and the new profit-*über-alles* ethic of the free market, on the other.

Yet the complexity and contradictions of translating ideals into policy illustrated the boundaries of ideal-driven politics in multiparty democracy. The immigration law, for example, was a far cry from the one Greens had envisioned. But, after drawnout bargaining and numerous draft bills, it was the best they could get. A government-sponsored report summed it up accurately: "The door [to immigration] is now by no means wide open but 'open a crack.' "[3] This was the price of power, of the "realo" way. In other areas, noble intentions were even harder to translate into practice. The abuse of the government's liberalized visa regime underscored the complications of an "open borders" policy without requisite precautions. The backlash ensured that nothing similar will be attempted in the near future, if ever. Likewise, the Greens' hallmark multiculturalism took an unexpected flaying. In Germany as elsewhere, multicultural policies have all too often led to the existence of parallel societies among migrant populations, in which patterns of cultural conservatism are preserved. In these niches, women remain subservient to men and are often the victims of domestic violence. In the aftermath of 9/11, as well as the 2004 and 2005 terrorist bombings in Spain and London, multiculturalism was cited as another example of starry-eyed idealism that ended in debacle. Today, the Greens, too, acknowledge that integration should be promoted, although, they argue, not forced upon immigrants. And then there were those areas of prime Greens concern in which the red–green government accomplished nothing at all: Germany's arms exports didn't sink, no highway speed limit was set, first-use nuclear weapons remained in European silos, and just as many cars were on the road as in 1998. And it turned out to be Al Gore—not Joschka Fischer—who became the world's spokesman for global environmental issues, though it certainly could have been otherwise.

Also on its account, though not to its credit, the red–green years saw Germany's social welfare system begin a historic restructuring. The government took a giant step in the direction of the free market and, as predicted, the reforms increased the gap between the haves and the have-nots.[4] In the Berlin Republic, job loss or long-term unemployment was more likely to cast one into the leagues of a growing underclass. One particularly damning report, commissioned by the government itself, calculated that between 1998 and 2003, the percentage of Germans living on the poverty line rose from 12.1 to 13.5.[5]

On the face of it, however, it was in foreign affairs that the Berlin state broke most dramatically with Bonn. The Berlin Republic demonstrated itself a confident, at times independent-minded international actor. An ironic twist, Germany's critically minded "culture of protest"[6] helped win the Berlin Republic the trust of its international allies, a confidence that enabled the red–green government to pursue a pro-active, interventionist foreign policy, one which bitterly divided the ranks of the protest generations themselves. The Germans' skepticism of institutional authority and probing collective conscience make the bar for German military endeavors relatively high; Germany touts a cautious "strategic culture"[7] with a built-in extra-parliamentary check. And, even in light of its deployments of German troops, the Berlin Republic proved itself an imaginative source of alternative, nonmilitary strategies to defuse conflicts and broker peace. In the spirit of both *Ostpolitik* and *Friedenspolitik*, the civilian power of conflict prevention mechanisms, creative diplomacy, and conditionally linked aid remain the favored tools of the republic on the Spree—means best employed together with European allies, as part of European Union security policy.

By far the biggest question mark looming over the Berlin Republic is developments in its eastern states, the former territory of East Germany. The 16 million-person citizenry there has not fused seamlessly with that of the old Federal Republic. During the Cold War years, Willy Brandt called Germany "two states, one nation." Today Germany is one state with two societies, divided along the old frontline of the East–West conflict. At the crux of the problem is the beleaguered economy there, which has neither rebounded from the shock of the market transition nor proved capable of starting up anew. Unemployment is over 30 percent in many particularly hard-hit regions, eastern Germany's "black holes." Those pockets are wastelands, emigration having drained the best young minds. Historical comparisons with the early decades of the Bonn Republic are disheartening: in 1965, for example, sixteen years after the Federal Republic's creation, the economic miracle had already run its course. At that time, the citizens of the postwar Federal Republic were waking up to democracy; the Easter Marches and Voltaire Clubs were in full swing; and the outbreak of the student movement was just around the corner. Today there is nothing remotely similar in the depressed, disillusioned east.

Blame for this bleak state of affairs has been cast about liberally. One candidate, certainly, is the Kohl administration, which orchestrated the overnight transition of the unprepared eastern economy to market competition. Many argue that the Treuhand holding company, responsible for selling off the east's state-owned enterprises, in fact oversaw the demise of these companies rather than their successful privatization. The easterners' own blind rush into the arms of the Federal Republic undermined the possibility of them bringing something of their own into the union, which later made unification feel all the more like a hostile takeover. Another factor is certainly the completely different politicization and socialization that the easterners experienced in the GDR. During the Cold War years, the populace profited neither from a Konrad Adenauer nor a Rudi Dutschke, from neither parliamentary democracy nor civic movements. The oft-cited contribution of the easterners to the Berlin Republic is the spirit of "freedom and civic courage" exhibited in autumn 1989. This is, for the most part, a *Lebenslüge* (self-deception), though perhaps a necessary one. Although East German citizens did eventually take to the streets in late 1989—and overthrew the regime—it was only after a very small number of truly courageous activists had opened the way. In fact, the history of communist East Germany is largely one of compliant (if grudging) submission to the state and a striking *lack* of civic courage. When this short burst of democracy from below did happen, it faded quickly; once unification was in sight, the answer to all of the easterners' problems and dreams were transferred to another, more benevolent state authority.

The thin democratic consciousness, collective inferiority complex, and economic desolation in the east have proved fertile ground for populism. The former East German communist party, now called the Left Party, has emerged as a permanent part of the republic.[8] Positively, this contributes to political pluralism—making the German party spectrum more resemble those of France and Italy, as well as of Hungary and Poland—and it gives the Federal Republic a democratic socialist party again. Yet the party's apologetic explanations of the discredited regime and its frequent recourse to populism taps illiberal currents. It is telling that easterners who describe themselves as leftist are drawn to the former communists and not to the Greens. That said, in every national election since 1998 over 60 percent of eastern voters opted for one of the three left-wing parties: Alliance 90/ Greens, the PDS/Left Party, or the SPD. There is once again a "majority to the left of the CDU" in the Federal Republic, and it could come to office if only the Social Democrats would agree to share power with the Left Party. While it does so in several eastern states including city-state Berlin, it rules out doing the same on the federal level. But then, the SPD once said this, just as adamantly, about governing with the Greens, too.

The Berlin Republic also has a far right, with organized intellectual and violent lumpen strains that contest the liberal consensus. Despite their marginality, they claim a place in the republic, sometimes by means as brutish as attacking darker skinned foreigners. The mere existence of these actors, in Germany of all places, attests to the fact that racist thinking and illiberal values still vie among the republic's competing discourses. While a few of the small extremist parties entered some regional legislatures in West Germany in the late 1980s and early 1990s, they were shut out of electoral politics during most of the red–green years. Unlike the national legislatures in France, Italy, and almost every other European country, Germany alone doesn't have, and never has had, a far right party in the national parliament. But, disturbingly, far right parties have begun to make headway in the eastern states, including the election of such parties to two *Landtags* in 2004 and 2006. Surveys show racism and intolerance consistently and substantially higher there than in the west.[9] In the past, the Bonn Republic reacted by banning rightist groups, symbols, and songs. In desperation the Berlin Republic has tried this, too. But outlawing Nazis doesn't address their sources; a stable democracy like the Federal Republic now has to battle these phenomena with democratic means. It has to win young Germans over through its ideas and achievements, convincing them they have the better future in a liberal republic.

As for the Greens, among its laurels the German party has inspired countless other ecology parties across Europe and beyond. Today there is an all-Europe Green Party with representatives of thirteen countries in the European Parliament (its co-chairman, Dany Cohn-Bendit). In sixteen European countries—eleven of them former communist states—greens have shared power in national governments. In the west, it was first in 1995 in Finland that a green party entered a national government. Since then, greens came to power in France, Belgium, and Italy, although always as smaller coalition partners and never as a major party. And sadly, the popularity of the first green parties in central and eastern Europe proved short-lived. In those countries, the material concerns of the economic transition took precedent over the post-materialist values of environmentalism. But there is cause for optimism: in 2006 the Czech Greens entered the national government there for the first time.

And certainly, the German Greens' ecological concerns are no less relevant today than they were in previous decades. Everywhere in the world, ecology, energy, and sustainable development are front-burner issues, as global warming illustrates so vividly. In the past, environmentalists were ridiculed as being "hysterical" and "fear-mongering" for saying what most scientists and world leaders admit to today.

Yet despite this, nowhere are green fortunes any more uncertain than in Germany itself. The political project of the protest generations has run its course and the Greens are now victims of their own success. So many of their ideas have become policy and their assumptions part of a broad consensus that they appear unsure where to go next. While the party's concerns have not been rendered obsolete by their partial adoption as policy, the Greens have lost their unique claim to them. All of the German parties now have environmental agendas, even if the quality of their commitment to them varies greatly. Also, in opposition again, the Greens find themselves fighting rear-guard actions to protect their projects from the successor government. The best example is nuclear power: conservatives are doing everything in their power to reverse the phasing out program—and now, audaciously, they do so in the name of scaling back on fossil fuels. This new defensive orientation of the Greens, basically conservative, drains the party of that pinch of utopia that had once separated it from the rest. The flat, bureaucratic face of their leadership today reflects this quandry; it's hard even to imagine one of today's top Greens soiling his or her suit to blockade a nuclear reactor site. Younger Germans gripe that the sixty-eighters *are* now the establishment, so ensconced at the top of the universities, media, and think tanks that it is impossible to get around them.

Furthermore, with Greens' antimilitarist credentials tarnished, the Left Party now poses as the republic's peace party. Understandably, the Greens' protestations against new German missions abroad—or upgrading those that the red–green administration approved—now ring insincere. On top of this, their coalition partner of choice, the Social Democrats, has forsaken them for the Christian Democrats. The Greens' options have dwindled, leading them to explore the possibility of "black–green" coalitions with the Christian Democrats, a model being tested in several smaller cities. As of 2007, there was just one red–green administration in all of Germany's sixteen states—in the little northwestern city-state of Bremen.*

Whatever the Greens do, they will now have to do it without Joschka Fischer. In 2006 Fischer resigned his seat in the Bundestag in order to accept an adjunct lectureship at Princeton University as the Schultz Professor of International Economic Policy. He has a little office, room 111, on the campus. Most of the students have no idea who he is. Fischer splits his time between Princeton and Berlin with his new wife, Minu Baruti, and her young daughter. He works on his memoirs and occasionally pens an op-ed for the international dailies. The German newspapers do an occasional light feature on him, his name still near the top of popularity polls. Although Fischer now has plenty of time on his hands, he doesn't lace up the running shoes anymore, presumably marathons being another one of those against-all-odds challenges that he doesn't have to accomplish twice.

Fischer has ruled out a return to domestic politics in Germany, saying that he has passed the baton to a younger generation of Greens. "I don't want to be the grandpa in the Muppets Show," he said. In a typically Fischeresqe parting shot at the party that took him to the top of the republic, he told the *Tageszeitung*, "I'm one of the last live rock 'n' rollers of German politics. Now in all of the parties come the 'playback' generation."[10] In other words, presumably, the heavy lifting of setting Germany on a peaceful, democratic, western course has been done—by Fischer and the other greats of modern German politics. Now all that follow-up generations have to do is keep it there. Although this kind of "end of history" thesis is far too undialectical for a former student of Adorno and Habermas, Germany is now out of the woods, its transition to the world of civilized states incontrovertible.

Although his name has been tossed around for international posts such as EU foreign minister and U.N. special envoy to the Middle East, he would probably have to have the backing of one of Germany's major parties in

* A sign that the Greens might indeed be around for some time, the party captured a stunning 17 percent of the Bremen vote in early 2007—their best election tally ever—and in doing so put a red–green government back on the country's political map.

order to land them. It wouldn't be too late for Fischer to assume the role of international spokesman and lobbyist for the global environment, perhaps even in tandem with Al Gore. There's a challenge with plenty of room for rock 'n' roll. Joschka Fischer is only in his late fifties, much too young for a *zoon politikon* such as himself to retire. If his past is any harbinger of the future, his next incarnation may be as surprising as that of Germany's own "in transit" self.

Notes

CHAPTER 1

1. Perttri Ahonen, *After the Expulsion: West Germany and Eastern Europe, 1945–1990* (New York and Oxford: Oxford University Press, 2003), 21. See also Angelika Königseder and Juliane Wetzel, *Waiting for Hope: Jewish Displaced Persons in Post-World War II Germany* (Evanston, Ill.: Northwestern University Press, 2001), 15.
2. *Flucht, Vertreibung, Eingliederung: Baden-Württemberg als neue Heimat*, Begleitung zur Ausstellung (Sigmaringen: Jan Thorbecke Verlag, 1993), 118–20.
3. Sylvia Schraut, *Flüchtlingsaufnahme in Württemberg-Baden 1945–1949: Amerikanische Besatzungsziele und demokratischer Wiederaufbau im Konflikt* (Munich: Oldenbourg Verlag, 1995), 69.
4. Sibylle Krause-Burger, *Joschka Fischer: Der Marsch durch die Illusionen* (Stuttgart: DVA, 1999), 37–40.
5. Ibid.
6. László Hubai, *Magyarország 20. századi választási atlasza,1920–2000*. Vol. 3. Magyarországi települések választási adatai (Budapest: Napvilág, 2001), 265.
7. John Erickson, *Stalin's War with Germany: The Road to Stalingrad* (London: Weidenfeld and Nicolson, 1975), 362, 454, 460. See also Erickson's *Stalin's War with Germany: The Road to Berlin* (London: Weidenfeld and Nicolson, 1983), 34.
8. See Norman M. Naimark, *Fires of Hatred: Ethnic Cleansing in Twentieth-Century Europe* (Cambridge: Harvard University Press, 2001).
9. Michael Schwelien, *Joschka Fischer: Eine Karriere* (Hamburg: Hoffmann and Campe, 2000), 162.
10. Theodor Schieder, *Dokumentation der Vertreibung der Deutschen aus Ost-Mitteleuropa*, Volume II, *Das Schicksal der Deutschen in Ungarn* (Bonn:

Bundesministerium für Vertriebene, Flüchtlinge und Kriegsgeschädigte, 1956), 124–26.

11. Ibid.
12. Konrad H. Jarausch, *Die Umkehr: Deutsche Wandlungen 1945–1995* (Munich: DVA, 2004), 49, 61.
13. Christoph Klessmann, *Die doppelte Staatsgründung: Deutsche Geschichte 1945–1955* (Bonn: Bundeszentrale für politische Bildung, 1991), 91.
14. Ahonen, *After the Expulsion*, 21.
15. Sebastian Haffner, *Im Schatten der Geschichte* (Munich: DVA,1985), 291.
16. Ulrich Chaussy, "Jugend," in *Die Bundesrepublik Deutschland: Geschichte in drei Bänden*. Volume II, *Gesellschaft*, ed. Wolfgang Benz (Frankfurt: Fischer Verlag, 1983), 35.
17. Krause-Burger, *Joschka Fischer*, 41.
18. Ibid.
19. "Er war als Bub schon schwierig,"*Express*, May 24, 1986.
20. Sigmund Freud, *Gesammelte Werke, Werke aus den Jahren 1917–1920* "Eine Kindheitserinnerung aus Dichtung und Wahrheit," Volume 12 (London: Imago, 1947), 26.
21. Krause-Burger, *Joschka Fischer*, 46.
22. Heide Fehrenbach, "Learning from America: Reconstructing 'Race' in Post-war Germany," in *Americanization and Anti-Americanism: The German Encounter with American Culture after 1945*, ed. Alexander Stephan (New York: Berghahn, 2005), 108.
23. Ibid., 109.

CHAPTER 2

1. Herlinde Koelbl, *Spuren der Macht: Die Verwandlung des Menschen durch das Amt. Eine Langzeitstudie* (Munich: Knesebeck Verlag, 1991), 19.
2. Manfred Görtemaker, *Geschichte der Bundesrepublik Deutschland: Von der Gründung bis zur Gegenwart* (Munich: S. Fischer Verlag, 2004), 194.
3. Peter Reichel, *Vergangenheitsbewältigung in Deutschland: Die Auseinandersetzung mit der NS-Diktatur von 1945 bis heute* (Munich: CH Beck, 2001), 83–84.
4. Edgar Wolfrum, *Die geglückte Demokratie: Geschichte der Bundesrepublik Deutschland von ihren Anfängen bis zur Gegenwart* (Stuttgart: Klett-Cotta, 2006), 58.
5. Nick Thomas, *Protest Movements in 1960s West Germany: A Social History of Dissent and Democracy* (Oxford: Berg, 2003), 24.
6. Konrad Jarausch, *After Unity: Reconfiguring German Identities* (Providence: Berghahn Books, 1997), 40.
7. Edgar Wolfrum, *Die geglückte Demokratie*, 161.
8. Jarausch, *After Unity*, 40–41.

9. David Bathrick, "Cinematic Americanization of the Holocaust in Germany," in *Americanization and Anti-Americanization: The German Encounter with American Culture after 1945*, ed. Alexander Stephan (New York: Berghahn Books, 2005), 140–41.
10. Ulrich Enzensberger, *Die Jahre der Kommune I: Berlin 1967–1969* (Colonge: Kiepenheuer & Witsch, 2004), 38, 46–47.
11. "Ein unheimliches Gefühl," *Der Spiegel*, May 18, 2002.
12. Kurt Sontheimer, *Die Adenauer-Ära: Grundlegung der Bundesrepublik* (Munich: Deutscher Taschenbuch Verlag, 1991), 163.
13. Sibylle Krause-Burger, *Joschka Fischer: Der Marsch durch die Illusionen* (Stuttgart: DVA, 1999), 67.
14. "Joschka Fischer," *Frankfurter Allgemeine Zeitung*, May 15, 1998.
15. Ruud Koopmans, *Democracy from Below: New Social Movements in the Political System in West Germany* (Boulder, CO: Westview Press, 1995), 40–41.
16. Rob Burns and Wilfried van der Will, *Protest and Democracy in West Germany: Extra-Parliamentary Opposition and the Democratic Agenda* (London: Macmillan, 1988), 5.
17. Konrad Jarausch, *Die Umkehr: Deutsche Wandlungen 1945–1995* (Munich: DVA, 2004), 35.
18. Ibid., 61.
19. Ibid., 54.
20. Joyce Marie Mushaben, *From Post-War to Post-Wall Generations: Changing Attitudes towards the National Question and NATO in the Federal Republic of Germany* (Boulder, CO: Westview Press, 1998), 167.
21. Ibid,166.
22. Jarausch, *Die Umkehr*, 212–13.
23. Otfried Nassauer, "50 Jahre Nuklearwaffen in Deutschland," in *Aus Politik und Zeitgeschichte*, Vol. 21, May 23, 2005, 27–31.
24. Manfred Görtemaker, *Geschichte der Bundesrepublik*, 192.
25. Dennis Bark and David Gress, *A History of West Germany: From Shadow to Substance, 1945–1963* (Oxford: Basil Blackwell, 1989), 407. Also Lorenz Knorr, *Geschichte der Friedensbewegung in der Bundesrepublik* (Colonge: Pahl-Rugstein, 1983) 108–110.
26. Günter Wernicke, Pax Report 3/1997, 4.
27. Karl A. Otto, *Vom Ostermarsch zur APO. Geschichte der aussenparlamentarischen Opposition in der Bundesrepublik 1960–1970* (Frankfurt: Campus Verlag, 1977), 41.
28. Alexandra Richie, *Faust's Metropolis: A History of Berlin* (London: HarperCollins, 1999), 682–687. Wolfgang Kraushaar, *Die Protest-Chronik 1949–1959: Eine illustrierte Geschichte von Bewegung, Widerstand und Utopie*, Volume 2, (Hamburg: Rogner & Bernhard, 1996), 795–846.

29. See the finest of several Brandt biographies: Peter Merseberger, *Willy Brandt, 1913–1992: Visionär und Realist* (Stuttgart: DVA, 2002.)
30. Hubertus Knabe, *Die unterwanderte Republik: Stasi im Westen* (Berlin: Propyläen, 1999), 234–61.
31. Willi Hoss, *Komm ins Offene, Freund* (Münster: Verlag Westfälisches Dampfboot, 2004), 80.

CHAPTER 3

1. Arnulf Baring and Gregor Schöllgen, *Kanzler, Krisen, Koalitionen* (Berlin: Siedler Verlag, 2002), 95.
2. Peter Merseburger, *Willy Brandt, 1913–1992, Visionär und Realist* (Stuttgart: DVA, 2002), 490.
3. Ulrich Chaussy, *Die drei Leben des Rudi Dutschke: Eine Biographie* (Berlin: Ch. Links Verlag, 1993), 145.
4. Siegward Lönnendoncker, et al., *Die antiautoritäre Revolte: Der Sozialistische Studentenbund nach der Trennung von der SPD* (Wiesbaden: Westdeutscher Verlag, 2002), 100.
5. See Arnd Bauerkämper et al., *Demokratiewunder: Transatlantische Mittler und die kulturelle Öffnung Westdeutschlands 1945–1970* (Göttingen: Vanderhoeck& Ruprecht, 2005).
6. Ingrid Gilcher-Holtey, *Die 68er Bewegung: Deutschland, West Europa, USA* (Munich: CH Beck, 2001), 30.
7. Todd Gitlin, *The Sixties: Years of Hope, Days of Rage* (New York: Bantam Books, 1987), 242.
8. Ibid.
9. Gilcher-Holtey, *Die 68er Bewegung,* 38.
10. Tilman Fichter and Siegward Lönnendonker, *Macht und Ohnmacht der Studenten: Kleine Geschichte des SDS* (Hamburg: Rotbuch Verlag, 1998), 55–72.
11. Konrad Jarausch, *Die Umkehr: Deutsche Wandlungen 1945–1995* (Munich: DVA, 2004), 228.
12. More broadly, historian Manfred Görtemaker argues that the election of the Social Democrat-Liberal coalition in 1969 and the 1967–70 student movement together constitute the "re-founding" of the Federal Republic. See Manfred Görtemaker, *Geschichte der Bundesrepublik Deutschland: Von der Gründung bis zur Gegenwart* (Munich: S. Fischer Verlag, 2004), 475–525. Politicial scientist Claus Leggewie refers to the anti-authoritarian revolt as one of a series of "founding acts" of the Bonn Republic. See "Verordnete Gründung—verfehlte Nachgründung—vertane Neugründung" in *Blätter für deutsche und internationale Politik,* 6 (1993), 698.
13. Frank Deppe (ed), *2. Juni 1967 und die Studentenbewegung heute* (Dortmund: Weltkreis Verlag, 1977); *Der 2. Juni: Studenten zwischen Notstand und*

Demokratie. Dokumente zu den Ereignissen anlässlich des Schah-Besuchs (Cologne: Pahl-Rugenstein Verlag, 1967); Lönnendonker, *Die antiautoritäre Revolte*; Hans Dieter Müller and Günter Hörmann, *Ruhestörung—Ereignisse in Berlin 1967*, film , directed by Hans Dieter Müller and Günter Hörmann (FRG: 1967); "Der Polizeistaatsbesuch. Beobachtungen unter deutschen Gastgebern," film, directed by Roman Brodmann (FRG: 1967) ; "Der nicht erklärte Notstand," *Kursbuch*, 2, no. 12, April 1968.

14. Bettina Röhl, *So macht Kommunismus Spass! Ulrike Meinhof, Klaus Rainer Röhl und die Akte Konkret* (Hamburg: Europäische Verlagsanstalt, 2006). Röhl documents that the magazine received funding from the GDR. It doesn't follow, however, that everyone who wrote for and read *Konkret*, was a "puppet" or admirer of the East German regime.
15. Lönnendonker, *Die antiautoritäre Revolte*, 334.
16. Nirumand interview in Röhl, *So macht Kommunismus Spass!*, 559.
17. Lönnendonker, *Die antiautoritäre Revolte*, 337.
18. Andrea Ludwig, *Neue oder deutsche Linke? Nation und Nationalismus im Denken von Linken und Grünen* (Opladen: Westdeutscher Verlag, 1995), 29.
19. Antonia Grunenberg, *Antifaschismus—ein deutscher Mythos* (Hamburg: Rowohlt, 1993), 129.
20. Chaussy, *Die drei Leben*, 171.
21. Sibylle Krause-Burger, *Joschka Fischer: Der Marsch durch die Illusionen* (Stuttgart: DVA, 1999), 77.
22. Ibid., 82–83
23. Frank Böckelmann, ed. *Subversive Aktion: Der Sinn der Organisation ist ihr Scheitern* (Frankfurt: Verlag Neue Kritik, 1979).
24. Günter Gaus, *Rudi Dutschke. Zu Protokoll: Fernsehinterviews*, Voltaire Flugschrift 1968, 14.
25. Rudi Dutschke, *Mein langer Marsch: Reden, Schriften und Tagebücher aus zwanzig Jahren* (Hamburg: Rowohlt Verlag, 1980), 22–23.
26. Chaussy, *Die drei Leben*, 141.
27. Ibid., 180.
28. Gaus, *Zu Protokoll: Fernsehinterviews*, 14.
29. Klaus Theweleit, "Wir alle diskutierten die Stadtguerilla," interview in TAZ Journal, *Dutschke und Du . . . verändern, kämpfen, leben: Was wir von Rudi Dutschke lernen können,*, 2006/01, 27.
30. Gilcher-Holtey, *Die 68er Bewegung*, 31–34.
31. Theweleit interview, "Wir alle diskutierten," 22.
32. "Ein unheimliches Gefühl," *Der Spiegel*, May 18, 2002.
33. Joschka Fischer, "Ein magisches Jahr," *Der Spiegel*, Spiegel Special Edition, 9 (1998), 59–61.
34. Ulrich Enzensberger, *Die Jahre der Kommune I: Berlin 1967–1969* (Colonge: Kiepenheuer & Witsch, 2004), 98.

35. Chaussy, *Die drei Leben*, 135.
36. Fichter and Lönnendonker, *Macht und Ohnmacht*, 126–28; Chaussy, *Die drei Leben*, 233–72.
37. Josef Bachmann was sentenced to seven years imprisonment. He took his own life in 1970.
38. Michael Baumann, *Wie alles anfing* (Giessen: Anabus Verlag, 1977), 46–47.
39. Stefan Aust, *Der Baader-Meinhof-Komplex* (Munich: Wilhelm Goldmann Verlag, 1998),72–73.
40. Gerd Langguth, *Protestbewegungen: Entwicklung, Niedergang, Renaissance seit 1968* (Cologne: Verlag Wissenschaft und Politik, 1984), 28. Across the country, 827 people were arrested in "violence-related incidents." In Munich, two protesters were killed.
41. Hans-Jürgen Krahl, "Römerbergrede," in *Frankfurter Schule und Studentenbewegung: Von der Flaschenpost zum Molotowcocktail, 1946–1995.*, Volume 2, *Dokumente*, ed. Wolfgang Kraushaar (Hamburg: Rogner & Bernhard, 1998) 384–85.
42. Dany Cohn-Bendit and Reinhard Mohr, *1968: Die letzte Revolution, die noch nichts vom Ozonloch wußte* (Berlin: Verlag Klaus Wagenbach, 1988), 143.
43. Ibid.
44. "Bei Arafat und Minztee," *Die Tageszeitung*, Feb. 23, 2001.
45. Leggewie, "Verordnete Gründung," 699.
46. Bauerkämper et al, *Demokratiewunder*, 15.
47. Jarausch, *Die Umkehr*, 200, 355.
48. Kraushaar, *1968*, 315.
49. "The Turning Point," *Time* magazine, April 24, 2005.
50. Kraushaar, *1968*, 323.
51. Fichter, *Macht und Ohnmacht*, 137–38.

CHAPTER 4

1. Paul Berman, *Power and the Idealists: Or, the Passion of Joschka Fischer and its Aftermath* (Brooklyn, NY: Soft Scull Press, 2005), 43.
2. Gerd Koenen, *Das rote Jahrzehnt: Unsere kleine deutsche Kulturrevolution,* 1967–1977 (Frankfurt: Kiepenhauer & Witsch, 2001), 184.
3. Ibid.
4. Sabine Stamer, *Cohn-Bendit: Die Biografie* (Hamburg: Europa Verlag, 2001), chapters 1 and 2.
5. Daniel Cohn-Bendit, *Wir haben sie so geliebt, die Revolution* (Frankfurt: Athenäum, 1987), 247.
6. Christian Schmidt, "*Wir sind die Wahnsinnigen . . .*" *Joschka Fischer und seine Frankfurter Gang* (Munich: Econ Verlag, 1998), 45–46.

7. Herlinde Koelbl, *Spuren der Macht: Die Verwandlung des Menschen durch das Amt, Eine Langzeitstudie* (Munich: Knesebeck Verlag, 2002), 20.
8. The night of Benno Ohnesorg's murder, Ensslin was reported to have stormed into West Berlin's Republican Club shrieking: "They want to kill all of us! You know what kind of pigs these types are. This is the generation of Auschwitz . . . They have weapons and we don't. We have to arm ourselves!" Tilman Fichter, quoted in Gerd Koenen, *Vesper, Ensslin, Baader: Urszenen des deutschen Terrorismus.* (Cologne: Kiepenheuer & Witsch, 2003), 124.
9. Stefan Aust, *Der Baader-Meinhof-Komplex* (Munich: Wilhelm Goldmann Verlag, 1998), 21–26. Butz Peters, *Tödlicher Irrtum* (Berlin: Argon Verlag, 2004), 177–84.
10. Ulrike Haider, *Keine Ruhe nach dem Sturm* (Munich: Rogner & Bernard, 2001), 176.
11. Peters, *Tödlicher Irrtum*, 286.
12. Koenen, *Das rote Jahrzehnt*, 335.
13. Ibid.
14. Ibid., 334.
15. Stamer, *Cohn-Bendit*, 164.
16. *Die Stille nach dem Schuss*, Director Völker Schlöndorff, (Potsdam: Babelsberg Film, 2000).
17. Wolfgang Kraushaar, ed., *Frankfurter Schule und Studentenbewegung: von der Flaschenpost zum Molotowcocktail 1946–1995* (Hamburg: Rogner & Bernhard, 1998), 523.
18. Schmidt, *Wir sind die Wahnsinnigen*, 66.
19. Hans-Joachim Klein, *Rückkehr in die Menschlichkeit: Appell eines ausgestiegenen Terroristen* (Hamburg: Rowohlt, 1979), 180–81.
20. Ibid.
21. Wolfgang Kraushaar, *Fischer in Frankfurt: Karriere eines Außenseiters* (Hamburg: Hamburger Edition, 2001), 163.
22. Ibid.
23. Peters, *Tödlicher Irrtum*, 397–494; Aust, *Baader-Meinhof*, 483–661.
24. Peters, 455–60.

CHAPTER 5

1. Arnulf Baring and Gregor Schöllgen, *Kanzler, Krisen, Koalitionen* (Berlin: Siedler Verlag, 2002), 122.
2. Edgar Wolfrum, *Die geglückte Demokratie: Geschichte der Bundesrepublik Deutschland von ihren Anfängen bis zur Gegenwart* (Stuttgart: Klett-Cotta, 2006), 315.
3. Ibid., 318.

4. *Offizielle Mitgliederstatistik der SPD.* Historische Kommission beim SPD-Parteivorstand, Willy-Brandt-Haus, Berlin. The new members were overwhelmingly young Germans. In 1972, for example, two-thirds of the 153,000 new members were under 35 years of age.
5. Joyce Marie Mushaben, *From Post-War to Post-Wall Generations: Changing Attitudes towards the National Question and NATO in the Federal Republic of Germany* (Boulder, CO: Westview Press, 1998), 157–79.
6. Manfred Görtemaker, *Geschichte der Bundesrepublik Deutschland: Von der Gründung bis zur Gegenwart* (Munich: S. Fischer Verlag, 2004), 620–23.
7. Karl-Werner Brandt, et al., *Aufbruch in eine andere Gesellschaft: Neue soziale Bewegungen in der Bundesrepublik* (Frankfurt: Campus Verlag, 1983), 87.
8. Görtemacher, *Geschichte der Bundesrepublik*, 628.
9. Wolfgang Rüdig, "Bürgerinitiativen im Umweltschutz," in Otthein Rammstedt, ed., *Bürgerinitiativen in der Gesellschaft* (Villingen: Neckar Verlag, 1980), 133.
10. Görtemaker, *Geschichte der Bundesrepublik*, 476. According to Görtemaker's calculations, the student movement comprised around 170,000 people.
11. Mushaben, *From Postwar*, 215.
12. Joschka Fischer, "Warum eigentlich nicht?," in *Von grüner Kraft und Herrlichkeit* (Hamburg: Rowohlt, 1984), 97.
13. Joschka Fischer, "Durchs wilde Kurdistan," *Pflasterstrand*, 47 (February 1979), 28–31. Notably, in this reckoning with New Left's anti-imperialism Fischer fails to mention the anti-Semitism that permeated the Third World movements in the seventies. Three years later, in a September 1982 article in *Pflasterstrand*, Fischer does address the German left's pro-Arab stances and insufficient sensitivity to Israel's plight.
14. AtomExpress, eds, "*. . . Und auch nicht anderswo!" Die Geschichte der Anti-AKW-Bewegung* (Hamburg: Verlag Die Werkstatt, 1997), 32.
15. Some of these initiatives had formed before the Wyhl campaign in 1973–74, to protest—and to stop—the construction of a lead factory in nearby Marckolsheim, France.
16. Sara Parkin, *The Life and Death of Petra Kelly* (London: Pandora Books, 1994), 79.
17. "Blick zurück—25 Jahre Grün," film, directed by Sigrun Schnarrenberger (Federal Republic of Germany: Heinrich Böll Foundation, 2005).
18. AtomExpress, "*. . . Und auch nicht anderswo!*," 70.
19. Wolfrum, *Die geglückte Demokratie*, 336.
20. See Alice Schwarzer, *So fing es an! Die neue Frauenbewegung* (Munich. DTV, 1983), 23–30.
21. Parkin, *The Life and Death*, 86.
22. See the website of Lower Saxony's Greens: www.partei.gruene-niedersachsen.de/cms/ueber_uns/rubrik/7/7388.1977_1979.htm [May 10, 2006].

23. Christoph Becker-Schaum, "Von der Protestbewegung zur demokratischen Alternative: Die Grünen Hessen 1979–2004," in *Hessen: 60 Jahre Demokratie*, ed. Helmut Berding (Wiesbaden: Historische Kommission für Nassau, 2006), 155.
24. "Die Grünen in der BRD," *Die Tageszeitung*, June 13, 1997.
25. Fischer, "Warum eigentlich," 92.
26. Sabine Stamer, *Cohn-Bendit: Die Biografie* (Hamburg: Europa Verlag, 2001), 176.
27. "Die widerspenstige Zähmung," *Pflasterstrand*, Nov. 18, 1980, 10–12.
28. Mushaben, *From Post-War*, 201.
29. See Lawrence S. Wittner's comprehensive *Toward Nuclear Abolition: A History of the World Nuclear Disarmament Movement, 1971 to the Present* (Stanford, CA: Stanford University Press, 2003).
30. Hubert Kleinert, *Vom Protest zur Regierungspartei: Die Geschichte der Grünen* (Frankfurt: Eichborn Verlag, 1992), 30.
31. Ulrich Chaussy, *Die drei Leben des Rudi Dutschke: Eine Biographie* (Berlin: Ch. Links Verlag, 1993), 328.
32. Die Präambel zum Parteiprogramm der Grünen. Available at www.dhm.de/lemo/html/dokumente/NeueHerausforderungen_programmPraeambelDerGruenen1980/index.html [June 1, 2007].
33. "Wir sind die Antipartei-Partei," *Der Spiegel*, May 14, 1982.
34. Ibid.
35. Parkin, *The Life and Death*, 97–102.
36. Brandt, et al., *Aufbruch in eine andere Gesellschaft*, 210.
37. Jeffrey Herf, *War By Other Means: Soviet Power, West German Resistance and the Battle of the Euromissiles* (New York: Free Press, 1991), 84–85.
38. Wittner, *Nuclear Abolition*, 144.
39. "Mit dem Herzen denken," Jürgen Gottschlich, in Taz Journal, *Die grüne Gefahr: Eine Partei auf dem Weg zur Macht*, 1998, 14.
40. Petra K. Kelly, *Mit dem Herzen denken: Texte für eine glaubwürdige Politik* (Munich: CH Beck, 1990), 104–11.
41. "Antinuclear Groups Seeking a Global Network," *New York Times*, December 6, 1981.
42. Wolfgang Kraushaar, *Fischer in Frankfurt: Karriere eines Außenseiters* (Hamburg: Hamburg Edition, 2001), 176.
43. Fischer, *Von grüner Kraft*, 109–18.
44. Ibid.
45. Kraushaar, *Fischer in Frankfurt*, 178.
46. "Die Raupe vom anderen Planeten," *Süddeutsche Zeitung*, February 18, 1983.
47. Kleinert, *Vom Protest zur Regierungspartei*, 76.

CHAPTER 6

1. "Strauß warnt vor Grünen und Alternativen," Associated Press, July 19, 1982.
2. Tagesschau interview with Helmut Schmidt, March 23, 1982.
3. "Börner—des Kanzlers letzte Hoffnung," *Bunte,* May 19, 1982.
4. Editorial, *Abendpost,* March 29, 1983.
5. "Schlicht illegal,"*Konkret,* April 1983.
6. "Muntere Zeiten," *Der Spiegel,* March 14, 1983.
7. "Die Angst der Grünen vor Amt und Macht," *Der Spiegel,* April 3, 1983.
8. Anne Borgmann et al., *Die Grünen entern das Raumschiff Bonn: Ein Lesebuch über den Start im Bundestag* (Hattingen: Flieter Verlag, 1983), 11. See also Charlene Spretnak, *Die Grünen: Nicht links, nicht rechts, sondern vorne* (Munich: Wilhelm Goldmann Verlag, 1985).
9. Brigitte Jäger and Claudia Pinl, *Zwischen Rotation und Routine: Die Grünen im Bundestag* (Cologne: Kiepenheuer & Witsch, 1985), 105.
10. Joschka Fischer, "Der Bundestag ist eine unglaubliche Alkoholikerversammlung," in *Von grüner Kraft und Herrlichkeit* (Hamburg: Rowohlt, 1984), 136.
11. Ibid., 140.
12. Joschka Fischer, "Die Schuld an Auschwitz," in *Von grüner Kraft und Herrlichkeit* (Hamburg: Rowohlt, 1984), 143–49.
13. Ibid.
14. Ibid.
15. Richard von Weizsäcker, "Zum 40. Jahrestag der Beendigung des Krieges in Europa und der nationalsozialistischen Gewaltherrschaft" in *Reden aus Deutschland: Zeitgeschichte von 1949 bis heute* (Hamburg: 1990).
16. Joyce Marie Mushaben, *From Post-War to Post-Wall Generations: Changing Attitudes towards the National Question and NATO in the Federal Republic of Germany* (Boulder, CO: Westview Press, 1998), 204–05.
17. "Sinnlos und gefährlich, gefährlich für alle," *Der Spiegel,* September 26, 1983.
18. Sara Parkin, *The Life and Death of Petra Kelly* (London: Pandora Books, 1994), 134.
19. Lawrence S. Wittner, *Toward Nuclear Abolition: A History of the World Nuclear Disarmament Movement, 1971 to the Present* (Stanford, CA: Stanford University Press, 2003), 145. Wittner's estimate is high. Other range from 350–450,000.
20. "Für die Mehrheit des Volkes," *Frankfurter Rundschau,* October 24, 1983, p. 2.
21. "Wir haben lange genug auf Sie gewartet," *Frankfurter Rundschau,* October 24, 1983, p. 3.
22. Mushaben, *From Post-War,* 213.

23. Steve Breyman, *Why Movements Matter: The West German Peace Movement and U.S. Arms Control Policy* (Albany, NY: SUNY Press, 2001), 228–34.
24. Mushaben, *From Post-War,* 147.
25. Ibid., 49.
26. Werner Hülsberg, *The German Greens: A Social and Political Profile* (London: Verso, 1988), 71.
27. Breyman, *Why Movements Matter,* 248.
28. Ibid., 253.
29. Simon Duke, *The Burdensharing Debate: A Reassessment* (New York: St. Martin's Press, 1993), 116.
30. Steve Breyman, *Why Movements Matter,* 228–34.
31. Mushaben, *From Post-War,* 81.
32. Wittner, *Nuclear Abolition,* 424.
33. Ibid.

CHAPTER 7

1. Hubert Kleinert, *Vom Protest zur Regierungspartei: Die Geschichte der Grünen* (Frankfurt: Eichborn Verlag, 1992), 105.
2. "Die Mehrheit links der Union," Jürgen Gottschlich, in Taz Journal: *Die grüne Gefahr: Eine Partei auf dem Weg zur Macht,* (Berlin: taz Verlag, 1998), 34.
3. "Wir müssen Machtfaktor sein,"*Der Spiegel,* February 27, 1984.
4. "Eine andere Machtkultur,"*Die Tageszeitung,* March 4, 1985.
5. "Nix mehr da,"*Der Spiegel,* September 16, 1985.
6. Matthias Geis and Bernd Ulrich, *Der Unvollendete: Das Leben des Joschka Fischer* (Berlin: Alexander Fest Verlag, 2002).
7. Christoph Becker-Schaum, "Von der Protestbewegung zur demokratischen Alternative: Die Grünen Hessen 1979–2004," in *Hessen: 60 Jahre Demokratie* (Wiesbaden: Historische Kommission für Nassau, 2006), 171.
8. "Das war's," *Der Spiegel,* October 21, 1985.
9. "Mobile factories," *Der Spiegel,* October 28, 1985.
10. Ibid.
11. Joschka Fischer, *Regieren geht über Studieren* (Frankfurt: Athenäum Verlag, 1987), 33.
12. Ibid, 37.
13. "Organisiert wie eine Fritten-Bude," *Der Spiegel,* March 17, 1986.
14. "Reaktorkatastrophe in der UdSSR," *Die Tageszeitung,* April 30, 1986.
15. "Die Sache hat uns kalt erwischt," *Der Spiegel,* May 12, 1986.
16. Ibid.
17. Ibid.
18. Ibid.

19. "Wenn der erste auf Demonstrationen schießt," *Der Spiegel,* August 21, 1986.
20. Fischer, *Regieren geht über Studieren,* 203.
21. Kleinert, *Vom Protest zur Regierungspartei,* 208.
22. Joschka Fischer, *Der Umbau der Industriegesellschaft: Plädoyer wider die herrschende Umweltlüge* (Frankfurt: Eichborn Verlag, 1989).
23. Matthias Geis and Bernd Ulrich, *Der Unvollendete: Das Leben des Joschka Fischer* (Berlin: Alexander Fest Verlag, 2002), 73.

CHAPTER 8

1. A 1990 opinion poll found that only 70 percent of West Germans and 43 percent of East Germans knew the first line of the German national hymn. "Den Neuen fehlt Selbstvertrauen," *Der Spiegel,* November 12, 1990.
2. Hubert Kleinert, *Vom Protest zur Regierungspartei: Die Geschichte der Grünen* (Frankfurt: Eichborn Verlag, 1992), 331.
3. "Jenseits von Mauer und Wiedervereinigung," *Die Tageszeitung,* November 16, 1989.
4. Andrei S. Markovits and Simon Reich, *The German Predicament; Memory and Power in the New Europe* (Ithaca: Cornell University Press, 1997) 91, 125–28. Poland was a notable exception with a sizable majority initially expressing opposition to German unification. The French political class, in contrast to the French public, initially voiced reservations about a united Germany.
5. Ibid., 60–61.
6. In German it was "*Wir sind das Volk*" and "*Wir sind ein Volk.*"
7. "Schwierige Wahlverwandte," Dieter Rulff in Taz Journal: "*Die grüne Gefahr: Eine Partei auf dem Weg zur Macht,*" (Berlin: taz Verlag, 1998), 73.
8. *Taz Journal*: "Die grüne Gefahr, 72.
9. Paul Hockenos, *Free to Hate: The Rise of the Right in Post-Communist Eastern Europe* (New York: Routledge, 1993), 38–40.
10. Ibid., 304.
11. "Sie kommen, ob wir wollen oder nicht," *Der Spiegel,* April 6, 1992.
12. "Hurra, Deutschland!" *Der Spiegel,* October 1, 1990.
13. Ibid.
14. Sibylle Krause-Burger, *Joschka Fischer: Der Marsch durch die Illusionen* (Stuttgart: DVA, 1999), 192.
15. "Vielleicht haben sie die grüne Bewegung besser repräsentiert als irgend jemand sonst," *Frankfurter Allgemeine Zeitung,* October 21, 1992.
16. "Wir trauern um Petra Kelly und Gert Bastian," Press release of Bundesvorstand Die Grünen. October 22, 1992.

17. Gregor Schöllgen, *Die Außenpolitik der Bundesrepublik Deutschland: Von den Anfängen bis zur Gegenwart* (Munich: Verlag C.H. Beck, 1999), 211.
18. Ludger Volmer, *Die Grünen und die Außenpolitik: Ein schwieriges Verhältnis* (Münster : Westfälisches Dampfboot Verlag, 1998), 497.
19. In a landmark decision in 1994, Germany's highest court declared that the country's participation in collective military operations outside of NATO territory did not violate the Basic Law. It must, however, be approved by a Bundestag majority.
20. Auswärtiges Amt (Hrsg.), *Außenpolitik der Bundesrepublik Deutschland. Dokumente von 1949 bis 1994* (Colonge: Verlag Wissenschaft und Politik, 1995), 793.
21. Sven Bernhard Gareis, *Deutschlands Außen- und Sicherheitspolitik: Eine Einführung* (Opladen: Verlag Barbaras Budrich, 2005), 172.
22. Brett Klopp, *German Multiculturalism: Immigrant Integration and the Transformation of Citizenship* (Westport, Conn.: Praeger, 2002), 3.
23. "Versager aller Länder, verteidigt Euch!" *Die Tageszeitung*, October 24, 1993,
24. "42 Kilometer Straßenkampf," *Die Tageszeitung*, April 4, 1998.
25. Markus Klein and Jürgen W. Falter, *Der lange Weg der Grünen: Eine Partei zwischen Protest und Regierung* (Munich: Verlag C.H. Beck, 2003), 152–53.

CHAPTER 9

1. Joschka Fischer, *Risiko Deutschland: Krise und Zukunft der deutschen Politik* (Cologne: Kiepenhauer & Witsch, 1994).
2. Ibid., 187–88.
3. Ibid., 220.
4. Ludger Volmer, *Die Grünen und die Außenpolitik: Ein schwieriges Verhältnis* (Münster: Westfälisches Dampfboot Verlag, 1998), 478–80.
5. Ibid.
6. "Bosnische Konsequenz," *Die Tageszeitung*, August 2, 1995.
7. Ibid.
8. "Greif' zur Waffe, fahr' nach Sarajevo," *Die Tageszeitung*, August 12, 1995.
9. Ibid.
10. Briefe, *Die Tageszeitung*, August 2, 1995.
11. Ibid.
12. "Ärger mit Fischers Reiselust," *Süddeutsche Zeitung*, May 31, 1996.
13. "Innenpolitik sucht neue Aufgabe," *Süddeutsche Zeitung*, July 4, 1997.
14. "Das Prinzip Fischer," *Die Zeit*, December 8, 1995.
15. Joschka Fischer, *Mein langer Lauf zu mir selbst* (Munich: Knaur, 2001), 47.
16. Ibid., 48.
17. Ibid., 58.

18. Ibid.
19. Ibid., 84.
20. "Permanente Revolution, " *Der Spiegel*, September 5, 2005
21. "Grüner Alptraum," *Bild-Zeitung*, March 9, 1998.
22. "SPD betont Distanz zu Beschlüssen der Grünen," *Frankfurter Rundschau*, March 10, 1998.
23. "Fischers große Oper," *Der Spiegel*, September 14, 1998.
24. Grüne Ambitionen diplomatisch gestärkt," *Die Tageszeitung*, June 20, 1998.
25. "Hinter allem ein Ausrufungszeichen," *Die Tageszeitung*, August 21, 1998.
26. "Eine andere Zeit," *Der Spiegel* Wahlsonderheft 1998, p. 11.
27. Ibid., 8.
28. "Schäuble wäre besser gewesen," *Die Tageszeitung*, September 29, 1998.
29. *Der Spiegel* Wahlsonderheft 1998, 9.
30. "Ein Kulturbruch, mit Links," *Die Zeit*, October 1, 1998.
31. Joyce Marie Mushaben, " 'Girl Power': Women, Politics and Leadership in the Berlin Republic," in *Germany at 55: Berlin ist nicht Bonn?*, ed. James Sperling (Manchester: Manchester University Press, 2004), 184.
32. "Wie Deutschland in den Krieg geriet," *Die Zeit*, March 10, 1999.
33. Ibid.
34. "Risiko Sonnenblume," *Die Zeit*, October 1,1998.
35. "Auf dünnem Eis," *Der Spiegel*, November 2, 1998.
36. Madeleine Albright, *Madam Secretary: A Memoir* (New York: Macmillan, 2003), 409.
37. "Auf dünnem Eis," *Der Spiegel*, November 2, 1998.
38. See Joschka Fischer, *Vom Staatenverbund zur Föderation: Gedanken über die Finalität der europäischen Integration* (Frankfurt: Suhrkamp, 2000).
39. "Hände von der Hosennaht," *Der Spiegel*, December 14,1998.
40. AFP, December 30, 1998.
41. Charlie Jeffery and William E. Paterson, "Germany, France—and Great Britain?," *Internationale Politik—Transatlantic Edition* (2000/1).
42. "Die Deutschen und der Krieg," *Die Zeit*, March 31, 1999.
43. *Frankfurter Rundschau*, April 21, 1999.
44. "Zweifel am Krieg," Der Spiegel April 5,1999.
45. "Showdown bei den Grünen," *Die Tageszeitung*, May 14, 1999.
46. Hans Jörg Hennecke, *Die dritte Republik: Aufbruch und Ernüchterung* (Munich: Propyläen, 2003), 119.

CHAPTER 10

1. Frank Brunssen, *Das neue Selbstverständnis der Berliner Republik* (Würzburg: Königshausen & Neumann, 2005), 14.

2. Gerhard Schröder, "Regierungserklärung von Bundeskanzler Gerhard Schröder vom 10. November 1998 vor dem Bundestag," *Frankfurter Allgemeine Zeitung,* November 11, 1998.
3. "Vorsorgliche Belagerung: Lafontaine greift die Bundesbank an," *Die Zeit,* November 5, 1998; "Lafontaines Vorstoß schwächt das Vertrauen in den Euro," *Handelsblatt,* November 13, 1998.
4. Franz Walter, *Abschied von der Toskana: Die SPD in der Ära Schröder* (Wiesbaden: VS Verlag, 2004), 17.
5. Brett Klopp, *German Multiculturalism: Immigrant Integration and the Transformation of Citizenship* (Westport: Praeger, 2002), 33–34
6. Ibid.
7. "Widerstand überlebt Atomkonsens," *Die Tageszeitung,* September 25, 2000.
8. "Grüne Opposition," *Die Tageszeitung,* August 29, 2000.
9. Available at www.bund.net/pressearchiv2000/ [January 12, 2005].
10. Kristine Kern, Stephanie Koenen, Tina Löffelsend, "Die Umweltpolitik der rot-grünen Koalition: Strategien zwischen nationaler Pfadabhängigkeit und globaler Politikkonvergenz," Wissenschaftszentrum Berlin, Discussion Paper Nr. IV, 2003, 15.
11. Ibid.
12. "Rot-Grün die Zweite: Eine umweltpolitische Bilanz," BUND, 2005, 6. Available at www.bund.net/lab/reddot2/pdf/bilanz_rotgruen.pdf [January 2007].
13. Kristine Kern, et al. "Die Umweltpolitik," 16.
14. "Reisen mit Joschka," *Der Tagesspiegel,* September 13, 2000.
15. "Mit Molotow-Cocktails nie etwas zu tun gehabt," *Der Spiegel,* January 8, 2001.
16. "Hier lebten Fischer und die RAF-Terroristin," *Bild-Zeitung,* January 24, 2001.
17. "Ich habe gekämpft," *Der Spiegel,* January 8, 2001.
18. "Ja, ich war militant," *Der Stern,* January 4, 2001.
19. Transcript U.S. Department of State, February 20, 2001. U.S. Department of State Office of the Spokesman
20. "Regierungserklärung Bundeskanzler Schröder," September 12, 2001. Available at www.documentarchiv.de/brd/2001/rede_schroeder_terror-usa.html [June 1, 2005].
21. "Die Reflexe des 'weissen Mannes,' " *Freitag,* October 12, 2001.
22. Hans Jörg Hennecke, *Die dritte Republik: Aufbruch und Ernüchterung* (Munich: Propyläen, 2003), 289.
23. "Streit um Einsatz der Bundeswehr: Fischer droht Grünen mit Rücktritt," *Berliner Zeitung,* November 8, 2001.
24. Reinhard Urschel, *Gerhard Schröder: Eine Biographie* (DVA: Stuttgart, 2000), 373–74.
25. "Kein deutsches Interesse in Kabul," *Frankfurter Allgemeine Sonntagszeitung,* December 17, 2001.

26. Martin Wagener, "Normalization in Security Policy? Deployments of Bundeswehr Forces Abroad in the Era Schroder, 1998–2004," in *Germany's Uncertain Power: Foreign Policy of the Berlin Republic*, ed. Hanns Maull (London: Palgrave Macmillan, 2006), 80–81.
27. "Der Streitfall Afghanistan-Krieg," *Leipziger Volkszeitung*, November 10, 2001.
28. "Abmarsch in die Realität," *Der Spiegel*, November 12, 2001.
29. "Das ist ganz, ganz heiß," *Der Spiegel*, November 5, 2001.
30. "Zur Verdrängung bereit," *Freitag*, April 5, 2002; "Solidarität ja, aber ohne Soldaten," *Rheinischer Merkur*, November 15, 2001.
31. German Marshall Fund report, *Transatlantic Trends 2005* (Washington 2006), 9. Available at www.transatlantictrends.org/trends/index.cfm?year=2005 [June 17, 2007]
32. "Solidarität ja, aber ohne Soldaten," *Rheinischer Merkur*, November 15, 2001.

CHAPTER 11

1. "Killer loses fight for life," *The Daily Telegraph*, March 4, 1999.
2. "U.S. Execution of German Stirs Anger," *New York Times*, March 5, 1999.
3. This was later, in September 2002, explicitly outlined in the National Security Strategy of the United States of America; see www.whitehouse.gov/nsc/nss.html [November 12, 2005].
4. Matthias Geyer, Dirk Kurbjuweit, and Cordt Schnibben, *Operation Rot-Grün: Geschichte eines politischen Abenteuers* (Munich: DVA/Spiegel Buchverlag, 2005), 177.
5. Gerhard Schröder, *Entscheidungen. Mein Leben in der Politik* (Hamburg: Hoffmann und Campe, 2006) 197.
6. "Stern Bush repeats warning to Axis,'" *USA Today*, February 1, 2006.
7. Ibid.
8. "A Nation Challenged," *Financial Times*, February 7, 2002.
9. Matthias Geyer et al., *Operation Rot-Grün*, 178.
10. "Wir sind keine Satelliten," *Die Welt*, February 12, 2002. These are the translations of the author, not of the *New York Times*.
11. This list of Germany's alleged motives, which include latent fascism, comes from William Shawcross's unapologetically pro-Bush administration book *Allies: The U.S., Britain, and Europe, and the War in Iraq* (London: Atlantic Books, 2003), 100–06.
12. Michael Staack, "Nein zur Hegemonialmacht: Deutschlands außenpolitische Entscheidungsprozesse im Irak-Konflikt," in *Europa nach dem Irak-Krieg*, eds. Michael Staack and Rüdiger Voigt (Baden Baden: Nomos, 2004), 203–27.
13. "Bush macht Europäern Zusage," *Frankfurter Rundschau*, May 24, 2002.

14. Wolfgang Thierse, Begrüßungsansprache. Available at www.bundestag.de/aktuell/presse/202/p2_020523.html [May 23, 2002].
15. "Grüne kritisieren US-Politik vor Bush-Besuch scharf," *Frankfurter Rundschau*, May 17, 2002.
16. *Transatlantic Trends 2005*, German Marshall Fund of the U.S., (Washington, 2006). Available at www.transatlantictrends.org/trends/index.cfm?year=2005 [June 17, 2007].
17. Ibid.
18. "Americans Grow More Doubtful About Iraq War," *Gallup News Service*, September 23, 2003.
19. "Das beschädigte Paradies," *Der Spiegel*, June 18, 2002.
20. Ibid.
21. "Der lange Weg zum lauten Nein," *Die Zeit*, January 23, 2003.
22. Available at 212.227.198.222/eic/Eichsfeld/Schrder%20Rede%20Wahlkampfauftakt Hannover.pdf [August 5, 2002].
23. Ibid.
24. Matthias Geyer et al., *Operation Rot-Grün*, 212.
25. "Vice President speaks at VFM 103rd National Convention," White House press release, August 26, 2002.
26. "German Stance on Iraq isolates Nation from ist Postwar Allies," *Wall Street Journal*, September 17, 2002.
27. "Joschka Fischer wirbt für sich," *Die Tageszeitung*, August 8, 2002.
28. For 1998–2002 Germany ranked as the world's fourth largest arms importer, behind the United States, Russia, and France. Berlin Institute for Transatlantic Security, Dokumente zum deutschen Rüstungsexport (1999–2004). Available at www.bits.de/main/topics.htm [March 1, 2007].
29. "Ich bin kein grüner Helmut Kohl," *Die Tageszeitung*, September 19, 2002.
30. Ibid.
31. "US condemns 'poisoned' relations with Berlin," *The Financial Times*, September 21, 2002.
32. "US will work around German leader," *The Guardian*, May 26, 2003.
33. Philip Gordon and Jeremy Shapiro, *Allies at War: America, Europe and the Crisis over Iraq*, (New York: McGraw-Hill, 2004) 176–77.
34. "Outrage at 'old Europe' Remarks," BBC News World Edition, January 23, 2003.
35. Available at archiv.bundesregierung.de/bpaexport/regierungserklaerung/79/472179/multi.htm [November 5, 2006].
36. "Mitgliederverluste für etablierte Parteien," available at de.altermedia.info/date/2004/12/21/ [May 13, 2006]. See also Franz Walter, *Abschied von der Toskana: Die SPD in der Ära Schröder* (Wiesbaden: VS Verlagfür Sozialwissenschaften, 2004), 9–10.

37. *Datenreport 2004: Daten und Fakten über die Bundesrepublik Deutschland,* Statistisches Bundesamt together with the Wissenschaftzentrum Berlin für Sozialforschung and the Zentrum für Umfragen, Methoden und Analysen, Mannheim, (Berlin: Bundeszentrale für politische Bildung, 2005), 650–652; "Viele Thüringer mistrauen der Demokratie als Staatsform," *Frankfurter Allgemeine Zeitung,* January 29, 2005; "Braune Kümmer," *Focus,* September 25, 2006.
38. "Was macht Joschka so sexy," *Bild-Zeitung,* October 29, 2004.
39. In fact, the 300-page *The Return of History: The World after September 11 and the Renewal of the West* was published in 2005 during his final months in office. It includes chapters like "Hobbes versus Kant: The Irony of American History." *Die Rückkehr der Geschichte: Die Welt nach dem 11. September und die Erneuerung des Westens* (Colonge: Kiepenheuer & Witsch, 2005).
40. "Fischer hält an neuer Gedenkpraxis fest," FAZ.NET, March 29, 2005.
41. "Das Gesicht der Rebellion," *Die Berliner Zeitung,* March 31, 2005.
42. "Der Fall des Hauses Fischer," *Frankfurter Allgemeine Zeitung,* March 27, 2005.
43. "Superstar a. D.," *Der Spiegel,* February 22, 2005.
44. "Schreiben Sie: Fischer ist schuld," *Die Tageszeitung,* April 26, 2005.
45. "Fischer ist Geschichte," *Die Tageszeitung,* May 30, 2005.

CONCLUSION

1. "Was es bedeutet, deutsch zu sein," *Die Welt,* September 10, 2005. Einstein was a German Jew who fled Nazi Germany in the thirties.
2. Edgar Wolfrum, *Die geglückte Demokratie: Geschichte der Bundesrepublik Deutschland von ihren Anfängen bis zur Gegenwart* (Stuttgart: Klett-Cotta, 2006), 500.
3. Available at www.migration-info.de/migration_und_bevoelkerung/artikel/010401.htm [December 2006].
4. "Lebenslagen in Deutschland: Der 2. Armuts- und Reichtumsbericht der Bundesregierung," Berlin, 2006. Available at www.bmas.bund.de/BMAS/Navigation/Soziale-Sicherung/berichte [June 7, 2006]. By 2005 the top wealthiest 10 percent of Germans owned 47 percent of total financial assets while the lower 50 percent owned just 4 percent.
5. Ibid.
6. Jan-Werner Müller, *Another Country: German Intellectuals, Unification and National Identity* (New Haven: Yale University Press, 2000), 261.
7. See Kerry Longhurst, *Germany and the Use of Force: The Evolution of German Security Policy 1990–2000* (Manchester: Manchester University Press, 2004).

8. From 1990–2005 this party was called the Party for Democratic Socialism (PDS). The PDS changed its name to the Left Party when it merged with an alliance of left-socialists from the western states.
9. "Braune Kümmer, " *Focus*, September 25, 2006.
10. "Ich war einer der letzten RocknRoller der deutschen Politik," *Die Tageszeitung*, September 23, 2005.

Index

Making Up Amelia

Marjorie Smith

Yokoi Books
Bozeman, MT
2012

Making Up Amelia

Library of Congress Control Number: 2012948929
ISBN: 978-0-9883096-0-9

THIS IS A WORK OF FICTION. Although a few historical characters appear briefly, their words and actions are the product of the author's imagination. As for the other characters, any resemblance to any person living or dead is coincidental.

Cover design: Marla Goodman adapted by M. Smith
Author photo: Linda Best
Internal Icons: Rob Rath
Map: M. Smith

In memory of my father, Roy E. Huffman,
from whom I learned many valuable things,
including the importance of going after your
dreams before they fade.

Making Up Amelia

Contents

In acknowledgement

Writing is a lonely calling, or so we always say. Yet I have been blessed with many friends who have read this story and made invaluable suggestions and bestowed encouragement at just the right times. I am particularly grateful for the support of my family: Menga Huffman, Jim Huffman, Betsy Miller and Kim Smith Unberhagen.

Special thanks to my aviation guru, Thomas Nagorski, who can think of an alarming number of ways to send an airplane astray; to my friend and first copy editor, the late and much missed Rex Adkins; to nit-picker par excellence Vance Ormes; and to the wonderful novelist Stanley Gordon West who saw how to tie up a complex plot with just two more words.

I am also beholden to artists Robert Rath, Marla Goodman and Linda Best for sharing their talent with me and to all the friends who have read the story through the years and made suggestions.

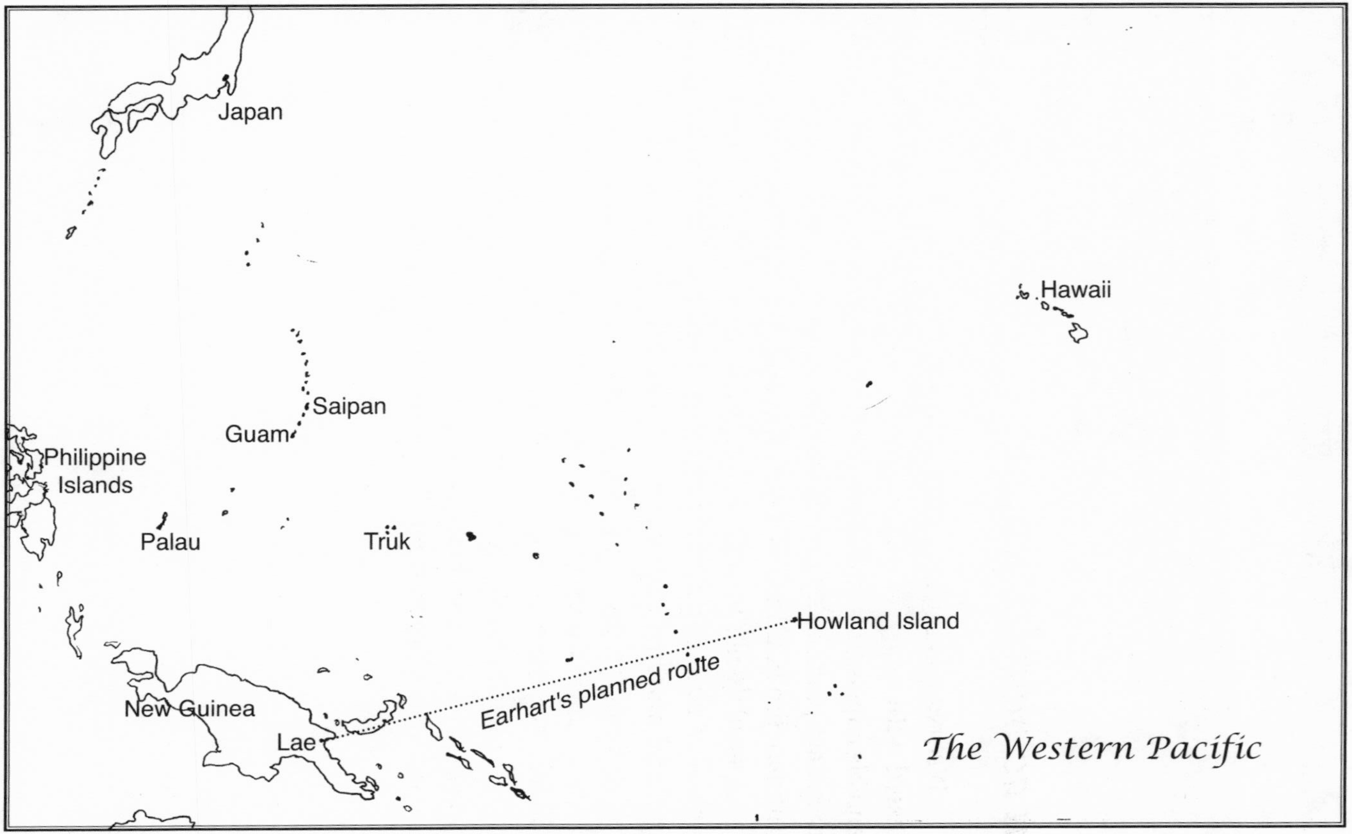

The Western Pacific

The past is never dead. It's not even past.

— William Faulkner, *Requiem for a Nun*

Making Up Amelia

BLUE. AS FAR AS SHE COULD SEE, BLUE. The ocean stretched endless below, and they would fly forever toward the night that was racing to meet them.

That was why she'd originally planned to go the other direction, to chase the sun, prolong the day's light. It hadn't mattered until today. But today there were many races under way. Racing against the night. And against the emptiness that was expanding in the fuel tanks. Racing against the ocean's ability to hide a tiny island behind piles of waves. Racing against themselves, against their own frailty.

Still, she loved the blue, loved being in the blue and of it. At this moment, there was nowhere else on earth she'd rather be.

Part 1

— 1983 —
Wednesday

AS WOULD BECOME CLEAR in the next day or two, a slight shudder of dread was entirely appropriate. It rippled through Laura Monroe that first night in Guam like a tiny earthquake when Teri asked her question.

"Mom, why is that man staring at us?"

Laura didn't turn to look in the direction her daughter had indicated with a jerk of her fork. So, it is him, she thought. She had seen him sitting two tables away as the hostess seated her, but he had been absorbed in conversation with his companion, so she'd seen only part of his face. It's only because I'm in the islands, she'd told herself. Half the white men in Micronesia might look like Gordon Hassler to me. But if someone seated at that table is staring at us…

"Now he's coming over," Teri whispered hoarsely.

The voice, low and mellow, was as much a part of Laura's memories as the scent of the plumeria blossom she'd pinned in her hair. "Don't tell me," Teri had said earlier, displaying a fourteen-year-old's carefully cultivated boredom, "I suppose you always wore flowers in your hair when you lived in the islands."

"It is you. Laura Monroe. What brings you back to Guam?"

Same round, friendly face. Thick wavy hair, entirely gray now.

"Hello, Gordon," she said. "I could ask the same of you."

"Oh, business prospects," he said. "Keeping my hand in. You know what they say, we're fast approaching the Century of the Pacific. And what are you up to? More investigative reporting?"

She warned herself not to tell him too much, not to give him too many openings. He had always been too easy to confide in.

"We're down from Tokyo for a few days' vacation," she said. "You remember my daughter Teri?"

Hassler radiated charm as he leaned across the table to take Teri's hand and hold it for a moment. "This glamorous young woman is Teresita? You mean this is that tiny baby you had just a few years ago in Washington?"

Yes, Laura thought, that's the way it always is. We don't talk about the times we've met more recently. Everything goes back to the original times, when Foster and I were still together, and Edwina was nearby to keep Gordon in line.

"How's Edwina?" she asked.

"Oh, she's fine, just fine. She'll be delighted to hear that I've seen you."

Laura was quite certain Edwina Hassler would never hear about this encounter. She'd certainly never heard about the others.

Hassler chattered on. "Tokyo, you say? Obviously you've got tales to tell. We'll have to get together for a drink. But right now, I've got to get back ... " He waved toward the table he'd left. A husky, sunburned man stood there, making a show of looking at his watch.

"Sure. Good to see you, Gordon." Laura turned back to her coffee, waiting for Teri to stop gazing after Hassler and return to her enormous slice of passion-fruit chiffon pie.

"Well," Teri said, her voice slathered with sarcasm. "You were certainly thrilled to see him. A face from your scandalous past?"

"Just someone I've known forever."

"Am I supposed to remember him?"

"I hope not."

"Oh?" In spite of herself, Teri seemed intrigued.

"He came to San Francisco once when you were about three. He wanted to take me out for dinner. I was a little worried about ... oh, his intentions."

Teri's quizzical grimace was eloquent: Oh? Tell me more.

"Men seem to think that a recently divorced woman is desperate for a man," Laura said, wondering whether this was something

a fourteen-year-old really needed to know. Oh well, too late to worry about that. Teri had been alarmingly precocious in some matters for most of her life. "I took you along for protection and you fell asleep with your head in your plate in one of the city's most expensive restaurants."

Teri grinned, looking for a moment like the little girl she used to be instead of the bored sophisticate she was trying to turn into. "Some chaperone I was."

"You were fine. You've always been fine." Laura smiled fondly at her daughter, at her thick, straight, honey-colored hair and tanned skin. Teri was the one sweet souvenir of a soured marriage.

She remembered Gordon's frustrated glances at the sleeping child that night in the San Francisco restaurant. Perhaps he had wanted to bring the conversation around to more personal topics but had feared the child would overhear. Of course, Teri's being there had also given him an excuse to come up to the apartment, carrying "that heavy child." After she'd tucked Teri in, he'd suggested she read him some of her poems. He said he'd even brought some of his own along.

She'd gotten rid of him after a cup of coffee—and without a word of poetry. She didn't remember exactly what she'd said, but she knew he had been annoyed when he left. After all, it had been an expensive restaurant and he'd made those long-distance calls in advance from Washington, setting up the date, urging her to get a babysitter so she could really "show him the town." Perhaps he'd guessed that she hadn't even tried, despite her claim that the sitter had backed out at the last moment. Then again, she was quite sure he hadn't charged those phone calls on his personal bill.

"Are you finished with your pie?" Laura asked, reflecting that Teri had the same ardent interest in desserts her father had always exhibited, while she herself seemed fated to spend her life in polite demurral, "Just coffee for me, thanks."

Teri smacked her lips theatrically. "Yes, I am. But are you finished wallowing in your island memories and this corny music?"

Laura tuned in again to the sounds wafting from speakers hidden somewhere in the dining room's tropical decor. It was a pop orchestra rendition of old Hawaiian classics, and it was pretty syrupy. Oh, dear, she thought, are my romantic island memories being eroded by Tokyo's hustle-bustle? Or is it that Casey Kaṣem and his Top 40 Countdown Teri always listens to on Armed Forces Radio that makes this music seem a bit—well, corny?

"How was your meal?" the hostess asked as Laura signed the bill at the cash register.

"It was surprisingly good," Teri said regally. "And the view of the sunset was divine."

Laura aimed a pretend kick in Teri's direction as they strolled across the hotel's breezy lobby, heading for the stairs that led to their second-floor room. She was delighted with Teri's clowning. For the first few hours after their arrival this afternoon, the girl had been pouting, dwelling on her annoyance at being dragged away from Tokyo and her boyfriend just so she could visit "your dumb islands." Not so very different, Laura reflected, from my own reluctant arrival in the western Pacific as a young bride many years ago. And now, like mother, like daughter—Teri seemed ready to be captivated, too.

Laura caught Teri by the hand and stopped her where an open doorway led out to the terrace bar. "Smell the flowers," she said and Teri sniffed deeply and pretended to swoon. "I told you what they say: Guam is good."

"Oh, Mother, that is so trite. Guam is good. I've heard the song. I saw the banners at the airport. How can you repeat a slogan like that with a straight face?"

"Did I tell you what they say in Saipan?" Laura asked as they headed once again for the stairs.

"No, but I can guess. Saipan is better?"

"No. They say: *Saipan mas mauleg."*

"Which means?" Teri asked with excruciating politeness.

"Saipan is better."

The girl's groan seemed to echo in the stairway. But she relented. "Of course Saipan's better. Didn't you and Daddy invent me there?"

Laura and Teri had just come from Saipan, an island that had always sung of ghosts and intrigue to Laura, but which Teri found simply sunny, scenic, and dull—definitely not worth having to leave Jonathan Waterbury ten days early, en route to her annual visit with her father in Hawaii.

In Saipan, Laura had found herself wondering whether she had really organized this trip to share her perplexing passion for these islands with her daughter or if perhaps she was searching for ghosts—the ghost of what had once seemed to be a happy marriage, the ghost of herself in her twenties, when anything was still possible. Having sidled past those elusive shadows on Saipan, what was she looking for now in Guam? Was she dragging Teri along on a pilgrimage in search of her own lost youth?

She thought of those years in San Francisco, when she had first struggled with the challenges of being a single, working mother, when she had cursed Foster Monroe for interrupting her life, for dragging her off to these improbable bits of Technicolor fantasy—and cursed the islands themselves for their debilitating hold on her soul. And yet, being back in the islands, breathing the soft, moist air and the flower scents, she was being seduced again.

In their hotel room she stood before the mirror, trying to see that younger Laura in the face looking back at her. She removed the fragrant, five-petaled plumeria blossom she'd tucked behind her ear after she'd snatched it from a small tree by the hotel doorway when they arrived. Then it had looked as though it were carved from ivory. Now it was as limp as yesterday's salad.

"Ah, sweet Teresita," she said as her daughter turned on the television, "I don't approve of this whole concept of getting older."

"Don't call me Teresita," Teri said automatically. Then she seemed to focus on her mother for a moment. "You always had long hair in the islands, didn't you?"

Laura touched her short, smooth cut and then pantomimed what once had been as she stood, looking into the mirror. "Long brown hair, flowing down my back, or piled on top of my head when it got too hot. Short dresses and tan legs and a flower in my hair. I was the belle of the Pacific."

"Jeez, I hope you're not going to get weird on me, coming back to the scenes of your great triumphs."

Great triumphs? Hardly. She had come to the islands those many years ago with the sense that she had put her life on hold—postponed her career as a journalist, given up her excellent ranking as one of California's better amateur tennis players—all sacrificed to this wild idea of Foster's that they move out to the farthest reaches of the Pacific. Then, much to her surprise, she had become entranced with the islands.

Foster, who had grown up in Arizona, used to claim that anyone who stayed in the Marianas too long would develop gills from breathing the humid air. But to Laura, raised in the moist cool climate of San Francisco, it seemed the best air she'd ever breathed, like the soft, friendly fog of her childhood, but warm as a comforting mug of cocoa.

She shook her head in disbelief, calculating: Nineteen years since Foster and I first arrived in Guam. My life is sliding away.

Teri sat on her bed, using the remote control device to flip through a dozen cable television channels. "In our day," Laura said, "there was only one channel on the whole island."

"Oh? Television had already been invented in your day?"

Laura tossed the small, fragrant corpse of the plumeria blossom at her daughter.

When the phone rang, Laura reached for it, willing it to be her friend, Charlotte Sablán, the only other person who knew she was on island. But, of course, it was Gordon Hassler.

"Hello, Laura." His voice was low, romantic. Good grief, she thought, don't men like Gordon Hassler ever outgrow these games?

"I was surprised to see you here," he said. "I thought you'd given up the islands in search of bigger worlds."

"I think islands may be addictive."

"They have been for me," he said. "Listen, why don't you come down to the bar and join me for a drink? Teri looks big enough to look after herself."

"Oh, I'm sorry, Gordon. I'm already in my nightgown," From the next bed, Teri rubbed one shaming index finger against the other. "I've got junk on my face already. I'm a mess."

Teri pretended to gag at her mother's disgusting appearance and Laura had to look away to keep from laughing.

"Well then, how about meeting me for breakfast?"

Laura hesitated. Charlotte was coming by later in the morning, which would give her an excuse not to prolong things. There was no reason she couldn't meet him for breakfast. Maybe Teri would come along. "Sure, Gordon, that would be nice. What time?"

"Eight o'clock not too early for you?"

"Eight would be fine."

"I'll meet you in the lobby then."

She hung up and told Teri, "I'm having breakfast with him tomorrow."

"Well, don't expect me to protect you this time." Teri smirked. "I'm on vacation. Eight is not fine for me."

Laura sighed in mock frustration. "Well, I guess I'll have to deal with him all by myself. But you've got to be dressed by ten when Charlotte Sablán comes to pick us up."

"Yes, Mother." Teri retrieved her over-burdened martyr's voice.

Laura gave her a quick kiss and went into the bathroom to change into her nightgown and put junk on her face.

– 1936 –

THE BOY WAS AT THE COUNTY FAIR that afternoon, doing his magic tricks, the sleight of hand he was so adept at. He'd taken an afternoon off from work at the garage to help out in a booth to raise funds for the Boy Scouts—people bought tickets to try to outguess the magician. Even though many of his tricks involved cards—and yes, even poker hands—it wasn't gambling, he assured his mother, it was show business. Not that it made her feel much better.

In the early evening he became aware of the pale eyes of a stranger staring at him. The man was tall and handsome, dressed in black like a gunfighter in a Western movie. Even his Stetson hat was black, despite the heat of the South Dakota summer.

After he watched for several minutes, the man spoke with a soft, twangy drawl. "Hey, kid, ever hear of the deadman's hand?"

The boy smiled to himself. He was fond of detective stories and he congratulated himself on knowing more about the stranger than he might suspect: From his voice, he was a Southerner. From his question, he was a tourist who had just come down the road from Deadwood where you could visit the very saloon where Wild Bill Hickock had been shot in the back while holding a certain poker hand.

The boy shuffled his deck and then solemnly dealt out the hand, face up so everyone could see. Two black kings and two black eights defined the deadman's hand, but because he had to be sure he didn't deal another king or eight—that would be a full house, something entirely different—he always threw in the nine of diamonds. It wasn't just any deadman's hand—those were the exact cards Wild Bill Hickock had held.

"Excellent," the stranger said with a grin. He seemed to reach toward the boy, perhaps to slap him on the shoulder, but he stopped his hand in mid-air. The boy was surprised at the man's hand with its shapely fingers and gleaming nails. He wondered: Do men get manicures?

"You're very good with your hands," the man said. "What else can you do with them?"

"I'm really a mechanic," the boy said. "I just do this for fun."

The man pushed his black hat back from his long face. "That mean you've graduated high school?"

"Yes, sir. This past spring."

"I'm having a little trouble with my car," the man said. "I don't suppose you could take a few minutes to look at it? When you get a break here?"

A few minutes later,. as they walked toward the parking lot, the man asked, "What's your name?"

"Garrett," the boy said. "Garrett Howland."

"It is a very great pleasure to meet you. Everyone calls me Tex and I hope you will, too."

He led the way to a gleaming black Rolls Royce, the biggest car Garrett had ever seen.

"Wow! Gee, Mister, I don't know if I can—"

"Tex," the man said firmly.

"I'm sorry. Uh, Tex. It's just that I've never even been close to a car like this."

"But you sure would like to be, wouldn't you, Gary?"

"Well, yeah, sure … but I don't know if I can be any help."

"Go on. Open the 'bonnet' as my British friends like to say. Take a look at her."

Slowly, almost with reverence, the boy raised the side of the long hood and gazed into the shiny engine compartment. He stared for a long time, mentally tracing the connections, wishing he had the right wrenches to just examine a few of the more intriguing bits up close. He turned toward Tex. "She is beautiful," he said.

The man's face had a strange look on it. "So are you," he said. "So are you."

Garrett didn't know what to say. He felt himself blushing.

"Well listen, I don't really think there's anything seriously wrong with the car. Tell you what, if you'll show me the best restaurant in this burg, I'll buy you dinner and tell you about my summer vacation. Why, I'll even let you drive."

Sliding onto the soft leather upholstery of the driver's seat, the boy felt a sudden chill. He shouldn't be doing this, he knew with strange certainty. He took a deep breath and the apprehension passed. How many chances would a boy in Spearfish, South Dakota, have to drive a car like this? With his mother nagging him about registering for classes at the local college, he wasn't likely to get out of Spearfish anytime soon. And what harm was there in eating dinner in a restaurant with a pleasant man? After all, the Black Hills were supposed to be getting ready to host hordes of tourists bringing economic salvation once the sculpture of the presidents was finished. Certainly Garrett Howland should do his part.

He turned the ignition on and the car purred to life.

— 1967 —
September

JODIE DESPAIN ASKED A CO-WORKER to drop her off beside the airstrip at Guam's Naval Air Station, near a Volkswagen minibus that bore a large logo in brilliant tropical colors: Micronesian Pacific Airways. She gripped her small suitcase and walked toward the minibus with a tremor of anticipation close to panic. She tried not to look at the small, yellow plane parked a few yards away. It seemed fragile as a dragonfly.

"When you come up to see us," Laura had said, "fly with Donnie MacDougal. He'll probably let you sit up in the cockpit." Flying with bush pilots in small planes is the sort of thing Laura Monroe would do, Jodie thought. She saw Laura as someone going through life saying, "Hey! I haven't tried that yet!"

But what am I doing here? Jodie asked herself. She'd never been on anything but 707 jetliners, and then only because she had to, to get to Guam where she'd managed to get a good job right out of college. For Jodie, flying was something that existed in the realm of the theoretical. Boarding a trans-Pacific flight was like consigning her body to an anesthesiologist so that her appendix could be removed, a process for which she bore no responsibility. She climbed aboard a jet, fastened the seat belt, opened a good book, and went away, leaving everything else up to the giant corporation whose business it was. On the other hand, Micronesian Pacific Airways was anything but a giant corporation. According to Laura, it consisted of a pilot, a plane, a minibus, and a telephone.

A disheveled, bearded man juggling several cameras stood beside the opened sliding door of the van, talking to a shadowy figure

inside. From photos in the Guam newspaper, Jodie recognized the man seated at a folding table in the van. He was lanky with dark, weathered skin and craggy features. She'd been reading about Donnie MacDougal's exploits ever since Laura weaned her from the staid military daily, *Pacific Stars and Stripes,* and persuaded her to try the local papers. The Guam press doted on the Hawaiian pilot's dramatic landings on islands whose airstrips had been blasted to craters during the war and left unrepaired for twenty years.

He looked up from his paperwork and asked, "Are you Jodie deSpain?" Jodie thought it didn't seem quite right for a romantic island legend to be completing bureaucratic forms but she handed him twelve dollars in cash. He scratched his head, his black hair cropped as close as velvet. "I suppose you need some sort of receipt?"

"Not really," she said. "It's a private trip."

The bearded man said, "Donnie, you should get tickets printed up as souvenirs—certificates of survival." He turned to her abruptly. "What takes you to Saipan?"

"I'm going to visit some friends for the weekend." Jodie was irritated by his question. She needed to concentrate all her energy on getting into that little airplane.

"What a coincidence," he said. "So am I. What do you do in Guam?"

"I'm a lab supervisor," she said. "Guam Naval Hospital."

"I'm Will Hildebrandt, of the *Daily Star,*" he said. Well, she thought, that explains the cameras. She'd seen his name in photo credits and bylines, first in the *Guam Daily Chronicle* and lately in the new *Daily Star of the Pacific,* whose name seemed as overly ambitious as that of Micronesian Pacific Airways.

MacDougal unfolded himself from the van. The epaulets, braid, and wings on his crisp white shirt contrasted with his faded chinos. He picked up a large tool kit from the floor of the van. "Will's my personal press agent," he said, almost in apology.

Hildebrandt seemed eager to establish his credentials. "Remember the story a couple months back, when the Feds tried to pull

Donnie's license because he brought an alien into the U.S. without the proper documents?"

She did remember something. "Wasn't it a Micronesian who was injured?"

"That's the one," Hildebrandt said. "Down in Ulithi. He crashed his motorbike and broke his head. And for some silly reason he hadn't thought to tuck his Trust Territory ID into his *thu*—you know, his loincloth—when he set out for his Sunday spin. Donnie was taking me and some other folks to Yap when he picked up the SOS call from the medic in Ulithi, so he diverted the flight, loaded the guy aboard, brought him to Guam, and they patched him back together at your hospital. But it was Donnie who saved his life."

"And Will who saved my license," MacDougal said.

She remembered that there had been indignant editorials in both Guam newspapers after Will's story raised a ruckus. She thought she remembered that Micronesian Pacific Airways had been grounded for less than 72 hours.

A tall teenaged girl emerged from the plane with a tiny vacuum cleaner, followed by a younger boy. "This is my ground crew, Cory and Jeff." MacDougal said. Both children had dark, golden skin and the semi-Asian features of mixed-race islanders. "You already spoke to the reservations department, my wife."

He pulled some car keys from his pants pocket and handed them to the girl. "Back about four, babe," he said. "Drop those papers off now, and pick up the immigration guy on your way past the terminal when you come back this afternoon."

Donnie MacDougal ambled toward his plane. As Will Hildebrandt wriggled into the straps of a bulging backpack, the boy, Jeff, said, "Excuse me, Miss. Check your baggage?" He took her bag and scampered away to stow it in the back of the plane.

MacDougal stopped beside the plane's folding steps. "You don't mind, do you, Will? I'll let Jodie sit up front this trip."

"Jeez," Hildebrandt said, "I'm not going to get any pictures from back there."

"Ain't no big t'ing." Donnie lapsed into Hawaiian pidgin, and his voice sounded like he was humoring a child. "What's to shoot? Rota? Saipan? How many times you been dose places, bruddah?"

In slow motion, Jodie climbed up the sloping aisle to the cockpit and plopped into the seat beside Donnie MacDougal. There seemed to be a full set of controls in front of her and when Donnie moved his "steering wheel" back, the one in front of her came back, too. She supposed there was a proper aviation term for the apparatus but she didn't want to interrupt the pilot's pre-flight checklist to ask for it.

Donnie spoke briefly into a microphone—then the plane raced down the vast Naval Air Station runway, becoming airborne on what seemed to be only a tiny segment of it. Sitting up front, she felt responsible for keeping the plane in the air.

They soared over the northern plateau of Guam, looking down on silver-green spiky heads of pandanus trees and dense green and brown growth of tangan-tangan. The jungle was punctuated by red gravel roads and the corrugated tin roofs of little houses. Then the large village of Dededo sprawled below them, soaking up the morning sun. Jodie felt as though she were perched on a kite caught in a perfect updraft.

They swept toward the palisaded cliffs where Guam plunged into the Pacific and down into the Marianas Trench, the deepest ocean on the planet. High above that infinitely blue depth, they flew toward Rota Island, easily visible across thirty miles of sparkling sea.

"Ever been to Rota?" Donnie asked over the loud rumble of the engines.

"No." She shook her head in case he couldn't hear her. She turned and saw Will Hildebrandt slouched in a rear seat in the passenger section. There were three pairs of empty seats in front of him.

"It's the last repository of Chamorro culture," Donnie shouted. "Uncorrupted by the Spanish or the Yanks. They still know how to count in Chamorro there, instead of *uno, dos, tres.*"

She hoped he wouldn't mind if she didn't answer. She just wanted to sit there, soaking up the flight. This was not remotely

like being on a jet where incomprehensible technology did its efficient job. This was real. Somehow she could feel the wind outside, feel how it flowed beneath the wings to lift the plane. She could see its power in the sinews standing out in Donnie MacDougal's bare forearms as he maneuvered the controls. Suddenly, she wanted to grab her set of controls, to lay her fingers on the plane's quick pulse. Instead, she jammed her hands under her seatbelt.

It was the first time she believed in flight.

Donnie must have seen something in her face. "You can see how folks get hooked," he shouted.

Behind her, the dark cloud of Will Hildebrandt's funk oozed out to fill the passenger compartment, with tendrils stretching forward to nudge her. But in the cockpit, with its bubble of window, all was light, and she sat at the cutting edge of the universe. There was nothing but blue sea and sky, the wonder of air, and the green encrusted island of Rota sliding rapidly toward them.

They flew over a peninsula that hooked southward with a village cradled in the crook of its arm, then on over the island's central plateau. A raw, white scar gouged in an endless jumble of green was the airfield. Donnie flew low over the runway once and then pulled the plane up abruptly. "Damn!" he said. "No one in sight."

Will Hildebrandt moved forward to the seat just outside the cockpit. "Supposed to be a passenger?" he shouted.

"I had a radio message. Someone needs a ride to Saipan." Donnie turned the plane in a sweep that took Jodie's stomach by surprise. He swung wide over the ocean, then turned back, diving toward the peninsula. They buzzed the village, flying so low Jodie wanted to hold her feet up. Out to sea again, Donnie turned the plane and buzzed the village once more.

"Look." Will pointed over Jodie's shoulder. A pickup truck emerged from the narrow streets of the village and sped toward the plateau in a cloud of white coral dust.

"See how accommodating this airline is," Donnie said as he turned toward the airfield again. "We even make wake-up calls."

On the coral gravel runway, Donnie made a game of dodging pools of rainwater, zigging and zagging, rocking from one wheel to the other as Will whooped and hollered and Jodie tried to clench her earlier exuberance firmly to her. He knows what he's doing, she told herself. This is a real runway, not like where he lands sometimes.

They taxied to a wide spot and, with practiced showmanship, Donnie stabbed a pedal, spinning the plane's tail so they reversed direction in the distance of a wingspan. Now pointed back the way they had come, he stopped the idling engines and he and Will exited for a smoke. Jodie sat alone in the cockpit, contemplating the new dimension the universe had acquired. She reached forward like a guilty child to pull the small wheel an inch toward her, then returned it to its previous position. She studied the dials and gauges arrayed before her as though they might hold an answer to the riddle of life.

"Hey, Jodie!" Will shouted.

She made her way to the doorway.

"Donnie says this is the first time you've flown in a small plane. Let me take your picture for a souvenir."

Apparently he was forgiving her for usurping his favorite seat. She stepped to the ground and stood beside the plane. A breeze ruffled her short hair, and she realized wind meant something new to her. She grinned as the shutter thwocked.

"Now one with His Eminence," Will said. As Donnie stepped beside her, she realized he was one of the few men who towered over her. He put his arm lightly around her shoulder, a brotherly embrace—but it set off an inexplicable electrical storm in her chest.

The pickup truck from the village appeared at the far end of the runway and raced toward them. When it skidded to a stop, its passenger—a plump islander—spilled out and hurried over to them, slapped Donnie on the back and babbled an apology. As the pickup sped away, Jodie hesitated at the door to the plane, wondering if she would be bumped from the copilot seat now. Donnie grinned and waved her forward, ahead of him. Will and the newcomer took seats at the plane's rear.

"Will's nose is back in joint," Donnie remarked as he ran through his pre-flight checklist. "He's got better news prospects back there now than he would have up here."

"Who is that?" she asked in a low voice.

"Senator Jesús B. Santos, the Terror of Tinian. They say he's *persona non grata* in Guam because of all the rubber checks he's written, but he's a really big wheel in the Congress of Micronesia, I do believe."

She'd heard about Santos somewhere. It was the sort of thing Foster and Laura Monroe might have mentioned, caught up as they were by the great spectator sport of island politics. She glanced back into the passenger compartment. The round-faced politician was leaning across the aisle, making a point in Will's face with his index finger. Will was scribbling in a small notebook.

Donnie took off after slithering once more between the puddles on the runway, and they headed north again. As they rose, the ocean stretched away forever in all directions.

"As a special introductory offer, I'll show you the best-kept secret in the Mariana Islands," Donnie shouted.

They continued to climb until they reached a layer of clouds several hundred feet thick. Donnie steered the plane into a channel that cut through the white fluff. On both sides of them, the clouds cascaded down, just at wing-tip, like endless waterfalls, falling, falling. The plane floated between vast banks of insubstantial substance, continuing to climb. Finally they burst out again into blueness above and on all sides, with the quilt of cotton foam below.

As they rose high above the cloud bank, Donnie pointed to the northwest where the clouds ended and the sea was visible. A series of islands, high, green-blue peaks, marched into the distance. She looked at him in astonishment. Her concept of the Mariana Islands, reading south to north, was: Guam, Rota, Tinian, Saipan. What were these?

"The Northern Islands," Donnie said. Even though he was shouting, his voice caressed the names of the islands. "That's Ana-

tahan right there, and Alamagan, then Sariguan, and just on the horizon, all those bumps, that's Pagan."

"Wow!" Though inadequate, it was the best she could do.

"There's more north of Pagan," Donnie said. "Agrihan—the highest point in Micronesia. The northernmost one is Maug. That's Guam spelled backwards."

Jodie looked to see if he was joking but he was as serious as a man could be while flying with such uninhibited glee.

After a time in the enchanted zone between sun and sea, they approached the long, tall island called Anatahan. "Now for the secret," Donnie said, jamming the stick forward. The plane dived toward the island.

"What the hell?" Will blurted from behind them.

"Little sightseeing bonus for you gentlemen!" Donnie shouted over his shoulder as he leveled the plane off. Now Jodie could see the crater in the center of the island's peak, see that Anatahan was a volcano that had grown up from the ocean's floor. They drew closer. A lake sparkled in the center of the crater, a sapphire in a setting of green filigree.

"Oooh!" she whispered.

Donnie swooped the plane down until they passed right over the crater walls and looked into the sapphire's depths.

"Son-a-bitch." Senator Santos' voice erupted from behind them. "I always heard there was a lake at Anatahan but a man gotta beat his way through the jungle for two days to see it. Son-a-bitch!"

Donnie shrugged what seemed a shiver of pleasure at being able to give them the lake. He pulled the plane up again and leveled off, heading south. Now they saw Saipan and its terraced twin, Tinian, seeming squashed and low after the tower of Anatahan.

"Okay," Donnie said, "Your turn."

Jodie's heart stopped.

"Go on, put your hands on the wheel."

Slowly, she reached out, touched trembling fingers to the small wheel, then tightened her grip.

"It's all yours." Donnie threw his own hands into the air, clasped them behind his head. "Okay, pull back, gently now. Turn it a little to the left. That's it."

She felt the force of the universe flow directly into her body, and she was filled with irrational love, love of flight, love for the crazy island pilot and the check-bouncing Chamorro senator. Even grouchy Will Hildebrandt seemed lovable.

Maybe it's oxygen starvation, she thought.

—1983—
Thursday

THERE'S NEVER BEEN ANYTHING between me and Gordon Hassler, Laura thought as she stepped into the shower. Nothing except all those strange, never-quite-acknowledged encounters.

The first incident remained vivid in her mind, even after—what—fifteen years? She had been in Palau on assignment for the Trust Territory government's public information office, staying at the old Royal Palauan, a picturesque hostelry cobbled together out of remnants of World War II barracks. A few days after she'd arrived, Gordon Hassler moved into the room across the hall. One evening after a party, he gave her a ride back to the hotel. As they strolled through the lobby with its slow-moving ceiling fans, decaying rattan furniture, and ambiance that was, to Laura, the epitome of everything Michener and Maugham had ever written about the South Seas, Gordon asked, "Can I buy you a drink?"

"No, thanks," that younger and more innocent Laura had said. "I've had enough for tonight. I'm going straight to bed."

He had followed her down the hall, their rubber zoris slapping softly on patchy linoleum. He had stood waiting as she struggled with her key in the rusty lock. "Well, goodnight, Gordon," she'd said, turning to face him as the door opened on creaky hinges. There had been an odd look on his round, boyish face.

"We have so much in common, Laura," he said.

"We do?" She was startled. In that instant she thought of Saipan gossip about Gordon Hassler's flirtations with various young wives, gossip she'd always scoffed at. Gordon was ... not a father figure exactly, more like a father-in-law. He seemed to take particular in-

terest in Foster's career within the island bureaucracy. Of course, he also seemed sincerely interested in Laura's journalism. But what was going on now?

"I don't tell just anybody this, but I write poetry, too."

"You do?" I sound like an idiot. Leave me alone. Go away.

"I thought it would be nice if we got together sometime, read our poetry to each other. It's so important to find a sympathetic listener."

She could not shake off the habit of friendship. "Well, that would be nice … "

He took a step forward, as though to enter the room. Her room. "No time like the present."

She moved to block the door. "No, Gordon, not now. I—I've got to get to sleep. I've got a lot to do tomorrow." Then she had pushed the door shut against him.

Now, standing in the shower in Guam in 1983, it occurred to her that she had established the pattern then for all their future encounters: Never admit what he was up to. And so, she never had reason to refuse his next invitation. They just went on being old friends. Come on, she thought, angrily lathering shampoo into her hair. Get with it! Tell that creep Hassler to get lost.

As she got out of the shower, she was startled for a moment by the large raised initials on the thick white bathmat. GH. The man is haunting me! She clutched the towel around her.

No, you idiot. After all, this is the Guam Hilton.

She toweled her hair dry and stood before the mirror, putting on eye makeup, still half-caught in that other place, that other time. She remembered how she had leaned on the door from inside, trying to laugh as though it were all a joke, shutting Gordon Hassler out of her room, trying to shut him out of her life.

He'd never said anything about it. Not the next morning when he had sat down across from her at the long table in the dining room of the Royal Palauan. Not after they had both returned to Saipan. It wasn't surprising that he hadn't mentioned it, she supposed. But

neither had she. She hadn't wanted to upset Foster, hadn't wanted to jeopardize her friendship with Edwina.

She combed her hair, put on lipstick, and tiptoed to her daughter's bedside. "Teri has to be ready by ten o'clock," she whispered softly into the girl's ear, trying to implant a subconscious alarm. She kissed her daughter's cheek and left the room quietly.

*   *   *

"Well, Laura," Gordon said as they took their seats outside under a shady umbrella. The tropical sun had already warmed the concrete terrace where it wasn't shaded. "It's been a long, long time."

Not that long, she thought, remembering the most recent time their paths had crossed. It was less than two years ago. But perhaps he hadn't seen her that time.

"Teri has become a real beauty," he said.

"Thank you."

"Where's Foster these days?"

"Honolulu." She was careful not to confide in him, not to mention that in a few days she would be putting Teri on a plane to spend the rest of the summer with her father. For a moment she wanted to tell him, this old friend, so caring, so gifted at listening. She could almost hear herself telling him how she had written to ask Foster if he could increase his contribution to Teri's support to help cope with the hefty tuition charges at the American school in Tokyo, and how he had countered with the suggestion that Teri stay with him, enroll in high school in Hawaii, have "an American experience."

It almost seemed appropriate to tell this friend who had known them all these years how desperately she hoped Teri would decide to return to Tokyo, no matter what financial bind it created. "I'm not ready to spend whole school years alone," she would have said. "I planned to have at least three more years with her before she goes to college." But she didn't want to let Gordon Hassler see her vulnerable, couldn't let him know that in just a few days Teri would be

gone and she would be here alone. I'm still hiding behind the kid, she thought.

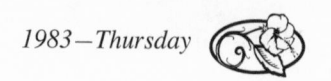

Anyway, I don't need his sympathy. Teri is going to be so eager to get back to that dreadful future insurance salesman Jonathan Waterbury she thinks she's in love with, her father will have trouble keeping her in Hawaii all summer. Unless she gets a crush on someone there. Then she's likely to take Foster up on that American experience. Oh, why does Mother Nature turn on teenagers' gonads when they're not ready to cope? Or is it the parents who aren't ready?

"So Foster's still in Hawaii. What's he doing there?"

"Some kind of consulting. I've never been quite sure what he does—it's really not my business anymore."

His eyes seemed to search for something in her face. Did he think she was faking nonchalance about Foster? It certainly felt sincere to her. Not wondering about what Foster was up to had been one of the most lasting pleasures of being divorced from him.

"A remarkably enlightened attitude for an ex-wife," Gordon said. After a pause, he added, "You know, I never understood why you left Foster."

"I didn't really understand myself for a long time."

"I always wondered if it had anything to do with Lionel Keating."

Laura smiled what felt like a Mona Lisa smile—from the inside at least. She hoped she looked mysterious. She conjured up a picture of the handsome Hawaiian she'd known so long ago. "Lionel? No, it was nothing to do with Neil. Well, at least it wasn't directly connected with him."

Many years ago, when she'd first known Gordon Hassler, she might have wanted to explain, to rationalize her decision. Back then she might have told him how she had always wanted to be madly in love, how she had married Foster because he was older and worldly and annoyed her mother—and how that turned out not to be enough. She might have told Gordon that she started think-

ing about leaving Foster when these islands made her realize how ill-matched they were—how she could be passionate, even about her role as a journalist in these fledgling democracies, while Foster had no particular passion for anything. Now she no longer needed to justify her choice. And she certainly didn't need to explain it to Gordon Hassler.

After a silence, Gordon said, "What are you up to these days?"

"Well, I got on with Associated Press a few years ago," she said, thinking: You knew that. We've had this conversation before. "I've been at the Tokyo bureau for about a year."

"I guess I do remember hearing something about the AP," he said. She could remember telling him about it twice. The first time was when she ran into him on a corner in Rosslyn, across the Potomac from Washington, and he had insisted on taking her out for a drink. She had accepted "for old times' sake," and it had led to another of his oblique propositions.

Two months later, he and Edwina had been two blankets over on the lawn at Wolftrap in Northern Virginia during a performance of *Don Carlo*. When Edwina had spotted her during the first intermission, Laura crept over to talk to them, and Gordon hadn't mentioned the other times he'd seen her, not the drink in Rosslyn nor the dinner in San Francisco years before. So she told her story again for Edwina—how she had escaped from the purgatory of the typing pools of San Francisco, launched once again into the journalistic whirlwind, the role in which the Hasslers had first known her in the islands, the role she'd always known she was meant to play. The islands had been just an interlude, she had assured them, but now she was back on track. She hadn't confided the despair she'd felt those years in San Francisco when her only salable asset seemed to be the speed of her fingers flying over typewriter keys.

"Did you have to learn Japanese for this Tokyo assignment?" Gordon asked now on the terrace of Guam's Hilton Hotel.

She wondered if he remembered that she had been studying Thai when he had bought her that drink in Rosslyn, or if he had any

idea she had seen him one night in Bangkok. "We don't get as much training beforehand as we need," she said. "It's really only courtesy level. But they do pay for my language classes in Tokyo."

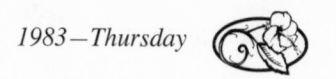

"You always were good at languages."

"Not necessarily good," she said. "Just fascinated by them."

"I remember you knew all those Chamorro words when we were in Saipan, and words from other Micronesian languages."

Immediately she thought of two words, the Trukese *finigogo* which meant "a big, complicated mess," and the Palauan *buulaak* which translated as "nonsense." Both apt words to apply to Gordon Hassler, she thought.

"How's Japanese going?"

Laura made a wry face. "Did you know that in order to read a Japanese newspaper you're supposed to know one thousand eight hundred and fifty *kanji*—those Chinese characters the Japanese still use?"

He made the sympathetic clucking sounds that she remembered. Such an understanding man.

"And how is life in Tokyo?" he asked.

He really means "love life," she thought. She was vague. "Fascinating."

His voice shifted into that Hollywood-romantic-hero octave. "Ah, Laura, we have so much in common."

"Well, we do seem to show up in all the same places." There, that is as close as either of us has ever come to acknowledging all these peculiar encounters.

"Yes, we do," he said. He seemed to narrow his eyes, appraising her. Does he wonder whether I will tell Edwina about his … what are they? Incomplete passes? Whatever, he apparently decided to back away from the personal, at least for the moment.

"So, are you still the great writer of exposés? Still seeking malfeasance in government?"

Is he afraid I'll write something about him? He isn't even in the government any more, is he? Of course, he had been interested in

her writing—or in influencing what she wrote—from the day they first met. She tried to keep her mind on the present conversation. "News coverage is pretty much cut and dried in Tokyo," she said. "The Japanese are so organized about it. But I do get to do some interesting features now and then."

"And I'll bet you still write poetry." His voice was throaty once more.

Here we go again, she thought. Next he'll invite me up to his room to hear some of his poems.

Later she would tell Teri, "He ordered banana fritters and I ordered pineapple fritters and we frittered our way through sticky, syrupy small talk." Gordon's voice switched channels to a light, gossipy tone but she had the feeling he had a question he hadn't figured out how to ask. He mentioned mutual acquaintances who were still in Saipan, people she affirmed she had just seen there. Despite ostensibly having come on business he seemed ill-informed about what was happening on Guam. Finally, he suggested they share the rental on a car and drive around the island but she quickly said that was on her schedule for today, with an old friend.

"So you still have friends in Guam?" Does he seem threatened by that? Perhaps it inconveniences his romantic fantasies.

"I've kept in touch with a few people, like Charlotte Sablán."

"Sablán? Is that the woman who set up that research center about the islands out at the university? I've often thought of contacting her about a research project of mine."

It was an opening she was probably meant to follow through on. What sort of research, Gordon? What are you doing these days? Within a few hours she would berate herself for not asking those questions, but right now she just wanted to end the encounter.

Gordon signed the bill, took Laura's arm, and walked her across the breezy hotel lobby to the stairs. They parted with vague promises to get together again during their time in Guam. As she climbed to the second floor, Laura couldn't decide whether she felt slightly menaced by Gordon Hassler, or just slightly disgusted. Or

did the discomfort come from his side of the equation? Is he, perhaps, uneasy about me? she wondered. Worried that I'll tell his wife about his propositions, if that's what they were? Or is there some other way in which I threaten him? Why has he always been so interested in my journalistic career?

If someone from my past is going to keep popping up in unexpected places, why couldn't it be someone dashing and handsome, she thought. Someone like Lionel Keating, for instance, instead of the obsequious Gordon Hassler?

For a moment, as she padded down the thickly carpeted hall in the Guam Hilton, she saw instead the crumbling linoleum of the Royal Palauan fifteen years before. Then, just as she reached the door to her room, she stopped with a new thought.

When she'd run into him that time in Rosslyn, he had expressed great surprise at her being back in the D.C. area, in Rosslyn of all places. Why had she never wondered what Gordon Hassler was doing there? She remembered clearly where she'd encountered him. Very near the Rosslyn Metro station, on a certain peculiar block, the one with a wedge-shaped gas station at ground level and a Methodist church above it, "Our Lady of High Octane," Foster had called it.

And next door, the one address you could find in the phone book for the Central Intelligence Agency, the one door just anyone could walk through and inquire about employment or, perhaps, about the going prices for secrets.

What had Gordon Hassler been doing in that particular place? What was he doing in Guam now? For that matter, what was he doing in the islands nearly twenty years ago, befriending naive young reporters from island newspapers?

Puntan Dos Amantes

THE CLIFF AT THE FAR END of Tumon Bay is so dramatic, so extreme, it demands an explanatory legend. And, of course, there is one.

Long ago in olden times—before the Spaniards came, before the Americans, long before the Japanese—long ago in Chamorro times a beautiful girl lived in Agaña, the daughter of proud and arrogant parents. The girl was so lovely that any man who beheld her was hopelessly smitten.

Her parents—ambitious and practical—were determined their daughter would marry well, to insure that they would rise in island society. Therefore they agreed to bestow their daughter's hand upon a wealthy elderly man of noble blood who seemed besotted with the young beauty.

The poor girl was already in love with a young man from a poor family who had nothing to offer her but his hard work and his utter devotion. The girl told her parents of her love and begged that they allow her to follow her heart and marry the man of her choice, to permit her this one chance at happiness. But like parents the world over, they were sure they knew what was best. They carried on with their plans to have the girl marry the rich old man.

It was a terrible choice for the girl to make, but although she loved her parents, she loved the young man more. The night before the day set for her wedding, she ran away from her parents' home in Agaña and met her young lover far outside the town. They fled deep into the jungle.

Keeping out of sight in the thick vegetation, they hurried past the villages of Apurgan and Socio. At last they came to Tumon.

The nobleman recruited men to search for his bride. They scoured Agaña from the sea to the cliffs. When daylight came, they found the trail the lovers had taken and pursued them. By midday, the search party had reached Tumon.

When the lovers heard the sounds of pursuit, they promised eternal devotion and swore they would never be separated from each other. Hemmed in, they came to the edge of the tall cliff overlooking the bay. They tied their long hair into a lovers' knot and, arm in arm, threw themselves off the cliff and fell down, down, down hundreds of feet to the sea below.

No bodies were ever found. Some say they see the spirits of the lovers, sparkling far above the sea on bright, sunny days. Others say they hear the sound of happy young voices, murmuring in the caves beneath the cliff.

Who knows? The power of love can be as deep and strong as the ocean, as soaring as the cliff, and as sweet and delicate as the ylang-ylang, quietly blooming in the warm, tropical night.

– 1983 –
Thursday

LAURA SMILED AS SHE WATCHED Teri get caught up in Charlotte's storytelling. Charlotte had a way of beginning as though she were delivering an academic report, but by the end, a legend seemed as intimate and juicy as a morsel of island gossip.

They had embarked on what Foster used to call "a rock around the rock"—a tour around the island. Although it had been many years since Laura had seen Charlotte Sablán, they had corresponded regularly, if not frequently, and there was little catching up to do. Charlotte's short curls might be grayer now, but her round, cheery face seemed unchanged, and her brilliant orange muumuu could have been the same one she'd worn nineteen years ago when she strode into the newspaper office where Laura worked and demanded a map to a waterfall Laura had described in a feature story. "I've searched for Tarzan Falls the entire time I've been on this island," Charlotte had said indignantly. "I thought it was the Guamanian version of a snipe hunt."

This morning, Laura had given her a hug in the hotel lobby and introduced Teri, who formally offered her hand. Charlotte took in the pastel T-shirt, neatly tucked in; the trim mid-thigh khaki shorts, and the carefully combed honey-colored hair. "Foster Monroe's daughter, all right," she said. "But it's much prettier on you."

Teri sat in the back seat of Charlotte's Toyota and practiced her bored look. But she was soon captivated by the dramatic view from Two Lovers Point, and by Charlotte's bottomless bag of Chamorro legends, snippets of island history, and political gossip.

"Charlotte invented the Western Pacific Research Center single-handedly," Laura told her daughter. "And if the library should ever

burn down, ain't no big t'ing, because she's got all the information in her head."

Charlotte professed shock at Laura's sacrilege. "Micronesia is a major topic," she insisted. "It's much bigger than me, or what I've collected."

In the days to come, Laura would recall only one relevant interlude in their itinerary that day—their stop for lunch at a restaurant on the cliff overlooking Pago Bay. A tall, slim woman with deep-set, dark eyes, jet black hair, and dark, golden skin greeted Charlotte by name and seated them at a table by a window. Outside, the branches of a purple-pink bougainvillea framed a spectacular view across the bay to the campus of the University of Guam and beyond to palisades of cliffs marching north. Even from this vantage point miles away, they could see the mist produced when waves that had crossed the Pacific and slid over the world's deepest ocean trench crashed against Guam's rocky foundation.

"Wow," Teri said.

"Very few Americans know this," Charlotte said, "although the Japs have figured it out. Guam is a very beautiful island."

Laura tried not to wince at the word "Jap." She must remember to explain later to Teri how Charlotte's anti-Japanese bias grew out of the experience of her Guamanian husband's family during the wartime occupation of their island.

Oblivious of any *faux pas*, Charlotte continued, "I don't suppose you recognized the hostess?"

Laura scrutinized the young woman who was returning to their table, wondering if she could possibly be one of Charlotte's daughters. She decided the hostess was darker-skinned than any of Charlotte's kids. "No, I can't place her."

The hostess asked, "Can I get you anything from the bar?"

"Laura Monroe," Charlotte said, "may I present Cory MacDougal? And this is Laura's daughter Teri."

"Cory," Laura said. "My goodness. The last time I saw you, you were a kid lugging a vacuum cleaner across the tarmac to clean out your dad's airplane."

"Monroe?" Cory seemed cautious. "I think I remember. You were a writer—took some trips with my dad?"

"Some exciting trips. Got some good stories flying around with that wild man."

Cory still seemed wary, perhaps even hostile. "You're not the woman he taught to fly?"

Laura laughed. "No, not me. I just liked to go along and see what kind of news Donnie MacDougal could stir up." No wonder Cory's hostile, Laura thought. The woman her father had taught to fly broke up his marriage before the lessons were over. Fragments of memory—people, places—came flooding back, as vivid as the flowers that framed every window of the restaurant. Laura shook her head to scatter the images. "What's your dad doing now?"

Cory laughed. "What do you think? Flying. Hawaii, mostly. Although he did give Alaska a try for a couple years. Too cold for him, though. He says a Hawaiian's meant to drown in warm water, not die crawling across the ice somewhere."

"I remember one night in San Francisco," Laura said. "It must have been what … 1972? I was listening to my favorite classical radio station and during the news break the announcer read an item about an American civilian pilot being captured in Laos. I really wasn't paying close attention, but I thought I'd heard the name Donald MacDougal. I called the radio station as soon as the music started again and I asked the announcer to read the entire news story about Laos. And sure enough, it was Donnie. I broke down and cried. I was so mad that we were still sending people into that hopeless swamp."

"Believe it or not, that's how we heard about him getting captured, too," Cory said. "Radio news. It seems the … uh … organization he hooked up with isn't as good at letting people know what happens to their loved ones as the military is."

"But he's okay now," Charlotte said hurriedly to Teri, as though to shelter her from more Vietnam talk after filling her ears with the sex and gore of Chamorro legends all morning. "And I bet you would like something to drink."

Teri asked for a Coke and Charlotte and Laura ordered San Miguel beer. As Cory MacDougal left, she promised to send a waitress to take their food order.

"It's just as well you didn't let us go on babbling," Laura said. "My next story would have been about the *San Francisco Chronicle* running a Reuters story on how Donnie bad-mouthed the U.S. when the Communists let him out of his cage. But it was only in the earliest edition, the one that went way out of town. All the later editions ran an AP story that had an entirely different slant. I always wondered how the CIA managed to make him change his story so fast. Or got the newspapers to change versions."

"We never heard the Reuters version here," Charlotte said. "But I remember something about it. Didn't you send me a clipping?"

"I probably sent you a clip of the story about Donnie I sold to a weekly in Oakland. It was a portrait of the last American out of Southeast Asia—which Donnie was supposed to be, at least at that time. Remember the old joke: Will the last man out of Vietnam turn off the light at the end of the tunnel? So I had Donnie standing there, silhouetted, flicking the light on and off, because of the conflicting reports on what he'd said when he got out."

"So what is this guy?" Teri asked. "Some kind of spy?"

"No, an adventurer," Laura said. "I don't imagine Donnie's time with Air America had anything to do with politics. Just a chance to fly in scary places."

Much later, as the waitress was clearing away their dishes, Charlotte grinned. "Well, Laura, more faces from your past. An odd couple indeed."

Laura turned to see Cory MacDougal showing two men to a table. She recognized the Guamanian instantly. He wore a crisp, white, short-sleeved shirt tucked into dark, neatly-pressed slacks.

"It's Rudy Terlaje! He looks like he's always looked." she said. "But who ... ?" The other man wore a brilliantly colored aloha shirt, baggy khaki shorts, and rubber zoris. She couldn't place his face at all but there was something familiar about the way he shambled across the polished ceramic tile floor.

"Imagine a lot more hair," Charlotte suggested, and Laura looked again at the man's round, red face and very short haircut.

"Good grief!" she said. "It's Will Hildebrandt."

"Bingo," Charlotte said. "Why don't you take Teri over and introduce her to your past and I'll take care of this bill. We've got to get on the road if we're going to do all the villages."

Laura strolled over to the table where the two men had buried their faces in the menus. "Hi," she said. From the corner of her eye she saw Teri hanging back, trying not to get involved.

Both men looked up. "Well, I'll be damned," said Rudy Terlaje, brushing back a shock of iron gray hair that had been falling into his eyes for at least nineteen years that Laura knew of. "If it isn't the latest hot byline from AP Tokyo."

"Laura?" Will Hildebrandt seemed as unsure of her as she had been of him. As he stared at her, she imagined those wide, pale blue eyes peering out from the mop of shoulder-length hair and unkempt beard with which the old Will Hildebrandt had celebrated the sixties.

"Will," she said with real warmth. "It's great to see you. And you, too, Rudy. Don't tell me you're still editing the *Daily Chronicle*?"

"No, of course not. I retired, what ... " He turned to Will for confirmation. "Two, three years ago?"

"At least that long," Will agreed. "And the new guy's even harder to get a gig out of." He winked at Laura and she remembered his years of trying to sell his free-lance work to Rudy—whose management style seemed based on strict penny-pinching.

"But I still read the paper," Rudy said, "and they do run your stuff from time to time. Anything from Japan is very big here, as you might have noticed. The island's diversified its economy just like we used to editorialize. So now we're almost as dependent on the damn

Japs and their fads and fashions in honeymoon trips as we are on the U.S. military." He sighed sadly and sniffed loudly. Laura glanced at Teri to see if she'd been shocked again by that three-letter word "Jap." Teri was doing blank, one of her most practiced expressions.

"I could tell immediately from the writing style, it was our very own Laura Monroe up there in Tokyo," Rudy said.

"Yeah, wordy as ever, ain't ya, Laura?" Will said, and Laura wanted to hug him for segueing so smoothly from the shock of sudden reunion into their old game of endless insults.

"So Willie-boy," she said, "how are you supporting yourself and the uncounted seed of your loins? Still meeting planes with your camera and peddling souvenir photos?"

"Don't knock it, Monroe," Will said. "Sell people what they want—it's the 'merican way."

"Will's doing okay," Rudy said with a paternal pride that was astonishing, given the years he and Will had circled each other, snarling like rival dogs. He sniffled again, a sound that took her back to her first month in Guam. Good old, glum old Rudy and his perpetual battles with allergies. "Will's very big in the outdoor rags now. Slick dive magazines. Haven't you seen his byline?"

"To be honest, I don't see dive magazines," Laura said. "I'll have to look for some." She pulled the reluctant Teri up to the table for introductions. Rudy, making small talk, asked where they were staying.

"The *Hilton*?" Will said. "Jeez, Laura, you used to pretend to be one of the real people. This Tokyo assignment going to your head, is it?"

Laura found herself considering the question seriously. "No, I don't think so. I think I believe in the whole thing as much as ever. You know, the value of the fourth estate in a democracy."

"Laura always insisted we had a sacred calling," Will reminded Rudy.

"You still believe that, even in the Japanese context?" Rudy asked.

"Oh, everything gets pulled askew when you factor in the Japanese press clubs, but, yeah—I still believe in what I do for a living."

Rudy was raising his iced tea glass to her in a silent toast when Charlotte waved from the doorway of the restaurant.

Laura and Teri followed her out of the air-conditioned building into the steaming afternoon and down a long concrete walk lined with scarlet-blossomed hibiscus. They opened all four doors of Charlotte's car to release the baked air before they climbed in.

"It's so much fun, seeing old friends after all this time," Laura said. "I wanted to hug Rudy just because he snuffled like always."

"It's fun seeing *some* old friends," Teri said. "You didn't seem to want to hug that guy last night."

"Oh, Gordon," Laura said. "Well, he's more complicated."

"Is Gordon Hassler here again?" Charlotte asked as she backed out of the parking place and turned down the winding driveway toward the round-the-island road.

"I had breakfast with him this morning. I didn't realize you knew him."

"Well, indirectly. He's been around forever—in Saipan, at least. I'm sure he was out here long before you and Foster came along to brighten up our parties."

In Laura's days as a news reporter here, Charlotte had always been an invaluable reference on personalities. One phone call and Laura could learn the dirt on anyone. Of course, Charlotte would have known Gordon Hassler, or known of him.

Charlotte turned south toward the more traditional villages, promising Teri a few glimpses of the Spanish-Chamorro culture that had been so abruptly interrupted by the Japanese invasion in December 1941, and by everything that had come since—including Charlotte's own arrival as the blushing "statesider" bride of the son of one of the island's best families.

* * *

It was nearly sunset when Charlotte pulled into the Hilton's sweeping circular driveway. There was an ominous cluster by the main entrance—an ambulance and three police cars.

"They need a police escort to take someone across the street to the hospital?" Teri asked.

Charlotte's curiosity was piqued. "What's happening?" She pulled into an empty parking place. "Come on, I'll walk you up."

Charlotte should have been the news reporter, Laura thought, remembering the time many years ago when she'd been awakened by her friend's phone call early on a Saturday morning. "Why aren't you up here on our patio watching the *Guam Bear* sink in the harbor?" And other calls, during the island's brief dry season. "Get up here with your press pass, Laura. There's a terrific grass fire on top of the mountain, and they won't let me cross the fire lines."

Now, as they walked toward the hotel entrance, Laura slowed her steps, a sudden premonition of peril seeping into her mind. She was about to see something she didn't want to see. Something Teri shouldn't see. She hung back.

Several blue-uniformed policemen crowded through the hotel's doorway, moving toward the gaping back door of the ambulance. They carried a stretcher bearing an ominous long shape covered by a sheet that was splotched with blood. A crowd of curious onlookers followed from the shady depths of the hotel lobby.

Teri whispered urgently. "What … what is it?"

Without a word, Laura and Charlotte closed ranks, shoulder to shoulder, trying to push the girl back so she couldn't see. A policeman with lieutenant's bars glanced away from his men's gory burden for a moment and saw them. He hurried over. "Good evening, Mrs. Sablán," he said. He stared at Laura. "Aren't you Laura Monroe?"

Laura looked into the friendly, round face of someone else she should know, if she could only tune her memory to the right channel.

"I'm Ben, Ben Guerrero," the lieutenant said.

"Ben! How great to see you." As soon as she said them, the words seemed inappropriate in light of what the police were loading into the ambulance.

"I wish I could just say welcome home," Ben Guerrero said. "But I've got to ask you to come down to headquarters with me. We need to ask you some questions."

"Mommy!" Teri's grown-up pretensions dissolved in a frightened squeak.

Ben Guerrero turned to her. "I'm sorry, Miss. I didn't mean to scare you. It's just that we've talked to everyone we can find here at the hotel, and about the only thing they've been able to tell us is that a hotel guest named Laura Monroe was seen with the victim this morning."

"The victim?" Laura said dully. The second half of the premonition slid into place. She was going to hear something she didn't want to hear.

"There's no identification on the body, or in his room," Guerrero said, "but he registered under the name Gordon Hassler. So, since you may have been one of the last people to see him alive … "

Laura's knees seemed to melt and she sagged against a car. Oh my God, she thought, what if he asks me to identify the body?

"Ben," Charlotte said sternly, drawing herself up to full height, hearing something else in the policeman's request. "Laura has been with me and her daughter since ten o'clock this morning."

"Okay, Mrs. Sablán, take it easy. I'm not accusing anyone of anything. I just need to find out whatever I can about this guy that's gotten himself butchered on my beat. Okay?"

Butchered! The word fits the red stains on the sheet. But Laura couldn't reconcile the word with the name Gordon Hassler, with the flirtatious face of the man who had once been such a good friend, a part of her island history.

Their paths had crossed once again, and once again things were awkward. Awkward? Upsetting in the extreme.

She wondered if she were going to faint but she managed to sound confident. "Sure, I'll be happy to tell you anything I can."

And find out whatever you can tell me, she thought quickly. I'm supposed to be a reporter. Her bureau chief had laughed as he wished her a good trip and said, "Send news, if anything ever happens in Guam." Murders were always news, if they were bizarre enough.

"Mother," Teri said reproachfully as Laura took a step or two toward the police car Ben Guerrero indicated.

"Excuse me," the policeman said, holding out his hand. "I'm Ben Guerrero. I've known your mom and dad since I was in high school. My older brother worked with your dad back then. Were you at breakfast with your mother and Mr. Hassler this morning?"

Teri shook her head numbly.

"If you want to come along … " Guerrero said doubtfully.

Charlotte stepped into the breach. "No, I think it would be better if I stay with her here. She doesn't need to hear all the details I'm sure Laura will be asking you for. Come on, Teri, I'll buy you a Coke." She took the girl's arm and headed for the hotel lobby.

"Are you sure you can stay?" Laura asked the back of Charlotte's muumuu. How did I manage to keep the child away from the less pleasant parts of my job until we came back to my beloved islands?

She corrected herself. It's not my job that's funneling me toward this Guam police car. It's Ben Guerrero's job. I suppose I'm some kind of suspect.

"Thanks, Mrs. Sablán," Guerrero said over his shoulder. He opened the front passenger door of the police car. "I'll wait to ask you what you know about Mr. Hassler until we get back to the station so the captain can sit in. He's on the squawk box every five minutes, saying 'Find out who this guy is.' Thinks it's another drug rub-out. And drugs bring the Feds, which always gets messy. So on the way back to town, you can tell me what brings you back to Guam. And what's Foster up to these days?"

Laura sank into the passenger seat as Ben Guerrero buckled himself in behind the steering wheel. She reached for the seat belt at her side. Does Guam have a seat belt law now? No, surely it's just part of a good cop's routine. Feeling almost defiant, she let her belt snap back into the retractor.

Drugs? Could the slight aura of weirdness that has always seemed to hover about Gordon Hassler come down to drugs?

She glanced back at the hotel to see Charlotte's fluorescent orange muumuu disappearing into the lobby. The colors were echoed by the sunset smearing itself across the waters of Agaña Bay as Ben Guerrero, looking the epitome of the well-trained cop, drove her toward Agaña.

— *1937* —

First of all was the green.

Then the air: Heavy, moist, full of smells that somehow seemed elemental.

And there was the heat. Oppressive, overwhelming. It enveloped Garrett the moment he stepped off the plane. He had a sudden, sharp premonition that this was his fate, that he would spend the rest of his life close to the equator, dissolving in sweat.

He was astonished at the bustling port. It was a genuine boom town. If he squinted, imagined away the soggy weight of the air, ignored the incredible, fecund blanket of green that crept up against shanties and villas alike, slowly digesting even the muddy streets. If he concentrated, he could imagine that he was in San Francisco watching forty-niners stream off ships on which they'd sailed around South America, gathering supplies, setting off for the foothills of the Sierra. Or perhaps this could be Seattle, with gold-crazed prospectors clamoring for passage to the frozen Yukon.

Folks said the boom had been going on here for over a decade. From this ramshackle shard of civilization, hardened miners and desperate dreamers traveled to the gold fields on airplanes that shrilled like mosquitoes as they climbed over the steep green wall of mountains jutting up just inland from the town.

Coming over from Port Darwin, their pilot had pointed down into the endless sea of green and said, "That's it, that's where you're headed!"

Tex had said they were on their way to Annie Creek to try their luck. It was, Tex had said before they made the deal with the

pilot, the only good reason to charter a flight to New Guinea. Garrett didn't know what their real mission was, but the gold fields sounded perfectly plausible to him.

After all, when they had first met a year ago, Tex had just come down the road from Deadwood, another gold rush town. Oh, he had told that story about making up his own tour, visiting the spots where all the legends of the Wild West had met their ends—Jesse James, Billy the Kid, Wild Bill Hickock—but Garrett had never quite believed him. It seemed too strange, even if Tex did look like he was trying to be somebody in a Western movie. Despite the black Stetson worn in every season, and the fancy vests, Garrett believed it more likely that Tex liked to go places where gold was found. Or at least where money was being made. He hoped that Tex was thinking of some more luxurious ports of call than Lae, New Guinea, when he'd said, "Stick with me, kid, and I'll show you the world."

They spent some hours at the airfield after they first arrived in Lae. Tex said the Waua District gold strike had done more for the development of land-based aviation than any other event in the history of the world. Tex was very interested in aviation development. Garrett supposed he had a lot of money invested in it. Tex clearly had a lot of money somewhere. And the power that went with it.

An incredible variety of planes were flying in and out of the big airdrome. Tex took delight in reeling off their names—Tri-Motors, Stinsons, Robins. Some, he said, were mongrels. Almost all were tired and battered. The very air around the airdrome seemed to churn with turbulence caused by all the planes, and Garrett thought he detected the faint taste of airsickness on the breeze.

What Garrett noticed mostly, though, was the heavy air, the unrelenting heat, and the menacing green—a threat that was startling to a boy who had grown up on the edge of the drought-haunted northern Great Plains where green was a promise, the only color in the rainbow that guaranteed a future.

One image haunted him. As they swirled down from their view of the highlands, down to the coastal plain, to the muddy, vibrant

boom town, the pilot told them how others seeking their fortune—"just like you fellows"—chartered planes to fly them up to Annie Creek or to Waua or even farther in, to look for their share of the Mother Lode. If they were lucky, they chartered flights back to town every so often for a binge, spending their hard-won gold dust on beer and women and maybe a bath, sending home what was left to families in Australia or America or Europe.

But if they were unlucky, they had only one way back. They walked. Or crawled. Through that tangled green mire of jungle, down four thousand feet to sea level, down cliffs, down waterfalls. Some of them never made it. "Their bodies might be hanging below right now," the pilot said, and Garret imagined them, impaled on the branches of trees or on rocky crags as the jungle wrapped them in its green shroud. "You know, there's meat-eating plants down there," the pilot added.

It wasn't just Tex's demands upon his body that kept Garrett from get a good night's sleep these days. The entire time he was in New Guinea, he dreamed about the green—creeping up on him, devouring him, making him a part of the tropics forever.

– 1983 –
Thursday

IT WAS HARD TO RECONCILE the plump, confident Lieutenant Guerrero with the scrawny, eager teenager who had sat at their kitchen table on long-ago Saturdays, wolfing down tuna sandwiches while besieging Laura with questions about the Beatles and other phenomena of the sixties.

She'd answered him as well as she could, even though she was more concerned back then about having abandoned the well-maintained tennis courts of California than about the cultural revolution she had left behind in the States.

Now Laura wanted to ask about the twists and turns of life that had led Ben Guerrero to be driving this patrol car along the road from Tamuning to Agaña. Instead, she fielded his low-key questions about Foster and her current job and what had brought her back to Guam.

Surely, she told herself, this summons to talk to the police was exactly what Guerrero had said it was: She was, at the moment, the last person known to have seen Gordon Hassler alive so she might have some valuable information. It certainly didn't mean she was under suspicion.

As Ben Guerrero negotiated the crowded highway along Agaña Bay where coconut palms made graceful black silhouettes against the fading sunset, she thanked her heavens that bureaucracy didn't come naturally to most Guamanians. Many times she had used, as an illustration of how common sense could prevail over blind obedience to bureaucratic regulations, the tale of their return—hers and Foster's—many years before from a shopping binge in Hong Kong.

Among their purchases had been a necklace of polished stone beads from India and a few pieces of Japanese-made Scandinavian-styled furniture. Looking unhappy with his assignment, the Guamanian customs officer on duty at the airport that evening had confiscated the necklace.

"You see, *paré*," he had explained to Foster, using the word that implied they were adopted brothers, "this is what U.S. Customs calls presumptive items." He shoved a fat manual toward them, his stubby brown finger indicating a paragraph of close-set type as he paraphrased, "Any semiprecious stone jewelry purchased in Hong Kong is presumed to be made in Communist China unless you got what they call CCO—Comprehensive Certificate of Origin—to prove this necklace is made in Hong Kong."

He had asked hopefully, "You got a CCO for this?"

"Of course not," Foster said. "Beggars beads are made in India, not Hong Kong. And as far as I know, Uncle Sugar hasn't called a trade war against India yet."

The agent nodded sadly, his eyebrows dancing to denote his understanding of Foster's points.

"So what happens to the necklace?" Laura had asked as sweetly as she could. It hadn't cost more than six or seven dollars, but she had spent a long time choosing the one with the prettiest stones and the colors that would best complement her wardrobe.

The customs agent scratched his head. "We put it in the safe at the office. So what you can do if you want to is talk to my boss about it."

"Would that be Dave Camacho?" Foster asked.

"You know Dave? He's always willing to talk."

As Lieutenant Guerrero maneuvered through knots of traffic at the two traffic lights that marked the heart of Agaña, Laura reflected that in many cultures, Dave Camacho's willingness to talk would imply a willingness to accept a bribe, but this was Guam. All she'd done the afternoon after the incident at the airport was drop in on the chief customs inspector and point out the knots between the

stone beads of the necklace. "See that gold and red string? That's something they use in India but not in China," she'd said.

"You're right," Dave Camacho had agreed. "I've seen that same thread in some of the stuff Rajiv Hermani brings in from India for his store. This sure ain't Chinese." He had given her the necklace without another question. And when they got word that their furniture had arrived, Foster had asked Dave to accompany him to the warehouse at Apra Harbor.

"Does that look like Chinese furniture to you?" Foster asked after they had pried open the crate.

"No way." Dave had laughed. "Chinese furniture is much heavier than that, with lots of fancy carving."

Foster had said it was clear Camacho didn't think much of the simple, slim lines of their Japanese-Danish chairs and benches but, after he made another comment about how Chinese craftsmen used prettier wood, he released the shipment to them. As far as Laura knew, the furniture still graced Foster's place in Honolulu.

Although the United States no longer banned imports from China, Laura felt confident that Guamanian bureaucrats remained reasonable, so she followed Lieutenant Guerrero into the police station without trepidation. But her optimism fled when he led her into a small office just off the police station's main room.

She instantly recognized the stern face of Sergeant, now Captain, Jesús Pérez. He'd been the first Guamanian cop she'd dealt with her first day as a reporter for the *Guam Chronicle*. He was the only Guamanian she'd known who was a basically hostile person.

"So what happened to Pedro?" he'd asked that afternoon long ago when she introduced herself as she came into the station to check the police blotter.

"He's doing sports now," she had responded.

"Then where's Fred?"

"They tell me he quit to start a magazine."

The desk sergeant had let a sigh hiss out between his teeth. "So Rudy Terlaje puts a statesider on the police beat. It figures."

He'd never warmed up, even when everyone else around the station had relaxed into a jovial kidding relationship with her. After she'd started studying Chamorro, she once made the mistake of greeting Sergeant Pérez in his native tongue. He jerked his thumb at the sign on the wall above his head. ENGLISH ONLY IS TO BE SPOKEN IN ALL GOVERNMENT OF GUAM OFFICES.

She had laughed, thinking he meant to be funny.

"Oh, sure—laugh, Lady Lily White," he'd said. "You probably think it was funny that your people fined me a nickel every time they caught me saying a Chamorro word when I was in grade school. You statesiders got no reason to learn Chamorro. *We're* bilingual."

She'd stepped back, embarrassed, thinking of the times she'd had to ask him to help her untangle some garbled swatch of English on the police blotter when she couldn't quite make it out. That must have really offended him. She was careful never to speak to him in Chamorro again.

Now Police Captain Jesús Pérez stood up behind his desk as she and Ben entered his office. "So you're right, Ben—it is the Laura Monroe we know."

"Hello, Captain Pérez," she said, trying for a breezy, confident tone. "How much of this empire are you in charge of?"

"Just a small part," Pérez said. "But interesting. Detective division. Ben here's our star. He's a regular Columbo."

Laura smiled at Ben, thinking that Pérez must have mellowed with the years and his promotions.

Then again, maybe he hadn't. "We've brought you here for a murder investigation, not for *auld lang syne,*" he said. "So if you don't mind, we'll go in the room where we can record your statement."

"Of course. I want to do whatever I can to help."

Pérez didn't bother to make small talk about Foster, she noticed, although he and Foster had been friends in the old days. They had organized the Guam Jaycees, she recalled. Pérez was one of the subjects she and Foster had always disagreed on.

"'Sús is okay," Foster had insisted. "His bark is much worse than his bite." Are Foster and Pérez still in contact, she wondered. Does Pérez already know Foster and I split up many years ago?

In the sparsely-furnished, overly-air-conditioned room, Ben Guerrero started the tape recorder and spoke into the microphone, identifying the time, place, and people present. Then he said, "Laura, can you tell us how you happened to have breakfast this morning with Mr. Hassler?"

"We're old friends," she said. "I've known him almost as long as I've known you two. He worked for the Trust Territory government in Saipan, even before I moved up there."

Pérez nodded. "I thought it had to be the same guy. Hassler. What sort of name is it?"

Laura shrugged. "German? I never thought about it. I really don't know what his ethnic background is. Was."

Pérez continued musing. "He was a big wheel in TT administration, I remember. Sometimes acted as a liaison on law enforcement matters between the two jurisdictions."

"That would have been Gordon," Laura agreed.

"Do you know when Gordon Hassler first went to Saipan?"

"Not really. I know he was there the first time I went. That was in 1964."

"When did he leave Saipan?" Ben asked. "Do you know?"

"Yes. Because he left before we did, transferred back to Washington. And then he got a job for Foster, my ex-husband, and we moved to Washington, too."

"So he left Saipan about when?"

"Late 1968, I think."

"Did he come back to the Marianas often?"

"I have no idea," Laura said. "I really haven't had much contact with him for many years. I don't even know what he does—what he did for a living."

"But you arranged to meet in Guam?" Pérez jabbed the question at her like a pointed stick.

Her jaw dropped. "No! He had nothing to do with me being in Guam. I ran into him last night in the Hilton dining room. We decided to meet for breakfast."

Pérez and Guerrero both nodded, silently. She worried, suddenly, that they might not believe her. *Thank God I spent the day with Charlotte—the Sablán family surely has the connections to untangle any wrong conclusions these detectives might leap to.*

"Did Mr. Hassler say anything about other appointments today?" Guerrero asked. "Or about what he was doing on the island?"

"He said he was here on business. He might have been having dinner last night with his business contact. I have no idea who it was. I just caught a glimpse of a man with what looked like a bad sunburn."

"Somebody new to the islands," Pérez murmured.

Ben Guerrero scrawled quickly on a pad of paper. "I'll ask the dining room staff again about Hassler's contacts last night," he promised. "Maybe they'll remember the sunburn."

"And his plans for today?" Pérez asked.

The policemen seemed to be keeping their minds on the conversation better than she was. "Uh, no—he suggested we rent a car, drive around the island, so I had the impression he really didn't have plans. But I was already planning to go with Mrs. Sablán."

When Pérez raised an eyebrow, Guerrero said, "Charlotte Sablán. She drove into the hotel parking lot with Laura and her daughter."

Pérez let his eyebrows provide the Guamanian equivalent of, "I hear you. Continue."

Guerrero asked, "What can you tell us about Mr. Hassler's family, his next of kin?"

Laura gasped. "Edwina," she said. *Oh, no! I hadn't even thought about her. How will Edwina take this?* All the years she'd known the Hasslers, Laura had been confident that Edwina was in love with Gordon despite his reputation for flirtations with other women.

She forced her attention back to the police officers. "His wife, Edwina Hassler. She doesn't know, does she? How will she find out?"

"Do you know where we are to find Mrs. Edwina Hassler?"

"Last I heard they were living in Bethesda, Maryland. Right outside Washington."

"We're having his address traced from the credit card he registered with at the hotel," Guerrero said. "I'm sure we'll locate her."

"Will you ask her to come here?"

"We can't ***ask*** her to come without paying her way," Pérez said. "But if she volunteers, it might be helpful if she came. Murder is always messy, and she might be able to answer some questions for us."

"What did happen?" Laura said. "Am I allowed to ask questions?"

Pérez kept his face deadpan. "You always did, didn't you? I have just one more for *you*: Can you prove where you were between noon and three-thirty p.m. today?"

The way her heart sped up, the flush she felt in her face, took Laura by surprise. Perhaps she overdid her indignation. "Of ***course*** I can. I was with my daughter and Charlotte Sablán, touring the island. At noon we were having lunch out at Casa Celinda. Then until about six we were driving the southern route—Talofofo Bay, Inarajan, Merizo, Umatac—"

Pérez raised his hand to fend off her outburst. She thought she detected a smile behind his stern cop demeanor. "Okay, and Mrs. Sablán and your daughter will confirm your alibi?"

To Laura, *alibi* sounded very much like *lie* but she maintained a calm tone. "Of course."

Pérez shrugged. "Go ahead, Ben, give her the quick outline."

Guerrero cleared his throat and flipped back several pages in his notebook. "The call came from the hotel at 1530 hours. A bell boy went to deliver some laundry Mr. Hassler had sent out. The kid used the pass key to go in, thinking he would leave the laundry on the

bed. The body was in the middle of the room, and there was blood everywhere. It looked like he had been chopped up with a machete."

Laura shuddered, then tried to make her face expressionless. She remembered one of the first times she'd dealt with Sergeant Pérez, when he had refused to show her photos of an accident scene. "You'd show them to Pedro if he were still on this beat," she'd said testily and Pérez had sighed and shoved the 8 by 10-inch prints at her. Then he'd made a narrow, I-told-you-so smile when she reacted to the gore. "Some things are too hard for a lady to see," he had said. I've confronted worse in the years since, she thought. That Christmas Day plane crash in Bangkok, for instance. I should be hardened. But I've never before personally known a victim of violence.

"Nobody in the hotel heard anything?" she asked.

"Seems like there's not much staff around that time of day, and the other guests along that hall were away, sightseeing like you, or down at the pool or the beach," Guerrero said.

"Are you going to write something about this?" Pérez asked abruptly.

"I don't know. It's terrible to say but if it's dramatic enough, my bureau chief might be interested."

"Most bizarre murder scene I've ever seen," Guerrero said. "The kid dropped the laundry on the floor when he saw the body and ran to the desk to get help. And those shirts turned out to be the only thing in the room that belonged to Mr. Hassler. Nothing else. No suitcase, no clothes in the closet, no wallet, no shaving kit, nothing. Whoever killed him had time to gather everything up and get out with the suitcases. Must have been looking for something but didn't know for sure if he found it."

Laura tried to contain the images within her mind. Gordon alone in his room, answering his door, letting someone in. Or did the murderer climb in from the balcony? And then what? Did Gordon know what hit him? Was it someone he knew? A jealous husband, perhaps? The man with the sunburn?

"Can you think of why someone would want to cut Gordon Hassler up like that?" Pérez asked.

Laura thought about the years of gossip, her image of a jealous husband creeping in from the balcony. But it was just island gossip, what they had always called the bamboo telegraph. The only husband she actually knew who could claim that Gordon had made a pass at his wife was Foster, but surely Foster wasn't capable of violence over it—then or now. Foster's problem, as far as she was concerned, was a lack of passion. But in any case, she wasn't going on the police record with fifteen-year-old gossip. "No, I can't imagine why anyone would do it," she said clearly.

"Someone must really hate this guy," Pérez said. "It's not typical of drug murders."

"No," Guerrero agreed. "They tend to be less impassioned, more like executions."

"And they stripped everything from his pockets?" Pérez asked. Laura thought that he was watching for her reaction.

"Nothing in his pants pockets," Guerrero said. "No handkerchief, no wallet, no keys. Even his hotel room key wasn't anywhere. But they missed one thing. They didn't check his shirt pocket." Guerrero fished something in a plastic envelope from between the pages of his notebook and leaned across the table to hand it to Captain Pérez, carefully shielding it with his hand so Laura couldn't see it.

"I'll be damned," Pérez said, staring at the flat rectangle. Now Laura could see that it was a small photograph. On the back there was a large bloody blot. Pérez shook his head. "What the hell can this have to do with anything?"

Guerrero's hand moved suddenly, slapping the tape recorder off, and both men laughed.

"The director of public safety thinks we swear too much," Pérez said. "Embarrasses him when they have to play these tapes in court." She wondered whether it was a photograph of a woman. She wanted to suggest that she could tell them if it was Edwina; if it wasn't, that could definitely constitute a clue.

Pérez continued to stare at the photograph in his hand, then gave Laura a searching look. "Seems to me, this might flush something out of the boonies." He handed the small packet back to the lieutenant. "Why don't you take it over to the *Chronicle*? See if they want to print it in tomorrow's edition, along with the murder story."

Guerrero carefully tucked the photo back into his notebook, again without letting Laura see anything except the blot of blood on the back.

"Well, I think we've disrupted your evening enough," Pérez said. "Ben'll get someone to drive you back to the hotel so you can have some dinner."

"I'm not sure I want any dinner," Laura said, finally acknowledging the queasiness that had taken residence in her stomach.

As she left the room with Guerrero, Pérez seemed almost friendly. "I hope we won't have to trouble you any more about this."

"Oh, please, if I can be of any help … "

"We know where to find you," Guerrero said. "C'mon, I'll drive you back. I've gotta see if I can find anyone who remembers Mr. Sunburn."

As they walked back to the police car, Laura wondered if Guerrero and Pérez worked as a team, good cop, bad cop. It was certainly a relief just to be with Ben alone again. He was silent as he drove out of the capital town's congested core. Then they were back on Marine Drive, passing along the curved bay shore with headlights of oncoming cars glinting on the black water, flickering through the palm trees that lined the beach.

"Aiii," Guerrero sighed. "This is all very strange. See, there's a problem with some of these old-timers … I mean, if Hassler was in Saipan before 1962. Sometimes they had extra connections, you know? Nowadays, we're always thinking drugs when something like this happens, but I don't know … it could be something else. Something bigger, and harder to get at."

Bigger than drugs? Laura assumed he had to be talking about the CIA.

— 1967 —
September

AS DONNIE MACDOUGAL'S PLANE TAXIED to a stop on the Saipan runway, Jodie could see Laura and Foster Monroe leaning against a small wood-and-tin shack that served the airport as a terminal building. Laura's long brown hair was piled atop her head, a plumeria blossom tucked into it. The breeze ruffled Foster's thinning blond hair as he looked at his watch with exaggerated theatrical movements. They must have arrived much later than expected after that scenic detour over Anatahan. As she stepped to the ground, Jodie felt a broad grin spreading across her face. Laura nodded smugly. "I was right about which plane you should take, wasn't I?" she said.

Donnie retrieved some triangular blocks of wood from beside the terminal building and chocked them under the wheels of the plane. In the parking lot, a small islander emerged from a shiny black Cedric, the Mercedes-Benz of Micronesia, and hurried over to greet Senator Santos. Santos turned and asked if anyone needed a ride.

Hildebrandt said, "I'm with them," and for the first time it dawned upon Jodie that the friends Hildebrandt was coming to visit were the same as hers.

"Join us for lunch, Donnie?" Foster asked.

"Sure. I gotta check down at the hotel and see who's riding back with me."

As they walked toward Foster and Laura's Datsun, Jodie turned to look back at the plane. It sat lightly at the edge of the runway, a golden dragonfly floating on a pond of asphalt. How does he know it won't take wing again, she wondered. How does he dare to leave it?

*　　*　　*

The Royal Taga Hotel had opened recently. The tablecloths and napkins in the dining room were stiff and smelled of newness instead of the mildew that permeated most fabrics in the islands. The windows looked out across a lawn still struggling to take hold, to a narrow white beach, and beyond to the water. A white line of surf marked the reef that separated the smooth turquoise waters of the lagoon from the deeper blue of the Pacific. In the placid lagoon two rust-encrusted amphibious American tanks sat incongruously, exactly where they had been stopped twenty-three years before when Japanese guns interrupted their assault on the beach. It was disconcerting to see a sunbather slathering lotion on her legs, oblivious to the once-deadly gun aimed directly at her.

As she ate, Jodie wished Donnie MacDougal would talk more and Will Hildebrandt less. Suddenly Will jabbed a fork at Laura, then at Jodie, talking around a mouthful of french fries. "It's not clear to me," he said, "how this lady got hooked up with you two."

He has his nerve, Jodie thought, demanding my credentials as though I'm horning in on something. She had been planning this trip ever since Foster and Laura moved to Saipan.

"Guam Theatre Guild," Foster said as he cut another bite of his steak sandwich. "We found Jodie running it when we hit the island."

Will and Donnie stared at Jodie. She knew she didn't look the theatrical type. She liked to think she appeared the epitome of the cool scientist.

"Jodie's a fantastic actress," Laura said. "She and Foster have done some great plays together."

Jodie had always marveled at Laura's complete lack of jealousy where Foster was concerned. Foster and Jodie had played some pretty torrid scenes together on the stage of the naval hospital auditorium, and Laura always remained sunny and detached, cheerfully doing publicity for the Theatre Guild, filling in on makeup or

costumes or props as required, never minding that another woman was making love to her husband on stage. From reading some of the opinion pieces Laura had written, Jodie knew that she held strong views on political issues. Yet, where her personal life was concerned, she seemed content to float, seeing life through romantic, rose-colored glasses and the cool-frosted haze of gin and tonic.

"Well, she may be an actress, but I'll tell you what else Jodie is," Donnie MacDougal said, hoisting his water glass toward her in a toast. "She's a future pilot."

Jodie's heart thudded. She hadn't dared to form the thought—but she knew it was absolutely true as soon as she heard it.

Donnie grinned at her. "You couldn't hide it if you tried, lady. Your hands were reaching for the stick all the way to Saipan."

"What is it with you, MacDougal?" Foster asked. "You take these women up in your little yellow plane and you seduce them."

"Oh, Laura likes flying, too," Donnie said, "but it's the geography that gets her, seeing the islands and the reefs laid out below her like a map. For Jodie, it's the flying itself, the air, the lift. Tell me, am I right?"

Jodie felt an airiness inside her head, a lift in her heart. This man has seen a part of my soul I didn't know I had, she thought. If he wants me, I'm his.

Donnie winked at Jodie. "We may be sitting here with the next Amelia Earhart."

Something far back in distant memory suddenly clicked into place. Jodie blurted, "Now I get it."

"Get what?" Will demanded.

"I had books about Amelia Earhart when I was a child. I loved her because she was independent and chose her own life. But I never understood why she flew, why she didn't put her energy into … something useful. Like working in a research lab."

Jodie felt humbled. She had spent many years convinced that the scientific quest to pry secrets from the universe was the greatest pursuit of humankind. She saved a little out of each paycheck

towards the day that she could go on to graduate school, get on with the search for knowledge. Yet today, somewhere in that canyon of clouds, she had discovered a higher calling.

"You never wondered why the U.S. Navy would build an airstrip on some godforsaken dot in the middle of the Pacific Ocean just so some broad could fly around the world?" Will said. "You thought that made sense?"

"You mean Howland Island? I guess I never thought about it."

"You thought the United States had nothing better to do with its money in the Great Depression than set up landing fields for stunt fliers?"

Jodie felt dazed. Why is this wild man attacking me?

"You said the secret word, Donnie," Foster said. "You should know better than to mention Amelia in Will's presence."

"May the *kahunas* forgive me." Donnie rolled his eyes upward.

"It's not Amelia he's hung up on," Laura said. "It's the U.S. government. What ***was*** behind the airfield on Howland Island?"

That's Laura, Jodie thought. Quick to zero in on the point. Maybe that's what makes her a good reporter.

Will sputtered at Jodie. "I'll bet you haven't even read the Verdun book."

"What book?"

"About the search for Amelia Earhart. It came out months ago."

Something nibbled at the back of her mind. "I do remember some stories in the Guam papers—"

"In one Guam paper," Will interrupted.

Laura tried to explain. "Will helped Shelby Verdun research the book and took some of the photographs. He's mad because the *Chronicle* buried the story. He questions their news judgment."

"I question their goddamn motives!" Will roared loud enough so that other people in the dining room turned to stare at them. He dropped his voice to a raspy whisper. "Some people know the truth, and one of them is the publisher of the *Chronicle*." He stared into Jodie's eyes. "This is the island, you know. This very island."

"Saipan?"

"The place the Japs held her prisoner after she crashed in the Marshalls. The place where she and Fred Noonan died."

The entire dining room seemed to pause so that Jodie could let the information sink in, so that she would always remember where she was when she heard where Amelia Earhart died.

Donnie MacDougal stretched and stood, pulled his wallet from his pocket, peeled off a few dollar bills, and handed them to Foster. "I've got to track down my Saipan agent," he said. "It's been real, folks." When he moved around the table to stand beside Jodie, she felt the hairs on her arms bristling. "I'll see you at the airstrip on Monday, Blondie. On the way to Guam, we'll talk about starting your flying lessons."

* * *

After they dropped Foster and Will off at the Trust Territory headquarters building on what seemed to be the top of the island, Laura told Jodie she was going to take her to the best beach on Saipan.

Jodie, who had accepted without question her government-issue apartment at the naval hospital housing complex, found Laura's explanation for the Monroes' housing quite surprising. Refusing to live in the lap of creature comforts ordinarily provided to government officials of Foster's rank, Laura had instead chosen a second-floor flat in the heart of the island's largest village. So it was fitting, Jodie supposed, that Laura's favorite beach was not one of the languid strips of white sand curving beside the tranquil lagoon—they had passed several of these postcard scenes between the hotel and the mountain road that climbed up to the headquarters complex—but instead it was a rocky cove on the windward side of the island.

The Datsun struggled precariously down a deeply rutted track that tunneled through thick vegetation until the ocean burst into view in a blaze of blue. Laura parked and Jodie climbed into the back seat and wriggled into her bathing suit.

"Keep your shoes on," Laura advised.

They walked across a rocky beach, then gingerly crossed a crumpled, razor-sharp lava flow to reach a large tidal pool. Laura slipped off her short, bright shift and eased into the sparkling clear water in her bra and underpants. Jodie followed slowly. The surf sizzled just behind them and splashed onto cliffs beside them.

"You know, I don't show this to just anybody," Laura said, sweeping her arm to encompass a rugged coast that seemed punctuated by geysers of spray where the surf pounded against the island's bare bones.

It occurred to Jodie that she had been living on an island for six years, and this was the first time she'd considered the ocean as a force. Here it was, trying to pound the island to sand, to push an obstruction out of the way so it could wave unhindered all the way to the Philippines. Another element, like the wind, she thought. Another higher calling.

Her mind focused on the Hawaiian pilot, shaking his image like a puppy with a toy. She tried to think how to bring the subject up. But no matter how well Laura knew him, what could she say? After all, he was married. The first thing Jodie was going to have to do about this flying business was figure out whether it was the flying or the flier that had captivated her.

"I'm sorry about Will," Laura said.

"Will?"

"I mean that he's here. It was Foster's idea. I'm not sure if he's matchmaking, or if he wants Will to keep me busy talking politics so he can flirt with you."

"Matchmaking?" Surly, disheveled Will Hildebrandt and Jodie deSpain? There was no denying she had entertained a fantasy or two about Foster Monroe in the past few years, but Will Hildebrandt?

"Will's pretty prickly," Laura admitted. "But he is a good soul—and we both worry about him. He's been in Guam ever since the Navy brought him out when he was twenty, and his love life has been one long disaster. He keeps getting Guamanian and Filipino

girls pregnant and marrying them, but nothing lasts very long. So he's supporting three or four kids around the island."

"And Foster wanted to get something going between me and this Casanova?"

Laura laughed. "Men have simple minds. They see two unattached people, they try to pair them up. I think it's called Noah's Ark Syndrome. Foster's been worried about you ever since you and Barry split up."

With a start, Jodie realized that she hadn't thought once today about Barry Edwards, the Navy doctor she had dated for two years. Two years waiting for him to propose. And then a few months ago he'd been transferred and left as though they'd been nothing more than a summer romance.

Since she couldn't figure out how to bring Donnie MacDougal into the conversation, she settled for another flier. "What's the Amelia Earhart story Will is so obsessed with?"

"I'll show you the book at home. Basically, the theory is that Earhart was sent on her trip by the U.S. government to spy on the Japanese. According to Shelby Verdun's book, she was supposed to depart from her announced route and fly over Truk. The Japanese weren't letting anybody into these islands after the mid-thirties. Then there's another theory that she was supposed to ditch the plane in the islands and give the U.S. Navy an excuse to mount this huge search for the world's heroine and find out coincidentally what the Japanese were doing."

"What were the Japanese doing?"

"Getting ready for war with somebody."

"I guess I saw the headlines a few months ago. 'Earhart on Spy Mission?' Do you think it's true?"

Laura spoke thoughtfully. "I'll go along with Will on two things. One is, why did the Navy go to all the trouble and expense to build an airfield on Howland for her?"

"If she was supposed to ditch, they wouldn't even have had to build it."

"Oh, they probably would have, for credibility."

"But it's still pretty preposterous. She very likely would be killed, ditching."

"Someone told me there's a Rosalind Russell movie made during the war that has exactly that plot," Laura said.

"But if they were making movies about Amelia being a spy more than twenty years ago, why is it controversial now? Why didn't the *Chronicle* run the story about the book?"

"Aha! That's Will's second point. If there's nothing to it but old movie plots, why are people still covering it up? It's been thirty years since she disappeared. What's to hide?"

– 1937 –

IT WAS UNBELIEVABLY, UNENDURABLY HOT.

Sweat drenched Garrett's forehead and leaked into his eyes, fogging his vision. He raised the back of his wrist to wipe his eyes, but it was no good. His wrists were slimy with sweat. He realized that he was panting, like an old dog back home on the hottest day in August.

But it never got this hot in South Dakota. He wanted to crawl out from under the plane and see if he could catch a bit of breeze. But Tex had been very clear. Garrett must look as though he were merely checking the tires and wheel struts. The powerful magnets he was installing in the right wheel well were, Tex had hissed, "top secret."

Until yesterday Garrett had remained perplexed about their journey to this improbable corner of the world. Then it suddenly became clear. At lunch, Tex had said casually, "If you wanted to make sure an airplane didn't stay on course, what would you do?"

Garrett had attacked that problem while he attacked the small, tough steak he had been served. He really didn't know that much about airplanes but, as always, he wanted to please Tex. Life was so much easier when Tex saw that he was trying. As he ate, Garrett began to outline a complicated mechanical adjustment. Then he interrupted himself. "No, wait, wouldn't this be better? Magnets. If you put really powerful magnets somewhere in the plane, that would throw the compass off … "

Tex had laughed indulgently. "Good work, Gary. I think you've got it. Now what if you thought you might have trouble getting into the plane?"

"What about … couldn't you put a magnet in one of the wheel wells?"

Tex nodded with approval. "Still, there are things to worry about. The pilot might notice the compass wasn't reading true as they took off."

"Oh, you mean because they would know what direction the runway was sitting?"

Tex looked like a proud father. "All the aviation maps have the runway headings on them."

"But isn't the pilot pretty busy when he's taking off? Maybe he wouldn't notice."

"That is our best hope," Tex said. For the first time Garrett realized that this was no idle mental exercise. Tex really wanted to send somebody's plane astray. Perhaps they weren't here to take part in the race for gold in the highlands after all.

"Actually," Tex said, "you don't have to throw it off by much. It's not as if the map says the runway points west, and the compass shows north. Look." He started to draw on a scrap of paper. "See, here near the equator, if someone is flying two hundred miles per hour and the compass is off just one degree, after five hours, they'll end up seventeen and a half miles off course. So if they fly twelve hours, and their compass throws them off by five degrees, they'll be over two hundred miles from where they thought they were going."

Garrett screwed up his face and did his best to follow the diagrams and calculations. It did make sense to him—he just didn't think he could explain it to anybody else.

Later that afternoon, he and Tex were at the airdrome, watching the Lockheed Electra set down, watching the woman step out as the waiting crowd cheered and an unofficial honor guard of half-naked natives stood at attention, many of them with cigarettes tucked behind their ears.

She was a beautiful woman. Although she might be old enough to be his mother, she projected youthful energy and strength. She was the most remarkable woman he had ever seen, and he felt a

pang in his heart which might be love. Perhaps those dark instincts he thought Tex had unleashed in him weren't really true —maybe they were only Tex's feelings, nothing really to do with Garrett.

Or maybe it was that she seemed as strong and clear-headed as a man.

Tex had been one of the dignitaries greeting her, which didn't surprise Garrett. Nothing surprised him where Tex was concerned. Garrett was close enough to hear Tex explain that he represented the Consortium to Promote Land-Based Air Travel, or some such, and that his group had made substantial contributions toward getting the airfield built on Howland Island. He told her that her flight was going to change the course of international air travel.

She had been friendly, gracious, not seeming surprised by the news that she had a sponsor she had never met before. "Yes, I think G.P. mentioned something about that," she had said. Garrett had read that G.P. was what she called her husband.

Now, doing Tex's dirty work, Garrett wondered whether her husband was in on it. Maybe he and Tex were partners. Maybe G.P. wanted to get rid of her because he had a girlfriend. No, maybe he would inherit a lot of money if she got lost in the Pacific. That was probably it. The past year, living and traveling with Tex, Garrett had come to realize that almost everything came down to money.

During the welcome ceremonies, Tex had pulled him forward. "Here's a young man you should meet, Miss Earhart. He's a genius mechanic, and if you don't object, I'd like to have him check out the tires on your plane, go over the wheel mechanisms. The consortium wants to keep tabs on how it's all holding up. But I also know you'll want to meet him because of his name. May I present Garrett Howland?"

She had taken his hand and held it firmly in her own, looking at him with those direct, blue eyes. "How do you do, Mr. Howland. It would be an honor to have you check things out. I trust your name will be a good omen."

Fred Noonan, the navigator, had emerged from the back of the plane and hopped down beside Miss Earhart. He had looked at the crowd, grinned suddenly, and flung an arm around Tex's shoulders. "Tex Arnold, you old son-of-a-gun, what the hell are you doing way out here on the edge of the earth?"

"Good to see you, Fred," Tex said. Damn it anyway, Tex knew everybody in the world. Maybe it was okay, after all.

No. Drops of sweat plopped beside him as Garrett made sure the magnets would stay in place.

It wasn't all okay. He and his island-sounding name were omens of doom. Perhaps that was why Tex had picked him up in South Dakota. Perhaps Tex hadn't been attracted to him and his long, sensitive fingers at all. Maybe it had been his name that got him the invitation to see the world. Maybe he was just part of some giant, sick jest.

Miserable and confused, Garrett crouched under the belly of her plane, ensuring he was the only Howland that Amelia Earhart would see on her long journey.

— 1983 —
Thursday

After Lieutenant Guerrero drove her back to the Guam Hilton, Laura sat with Charlotte Sablán and Teri in the hotel coffee shop, toying with a salad. She had answered Teri's questions about her session at the police station with the barest possible explanations, trying to shield the girl from the images that were growing more vivid in her own mind with each passing moment.

"Charlotte, you said something earlier today about Gordon, about how long he'd been out here. Do you know when he first came?"

Charlotte laughed nervously. "When it suddenly becomes a matter of life and death, I'm not sure anymore. But … well, the impression I had is that he was in Saipan before they moved the Trust Territory headquarters up there. He wasn't part of the TT establishment when it was here on Guam, but somehow I have the idea that he was there from the moment they got to Saipan. Maybe sort of a liaison between TT and the previous occupants." She pronounced the words "previous occupants" in such a sinister whisper that Teri perked up.

"Who were the previous occupants?"

"I told you when we were in Saipan, honey," Laura said. "The CIA ran an operation there, training nationalist guerrillas to invade the Chinese mainland."

"Oh, that's right. And you said they weren't supposed to be doing that," Teri said, sounding almost as though she were reciting a lesson.

"***We*** weren't supposed to be doing that," Laura said. "We Americans. Not in a United Nations Trust Territory. So, when the U.N. found out about it, the CIA had to move out."

"Leaving behind a lovely office building and a lot of houses, so the Trust Territory government moved up," Charlotte said. "The U.N. had been pushing the TT to move headquarters into the actual territory they were supposed to be running anyway."

"And Gordon Hassler was there when they moved there?"

"Laura, it's only my impression. Things Ricardo, my brother-in-law, may have said. It had to do with filling orders for liquor or something—or maybe ordering films for the theater up there. They were changing from getting things through the Navy to civilian sources. Someone in the Sablán clan was usually involved. And my impression is that Ricardo dealt with Gordon Hassler."

Laura tried to remember what she knew about the Hasslers' arrival in Saipan. She had known that they were old-timers compared to most Americans on the island. But if Gordon had been a liaison between the CIA and the TT administration—well, that must have been what Ben Guerrero had been musing about: There might be secrets besides drug dealings that people could be murdered for.

"So, Mom, did the policemen believe your alibi? Do they want me to vouch for you?"

"Don't be silly," Laura said. "It's just because I had breakfast with Gordon. They thought he might have said something about an appointment or something."

"Who did you talk to, besides Ben?" Charlotte asked.

"'Sús Pérez."

Charlotte shook her head in sympathy. "There's a cold fish for a tropical island," she said.

"Soos Paris?" Teri giggled. "That's a guy's name?"

Laura started to laugh, a little shakily. "It's short for Hay-soos, spelled J-E-S-U-S. And I got off to a bad start with him nineteen years ago. My first day at the *Chronicle*, they had me writing the

Observation Post, which was a calendar of local events. And one of the first calls I took, this man read an announcement to me, something like 'The Guam Coin Club will meet Thursday at the home of Soos Paris in Ma-knee-low.' I had never heard of a village called Mangilao so I had to ask the guy about three times 'Where is the meeting? Is that a village? Can you spell it for me?' And then I had to tackle the man's name. 'Whose house is it?' I asked. 'Soos Paris,' he said. 'What's the last name again?' 'Paris,' he says. "P-E-R-E-Z.' I looked at what I'd written down and bit my tongue before I could say, 'But that spells Puh-REZ.' Then I still had to extract that first name from him. 'Could you repeat the first name?' 'Hay-SOOS,' he says, like a sneeze. 'I'm sorry,' I say sheepishly. 'How do you spell that?' Finally he just explodes. 'JEE-ZUZ, Lady!' he yells. 'Can't you spell Jee-zuz?'"

They all laughed, more than the story deserved. We're all on the edge of hysteria, Laura thought.

"I've never heard that story before, Laura," Charlotte said.

"Poor silly Mommy," Teri said.

"And, of course, late that same afternoon Rudy sends me over to the police station to get the stuff from the police blotter, and there sits the desk sergeant with this nameplate in front of him that's screaming Hay-Soos Paris at me. I never asked Sergeant Pérez if he was the 'Sús Pérez that collects coins. I just assumed he did."

Charlotte said, "I never thought of 'Sús having any kind of hobby, but he does live in Mangilao. And coins would be cold and dead enough for him." She regarded Laura for a moment. "You know," she said, "I'll bet you're going to have trouble getting to sleep. I think you need a drink."

"Maybe two or three," Laura said. They paid the coffee shop bill and strolled toward the patio bar.

* * *

Two mai tais did the job. Laura didn't have another conscious thought about Gordon Hassler until she woke up the next morning

and picked up the *Guam Chronicle* from outside her door. At the top of the tabloid-sized front page, he stared out, thick curly hair, pleasant smile—a file photograph of him looking about the way he'd looked when she first met him. FORMER TT OFFICIAL SLAIN AT HILTON, the headline bellowed. Quickly she sat down on the foot of her bed to read the story, word by word. It wasn't until she had ascertained that her ill-timed breakfast date was not mentioned that she noticed the boxed article at the bottom of the page. Her shocked shriek awakened Teri.

"What's wrong?"

Laura stared at another photograph, what she assumed was an enlargement of the snapshot Guerrero and Pérez had not let her see last night.

AN EARHART CONNECTION? asked the headline in the box.

> Police found this photograph of famous aviator Amelia Earhart in the shirt pocket of former Trust Territory Administrator Gordon Hassler when they examined his body at the Guam Hilton yesterday. Although the photo's origin is uncertain, the building behind Earhart looks like the old Japanese hospital in Saipan, according to Guam police lieutenant Vicente Guerrero, who is heading the murder investigation. Earhart disappeared somewhere in the Pacific while on an around-the-world flight in July 1937.

Teri stumbled groggily over to Laura's bed. "That's Amelia Earhart, isn't it?" She leaned over her mother's shoulder, reading. "And that ***is*** the Japanese hospital, isn't it? We went there right after we saw the jail, right? You said Amelia was supposed to have been kept in the jail by the Japanese."

Laura continued to stare. In the slightly blurry photograph, a tall, slender woman with short, dark blonde hair stared at the camera with clear directness. She wore a rumpled plaid shirt and squinted a little, looking into the sun. Behind her was the domed entrance to one of the small hospitals the Japanese had built on several islands during their days in Micronesia. Laura had once visited an identical

building on Dublon, in the Truk lagoon, and had seen remnants of another in Koror, Palau. But she had reason to know that the building in the photo was the old Saipan hospital.

In the photograph, a hand gripped Amelia Earhart's right arm. At the left edge of the photo there was a shoulder and sleeve, crisp white, a uniform of some sort, with epaulets. A Japanese naval officer, perhaps, forcing his prisoner—the world's darling—to pose for a picture.

Laura Monroe's eye fastened on the left edge of the photograph, on that shoulder in white, on the gripping hand. She felt as though she had been kicked in the stomach.

After all these years! Her mind seemed to scream in panic. Will this be the end of my journalism career? What am I going to do?

— 1937 —

AMELIA EARHART DIDN'T LEAVE the next day as she had planned, because of the weather. A typhoon to the northeast had created some bad headwinds. She had to fly so far, she needed the wind with her. On the following day, Garrett stood with the others, watching the heavily-laden plane scream down the runway until, at what seemed the last possible moment, it struggled into the air. There was a collective sigh of relief as the plane climbed higher above the sea and began the long journey east.

Walking away from the runway, Garrett thought almost every face but his own reflected the exuberance of the woman's brave and crazy plan. He didn't look at Tex. He didn't want to know what his face reflected.

Garrett had been wondering why they—Tex, perhaps, or someone in the government—hadn't persuaded her to fly over the Japanese islands and take some pictures. He had heard the talk. Here, where the Japanese had occupied the western half of the giant island of New Guinea, the white people were especially worried. No one knew what the Japs were up to in all those islands scattered across most of the western Pacific. Earhart and Noonan might have been able to get some revealing pictures if they rigged their plane right.

Tex drank more than usual that night at dinner, urging Garrett to match him, one glass of wine after another. Garrett wondered if the hotel would run out of wine because of them—no one else in the dining room seemed to be drinking it. Tex had introduced him to wine. Before last summer he'd had a few illicit beers with a buddy, but he had never seen people consume alcohol like Tex and

his friends did. Perhaps it was the only way they could sleep, considering how they lived their lives.

As he ate and drank, Tex talked about the Japanese and their intentions. Garrett had become used to these conversations. Tex didn't expect him to respond and, Garrett had begun to realize with relief, Tex wasn't talking to educate him. He was supposed to learn about good food and wine, Tex told him, but politics was outside his area of responsibility. Garrett thought perhaps Tex needed to listen to himself talk out loud to be sure of the thoughts inside his head. Usually Garrett would listen, nod thoughtfully, and concentrate on eating while Tex pontificated.

Tonight, however, the boy was struck by a sudden thought. "You know, if someone important got lost in those islands, then maybe their government would have an excuse to go looking for them. Then they could see what the Japanese are up to."

Tex straightened abruptly in his seat and Garrett saw that the pale eyes fixed on him had turned icy cold. It was as if Garrett heard then the words he had spoken a moment before. He had been wondering if Tex was important enough for the U.S. government to search for if he got lost in the Japanese mandate. In the chilling glare of Tex's eyes, he suddenly thought of Amelia Earhart.

Tex's voice was as icy as his eyes. "Sometimes, boy, you're too clever for your own good."

The voice, the words, the look sent a chill down Garrett's spine and, despite the steamy humidity in the dining room, he shivered violently.

— 1983 —
Friday

RUDY TERLAJE OPENED THE FRONT DOOR of the concrete block cottage he had built twenty years ago, right after Typhoon Karen persuaded him to compromise his architectural standards when it demolished his old wooden home. He stepped out onto the shady lanai, inhaled the scent of plumeria, and looked down his hibiscus-lined driveway toward the one paved street in the village. Mongmong was his hideout. The cramped valley had kept the developers out and, except for his house, this corner of the island had hardly changed since the war.

Rudy bent stiffly and retrieved the newspaper that had been flung onto the lanai. He carried it to the kitchen and put it down beside his place at the small table. He crossed to open the wooden louvers that blocked his view of the back garden, the center of his life since his retirement from the newspaper two years earlier. He peered through the screen—yes. The bronze cymbidium orchid was in bloom at last.

In nearly forty years of marriage, he and Rosa had come to an agreement: No words before at least one cup of coffee. She padded over from the stove and set a steaming mug down beside his place, brought the cream pitcher from the refrigerator, then retreated to the stove.

Rudy sat down, snuffled loudly—his allergies bothered him the most in the morning—and took a careful sip of the hot coffee. Then he spread out the tabloid-sized newspaper on his place mat.

The headline was riveting. FORMER TT OFFICIAL SLAIN AT HILTON. Even as he registered the thought that there couldn't be a Trust Ter-

ritory official he didn't know, he recognized the man in the photo. "*Jesús MariaJosé!*" he swore softly.

"*Hafa*?" asked his wife.

He waved at her as he might fend off a mosquito. Then he read the story, shaking his head, his mind crowded with fragments of memories, the many, many times he had spoken with Gordon Hassler. And now he was dead? How could this be? Even on an island as small as Guam, murder happened to strangers.

The other photograph at the bottom of the page caught his attention. The Chamorro expletive boomed out. "*Lañ*!" His hand jerked convulsively, tipping over his mug so that coffee flooded the newspaper, drowning the lower right-hand corner.

But he had seen it clearly. Damn, he thought. After all these years, the stupid thing slipped through.

He thought of Will Hildebrandt. For a long time he had considered Will a fool but, in recent years, Will had become the closest thing to a friend Rudy Terlaje allowed himself. The Guam Rehab Center had brought them together. Rudy had been on its board of directors for many years because his only son was a permanent client of the organization. Will had gotten interested in the facility while researching a story a few years earlier and joined the board as public relations director.

Despite their current friendship, Rudy still remembered the younger, wilder Will, the one who believed in conspiracy theories, especially about Amelia Earhart, the Will who could be such a pest to a managing editor who was just trying to keep things on an even keel. He bet Will was having a good laugh now, probably believing this photo proved all his half-baked theories.

Rudy scraped the chair loudly as he pushed it back and started for the door.

"Where are you going?" Rosa asked.

"Gotta drive into town and get another copy of the paper," he mumbled and hurried out.

*　　*　　*

When Will Hildebrandt got his copy of the *Chronicle*, he skipped—as was his wont on Fridays—to page 5 to check his column and see how many typos had been inserted to befuddle his readers today. He read through his paragraphs with satisfaction, chuckling in the appropriate places while gulping coffee from the mug he balanced precariously on a pile of books and papers beside his chair. I guess I'm mellowing, he thought. Imagine, Will Hildebrandt, the angry young Turk of yesteryear, writing a humor column about life on the rock.

But then, he thought, I'm not so young anymore.

He raised his eyes, looked around the chaos that was his home, a decaying Quonset hut on a muddy back street in Sinajaña village. No, you're not so young anymore, he told himself. And if you don't get organized, you'll never get another woman to move in here and clean this joint up for you.

His last wife, a Palauan bar-girl nearly his own age, had moved out more than eight months ago. At least he hadn't gotten her pregnant—he must be learning something from the succession of mishaps he'd strung together to approximate a life.

He sighed and folded the paper back to begin reading it properly from page 1. That's when he nearly passed out.

That photo. After all these years. Where did it come from? Why?

He read the lead story. Hassler, he thought. Yeah, I remember him. The guy was always good for a backgrounder, never eager for glory, never wanting to be quoted directly. Not like most the other clowns up there.

Strange. Hassler never seemed like a guy who would be into drugs. He was too—what? Too soft? Too accommodating, maybe. But why else did people get murdered these days in Guam?

That photo. He peered at it closely. No mistaking it. This was the one. The photo I sent to the Chronicle … what? Fifteen years ago? Maybe sixteen. And it ends up still on the island, in some dead man's pocket.

Damn! He mused. What's going on here? And how strange that I saw Laura Monroe just yesterday for the first time in more than a dozen years. She's staying at the Hilton, the murder site. Maybe she killed Hassler? No. Laura might have stolen the photo if she'd had the chance, but she couldn't kill someone. Unless … could she have planted it on him? But how could she have it? Maybe I should call her, suggest we synchronize our stories. Then again, maybe she won't even recognize the photo. That's what I should do. Hope that Laura Monroe has forgotten all about the photo. Hope nobody else recognizes it.

Hell, he thought. I need a drink.

* * *

Laura was sure that Teri knew something was wrong. Maybe she attributed it to delayed shock about Gordon's death. Laura sat with her on the dining terrace, trying to make coherent conversation while asking herself how she could protect the girl from whatever was brewing on the horizon like a typhoon. Should I send her to Foster in Honolulu on the next flight? But Foster used to be a very close associate of Gordon Hassler's. Is he in danger too?

Why was that photo on Gordon's body?

She picked at her breakfast and stared across Tumon Bay at Two Lovers Point. A man at the next table refolded his copy of the *Chronicle* and the large photo of Gordon Hassler as he'd looked in the mid-sixties jabbed into Laura's line of sight. She remembered the first time she had seen that face, the friendly smile, the way the breeze ruffled his thick, wavy hair without messing it up. He had been standing beside the little shack that had served as Saipan's airport terminal back then. Donnie MacDougal had helped her down from his Beechcraft plane and carried her bag as they walked across the tarmac.

The friendly man beside the shack appeared to be the only other human being on the breezy plateau where the runway was a long asphalt island in a sea of the scrubby brush the Chamorros

called tangan-tangan. Folk wisdom said that after the Americans captured the island from the Japanese in 1944, it had been so blasted by bombs and offshore shelling that an American commander ordered the entire island sprayed from the air with tangan-tangan seed in hopes of anchoring the soil so the tropical downpours wouldn't wash the island away.

"Hello, Donnie," the waiting man had said to the pilot. "And you must be Laura Monroe." He took a letter from his shirt pocket and she recognized the *Chronicle* envelope. It was the letter she'd written to the Trust Territory's public information officer requesting an interview with the high commissioner. "I'm Gordon Hassler, assistant commissioner for administration. Jack Picket asked me to meet you."

Many months later she would learn that Jack Picket had never even seen her letter, but that day she was simply relieved to be greeted at this lonely place by such a friendly face—and a high ranking Trust Territory news source at that.

Gordon Hassler had taken her suitcase from Donnie and wished him a safe trip back to Guam when he declined a ride "to town, as we so optimistically say." Hassler slapped his forehead. "My gosh, I almost forgot the bills. You don't mind posting some letters, Donnie?"

"Of course not. Especially when they're already stamped."

Gordon had hurried to his car and returned with a handful of letters. "My wife likes to wait until the last possible moment to pay bills," he told Laura. "Then I start to worry about late charges." He handed the envelopes to MacDougal, who tucked them into the breast pocket of his white pilot's shirt. "I figure having Donnie mail them at the Guam airport saves at least three days transit time."

Donnie had promised he would be back as scheduled to collect Laura. They watched him amble back across the tarmac to his plane. Donnie's distinctive gait made Laura think of one of those very long-legged birds that should be wading in a pond. A crane? Or maybe a heron.

"Listen," Gordon had said as he helped her into the passenger seat of his car, "the hotel's a real dump. Have you ever stayed there? Edwina — that's my wife — she insists you stay with us up on the hill. I think you'll find our guest room comfortable — and far cleaner and quieter than the TT Hotel."

"So, Mom, what are we going to do today?" Teri's voice cut through the memories and brought Laura back to the Guam Hilton where Gordon Hassler had carried something much more ominous in his shirt pocket than a letter from an eager girl reporter.

"What do you want to do? Should we play some tennis? You've got your racquet, and I'm sure I could borrow one."

Teri shook her head. "No, my father's right—it's too hot for tennis here. Remember? You said we'd go down to the beach and stay as long as I want. And I think you could use some time in the sun. Get your mind off unpleasant things."

Laura recognized that tone. Teri was slipping into the mothering-her-mother role she used to assume when she was very small and Laura's love life went awry.

"Okay, we'll go to the beach."

Laura let her mind drift away again. Who else would recognize the photograph if they saw it?

Well, Foster, for one. So much for sending Teri to him to get her away from trouble. That photo could mean trouble for all of us. For me, Foster, Jodie, Will—Will! Of course, he knows more about the photo than anyone. The rest of us never saw the final print. I need to talk to Will.

When they went back to their room to change into bathing suits, Laura riffled quickly through the small phone book. No Hildebrandt. Will had always been paranoid about readers being able to track him down if he wrote something they didn't like.Perhaps Charlotte would know how to reach him. No, she decided she didn't want to talk to Charlotte yet. She wanted to be calmer about this photo thing, so she wouldn't scare Charlotte away. She felt certain

she was going to need Charlotte, but first she had to decide what she needed her for.

Another thought. Rudy Terlaje would know. He was having lunch with Will just yesterday.

"Are you coming or not?" Teri asked impatiently.

"Oh, you go ahead. I'll be down in a minute. I need to make a phone call."

"I'll need a couple of quarters," Teri said, holding out her hand. "That's my get-lost-kid fee for today. Make it four quarters for the Galaxians game in the lobby."

Laura rummaged through her purse for change. "Okay, you little gold digger," she said, handing Teri some coins. "I'll be right down."

"You'd better be down before I run out of money, or I might start begging from Japanese tourists and confirm their worst suspicions about *gaijin* teenagers."

As soon as she heard the door click shut behind Teri, Laura wanted to scream after her to come back. Just because it was 9 a.m. didn't make it safe. Gordon Hassler had been murdered in broad daylight in this very hotel.

Stop it, she told herself. You're overreacting. She turned back to the phone book.

Terlaje, Rudolfo. Mongmong Village. Laura dialed the number and a cheery-sounding woman answered. Strange, Laura thought, I never once met Rudy's wife. Didn't we ever attend the same fiesta or wedding fandango? The woman's English was perfect, like Rudy's. "No, I'm sorry, he left for a bit. No, wait, I think I hear the car in the drive. Yes, here he comes. Please hold the line."

Rudy's voice was cold, cautious. "Terlaje," he said.

"Rudy, it's Laura Monroe," she said, congratulating herself, thinking she sounded as bright and friendly as his wife. "I want to get in touch with Will Hildebrandt. Do you have a phone number for him?"

Rudy sniffed and sighed. Somehow, he sounded annoyed, but he gave her the number, apparently from memory.

She thanked him, apologized for interrupting his morning, reflecting that Rudy always had been something of a grouch.

Then she dialed the number. The voice was more clearly Will Hildebrandt than the clean-shaven apparition she'd seen yesterday. "Yeah, Hildebrandt," he said.

Slowly, without breathing, Laura hung up the phone, sliding it gently into its cradle. Let's take this slowly, she told herself. I don't know what became of that photo after it left Saipan. Will is the only one who knows what happened to it after the film was developed and the contact prints made.

Maybe he knows how it got in Gordon Hassler's pocket.

Maybe he put it there.

She went back to her mental list. Who had been there?

Will.

Me.

Foster.

And of course, Jodie deSpain.

Oh, yes. And Donnie MacDougal. He'd been there, too. How odd that I ran into Will and Donnie's daughter at the same place yesterday.

Donnie is back in Hawaii, Cory said. And Foster is in Hawaii. Will and I are here in Guam.

But whatever happened to Jodie?

Foster might know. He and Jodie had always been buddies. I'll call him later, let him know about Gordon and the photo. Ask him what became of Jodie. Maybe Jodie is the key.

— 1967 —
September

JODIE LAZED IN A LOUNGE CHAIR on the shady balcony outside Foster and Laura's apartment in Chalan Kanoa village, skimming the book about Amelia Earhart. Suddenly, a voice brought goose bumps to her arms.

"Well, we meet again," Donnie MacDougal said as he climbed the last of the stairs leading from the village street to the balcony.

"Back again so soon?" Jodie felt her heart pound. Down girl, she told herself.

"I haven't left yet. They've got typhoon warnings down in Guam and, until I know for sure which way it's going, I'm better off here. I haven't got a hangar for my plane."

"What do you do when a typhoon comes?"

"Fly to some island where the typhoon ain't." He slid into the chair beside her. "Which is where I am right now, knock on wood." He glanced around, clenched fist at the ready, taking in the decorative concrete blocks of the balcony railing, the aluminum and plastic porch furniture, the concrete wall of the house. No wood in sight. He shrugged, beat his fist gently on his own head. "Oh, well. Whatever's blowing up is supposed to go south, between Guam and Ulithi."

"I hope they're right," Jodie said.

Donnie stretched luxuriously. "Someday Foster and Laura will learn that, living downtown, they're gonna get a lot of riffraff dropping in they wouldn't have up on the hill."

"I think that's why they're here," Jodie said.

For dinner that night, Laura made her spiciest curry, which provided an excellent excuse to consume many cans of icy beer on

top of the gins and tonic Foster had plied them with before dinner. After they cleared the table, Will Hildebrandt suggested they take Jodie sight-seeing.

"I've seen the sights," she said. "Laura took me to Marine Beach." She wanted to go on listening to Donnie MacDougal talk about his adventures flying small planes over huge expanses of ocean.

"Marine Beach." Will sounded disgusted. "Come on! This island's got relics of past civilizations." So it was that the five of them crammed into the Datsun and Foster drove up a steep road, climbing away from the narrow coastal plain. Instead of the concrete ranch homes of Capitol Hill, this road brought them to a colony of Quonset huts.

"Navy Hill," Foster said. "This is where they kept the Navy contingent that was fronting for the CIA, which was up on Capitol Hill, which was then called Army Hill."

"Who lives here now?" Jodie asked. Obviously the houses were occupied.

"People who don't have the pull to get housing on Capitol Hill," Foster said.

"Or the sense to live in a village," Laura added.

On the edge of the cluster of hump-backed tin houses, a tall white building glimmered in the moonlight. "The German lighthouse," Laura said, as though she were introducing Jodie to it.

Foster parked beside the abandoned lighthouse and they entered the large room that constituted its ground floor. Their voices echoed oddly as they lurched up the concrete staircase that spiraled inside the building, round and round to the room where the lamps had once been. Warning each other to take care, they stepped out onto a narrow circular ledge high above the housing area. A metal dome balanced on narrow metal poles above them, rattling in the wind. With the clumsy deliberateness of the inebriated, they eased down to sit on the ledge facing west, dangling their legs into space. Behind them the Quonset huts leaked warm lamplight into green

yards, but there were no lights far below them on the coastal plain—the dark expanse that had once been the thriving Japanese town of Garapan. Farther west, faint lights marked the presence of a small inter-island freighter in the harbor and the moonlight highlighted the pale line of surf that edged the broad lagoon.

"What a view." Jodie swept her arm out to encompass it and nearly lost her balance. As she realized with a thrill of fear that she was not really in control of her body, Donnie gripped her upper arm to steady her.

"Watch it, Blondie," he said. "How am I going to teach you to fly if you're in a body cast?"

The wind seemed to intensify and the dome above them creaked and groaned.

"The ghosts of Saipan are rattling their chains," Laura intoned in a slow, portentous voice.

"Don't get spooky," Jodie said.

"No, Saipan is full of ghosts. That's why I love it. Ghosts of the Chamorros the Spanish massacred. Ghosts of Japanese and American soldiers who fought each other to the death."

"And the Japanese civilians who jumped off the cliffs to escape capture," Foster added.

"Ghosts of the Chinese guerrillas who trained at Kagman to sneak back into Mao's empire and were never heard of again," Will said.

"Ghosts of the spooks who trained them," Foster said. "I trip over them everyday in the corridors at headquarters."

"Ghost of Amelia Earhart," Will said.

A bank of heavy clouds skidded across the moon, plunging them into darkness. Somehow that seemed funny and they started laughing. Then Foster began to sing, "Come back, come back, harvest moon." They joined in, improvising words or filling in with la-la-las until the moon burst out of the clouds.

"My God," Will said in a low voice. "Look at her." He pointed at Jodie and she felt a sudden chill of apprehension.

"Look. The hair, the cheekbones. It's uncanny. She's the ghost of Amelia Earhart."

The others stared at her.

"You're right," Foster said slowly. "Jodie, you could be her reincarnation."

Will seemed really excited now. "I noticed it on Rota, when I took your picture by Donnie's plane. I kept thinking I've taken this picture before. But I hadn't. I'd just seen it a hundred times—Amelia standing beside her plane."

"We've all had too much beer," Jodie suggested nervously.

Will was adamant. "I can't believe people don't stop you on the street and ask for your autograph," he said.

"If you wore a leather flight jacket … " Laura lowered her voice mysteriously. "Maybe you *are* Amelia Earhart. She disappeared in 1937. When were you born?"

"1939," Jodie said. "In Colorado. Sorry."

"So she waited a couple years for just the right baby to be born," Laura suggested. "Or maybe that's how long she survived after they captured her."

As the wind howled itself into a new key, Donnie suggested they get off the lighthouse before they were blown off.

"Is your plane going to be okay?" Jodie asked.

"I tied her down. She can ride this breeze out." He gave her a disconcerting little hug.

"Let's go see the old Japanese jail," Laura suggested. "That's where they kept Amelia. You can see if it seems familiar to you."

They spent what seemed like an hour thrashing through the underbrush of Garapan like a herd of demented water buffalo, following trails punctuated with fungi that winked green like cats' eyes in the darkness. The trails doubled back upon themselves, or disappeared altogether. Finally, finding themselves back near the car, they gave up and drove back to the Monroes' apartment for more beer. They took it down to the beach behind the village and stood waist deep in the lagoon drinking it, still in their street clothes.

"This water is much warmer than at Marine Beach," Jodie said.

Foster laughed. "That's because the entire town of Chalan Kanoa dumps its sewage into the lagoon about fifty yards from here."

"I thought you planners were supposed to fix that," Donnie said.

"*'Ey, bruddah,* that's not where the plan says it goes. That's where gravity and rotten sewage pipes say it goes."

Jodie watched the water glimmer with green fire whenever Donnie moved his legs, and imagined him as an enchanted Hawaiian god. Then she noticed it happened when any of them moved and the scientist in the back of her mind hypothesized phosphorescent algae.

"We should take a picture," Will said abruptly. "A picture of Jodie in front of the old Japanese jail, in Amelia Earhart-style clothes. Send it to the goddamn *Chronicle* and wait for them to publish it."

They were so drunk, it seemed like a brilliant idea.

"Sure," Laura said. "You could print it sort of sepia, couldn't you? Make it look old."

"We'll scrawl a note that this photo just turned up in some old papers on Saipan," Foster said. "See what they do with it."

Like a gang of rowdy teenagers, they dripped back through the village, plotting Will's revenge upon the *Guam Daily Chronicle.*

— 1937 —

GARRETT AWOKE DRENCHED IN SWEAT.

What if his meddling didn't work? What if news came that she had landed safely on Howland Island? What would Tex do to him?

No. That wasn't what had awakened him.

He tried to reach through the curtains of consciousness, to touch again the ice cold kernel of truth that had filled his soul with terror.

There it was!

Now he was dispensable. He had done the job Tex had brought him here to do. Tex would have no further need of him. In fact, he knew too much to be allowed to live.

What was Tex's plan? Hire a pilot to fly them back to Port Darwin—and push Garrett out as they climbed over that greedy, voracious jungle? No, that would mean he would have to shove the pilot out too—or pay blackmail forever.

Fishing. Tex had talked of introducing Garrett to deep sea fishing. That's when it would happen, on a fishing boat. Out of sight of the skipper, a quick blow from behind, knocking him out. Then, throw him overboard. Wait until they had traveled too far, then raise the alarm, shouting, "Man overboard!' That was how it would be. He could see his fate as if it were projected on a movie screen.

No. That wouldn't be his fate. Garrett rose gingerly from the narrow bed, heard Tex snoring gently in the next bed. The bastard was sated with too much wine and food and the passionate—no, violent—sex he had lavished upon his compliant toy, his obedient pet appliance, his degraded servant. And then, hadn't there been

almost a hint of sadness, of farewell, in the gentleness at the end, before Tex fell asleep?

Garrett felt like a small child, sneaking into the bathroom, rummaging in the dark among his father's personal belongings.

But he felt much older—a grown man—when his hand felt the cool bone handle of Tex's old-fashioned straight razor.

Childhood and dependency would end tonight.

— 1967 —
September

THEY WERE HUNG OVER SATURDAY MORNING, but it still seemed like a good idea. Perhaps, Jodie thought, a special camaraderie is born when people drink too much and consort with ghosts.

At breakfast, Donnie and Will griped about each other's sleeping habits. They had ended up sharing the double bed in the guest room while Jodie lay on the living room couch, her mind constructing elaborate scenarios in which she and Will changed places. In that drowsy, just-before-sleep stage, she had tried to remember the feeling of the little yellow plane under her hands, but everything was mixed up and her hands seemed to be groping for Donnie's velvet hair.

Foster drove Donnie off after breakfast to find the latest weather information while Laura ransacked closets until she found an old plaid shirt of Foster's that Will approved, a shirt much like one Amelia had worn in a photograph he'd seen. With the same quick competence she had applied to costumes for Guam Theatre Guild productions, Laura quickly set up her sewing machine and altered the shirt so it would fit Jodie. Will dragged what he called his dress trousers from his backpack and suggested Jodie try them on. He was an inch or two shorter than she but after Laura let down the hems, the pants were perfect: a little baggy, just like clothes had been in the thirties.

Foster and Donnie returned to report that Guam was still in typhoon condition two, which meant the typhoon could strike within 24 hours, but the storm was expected to pass south of Guam, leaving the rest of the Marianas in the clear.

After Jodie put on her costume, they drove again to what had once been Garapan. In the daylight they easily found the old Japanese jail. Saplings sprouted through some of the barred windows and there was no roof. Will circled the building, trying to frame a shot that would look as though the building were still in use. Finally he told Jodie to go into one of the least ruined cells so he could photograph her looking out, her hands clenching the bars.

It was very hot and oddly still. Suddenly Jodie was swept away by the same feeling that sometimes overtook her on stage when she completely lost herself in a role. Now that I have flown, she thought, I am Amelia.

She began to think Amelia's thoughts: the long hours Fred Noonan and she had spent suspended in the sky, flying here, to this tiny cell, sweltering now in the tropical heat, beset by voracious insects, surrounded by an enemy that knew exactly why the Americans had dropped out of the sky into this secret kingdom.

Will's voice came from far away. "That's enough." Feeling dizzy, she left the cell to find her co-conspirators agreeing that the old Japanese hospital would make a better set for their production.

In another part of the obliterated city, Laura led them to another ruined building. Two long one-story wings stretched at right angles from a domed entrance lobby.

Will squinted into his camera. "This is much better," he said. "Say Amelia got sick. She's going to die of dysentery before they can execute her. They bring her here for treatment. Look sick, Jodie."

He took some photos of her standing alone in front of the hospital but Laura argued that Amelia would have been brought to the hospital under guard. Donnie was still wearing his white pilot's shirt, but they agreed he was too tall for a Japanese so Laura tried it on while Jodie tried not to stare at the warm brown skin of Donnie's bare chest. Will framed a photo that would show a tall American woman standing on the steps of the hospital, with an officious shoulder and arm beside her.

With Laura's nails digging into her left arm, Jodie thought of the Amelia who had known such absolute freedom in the sky, who had thought the whole world was hers, suddenly imprisoned on this tiny island, deathly ill, knowing she had become a pawn to an enemy who didn't care that she had met kings and queens. In Jodie's body, Amelia straightened, stared defiantly at the camera, at the ugly, hairy man who held it.

"That's fantastic," Will said. "*Voila*! Instant history."

"You really are an actress," Donnie said quietly as they clambered, all hot and sticky, back into the Datsun.

"Now, we've got to process the film," Foster said.

"Oh, I'll take it back to Guam," Will said.

"No you don't," Foster said. "We're all in this. We'll sneak into the darkroom up at headquarters tonight."

"Foster!" Laura seemed shocked but everyone else agreed with Foster. It was all part of the game. They would use U.S. government chemicals to develop the film in the former CIA building.

"Call it our contribution to the anti-war movement," Foster said.

"And, after all," Donnie said to Jodie, "there's not a heck of a lot to do on a Saturday night in Saipan."

Well after dark that night, they drove up the twisting mountain road to the Trust Territory headquarters complex. Foster's key unlocked the front door of the building, and the conspirators made their way slowly up the dark stairwell to the public information office on the second floor where Laura sometimes filled in for people who were on vacation.

The door to the outer office was not locked, and neither was the darkroom. Will scurried in, turned on the red work light, and told them to keep guard.

Leaving the rest of the lights off in the office, the others whispered about how to keep watch. Should someone be stationed out on the stairway and someone else down by the front door? What

about the door at the end of the long back wing? Foster insisted their chances of being discovered were minimal because the janitors would have done their work Friday night.

Suddenly there were footsteps slapping up the stairs. The four sentries dived under the four desks in the outer office, crouching in the knee holes. The door from the hallway opened and the fluorescent lights buzzed on. A pair of leather sandals and sagging blue socks flapped right past Jodie's desk, so close she could smell the feet. The feet passed the darkroom door and went into an inner office. A click followed — another light being switched on. Then a sound that might be the shuffling of papers. Another sound, a sort of muffled jingle. Coins deep in someone's pocket? Trying to keep her long body crammed into the tight space under the desk, fighting to quiet her breathing, Jodie thought she heard Laura giggle under the next desk.

Jodie could just see the edge of the darkroom door. She concentrated, trying to send a telepathic message to Will to stay inside. Papers shuffled in the inner office. The darkroom door cracked open, but quietly jerked shut. Good, she thought, Will realized something was wrong when he saw the lights on in this room.

There was the soft click of a light switch again, and the sandals and blue socks shuffled past once more. The lights in their room were doused, the hall door clicked shut, and the footsteps slapped down the hall.

"Quick," Foster whispered. "While he's going through the papers in the next office."

They crept out from under their desks and Foster tapped lightly on the darkroom door, a shave-and-a-haircut beat. The door opened a crack and Foster whispered, "All clear, but hurry."

Light spilling out of an office down the hall helped the conspirators find the stairway. Outside in the soft, warm night they dashed across the parking lot toward the Datsun which Foster had parked on the far edge. They clambered in and Foster drove without headlights until they were on the road leading back down the steep hill.

"Whew," Laura said. "That was more exciting than the last Saturday-night Palauan bar fight we went to."

Foster burst out laughing.

"Who the hell was it?" Will demanded.

"I couldn't see anything but feet," Laura said, "but it had to be either Hassler or Trianovich."

"Who're they?" Jodie asked.

"Assistant high commissioners," Will said. "Just two steps below the high commissioner. But what was the guy doing?"

"Reading in-baskets," Foster said. "The rumor is that they sometimes show up at 5 a.m. to skulk around and read the stuff in each other's in-baskets. I guess since there was a flight from Guam this morning, somebody wanted to check and see if the mail had been distributed."

"Must have been Hassler," Donnie said. "If it were Trianovich we would have smelled that foul cigar he's always sucking. It took three days to get the stink out of the plane when he flew with me once."

"Yeah, I agree. Hassler," Laura said. "Did you hear the coins jingling? Gordon's always jingling change in his pocket. And anyway, that's how I first met him. Remember, Donnie? He met me that first time you flew me up from Guam. He had my letter to the public information officer and later, when we moved up here, I found out that Jack Picket never even saw my letter."

"But anyone could tell someone's going around in the building," Jodie said. "The lights going on in one office after another."

"Bureaucrats get weird," Foster said, "especially out here. But Gordon's a good guy. It's just his way of keeping on top of things."

"Even so," Laura said, "as good a friend as Gordon has become, I'm glad we didn't have to explain what we were doing in there."

"Well," Donnie said, "how are the pictures?"

"They look great, at least in the contact prints," Will said, patting the damp folder of paper towels clutched under his arm. "But I

think I'll have to wait until I get back to Guam to find the right kind of paper to make the final print."

When they had negotiated the steep mountain road again and were back on the beach road, Foster suggested, "Let's stop at the Palauan's for a drink."

The bar was a ramshackle tin-and-wood building right on the beach. Their entrance caused some excitement behind the bar.

"MacDougal!" A large, dark-skinned woman in a bright muumuu threw her arms wide in welcome. "You're back!"

As they slid onto rickety folding chairs around a small table covered with oil cloth, Jodie thought Donnie looked embarrassed. She wondered whether he had some sort of romantic relationship with the Palauan woman.

"*Alii, ruubak!*" The woman was at their table, grinning broadly at Donnie.

"How's it going, Bernie?" Donnie said. The others all greeted the woman like an old friend and Jodie made a point of smiling warmly.

"Tell you what," Bernie said. "First round's on the house if MacDougal sings."

"Sounds like a deal to me," said Will. They all turned toward Donnie.

"What do you want me to sing?" he asked, seeming resigned to his fate.

"Ooh, great. I'll hook up the mike," said Bernie. "Come with me, Donnie. Yoshi," she shouted at the young man behind the bar. "Get over here and get these folks' orders!" She bustled off to a back room with Donnie following sheepishly in her wake.

The two reappeared just as Yoshi returned with the drinks. Bernie pushed a microphone into Donnie's hand and fiddled with a dial on an ancient amplifier while he repeated, "Testing, testing, one, two, three, four." Finally satisfied with the volume achieved, she turned to a tape recorder beside the juke box and started run-

ning a tape through it, playing fragments of songs, looking for the one she wanted.

"Bernie gets live music in here once in a blue moon," Foster said, "and when she does, she records it for moments like this. If she'd been born in L.A. instead of Koror, she'd probably be a rock-and-roll impresario by now."

"Okay, this is it," Bernie said. "Here we go."

The sound quality was a little tinny but the instruments were recognizable: guitar, bass, and an electric piano.

Donnie grinned sheepishly and began to sing in a strong baritone voice.

I don't want to leave Palau,
I like this place so,
I've fallen in love in Palau,
And that's why I've got to go.

Jodie felt herself shivering with desire. All that animal magnetism and a great voice, too.

"Personally, I think he's as good as Don Ho," Laura whispered.

If ever there was a place,
Where love had to grow,
Palau was that special place,
And that's why I've got to go.

The sentimental lyrics in the song's bridge were balanced by a jangly Jerry Lee Lewis effect on the keyboard.

For life goes on outside
This sparkling lagoon.
Life has its ups and downs,
It's not all moonlight in June.

Then back to the more sentimental tune of the verse:

I don't want to leave Palau,
But I've come to know.
That beauty and love grow routine,
And that's why I've got to go.

Jodie closed her eyes as Donnie repeated the bridge and the last verse, wishing she had been to Palau so she could ask him about it, if it were true that beauty and love did grow routine. I'll never be able to settle for another man again, she thought. Not unless he can sing like that and teach me to fly.

When Donnie finished, there was loud applause from everyone in the bar. Bernie stood beside him, grinning broadly, shouting, "More! More! Give us another one!" in her throaty voice.

"One song, one drink. That was the deal," Donnie said. "You got plenty of Don Ho on the jukebox."

"You were wonderful!" Jodie said as he came back to their table.

He touched her lightly on the shoulder. "Thanks, Blondie. Ain't no big t'ing. All us Hawaiians can sing."

"Don't let him kid you," Will said. "If his airline goes bust, he could make it on the nightclub scene."

"In Guam?" Foster asked, pretending innocence.

"Well, in Waikiki," said Will.

"No way," Donnie laughed. "Don Ho would break my legs if I got in his territory."

Much later, back at the Monroes' apartment, they looked at the tiny contact prints Will had made, even making use of a magnifying glass Laura managed to unearth. Jodie began to feel uneasy. The pictures were almost too good. It was like Donnie's singing, copying another person's style almost perfectly. Was that really me in those little frames, she wondered. Or was I possessed by a ghost? Did I—for a few moments—become Amelia Earhart?

And what, after all, did become of Amelia Earhart?

— 1937 —

IT HAD ALL BEEN SO SIMPLE. First, getting away from the hotel without being seen, a few clothes stuffed into a pillowcase along with all the cash he had found in Tex's luggage. Then in the vague, earliest morning light, slipping aboard the *Wallaby*, an ancient freighter he had noticed taking on cargo at the dock the day before. He stayed hidden for hours as the freighter steamed he knew not where, and he worried about the reception he would receive when hunger finally drove him to announce his presence. The alarm might have gone out from Lae by then, a bulletin to arrest the young companion of a very important murder victim.

Eventually, he decided the sooner he came out of hiding, the better. He eased out of his corner in the hold and slipped up a ladder to the deck to find the sun still a couple of hours above the horizon.

The first seaman he met seemed unsurprised, as though strangers emerged from below decks about this time everyday. He had a broad Australian accent Garrett could barely understand. "Waal, myte," he said, "best I show ye to the cap'n."

The captain was middle-aged with a blotchy complexion that Garrett guessed bespoke too much alcohol as well as too much sunshine. He didn't sound Australian to Garrett, but he certainly wasn't American.

"And who might you be, m'lad?"

"My name's John Doe," Garrett said solemnly.

"Sure and it would be, wouldn't it? And ye've barely got out of the gold fields with the clothes on your back, and you're a wee bit embarrassed not to be going home with a fortune. Am I correct?"

"I'll work for my passage," Garrett said.

The captain gave him a wry smile. "Your passage to where?"

"Aren't you headed for Australia?" Australia was the land of second chances for criminals. Wasn't that what he had learned in his high school geography class?

"In another month or two. But we've got many islands ahead of us before we see the land of the wombat again." The captain laughed, one short bark. "Hah! Afraid ye've caught the local, m'lad, not the express."

"That's okay. I'll work."

And he did. He swabbed decks and hunted vermin in the hold and scrubbed pots and pans in the galley. He wondered whether the ship always set out from Lae shorthanded, knowing someone would stumble along to do the dirtiest work. He daydreamed about the large bundles of cash in his pillowcase, longed to buy his way out of this indentured servitude, but knew that having any cash at all would arouse suspicion. And so he sweated in the equatorial sun and remembered his premonition that day flying over the New Guinea jungles, that he would be trapped forever in the tropics.

The second night out of Lae, the radio operator stopped at the crew's table in the mess after dining at the captain's table with the other officers. "It's official now, lads," he said. "She's lost."

"Who's that, Sparky?" asked Leander. He was the sailor who had first seen Garrett and who seemed to have special rights to use him as a personal servant.

"That balmy sheila trying to fly around the world."

"Amelia Earhart?" Leander said. In the nick of time it occurred to Garrett that, as an American, he'd better express concern, too, so he chimed in just a beat behind, "Not Amelia!"

"Yup. Finally got my damn shortwave working again and the first thing I hear is that the lady never made it to that rock she was heading for. I suppose they'll have your whole navy out scouring the seas for her, won't they, Yankee Doodle?"

"Well, we're pretty crazy about Amelia," Garrett let John Doe acknowledge.

"Pretty crazy about a lot of things," said the radioman, smoothing his crisp white collar as he strolled away.

Garrett found his fellow seamen's responses interesting. They were all concerned about Amelia, as though she were a special heroine to them. A wave of guilt surged through him. He was responsible. He had killed Amelia Earhart! As surely as he had slit Tex Arnold's throat, he had condemned that vibrant, magical woman to death by drowning, or by starvation and thirst on some forsaken island.

That night he lay in his bunk, his head on the lumpy pillowcase that held a small part of Tex Arnold's fortune, and thought of a word he had heard years ago in Sunday school. Redemption. Was it possible for him to redeem himself? If he confessed his involvement, if he told right now how he had put her off course, if he told them where to begin the search, perhaps she could still be saved.

But he was afraid. Connecting himself to her, to her flight, would connect him to that disgusting corpse in Lae that was surely beginning to attract flies and attention by now, despite the Do Not Disturb sign Tex had hung on the door knob that night.

No, he was a coward. Having just saved himself from the fate Tex had planned for him, he couldn't sacrifice himself to try to save Amelia.

Then he thought of another way he could redeem himself. He would find out who Tex had been working for—who had decided to sacrifice Amelia Earhart so the Yank navy could invade the Japanese Mandate in search of her. He would find out—and make them pay. It might take a long time. It would probably take all of the cash in his pillowcase. But he had nothing but time, a lifetime ahead of him. And now, at last, he had a purpose for his life.

— 1983 —
Friday

FOR MUCH LONGER THAN WAS PRUDENT, Laura lay on the beach, toasting her back, knowing she would regret this tomorrow but unable to force herself to move. There was so much to do—so many people she should talk to. But where to begin? The crumbled coral of Tumon Beach grew ever more abrasive beneath her thighs and stomach, digging through the beach towel, just like the terrors that were forcing their way into her consciousness.

"Mother, you are turning absolutely orange," Teri said suddenly. Laura rolled over and sat up.

"I've been snorkeling for hours," Teri said. "I thought you were coming swimming, too. Did you fall asleep?"

"Yes," Laura lied, fumbling in her beach bag for her watch, finding suntan lotion instead. "Here, honey, would you rub this on my shoulders?"

The lotion felt almost cool as Teri dribbled it across Laura's shoulders and the scent invited her back to all the simpler times she had spent sunning on beaches in the western Pacific. She flexed her back, felt the tightness of her skin, and winced as Teri began to smear the lotion around. "Uh, maybe 'rub' was the wrong word. Can you just sort of slide it over my skin?"

Laura rummaged again in the bag and found her watch. "What time does your father usually get home from work?"

"It depends on whether he and Lolita are fighting or not," Teri said. Teri's current stepmother was only eight or nine years her senior. Had calling her Lolita been the child's own idea or was it something Laura had said when she first heard about the marriage?

She did take a certain mean pleasure in seeing Foster as Nabokov's hapless Humbert.

"Let's be optimistic and assume they're not fighting."

"Oh, I guess he makes it home by six," the girl said.

Laura peered through sun-bedazzled eyes at the tiny face of her watch. "Two o'clock. There's four letters in Oahu, four hours later there. So it's six. Let's go up so I can make a call to your dad."

Teri, she was confident, would spend a long while in the shower, washing the salt water out of her hair, giving Laura plenty of time to talk to Foster. If only he was home.

"You gonna tell him what happened to your gentleman admirer?" Teri asked as they trudged up the road toward the hotel.

"You mean Gordon Hassler? Well, he'll want to know. They were pretty good friends once upon a time."

The midday heat was a tangible weight upon their bodies. "I told you we should drive down to the beach," Teri said. "We haven't used that rent-a-car since we brought it from the airport two days ago."

"I've been in Tokyo too long," Laura said, thinking of mile-long stretches between bus stops in the megalopolis. "I forgot it's hotter here."

"Daddy never walks anywhere in Hawaii," Teri said. "Not even when he goes down the block to borrow a cup of sugar."

Puffing at the steepness of the last few yards to the hotel, Laura was nevertheless glad she'd chosen to walk. It was good for the kid to be reminded that her parents were two very different people.

When they stopped at the desk for their room key, the clerk said, "Oh, Mrs. Monroe, some phone messages came for you." Laura winced at the "Mrs." but she had long ago given up preaching to people in other cultures on the distinction between Ms. and Mrs. Since yesterday, all the staff in the hotel seemed to know her by name. Of course. She was the last person to "see him alive."

Walking up the carpeted stairway to the second floor, she glanced at the two message slips. Charlotte Sablán had called shortly

after they'd gone down to the beach. And Jerry Bosley, her bureau chief in Tokyo. What could he want? Well, they would have to wait—she needed to talk to Foster. Somehow he would have to provide the footing for any future action.

The phone was ringing as they entered the room. Laura answered cautiously. "Hello?"

"Laura, it's Charlotte. Listen, did you know about the photograph last night? Did Ben tell you anything about it?"

"Only that they found one clue on the body. He showed it to 'Sús while I was there, but they were careful not to let me see what it was."

She watched Teri stroll into the bathroom, remembering that they hadn't let her see the photo because they considered her a suspect. And that had been before she knew about her strange, photographic connection to Gordon's death. What would Ben Guerrero and 'Sús Pérez see in her responses if they were to interrogate her now?

She felt that chill of apprehension again. Still, it was not surprising that Charlotte would phone. Charlotte and her insatiable curiosity.

"I wonder if they checked the photo for evidence of age?" Charlotte said. "I'm not an expert on the subject, but I think I could tell if it was old enough to have been made in 1937."

"Old enough?"

"I'm wondering if they've considered the possibility of a hoax? I've seen dozens—maybe hundreds—of photos from Japanese times in Micronesia. We're building an excellent collection at the research center, if I do say so myself. Every time I see some Japanese tourists I ask them if they had any Micronesia colonists in their family and, if so, have they got any pictures? You might be surprised how many photos survived the war, and how many people will send copies to a historical research center if you give them your address."

Laura stood paralyzed. She heard Teri turn on the shower. No, Charlotte, she thought. Don't start talking hoax. Not so soon.

"I really don't know what they know about the photo, Charlotte. Just that it's a clue. And I guess they hope it will stir something up. I suppose you could talk to Ben. Or 'Sús Pérez."

Charlotte clearly was unconcerned about being drawn into the investigation. In fact, Laura was certain she would welcome it. "I'll give 'Sús a call," Charlotte said. "Offer to take a look at it for him."

After Charlotte said good-bye, Laura sat down on the bed and took some careful, deep breaths. More than ever, she needed to talk to Foster. She dialed his number in the Honolulu suburbs, remembering how in the old days in Guam, they'd had to drive to the RCA office in Agaña to place calls off island. And now you could direct dial anywhere in the world from your hotel room. The islands really were a part of present time now instead of that magical never-never land she used to love so much.

The idea of leaving Foster had first occurred to her when he got the offer from Gordon Hassler of a Washington, D.C. job. She had realized she wanted to stay in these islands, that they were becoming hers. Having come of age here, just as the islands were coming of age politically, she belonged here. But she hadn't been able to make a solid decision to leave him by the time she found out she was pregnant. And then it was just so much easier to pack up and move to Washington, to let Foster keep being in charge.

A sweet young voice with a soft southern drawl answered the phone. Lolita, Laura thought, trying desperately to remember her real name.

"Uh, may I speak to Foster?"

"Ah'm sorry, ma'am, he isn't home yet." There was an unspoken question in her voice: And who might you be?

"Uh, Andrea?" That was her name. "Andrea, this is Laura, Teri's mother?" She'd never met the woman, only seen a couple of blurry snapshots Teri had taken, but they'd had these conversations every summer for—what—three years since Andrea married Foster?

"Oh, hi," Andrea's voice softened, warmed. "Wheah are y'all?"

"We're in Guam."

"And Teri's still coming? When is it—Tuesday?"

"Yes, well, I wanted to talk to Foster about it. There's a complication—I'm not sure ..."

"Waal, if you aren't in luck. I hear my dearly beloved comin' in from the garage right now."

Garage? Why on earth does Foster have a garage in Hawaii? Laura didn't know if she'd ever seen one there. She would have to remember to ask Teri about it.

She heard Andrea's muffled, musical voice, heard the word "Guam" and something about a problem with Teri's plane ticket. Did I say anything about a ticket problem? Laura felt herself growing rattled and tried to tune into the soothing sound of Teri singing ballads in the shower.

"Hey, babe, what's up?" Foster's hearty voice nearly zapped her into the girl she'd been at Andrea's age, here on this island, depending upon her big, strong man.

"Oh, Foster." Her voice caught a bit in what she prayed was not really a sob. "Something terrible has happened."

"Teri!" His voice was pure panic. Laura reminded herself that she was the one who was always cool and collected in emergencies.

"No, no, she's fine. She's singing in the shower even as we speak."

She heard relief float his voice down an octave. "So what's wrong?"

"It's Gordon Hassler," she said. "He was murdered yesterday. Right here in the Hilton."

"Jesus," Foster breathed.

"I'd had breakfast with him that morning and people seem to think I was the last one to see him alive. So I had to go in for questioning—"

"I bet Teri got a kick out of that," he said.

"Fortunately Charlotte was here to look after Teri—"

"How's Charlotte doing? Still playing mother hen to the whole damn rock?"

She's even trying to mother the police, Laura thought. "She's fine." It was always like this with Foster. She could never direct the conversation, keep it under control.

"I had to be interrogated," she said. "By your old buddy 'Sús Pérez. And you know who's the No. 2 detective here? Ben Guerrero."

"Always knew that kid was going places," Foster said. She wanted to argue. You call being on the Guam police force going places? For a kid with Ben's brains?

"It was a pretty grizzly murder," she said, trying to stick to her subject. "Lots of cutting up with a sharp instrument. Ben seemed almost undone by it."

"But you're in the clear, I assume."

"Yes." She laughed, a little too loud. In the background, the shower concert continued. "My alibi was watertight. But Foster, something really bizarre— "

She stopped herself just as she had when Will Hildebrandt had answered his phone that morning. What if there were a police tap on her phone? She didn't dare mention the photo. That's why 'Sús Pérez had wanted it published—to see what it would stir up. Maybe she'd given away too much already, opening her conversation with the murder instead of slipping it in as a casual aside.

"What is it? You sound shook, babe." Great, Foster, focus the cops on me. Go ahead, I'm just the mother of your only child.

"Foster, do you know whatever became of Jodie?"

"Jodie?"

"Jodie deSpain." Come on, Foster, sharpen up. Maybe there was a way to get him thinking about the photo without mentioning it—but then how would she keep him from blurting something out?

"Jodie. Christ, I haven't seen her for years. She was here a few years ago—hey, we went out, had some laughs, some drinks. What the hell, I was between wives, as it were." That must be for Andrea's benefit. It was almost funny, the image of them trying earnestly to communicate with hostile ears listening in on every side. But then,

she and Foster had never really managed much communication in the years they'd spent together.

"I was just thinking about Jodie," she said. "Wondering what had happened to her. I ran into Cory MacDougal yesterday, of all people."

"Is that Donnie's daughter?"

"Yeah. She says her dad's in Hawaii. I don't suppose you ever run into him."

"No, although I had heard he was here. He doesn't get the press here he used to get out there in Wonderland. But I'm sure Jodie's not here with him, if that's what you were thinking. I'm sure she would have called me if she were."

"You know who else I ran into yesterday? Will Hildebrandt and … " She started to mention Rudy Terlaje, too, but stopped herself. No. I want him to focus on the five pranksters. Jodie. Donnie. Will. Laura. Foster.

"Will's still hanging on out there, is he? What's he up to?"

"He seems to be making a living writing for dive magazines."

"Well, that clever bastard. I just can't see Hairy Hildebrandt as a diver." Foster's voice shifted gears. "Remember that time in Saipan, when he and Jodie—"

"Yes, I was just thinking about that."

There was a pause. "Too bad about Gordon," he said finally. She wondered if, in his memory, he was crouched under a desk, watching those sagging blue socks and sandals slap past. Why had Gordon Hassler come snooping around that Saturday night? "So do they have any suspects?"

"They've only got one clue," Laura said carefully, wondering if the phone tap was being recorded for later transcription or if someone was listening to her in present time. "And it's really weird. They published it in the *Chronicle* this morning. It's something they found on the body—a photograph."

"A photo of what?"

"A photo of Amelia Earhart. Taken in Saipan."

"Saipan?" Foster's voice was absolutely neutral. After all, she thought, he is an actor. "So she really was in Saipan?"

"Apparently so. The picture very clearly shows the old Japanese hospital behind her."

"That is strange." Foster paused, then changed the subject, or at least so it would seem to anyone listening. "But what about Teri? Andrea said something about a problem."

"Not exactly. It's just that—well, I've been a little shook up by the murder. I mean I just had breakfast with him yesterday morning, for God's sake. And I guess I just wanted to talk to someone who would understand. A little."

"I'm sure it has been upsetting," Foster said. "And for whatever it's worth, I think I understand how you're feeling. Kind of betrayed? You always had that romantic, rose-tinted view of the island. You used to get shook every time Guam rolled over and showed us its slimy underbelly."

"Yeah, maybe you're right." She would have hugged him if he'd been within reach. Good old Foster. He can still come through when I really need him.

"Geez," he said. "I wonder how Edwina's going to take this. I always thought she really loved the guy."

"I was thinking about that. 'Sús Pérez hopes she'll come to Guam and help him figure this out, but I guess the police don't have the budget to summon her legally."

"S'pose it was a jealous husband? How embarrassing for her."

"I don't know. You never—you wouldn't have even given him a black eye if you—if he'd seduced me."

Foster hooted. "You? Fussy little Gordon Hassler seduce the great Laura Monroe?"

Sharp annoyance stirred in her. What does he mean by that?

"Now if it was Andrea," Foster said, "that might cause me to get out my whetstone and sharpen up my Swiss Army knife … "

Damn. Why do I let him get to me like that? Why do all these—these shoelaces from the past keep tripping me up?

"Listen, Foster, I'd better stop pouring my hard-earned yen down this trans-Pacific speaking tube … "

"I knew you still had a yen for me, Tater-pig," he said.

"Oh, shut up."

"Listen, babe, if you'd feel better getting Teri out of there, send her earlier. Tonight if you can get her on the flight."

"No, no … I'm sure everything will be okay. I just needed someone who knew Gordon to know … oh, the shower's stopped. I'll let you say hi to the bathing beauty."

Teri emerged from the bathroom with one towel wrapped around her slim, tan body, another encasing her head, turban style. Laura suspected that was the extent of the fluffy dry towels. She handed Teri the phone and strolled into the bathroom to give her some privacy.

Wasn't that why I called, to get Foster to offer to take Teri out of harm's way? Then why not take him up on the offer?

Because, she realized, her subconscious was more careful than her conscious. Her subconscious must have focused on what she had never confronted. Foster had worked with Gordon Hassler in Washington. Gordon was the one who had brought them to Washington. If someone had eliminated Gordon because of something he knew, might Foster know about it, too? She hadn't been very curious about Foster's job during those two years in Washington—she had been so swathed in her own problems, in her disappointment that having a baby had not revived the marriage, then in the growing understanding that she had to get out of the marriage to save herself and to save Teri.

She'd had only the vaguest idea where Foster was going when he left their Alexandria apartment everyday. The Interior Department, ostensibly. Both he and Gordon had been working in the Office of Territories, trying to get the infrastructure in the Trust Territory islands improved so the natives would stop being restless, so that they would want to remain a U.S. territory. That wasn't so sinister, was it?

She found herself staring at the rumpled bath mat, smoothing it out to confront those initials again. *GH.*

But if Gordon had been working in Saipan before 1962, that meant he'd had a CIA connection back then. And then hadn't she run into him near the CIA office that time in Rosslyn? And, she was now certain, she had seen him that night in Bangkok, having dinner with the CIA station chief.

She had become much more conscious of the CIA in her new incarnation as a foreign correspondent. It had been a favorite game at the Foreign Correspondents Club in Bangkok, trying to guess which of the U.S. Embassy officials applying for associate memberships were really spooks under cover. It wasn't just the Americans, of course. The Soviet members were all suspect—working press or diplomats. And although her assignment in Tokyo kept her focused on social issues—the fledgling women's and consumer's movements—she suspected the correspondents who covered political issues and security affairs could draw up a pretty good roster of which political or economic officers at the embassy were merely diplomats of convenience.

So why wouldn't the CIA use the Interior Department and the Office of Territories as cover if that suited them? Maybe the business Foster was running now in Hawaii was just an elaborate cover.

As she heard Teri say, "Bye, Daddy, I love you. See you soon," she tried to remember exactly how Foster had reacted when she'd told him Gordon had been murdered. "Jesus," he'd said. Quietly, with none of his usual sarcasm. Could it have been something he expected to hear? Could it be an occupational hazard he also faced?

The phone rang almost as soon as Teri had finished talking. "Mom, it's for you."

The voice on the line was gruff with tension, but instantly familiar.

"Laura? Will Hildebrandt. We need to talk."

Part 2

— *1937* —

ALL GARRETT KNEW ABOUT THE ISLAND when he jumped ship was that it was somewhere in the Solomons, and it looked big enough to hide him for a week or two while he re-invented himself. He had figured most of it out. He had agonized for days over his passport but decided at last it could only be a liability with its dated entry stamps that established his arrivals in Darwin and Lae on the same days as Tex Arnold. As he flushed the torn bits of the document down the head on the freighter, he acknowledged that it might be difficult to get a new one, but surely he could talk his way into one once he decided what name he wanted to use.

He believed that since he didn't know a word of French, he would be better off on an island run by the British than he would be staying on the *Wallaby* until it reached the French outpost in the New Hebrides. As far as he could tell, they were about to leave the British protectorate, so this had to be his island.

From a narrow space between two warehouses beside the dock he watched the *Wallaby* sail away, already homesick for its simple safety, lonely for John Doe, the man with no attachments who was sailing away from him with the ship.

John Doe. That was a perfectly good name. But he didn't dare use it. It would automatically create suspicion. He needed a name that would let him blend into the masses until he learned what he needed to know, until he was ready to strike.

He thought of his parents, his mother and the father he had barely known. He pictured them sitting together in that crowded little parlor in the little white house in Spearfish, trying to decide

what to name the baby. Garrett. It wasn't a family name, he knew that for sure. It was his impression that his mother had found it in a story. It must have seemed a romantic choice to her. He wondered what name she would have chosen if he had been a girl.

Sprawled in the shade of a palm tree on a postcard-pretty beach a couple miles from the port town—an idyllic spot he had retreated to in order to create himself anew—it struck him: he would never see his mother again. She would never know what had become of him.

As a youngster, Garrett had known what he wanted to do with his life: he wanted to be a mechanic and keep beautifully intricate machines running smoothly.

But his mother had other ideas. She wanted him to go to the local teachers college and make something of himself. It had been her plan since she first got pregnant, had been what caused her to nag her husband until he finally gave up his relatively well-paid job as a miner and accepted much less to be a janitor on the college campus. "It will be so much better for the child to grow up in a college town than in Deadwood," she had told him. (Once Garrett was in school, she had repeated the phrase, so he would know that they had made sacrifices for him.) And then, of course, she had felt guilty and martyred when her husband—having given up the dangers of hard rock mining—was killed by an exploding boiler in the college heating plant, leaving her to raise their eighteen-month-old son alone on her widow's pension and the sewing she took in.

When Garrett accepted a full-time job working at the garage where he'd helped out while still in high school, she had been especially annoyed because he didn't tell them he would be leaving to go to college in September. Then she had been devastated when, shortly before it was time to register, he told her he had decided to take a year off to do some traveling.

She had predicted the worst—and hadn't she been right?—and was horrified at his decision to go off with the rich, handsome stranger who had suddenly appeared." What do you know about him?" she had asked. "What does he want you to do for him?"

She had answered his artificial, jaunty postcards with stiff little notes that began, "Thank you for remembering me," then went on to urge him to work hard and behave himself. He had sent his last card from Port Darwin—he hadn't seen any picture postcards in Lae and hadn't been quite sure how to fill a sheet of hotel stationery. Thank God, she had no idea he had been anywhere near New Guinea.

Oh, mother, he told the blue tropical sky, I promise you will never be poor. As soon as it was possible, he vowed, he would send her a significant part of Tex's money. Anonymously. But she would know.

Garrett had never figured out what Tex Arnold was doing at a county fair in South Dakota that day. He had said he was on vacation. And he liked Garrett's looks. Perhaps he had been deserted by another young man whose looks he'd liked. Maybe he needed to go to really small towns to find naive boys who were eager to get out into the world. Things were hard in South Dakota in 1936. Perhaps he had come to feed upon their rural poverty. Sure, there was that story about seeking out the places where the legendary characters of the Old West had died. Maybe there had been something to that. Whatever his motive, Garrett was certain that Tex hadn't come to South Dakota looking for a good mechanic. That had just been a lucky coincidence. No. Unlucky. Unlucky for Amelia Earhart. Unlucky for Tex Arnold. Unlucky for Garrett Howland.

Now, he told himself, he must never demonstrate his mechanical skills again. He had to become a completely different person so that he could never be tied to Garrett Howland, the young companion of a murdered man.

Never again would he use his good hands to coax an engine into a sweet purr. And no more card tricks. Definitely not. More than once Tex had made him show off his tricks for powerful, important friends. What had they taken him for? A valet, perhaps? Or did they just accept the fact that Tex always kept a young plaything?

As Garrett dug into his pillowcase, groping for his playing cards, his fingers brushed the smooth metal of his pocket watch.

He drew it out and looked at it thoughtfully. It had stopped keeping time because he had given up trying to wind it each day. He turned it over. It was engraved on the back: GH ALL MY LOVE, R. JUNE 10, 1910. His mother had given it to his father on their first anniversary and his father must have carried it in his pocket for more than a decade—but not, apparently, on the day he died.

They'd had to wait a long time for their first child, their only child—almost ten years. And then their child turned out to be …

Garrett studied the watch. He had to keep this. It was the only connection he had to his father. His mother had taken the watch to an engraver, had him change the "C" for "Charles" to a "G" and given it to Garrett as his high school graduation present.

For a long time he stared at the letters GH and tried to see how they could be changed again. It had been easy to change a C to a G. But what could you change a G to? And what about the H? Could you make it into a B? With his finger, he traced letters in the sand. No, an H would make a dreadful B.

Well, what was wrong with keeping the same initials? As long as the names were very different.

So, G. What should his first name be? Not Gary—that was what Tex had called him. George was the only other name he could think of. But he couldn't be George. It sounded like a king. Or a joke. By George, no, I won't be George.

Then he remembered a boy who had lived down the street when he was small. He heard the shrill voice of the boy's mother calling him. "Gordie! You come home now, Gordie! Go-o-or-die."

He hadn't really known Gordie, who was several years older. He wouldn't call himself Gordie, anyway. Gordon. That was a nice, solid-sounding name. It had dignity. Gordon was a man who took life on his own terms, not a joke, and definitely not a Gary who let himself become another man's plaything.

Gordon. Gordon who?

He thought of the rest of his life, how he intended to be a hunter, to find out who had decided to destroy Amelia Earhart. Gor-

don Hunter? He tried it out. It didn't sound right. Gordon Hunter sounded hunched. He would hunch down, of course, until he found what he needed. But then he would fly out and take his revenge.

If not Hunter, what? Hassler. That sounded better. It had a hint of menace about it. Was it a proper name? Could someone be called Gordon Hassler? He liked the sound of it. He leaned over, wrote it carefully in the sand. He liked the looks of it.

Gordon Hassler. Okay, now what does Gordon Hassler do? What was he doing here on this beach in the South Pacific? The refugee from the gold fields story was good, very believable. But it tied him back to Lae. No. There had to be another route to this island for Gordon Hassler.

He had been crewing on a yacht, perhaps. It sank and he swam ashore. Everyone else was lost. Would the yacht need a name, a registration number? Would he have to file a report with some sort of international coast guard?

He had to take his time, get this right. Whatever he came up with, he was going to have to live with it. Just like the name. He liked the name. He decided to like everything about Gordon Hassler.

So Gordon Hassler was not a mechanic. He didn't know one end of an engine from another. And Gordon Hassler didn't do card tricks. He fingered the deck of cards, fanned them out, shuffled them quickly. He looked up and down the deserted beach. Not a soul in sight. He strolled to the edge of the water and flung the whole deck as far as he could out over the lagoon. The cards fanned out and floated down, fluttering in the light breeze, turning over, some hitting the water on edge, disappearing into it, others floating on the surface. Perhaps, if the cards were closer, he could read his fortune in their faces.

Not that Garrett Howland had ever read fortunes with his card tricks. And Gordon Hassler certainly didn't read fortunes. Gordon Hassler didn't even own a pack of playing cards.

— 1967 —
October

AFTER HER FIRST FLYING LESSON—the most exhilarating afternoon Jodie had ever spent—they stopped at the bowling alley bar for a drink. While they were there, at least three men stopped by their table, one by one. They each slapped Donnie on the back, said, "How's it goin', Buddy?" if they were statesiders, or *"Hafa, Gatchong!"* if they were Guamanian. And then they waited until Donnie introduced her.

"You know Jodie, don't you? No? Oh, Jodie deSpain, this is Carlos Guerrero. He does something for GovGuam—no one's ever figured out what. Jodie's my new student, Carlito. I'm going to make her into the next Amelia Earhart." The men congratulated her on signing up the best damn pilot in the Pacific as her teacher, and looked her over, fitting her into their own ideas of what women were allowed to do, and with whom.

She and Donnie talked about flying that first evening, only flying, although Jodie felt sure he was as aware as she of the other possibility that shimmered in the dim, smoky air between them. Donnie doodled on the back of a paper coaster with a ballpoint pen, creating a birdlike swoop of ink.

"What's that?" she asked.

He shrugged. "A map, maybe. A guide to the joy of flying."

"Can I have it?"

"For what?" Sounding surprised, he pushed the coaster toward her.

"I'll put it on my business stationery when I'm a professional pilot," she said.

He laughed with delight. "You do that," he said. "Jodie de-Spain, pilot. The joy of flight."

Very carefully, she tucked the slightly soggy coaster into an inner pocket in her purse.

She took more lessons but they were not followed by a stop for drinks afterwards. Instead, he would say he had to hurry home to keep some promise to his kids or to his wife, Panda. Panda—a disconcertingly engaging name for a woman Jodie found herself wishing nothing but ill.

Francesca MacDougal was called Panda, Donnie had explained with a grin, because her Filipino immigrant parents couldn't pronounce "F" and thus couldn't say the name they bestowed upon their own daughter. "They just followed ol' Ferdie Magellan's example when he called those rocks the Philippines," Donnie said. "He gave their whole damn island chain a name the poor Pilipinos can't pronounce."

His obvious fondness for his wife made Jodie wonder whether she had been imagining the whole thing. Perhaps he didn't feel any sparks when they were in the cockpit together. But he had to feel them—they made the hair on her arms stand up. Maybe he didn't ask her to go out for a drink again because he was afraid of what could happen. Maybe he was too sensible to let it happen.

Jodie suggested to herself that she too could be sensible. She usually was, living up to her self-defined image as the cool, competent scientist who let her true fire spill out only when she was on stage pretending to be someone else.

Yet somehow, the flight to Saipan had set her on a new course, slightly askew from the reality of her previous existence. If it were true that she could fly, what else could she do? What other unimagined treats did life have in store for her?

Damn it, she told herself one night in her cold, barren apartment. I'm 28 years old and what have I done in real time, in my own clothes? There's a world to be experienced firsthand, not just acting lines written by someone else. And I've barely begun.

She turned off the air conditioner and opened the glass louvers so the warm, humid night air washed in over her. What was the point of living on a tropical island all these years if she breathed artificially conditioned air? The real air was like the vacation trips she took, journeys to exotic Asian capitals she had never expected to visit. But then she returned to Guam and to this artificial existence, living on a Navy base, working in a naval hospital, acting in a theatre group that was entirely made up of people from the States. What did her life have to do with the life of these islands?

She put a favorite record on the stereo and sat down to listen. Berlioz, *Symphonie Fantastique*. All about witches, unrequited love, and the gallows, or so the liner notes insisted. But she had a new idea as she lay back on the couch and found herself clutching a sofa pillow to her chest. This was a composition about sex. Someday she would put this record on and he would be here. She could almost feel the soft velvet of his close-cropped hair beneath her hands and she imagined the weight of that lean, sinewy body on top of hers.

She sat up straight on the couch. "Jodie," she told herself sternly. "He's a married man. What are you trying to do?"

The music swirled, swooped; the insistent throb that made up its spine seemed to catch her, pulled her back down on the couch, back into her fantasy.

"So what?" It was almost a sob. "Some things in life are bigger than…than staid conventions. Sometimes there is magic."

* * *

Then one night, perhaps three months after she'd first met Donnie MacDougal, she was at the Top o' the Mar, the officers' club on Nimitz Hill, dining with some people from the hospital. Because it was a couple of weeks before Christmas, the club was decked out in red and green tinsel garlands. Even after six years on this tropical island, that touch of half-remembered winters seemed incongruous. She was sitting there, wondering why red and green tinsel should

make her think of snow, anyway, when Donnie MacDougal walked in the door with a group of men, two of whom she recognized as civil service folks from the Navy base down by the harbor. He spotted her the moment he entered the dining room—his dark eyebrows leapt up in that peculiar Guamanian greeting he'd adopted. Her heart jumped convulsively and she lost her train of thought, right in the middle of a sentence she'd been delivering to the doctor's wife across the table. Is he alone? Where is Panda?

The woman she had been talking to looked back over her shoulder, trying to see what had caught Jodie's attention in mid-word. "I'm sorry," Jodie said. "I just saw someone—I was startled to see him here." Damn, she thought, I sound like one of those bigots who thinks brown people should all be waiters.

"From the look on your face, I thought Barry Edwards had landed back on the island," her companion said. "You turned absolutely white."

It took Jodie a few seconds to remember. Ah, yes, Barry—the Navy doctor I was so in love with. The guy who dumped me only a few months ago, before my fateful trip to Saipan.

The people at Jodie's table were finishing their desserts and after-dinner coffee when she felt the hand on her shoulder, heard the quiet voice say, "Dance?" Without a word, without a thought of introducing him to her friends or explaining, she rose in a sort of trance, took his arm, and followed him to the small dance floor. A three-man Filipino combo had just begun playing on the tiny platform that passed for a stage.

"I never thought of you as a dancer," she said as he took her in his arms. Oh no, she thought. I sound so inane. But what should I say? She worried that she was trembling.

He laughed. "I wouldn't call myself a dancer," he said, "but sometimes it comes in handy to know how to put your feet down to the music without tromping on a lady's toes. It's the one way I've figured out of giving pretty girls a hug without getting slapped." He pulled her a little closer. The combo was playing one of those

cheery Hawaiian numbers—"Tiny Bubbles" or "Pearly Shells," she could never tell them apart—that encouraged the dancers to bounce around brightly on the small polished floor. She tightened her grip on his right hand and he squeezed back.

"So—uh—what are you doing at the Top o' the Mar?" There I go again, she thought. I sound like I think he doesn't belong here.

"Oh, I took some Navy guys up to Tinian today—just a joy ride. So they invited me to dinner afterwards."

"Tinian? What do people go there for?"

"See the pits," he said. She stared up at him, not understanding the words, thinking how she loved that bony face, that dark throat. He still wore his pilot shirt but with a couple of extra buttons open revealing part of his brown, smooth chest.

"The A-bomb pits," he said. "Where they loaded the bombs they dropped on Hiroshima and Nagasaki. You know they took off from Tinian?"

"I guess I knew that. I forgot. I guess … maybe you're making me flustered."

He held her back at arm's length for a minute and laughed, a man without a care in the world, a man who loved to dance and fly. "That's bad news," he said. "I don't see how you could possibly learn something as technical as flying from a guy that flusters you."

"No, just … dancing with you flusters me."

He stared at her closely. "Wow," he said. "I hope I didn't get the signals wrong. I'd have bet money that you wanted to dance with me almost as much as you wanted to fly with me."

"Oh, I do," she said quickly.

His smile was satisfied, almost smug. "Okay. That's what I thought."

He pulled her close again as the musicians segued into a slower tune. She thought she recognized it—another song by Don Ho, that Hawaiian singer whose song Donnie had performed at the little bar in Saipan.

"Where's your wife?" The question had popped from her lips unbidden but, once out, it seemed the most important piece of intelligence to be gained at this moment.

"Hawaii. Had to go to a funeral for an uncle. She left four days ago."

"Oh." She tried not to wonder how he had spent four days and nights on his own. Were there other women he danced with other nights?

"She left four days ago," he repeated. "I know exactly because every night I tried for hours to get my courage up to call you and see … see if I could buy you a drink or something. And I couldn't do it. Four nights, wasted. They'll never come back, you know."

"Oh, they might," she said, a sense of limitless possibility burgeoning in her chest like the sunny space that swept her endlessly up when the plane she was flying burst through the cloud cover. "You never know. You might get those nights back some time."

His voice was low and serious. "I convinced myself I ain't cut out for this sort of shenanigans," he said, "but I walked in that door tonight and saw you sitting there and I said, 'MacDougal, that's a sign if I ever saw one.' And here we are."

"Yes. Here we are." She moved even closer and he tightened his arm around her back so she was pressed against him, could feel his heart pounding. And very quietly, his breath warm in her ear, his voice throaty, he began to sing along with the music.

For endless months and years I heard
Those dreamy tales of love
I never found that sweet someone
Who fit me like a glove.
Now here you are before me,
The story's coming true.
I'll spend one month of forevers
In paradise with you.

I could die happy right now, she sighed to herself.

When the song ended, he held the embrace for a moment at the dark, far corner of the dance floor. "You got your car?" he asked. "Or can I give you a ride home?"

"Yes," she said. Although it was so dark she couldn't see his face clearly, she sensed that he raised an eyebrow, a question. "You can give me a ride." She saw the people she'd come to the club with milling around by the cashier, looking towards the dance floor, wondering what they should do. She stepped away from Donnie, shook her head to clear it, asked him to wait a minute, and walked toward them. What do I say?

The woman she'd been talking to across the table met her halfway. "I take it you don't need a ride back?" If there was anything in her voice, Jodie decided, it was envy, not disapproval.

"No, you go ahead," Jodie said. "I'll be fine."

"I'm sure you will," the woman said as she turned to join her husband and the others.

Jodie returned to Donnie on the edge of the dance floor. "All set?" he asked. She nodded. "We'd better dance another one," he said. "Let them get started."

Moving back into his arms felt as natural and right as slipping into a warm bath. She no longer heard the music—it was a current, like the air beneath the wings of a plane. She let it lift her, moved with it, moved with him. And when it stopped he leaned over and spoke close to her ear.

"I know my line is supposed to be 'Your place or mine?' But it can't be mine. My kids are there."

"My place is fine," she said. "I've even got some beer."

"Let me say good-bye to my guys," he said. "And I'll have to make a phone call to my daughter."

"What will you tell her?"

He frowned thoughtfully. "I think I just got involved in an all-night poker game," he said. "I've got to get up to the airport early and meet Panda's flight, anyway. I just don't want the kids to worry."

Jodie took her time in the restroom, combing and fluffing her short hair, staring at her face in the mirror. She was glowing, positively glowing. She laughed out loud. She looked like the painting on the cover of some lurid paperback novel.

Donnie drove slowly down the winding road off Nimitz Hill. They followed a cool, fragrant valley for half a mile before turning up another hill toward Guam Naval Hospital. Jodie smelled the night-blooming flower she had never seen, but whose scent seemed to cascade into the island's low valleys at night. "What is that? I've never known what that wonderful perfume is."

"Ain't that something?" he said. "Guamanians call it ylang-ylang. To the Filipinos, it's *sampaguita*. At home we call it *pi-ka-ke*. It's got something to do with peacocks, but I never can remember what."

"I'd like to call it *pi-ka-ke*," she said.

He reached for her hand on the seat of the van and squeezed it. "You go right ahead," he said. "I'm making you an honorary Hawaiian tonight."

– 1983 –
Friday

LAURA DROVE THE RENTAL CAR through Agaña's Friday evening traffic, heading toward the Mexican restaurant in East Agaña.

"Where shall we meet?" Will had asked. "Kinney's or Joe and Flo's?" Somehow it was comforting to know that both restaurants still existed on this transformed island. She and Foster had gone to them often with Will and other friends back in the sixties.

"You decide," Will had insisted.

She considered the long drive through the boonies toward Kinney's, up near the Air Force base, where it thrived as an escape into village culture for military folks. Did she even know the way any more?

"Oh, let's do Joe and Flo's. It's been years since I've had a tamale wrapped in a banana leaf instead of a cornhusk. Teri likes Mexican food and we never get any in Tokyo."

"Your daughter? She'll come?"

What can I do? Laura had thought. We'll have to talk carefully, that's all. "This is her vacation too," she told Will.

"Hmmpph."

She'd promised herself to think of ways to discuss things with Will without alarming Teri. She needed to ask Will what he had done with that photo. Back then he had said he'd mailed it to the *Chronicle,* and they all believed they'd seen the result—nothing. But had he actually mailed it?

Then just before she had left the Hilton for the restaurant, her boss had called from Tokyo and thrown her into a new state of confu-

sion. "I assume you've been out on the story already," Jerry Bosley said. "That why you didn't call?"

"Story? What story?"

"Amelia Earhart. The photograph. This is big stuff. For Japan, for Americans …"

"The photograph was on the wire?" She wanted to protest. It wasn't meant to go out to the world. It was supposed to flush something out on Guam.

"It came over first thing this morning. I called earlier … didn't they give you the message?"

"No," she lied. "I was at the beach … I just got in. I'm sorry. See, I knew the guy that got murdered and I just didn't think beyond that. I mean, how weird it was that this old photograph … I can't imagine what he was doing with it …" Am I babbling?

"Well, hey, I'm sorry about your friend and all that. Maybe he was trying to sell the photo to someone? Asking too much for it? But then the murderer wouldn't have left it behind. Well, anyway, the murder's not the story. The photo is. Think of it! After all these years, knowing where she really ended up. The Japanese did have her, right? That's who was running Saipan then. It is Saipan, isn't it?"

"Well, it sure looks like Saipan to me," she said. She took a deep breath. She was a journalist. Her business was truth. That's what Jerry Bosley expected from her. "But have you considered … I mean, what if the photo isn't genuine?"

"Naw, it's real. I'm sure. That's her. You probably didn't know this about me but I've always been kind of an Amelia buff. I've read all the books about her. There's no mistaking that face. Those cheekbones."

"Maybe some kind of darkroom trick?" Laura said feebly. "Super-imposing a photo of Amelia over a background of Saipan?"

"Have you talked to the authorities there? Do they suspect it's a hoax?" Bosley sounded contentious. He wants to believe, she realized. Everyone wanted to believe. People want mysteries solved. Or at least they think they do.

"No, I haven't heard anyone question it," she said.

"Why don't you run up to Saipan and see what you can find?"

"I just came from Saipan two days ago." Her mind was flying through scenarios. If the photo does portend danger for Teri and me, we might be safer in Saipan. But will the Guam police let me leave?

"We'll pick up the tab, of course. Look, Laura, I know you're on vacation, but what a break! I mean, you know those islands, you used to live there. You must know all the people in charge. You can get a story no one else can touch."

"You're right. I could." She kept her voice flat so he wouldn't hear the irony.

"Get right on it," Bosley said. "Call me in the morning. Let me know what you've found."

"Yeah," she promised. "I will."

She drove through Agaña seeing her journalistic career crumble before her eyes. How could she, as an ethical reporter, write anything about a photo she knew to be a hoax? Especially since there were four other people in the world who also knew.

"The amazing thing about Laura," Foster used to say, "is she really believes journalism is a sacred calling. Not only does she believe in the existence of truth, she thinks she can ferret it out—and recognize it when she sees it."

She let an irritated sigh escape. "Yes?" Teri said.

Laura shook her head. "There shouldn't be traffic jams in Agaña."

"You call this a traffic jam?" Teri feigned astonishment, "Well, personally, I'm from Tokyo and I call this the open road."

"And another thing," Laura could still hear Foster's voice, continuing some long-ago conversation in the back of her mind, hear him summing up his wife as though he were a director explaining a role to an ingenue cast in the part of Laura Monroe, girl reporter. "The more she sees of the slimy underbelly of politics, the more she believes in the whole system. If A. J. Liebling hadn't put it into words first, I would have come up with it, just watching Laura: Democracy

is the theory that the people know what they want—and deserve to get it, good and hard."

"Mencken," Laura had protested.

Foster had raised a sarcastic eyebrow. Yes? Your point?

"It was H. L. Mencken who beat you to that."

"Well, pardon me, Miss Baedeker."

"Bartlett," she had said very softly. "Bartlett's the quotes guy." Perhaps that was when I decided I'd have to leave him. Or maybe Gordon was right. Perhaps knowing Lionel Keating, I focused on the islands first, because Lionel made a passionate concern for them seem so ... so noble, so complete. And Foster made caring strongly about anything seem silly.

She pulled up in front of a low, concrete block building. The names "Joe" and "Flo" flashed in orange neon swirls—the same sign she remembered from years gone by. She thought about the very different Laura who used to come to Joe and Flo's. She sighed loudly as she turned off the engine and set the brake.

"I thought you liked this place," Teri said. "I thought this guy Will was an old friend."

"It's great. He's great. I'm just trying to figure out how to do what Jerry wants me to do and not mess up our vacation."

"Yeah, well so far everything's gone pretty much according to plan, hasn't it? You wanted me to see the islands 'cuz they're so quiet and peaceful, right?"

Teri might be a smart aleck, but Laura was glad her kid had a sense of humor. She linked her arm through Teri's and they sauntered into the restaurant. Laura noted with approval the electronic game tables by the windows—a useful change from the old days. She could slip Teri some quarters and get plenty of time to talk privately with Will.

"Hafa adai," said a waitress in a bright, flowered dress. "You can sit anywhere you want." She waved her hand toward the almost empty room. Will was there already, at a table close to the bar.

Laura took a step toward him and froze, just for a moment. Quarters for Space Invaders might take care of Teri, but what do I do about the guy at the bar?

He had glanced her way when the waitress greeted them, then looked quickly back to his beer. But her glimpse of him had been enough. She'd seen that face the night before, remembered it because the young man was almost movie-star handsome, with high cheekbones and chiseled features unusual for a Guamanian. Last night he'd sat at a desk in the police station. Just outside 'Sús Pérez's office.

Well, now I know: There is a live tap on my phone.

She greeted Will, perhaps with too much long-time-no-see for someone she'd seen just yesterday. Teri was sure to comment on that when they were alone again, but she was more concerned about what the cop would think.

As they slid into chairs at Will's table, Laura glanced around the room and said, "This place hasn't changed a bit—well, except for the machines." When that sent Teri over to inspect the game tables, Laura leaned close to Will, her head turned so her face wasn't visible to the bar.

"The kid will drive me to the poorhouse with those games," she said clearly. Then, whispering, "The guy at the bar works for 'Sús Pérez."

Will glanced at the bar, nodded, and suddenly doubled over in an intense, quite believable coughing fit. "I've got to move, Maria," he told the waitress who arrived with his beer. "The smoke's getting to my sinuses."

"Will Hildebrandt, you smoke more than anyone I know," the waitress said.

"Not anymore. Trying to quit." Maybe it's true, Laura thought. She didn't see the inevitable pack-sized bulge in the pocket of his aloha shirt.

Will grabbed his beer and moved to a table directly under an air conditioner jutting out of a hole in the concrete block wall. The table placed them exactly midway between the bar at the back of the

room and the game tables at the front. "White noise," Will mouthed to Laura.

"Oh, this is just terrific," Teri said as she returned from the game tables and slid onto a chair. "I always wanted to catch pneumonia in the tropics."

Will made an obvious attempt at small talk with Teri. "So are you a tennis nut like your mother?"

"I play," Teri said, sounding very bored by the fact.

"I remember your mom was always running all over the island trying to find a court and someone to play with."

"Couldn't you get Daddy to play with you?" Teri asked.

"Hah." Her own bitterness surprised Laura. "Funny thing about Foster," she said. "He pretended he liked tennis when we were dating but later he made it obvious it was too much work. Actually, when we lived here, I used to play with a couple of Charlotte's daughters on the Navy courts up on Nimitz Hill. The Sabláns had a permanent guest pass."

"And well they might," Will said. "The Navy confiscated the entire base from that family."

"Lolita and I play sometimes when I'm in Hawaii," Teri said. "She says she likes having me there because I play tennis. Daddy doesn't even have a racquet any more."

It was a new glimpse of Teri's other life, when she was visiting her father. Laura imagined her playing a frenzied set with her young stepmother. "Is she any good?" she asked.

Teri shrugged. "She probably would be if she practiced more."

So Foster had dragged another woman away from her tennis aspirations. And then Laura wondered what she was dragging Teri away from by taking her to Asia, following her own journalism career.

The air conditioner was blasting gusts of icy air right on them. Laura tried to control her shivers. "Why don't you decide what you want, honey, and then I'll give you some money to play Invaders or whatever they have."

Teri sighed. "They're not *that* far behind here. It's Galaxians." As soon as she had made her menu choice, she moved over to a table by the window and was soon engrossed in the game.

"In Japan they eat right on the game tables while they're playing," Laura said.

"I'm sure that can be arranged here too," Will said, and when the food arrived he asked the waitress to serve Teri at the game table.

Other people had come in, filling the tables between them and the bar, so Laura and Will were able to dispense with the facade of small talk. But the cop at the bar seemed determined to keep them under visual surveillance, even if he couldn't hear what they were saying. He ate his combination plate with his head turned toward them.

"That damn photo got put on the wire," Will said, crunching into a taco, red oil dribbling over his stubby fingers.

"I know. My bureau chief saw it in Tokyo. He wants me to fly up to Saipan and check it out. I've got to figure out something to tell him."

"Apparently the *Chron* sent it out last night," Will said. "It made the late afternoon edition of the *Examiner* in 'Frisco."

Laura tried to maintain their old bantering rivalry, grasping for some sense of normalcy. "If you were half as worldly-wise as you'd like people to think you are, Mr. Hildebrandt, you'd know enough to say S.F. instead of 'Frisco."

Will mimicked her tone. "It made the *Examiner* in S F. How I know is, Shelby Verdun called just before I called you. He's taking the flight that gets in first thing in the morning."

"That's Verdun as in —"

"*On the Earhart Trail,*" Will said solemnly.

If Will Hildebrandt has a hero in his life, Laura thought, it has to be Shelby Verdun. Verdun was the investigative reporter who had written the first book proposing that Amelia Earhart had been held prisoner by the Japanese and had died on Saipan where he believed they brought her after picking her up in the Marshall Islands. Will

had accompanied Verdun on his trips to Saipan, photographed the exhumation of remains that turned out not to be those of a tall Caucasian woman. It had been his loyalty to Verdun that fed his frustration when the *Guam Chronicle* refused to publish stories about the book, and subsequently inspired their prank of sixteen years before.

"I see," Laura said. "So we're both about to betray the confidence of our patrons."

"Or of our co-conspirators," Will said grimly. They stared at each other for a long moment.

"No," Laura said. "Not me, at least. Hey, it's just a career. I can always go back to the typing pool. I'm very fast."

"Well, I don't intend to meet Shelby's plane and blurt out a confession. What I've got to do is think of an excuse for not going up to Saipan with him. I don't think I could handle that. I've got calls in to my dive guys to see if they've got a good story I absolutely need to photograph."

They asked for more beer and Laura sent an order of ice cream over to Teri who must have been doing very well at the game—her coins were lasting unusually long, and a couple of Guamanian teenagers had moved from their own table to stand behind her chair, watching her play.

"There's some really heavy stuff going on here," Will said. "Not just who bumped Hassler off and why, but how Hassler got hold of that photo."

"Or who planted it on his body."

Will stared at her. "I hadn't thought of that. If that were the deal then it might be ..."

"One of us? One of us wanting to frame another of us?"

Will shuddered. "Someone who hates Hassler and me? No way, I'm not ready for that idea. Let's go back a ways. Say Hassler had the photo on him when he was snuffed."

"They took everything else in the room. Everything. The photo was the only thing they missed. If they missed it."

"How do you know that?"

"Cops told me. 'Sús Pérez and Ben Guerrero. I was interrogated last night as the last person to see the victim alive. Gordon and I had breakfast together yesterday."

"*Lañá*!" Will swore. "You really are in the middle of this."

"Yeah. Shoulder and all. But I didn't pull the trigger."

"I thought it was a machete."

"I mean the camera trigger."

Will was silent for a moment. "Right," he said finally. "Okay, I get you. We two have the most to lose."

"Unless you want to count Jodie," Laura said. She was sliding back in time, to those days when she and Will had often ended up covering the same stories, when she had been the one to calm the waters he had troubled in a press conference, when she had inserted the cool voice of reason into his rantings over conspiracies and plots.

"Yeah, of course. Jodie. You know, even looking at it in the paper this morning, I didn't see Jodie. I saw Amelia Earhart."

"Me too," Laura said. "I never saw Jodie get into a part so well. She'd always been a very good actress, but that morning she was exceptional. So far, I haven't even been able to find out where she is. I know Foster and Donnie are in Hawaii."

"Okay, so they weren't here slicing up poor old Hassler. But what concerns me is how the photo got here. And I'm pretty sure I know who's involved." He paused dramatically. She gave him the raised eyebrow. "Who quashed the story on Verdun's book?"

"Rudy Terlaje?" She was a little surprised. Will and Rudy had appeared to be close friends just yesterday.

"No, Rudy was just a minion. Who was the *Chron*'s publisher at the time? And who was the first Guamanian governor of Guam?"

"John dela Cruz?"

"One and the same!" Will shouted in triumph.

Laura glanced at the young policeman at the bar. She was sure he had caught every word of that phrase, despite the chilly white noise that enveloped them. "Careful," she cautioned quietly.

Will's voice dropped to a hoarse rasp she had to strain to hear. "Think about it, Laura. How did John dela Cruz get to be governor? Who appointed him?"

"Eisenhower, I suppose. It was before I came out here."

"Right. Eisenhower. A Republican. And who else did Eisenhower appoint—say, as Ambassador to Italy?"

"Geez, I haven't the slightest … oh, wait. Clare Booth Luce?"

"Bingo. And how much do you know about her hubby, the ubiquitous Henry R., greatest press emperor since Citizen Hearst?"

"Well, quite a bit, actually. I wrote a paper about him and the *Time* and *Life* coverage of Asia in a class I took a few years ago."

"Well, there you are," Will said firmly.

"Wait a minute. Are you trying to say Henry R. Luce was involved in Amelia Earhart's disappearance, so somehow he got the *Guam Chronicle* not to cover the Verdun book?"

"No, not that. At least I don't think that's what it is. No, Henry R. Luce was obsessive on the subject of China. His folks were missionaries there, right? And he would back Chiang Kai Shek to the bitter end."

Laura nodded. "That's true."

"Okay, so what was going on up in Saipan? They were training people to invade the mainland, take it back from the Commies. I bet Henry R. Luce was in on the plan as some sort of consultant. Now the last thing Henry and the rest of the Republican anti-communists want is some investigative reporter digging around up in Saipan, finding out about the CIA operation up there. So he puts the arm on his colleague, the publisher here in Guam to keep a lid on Saipan stories, deflect attention from that particular island, so the CIA can do its thing in peace. John gets to be governor because of his cooperation." Apparently Laura's face betrayed her doubt. "Oh, c'mon, Laura, what kind of Guamanian calls himself John instead of Juan? I've never trusted that son-of-a-bitch dela Cruz."

Laura shook her head. "Oh, Will, I think you're making it too complicated. I mean, I can see that the CIA might try to get the *Chron*

to keep attention away from Saipan during those years. But Henry Luce? Isn't that taking things a little too far? I mean, did you ever go to a library and check back copies of *Time* and *Life*? Did they cover Verdun's book when it came out? I bet they did. And anyway, I think Henry Luce died just about the time we were taking that photo. That same year anyway."

Will sputtered into the dregs of his beer. "Laura, you always do that, douse the best stories with ice water."

"Well, have you checked *Time* for items about Verdun's book?"

"No," he said, only slightly chastened. "But I don't necessarily think he had to be pulling strings by then, in 1967. Just that he might have established the pattern, sucked dela Cruz into his orbit, so by that time it was a habit."

Laura was silent for a few moments. "It's not a bad theory, Will. Oh, I don't buy the Luce connection, but the idea that the *Chron* decided to be quiet about Saipan stories to protect the CIA operation … I can believe that. But what has it got to do with Gordon Hassler getting killed?"

Will shook his head. "I haven't figured that out. But I'm sure there's a CIA connection to this. And I don't want to be rude, or intrude or anything but … " he took a deep breath, glanced toward the bar and then at Teri who was still plugging away at the electronic game. She was gathering quite a crowd of onlookers.

Will cleared his throat, lowered his voice almost to a whisper. "What about Foster? Exactly who did he work for in Washington?"

Despite her own train of thought earlier that afternoon, after she'd talked to Foster, Laura felt protective. She tried to laugh, but it didn't come off convincingly. "As a matter of fact, he worked for Gordon Hassler."

"I know. And who did they both work for?"

"Will, you know. Office of Territories, Department of Interior."

"Or so they said. And what's Foster doing in Honolulu?"

"He's got some sort of consulting business. I don't know. It's got nothing to do with me anymore."

"Laura." His voice was stern, his wide eyes fixed on her face. "Are you absolutely certain that Foster Monroe doesn't have and has never had a connection with the CIA?"

Unbidden came the thought that she had forgotten to ask Teri whether it was true that Foster had a garage in Hawaii. Or is it just a word Andrea uses, instead of carport? And even if he does have a garage, that doesn't mean anything sinister. She sighed. "How the hell can you be absolutely sure about something like that? Did Marina Oswald know her husband was going to shoot Kennedy? I have no reason to believe that Foster was ever into anything like that. And I just can't see it."

"But he would go so far as to fake an interest in tennis when he was courting you," Will said.

"Touché," she said quietly, disturbed. Am I not looking at Foster clearly? But he is Teri's father, for heaven's sake.

"I'm just saying we have to think of every possibility. I'm absolutely certain I had nothing to do with that photo coming out in such a gory way, and I'm almost as sure about you. We've both got too much to lose. But how can we be sure about Foster? All the island politics, here and in Saipan—it was all just such a joke to him. He never seemed to take it seriously, like we did. Wouldn't you agree? Foster's island years were pretty much just fun and parties and laughing at the quaint customs of the natives?"

"Yeah, you could say that. So how do you reconcile that with him being a spook?"

"Well, what if the happy-go-lucky stuff was a facade? Part of his cover?"

The group around the electronic game table suddenly erupted into loud yelling. Laura's heart thrashed in her chest and she lurched toward the windows. Then she saw Teri standing up slowly, shaking both her hands rapidly as though to fling cramps out of her wrists and fingers. She met Laura's gaze.

"I did it, Mom, I did it! I went over twenty-thousand points. It's the best I've ever done." Her triumphant expression startled

Laura. She looked like Foster, taking a curtain call after a particularly dramatic performance.

"Her name goes up on the wall now," said one of the Guamanian boys. "Highest score anyone ever got in this place."

Another young man was carefully writing down Teri's name, checking the spelling, showing her the signboard where she would replace the current champion. Teri glowed with excitement and triumph. "Mom," she said, "they want my hometown? Where shall I say I'm from?"

Laura laughed, catching the spirit of Teri's moment of fame. "Tokyo, Japan, I guess," she said.

"Tokyo." One of Teri's fans nodded. "That explains it."

Laura looked at the cop at the bar and wondered whether he would report Teri's success at electronic games to his boss as possibly relevant. Suddenly the young man was on his feet, a happy grin spreading across his face as he looked toward the entrance door.

Laura caught her breath. But there was no sour police captain coming in. It was a woman, perhaps in her mid-30s, with a wondrously bushy mop of long black curls that swirled around her like a cape. She wore elaborate makeup and a short, skin-tight dress. She hurried over to the young cop who was beaming like a little boy receiving a personal visit from Santa Claus.

"You came," he said with such delight that Laura heard him across the room. The woman walked very close to him and put her brilliantly colored lips to his ear, whispering something that made him giggle. With one arm he pulled her up tight against him.

Will clenched Laura's arm. He was choking back laughter. "Do you know who that is?" he said hoarsely. "No, of course you wouldn't. 'Sús Pérez's long-suffering wife died a couple years ago and he shocked the whole island by doing something very impulsive. He married that flashy bit of trash about two weeks after the funeral. I could have told him the folly of marrying a Filipina bar girl but he never thought to ask." He chuckled as he reached for his wallet.

"You mean that kid is stepping out with—"

"His boss's wife." Will had difficulty keeping his voice and his pleasure in check.

"Well." Laura dragged money out of her own wallet, insisting that she pay two-thirds of the check. "So I guess the young officer won't be making any reports to Captain Pérez about this evening."

They watched the policeman extract his own wallet from a hip pocket, a maneuver that involved slipping his hand under the woman's hip which seemed glued to his. After he paid his bill, they went out the door, two bodies apparently determined to occupy the same space.

Will was still laughing. "People call *me* paranoid," he said. "You're as bad as I am."

Laura felt a little silly. "I guess I got carried away. I was sure they were tapping my phone."

"Who on the Guam police force would ever have the time to listen to phone taps in the remote event they knew how to set them up?"

When they left the restaurant, two Guamanian boys escorted Teri to the passenger side of the rental car and stood chatting with her. Laura said quietly to Will, "I can't really see Foster as a spook. But you know who did have a CIA connection?" She waited for him to pick up on the clue, but he seemed deliberately obtuse. "Donnie MacDougal," she said.

"No." Will shook his head, his face indignant.

"Will, he flew for Air America in Laos," she said, keeping her eyes on the three teenagers on the other side of the car.

"I know that. But Donnie isn't in on this. I know that man. Not a devious bone in his body."

Laura amended her earlier thought. If Will Hildebrandt has a greater hero than Shelby Verdun, it has to be Donnie MacDougal.

"No way," Will insisted. "Donnie's nowhere near this stew."

"Okay," she said, standing beside the door to her car, ready to get in. "Then what about Jodie? Maybe Air America hired her too."

"That's right, she is a pilot. Maybe she could have worked for them. Soon as I get Verdun off to Saipan tomorrow, I'll give you a call. We'll see what we can find out. What the hell ever became of Jodie deSpain?"

As she drove back toward Tamuning and the hotel, Laura was only half aware of Teri's excited chatter about her triumph at the electronic game, her delight in the astonishment her boyfriend Jonathan would feel when she wrote to tell him her score. "He's never gotten close to that," Teri said with satisfaction. But Laura's mind was fastened on a refrain, a refrain beat out to the tune of "The Rain in Spain."

What the hell ever became of Jodie?
Jodie deSpain. Jodie deSpain.
Oh, what the hell ever became of Jodie?

— 1944 —

THE NIGHT BEFORE THE LANDING, Gordon Hassler lay stone still in his bunk in the vast belly of the transport. All around him, above, below, other men slept fitfully, or perhaps like him, stared into the darkness, desperately holding on to what might be the last night of their lives. But, for himself, he no longer feared death.

For weeks he had been haunted by a wisp of an image from a past that sometimes seemed so distant it must belong to an ancestor rather than to him. It was a single, recurring apparition like a bell tolling forever on one note: that nightmare he'd had his first nights in New Guinea about being trapped in a tropical jungle, of the green creeping over him, devouring him.

More than once these past two years, as the war seesawed back and forth over tiny bits of land that floated near the equator, he felt death's icy breath on the back of his neck. He had felt it at Torakina nearly nine months ago, watched men die around him, wondered why he lived when others perished.

Then three nights ago, as the ship plowed through the waves—before he knew where they were going—he had an unusually vivid dream. He fell, mortally wounded, on a beach of blinding white crushed coral. His blood seeped slowly over the sand, dyeing it pink. A green vine grew rapidly across the beach, flowing almost like a thick liquid. It enveloped his corpse, hiding him for the rest of time. The islands, the tropics, had a revenge to extract.

But he had his own revenge to seek. For that reason, he had taken care to enlist in the Marines and get assigned to the Pacific theater. He had never considered trying for Europe, where he could

fight the blatant evil of Hitler and Mussolini. Yet, unlike many Pacific volunteers, his was no indignant reaction to Japanese perfidy at Pearl Harbor. He had no particular quarrel with the Japanese, felt no racist disgust with smaller people who didn't know their place in the world. It was a personal agenda that drew him back to the Pacific.

As he had waited endless months on Bougainville, listening to news of the war surging from island to island, he'd begun to feel that a force was gathering to draw him toward a special fate. What if he ended up landing on the very island where Amelia had perished? What if he found some small bit of her plane there, something only he could recognize?

What if he died there too? Wouldn't there be some sort of poetic justice in that?

Otherwise, it had all been so pointless. Although the search for Amelia had been touted as the largest in the history of the world, the U.S. Navy hadn't gotten into much of the Japanese mandate because the Japanese insisted on doing their own searching there. And even if Americans had gotten into the forbidden islands, what difference would it have made? So the Japanese were fortifying the islands, contrary to the provisions of the League of Nations mandate. So what? The United States didn't even belong to the League of Nations. What could it have done about Japanese scheming?

The delay of the United States' entry into the war accomplished one thing for him—it gave him time to earn a college degree. With what he had come to think of as his inheritance, he had enrolled at San Francisco State College and earned a degree in accounting. At the time, he thought that would be his ticket into all the government records he needed to see. He would go to work for the government, start clawing his way higher and higher through the bureaucracy until he was in a position to learn what he needed to know to finally put Amelia and Tex to rest.

Then, before he graduated, the U.S. was in the war. He had enlisted the day after commencement. Although the Marine recruiter assured him he could get a commission as an officer if he would go

to an officer training school, he was too eager to go overseas. He elected to begin climbing up the ranks from the bottom.

Even though not a soul in the audience had come to watch him, he had gone through the college commencement ceremony. Actually being there seemed an essential part of building a résumé for Gordon Hassler.

He had thought wistfully of his mother, of her plans for him to go to college back when his only dream had been to become a mechanic and earn money to start his own life. How she would have loved being at his commencement. But as far as his mother knew, he had gone to Australia in 1937 and disappeared. She had never received another communication from him.

He felt guilty about the money. He had really meant to share it with her but, before he could figure out how to go about it in a way that would protect her from knowing where it came from, he figured out what it would cost him to go to school and live while he got a degree. It was almost exactly as much money as he had left—and that seemed to be an omen of what he ought to do. Why had Tex had so much cash with him anyway? Perhaps he had meant to charter a plane, to join in the search for Amelia himself.

If he survived the war, he would get a good job—college degree, military service on his résumé—and then he would start sending money to his mother.

Just before evening mess tonight, their target was confirmed, although anyone with a strong sense of direction and an idea of their traveling speed could have made a good guess. The assault would begin at dawn tomorrow, July 21st. The objective: retake Guam, the American territory the Japanese had occupied the same day they attacked Pearl Harbor.

He contemplated the island's name with deep disappointment. Guam. It was too far north and west. She wouldn't have come near Guam. Oh, it was covered with green all right, but it had no place in his nightmare, he was sure.

No, Gordon Hassler was certain he had no rendezvous with destiny in Guam. He hit the beach the next morning minus that haze of terror that had clung to him nine months ago at Torakina.

Guam. Just one more hoop to jump through. It was not an island to die on.

— 1968 —
July

JODIE FOUND THE PARADE honoring the 24th anniversary of Guam's liberation from the Japanese to be much like the parade for the 23rd Liberation Day. And the 22nd. And the 21st. How long had she been on this rock, anyway?

She went to the parade with two women friends, nurses from the naval hospital, and they sat where they sat each year, on the pleasant, shady second-story balcony of the Agaña Ford dealership. The building faced Marine Drive, resolutely turning its broad concrete block back to Agaña Bay, sparkling in the brilliant sun. It was in East Agaña, just a few hundred yards from where the parade would disband, so the marchers and the floats were rather wilted by the time they passed, but the man who ran the Ford dealership was a founding father of the local Navy League group, and he offered this vantage point to hospital staff every year. No one in her right mind would turn down such a shady spot for the Liberation Day parade. Across the wide expanse of Marine Drive, people sat on the hoods and tops of parked cars, blankets protecting their legs and bottoms from frying on the hot metal, hands or hats shading their eyes. Jodie even spotted a couple of Guamanian boys perched precariously in the limbs of a typhoon-battered breadfruit tree between the highway and the gravel road that provided parking and access for the shops across the way.

Of course, no one forced me to come to the parade, Jodie reminded herself as she watched one more float trundle by with buck-toothed caricatures of Japanese threatening a huddled group of giggling Guamanian children. She had come to prove a point to herself,

if to no one else. She did exist in her own right—she was not merely a box on the Guam Naval Hospital organization chart who came to life only during those all too rare hours she spent with Donnie MacDougal.

When he'd called her last night, she had pictured him hunched over one of the pay phones in the new airport terminal. He was more tangible and real through his voice than anything in her suddenly sterile apartment, including her own body.

"Just thought I'd better warn you, Blondie," he'd said. "In case you're planning to go to the parade tomorrow."

"Warn me?"

"Maybe it wouldn't bother you, but just in case … "

"What is it, you big goof?" God, she wanted him, wanted him here in this concrete block, white-painted, too-cool cell she inhabited.

"Panda's got us in the parade."

"In the parade?" She heard her voice flatten as though a balloon had been punctured inside her chest. All it took were those two syllables: Panda.

"It's one of her promotion schemes," Donnie said. "She registered us—the van, the kids, and all. We'll be one of the business entries."

"What, no plane?" She wanted her voice to sound amused, light. Instead, it sounded sharp and bitchy.

Donnie laughed sheepishly. "Yeah, a toy plane. Not *the* plane. But I thought I should let you know. Ain't no big t'ing, but … "

"Yeah, thanks. It's sweet of you to worry about me."

And it was sweet, she insisted to herself when she hung up, her arms clenched to her chest, bereft, lonely, desperate. She wanted him, not just his voice, low and longing in her ear. Quickly, before she could change her mind, she dialed her friend Elise, confirming that she would meet her in the parking lot at ten in the morning, reminding her that they would have to take Elise's car if Sonia was also coming—Jodie's little Mazda coupe could carry only two.

Donnie MacDougal is too sweet to have an affair, she reflected. He doesn't want to hurt anybody. Not me. Not Panda. But someone was bound to get hurt when a force as fiery as what happened between them was unleashed.

It had been clear from the beginning that Donnie's wife was not going to relinquish her property rights without a fight. Francesca "Panda" MacDougal had always been Donnie's business manager and, when he finally looked into some of the details, he discovered that when he had bought the new plane two years earlier, Panda had registered separate interests in it for herself and for each of the two children. Telling Jodie about it, Donnie shook his head in rueful admiration. "Damn, Panda is some business manager. Until I met you, I never even thought of playing around, but she was prepared. She's probably ready for anything."

What it meant, he had explained, stretching his long legs out on Jodie's coffee table, holding up his bottle of San Miguel to let the lamplight shine through it, weaving the long brown fingers of his other hand through Jodie's fingers, what it meant was he was a minority stockholder in his own airline, and thus an employee of his wife and children.

Getting her pilot's wings, falling in love, those had been ridiculously easy. The rest had been very difficult. After all, Guam was a very small island, and Donnie MacDougal was a fairly well-known public figure.

There were only two places they could be alone together: in the cockpit of his small yellow plane when he had no passengers—and there they kept their attention on flying, which was pretty wonderful in itself; or in her apartment on the naval hospital grounds where they investigated other forms of flight. But opportunities to fly together were limited by the cost of fuel for the Beechcraft and trying to coordinate their off-duty hours. His coming to visit her at night entailed passing through a gate and registering his name, car license number, and destination with a young, bored Navy security guard.

Somehow realizing her marriage was in jeopardy, Panda had gone into frenzied promotional gear the moment she came home from that trip to Hawaii. She booked flights constantly and kept Donnie so busy ferrying paying customers to Saipan, Tinian, Rota, Ulithi, and Yap, he barely had time and energy left for rescue missions, let alone to give flying lessons. Not that he would turn down a medical emergency if an SOS came in—it was Donnie's style to act now and deal with the consequences later. But flying lessons, even for Jodie, were more deliberate decisions, allowing too much premeditation, and usually she lost out to Panda's industrious sales jobs, or to maintenance required by the plane, or to the vagaries of the weather.

In the end, Jodie had scraped money together from her salary, hired a young Navy pilot, and chartered the one other privately owned plane on the island so she could get her pilot's license. The single-engine Skyhawk used less fuel and, as Donnie had told her often enough, learning to fly in a twin-engine workhorse like his was more difficult than learning to fly had to be. She would earn her single-engine pilot's certificate first. Getting an add-on for multi-engine later would be a breeze—or so Donnie promised. It was good to know that she could get the wonderful exultation from flying even without Donnie's magnetic body beside her in the cockpit. But it was frustrating in the extreme to be kept away from him.

Panda MacDougal's resourcefulness knew no bounds. Jodie was convinced that Panda had scripted the lines uttered by the naval hospital commanding officer when he called her into his office one morning not too many weeks after that night at the Top o' the Mar.

"Miss deSpain," he had said stiffly, "I don't know of a delicate way to say this, but I'm instructing security not to admit any non-resident vehicles except ambulances after twenty-two-hundred hours, and to keep records of license numbers of any that leave the compound between then and oh-six-hundred hours. I would ask you to consider carefully whether any of your actions are reflecting badly upon the United States Navy or this hospital."

And it wasn't as if they could park in Donnie's van on some lonely road, not with the flamboyant Micronesia Pacific Airline logo emblazoned on its sides. Jodie's tiny Mazda coupe—which she drove with the seat pushed almost back into the engine, wouldn't allow midget contortionists much more than a chaste kiss. So they took to parking her car in the undergrowth of *tangan-tangan* beside the round-the-island road and creeping down to one small beach or another, stumbling over rocks in the dark, tripping on beach vines, flailing about until they could find space between outcroppings of rock to spread the straw mat on the crunchy bits of coral that had not quite been reduced to sand, to crawl beneath the flimsy madras plaid bedspread she had bought at the Hermanis' India Bazaar store in Agaña.

For those stolen minutes on the beach, the world became huge. All the stars in the universe were suddenly flung across the sky, and the moon was soft and always full—even though her head was under the madras spread, her body pinned securely under Donnie's. Sometimes she even thought she heard a few strains of Berlioz wafted on a sea breeze.

One night a few weeks before Liberation Day, they had sat on the beach, listening to the surf. Donnie's cigarette tip was the only thing visible in the soft black air of the cloudy night. Jodie's entire body still tingled. She felt she should be glowing like phosphorescent fungi on a jungle trail.

"Problem with Panda," Donnie said with a gentleness that made Jodie ache for his bewilderment at this tack his life had careened onto. "Her problem is she's Filipina and Catholic. Us Hawaiians are Protestant and allowed to have some thoughts of our own. But she really believes we'll both burn in hell if we divorce. She's not really mean. She's just got the bejeezus scared out of her."

"Well, she's creating a hell for me right here," Jodie said, a tear creeping down her cheek in the dark. She hoped he couldn't tell she was crying. One of the things he loved about her, he often said, was that she wasn't a clinging vine.

What had happened between them was too big to fight, they agreed on that. There was no going back—not since that first night they danced. They talked about leaving the island, starting a flying business somewhere else, Hawaii, perhaps, even Alaska. But where would they get the money to buy a plane?

Elise's elbow in her ribs brought Jodie back to the balcony of the Ford dealership in East Agaña. "Would you look at that!" Elise said as she stared at Jodie, perhaps waiting to gauge her reaction.

The brightly painted Pacific Micronesia Airlines van was passing below, the entire MacDougal family arrayed on its roof. Panda wore a flattering Filipino dress, the fitted kind they called *sampaguita.* She was leaning toward the cars parked across the street, waving like a prom queen. The two kids sat at the front of the van, riding backwards holding a banner between them that advised FOR YOUR NEXT FLIGHT, CALL US. WE KNOW THESE ISLANDS! With their free hands, they waved sheepishly at the spectators lined up along the street.

Donnie sat beside Panda. Her hand gripped his wrist, to steady herself? To demonstrate her possession? Donnie wore his pilot's hat and shirt, and looked as though he felt foolish, waving a toy airplane back and forth. Somehow he spotted Jodie on the balcony, she was sure of it. He made a sweeping motion with his arm and let go of the model plane. It swooped upward, caught a tiny whiff of a breeze and drifted neatly down onto the floor of the balcony near her feet.

"Well," Elise said, obviously impressed.

Jodie stared as Donnie extracted his arm from Panda's grasp, and clambered down off the slowly moving vehicle, stumbling just for a step or two as he touched the pavement. Then he was running toward the stairway at the side of the Ford building. Jodie scooped up the model plane and hurried to meet him at the top of the stairs.

"You dropped something," she said clearly, in case anyone was listening, in case anyone didn't already know about them.

He took the plane from her and pulled her down two steps so they were alone on the stairway, pressed up against the hot concrete block wall of the building.

"Perfect landing, huh?" His dark eyes sparkled.

He's like a little kid, she thought. He's just delighted with himself. "It was a great shot," she said.

"I'm a great pilot," he said. His face grew serious. "Blondie, I feel a poker game coming on."

"You mean you are allowed out on the night of the Liberation Day Ball?"

He waved his hand scornfully. "I told her it was the parade or the ball, I wouldn't do both. She's a businesswoman, she wanted to do the parade. So pick me up at the bowling alley, okay? Nine o'clock?"

He hurried down the stairs and ran after the van. She returned to her place with her friends, trying not to grin and glow like a silly school girl.

"Are you sure he's just your flying teacher?" Elise asked.

"Well, he's also a friend," Jodie said.

Their companion stared at them sternly over her dark glasses. "Elise," Sonia said, "obviously the guy's a married man."

* * *

They were too impatient that night to drive for miles to an obscure beach on the windward side of the island. "Too many drunks out on the round-the-island road," Donnie said. They left Jodie's little car at the far edge of the crushed coral parking area at Tumon Beach and crept back through the *tangan-tangan* to reach a little patch of grass set back from the main sweep of the beach.

They were in the midst of a particularly inspired act of love when they heard the muffled burp of a police siren that seemed almost on top of them. Brakes screeched—it sounded like more than one car—and then the red flash of the police car light swept overhead. Before they had time to do anything but freeze their own movement, a voice shouted a few syllables only to be drowned out by several blasts of gunfire. A cry of pain, almost a bark, ended as abruptly as the siren's sound had.

Donnie and Jodie clung together, the sweat on their bodies growing clammy in the slight breeze from the lagoon. Then they heard the popping-gravel sound of a car leaving the parking area at a high speed. While the red light continued to rotate, highlighting one pink palm tree after another, they scrambled into their clothing, debating what to do in quiet, frantic whispers. Was anyone still out there, ready to shoot again? Someone must be hurt. Could they help? They must try.

Donnie had flown thousands of miles to save accident victims and women locked in difficult births, but now he seemed paralyzed by his own guilt. Jodie's mind squirmed, focusing on the disgrace this might heap upon her and Donnie and the naval hospital.

As they moved slowly in the flickering, ruddy darkness toward the police car, they heard another siren, saw another police car speeding down the steep road from the cliffs, its rotating light entangling the beam from the first car.

The couple melted back into the thick growth of *tangan-tangan* and stayed so still they couldn't hear their own breathing. Clearly they heard the horrified voices of two police officers who discovered a fallen colleague and radioed for help even as they assured each other he was dead.

Like eavesdroppers from another plane of existence, Donnie and Jodie crouched in the underbrush for an hour as other policemen gathered, as searchlights stabbed the night, as an ambulance screamed down from the public hospital up on the cliff, as flashbulbs popped. They heard the license number of Jodie's Mazda dispatched via car radio to police headquarters.

They also learned from their awkward vantage point that the slain patrolman had radioed in the license number of the car he had pursued to the beach, a car apparently occupied by drunken teenagers, and they heard the shouts of vengeful triumph when the message came that the car had been found and its occupants arrested.

They stayed hidden after the police cars drove away until finally—when quiet had descended upon the beach and they could

hear the surf breaking on the reef beyond the shallow lagoon—they crept back toward Jodie's car, giving a wide berth to the place where the patrolman had died.

They were in the Mazda coupe, and Jodie had started the engine when the light came on atop the police car they hadn't seen waiting at the other end of the parking lot. They froze and waited, wordless, while the officer approached, gun drawn. Jodie rolled down her window and Donnie leaned across her to say in a voice almost normal, "Evenin', 'Sús. Do you know Miss deSpain?"

"MacDougal? What the hell are you doing here?"

"I'm sure you can figure it out, 'Sús," Donnie said. "This here's Sergeant Pérez," he told Jodie. "He's my *compadre*."

Unimpressed by Donnie's attempt to adopt him, the policeman shook his head in apparent amazement, squatting so he could look directly into the car, shining a flashlight on them with one hand, his gun held steady with the other. "Figure out what you're doing at a murder scene? I could make some interesting conjectures…"

"Now, 'Sús, we … uh … Miss deSpain and I just came down to the beach to … uh … find some privacy. We were a ways down the beach there—" he waved his long arm and his wrist crashed into the windshield. "Ouch!" he said.

Startled, the crouching cop lost his balance for a moment, grabbing at the door handle to regain it, causing the little car to rock. The thought came unbidden, inappropriate. Someday I am going to laugh at this scene. Jodie saw herself sitting in Foster and Laura Monroe's living room somewhere at some future time. She and Donnie would be there, safe together, reminiscing about old times, describing the humorless cop crouched beside her car, his pistol on her, Donnie trying to keep his long arms and legs inside the miniature vehicle, trying to figure out how to keep Panda the Filipina Valkyrie from finding out they had just been inadvertent witnesses to Guam's first cop killing.

Someday it's going to be funny, Jodie promised herself. A tear squeezed out of her eye.

– 1983 –
Saturday

INSIDE THE TIGHT SLEEPING BAG of her sunburned skin, Laura watched the dream. She seemed to be a spectator in a box seat at the San Francisco Opera House. She was watching a contemporary ballet performed by people she knew well: Jodie deSpain, Donnie MacDougal, Gordon Hassler—the Gordon she had known in the sixties, not the older man of their most recent encounter. And there was the hairy, hippie Will Hildebrandt of the late sixties and a trim, handsome Foster Monroe with a flirtatious twinkle in his eye, a carefree but somehow silent laugh issuing from his throat.

Completely detached from the watching Laura, a younger Laura moved gracefully on the stage, the island-dweller with long brown hair swirling about her shoulders and arms as she wove in and out of the dance pattern, a large sprig of dark pink flowers pinned behind one ear. The watching Laura squinted, sniffed. Yes, dancing Laura was wearing oleander flowers, beautiful, fragrant—poisonous. Even the smoke was poisonous if prunings of the oleander tree were burned.

It seemed to be an important clue. Why did Laura dance wearing poison flowers?

Another clue. A shadowy figure appeared dancing in the wings, barely emerging into the stage lights long enough to beckon to one of the other dancers at center stage. Whose attention was he trying to get? Will's? Gordon's? Or perhaps Laura's? The watching Laura peered harder. If she could only figure out who the shadow man was … if she could identify him, she might understand everything.

She leaned forward in her seat. Who was he? And what was that music they were dancing to?

She was straining her ears, trying to place the familiar melody, when the music abruptly changed to an insistent off-key note that shattered the dream image, sent its shards swirling into a funnel that drained away from her. As she tried to peer into the vortex, then grabbing for the shadow man, her hand encountered the brilling telephone.

"H'lo?"

"Laura?" It was Charlotte Sablán, her voice as bright and cheery as a new day. "I'm sorry—you sound sleepy. Is it too early?"

"I don't know." Laura fumbled to find her watch on the bedside table. Half-past midnight? That can't be right. She turned the watch around. Seven a.m. seemed more likely, given the daylight trying to squeeze through a narrow gap in the heavy draperies. In the next bed, Teri groaned slightly in her sleep.

"I waited until I thought you'd be up." Charlotte chattered on. "I'm sorry if I woke you. It's just that it hit me in the middle of the night, and I couldn't wait to call you. If you remind me what her name is, I'm sure I can fit it all together ..."

"Name? Whose name?"

"The woman in the photo. The Amelia Earhart look-alike. I know where I've seen her. I just can't remember her name."

Laura's heart thudded in alarm. She was suddenly wide awake, but she coated her voice with a slur of feigned sleepiness. "What are you talking about, Charlotte?"

"Your friend. Remember the woman who worked at the Navy hospital? The one that got caught making whoopee on the beach with Donnie MacDougal? Long before that happened, you and Foster brought her to our New Year's Eve party one year, remember? Tall, blonde, cheekbones. That's who the woman in the photograph looks like. But what's her name?"

Laura mumbled a yawn that became satisfyingly real. She remembered Charlotte bragging about her encyclopedic memory: As long as she could see something written, she liked to say, she would

never forget it. Faces blurred for her, she couldn't even hear music. But once she saw something spelled out it entered her mental computer forever.

"Gee, Charlotte, I can't think ..." Laura began, imagining Will in the corner of the room by the closet, brandishing something at her—could it be a machete?—the hairy, sixties Will. Oh, hell, she thought, it's too early to figure this out. I might need Charlotte's help. She'll know immediately anyway if I'm lying... "Oh! Jodie," she said. "We brought Jodie deSpain to your party one year."

Charlotte's voice was triumphant. "Jodie deSpain. Of course. It all comes back to me now. We had some correspondence later, after she and Donnie skedaddled off the island. She wrote to me, said she was doing some research, needed my help."

"Well, if anybody is doing research about the islands, I bet you're the first person they contact."

"Ah, but Jodie deSpain was doing research on ... " Charlotte paused dramatically.

Laura sat up straight in her bed. "What was she researching?"

Charlotte's voice sounded like a fanfare: "Amelia Earhart."

Laura sat still for a moment. If Jodie had been researching Amelia, could she somehow have gotten hold of the photograph? Didn't Will have a crush on her once? Would he have given her the photo, despite what he said last night? She shook her head. So much to do. So much to figure out. "Listen, Charlotte, I'd like to talk to you about this. Could we do lunch?"

"Do lunch?" Charlotte sounded amused. "I thought people only said that in the movies. Well, why don't you and Teri come up here, and we'll 'do' lunch here. I know Vicente will want to see you and meet Teri."

"Don't you have to go to work?" Laura found herself clinging to an image of Charlotte and her library of books and correspondence at the University of Guam. Somehow Charlotte should be able to find the missing pieces that would put everything into a logical order.

"Not on Saturday," Charlotte laughed. "Come about eleven-thirty. We'll have a nice drink before lunch."

* * *

Laura managed to get Teri up, dressed, and down to the patio restaurant by eight-thirty despite Teri's insistence that breakfast in bed was the ideal way to celebrate a vacation.

Quickly Laura scanned the very slim Saturday edition of the tabloid-size *Guam Chronicle*. Not a word about the murder investigation. Did that portend laziness on the part of *Chronicle* reporters? Or was 'Sús Pérez limiting coverage for reasons of his own?

She stared absently toward Two Lovers' Point, still debating whether she should satisfy her bureau chief's request and fly up to Saipan or if she should try to convince him there was no story. It wouldn't help to tell him she had reason to believe the photo of Amelia Earhart was a hoax. Then he would want her to expose the hoax. But if she went to Saipan, sent him any kind of story, could she ever look Jerry Bosley in the eye again? He trusted her to use her island contacts to get to the truth, not cover it up.

Teri extracted the page of comics and features from the newspaper and began on the small crossword puzzle while Laura continued to stare vacantly, barely aware of the idyllic view of beach, lagoon, palm trees, and stark cliff.

"*Hafa adai*!"

Laura turned to find Will Hildebrandt standing beside their breakfast table with a thin, balding, lugubrious-looking man beside him. "Here's the lady I was telling you about," Will told his companion. "Laura Monroe, Associated Press, meet Shelby Verdun, investigative reporter par excellence."

Perhaps it was weariness after the long flight from San Francisco that gave Verdun such a sour expression. He had a small, bristly, gray mustache and hadn't shaved recently. She thrust out her hand.

"Hello! I've heard about you from Will. I think you're one of his all-time heroes." She found herself staring. Is this the shadow man from my dream dance? Does Shelby Verdun hold the key?

Ignoring her hand, Verdun pulled out the vacant chair at their table and slid into it without a word. Will dragged over a chair from another table and plopped into it, effectively blocking the service staff's route across the patio toward the indoor dining room and the kitchen beyond. He sat oblivious as two waitresses shoved a neighboring table out of the way to clear a new path.

"I just caught a glimpse of you as we were leaving," he said. He seemed to notice Teri for the first time. "So how's the Galaxians champ this morning?" Teri shrugged and continued with her puzzle.

"I'm sorry," Laura said, apologizing to Teri more than to Shelby Verdun. "This is my daughter Teri." The two gave each other quick, silent nods. "Did you have a good flight?"

Verdun was abrupt and to the point. "Listen, Will says you might be interested in flying up to Saipan on this story. We talked to a pilot at the airport, and he can make a run later today. You want to share charter expenses?"

That voice. Of course. "You know, I grew up in San Francisco. I'm sure I used to hear you on the radio," she said.

"Most people did," he said.

Good God, she thought, maybe I even heard some of his reports about his Amelia research before I was married and came out here.

"So what do you say? Want to make the trip to Saipan?"

"Well, uh—I have an appointment at noon," Laura said, still trying to decide if she really had to make the journey.

"S'okay. I won't take off until about three. That would still give us a couple of hours of daylight after we get there. We'll be back here in time for dinner. All I want to do is take another look at that Jap hospital. I don't need to do any interviews. I talked to everyone 'til we were all blue in the face twenty years ago. Anything they remember at this point is going to be something they just made up to get their mugs in the newspapers."

Laura found herself put off by Verdun's cynicism, although he was right in this particular instance: nobody living in Saipan today would have any valid information about the photograph that had just appeared in newspapers all around the world. But was his closed mind the proper tool for a reporter?

"Are you covering the story for anybody?"

"No, I'm retired from the daily grind," he said. "But I'm always open to subjects for a new book. An update on the Amelia story would be pretty fast to write ... with a guaranteed market. But I'm sure there's something fishy about that photograph."

"Shelby's convinced the hospital in the photo looks older than it should if the photo was taken during Japanese times." As Will spoke, Laura tried to assess how well he was holding up. He seemed remarkably calm, all things considered.

"Yeah," Verdun said. "The oldest that building could have been in 1937 was about twenty years. More likely ten. After all, the Japs only took over the islands in 1914. When the Brits declared war on Germany, the Japs used their so-called alliance with the Brits as an excuse to glom onto all the German possessions in the Pacific." He seemed to address this capsule history lesson to Teri, who smiled politely and returned to her crossword puzzle.

"In the photo, as published in the *San Francisco Chronicle*, the building looks a lot older than ten or twenty years," Verdun said. "Although those black blotches obscure part of it."

"Red," Laura said, stubborn on this one point. "The blotches are actually red. Gordon Hassler's blood."

"Oh, I suppose so. I'm hoping the cops will show me the actual photo, let me have a closer look at that building."

"Buildings do age rapidly in this climate," Laura said.

"Will said the same thing," Verdun said, stroking his mustache. "I know, when you live out here you get that impression. Mildew grows on leather shoes overnight. But there's bound to be a difference between a ten-year-old building and one that's over fifty years old and has been abandoned for many years."

"So you think the photo is … a recent fake?" Laura wondered if she sounded hopeful. If the fake is thought to be recent enough, that would let me off the hook.

"That's why I want to take a look at the hospital today. I remember what the jail looked like in the sixties—I spent quite a bit of time there because we thought Amelia had been held there. I was trying to pick up her vibes, I guess."

Shelby Verdun didn't seem like the sort of person who would acknowledge the existence of "vibes," but then, he *was* from San Francisco. She wished suddenly that she had a copy of his book. Maybe Charlotte had one she could borrow.

"Even though the Saipanese story was that she died of dysentery, I didn't really focus much on the hospital," Verdun continued. "Wish I had. It's possible they might have taken her there when she got sick. But then who took the picture?"

"Some Japanese?" Will offered.

"But how did it get to Guam in 1983?" Verdun said.

"Maybe the guy who took it came to Guam as a tourist?" Will said. "Brought some snapshots with him to show the island folks. Elderly Japanese show up from time to time, looking for islanders they knew in the old days. The Guamanians and Saipanese stopped hating the Japanese as soon as they realized how much money Japanese tourists had to spend."

"So this Japanese brings the photo down to Guam and, for some reason, he gives it to Gordon Hassler," Laura said, trying to help the alternate explanation along.

"That guy he was with that night sure wasn't Japanese," Teri said. She looked up from her puzzle. "Mom, what's an eight-letter word for 'Benedict Arnold's act'? Treason only has seven."

"Betrayal," Laura said sharply. Thanks a lot kid, she thought.

"You knew this guy Hassler?" Verdun said to Teri.

"Friend of my mom's," Teri said. "Apparently I knew him when I was a little kid, but I only remember the other night. And the next afternoon." She shuddered dramatically.

"We saw them moving Gordon's body into the ambulance," Laura explained. "We had seen him the night before, over there in the dining room. Then I had breakfast with him the next morning, which the hotel staff reported to the cops, so I had to go in for questioning as the last person to see him alive."

"The last person *known* to see him alive," Will said.

Verdun waved impatiently at Will. "So who did you see him with that night?" he asked Teri.

"I have no idea. Just a big man with a sunburned face. He definitely wasn't Japanese."

"She lives in Tokyo," Will told Verdun. "She probably knows Japanese when she sees them." Teri rolled her eyes, her face a mask of disgust for the entire race of adults.

"Well, you may be able to fill in some blanks in this story," Verdun said to Laura, "since you knew the murder victim. What do you say? Will AP split the charter costs on the plane?"

It seemed the easiest way to satisfy Bosley's request that she get on the story. Maybe she could quote Verdun on the dubiousness of the photo to discourage her boss from further pursuit of the story. She had to do something. And perhaps she could help ensure that Verdun didn't figure out precisely when the photo had been taken. "I'm sure they will. How big's the plane? I'd like to bring Teri along. We're supposed to be having a vacation." Teri was rolling her eyes once again, but Laura couldn't leave her here playing Galaxians on an island where a madman was running amok with a machete.

"Yeah, there's room. Will isn't able to come," Verdun said, curling his upper lip so his mustache brushed his long nose. Will shrugged helplessly as Verdun continued, "which means I'll have to take the photos myself. Unless you ... ? "

"Well, I used to do a lot of photography when I lived here," she said. "But I'm rusty and I don't have a decent camera with me."

"I'll loan you one of mine," Will said, suddenly coming alive. "I'm taking my underwater gear on the dive assignment, but I can let you use my old Pentax. Isn't that what you always used?"

Laura agreed to meet Verdun at the airport at a quarter to three. Will gave her explicit instructions for finding the charter pilot. He promised to return to the hotel shortly with his extra camera. The two men left, saying they were heading for the police headquarters in Agaña.

As she sat sipping another cup of coffee, Laura had a delayed reaction. The police. Was Charlotte likely to call 'Sús Pérez and confide her theory on the identity of the woman in the photo? Surely not. Still, what suited Charlotte so perfectly for her job organizing the Western Pacific Research Center was not just her hunger to collect everything ever written about the islands. She loved to share information with anyone who expressed interest in it. If Jodie deSpain had written asking Charlotte for information about Amelia Earhart, she probably received bales of material in the next mail.

Charlotte hadn't said anything this morning about getting to see the photo. If she had asked 'Sús Pérez to let her see it to determine whether it was old enough to be of Amelia Earhart, would he have shown it to her? If he hadn't, perhaps she would be annoyed enough with him not to share her latest insight.

At least she could begin with Charlotte in her quest to track down Jodie. How long since Charlotte had last heard from her? She hadn't said when their correspondence had occurred.

Was Jodie really the key? What about the shadow man in her dream? It hadn't been Gordon, Donnie, Will or Foster. Who else could be involved?

— *1950* —

GORDON HASSLER DIDN'T DO CARD TRICKS. In fact, he didn't even play cards. It wasn't a religious thing, nothing like that. He just said he found games a waste of time when there was so much else to do. It was really his only bad point, Edwina Thompson thought. She loved playing bridge more than almost anything, and it would have been wonderful to have another skillful partner. At the end, bridge had been the only thing right about Kenneth, her ex-husband.

As far as she could see, Gordon really didn't do anything with the time he was careful not to squander on cards—except work. Washington, D.C., was full of ambitious young men working long hours in the rabbit warrens of the bureaucracy, but Gordon was a regular working fool, hauling fat files home from the office most nights, poring over them, taking notes.

Another interesting thing: Gordon Hassler didn't know one end of an engine from another. It struck her as odd, in a way. Kenneth had had absolutely no mechanical aptitude, but he was interested in machines. He was always trying to fix his car—usually doing it some sort of damage in the process. But Gordon was content to hire mechanics to do everything, never asked any questions about what they did, and paid them with an innocent faith that they had fixed what was wrong and had charged him fairly.

And one other thing: Gordon Hassler could never be accused of being queer. Gordon Hassler was very fond of women. Overly fond, some of her friends thought. Some even called him a womanizer. But from Edwina's point of view, that was one of his virtues. She had married her high school sweetheart at eighteen—and had been dis-

carded years later when he decided that female flesh disgusted him. That leaves a mark on a woman. She liked knowing that Gordon was attracted to her because she was female. The fact that he singled her out to spend more time with than the younger women he flirted with was flattering, reassuring somehow. Even though she was a few years older than he, she hadn't lost everything, hadn't wasted all her hopes for happiness on her fifteen years with Kenneth.

*   *   *

To his great pleasure, Gordon Hassler found women to be an easily acquired habit. Whatever else it had done to him, the past thirteen years had cured him of the debilitating shyness that had paralyzed Garrett Howland around girls. For Gordon, flirting with women was very pleasant. The only problem was, each conquest took a lot of time. And while the courtship phase was exhilarating, the breaking-off-connection part was depressing. It seemed to take him back across the years into the core of his guilt—his complicity in the destruction of the most beautiful woman he had ever seen—his direct responsibility for Tex Arnold's death—his disappearance from his mother's life. Not that he—or that poor kid Garrett Howland—had had any choice in any of those matters. And he had done his best to redeem himself. For several years now, he had been sending money to his mother in a way he had figured out so she would never know he was still alive. But in his heart he knew the money didn't make up for her loss.

He fingered the silky-smooth gold watch in his pocket. He wished he had sent the watch to her when he'd first made contact. It belonged to her—the one link with her lost husband and son. But he hadn't sent it. He wasn't even sure he could part with it.

Edwina reminded him a bit of his mother. She must be now about the age his mother had been when he was born. But Edwina couldn't have children. That was one of the things Gordon found appealing about her. He knew he couldn't muster the concentration

to be a father, to be the father he himself had never had. He needed to save his attention for the central project in his life.

But a wife—if she were a mature, self-sufficient woman—wouldn't dissipate his concentration too much. And if a man were married, it might solve several problems. For one thing, a married man was assumed by society to be heterosexual—although Edwina herself might argue the point based on her own sad experience. A married man could still have the fun of flirting now and then—if he chose a wife who was patient and grateful. But he wouldn't have to follow through, and the breaking-off should be much simpler. Even the most naive young clerk or secretary wouldn't expect much from a married man.

And anyway, he had to cut down on the flirting, spend more time on his special research. He seemed to be making progress after all these years. Getting hired by the auditor's bureau in the State Department had been a lucky break. Although he had been there less than a year, already he had managed to track down a number of references to the Earhart flight. Her ambitious plan to fly around the world had involved negotiating for landing rights and support in a large number of colonies and nations around the globe.

He made his decision. He would be thirty-one in a few weeks. It was time to make his résumé even more solid. He would ask her tonight.

"Edwina, I want you to share my life, my future." Yes, that was it.

His future. But never his past. She didn't need to know a thing about that.

— 1983 —
Saturday

Laura and Teri pulled up in the driveway of the Sabláns' hilltop home at precisely eleven-thirty. Charlotte leaned out of an upstairs window. "Come on up," she shouted. "The door's open."

They entered the house and climbed a wide stairway. Laura named the Sabláns' numerous offspring whose large colored photographs lined the stairwell. "You recognize them all?" Teri whispered.

"Actually, I'm faking it," Laura said.

At the top of the stairs, Charlotte's husband Vicente waited. He grasped both Laura's hands and stared into her face. "So, Laling, you have come back to us at last. Welcome home!"

Vicente looked much grayer than Laura remembered but he seemed as spry and animated as ever. He dropped Laura's hands and turned to Teri. "And this must be the famous Teresita Monroe," he said. "Welcome to our eagle's nest."

Teri was already taking in the view. On both sides of the living room, huge windows overlooked what seemed to be the entire island. "Come see." Vicente took her hand. "I'll give you the bird's eye KGB tour of the U.S. Navy and its secret harbor. Then we'll get out the telescope and see if we can find your hotel."

They moved to the windows on the south wall of the room, and Laura stood beside them, admiring the sweeping scene. Beyond the wide, manicured lawn, the grassy, knobbly hills of the island's central spine marched southward. To the west, a dark growth of trees on the island's coastal plain connected the hills to the vast, turquoise-tinted bowl of Apra Harbor, peppered with ships and rimmed by warehouses and trim white military buildings.

Laura heard the slow shuffle of zoris on the polished terrazzo and turned to see Carmelita, the ancient Filipina maid, beckoning to Charlotte. "Ah, yes, Carmelita. We'll have our cocktails now. Gin and tonic, Laura?"

Laura started to protest that she never drank hard liquor anymore, but the scent of plumeria wafting across the terrace seduced her, reminding her of all the times she had drunk gin with the Sabláns. "Only one," she stipulated. "I've got to be at the airport before three."

Charlotte hurried after Carmelita into the kitchen and returned with three gin drinks and a cola for Teri.

"So Carmelita is still with you?" Laura reflected that the Filipina must be well past eighty. She had been the nanny for Vicente and his brothers and sisters when they were children.

"We're her only family now, after all these years, Charlotte said. "We try to get her to take it easy, but she keeps taking care of us."

Lunch was a feast of Guamanian and Filipino delicacies. "I knew you wouldn't get to try some of this at the hotel," Charlotte told Teri, introducing her to the various dishes. "And this is your mother's favorite."

Laura examined the salad. "Heart of palm. Charlotte, you haven't murdered a coconut tree on my account?"

"No, actually, Vicente had a big Rotary Club do—I just saved the choice end of the heart for us."

Working her way through the spicy food—redolent of her days of youth and adventure—Laura reminded herself that eating was not really why she was here, that she had wanted to pump Charlotte's memory about Jodie. But how to begin with Teri and Vicente here?

"Who's flying in this afternoon?" Charlotte asked.

"Oh, we have to fly up to Saipan. My bureau chief wants me to check out the hospital and that photo."

"Ah, yes, the photo."

Somehow Charlotte seemed to have passed Vicente his cue. "Tell you what, young lady," he said to Teri. "Let's go out in the

kitchen and see about dessert. I bet you can put together a mean Dagwood sundae."

Grinning, Teri followed him out of the room.

"So," Charlotte said. "you're off to Saipan on the trail of that photo. What do you think of my theory about your friend Jodie?"

"Well, I looked at the picture in the newspaper again and you're right—it does look a little like Jodie. But it looks more like Amelia Earhart. Do you think since you knew Jodie was researching Amelia Earhart, that may have caused you to see a resemblance?"

Charlotte shrugged. "I suppose it might have."

"Did the police let you see the original photo?"

"That officious bastard 'Sús Pérez. He said he didn't need any help deciding how old a piece of evidence was. I'm quite sure it hadn't even occurred to him to check on the age of the photo until I mentioned it."

Laura was reassured. Charlotte surely would not confide her insight about Jodie deSpain to an officious bastard.

Vicente appeared in the kitchen doorway. "Laling," he said sternly, "your daughter tells me you don't eat ice cream."

"Sorry," Laura said. "I'd drink some coffee if you have some."

Charlotte nodded brightly. "Just coffee for me too, Ben."

Vicente went back into the kitchen, muttering to Teri, "I had no idea those women were so un-American."

"So you and Teri are going up to Saipan by yourselves?"

"No, actually, Shelby Verdun came in this morning from San Francisco, and he's chartered the plane—just for a quick trip. He thinks the hospital looks too old to have been photographed in 1937—wants to take a look at it today. So I'm sharing expenses with him—at least I can write a story about him revisiting the scene of his earlier investigations."

"Yes, his book was the first to propose that Amelia might have made it to the Marianas," Charlotte said.

"Which reminds me—do you have a copy of his book here? I'd really like to refresh my memory about some points."

"Yes, of course. I may even have an extra copy." Charlotte stood and slip-slapped down the long hall toward her home library. Laura followed. The room was crammed with books. Piles atop low shelves under the windows threatened to entirely obscure the view of the terrace and the island beyond. Charlotte walked directly to a shelf and removed a book without hesitating. "Yes. Two copies here. That's in addition to the copies out at the Center at the university. I don't know where they all come from. Even after all these years, my old college friends send me treasures they discover in used-book stores. They can't imagine that I might already have the book or that Guam has a bookstore."

Laura riffled through the volume, looking for the photo pages. She paused at a photo of the author leaning on a shovel in the old Chamorro graveyard where they had exhumed remains that did not turn out to be those of Amelia Earhart. Yes, that was what Shelby Verdun would have looked like twenty years ago. She flipped back to a close-up portrait of Amelia Earhart wearing a plaid shirt. "I don't know, Charlotte," she said, feeling like a manipulative sneak. "That sure looks like the woman in yesterday's newspaper."

Charlotte looked over her shoulder. "Hmmm. It also looks a lot like Jodie deSpain. At least as I remember her."

Rubber zoris slapping down the long hall announced Vicente's arrival with a carafe of coffee and two mugs. "Yup," he said over his shoulder to Teri, silent-footed in her tennis shoes. "As I suspected, they are in the library."

Teri carried a small platter of deep-fried turnovers that set Laura's mouth watering despite the large lunch she had just consumed.

"Carmelita must have made empañadas this morning," Vicente said. "Tried to hide them from me but no morsel of food can go undetected in the same house as Vicente the Great. I remember now that you never eat sweets, Laling, only savories."

Laura sank her teeth into the fried cornmeal crust and spicy pumpkin filling squirted into her mouth. "Mmm! It's been at least a hundred years since I've had an empañada!" Teri watched her mother with a slightly disgusted grimace.

"Come along, Tering," Vicente said. "Now we'll do the Dagwood sundaes."

When they had gone, Laura said, "You heard from Jodie recently? I haven't heard a word for—oh, more than ten years. I'd love to know where she is, what she's up to."

"Well, not recently. It was a couple years ago." Charlotte settled into a comfortable easy chair and poured the coffee. Laura slid into the other chair and took the offered mug. "I'm trying to think when I last heard from her. We exchanged several letters and then after a while I didn't hear from her again. I'll have to check—it will all be in my files out at the university."

"Do you think I could see her letters?" Laura asked. "Given your theory about the photograph, and my bureau chief's interest in this story …"

"Of course," Charlotte said. "We could go out to the campus now. Oh, that's right. You're going to Saipan." She pulled up a watch that hung from an elaborate brooch on her bosom and squinted at the tiny face. "What time are you due at the airport?"

"Two forty-five. How long will it take me from here?"

Charlotte shrugged. "Vicente says it's only twenty minutes but he drives like that proverbial bat. I always give myself forty-five minutes."

Laura glanced at her own watch. I'll leave here at two, she decided, and settled back to thumb through the Verdun book.

Vicente and Teri reappeared in the doorway. "Listen, Laling," he said, "does Teri have to go to Saipan with you? She just discovered my stash of rolls for the player piano."

"What a good idea," Charlotte said. "Why don't you let her stay with us? She's already seen Saipan."

"Couldn't I stay here, Mom?" Teri said.

Laura tried to think carefully. The hazards she imagined seemed far away, centered at the Guam Hilton if anywhere. Charlotte's passionate curiosity and love for sharing tidbits of information seemed entirely benign in the warm flood of her hospitality. "Well, if the Sabláns are sure you won't be in the way …"

Teri was visibly relieved. "Thanks, Mom," she said. "I'm not too crazy about getting on some little, bitty plane."

Vicente shuddered. "No one is ever getting me on anything smaller than a Jumbo Jet," he said. "As far as I'm concerned, the closest islands to Guam are Hawaii and the Philippines—where the big jets go. Okay, now for the old-time piano concert." The two hurried down the hall again like a pair of kids just let out for recess.

"Gosh, that's great of him," Laura said.

Charlotte waved her hand in dismissal. "He's thrilled. He hasn't got enough to do since he retired, and keeps complaining about our kids taking the grandchildren off-island to live. Teri is a gift from the gods."

Charlotte promised to meet Laura at the university Monday and share her file on Jodie deSpain. She also suggested that Laura retrieve Teri by meeting them for dinner at Kinney's Restaurant when she came back from Saipan.

At two, Laura gave Charlotte a hug and left, clutching the Verdun book to her chest like a shield. Vicente and Teri barely looked up when she shouted her farewell. They were sitting side by side on the wide wooden piano bench with Teri's feet frantically pumping up and down and Vicente swaying in time, his crackly voice singing as the piano keys danced magically, untouched, and "Darktown Strutter's Ball" tinkled forth.

The song remained with her down the narrow gravel road to the wide, palm-lined boulevard through the naval base, past the big white building that was headquarters for the Commander of Naval Forces Marianas, and down off the airy heights of Nimitz Hill. As she turned onto the road that led toward Guam Naval Hospital, she tried to force a musical segue, tried to recapture the feel of her early

morning dream. What was the music those apparitions had danced to? It had seemed so right to her in context, but later she could remember only that it was very odd music to accompany a ballet. If I could only recapture that dream and figure out who that man in the shadows was, she mused.

* * *

Laura was early when she pulled into the airport parking lot. She stuffed the Verdun book into her bulky shoulder bag and slung Will's old camera bag over her other shoulder. In one corner of the terminal she found a young man wearing a pilot's hat, with wings pinned on his crisp white shirt.

"Are you the charter pilot?" she asked.

"Are you part of my Saipan party?" He was handsome in a slim, angular way and there was something almost familiar about his hawk-like features. "I expect Mister ... what's his name?" He glanced at a scrap of paper in the palm of his hand. "Mr. Verdun. He will be here any minute."

There is even something familiar about his voice, Laura thought. "Excuse me," she said, "you're not ..."

"No, you're right. Mr. Verdun made the deal with my boss. But then he looked at his hours for this month and decided he'd better let me fly this one. I'm Jeff MacDougal."

"MacDougal. You're Donnie's boy. I just saw your sister the other day."

The young pilot grinned broadly. "You know my dad?"

"Took some of the best flights of my life with him," she said.

"In Hawaii?"

"No. Here in the Marianas. I used to live out here — when you were a little kid. I'm Laura Monroe. I worked for the newspapers out here for a while, and then we lived in Saipan."

"Well, nice to meet you," he said.

"So is this the same flying business your dad started?"

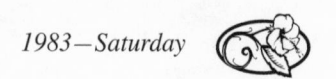

"Well, not quite. See, when he left the island, my mom still owned the plane but she had to hire somebody to fly it for her, right?"

Laura saw Donnie's zest for life and people in his son's unassuming candor. She had presented herself as an old friend of the family and he had accepted her, no questions asked. "So then she kept giving the guy more shares in the business when she couldn't pay all his salary, and the first thing she knows, he's got a half interest, which he sells to this other guy—my boss, now—and my mom really couldn't get along with him, so he bought her out and she started her travel agency."

Laura nodded. "I've seen her ads. Panda's Pacific Adventures, isn't it?"

Jeff smiled. "Something like that."

"So where did you learn to fly?"

"It was my high school graduation present. I hadn't seen my dad for about seven or eight years, right? So my mom gave me a ticket to go see him in Hawaii. And he gave me flying lessons."

"How long ago was that?" Laura didn't want to pry, but Jeff MacDougal seemed like a good source of potentially useful information.

"I graduated in '76," he said. "It wasn't too long after Dad got out of Laos."

"How was he after Laos?"

The young pilot shrugged. "He seemed the same to me, but what do I know? I mean I was only eleven when he disappeared outta my life. So, of course, my dad was always my biggest hero. No matter what. It used to drive my mom crazy."

"When you went to Hawaii was your dad … uh … was he alone?"

The young man's cheerful face darkened. "Oh, you know about her? No, she wasn't there with him. I kind of imagined maybe he left her so he could spend that summer with me. Guess I liked to think they'd broken up about it, you know? See, when he first got

out of Laos he had an address in California. San Francisco, I think. But then when Mom said she would give me a round-trip ticket as far as Hawaii, he wrote and said, 'Let's spend the summer flying in Hawaii.' And we did."

"So you don't know what became of … the other woman?"

Jeff MacDougal shook his head and smiled. "Ain't no big t'ing, far as I'm concerned. Although I guess she made him happy at the time. And I have a feeling they got back together again, at least once. I think that's why he went off to Alaska for a while. But I guess it didn't work 'cuz pretty soon he was back in Hawaii, and no sign of Miss Jodie deSpain anywhere in the Pacific. Say, is that the rest of our party?"

Laura turned and saw Shelby Verdun hurrying across the polished terrazzo of the nearly empty terminal lobby with an elderly Caucasian woman hurrying after him.

"Sorry to be late," he said, looking suspiciously at Jeff MacDougal. "Where's Johnson?"

"We're in luck, Shelby," Laura said. "Mr. Johnson assigned Jeff MacDougal to fly us. He's the son of Donnie MacDougal—the most celebrated pilot in Micronesia."

For once Verdun showed some real interest. "Is that so? Well, I'm sure I flew with your father when I was out here in the early sixties, doing my Amelia Earhart book."

"If you were hanging out with Will Hildebrandt, I'm sure you weren't allowed to fly with anybody else," Laura said.

"So where's your kid?" Verdun asked, looking around.

"Oh, I'm sorry. She decided she would rather stay here with some friends."

"No problem. Anyway, I found a new recruit for the expedition down at the police station. Says she's an old friend of yours."

Laura focused on the woman who seemed to be hanging back uncertainly, just beyond range of their conversation. She looked like someone who hadn't slept for days, who was terribly sick or terribly sad. But she also looked like …

"Edwina!" Laura dashed across the space that separated them and enveloped Edwina Hassler in a hug, remembering as she squeezed her old friend's thin shoulders that she had worried about what to say if and when she saw Edwina. But it was not a time for words.

Jeff MacDougal cleared his throat self-consciously. "S'cuse me folks, but maybe we should go out to the plane? We probably better stick to the schedule if you want time to look around up there."

They left the terminal to walk across the tarmac toward the small plane parked a hundred yards away. Laura counted carefully. *It's only been three days since Teri and I flew in from Saipan—and the tangled, incestuous life of the islands has completely engulfed me. Here I am, with a dear old friend whose husband has just been murdered, with the son of the man who flew a group of friends together sixteen years ago, and with the author of the book that inspired our stupid prank.* And, she thought with sudden certainty, feeling its weight on her shoulder, *I even have the camera that took the photograph that has something to do with Gordon Hassler's death.*

– 1974 –
July

JODIE DESPAIN, PILOT.

She rolled the sheet of stationery into her typewriter and paused to admire the design. Dark blue ink on pale blue linen paper: her name, address, phone number, all trailing behind that swooping figure that Donnie MacDougal had doodled on a paper coaster after her first flying lesson, his map to the joy of flight. She had kept the coaster safe until she could finally settle somewhere long enough to get stationery printed. The design said Donnie to her, and flight—the central facts of her existence.

Even after all these years, her eyes lingered on that magic word: *pilot*. It seemed to draw a line between the two phases of her life—Jodie deSpain, girl scientist who escaped her neatly defined life by acting in amateur theatricals, and Jodie deSpain, pilot who was true to herself, who did what she knew she had to, who grabbed life with both hands.

"Jodie, honey?" The voice from the living room broke into her mood, dragged her into the present. *True to myself? Like hell.*

"Hey, Jo," Reggie called again. Heavy footsteps in the next room moved away, toward the kitchen. "You awake in there? You want a beer?"

"No, thanks," she said loudly. "I'm fine."

She heard his footsteps returning, heard him pop open a can of beer, and crank up the volume on the TV baseball game. Outside on the bay, sailboats scudded swiftly across the water between her and the gray-green hills of Angel Island. Farther in the distance, she could see the blocky rocks of Alcatraz, but the white walls and red roofs of San Francisco were entirely lost in the city's shroud of fog.

Jodie turned back to the typewriter, to the still blank piece of stationery in it. Goddamn Panda, she thought, irrationally wanting to blame her old nemesis for everything. But Panda had nothing to do with her current discomfort, with the gentle, fleshy man sitting out there in his living room while she hid here in his bedroom, trying to find the way back to a life she seemed to have misplaced.

Suddenly she thought of the flimsy madras plaid bedspread she kept hidden in a drawer here in Reggie's house, touching it surreptitiously now and then when her loneliness overwhelmed her. She wanted to abandon the typewriter and her resolutions, get the madras spread out and wrap up in it, hide in sleep and memories. Instead, she stared out the window until, slowly, San Francisco Bay and the menthol scent of eucalyptus that permeated Northern California vanished and she felt the soft moist air of Guam, heard the surf, tasted the salt of the sea and Donnie's sweat, remembered how huge the world became for those minutes they had stolen together.

She remembered then that nightmare at Tumon Beach, sitting with Donnie crammed into her tiny car while the officious Guamanian cop teetered on the balls of his feet, squatting outside the car, his gun on them, ready to execute them for their adulterous crime.

"Someday it's going to be funny," Jodie muttered to the silvery air in a bedroom in Belvedere, California.

"What'll be funny?" Reggie's voice was quiet but his hands were on her shoulders. She screamed.

"Jodie, darling, stop it!" He dragged her to her feet, clutched her to him in a bear hug, and patted her head awkwardly. "Even in broad daylight you get your nightmare?"

When they first got involved, she had told him about that night on Tumon Beach, exaggerated its impact if the truth be known—it gave her an excuse for being unresponsive in bed. "I'm sorry," she would say through her tears, "I'm just so haunted by that night."

"It's okay, baby," he had said more than once. "I can understand it. To be right in mid-stroke and have all hell break loose a few yards away, sure it's gonna have an effect. But you'll get over it. Won't

you? Do you think maybe you should see a shrink about it?" And all the time her tears were because he wasn't Donnie, because she hadn't been able to hold out for Donnie, hadn't been able to wait until he came back from Southeast Asia, because life wasn't turning out the way she had known it could be ever since that first flight to Saipan seven years ago.

"Sometimes even in the daylight," she said into Reggie's soft shoulder, feeling her leanness sink into the pillows of his chest and belly. "But I'll be okay. Really, I will. I'll get my letters written."

From the other room the television's tone changed. "I think the game's coming back on," she said. "I'm okay, Reggie, really."

"You're sure you don't want a beer?"

"No, no, I'm fine." She tried to soften the edge on her voice, to squelch the screaming inside her head that said, "Get the hell out of here! Leave me alone!" Whatever message Reggie got, it was enough to send him lumbering back into the living room.

The thing to be said for Reggie, besides his gentleness and this safe and cozy house on the bay, was that he owned—but didn't fly—a small plane. The fast-food franchise business he had started a few years ago had succeeded beyond his dreams and now required him to fly throughout California and Nevada, peddling tacos and burritos.

Jodie had just gotten her stationery printed and was getting ready to buy ads in the Bay Area papers when she spotted Reggie's ad looking for a pilot. She needed some work to tide her over until she got established, so she jumped at his job offer. His later suggestion that she move in with him wasn't so appealing but she had succumbed. Reggie's timing had been in his favor. The woman she had been sharing an apartment with in the City had wanted to have her boyfriend move in and made it clear that three would be a crowd. The roommate offered to forward mail and phone calls until Jodie could get her stationery reprinted. So, in the end, it had been easier to move in with Reggie than to find a new place. And, in a way, she supposed she was getting even with Donnie for abandoning her.

She and Donnie had stuck it out in Guam for months that dragged into years, through the murder trial of the delinquent teenager who was eventually convicted of killing the cop. Their status as witnesses was splashed across the island press for many days—first the rumored existence of witnesses who were illicit lovers, seeking an out-of-the-way spot for their tryst—then more specific descriptions as the prosecution leaked more information to the island's tiny crew of journalists. They had run with every innuendo, Jodie remembered, all except Will Hildebrandt. He had held back, tried to avoid the story out of his loyalty to Donnie. When he wrote about it, it was with lines like: "Murder witnesses said to be a well-known island businessman and a civilian employee of the Navy … "

Then, finally, at the trial, their names had been revealed, along with insulting views of their faces sketched by a particularly vicious cartoonist hired by one of the newspapers.

"Here," Donnie had laughed, handing her a clipping of the sketch, "maybe you can use this sometime for an ad." She hadn't been able to laugh with him. The caricature was bad enough of him, emphasizing the beak shape of his nose, exaggerating his crewcut. She had looked like a long-necked chicken with false eyelashes, her short hair ruffled like feathers.

Panda had gotten a lot of press attention, and a very flattering photograph taken on the steps of the courthouse as she played the loyal helpmate. "Of course I will stand by my man," the picture caption quoted her as saying. "I know how to forgive."

"Fat chance," Donnie had said, reading that. "She'll be taking it out of my hide for as long as I live."

Jodie wasn't at all surprised when the Navy found a way to abolish her job, decreeing it required a commissioned officer's attention to supervise her lab. As she packed for her move—to where she hadn't decided—she went more than a week without hearing from Donnie, the most awful week of her life. Panda has won, she told herself again and again. Those words screamed inside her skull until, at times, she was afraid she had screamed them out loud and

was hearing echoes falling from the painted concrete walls of her apartment.

Then, the night before her movers were due, he had showed up at her door, waving airline tickets.

"Aloha, Blondie," he'd said. "We're leaving for Honolulu on tomorrow's flight. Tell 'em to ship your stuff there."

He had turned over everything to Panda—the plane, the business, the house, the van, total custody of the kids. Panda had given him two-thousand dollars to get him started again and he had blown most of it on the pair of tickets to Honolulu. His daughter Cory had dropped him off at the gate to the naval hospital—the last he would see of either kid, Panda told him, until they came of age and could decide on their own whether to re-establish contact. He had all his belongings in one large duffel bag. And he looked like the happiest man on the island.

"You big idiot," she had said through her joyful tears. "You didn't have to buy a ticket for me. The Navy owes me a ride home."

"I want you with me. I've made a couple of sacrifices for you, and I'm not going to let you out of my sight."

But of course he had. After a few lean months in Hawaii, he had decided that the one way he could save enough to buy another plane was to go to work for Air America, flying CIA missions in Vietnam.

"I'll dry up and blow away without you," she had sobbed.

"No, you won't, Blondie," he said, ruffling her hair. "You'll fly."

She had hung on in Hawaii for a few months. She had even looked up her old friend Foster Monroe, who introduced her to the folks who ran one of Hawaii's community theatre groups, but she never quite felt at home in Hawaii. Anyway, she wasn't getting enough paying flights to stay proficient.

"I've got to make a place for myself in the flying world," she wrote to Donnie. "I'll try San Francisco. I've heard there's a lot of work there right now."

Two days after she'd heard a news item about Communists capturing a civilian pilot in Laos, she answered Reggie Barton's ad.

Only recently she had heard from someone passing through from Honolulu that Laura Monroe was living in San Francisco now. Jodie had gone so far as to check the phone directory and find Laura's number—but she couldn't bring herself to call. She had always been perplexed by Laura, wondering how she could be so off-hand about her relationship with a charmer like Foster Monroe, taking him too much for granted.

Or perhaps, Jodie admitted, she felt a little guilty, because she had flirted outrageously with Foster in the pre-Donnie days, when she was trying to make her doctor boyfriend jealous. What was his name? Barry, that was it.

The main problem now, she thought, was that Laura knew Donnie, knew how they enriched and complicated each other's lives. How could she talk to Laura without admitting her nightmares about Donnie, caged in some jungle, being tortured if only by being kept out of the sky? More to the point, how could she explain to Laura why she was living with another man?

* * *

In the living room, Reggie erupted into angry shouts at an umpire. Jodie shook her head to clear it, turned away from the gray-green view in the window and brought her pale blue stationery into focus.

Yesterday she had been reading a book about Amelia Earhart and learned that she too had been drawn to science first—that she had studied medicine and worked as a nurse. And something had clicked. Jodie had made a promise to herself. She was going to regain control of her life. She needed to work on something that could engage her mind, take her out of the trap of herself.

"Charlotte Sablán," she typed. "Western Pacific Research Center, University of Guam, Mangilao, Guam. Dear Mrs. Sablán."

She paused, wondering how to begin. Better make it personal, so the lady will be sure to answer.

"I'm not sure if you'll remember me," she typed. "Laura and Foster Monroe brought me to one of your wonderful New Year's parties a few years ago.

"I'm doing some research on the disappearance of Amelia Earhart and I wondered if there is any unpublished material on deposit in your archives. I remember Laura saying that whatever had been written about the western Pacific, you'd know about it."

She felt a weight lifting from her mind as she typed. Yes, this was how she would deal with her obsessive concern for Donnie's well-being and her guilt about her manipulative relationship with Reggie. She would develop a new obsession, one that couldn't possibly touch her personally.

— 1983 —
Saturday

JEFF MACDOUGAL HESITATED AT THE DOOR of the small plane to look over his passengers. It was a moment Laura remembered from flights years ago with his father. Who gets to sit up front? Much as she loved to sit in the cockpit on inter-island flights, good manners dictated that she defer to Shelby Verdun since he had made the original charter arrangements.

"Do you want to flip coins for the copilot seat?" Jeff asked. "Play a few rounds of rock-paper-scissors?"

"You have first claim, Shelby," she told Verdun. She thought she saw a tiny wisp of fear dart through his bored eyes.

"Oh, no," he said quickly. "But perhaps Mrs. Hassler … "

Edwina seemed to shrink back into herself. "Oh, not me," she said. "In fact, I was just wondering why on earth I came along." She stared at Laura, wistfully perhaps. Had she come along to the airport just to see her old friend, then found herself trapped into this joyride?

Jeff's eyebrows lifted into that all-purpose Guamanian question mark as he smiled at Laura.

"I'd love to be your copilot," she said. She waited outside the plane until he got the other two settled into their seats in the tiny cabin, then she wriggled into the cockpit as he secured the door.

"I bet you thought we were going to flip coins to see who *had* to sit up front," she said.

"No way! I could tell you were a flier from the minute I laid eyes on you in the terminal." His dark eyes were warm, almost flirtatious, and his hand seemed to linger on hers as he helped her fasten the seat belt.

What the heck was going on here? She thought of the handsome Hawaiian beach boys who loitered at Waikiki, offering to teach lady tourists to surf, willing to oblige them in other ways too. Is that what Jeff MacDougal is—a high-flying Hawaiian beach boy? What does he see in me? Loneliness and need?

Almost surreptitiously, she watched him as he ran through his pre-flight checklist. His profile was very like his father's and it was hard to reconcile him with the cute, button-nosed little boy she had seen hanging out around his father's plane years ago.

"There's two kinds of people who charter small planes," he said, turning that gleaming smile on her again. "There's folks who need transportation to get some place and then there's folks who need to fly. And you … " he reached over and patted her arm, "you need to fly. Am I right?"

Laura cleared her throat, afraid her tone of voice might say something she didn't intend. "I do enjoy flying. But your father once said I liked the geography of it, liked seeing the world laid out below me so I could analyze it, while Jo…"

One black eyebrow shot up on the young man's handsome face. "Joe?" he asked.

"Jodie. Jodie DeSpain. It was the day they met. He flew her up to Saipan to visit us, and he seemed to know from that first moment that Jodie wanted to fly, felt about flying like he did."

Jeff stared at her for a few seconds. "So, she was a friend of yours," he said stiffly. "And was my dad right? Did she have a thing about flying? Or was it just a thing about him?"

Laura felt suddenly, strangely bereft. The flirtatious tone was gone from his voice—if it had ever been there. She'd broken the spell, placed herself securely in his father's generation, allied herself with his mother's sworn enemy.

"Oh, Jodie loved flying," Laura said. "There was never any question about that." She watched as Jeff made more adjustments to the array of levers and knobs before him. He reached for the headset

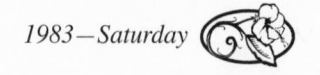

and started to pull it over his ears and she hurried to add, "But she really had a thing for your father too."

The young man nodded and pulled the earphones on. He punched a button on the wheel and spoke into the microphone at his chin, stating flight details and destination in a businesslike voice.

And how I envied her that, she thought. I always wanted to feel as passionate about a man as I felt about my career.

Even when the Marianas grapevine had hummed in shocked delight over the scandal of the Navy nurse, as Jodie was usually characterized, and the Hawaiian hero, Laura had envied Jodie her obsession with that tall, golden pilot. She'd felt cheated, somehow, that she had never felt that way about anyone, never been in a relationship where sparks flew between her and someone else, sparks that other people could trace like a trail of fireflies. My marriage, my love affairs—they've always been so—comfortable. No one could ever write an opera about any relationship of mine. Nor a ballet.

Jeff MacDougal taxied the plane onto the runway, reset something, double-checked something else, and started a clock in front of him. Then he turned to Laura, smiled and said, "Here we go, *Cara Mia*," as he reached over to pat her hand again.

He pushed the throttle forward and she heard the engines sing a staccato duet. When the plane seemed to wobble, he moved levers slightly and their race down the runway smoothed out. Then a slight tug, and the world fell away from them. The propellers whined, out of harmony until the pilot adjusted them. As the two engines synchronized, she heard music at the back of her mind, an orchestra playing the introduction to a Broadway musical number. Then came a voice only she could hear, a deep baritone, singing about an enchanted evening and seeing a stranger across the room.

South Pacific! Was that it? Was that the music those dream ballet dancers performed to this morning? Rodgers and Hammerstein? She closed her eyes, tried to fit the memory of the dream with the tune fading away as the small plane's engines droned loudly into her consciousness.

No. That wasn't the ballet music. It was the background music for this scene, for this moment.

From the corner of her eye, she admired the proud, strong profile of Jeff MacDougal, glanced down at his brown arms holding the plane steady as it climbed up over a plateau starred with the asterisk marks of pandanus trees. He seemed to fly in the airy footsteps his father had carved through this heavy blue air, these soft clouds.

Why had she never thought to take flying lessons?

The day was bright and the world completely suffused with blue. Laura remembered some ad agency people who had arrived in these islands when she lived here, people from Los Angeles who had come to design an advertising campaign for the newly created Air Micronesia. At a party, she had suggested a slogan to them: "Don't come if you don't like blue." They had told her that negatives were a very bad idea in a promotional campaign. Then later, a friend who worked with the little Micronesian inter-island shipping company used Laura's idea for a very modest brochure she mailed to people who loved freighter travel. "Our ships travel to some of the Pacific's most beautiful, loneliest islands. But don't come if you don't like blue."

Not liking blue was—at this moment, in this place—incomprehensible. Not like blue? What else is there? The universe is blue.

They had flown across the thirty-mile swath of the Pacific that separated Guam and Rota Island. Below and to their right the plane's tiny dark shadow leapt onto the shore of Rota and skimmed gracefully atop the crowns of coconut palms far below them.

The horizon traced a shimmering blue line and, like tarnished metallic brooches clipping the darker blue sea to the paler blue sky, the green islands of Tinian and Saipan rode the line. A tiny bit of rock seemed to have broken off from Tinian's westernmost point. Was it called Goat Island? Laura tried to tune her island memory clearer.

She glanced at Jeff, wondering whether he could hear her if she asked the islet's name. To her surprise, he was watching her, a slight smile on his lips. It broadened into a grin as their eyes met.

"Beautiful day, isn't it?" he shouted above the engines' high-pitched scream.

"Beautiful world," she shouted back. She wriggled back deeper into her seat, like a cat, settling in. Even as she did, she wondered whether it didn't look provocative.

Jeff's eyes narrowed slightly, as though he were processing new information. Then he turned back to his task, floating them between blue and blue, toward the pointy green coolie hat that was Saipan.

They landed on the airstrip in Saipan's southeastern corner and pulled up close to the sprawling complex of swooping roofs that was the Saipan International Airport.

Jeff unbuckled and unfolded from his seat, helping Laura to her feet. In the cabin Edwina and Shelby were gathering their belongings, congratulating Jeff on the smooth flight. He shrugged. "How could I go wrong, on a day like this. Say, did you folks charter a car too?"

"No," Shelby said, "I was assured we could rent one at the airport."

"Don't bother, not for just a couple hours," Jeff said. "We keep an old jalopy up here. I'll drive you wherever you want to go. *Saabisu.*"

Verdun frowned. "What?"

"You speak Japanese," Laura said in delight.

"Well, a word or two. We get a lot of Japanese customers."

"Well, what's it mean?" Verdun asked.

"*Saabisu*? It's what we call Jinglish in Tokyo," Laura said. "Service. But to the Japanese it means it's free, comes along with the price of what you've already bought."

Verdun's thin lips stretched into a grin. "Well, all right. We'll take you up on it!"

Edwina trailed along, marveling at the huge terminal building, comparing it to the shack that had served the purpose during her years in Saipan. Jeff led them into the building where a bored immigration clerk waved them through. They crossed the spacious lobby

and were outside again, walking across a parking lot that radiated heat like a giant pancake griddle. The car was an ancient Datsun, its body badly rusted from years in the island's salty breezes.

"I believe I know this car personally," Edwina said. "I think it's the one we sold when we left the island in '68."

"Really?" Verdun sounded almost excited.

"No, no," Edwina said hurriedly. "It's a joke. I'm sorry, Jeff. I didn't mean to impugn your car's integrity."

Laura looked at Edwina with admiration. She was clearly devastated by Gordon's death, yet here she was providing a slimpse of the wry, slightly sarcastic Edwina of the old days.

"Ain't no big t'ing," Jeff said, and Laura could have sworn it was his father talking. He unlocked the driver's door and stretched to unlock the other doors, winding down windows. "Better let some air in before we get in," he advised. "It's an old heap but it gets the job done. We put our maintenance money into the planes."

Shelby Verdun seemed positively buoyant. "No problem," he said. "The price is right." With proprietary stride he stepped to the front passenger seat. Gingerly, Laura and Edwina edged onto the searing hot back seat.

"Only thing is," Jeff said as he started the engine, "I hope you know where we're going. I don't usually go anywhere but the hotels on this rock."

As Laura played navigator, she thought how odd it was, with all the construction that had gone on in Saipan in the years since she lived here, that finding the old Japanese hospital involved the same process it had in the sixties. Choose the right grassy bay in the jungle that edged the inland highway, park on the grass and find a faint path that was all that remained of what must have been a major street in the Japanese metropolis of Garapan in the 1930s.

Laura tried to imagine back through the years. Fifty years ago, before Amelia Earhart embarked upon her flight, before the Japanese used the word "*saabisu*" to mean anything at all, what would have been here? She'd seen old photos of Garapan. A muddy street, lined

with small shops with living quarters above them. People hurrying to and fro. Japanese housewives in kimono, wearing wooden *geta* on their feet like miniature stilts to raise them above the mud. Japanese police officers striding along in starched authority. Chamorro men in loose shirts and pants, wearing hats woven of palm fronds. Chickens skittering across the street.

Had she actually seen these things in an old photograph? Or was she tuned in to the past as she led the small expedition through the hot, fecund jungle that had once been Garapan?

When the path broadened into a wider clearing, she hesitated for a moment. "I think we want to turn right here," she said, peering into the green growth of banana trees and ubiquitous *tangan-tangan*, trying to catch a glimpse of the hospital's once-white walls through the leaves.

"I'd say so," Jeff MacDougal said. He pointed at a small bit of wood nailed onto a coconut trunk. JAP HOSPITAL was painted in jagged letters with a stubby arrow pointing right, exactly where Laura had indicated.

"Oh," she said sheepishly. "I didn't even see that." She didn't mention that she had also missed it when she and Teri had been here a few days ago. Jeff reached over and poked her gently in the shoulder. "Hey, we couldn't have gotten this far without you."

The path to the hospital was narrower than the trail they left, just as it had been sixteen years ago when she had come here with Jeff's father in his crisp white shirt, with Jodie wearing Foster's plaid shirt and Will's baggy trousers. Laura let her mind slip back. I was—what? Twenty-five? Jeff's approximate age now. And at twenty-five I agreed with the rest of them that it would be a great idea to trick the *Guam Chronicle* into running a false photo of Amelia Earhart. To run it then, in 1967, not in 1983.

And then what? What would we have done if the *Chronicle* had used the photo? She couldn't remember what the plan had been, if there had been a plan. Would we have revealed the hoax to embarrass the newspaper? Or would we have kept it to ourselves?

She was never going to fit the pieces together if she couldn't bring herself to ask Will if he really had sent the photo to the *Chronicle* and if he had made any other prints. A copy for Jodie, for instance. Whenever she'd seen an opportunity to ask him, she'd decided not to feed his paranoia. But darn it, if he was going to stick her with spending an afternoon with Shelby Verdun, she should at least demand some information from him.

And what, exactly, am I going to write about the photo to send to Jerry Bosley at the AP Tokyo bureau?

Now there it was—the ruined hospital. They stopped at the edge of the clearing. Laura tried to compare the present state of the building with what she had seen sixteen years ago. In some places chunky concrete flakes had fallen from the walls or hung on steel reinforcement rods like patches of skin peeling from a severe sunburn. The thought made her own day-old sunburn seem to blaze anew. But the domed lobby that anchored the corner of the L-shaped structure looked as she remembered it from 1967—or from yesterday's *Chronicle*.

Shelby Verdun stopped beside her, staring at the building before them. He rummaged in a zippered folder he carried and extracted a clipping of the photo that must be from a San Francisco paper. They had run it as a four-column cut, larger than the *Guam Chronicle* had used it, which was in turn, larger than the original snapshot she had seen in police detective Ben Guerrero's hand. The photo in Verdun's clipping was immense next to the contact print Will had made those years ago in the photo lab up in Trust Territory headquarters. This photograph was out of control, growing and expanding until it would swallow them all.

"Hmmm," Verdun mused.

"What do you think?" she asked cautiously.

"Well, I still say there's no way this building … " he poked his index finger at the clipping " … is only ten or twenty years old. But it's not a really recent picture."

"Oh?" Laura and Jeff crowded closer to him.

"No." He pointed out a missing patch of concrete beside the building's open lobby under the dome. In the photograph, the same wall was smooth and even. "And look at this tree branch that just comes into the photo on the right edge. That tree is much taller now, if it's the same tree."

"Wouldn't that depend on how tall the photographer was?" Laura asked. "I mean if the photographer was a really short Japanese ..." She paused to reconsider.

"Then the tree would look taller than it would from my height," Verdun said as though that settled the issue of the photo's age for once and for all.

"You know, Laura," Edwina said softly, "I think I remember the first time you saw the hospital."

"Really?" Laura tried to think back.

"Remember, you came up to write some stories about the Trust Territory? And you stayed with us?"

Ah, yes, that first trip, when Gordon met Donnie's plane. "And you took me on a picnic at Marine Beach."

"But before that, didn't we take you on a tour of Garapan? The locomotive and the statue at Sugar King Park? The Japanese jail?"

"Yes," Laura said, suddenly remembering. "And the hospital. That *was* the first time I saw it." Now she remembered—walking down the overgrown trail, how Gordon's hand had brushed across her back as he held a branch of *tangan-tangan* aside for her to pass. Even then, the first weekend she knew him, she had wondered how his wife felt when he flirted with other women.

"When would that have been?" Verdun asked. "When you first came here?"

"I think it was 1965," Laura said.

"So, what do you think? Is the hospital different from then?"

"Oh, I'm not sure," Laura said. "Obviously someone's keeping the vegetation trimmed back now—I don't think there was so much of a clearing then. And I remember—I think it was here and not the hospital on Dublon in Truk—there was a young tree growing out of

a window down at the end of that wing, where there was no floor in a room."

"So, do you think the photo in the papers looks more like what you saw in the sixties or like now?"

"Oh, geez, Shelby, I don't know—I recognized the place when I saw the photo in the paper. But I recognized it when we saw it right now too."

"You want to take my picture?" Jeff asked. "I'll send it to my dad. He'll get a kick out of it. I bet he never even saw this place."

I'll bet he did, she thought as she focused Will Hildebrandt's Pentax on the scene it had photographed at least once before. *And what would this young man say if I told him it was the sleeve of his father's shirt that showed at the left-hand edge of the photo in Shelby Verdun's clipping. Plus my forearm and hand?*

It was strange, looking through a viewfinder again. When she had first lived in the islands, she'd been a real camera nut, taking photos not just for the newspapers she worked for, but as a hobby. And then, abruptly, she stopped. It had suddenly seemed as though the very act of framing a photo in the viewfinder had cut her off from life, limited her to experiencing things only after the photos were processed. Had that been her own idea? Or was it another bit of the philosophy of Lionel Keating, her island guru? Like his notion that where you lived shaped your soul and the most coherent, integrated souls were island-shaped.

"What do you think?" Shelby asked Edwina. "Is this a picture of the building in the thirties or in the sixties or the eighties?"

"I'm sorry. I can't look at that picture." Edwina whispered so her voice could hardly be heard.

The blood splotches. Edwina's husband's lifeblood was recorded on that clipping. Laura hurried to her old friend's side just as Edwina's legs seemed to give way. She sagged into Laura's arms.

"I shouldn't have come," she sobbed. "I knew I shouldn't come."

Did she mean she shouldn't have come on the Saipan jaunt or that she shouldn't have come back to the Marianas at all?

Almost in slow motion, the two men began moving. Jeff MacDougal was coming toward them, a look of concern on his face, while Shelby Verdun melted back and away, toward the ruined building.

When Edwina's sobs grew until they were howls, Laura slowly sank to the ground, still supporting the older woman. Was this the first time Edwina had let herself cry since she heard the news of her husband's murder? Had 'Sús Pérez made her officially identify the body?

"There should be a first aid kit in the car," Jeff said. "I'll get it."

Edwina's sobs had subsided into hiccups when he returned in a few minutes, carrying a small metal case. "I'm not sure what a first aid kit can do for me," she said. Her voice was shaky but Laura saw her trying to make light of her situation. "They don't put smelling salts in them anymore, do they?"

"Almost," Jeff said as he removed a one-shot whiskey bottle. "Try this." He twisted the cap off the bottle with a snap.

Edwina frowned but accepted the little bottle. "Maybe you're right," she said. She squeezed her eyes shut as she took a gulp. "Ah," she said. "That's good scotch. Too good to gulp like that. This is sippin' whisky."

"Nothin' but the best for Micronesian Pacific Airlines." Jeff grinned at Edwina.

"Laura," Verdun said from across the clearing, "if your friend is going to be okay, do you think you could shoot some pictures?"

What a guy, Laura thought as she rose to her feet and started toward him. He brings Edwina along as some sort of reporter's asset but when she looks like she might be a drag on the party, she's my friend.

For twenty minutes they posed and snapped several pictures—Shelby alone in front of the hospital, Shelby pointing out the recently flaked concrete facade to Jeff, Jeff grinning "Hi, Dad" at the camera. Edwina flatly refused to pose, to Shelby's disappointment.

At last they trekked back toward Jeff's car.

"Funny thing happened when I came to the car to get the first aid kit," Jeff said as he opened a rear door for Edwina. "A car had just pulled up right here in front of our car and two men were getting out. A Saipanese guy, I'd guess, and a big *haole*. But when they saw me come out of the boonies, the *haole* said something and they jumped in the car and drove away in a big hurry."

"How strange," Laura said. "They must have seen your car here. And you don't look that scary to me." As she grinned up at him, a small voice at the back of her mind said, Uh-uh-uhh, you're flirting with this boy.

"Did they have cameras?" Shelby asked.

"I really didn't notice," Jeff said. "I only caught a glimpse of them, they left in such a rush."

"Reporters, I'll bet," Verdun said. "Someone trying to beat our story."

With the four of them packed into the small car once again, Jeff pulled out of his grassy parking space onto the highway. "Where to now?"

"Why don't we drive up to Army Hill," Shelby said. "I'll never forget how amazed I was to find that modern concrete town up there on top of the mountain. I didn't even know it was there until my third trip to the island."

Laura remembered the story from Verdun's book—how he had been invited to give a talk on his Amelia Earhart research to a group of Americans and found himself in the middle of a top-secret CIA base.

Jeff turned onto the highway heading north but Edwina said, "Please, no, I can't go up there. It's too close."

Too close to her memories? Laura wondered. After all, she and Gordon had lived on the hill—called Capitol Hill once the CIA moved out—for several years. Or is it too close to her husband's true occupation, which led to his murder?

Jeff slowed the car and turned off into a small road that would have been just two blocks from the hospital's turnoff if Garapan

still had blocks. He turned to Shelby and then Laura, his eyebrows asking what he should do.

"Oh, what the hell—let's go to one of the hotels. Find some Saipanese to interview. I could use a drink too," Verdun said, disgust obvious in his voice.

Jeff sat still for a moment, staring through the windshield. Up ahead, a car had turned onto the side road and was approaching.

"I'll be damned," Jeff said as he put his car into gear and whipped around and back onto the highway, heading south once again. "That's the car." He jerked his thumb over his shoulder toward the car that was pulling onto the highway behind them, a bright red, late-model Toyota. "The people who didn't want us to see them going to the hospital."

Laura watched the red car behind them. It seemed to slow down. Are they looking for the path to the hospital? A sudden chill swept down her spine. Who are they? All she could see were two people, probably men, but maybe she thought that because Jeff had already told them that—a statesider and an islander.

"Where you turned around back there—that was the road up to Sugar King Park," she said. Just a few days ago she had taken Teri to see the large bronze statue there of the Japanese industrialist who had founded Saipan's short-lived sugar industry. "They might have gone up there because it's on a hill and, if they walked over by the old locomotive, they could see our car when we left the hospital area. But they wouldn't see that we turned onto the road that goes to the park, because they had already gotten back in their car."

"Weird," Jeff said.

* * *

Because the idea of a revolving restaurant on Saipan was so incongruous to Shelby and Edwina, Jeff drove them to the Nauru Building. At eight stories, it must have been the tallest building in Micronesia but sitting beside its nearly empty parking lot with tan-

gled green growth stretching away in all directions it seemed squat, shaped like that pet robot in the Star Wars movies.

They rode the slow elevator to the top. At a table by a window they sipped drinks while Laura talked about the tiny republic of Nauru to the south, near the equator, and how its income was based solely on the phosphate deposits that blanketed the tiny island.

"They are destroying their own home in order to be rich," Laura said. "So they have to buy real estate on other, poorer islands. I've always thought there was an analogy there, an environmental warning for the world."

"Like we always tell our passengers," Jeff said, "this skyscraper is built entirely of bird shit."

Apparently Donnie MacDougal had taught his son one of his own paramount rules—drink only after your final landing for the day. While the others ordered gins and tonic, Jeff ordered iced tea. Below them, the island slid past, first the multi-green tones of *tangan-tangan* thickets and palm groves, then the dazzling turquoise of the lagoon with the deep blue ocean yawning beyond.

"This is almost unreal," Verdun said. "When I made my trips here, the only hotel was an old, tumbledown World War II barracks."

"That's all that was here the first time I came too," Laura said.

"So what were you gals doing here in the sixties?" Verdun asked. "Were your husbands both with the CIA?"

Laura shook her head emphatically. "No. Trust Territory Government." At least mine was. And who am I trying to convince? Who cares what Shelby Verdun thinks? "Actually, the first time I came, it was on assignment. I was writing some stories for the *Honolulu Star Bulletin*. We moved up here later."

Edwina did not explain her reasons for living in Saipan, but it occurred to Laura that she must have been here when Verdun was doing his research. Perhaps Gordon had dealt with Verdun's request to visit back when Saipan was closed to casual visitors. Well, she wasn't going to mention it, if he didn't think of it himself. It would only make it more difficult for Edwina to maintain her composure.

"Did you get a story out of this?" Laura asked Verdun.

"A story, maybe. Certainly not a book yet. How about you?"

She shrugged. "I guess I can write a long caption for a photo."

"Will promised to meet us at the airport and take the film home to process," Verdun said. "Maybe you can get the folks at the local rag to wire it up to your bureau."

They finished their drinks slowly, then jiggled back down in the balky elevator. At Laura's suggestion, they drove over to the small shopping center nearby and asked the people in the grocery store check-out line if they had heard about the new Amelia Earhart photo. Edwina waited in the car with Jeff, having whispered to Laura she was afraid she would see someone who remembered her and might ask about Gordon. Someone who had heard the news of the murder—or worse yet, someone who hadn't.

It wasn't a scientific survey but people in Susupe Village seemed very blasé about the photo.

"Yeah, sure I seen it," one man said. "So what? Statesiders are always trying to dig Amelia Earhart up on Saipan. Why don't they let that lady sleep in peace?"

* * *

The sun was nearly down when they got back to the airport. Jeff was parking in his regular place when Laura saw a red car pull up at the departure doorway. The passenger climbed out and then leaned back into the car to speak to the driver.

Laura kept her eyes fixed on the man as she got out of Jeff's car. "Isn't that the same car we saw back near the hospital?" she asked Jeff quietly as he locked doors and wound up windows.

He squinted across the intervening space. "Sure looks like it. You don't see that many red Toyotas around here. And that's for sure the same *hombre* I saw getting back into the car when I went to get the first aid kit."

Laura dawdled, trying to get the others to slow their progress toward the terminal building. She wanted the man to be well inside,

in line at the check-in counter so he wouldn't notice her. She was sure she knew who it was, but she wanted a closer look.

Yes. His sunburn was somewhat subdued after three days but the large man in the bright aloha shirt waiting to check in for the Air Micronesia flight to Guam was the same man she had seen dining with Gordon Hassler at the Hilton the night she first arrived in Guam.

— 1956 —

HE SAT ON ONE OF THE BEDS in the cheap hotel room, waiting, his right hand in his pocket doing sleight-of-hand exercises with quarters and dimes. Funny how his fingers never forgot the tricks they had learned when he was a boy.

The hotel room was probably like a thousand others in the city: Drab, slightly dingy walls. Two badly framed *Saturday Evening Post* covers on the walls. Furniture meant to look modern, succeeding only in looking tired. Chenille bedspreads in a faded, orangey- pink. No TV, no phone.

He supposed rooms like this were often occupied by business travelers, salesmen for less prosperous companies or supplicants from the hinterland come to lobby members of their congressional delegation. But he couldn't imagine staying longer than he himself did in a room like this.

It was ideal for an afternoon—just a couple of blocks from several decent restaurants where a young lady could be courted with wine and flattery. Having obtained her consent to find a hotel room he would, of course, apologize that it was so modest. But, he would assure her, it was clean. And very discreet.

And why not? Certainly it was all to the hotel management's advantage to nod agreeably when a couple arrived at, say, two o'clock in the afternoon without luggage, registered as Mr. and Mrs. Jones, and offered to pay in advance.

And, Gordon thought, what difference does it make to me if the staff slips in after five, changes the sheets, and rents the room again? I always get my money's worth.

For many years, he had only flirted, using his marriage as an excuse to avoid consummating his flirtations. But gradually he let it escalate. He seemed to need more excitement in his life. First it had been quick nuzzles and occasional long, deep kisses in the office supply room. Then he discovered the pleasures to be had in the janitor's closet. A person could do some very heavy petting crammed up against that big square sink, shed some clothing, really get the blood pounding.

Eventually, though, he began to long for the horizontal, for more time and space, for a bed. This was what happened to drug addicts, he had heard, starting out with marijuana, then escalating, always needing a bigger thrill.

Not that he and Edwina didn't have a very satisfactory sex life. In fact, he had learned that she could be a real tiger, sometimes raking his back with her nails, leaving scabbed scratches that a sweet young thing might discover in the janitor's closet as her hands crept beneath the layers of his clothing. "Well!"she might say and he would shudder and try to sound sheepish. Of course he didn't tell them it was his wife who had done it. But he was scrupulous, never letting them think they were his only extra-curricular activity. He might say something like, "Yeah, I have to give that lady up before she tears me to shreds."

"Poor baby," his current conquest would coo, gently stroking his back while he bent her against the sink, slipping his hands under her sweater, letting his fingers move upward in delicate strokes until he could work his sleight of hand on the hooks on her bra.

He let things escalate because he knew how to be careful. And because—although discretion was essential so as not to hurt Edwina—he wanted word to get around a bit among male co-workers so they would nod knowingly when he confided that he would be taking the afternoon off because he had important business to attend to. This was, he never forgot, his best protective coloring.

In almost ten years of research, he had never found a mention of Tex Arnold in any government documents, but he needed to be

sure. If anyone in the world was still looking for the young man who had shared that New Guinea hotel room with Tex Arnold, they would surely know what kind of young man he had been, knowing that Tex always had a young man around, that he was never seen with women.

One day not long ago, it had occurred to Gordon that Tex Arnold's desire to do away with Amelia Earhart might have been personal rather than political. What if she had raised some of the money for her flights through blackmailing someone like Tex? But no, Tex had introduced himself to her when she arrived at Lae and she hadn't shown a sign of recognition. And she never would have let Tex's personal mechanic near her plane if she'd had an earlier unpleasant experience with Tex.

Perhaps Tex hated her because she was a strong, successful woman. Did she remind him of his mother? Tex had never said a word about his mother—did that mean he hated her? But then, had the boy Garrett Howland ever said anything to Tex about his own mother?

Though it showed no special promise, Gordon decided this tack of seeking a personal motive should be his next line of investigation—all the other trails he had tried were cold as ice.

The door from the bathroom opened and a young woman emerged. Diann, Diann, he repeated to himself. It was very important to use her name at the key moments. She was a fairly new clerk in an office down the hall from him. A tall woman, as tall as he, with a plain face that likely caused most men to ignore her. But Gordon had discerned that despite her dowdy clothing, she had a body that might be worthy of worship. He already knew from an encounter in the janitor's closet that it was a body that ached to be touched. Never had that tiny room grown so steamy so fast.

Now she sat primly on the other twin bed, her hands clenched in her lap, her mouth in a tense, straight line. His mind was completely at ease. She knew exactly what they were here for—why he had encouraged her to drink most of that expensive bottle of wine

he had ordered to go with lunch. But she was shy—inexperienced in this sort of thing. He would become her professor in the art of stolen love. For a time.

He patted the bed beside him. "How am I going to kiss you if you sit over there?" He kept his voice gentle yet sexy. She giggled nervously but moved across the intervening space. He had decided that it was never worth paying for a decent double bed until later encounters when more variety was needed—double beds in a cheap hotel like this were murder on his back. Later, if an affair stretched out, when an expensive lunch and good wine were no longer necessary, then he would invest in a better room with a better bed.

He put his arms around Diann, began by kissing her very softly, sweetly. Her mouth was hot, tugging at him, demanding. His hands moved slowly, surely, dealing with the zipper at the back of her dress, dragging the dress down over her substantial bosom. Slowly, gently tormenting her, his sure fingers pretended to fumble with the bra hooks.

His conscience was entirely clear. Edwina loved him. If she knew how what he was doing protected him, she would want him to do it. And the cost of these little adventures—well, he had come to think of the expense as a sort of insurance payment.

He certainly felt no guilt toward these women who so willingly invited him to explore their bodies. Diann was entirely nude now, a Rubenesque beauty he almost felt that he had created by helping her out of her clothes, by stimulating that ruddy glow in her skin. What pleasure to compare Edwina's lean, taut body with one like this. Life was very full and rich.

She quivered on the bed beside him, her arms pulling him down to her. "Come," she whispered. "Please. Hold me close." Slowly he undressed, keeping his eyes on her the whole time, letting her know how beautiful she was.

"You have a glorious body," he told her as he traced with one finger a route from her throat over one large breast and down slowly across her belly. "I wish I could—but I'm a married man. Really, I'm

happily married. I just—I can't get you out of my mind. I just had to touch you—to see if you are real. But you have to understand—this has to be for today only. For us there may never be a tomorrow. Can you accept that?"

As he murmured words that had almost become a litany, his two hands—those hands that used to do magic with engines—stroked the girl's body, cradled the heavy breasts that seemed to grow even larger. His long, sensitive fingers flitted across the round belly. He stopped the hands abruptly.

"Do you understand that, Diann? You have to understand. For us there may be only today."

He stared into her face, into the wide blue eyes that filled with tears. "I understand, I understand," she whispered. "Please. Please take me."

With his left hand he began to massage her right breast. He lowered his mouth to her left nipple. His tongue traced the hard knob, large as a marble now, and gently he began to suck. She was moaning, writhing beneath him. His right hand crept down toward the soft pubic hair, finding the way.

Could he help it if—knowing he and Edwina had no children, that Edwina was older than he—could he help it if some of these young women dared to hope?

He made no apologies. He was an excellent lover. Beneath him, Diann was making a deep throaty sound, a primal growl. Almost time to finish this first round.

Being a good lover came easily. He had a sure system for making it last as long as possible.

Even with his wife, he always imagined he was making love to Amelia Earhart.

—1983 —
Saturday

WILL HILDEBRANDT WAS LOUNGING in the arrival area of the terminal building when they returned to Guam. "So how'd the hospital look?" he asked Verdun.

"Oh, it's older now than in the photo, all right," Verdun said. "But not forty-six years older. I'm almost sure of that."

"So what do you think the story is?"

"Well, I'd sure like to see the original photo, but I'm wondering about some darkroom shenanigans. Use a picture of Earhart—superimpose it on a photo of the hospital …"

"But why would anyone do that?" Edwina spoke softly.

"I don't know. But there's bound to be a story in it."

Laura tried to help develop an explanation for the photo. "So maybe someone who knew what happened to Amelia was trying to prove that the Japanese did have her in Saipan?" The CIA, she was thinking. And Gordon had very likely been connected with the CIA. "So whatever the pre-war spy agency was called—what if they sent her to spy on the Japanese? …" You're getting carried away, she told herself. Yes, maybe it would make sense for Gordon to be trying to plant a picture that blamed the Japanese for Earhart's death if he was indeed connected with the CIA and the agency was connected to her disappearance. But how did he get that picture? And why is he dead?

Jeff chimed in. "Okay. But if the photo *is* a composite, who's hanging on to Amelia's arm? Doesn't the photo mean she did survive the ditching or whatever happened to her plane?"

Not only did the boy reek animal magnetism, he was smart. She'd flown back from Saipan beside him in the cockpit and was ure she had not imagined it—for some reason, he was attracted to her.

Verdun regarded Jeff with interest. "You're right—unless it was a photo taken before her trip, or at an earlier stop on the trip. But I can't imagine a situation where anyone would be holding on to her like that. Unless that's a composite too."

No one ever asks whether it's actually Amelia in the photo, Laura marveled. Except for Charlotte. Laura removed the camera strap from her shoulder and handed the camera to Will. "The film's still loaded. Nothing very exciting, I'm afraid."

"Why don't we all go get something to eat?" Will said. "Then I'll go home and process the film."

"I've got to drive up to Kinney's and meet the Sabláns," Laura said. "Teri stayed here with them."

"Oh, yeah," Will said, looking around. "I wondered what you'd done with the kid." Laura was certain he hadn't given the girl a thought. "Well, Kinney's sounds good to me. Why don't we all go up there for dinner?"

Oh, great. Let Charlotte tell Shelby her theories about the photo.

"Is it anywhere near the Hilton?" Edwina asked hopefully. "I'm really exhausted."

"I'll take you back to the hotel," Jeff said. "I'd love to join you folks for dinner but I've got a—uh, an appointment."

There! Laura felt an odd flare of triumph. He doesn't want me to know he has a date. How have I managed to bewitch this boy while I'm so distracted?

"Maybe I can get a taxi," Edwina said tentatively.

"Don't be silly," Jeff said. "The hotel's right on my way. It's no trouble." He winked at the older woman. "It's *saabisu*."

"Good man, Mac," Will said. "Say, what do you hear from your dad?"

"Not much and not often," the young man said easily.

"That's our Donnie," Will said. "Well, I suppose it's silly to take three cars all the way out to Kinney's, but ..."

"Let's keep our flexibility," Verdun said. Laura felt relieved she wouldn't have to share a car with him.

"You take the lead," Laura said to Will. "In case I've forgotten the way." As she turned toward the parking lot, she found both Jeff and Edwina close at her side.

"Laura, could I see you later?" Edwina asked. "I've got to get some rest now—I really feel the jet lag. But I would like to talk to you—maybe in the morning?"

"Sure, Edwina. Anytime. Just ring Room 233."

"Maybe breakfast?"

Laura felt a tiny shudder of apprehension. Was it just three days ago when I agreed to join Gordon for breakfast? She tried to put the spooky feeling aside. "Do you want to meet me in the coffee shop tomorrow? How early?" At least they could have breakfast in a different part of the hotel than where she had met Gordon.

"Is eight o'clock okay?"

"Eight would be fine," Laura said. Then a real chill ran down her spine. Wasn't that exactly what I said to Gordon? She patted Edwina's hand in farewell and then found Jeff MacDougal touching her other arm.

He looked a little sheepish. "Listen—could we maybe have a drink sometime or something? I'd like—I want to see you again."

Laura felt color rising in her face. "Of course," she said. "I'll be here a few more days. Give me a call. I'm at the Hilton."

As she stood beside her rental car, waiting to see what vehicle Will was driving, an Air Micronesia plane screeched down onto the runway beyond the parking lot. Was it the plane from Saipan with the sunburned man on board?

She was soon driving the long road north toward the air base with Shelby's rental car sandwiched between hers and Will's ancient Volkswagen van, but she couldn't get her mind off the handsome

young pilot and the chemistry that surged between them. What's going on? Am I trying to duplicate Jodie's feat and shock the whole island?

She tried to picture the Canadian diplomat she'd been seeing in Tokyo—visualized his elegant apartment, the exquisite sound system for his classical music, his distinguished silver-gray hair, his kind mouth. But the golden brown skin and dark eyes of this grown-up island child kept thrusting themselves into the foreground.

Okay, she told herself, I've been under a lot of stress lately. But what's his excuse?

* * *

Teri and the Sabláns were seated at a small table in the crowded, noisy restaurant. When he saw there were two others with Laura, Vicente stood and stretched to his fullest height, looking for a larger table. The best he could do was to scrounge a couple of additional chairs and crowd them around the small table.

"I think I've heard about this place in some of my father's tales of the islands," Teri said. A quick grin had conveyed her relief at her mother's safe return. "The entire menu is fried chicken, fried shrimp, or grilled steak."

"Yup," Will said with satisfaction. "Some things never change, thank God."

"Actually, your father's story is about Saipan," Laura said. "When we moved up there, chicken, shrimp, and steak were the only thing on the menus there—at both restaurants on the island. Your father was so excited when they opened the restaurant in the new hotel—well, it was new then. They had these huge menus, so he couldn't wait to order something exotic and sophisticated. He succeeded in being the first person seated in the dining room the night they opened it but, as he picked things out to order, the waitress kept sighing and saying, 'No, we don't have that yet. Sorry, we don't have that yet either.' Finally Foster said, "Okay, let's start over. What do you have?' And of course the answer was …"

"Chicken, shrimp, or steak," the others chorused.

They placed their orders, carefully specifying how they were to be billed, and then the table exploded into questions and comments about how long it had been since Shelby had last been in the Marianas and how the Japanese hospital looked and how many piano rolls Vicente had for his player piano.

At first Laura thought there was no danger of Charlotte making any unfortunate confidences about whom she thought she saw in the photo—no one could hear a word anyone else was saying. But eventually orderly conversation was achieved and Shelby began to dominate it with his convoluted reasons as to why the photo wasn't authentic.

"But I thought you believed she died in Saipan," Vicente said.

"I did for a long time, when I was working on my first book," he said, "but in the end my only real conclusion was that the government was hiding something. Now, this guy Hassler, he worked for the government, right?"

"Oh, yes," Charlotte said. "At least while he was out here in the islands."

"So I've got him pegged as some sort of a cover-up artist for the government. Even at this late date, he must have been out here, trying to keep us from finding the truth about Amelia."

"So then who do you think killed him?" Charlotte asked.

Laura glanced at Teri who was looking bored, despite the suspenseful nature of the conversation. Of course, bored was Teri's look for the season.

"What if someone was trying to blackmail him?" Verdun said. "Someone who had found evidence that contradicted what the government has said all these years—that it had nothing to do with Amelia's disappearance other than arranging for some of her landing places."

"What kind of evidence could it be? You mean the photo?" Will seemed so caught up in Verdun's story, Laura wondered whether he'd forgotten where the photo had come from.

"It could be the photo, if it were authentic," Verdun said.

"Ah, yes, the photo," Charlotte said. "I have some thoughts about the photo … "

Laura waited a half beat or so, hoping Will would save the day, but he seemed to be waiting to hear what Charlotte was going to say. It was up to Laura.

"Whoops!" She lurched across the table awkwardly. Her aim was perfect—her elbow sent her full glass of ice water cascading right into Shelby Verdun's lap.

"Mother!" Teri sounded mortified.

"I'm so sorry," Laura said, starting to dab at Verdun's trousers with her paper napkin. He wrenched it from her hand, sputtering in surprise, anger, agony—she couldn't tell which.

During the chaos—Vicente trying to signal a waiter, Will grabbing napkins from other tables and handing them to Verdun—Laura was conscious of two pairs of eyes fastened sternly upon her: Teri's and Charlotte's. They know, she thought. They know everything. Or that I did it on purpose, and that's next to everything.

"Geez, Laura," Will said. "I thought you were this great athlete. That was pretty klutzy." He offered to show Verdun the way to the restroom. "I think they have one of those godawful hot-air dryers," he was saying as he shambled away between the tables, Verdun hunched over almost like a man who had been kicked in the groin. Good grief, Laura thought. it was only a plastic glass. Nothing heavy.

She was still calling, "I'm so sorry, I'm so sorry," after them as she turned her eyes back to those still at the table. Charlotte was still staring at her. Her eyebrows lifted the slightest bit, acknowledging the line Laura had gouged in the conversational sand. Laura suspected she would hear about this when they were alone.

As for Teri, she was smiling sweetly. "Maybe I could find a video game until the food comes, if I had some quarters."

"Have you seen any here?" Laura asked.

"Oh, you mean those Japanese games?" Vicente asked. "I heard Teri's a grand champion. I'm afraid the only device they have to steal

your quarters here is the jukebox. Here, Teri, pick out some music. We should be able to hear from that speaker." He pointed at a large box fastened to the rafter above their heads.

Teri returned to the table at the same time as Will and Shelby, as well as the waiter with their order. "That jukebox must be from a museum," she said. "They've got songs from my mother's youth."

Conversation ceased as they tackled their large platters of food. In the near-lull, Laura heard familiar chords. A guitar and … was it a ukulele? Then came the mellow, island voice, singing about pearly shells and love.

Charlotte clapped her hands. "Oh, Don Ho. My goodness, I haven't heard this for ages."

"My mother loves this guy," Teri said with amusement verging on wonder. "She used to listen to this music all the time when I was a little kid."

"What can I say?" Laura said. "I missed the islands."

The music was a magnet, drawing her into another time if not another place. It was party music from the sixties, and she remembered being in bars in Palau and Saipan, listening to the music, singing along, drinking, and laughing. Being silly. Being young.

She looked at Will, wondering whether he felt the same nostalgia, but he was concentrating on cutting a rather tough Australian steak. Shelby Verdun sat stiffly, silently, peeling the crust from his fried chicken.

When the second Don Ho song began, Verdun said to Teri, "How much of this island magic will we be subjected to?"

"Three songs," she said. "Three for a quarter. That's all I picked." She reached into her pocket and passed two quarters to Vicente. "Sorry, I didn't mean to keep these."

"Ain't no big t'ing, brudduh," Vicente sang along with the Hawaiian star. Laura's mind segued from her own youth to the youth she had spent the afternoon with. He'd said the same thing. So had his father many years ago. Which brought her back to Jodie, and the dilemma of the photo.

It wasn't until the third song began that she felt the chill of recognition. The other songs had been faster, lively numbers. This was slower, a sad song. You could slow-dance to this music.

I remember last June, I was alone
Wishing I had someone
I could hold and kiss and love
On the Fourth of July,
You burst upon my scene
Fireworks and flowers filled the sky.

And they had danced to it. This morning in her dream. This was the improbable ballet music she'd heard. She closed her eyes for a moment to recreate her viewpoint from that orchestra seat at the San Francisco Opera House. Yes, they were dancing to a Don Ho song, that's what had seemed odd.

But you had to go
A prior commitment
Keeps you out of reach,
Not out of sight, not out of mind
And when autumn comes, I'll be alone
Guess alone is how I'm gonna be.

She also remembered the man hovering in the wings just beyond the stage lights in her dream. And now she recognized him.

"Will," she whispered urgently, leaning toward him, across Verdun's plate. Verdun leaned forward to steady her water glass and his. "Watch it," he cautioned.

"Hmmm?" Will was enjoying his steak with a look that came close to a purr.

"We need to talk to Rudy."

He raised an eyebrow, continued chewing. Charlotte had begun to chatter about the time she and Vicente went to see the Don Ho

show at Waikiki and how disappointed she had been to find that he was such a short man when he had such a tall voice.

Vicente said with mock indignation, "I didn't realize you had a problem with short men!"

They finished their meals and their beers, went through elaborate calculations to divide up the bill and tip, and eventually made their way to the parking lot. Will brushed against Laura.

"You're right," he said. "Rudy's gotta know something."

"I had a dream," she said. "Almost a vision. He's the key—only I didn't figure it out until I heard the music."

"We could go tonight," Will said. "It's not ten yet. Rudy's a night owl."

"What are you two plotting?" Charlotte boomed in a hearty voice right behind them. Then she looked guilty, perhaps wondering whether she had transgressed that invisible line in the sand.

"Think you can find your way back to the hotel?" Will asked Verdun.

"I'd feel better following someone," he said nervously. Ever since the ice water hit his lap, he had been a subdued and humbler man.

"Follow me then," Will said, and the two cars left the graveled parking lot as Laura and Teri stood thanking the Sabláns for their hospitality and friendship.

"Come on out to the Center Monday morning," Charlotte said. "I'm sure we can find some interesting stuff in my files."

Teri pounced the minute they were alone in the car. "Mother, why did you dump your water on that poor man! I knew something strange was going on. What is it?"

Laura sighed. She was afraid that anything Teri knew could add to her peril, but she certainly wasn't going to leave the girl at the hotel while she and Will visited Rudy Terlaje. And she certainly couldn't trust Will to do it alone—his history with Rudy was too long and tangled.

"It's that picture—Will and I have seen it before."

"I knew it. I knew it was the picture," Teri said in triumph.

"So we need to talk to the guy that we know also saw it … before."

"When? When you lived here before? Did you find a picture of Amelia Earhart and you never told me?"

"Well, it's complicated. But please, you have to promise me, don't say a word. I want you to come with us, but wait until you and I are alone before you say anything, okay?"

"Okay," Teri said, and there was no trace of her bored and sophisticated voice. "This is great. We're going to figure out what happened to Amelia Earhart."

Or Gordon Hassler, Laura amended silently, keeping that connection to herself.

— 1960 —

DESPITE GORDON'S INITIAL DOUBTS, grabbing the liaison job in Saipan had been a stroke of genius. At first he had simply seen it as a chance to get into the CIA, get close to their archives. However, living in the islands seemed to bring him closer to everything. The answer to the mystery was still here, swimming in the almost liquid air. Things never change in the seasonless tropics. Something that happened twenty-three years ago is still happening, in a way.

An important part of the liaison job was to keep the press unaware of the operation in Saipan. It was unlikely that the CIA's program to train Chinese guerrillas for an eventual assault on Mainland China would fit within the United Nations' definition of defensive use of a part of the Trust Territory. On his twice-monthly trips to Guam, Gordon's regular rounds included the Navy and the Air Force commands, where he arranged for consignments of duty-free liquor and other necessities for the CIA community in Saipan. He also called on a local film distributor, where he ordered movies that would be shown in the base theater. His bosses had decided that the prints they obtained from the military entertainment division were in such bad shape from too many showings, they were better off getting slightly older films from the Guamanian commercial distributor which also had access to foreign films the U.S. military establishment had apparently decided were of no interest to the troops.

Last on his rounds was the press. First he would stop by KUAM, the radio-TV station, and chat with the news director, a garrulous, good-hearted old guy who—Gordon learned after several months—had come to the Western Pacific to spread the gospel according to Baha'ullah.

"Baha who?"

"We're Bahais," Arne Knudsen said. "Here, you might find this interesting." He handed Gordon a small folder that included a calendar for a year with seventeen months. "Our Bahai calendar, with the holy days marked."

"Does that mean I won't find you here at work some days?"

Knudsen shook his head. "No, this job doesn't allow that much flexibility. I get my devotions taken care of before working hours. But I think it's always good to let people know we exist, that we have another way of looking at things, another way of counting time."

Yes, a new perspective was healthy in most things.

"So how's everything in Saipan?" Knudsen asked. "When are you going to let me come up and do a story?"

"A story about what?" They had this conversation every time they saw each other. Gordon wasn't sure if it was the newsman's curiosity about what lay behind a closed door or the desire of a missionary to make new contacts that made Arne Knudsen think he wanted to go to Saipan.

"Whatever's happening up there. Just to remind ourselves that Guam is not a world completely unto itself."

"I wish there were something interesting going on in Saipan," Gordon said. "Then my wife wouldn't be going crazy."

He left the radio station and drove down to Agaña in the car the Navy supplied him for each visit.

It was his job and he did it well. He portrayed Saipan as such a dull place no one would ever want to go there. But the truth was, Edwina had never been happier than she was in Saipan. Oh, true, she had those sharp, cynical turns of phrase that might make some people wonder if she were bitter—perhaps about his habit of flirting with other men's young wives. But she had never before lived where she didn't have to hold a job, where she could spend her days on her beloved bridge games, where she had a maid for the housework and could plan an occasional elegant little dinner party. Being a lady of leisure suited Edwina, and Gordon found it relaxing to be with her.

So much so that his flirtations remained just that. Besides, the island was so small, there was no way to be discreet about an affair. He couldn't even imagine sneaking away to Guam with a paramour. He would probably run into Arne Knudsen at the airport and get roped into attending a Bahai religious ceremony.

Gordon parked across from the *Daily Chronicle* building. He would spend fifteen minutes chatting with the glum Rudy Terlaje and still have plenty of time to get back out to the airport for his flight home.

The girl at the advertising department counter nodded at him in recognition and he climbed the stairs to the editorial office on the second floor. Rudy Terlaje sat at his desk near the top of the stairs, sorting through stacks of yellow Teletype copy weighted down with oddly shaped chunks of coral.

"Ah, Gordon," the editor said, almost as though he expected Hassler. "I was hoping you'd come along. Something about Saipan came over the wire a couple of hours ago."

Gordon heard a tiny alarm bell at the back of his mind. Anything that called attention to the island was bad, according to his bosses, and a reflection upon his work.

"What's the story?"

"Something out of San Francisco." Terlaje shuffled through the stories on his desk. "It seems a Saipanese woman living somewhere in California told some radio reporter that she saw that woman flier, Amelia Earhart, on Saipan when she was a kid. Says the Japanese were holding her prisoner."

Gordon's heart thudded. "It can't be true," he said.

Terlaje shrugged. "You've never heard anything up there about a white woman seen in Japanese times?"

Gordon reflected that he actually heard very little at all from the Saipanese with whom he had contact. His civilian liaison assignment dealt with the logistics of getting day workers transported to the CIA enclave each day, seeing that their security clearances were up to date, and alerting his bosses if there appeared to be any dis-

enchantment brewing among the island workers. He never had the sort of conversations with the Saipanese in which they might confide tales and legends of their youth.

"No," he told Rudy with a carefully careless chuckle, "I've never heard such a thing."

Rudy read from a sheet of yellow Teletype paper. "Mrs. Cortez said the woman was a prisoner of the Japanese and that she heard the woman later died of dysentery. She described the American woman as tall, thin, with blonde hair cut quite short."

"Certainly her hair would have grown," Gordon said.

Rudy raised an eyebrow, either in question or comment — Gordon couldn't be sure. He jammed a hand into his pocket where his fingers began practicing on the coins, making a jingling sound. With effort, he stilled his fingers. "I mean if it were Earhart and she had been held prisoner for a while, don't you think it sounds a little too perfect if she's described as looking exactly as she did when she disappeared?"

That face flashed vividly onto the inner screen of his mind: the sparkling eyes, the high cheek bones, the feathery hair, tousled by a breeze as she turned to wave before she stepped into the cockpit. Just as she looked before she disappeared.

"Yeah, you've got a point," Rudy said. "First thing I thought of was I never heard of any Saipanese called Cortez but it turns out the lady is married to a Filipino—I'm not sure what they're doing in California. Like you say, it all seems very unlikely that Earhart would have ended up in Saipan. But we may get a query from UPI or the AP or someone ... " His eyes scanned the Teletype story. "Yeah, here, this is what I thought might interest you ... 'Verdun says he plans to visit Saipan and check out the Cortez report as soon as possible.'"

"Verdun?"

"The San Francisco reporter who unearthed Mrs. Cortez. He works for some radio station."

Gordon closed his eyes. Now what? Surely there was some way the Navy could keep a reporter off the island. After all, no one could come to Saipan without permission of the Commander of Naval Forces Marianas, the nearly omnipotent ComNavMar. Still, any kind of press interest in Saipan was going to alarm Gordon's bosses.

He opened his eyes to find Rudy staring at him with an odd look. Was it hunger?

"What I wanted to say, Gordon, is I expect I'll be getting a query from the wire services on this … any that still remember we're here. And it's going to be a little strange if I say, sorry, I'm sure the Navy and their friends don't want any visitors."

"Yes … " What the hell was Terlaje leading up to? Gordon had never seen him look so alert, so intense. Perhaps he really was a newsman under the bored, sniffling exterior.

"What I thought was maybe you could arrange for me to go up to Saipan, talk to a bunch of Saipanese, get a story out that squashes the whole thing."

"Hmm." Gordon supposed it was possible. But what if Rudy found a bunch of other people who said they remembered a tall, blonde white woman on the island in 1937? Ridiculous. She couldn't have made it that far north. Unless the Japanese had picked her up somewhere else and brought her to Saipan. After all, Saipan had been their headquarters in the western Pacific.

"Well, Rudy, it is my job to keep the press away from Saipan … "

"I know, I know. But if you had a bona fide newsman, and you knew what he was going to write, it might fend off the others."

"But would I know what he was going to write?"

Rudy lowered his voice to a whisper. "You sure would. Look, I'm very anti-communist and there's no way I want to see whatever it is you guys are trying to accomplish get fouled up. So my own bias would dictate what I wrote. But also, it would be work for hire. If you pay me to write something, I write what you want."

"Pay you?" Gordon felt genuinely shocked.

"I'll be straight with you. There's no way the old man," he jerked his head over his shoulder toward the publisher's private office, "will pay for any off-island coverage. If I'm going to take a few days, I'll have to use vacation time. Plus I have a special need for some cash right now. My wife's heard about a drug that might help our son … he's retarded, you know. There's a doctor here in Agaña who can get the drugs and will let us try them, but it's gonna cost me a bundle. A bundle I don't have."

"How big a bundle?" Gordon had access to cash to use when necessary to make sure things went smoothly for the CIA operation—but how high could he go? He had never been told.

Rudy hesitated.

He's trying to gauge me, Gordon thought, trying to guess what the traffic will bear.

"I'll do it for two thousand," Rudy said finally.

Two thousand? Gordon hesitated. If it quashes this Amelia Earhart nonsense it would be worth it. And if the CIA won't pay that much, I'll make up the difference myself. "I'll have to check, but I think we could handle that," he said.

Rudy's face lit up for a second, more alive than Gordon had ever seen it. Then it seemed to fall.

He's thinking he should have gone for a bigger number. With sudden generosity, he added, "You buy your ticket, but we'll reimburse you. And put you up in the guest house. Two thousand plus expenses."

Gordon felt like rubbing his hands together in satisfaction as he hurried down the stairs afterward, so he jammed them into his pockets. Once again, his right fingers found coins and started shuffling them about. This time he barely noticed. He got into the car and headed for the naval air station.

Amelia Earhart in Saipan?

It couldn't be. And yet … what if she had already planned to stray into the Japanese mandate? Then my sabotage would have put her even farther off course—maybe as far north as the Marianas.

Deep in Japanese territory, beyond where the U.S. Navy would be searching for her.

But then whose interests would Tex Arnold have been serving? The Japanese?

— 1983 —
Saturday

LAURA PULLED INTO THE PARKING LOT at the Hilton and saw Will shaking hands with Shelby Verdun near the main entrance. She turned off her headlights and let the car idle at the edge of the hotel driveway.

"What are we waiting for?" Teri said.

"Shhh."

After Verdun disappeared into the hotel, Will turned and stood shuffling his feet, looking around the parking area anxiously.

"Wind down your window," Laura said. She turned on the headlights, pulled up beside Will, and leaned across Teri to say, "Get in. You navigate and I'll drive."

Will stared in the window at the mother and daughter for a moment, shrugged, opened the back door, and got in. "So this is a team effort?" he said.

Laura pulled out of the parking lot. "Teri's cool," she said. "She'll keep quiet."

The girl turned around and grinned at Will. "Who knows? You might even get to like me."

Will laughed nervously. "Listen, Laura, when we get down to Marine Drive, we need to stop somewhere so I can give Rudy a call. I didn't want to chance doing it at the hotel with Shelby there."

Laura parked in front of the Panciteria, a sprawling Chinese/Filipino restaurant she remembered from her first day on the island all those years ago. "They must have a phone somewhere in there," she told Will. While he was gone she reached over and patted Teri's hand. "Actually, I think Will is terrified of anyone of the female persuasion."

"I thought he'd had all sorts of wives."

"That's why he's terrified of women."

Will returned to the car. "Okay, he's expecting us."

"Does he think we're crazy?"

"Rudy knows I'm crazy," Will said. "He probably won't be sure about you until he hears our story. Do you remember how to get to Mongmong?"

Rudy Terlaje greeted them at the doorway of his dark house before Will could tap on the door. His face was impassive. As always. "Come in. We'll go out to the kitchen so we don't disturb my wife."

Through an archway off the entryway, Laura saw the blue light of a television in a darkened living room. A chair with a tall back faced the set, its occupant invisible.

In the kitchen, Rudy turned on the ceiling light and pulled out chairs around a small table. Silently they slid onto the chairs. There was what seemed to Laura a very long, tense moment of silence.

"So you need to talk to me about Gordon Hassler? Who's writing the story or is this a collaborative effort?"

Laura and Will exchanged a glance and Laura said, "Did you know him well?"

"Oh, I wouldn't say I knew him. I used to see him a couple times a month back in the old days, when he was liaison for the old outfit on Saipan."

"For … what did they call it? The Company?" Laura tried to create that sense of being in league together with her subject that often served her well in interviews.

Rudy snorted. "I guess that's the trendy way to refer to it." He gazed at Teri. "Do you usually help your mother on her reporting assignments?"

"When I was little she used to take me with her sometimes," Teri said. "Lately she just gives me money to play Galaxians."

Rudy lifted a quizzical eyebrow.

"You know those Japanese electronic games?" Will said. "Teri was the big winner down at Joe and Flo's last night."

"Well, I have to give you folks credit," Rudy said. "I'm a little disappointed in 'Sús Pérez. He hasn't been out to talk to me about Hassler. You'd think if you were investigating a murder, you would want to know if the victim had any skeletons in his closet."

"And you think Gordon did?" Laura asked.

"I wouldn't call it a skeleton. He was doing a job that needed to be done. But in that business you're bound to make enemies. I mean, we wouldn't need things like the CIA if we didn't have enemies. And who knows what sort of projects he worked on after he left here."

Laura felt a small chill. After he left the islands, Gordon worked in the same office as Foster Monroe. Did Teri know that? Did she know her father had a job in which he was bound to make enemies?

Will must have decided to play the investigative reporter a little longer. "So, Rudy, do you have any theories about what happened to your old acquaintance?"

Rudy shook his head. "Nary a one. And that wouldn't perplex me at all … not knowing what Hassler got up to after he left the islands. Except for one thing."

"The photo," Laura said softly.

Rudy looked almost surprised. "Yes, the photo they found on his body."

"You've seen it before," Will said, making it a clear statement of fact.

Rudy was instantly wary. "What makes you say that?"

"I sent it to you." Will's words rang like a bell, pure and piercing. Even Laura stared at him, surprised to hear the issue suddenly in the open.

Rudy was silent for several moments. Finally he spoke. "Will Hildebrandt. The conspiracy nut. Of course. I should have guessed. And where did you find a photo of Amelia Earhart taken in Saipan?"

Will took a deep breath and spoke again, staring directly into his friend's eyes. "I took it."

There was a tense pause.

"I mean, I framed the shot, I clicked the shutter. I developed it. I printed it. I addressed the envelope. I stuck on the stamp."

Rudy's face remained paralyzed but Teri's jaw dropped and she jerked her face back and forth, looking at Will, then her mother, and back at Will. Rudy stood so suddenly his chair tipped over with a clatter. He strode across the room and pulled open a drawer and rummaged in some papers. Very quietly, Laura leaned over and righted his chair. Teri was still looking back and forth. She seemed awed. Or maybe scared.

Rudy returned to the table and slapped yesterday's newspaper down on it. His index finger was trembling as he pointed to the photo in the lower right corner. "You took this picture. And this is not Amelia Earhart, is that what you're saying?"

Will nodded slowly, still staring at Rudy.

"Then who the hell is it?"

Laura couldn't leave Will alone at the end of his limb any longer. "It was a friend of ours. She bore a striking resemblance to Amelia … and we all got drunk one night and had this crazy idea … "

"To fabricate a news story?" For the first time in all the years she'd known him, Laura heard Rudy Terlaje raise his voice. "Two reporters—still working as reporters today, if I'm not mistaken—fake a news story. Did you send it out all over or was I the only target of your little prank?"

"I only made one print," Will said.

"Why? Why me?"

"I was pissed off, Rudy," Will said. "You totally ignored Verdun's book when it came out. The *Chronicle* didn't seem capable of printing the name Amelia Earhart. I wanted to see if you would publish her picture."

"And I was delighted not to publish it," Rudy said. "One of my first thoughts when I opened that envelope was: If Hildebrandt sees this, he is going to be crowing, 'I told you so, I told you so.'"

"Is that why you didn't run it?" Laura said, amazed. "Just to bug Will?"

"I didn't run that photo for the same reason I didn't run anything about Verdun's book—to keep people from overrunning Saipan."

"Were you an agent?" Will asked. "I thought John dela Cruz … I thought the publisher … "

Rudy's mouth opened as though he were caught by surprise, or ambushed by a memory. "I suppose I was an agent, in a way, ."

"But the CIA was long gone from Saipan when the book came out in '66. And we took the photo in '67," Laura said.

"It was dela Cruz, wasn't it, Rudy?" Will said. "John dela Cruz wouldn't let you run an article about the book or use the photo because of his connections with the China Lobby. Am I right?"

"Dela Cruz never saw that photo," Rudy said in a low voice. "I decided not to run it. On my own."

"But I thought—I mean, dela Cruz was a fanatic anti-communist. On a par with Henry Luce as I recall."

"Did you ever wonder what I thought of the commies?" Rudy asked and Will fell silent.

There's some other reason he didn't run the photo, Laura sensed. Not just because he hated communists. Something personal, something that's making him feel uncomfortable. But she couldn't guess what it was.

"Maybe I didn't run it out of force of habit. I had been asked a dozen times not to run this sort of stuff, not to endanger the operation in Saipan."

"By John dela Cruz," Will could not let loose of his pet theory.

Rudy took a deep, slow breath. "No. By Gordon Hassler. In his role as liaison between the operation and the rest of the world."

Laura let out the breath she suddenly discovered she was holding in. It made a small but piercing whistle. "Okay," she said. An answer to the mysterious reappearance of the photo had to be two feet in front of her, as close as Rudy Terlaje's face. "Then what did you do with the photo? Did you give it to Gordon? Is that how it ended up in his pocket?"

"How that photo ended up on his body—that's for you to figure out. You took the photo. You must have the negative. I tore the print you sent me into tiny pieces and burned it in my ash tray."

Laura stared at Will a moment, then turned to find Teri's mouth gaping in her direction. We're like the Three Stooges with these double takes, she thought.

"You … burned … the … photo," Will said in a monotone, apparently trying to grasp the implications.

"You clicked the shutter," Rudy said. "You developed the film. You made the prints. You must know who you addressed them to."

Part 3

— 1975 —
March

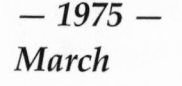

THE APARTMENT WAS TOO SMALL and far too expensive and Jodie hated the furniture—she imagined Foster Monroe proclaiming it neo-plastic Mediterranean. But she had to have a place of her own, a San Francisco address, so that Donnie would never find out about Belvedere.

The cable arrived the same day the item had appeared in the *San Francisco Chronicle* about the last American in Indochina being freed.

BLONDIE: THEY'VE SPRUNG ME. CALIFORNIA HERE I COME.

How much time do I have? Surely there would be a debriefing for him somewhere before the U.S. government turned him loose. Where? In Hawaii? Would he have to go to Washington?

"I'll take it," she told the rental agent. The other two apartments she'd looked at had even more outrageous prices. At least this one had a bit of a view, a sliver of the bay glimmering between the ranks of low apartment buildings across the street.

"I'll need a check for nine hundred dollars," the agent said. "Better give it to me now if you want to hold the apartment."

Jodie gulped. "N-nine hundred?"

"First and last month's rent plus damage deposit."

With shaking fingers, Jodie wrote out the check. "Can you give me a half day before you deposit this?" she asked. "I need to transfer some funds."

The agent shrugged. "I'll do my best, sweetie, but you'd better have the dough."

"Oh, I've got it," Jodie lied, dreading what she was going to have to do to get it. It was going to be hard enough telling Reggie she was moving out. Asking him for money would be even worse. If only she hadn't bought the car with the money she'd managed to accumulate. But the car had seemed essential, the only way to get away from Reggie's constant, smothering caring.

And it comes in handy now, she thought, speeding across the Golden Gate Bridge, hurrying to the house in Belvedere. How would I have moved out without a car? Asked Reggie to lend me his?

She was loading the madras plaid spread and some books into the passenger seat—her last load from the house—when she thought to call Maryann, her former roommate, to give her the new address. Donnie could be there any minute, trying to contact her.

Maryann was away from her desk—for thirty minutes, it turned out, while Jodie tapped her fingers and read and reread the same items in the alternative weekly newspaper Reggie had subscribed to in a doomed effort to be trendy. She wished she dared to go out to the garage to organize her boxes there but was afraid of missing Maryann's call. She tried to rehearse a speech for Reggie. What if Donnie was already at the airport, calling Maryann's apartment? What if Tony, Maryann's boyfriend, answered and gave him Reggie's number? She could imagine Tony saying, "Jodie? No, I guess she used to live here, but she moved out months ago. Shacked up with some guy over in Belvedere."

Maryann finally called. She pretended to be impressed by the new address. "Once you've lived in Bel-vuh-deah, my deah, I suppose you're just too grand for the Inner Richmond anymore."

"No," Jodie said. "It's not that I can afford to live in the Marina—it's all I could find."

"Phone number?"

"Oh, damn," Jodie said. "I wonder how long that will take?"

"Call them and set up the installation," Maryann said. She had many years experience constructing scenarios for the benefit of boyfriends, Jodie had discerned. "They might be able to assign the num-

ber right now and we can just pretend it's out of order. Otherwise, I'll tell him you've had to change your number because of crank calls or something, and you might be between numbers. That will make it sound like you've been there for a while."

"Great," Jodie said. "What about Tony?"

"Hmm," Maryann said. "It's hopeless to try to make him learn a script. Let's pray I take the call."

Out at her car, Jodie rummaged through the brown paper grocery bag into which she had tossed her entire shoe wardrobe. She changed into the outrageous platform shoes she had bought a few months ago—her own effort, perhaps, to be trendy. They were painfully uncomfortable and it probably wasn't safe to drive wearing them, but they did make her feel self-confident. They also made her at least two inches taller than Reggie.

Driving to his office on the edge of San Rafael, Jodie tried to think through her speech. She was determined—for once—to be completely honest with him. But where to begin? Tell him she had moved out? Or ask for the money first?

She parked in the shade of menthol-scented eucalyptus trees and clumped into the small office building. Reggie told his secretary to show her right into his private office the minute he heard she was there. He looked a little startled when she turned back to close the door to the outer office. "What's up, kid?"

"Reggie, I need some money," she said, blurting it out. "An advance on future pay. Only after you hear the rest of what I've got to say, I probably won't be working for you anymore."

He sighed and lumbered to his feet. "Sit," he said, pointing at one of the easy chairs at the side of the room. He lowered himself into the next chair. "How much do you need?"

She sank into the chair. "Five hundred," she said. No. There will be installation charges on the phone, deposits on utilities. "No, better make it seven hundred."

He wrestled his checkbook out of his hip pocket. "Okay. And the bad news?"

She took a deep breath. "I'm moving out. I have moved out. I've got an apartment in the city."

He closed his eyes and for one frightened moment she thought he might cry. He nodded slowly. "He's back, isn't he? The guy who taught you to fly. I saw an item about Laos releasing an American pilot. That's him, isn't it?"

She nodded, surprised. She had never said much about Donnie to Reggie. She had never even mentioned that he was the man she had been making love to when the cop was shot, although she had described the rest of that event in melodramatic detail. Reggie was more aware and sensitive than she had given him credit for being.

"I knew eventually I'd lose you," Reggie said, handing her the check. "No. I knew I'd never really had you. You don't have to pay me back. Consider it ... severance pay."

For a second her heart sank. Once again, she was being fired. Never again would she fly that sweet little plane over the sparkling bay, heading off toward the brown and green Central Valley.

But then she felt as though a helium-filled balloon were pulling her up. She was free. It was over.

She thanked Reggie profusely and floated out to her car despite the brick-thick shoes strapped to her feet. Freedom. And just enough room for some groceries. No, she would get her things into the apartment, go back to Reggie's garage and get her dishes and her paltry collection of art, hang some things up on the apartment's stark white walls. She had to make it look as though she had been living there for ages. Then she would go out for some food. But first, she had to deposit Reggie's check.

It was dark when she wearily climbed the stairs one more time to the new apartment, her arms laden with food, wine, beer and a bouquet of flowers. He was beside her door, sitting on the stairs that led up to the apartment on the third floor. He looked terribly thin and haggard but his eyes lit up like headlights.

"About time you got home, Blondie," he said.

Very carefully she set the bags of groceries down on the floor by the door, laid the flowers on top of one bag. Then she screamed and ran into his arms just as he rose to his feet. She felt her body trying to swallow him, trying to make him part of her. She was crying, laughing, squealing with joy.

Laughing, he peeled her limbs away and said, "I'm glad you're glad to see me, but shouldn't we do the rest of the welcome ceremony on the other side of the door?"

Her hands had lost their ability to manage details. She couldn't find the right key, couldn't get it into the unfamiliar lock.

"Take it easy, Blondie," he said, stroking her arms gently. "Take a deep breath. A pilot needs to keep cool. Didn't your flying teacher ever tell you that?"

The next morning she found the beer, wine, milk and eggs lined up neatly in the clean, nearly-empty refrigerator. She had no memory of bringing the groceries in. Then she noticed the flowers stuck rather unceremoniously in water in a Pilsener glass that bore the logo of the Top o' the Mar, the Navy club in Guam where they had first danced. Donnie must have put things away—she would have found a vase. Good thing she had made the second trip out to Reggie's and gotten her other boxes from his garage. Donnie could certainly believe this was her apartment, that she had been living here for some time, when he found the glass from Guam in her cupboard and put the flowers in it.

She didn't remember anything about the night except him, the weight of his body, the blessed leanness of him, the sense of completion, the first peace she had known since he'd left her in Hawaii nearly four years ago.

Now everything was going to be fine. Surely they would live happily ever after. They had earned it.

*   *   *

The trouble with perfection is it's only momentary. He tried to play her game for a few days, giving every appearance of believing her when she pretended to call from a neighbor's phone and arrange to take several days off from a job she no longer had. Her story about having the phone number changed seemed to satisfy him and very quickly the refrigerator took on the look of long-time residence. But something was wrong.

"Do you think being in that prison changed you?" she dared to ask, trying to find a way to talk about what was different. She needed to decide whether she should look for a job to make the next rent payment, or whether to ask him if he could pay.

Donnie shrugged. "Well, I quit smoking. That should be an improvement."

Then one day he came out with it. "Okay, Blondie, I need to know. Who exactly lives in Belvedere?"

"My boss," she said quickly. "The guy I fly for."

He nodded and for a moment she thought she had made it past the chasm, that perhaps she could go on to say that she didn't like working for Reggie, giving Donnie the chance to say, "Look, you don't need to work for anyone. I've got my grubstake. Now let's buy a plane and go into business." How much would they pay him for the years he spent imprisoned? Surely someone was going to pay big for that.

But he didn't give her a chance to steer the conversation.

"Jodie, I know it's more than that with this guy. That first night, I came in from the airport in a taxi, went racing to that address on Tenth Avenue. Your friend Maryann was really friendly, said you'd gotten your own place some time ago, gave me the address. I asked about the phone number. I was beginning to get cold feet — scared I'd find you with someone else. She said you'd just gotten your number changed and then she says to the oaf across the room, 'Did Jodie call with her new phone number?' and he says, 'What? Did she leave the guy in Belvedere? I thought she had a good set-up there.' She shoots him a killer look, told me they must have gotten their

Jodies confused. I said, 'That's okay, I'll just find a cab and surprise her at her apartment.' And, oh Jodie, when I saw you I wanted to believe you'd waited for me."

Jodie thought her heart had stopped. There was no sound in the apartment except the humming of the refrigerator out in the kitchen. They needed background music for this scene. She willed the radio to come on, play some sad yet hopeful music to get them past this crisis. But the silence continued, unrelenting, until Donnie shattered it.

"Damn it, Jodie, what kind of idiot do you take me for?"

She felt tears welling in her eyes, tried to stop them, then hoped they would soften his anger. "Please don't," he said, and then let the silence stretch out until she wanted to shriek. Finally she said very quietly. "I told you when you left for Southeast Asia: I can't make it without you."

"Oh, come on, Blondie, you were fine before you ever met me. Don't dump that load on me."

"I was different before I met you," she said. "I need more out of life now." She waved her arms hopelessly. "I need … I need to fly."

"Flying I can understand. But screwing? While I was locked up in a cage in Laos you needed to roll around in some other guy's bed? Jesus H. Christ, Jodie."

She started to cry, to sob so hard she thought she might suffocate. He seemed to grow alarmed, and held her tightly in his arms until she calmed down. She felt about the size and shape of a potato and wondered whether he would ever bring himself to kiss her again.

Finally he spoke, "I suppose it's only fair."

Her heart surged with hope. Perhaps he could see her dilemma.

"I betrayed Panda — so you betrayed me."

No, no, her mind objected. That idea of balance completely leaves me out. "Donnie, you left me. I had to find a way to live."

"I had to live in a cage. And every stinking, sweaty night I thought about you, babe."

"Every stinking, sweaty night with Reggie I thought about you, I swear to God I did."

Rationally, he said, he could believe her, he could understand. But that understanding didn't incorporate itself into his body. Their love-making now seemed contained by fragile glass walls they had to be careful not to crack. He paid the next month's rent. She saw an ad for part-time relief for a corporate pilot and sent in her résumé.

And then the heavy, square envelope came from Guam.

"Hot damn," Donnie said, his eyes sparkling with their old verve. "My boy's graduating high school. And his mother's giving him a trip to Hawaii for a present. I know what I'm going to give him."

"What?" Jodie made the question as neutral as she could, trying not to betray the trepidation she felt.

"Flying lessons. I'll go home for a while and teach the kid to fly."

Home. I wanted your home to be with me.

But the man had been caged with Panda as well as in Laos. The one thing she could still do for him was let him go without reproach.

And she did, although her heart was breaking.

— 1983 —
Saturday

LAURA DROVE SLOWLY DOWN MONGMONG'S single dark street. Teri and Will were silent. Finally Laura spoke.

"What now?"

"I can't believe it," Will said. "I made the contact prints, up in Saipan. I came home and I made one print. One."

"So what did you do with the negatives?" Teri asked impatiently. Even a fourteen-year-old knows a photo is not a one-time thing.

"I suppose I've got them on file," Will said. His voice was tinged with wonder at this new direction, this grand conspiracy suddenly laid on the doorstep of his own darkroom.

"Why does the idea of your files fill me with fear?" Laura said, trying to make her voice light.

"Hey," Will said defensively, "it's not as bad as you think. I set up a system years ago and I've been pretty good about sticking to it. So I guess we'd better go over to my place and take a look."

The clock on the dashboard said 10:45 as they pulled up beside a decrepit Quonset hut in Sinajaña Village, just a couple miles from Rudy Terlaje's trim bungalow in Mongmong. Laura left the headlights on for a few moments, shaking her head in mock amazement. "Will, I can't believe this place is still standing."

"Were you here back then? I don't remember."

"Of course, dummy. Any number of times. Bringing you home when you were too drunk to find the ignition."

"Oh, of course," Will said, getting out of the car and opening the front passenger door for Teri. "I don't know if you realize this about your mother, but she was a terrible prude in her youth. She

was always sober when the rest of us were feeling no pain. She invented the concept of the designated driver."

"What about all that gin I heard you used to drink?" Teri asked Laura.

"I'm afraid my sobriety was only relative," Laura said. "Like I said, Will couldn't find the ignition on his best nights."

"Only because you hid the keys from me," he said. "Finding the car the next day was the real bitch."

They walked on a path of crumbling concrete. Laura laughed. "I remember dragging you up this walk one night, Foster and I on either side of you. You were falling down drunk and singing some rude song in a very loud voice. And your wife, whichever one it was, appeared in the doorway and started lobbing things at us. Dishes and books as I recall. And screaming at us at the top of her lungs."

"Cassandra," Will said. "She was the one who threw things." He shuddered audibly. "Boy, did she live up to her name!"

"Why? What does Cassandra mean?" Teri said.

"Oh, I don't remember. Some myth. Something about foretelling disaster. Only in her case, she was the disaster." He fumbled with the door knob, mumbling, "Gotta hold this just right to get it open."

"That must be fun when you're tiddly," Laura said.

"Excuse me, Mrs. Monroe, maybe you haven't noticed the last couple nights, but I've cut back. A couple beers do it for me now." Slowly he moved into the room. They could sense him swatting toward the ceiling. "Should get a switch put in by the door sometime," he said. His hand must have struck the light chain for, in an instant, they were flooded by light from a large, naked lightbulb that swung from the arched metal roof. Laura looked around the crowded room. Piles of books and papers dominated the place, with a few bits of furniture peeping out here and there. A card table had the only clear surface in the room, and it bore a typewriter on one side and a place setting with sticky dishes and flatware on the other.

"Good grief, Will," Laura said fondly, "this place hasn't changed a bit."

"One thing is different," Will said. "I don't pay rent anymore."

"You bought this?"

"Nope. Ol' Pedro Santos, my landlord, left it to me in his will. Mostly 'cuz he knew it would piss off his cantankerous and multitudinous offspring."

"So you're a homeowner."

"Well, it's kind of up in the air. Has been for years. See, he left me the Quonset and the land on which it sits. Nothing else. No setback, no front walk, no parking place. It's driving Foster's successors in the planning division bonkers because it doesn't fit into the zoning, such as it is. The first couple years, two of Pedro's daughters came and planted a garden between the house and the street, to prove their ownership, I guess. I literally had to tiptoe through the squash and onions to get to my car. But they got tired of driving halfway across the island to weed it, so it reverted back to the tropical wasteland God intended. The really great thing is I don't pay rent and I also don't pay property taxes 'cuz the assessor can't figure out what's going on. Want a beer?"

"Yeah, I think I could handle one now and still get us back to the hotel."

Will led them into a tiny galley kitchen, cluttered with piles of unwashed dishes and pots and pans. He opened the refrigerator door and grabbed two cans of beer. "I don't have any soft drinks," he told Teri apologetically. "Do you like tomato juice?"

She made a face. "Water would be fine. If you have water."

He laughed and rummaged deep in a cupboard for a glass. Looks surprisingly clean, Laura thought. "Yeah, the public utilities folks had no problem with Pedro's will. They send me water and electric bills just like they always did."

He led them through a room that was probably a bedroom—they could see a bit of bare mattress sticking out from under piles of books and stacks of old newspapers. "This is where my kids could sleep," he said. "If any of them ever bothered to visit their old man." Laura was touched by his wistful tone.

In the adjoining room he flipped a switch. A red light cast an eerie glow onto their faces. He pulled another ceiling cord and a regular light revealed the darkroom — small and remarkably neat. On one wall a sink was surrounded by clear counter space. Will took the camera from his shoulder and set it down. "Ever seen film developed?" he asked Teri.

"Yeah," she said. "Actually, I took a photography class last year at school."

"Oh, well, then maybe I should let you process the film your mom took today."

"I thought we were looking for that old negative," Teri said.

Will shook his head. "Jeez, the kid's just like her mother," he said. "No time to dawdle. Get to the point."

The opposite side of the room was lined with shelves full of loose-leaf notebooks, labeled by years. Will reached up for a black binder with 1967 on its spine.

"Will, I am amazed," Laura said, staring at this island of orderliness.

"Yeah, it's a good system. Black binders have black and white negs and contact prints, the red and blue ones have colored slides. Remember Gloria? She was that Guamanian girl I was married to—my first wife, as a matter of fact, when I was just out of the Navy. No, she was probably before your time. Anyway, Gloria set it up. God, she was good." He shook his head, staring off into the past, remembering. "Anyway, I keep it up, kind of to remember Gloria. And you'd be surprised what you can get for an old photo, now and then, if you can find it when you need it."

"Is Gloria still in Guam?" Teri said, her attention straying at last from the search for the negative.

"Hell, no. She took off with a lieutenant commander, headed for Guantanamo Bay. Gloria liked Navy guys. I didn't hear until years later, when her sister let it slip, that after she left she had a kid. My kid, I'm pretty sure. You never knew about that, did you, Laura?"

"I may have heard some maudlin moaning once or twice."

"Shit. Good old Gloria. Wonder where she is now? I bet she's fat and old like a Guamanian grandma. The kid—it was a boy—would be … hell … twenty-five by now." He shook his head and looked back at the binder he was holding. "Okay, when did the great photograph get taken? What month?"

"September? I'm almost sure it was September."

Will set the heavy book on the counter by the sink and began flipping pages. Some were sheets of contact prints; others were transparent sleeves with strips of negatives in special pockets. At the top of each page, a month and year were written in grease pencil.

"July, '67; August, '67; okay here we are, September." The first page of contact prints showed traffic on Marine Drive in Agaña. Will flipped past a few more pages slowly and suddenly stopped. "Damn," he said. "It's gone."

A sheet of contact prints had been torn from the binder, leaving behind only the edge of the page with holes punched in it. Part of one frame remained from the bottom row of pictures.

"Are you sure this is the one?" Laura asked.

"Yeah." Will jabbed his finger at the tiny scrap of photo remaining in the book. "See? One wing of the Japanese hospital. You can't see anyone in front of it because the rest of the photo is gone."

"Are the negatives gone, too?" Teri sounded as distressed as Laura felt.

"All but the first strip." Will slid the strip of film from its sleeve and laid it on a small light box. They peered at the tiny images. A small plane sat on a large runway in two shots. Then the plane was on a rougher surface with a person beside it.

"Is that Jodie?" Laura asked.

Teri leaned forward eagerly, squinting at the tiny negative. "It does look like Amelia Earhart," she said. "At least the hair does."

"The cut is like Amelia's," Laura said. "I think Jodie's hair is actually lighter than Amelia's."

"We stopped in Rota on the way to Saipan in Donnie's plane," Will said. "It was her first flight on a small plane so I took her picture

with the plane. I was kinda hoping to curry favor with her—you know, the moment I met her it occurred to me that I had never dated a blonde. Boy, some people's lives would have been a lot simpler if Jodie had fallen for me instead of Donnie, huh?"

"But probably not yours," Laura said. "Or Jodie's."

"Well, anyway, the rest of these ... " He poked at the remaining empty sleeves. "No, wait, I took one or two of Jodie and Donnie together in Rota. Then the rest would be the ones I took in Saipan. Remember, first we went to the jail and then we went to the hospital."

"Wow." Laura leaned against the counter, letting it sink in. "The negs are gone. But don't you see—they had to be. When Rudy said he destroyed the print you made. Unless you had made another print and forgotten about it. Or unless ... "

"Unless I was lying," Will said. "I assure you, I am stunned."

"I can see that," Laura said gently.

"So who stole it?" Teri asked.

"I don't know," Will said. His voice was flat.

They carried their half-emptied drinks back into the living room where Will swept books and clothing off furniture so they could sit.

"I can't understand it. I mean, I never lock my front door. My front door doesn't have a lock. Anyone could come in. But why would they? And why would they look in that particular book? And take those particular shots?"

"What about your other wives? Did any of them help in the darkroom? Help with the filing?"

"No. Gloria was the only one who was the least bit interested. The others thought the place smelled bad. And when there were kids living here I did keep a padlock on the darkroom door so they couldn't get into the chemicals. This just doesn't make any sense!"

"And you never had anyone help you in the darkroom? Never had an assistant?" Laura asked.

"Oh, my God," Will said.

"Did you?"

"I did once. Hired a high school kid to help out, keep up the files, do some routine printing for me. It was when I was taking those arrival and departure shots out at the airport. People actually ordered copies."

"So could this kid have taken the negatives?"

"I don't know why, but I'm sure she did. Damn. Her father asked me to take her on as sort of an apprentice. She was getting a little wild and hard to handle, and he was trying to get her to focus on something she was interested in. Damn, damn, damn."

"Will, who was it? This may be the answer to everything. Who was your apprentice?"

He was biting his lip and shaking his head. Finally he spoke. "Cory MacDougal," he said. "Donnie's kid."

— 1968 —

AFTER GORDON HASSLER FILLED OUT and signed the brief registration card—name, island of residence, TT employee yes or no?—he glanced at the blackboard that hung on the wall behind the cash register. The numbers 1 through 16 had been painted down the left edge, representing the rooms in the Royal Palauan. The current occupants' names were scrawled in chalk beside the numbers—the most public hotel register in the Pacific. But it was always good to know who else was staying at the hotel.

He felt a small thrill of excitement as he read the name assigned to room 11. Laura Monroe. So she was still here.

"Excuse me, Annie," he said to the woman behind the bar. "Can I change rooms?" He had been given one of the large rooms in the north wing, out of deference to his status as one of the top officials at Trust Territory headquarters. "I see Number 10 is vacant. I don't really need to take up a big room. I'll only be here a couple of nights."

The large Palauan woman shrugged, her face impassive as ever. He wondered whether it remained that straight and stern when she was in the throes of passion. "Whatever you want, Mr. Hassler. That room's on the sunrise side, so you'll be cooler in the afternoon."

Gordon smiled at the idea of one place being cooler than another here four degrees from the equator. He carried his bag down the linoleum-carpeted hall to room 10 and struggled with the key in the lock. He glanced at the door to room 11 across the hall and tried to remember what Laura was down here for. She had been away from Saipan for several weeks. *Well.* He almost rubbed his hands together in anticipation. He had always been certain that the girl was

looking for something Foster couldn't satisfy in her. And he thought that if fate ever provided an opportunity—away from Foster, away from Edwina—something very special might happen.

Once he had gone to work for the Trust Territory Government and no longer felt constrained by the limitations of CIA employment and life on one small island, he had begun to think again about having an affair. Just to keep his edge, he told himself. And Laura Monroe had always been especially appealing to him.

He hung his shirts and other pair of slacks on the hooks on the wall—no chance of clothes getting moldy in closets at the Royal Palauan—there were no closets. Then, after another almost wistful glance at the door to room 11, he returned to the lobby, where the district administrator's Palauan assistant waited to drive him the quarter mile to the government administration building.

Koror—more than most towns in the Trust Territory—still retained a Japanese flavor: narrow streets, small buildings crammed in wall-to-wall, even an occasional concrete-lined benjo ditch left from before the war. Of course it helped that Koror had been unscathed in the war, unlike its sister islands, Peleliu and Angaur, not far to the south. They had been the scenes of bitter battles.

As the dark green government Datsun bucked and rocked along the abysmal main street, Gordon mused that it would be easier on his backside to walk to the district administration building—but that simply wouldn't do, not for someone in his position.

He thought of the Jesuit priest who had been living here since right after the war. When Peace Corps volunteers began arriving to work in Micronesia, Father Ned had said that the most revealing thing the Palauans would learn from the volunteers was that Americans could survive without flush toilets. And that they can walk, Gordon thought, as the car overtook a pair of volunteers sauntering along the main street.

He managed to slip his question in during the first ten minutes of his meeting with Lionel Keating, the affable Hawaiian who was the dean of the district administrators in the Trust Territory.

"Is Laura Monroe still down here?"

Keating grinned and leaned back in his chair. There was something almost possessive in his voice, Gordon thought. "Sure is. She came down to write a story about the Palau Fair, but then we worked out a deal for her to stay until the South Pacific Fisheries conference at the end of this week. Managed to convince her boss in Saipan that it's cheaper to pay Laura's per diem at the hotel than to fly her or someone else back down for the conference. And since she only works for them on a per project basis, there's no salary cost involved. But, hey, didn't you have to sign off on it?"

Hassler laughed. "No, the information office's got its own travel budget. We really don't ride herd on every dime in the TT budget."

Keating snorted, a mock-serious sound. "Sure couldn't prove it by me, *brudduh*. You look over my shoulder at every nickel."

As they went on to talk about the various budget issues pending between Saipan and Koror, a part of Gordon's mind puzzled over that glimmer of possessiveness in Keating's voice as he spoke of Laura Monroe. Could there be something between them? No, certainly not. Lionel was a family man. And far too old for Laura.

But, Gordon reminded himself, he was also a married man. And, he recalled, he and Keating had been born the same year.

Surely it was just Keating's personality—that Hawaiian hospitality that made him seem to adopt anyone who set foot in his realm. From a bureaucratic point of view, he was probably glorying in having his own public information officer for a month or so.

At four-thirty, Gordon left the government building in a rental car Keating assigned to him and drove back to the Royal Palauan. He saw her as he turned in at the hotel's sweeping driveway. She was strolling up the street, dressed in a short, pale dress that fluttered around her tan legs, a wide-brimmed hat atop her long brown hair. She could be taken for a Peace Corps volunteer herself—except that she looked too neat, as though she had access to daily showers and an ironing board. He stopped and waited in the car at the base of the driveway.

She took off her dark glasses and leaned into the car to greet him. "Gordon Hassler. What brings you to Palau?"

He squinted in the sun. "Actually, Foster asked me to come down and see if you are still alive." He watched carefully for a reaction.

"I'll bet he's getting pretty sick of his own cooking," she laughed.

"Oh, I don't think so. Word has it he's taking all his meals at the Royal Taga."

Laura groaned. "And me down here not earning any dough to pay off the bill." She said the words but seemed completely unconcerned.

"Let me buy you a drink. Are you by any chance invited to the Keatings' for dinner tonight?"

"I sure am."

"Then I can give you a ride?"

"Thanks. That would be great—then Neil won't have to send somebody down to pick me up." He almost winced at her obvious familiarity with the handsome Hawaiian. He had heard very few people address Lionel as Neil.

They sat in the thatched-roofed gazebo centered in the large lawn of the ramshackle hotel and sipped gins and tonic. "I've been wracking my brain," Laura said. "I wanted to take Neil a present—something funny. It's his birthday, you know."

"No, I didn't."

"Well, he wouldn't have told you—he wants to ignore it. Dorie told me. This is the big one. The big five-oh." Her green eyes sparkled over the rim of her glass. "Hard to believe Neil's that old, isn't it."

The young could be so tactless. Surely she had no idea he would be turning fifty himself in a few months. "So what have you been doing down here all these weeks?"

Laura leaned back in the wobbly wicker chair and let the icy liquid slide into her mouth.

"I'm remembering simple things. Like how to be alive. How to smell the plumeria, how to feel the sun on my skin, how to hear music in people's voices."

"You like Palau," he said.

"I think it's my favorite place in the world."

"But doesn't it get boring after a while, just sniffing flowers and listening to people chatter in a language you don't understand? Or is Palauan one of your remarkable skills?"

Laura laughed. "Not really. I know a few phrases. *Alii ruubak. Alii ruudiil.*"

"Which means?"

"Hello there, you big handsome man. And hello yourself, you sweet young thing. Or so I gather."

Alii ruudiil, he thought. Remember that—it may come in handy sometime.

"Look at that poinciana!" she said, changing the subject abruptly, waving her hand vaguely toward the lawn, or the village beyond. He tried to remember: was poinciana flora or fauna?

She must have understood his confusion. "The flame tree. Right here."

He focused his eyes on the huge tree sprawling above the gazebo. "That's a flame tree?"

"Yes. You know how they bloom in Saipan, all flowers, no leaves."

"So it looks like a New England autumn when you fly over the island."

"Exactly. But they're different down here. See? All the leaves are out and the blossoms are like giant orange orchids scattered here and there. I love that about Micronesia. The differences. Think about how different the Palauans are from the Saipanese. Doesn't that fascinate you?"

He shrugged. "Maybe for a couple of days. But you've been down here for weeks. Your fans in Saipan are bereft."

She laughed. "Well, I don't get bored. And I'm getting a lot of reading done—I brought the whole Sigrid Undset tetralogy with me—*The Axe*. Have you ever read it?"

"Undset? Is that Swedish?"

"Norwegian. A novel of medeieval Scandinavia. Very dark."

"You're reading novels about medieval Norway here in Palau?"

"Crazy, isn't it? But the paperbacks showed up in the gift shop at the Royal Taga just before I left Saipan, and I thought 'These must be here for a reason.'"

"You don't think Somerset Maugham might fit into the ambiance a little better? James Ramsey Ullman? Something set in the South Seas?"

"I've read them already. And Undset is great. It's so cold and bleak in those novels it really enhances everything about being in Palau."

He shook his head fondly. What an extraordinary young woman she was. And her body was as intriguing as her mind. His finger tips tingled, wanting to touch that golden skin.

"Whoops," she said, gulping the last of her drink. "I've got to get something together as a present for Neil. Guess I'll try to write a funny poem. Thanks for the drink, Gordon. I'll be ready in ... What? An hour?"

And she was off in a flash of golden thighs and green eyes, hurrying across the wide gravel driveway, letting the screen door slam behind her as she entered the dim cave of the hotel lobby.

*　　　*　　　*

When they returned from the dinner party at the Keatings, the lobby was ablaze with the light of the fluorescent fixtures that seemed to flicker above the slowly revolving ceiling fans. He had felt encouraged during the party, detecting no particular chemistry between Laura and Lionel Keating. She treated Keating with the familiar fondness she might apply to a favorite uncle.

Rather the same way she treated him.

He had hoped she'd had enough to drink that she might slide across the front seat to lean against him as he drove the few short miles down from the district administrator's hilltop residence. But instead she leaned against the passenger door and chattered about the other people who had been at the party.

As they strolled across the driveway toward the hotel he winced at the blazing lights of the lobby. A bit off-putting after Dorie Keating's candlelit table, but what other possibility did he have? He put his hand on her arm. "Let me buy you a nightcap?"

She laughed. "No thanks, I've had enough for one night. I'm ready to go to bed."

So was he.

He walked with her down the long south hall, lit only by the light overflowing from the lobby and dim fluorescent fixtures above the doors to the bathrooms midway down. Her key made a grinding sound in the lock for room 11. She switched on the light—a blinding, bare bulb, swinging from the ceiling. "Thanks for the ride, Gordon," she said.

He almost lunged so that his shoulder was in the doorway, his chest almost brushing hers for a moment before she took a step backward into the room, her eyes widening. Firm young breasts. I have to touch them. "We have so much in common, Laura."

"We do?" Her face seemed blank, as though she had no idea what he was leading up to.

"I don't tell this to just anybody, but I write poetry, too."

"You do?"

"We should get together sometime, read our poems to each other. It's so important to find the right listener."

"Oh, yeah, that would be great." Her voice was flat. He had never heard it like that.

He took a step forward, so he was almost in the room. "There's no time like the present," he said, trying to decide if the poems were really necessary. They were just across the hall. Perhaps he didn't

have to physically save his space here in her doorway. He could get the poems and she would let him in—surely she understood what was happening between them tonight, romantic soul that she was.

When she moved into position, closely facing him, he could almost feel those breasts against his chest. Except she was not moving into an embrace. Her hands were up, pushing him away, laughing a little shakily. "No, Gordon, not now. I … I've got to get to sleep. I've got a lot to do tomorrow." And she was actually shoving him out into the hall, using the door now to shut him out.

He stood there staring at the black numbers painted on the mildew-green door. Eleven. One one. One plus one doesn't always add up to two. One minus one.

He stood there for a full minute before he heard the bolt turn in the lock. She must have been leaning against the door, that untouchable bosom heaving, perhaps with a tear or two running from those green eyes. Next he heard her footsteps, the slap of zoris as she crossed the room. Then the sound of water in the sink.

He found his key and opened the door to his room, shutting his eyes as he turned on the light. He sat on the bed. He had seldom misjudged his moment so badly. What was it about the girl that had put his timing off? For a long time he sat, doing nothing, thinking nothing. At last he roused himself, crossed to his suitcase and removed a loose-leaf notebook.

Maybe he shouldn't have used the poetry gambit. He had never tried that on any other woman. Perhaps the poetry—he patted the notebook in his lap—was too revealing. It made him vulnerable.

So what approach should he have used? What about those Palauan words she'd said this afternoon. "Hello there, you sweet young thing. *Alii ruudiil.*" And then she might have answered, "Hello, you great big man. *Alii ruubak.*" Why hadn't he tried that? She'd given him the cue before the party. And Palau was her favorite place in the whole world—the perfect place to discover new dimensions to old friends.

He began to flip through the poems in the book. He was in here, every bit of him, but in deep disguise. Why do I write these, anyway? Who am I communicating with? That boy I abandoned on a beach thirty years ago?

He remembered when he first bought the little binder, during his first year at San Francisco State. And then how painstakingly he had re-created from memory his early poems—the handful of good ones—the ones he had written as a teenager and during his time with Tex. Poems he had torn up and flushed down the head with his passport on board that tramp steamer, the *Wallaby*. But poems that needed to be on paper, to get them out of his mind.

I'm going to be fifty soon, he thought. Will Laura write me a funny poem like she did tonight for Lionel Keating? He's looking awful nifty as he faces up to fifty … that had been one line. Doggerel, sure, but she did it to perfection.

Write your own poem about turning fifty, he told himself. Turning fifty without accomplishing anything in your life—anything except … but here his mind turned away.

He moved a clean sheet of paper from the back of the notebook to the front and stared at the spaces between the blue lines. Fifty, he thought. Fifty.

His pen began to move.

Those breasts.
Those breasts wanted out,
screamed to me for release
from their imprisoning hammocks,
screamed to be touched
to be caressed,
to bloom beneath my hands.

Those breasts,
I was meant to be their liberator

to teach them things they never knew,
put my mouth over them
to taste their stories,
and every year on this day
we—those breasts and I—
would celebrate liberation day.

But no,
you shut me out,
shut them in,
leaned against the door,
leaned those breasts against the door,
between us.

He re-read it. Not perfect, of course, first drafts never were. But it had promise. Yes.

And now he could sleep.

* * *

The next morning he waited inside his room until he was sure he heard her leave the room across the hall. He would join her at that long community table in the dining room and under the stern gaze of the waitress he would try to gauge how she felt about him this morning.

She was there alone near one end of the table, wearing a blouse or a dress that bared her arms and even a bit of her shoulders. He took a deep breath before he started across the lobby.

But someone was ahead of him, moving toward her on a different tangent, coming in from the hotel's front door—Lionel Keating, strolling with that easy, almost insolent island gait of his. Laura looked up from her tomato juice and her face broke into a warm smile.

"*Alii, ruubak,*" she said in a throaty voice that seemed more appropriate to late night in a Palauan bar.

Lionel Keating's back was toward Gordon but he saw the man's bare forearm reach out, caress her shoulder, the long brown fingers lingering on the smooth golden skin of her arm. His voice came across the lobby clearly, although it seemed low, very personal: "*Alii ruudiil.*"

For the life of him, Gordon couldn't decide whether they were just playing a game or if there was something real happening here, something that should have happened last night in room 11. But he had to have breakfast, and there was only one place to do that. Resolutely, he continued into the dining room and pulled out a chair across the table from Laura.

"Good morning," he said to the two of them, pleased at how normal and everyday his voice sounded.

— 1983 —
Sunday

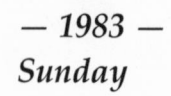

LAURA DIDN'T SLEEP WELL. Her mind was like a hamster in a wheel, racing around and around.

Cory MacDougal had stolen the negatives. She must have wanted the picture of Donnie and Jodie on Rota, so her mother would have photographic evidence of Donnie's connection with Jodie. How was the kid to know it was taken the day they met?

That must mean Panda had the negatives. She might have used them to try to hold on to Donnie, or hurt him, or hurt Jodie somehow. If she had all the contact prints from that page, would she guess what we were up to when we set up the photo in front of the hospital? Having an obsessive interest in Jodie deSpain, would Panda MacDougal even think of Amelia Earhart?

No, maybe not. So the photo became a picture of Jodie deSpain, not Amelia Earhart—a photo in the possession of someone who hated Jodie.

How did Gordon Hassler end up with it? Why? What would be the connection between Panda MacDougal and Gordon Hassler? When Gordon was the CIA's liaison, flying to Guam regularly, would they have met? Were the MacDougals even in Guam then? Before Saipan was opened to civilian traffic in 1962, where could Donnie have flown to?

Another thought. Perhaps Jeff remembers when his family moved to Guam. She'd have to ask him, if she saw him again.

Jeff, she mused. What an attractive young man. And what amazing chemistry there seems to be between us. But what can he see in me? The appeal of the forbidden? Young men in their twenties

aren't meant to chase women over forty? Young islanders shouldn't lust after white women?

Jeff. Hmmm. What if he did want to … to do something about that chemistry? Should she? No, it's impossible. Where would Teri be while we were having our tryst?

Of course, Teri was supposed to leave for Hawaii Tuesday. Perhaps if she delayed her own flight to Tokyo for a couple days …

Hawaii. Foster. What did Foster and Gordon do when they worked together in Washington? Would Teri be safe with Foster?

She had to talk to Foster again. He must find out where Donnie was. And Jodie, if possible. Was he concerned enough about the photo's reappearance to have done some checking already?

If Foster were part of the CIA and he saw Gordon's murder as connected to that affiliation, wouldn't he have insisted that I get Teri out of harm's way? Send her to Hawaii? Unless he felt that he was also in peril. Then where would Teri be safe? Here, in the same hotel where Gordon Hassler was hacked to death, with a mother who knew the origin of the photo in his pocket? Or in Hawaii with her father who had once been a colleague of the murdered man?

Her mind shifted tracks again. The photo. Panda MacDougal must have had the negative once. Someone needed to talk to her. Should it be Will? But she herself had always been the diplomatic one, the one who always got people to say more than they meant to.

Or was it Cory they should talk to? After all, Cory must have stolen the negatives. And Laura knew where to find her—she worked at that restaurant overlooking Pago Bay.

She finally fell into a sound sleep, only to be awakened by a flare of light from the bathroom. "What?" she yelled, sitting bolt upright, her heart racing.

Teri giggled and peeked around the bathroom door. "Sorry," she said. "I should have shut the door before I turned on the light."

"What are you doing up so early?" Laura was regaining her bearings. "I thought you were on vacation."

"I've got a date," Teri said, closing the bathroom door. Laura heard the shower start.

Teri had a date? How could that be?

No, she thought. I have a date. She was to meet Edwina Hassler for breakfast. She scrabbled for her watch on the bedside table. Seven-thirty. She had half an hour.

She tried the bathroom door. Locked, of course. No matter how many times she described the dire possibilities to Teri—you could slip, hit your head, how could anyone help you?—Teri insisted that the reason bathroom doors had locks was so she could protect herself from the voyeurs and molesters who undoubtedly wandered through the world trying random bathroom doors.

"Teri. Let me in. I need to use the toilet." Laura rattled the doorknob, but above the sound of running water she could hear Teri singing—some mushy song from the country music hit parade.

Date? How can she possibly have a date? Jonathan Waterbury was safely thirteen hundred miles away in Tokyo.

According to Laura's watch, Teri's shower lasted seven minutes, although it seemed much longer to Laura. The girl finally emerged, glowing and fresh, wrapped as usual in two towels, one for her torso, one for her hair. "Good morning, Mother," she said elegantly.

Laura prepared to get in the shower, talking over her shoulder. "Who on earth do you have a date with?"

"Nashi," Teri said dreamily.

"Nashi? Who the hell is Nashi?"

"Ignacio Ramírez." Teri left a long pause. Standing naked beside the tub, Laura waited to hear more, not turning on the water. "He's one of the boys who was watching when I became the Galaxians champ at your Mexican restaurant the other night."

As she climbed into the shower, Laura tried to picture the boys who'd been at Jo and Flo's. Were they Guamanian? Filipino? What difference did it make? Ramírez could be a Guamanian name. She had worked with a Ramírez in the old days at the *Guam Chronicle.*

But when did Teri have a chance to make a date? She had been with Laura or the Sabláns every minute yesterday.

Her shower finished, Laura flung on her clothes and makeup, still firing questions at her daughter who was sitting at the dressing table combing her hair with a faraway look in her eyes.

"Which one was Ignacio?"

"Nashi. He hates his real name, just like me, but he had to write it down so that when I called, his mother would let him know. At least you don't refuse to let people talk to me unless they ask for Teresita."

"You called him?" Laura tried unsuccessfully to keep the surprise from her voice.

"Yes, Mother. It's the new age, remember? Women have equal rights."

"But when ... how ... "

Teri sighed with exaggerated patience. "From the Sabláns' yesterday. I was telling Vicente about my high score on Galaxians and these cute boys who were watching me, and that one even gave me his phone number and told me to call him so we could try competing with each other."

Laura found herself surprised and somehow gratified that Teri found the island boys attractive. So many of the American kids at the American school in Tokyo seemed to have adopted a racist — or was it colonialist? — outlook. Jonathan Waterbury for one.

Teri bubbled on. "You know, Galaxians is great for two people at a time if they're both good. Vicente asked what the boy's name was and said he knew Nashi—he's Roberto's son, and you used to work with Roberto so he must be a nice kid, and I should call him and see if he wanted to come up to Sabláns'. I think Vicente was afraid I'd get bored with him and Charlotte. So I called Nashi, and he couldn't come then but we made a date to play Galaxians here at the hotel this morning. Right under your nose if you feel the need to chaperone. Okay?"

"How old is Nashi?"

"I knew you'd ask me that. I asked him how old he was because I just knew you'd have to know. He's sixteen. That's why we have to do this so early."

"What's his age got to do with it?"

"He doesn't have his own car and his brothers won't let him use theirs, so he always has to hitch rides. That's why he couldn't come up to Sabláns'. But this is Sunday morning, right? So his whole family goes to a church every Sunday that's really close to this hotel. They take a bunch of cars and it's very confusing so he'll just slip away and meet me in the lobby."

Yes, Laura thought, there is a Catholic church a half mile or so down the road toward Tamuning. Is it called San Antonio? "He'll sneak away from church to come play video games?" Laura asked. And with a statesider girl? She remembered Roberto Ramírez well. He had been the most articulate Guamanian she had known—at least, after 'Sús Pérez—on the subject of the demolition of Chamorro culture by Americans. Once when she was trying to explain to him why he should use the subjunctive mood in his editorials, she remembered his saying he didn't care if having Chamorro as his first language had handicapped him as a writer of English. "I gave my kids this Chamorro blood," he once said, holding out his arms, staring at his smooth brown skin. "The only bit of culture left I can give them to go with it is our language."

"They only speak Chamorro in his home," she told Teri. "Did he tell you that?"

"You do know Nashi," Teri said in delight.

"Not Nashi specifically, just the family," Laura said. If the boy was sixteen, he would have been born after she moved to Saipan. "Did you tell him what 'nashi' means in Japanese?"

"You mean 'pear'? He got a kick out of that. I suppose he wouldn't have thought it was funny if he was shaped like his friend—the chubby one, remember?"

Laura tried to remember. She wished she had paid more attention to the boys who'd been watching Teri play the video game. At

the time, she'd just been grateful the girl was involved in the game and distracted a bit by an audience, so she and Will were free to talk.

She hesitated by the door, staring at her daughter who was still wrapped in her towel, primping before the mirror. "So when is Prince Charming coming?"

"I'm meeting him downstairs at eight-thirty."

"And you'll stay in the hotel?"

"Yes, mother," Teri said with weary patience.

"Well, uh … have fun. Ask him what his father is doing these days." Laura still kept one foot in the room, the other in the hall, ready to hurry downstairs and find Edwina.

"Teri?"

The girl turned large brown eyes toward her and waited.

Laura couldn't tell her not to mention the photo, that wouldn't be fair. Teri had promised.

"Be careful."

"Don't worry, Mother. I'm very good at Galaxians. I won't let him beat me."

That's not what I mean, Laura thought, hurrying along the thickly carpeted hallway.

* * *

She found Edwina hovering by the hostess station at the door to the coffee shop. She looked terrible—as though she had been crying for hours, and had put on too much eye makeup to compensate.

"I'm sorry I'm late," Laura said. "Teri beat me to the shower."

"Oh, don't worry about it. I was early because I couldn't sleep. My body is very confused right now as to what's night and what's day. Of course, I haven't slept much anyway since I got the phone call from Captain Pérez."

As the hostess led them to a booth, Laura thought how dreadful it was that a cold fish like 'Sús Pérez made the call. Why hadn't he asked Ben Guerrero to do it? Maybe 'Sús enjoyed delivering bad news to statesiders. He always had had a chip on his shoulder.

"That must have been the worst phone call you ever got," she said.

Edwina sighed and took a deep, trembling breath. But when she finally spoke, her voice was clear and sure. "It was. And the scary thing is, I knew. I knew the minute the phone rang that it was a call from Guam, and that if it wasn't Gordon, the news would be terrible. I'd had this uneasy feeling about him for hours. I don't know—maybe since he'd left home. As soon as I heard … uh … heard the news, I began thinking that I must have known, that my subconscious must have known the moment he died. Anyway, when I heard an unfamiliar voice with an island accent asking for Mrs. Edwina Hassler, I knew, even before I heard the words."

Laura reached across the table and patted Edwina's hand. When a waitress arrived, they accepted her offer of coffee and placed their orders. Laura took a sip of coffee. Is it fair for me to begin digging for information right from the beginning? After all, Edwina made the date—there's something she wants to talk about.

Edwina began with yesterday. "I do remember when he first came to Saipan, you know."

Laura found herself raising an eyebrow, Guamanian-style, indicating, "Yes? Go ahead." She remembered a former boyfriend from her early post-divorce days who used to get furious with her about that. "How do I know you're listening to me?" he would fume. "You're so unresponsive."

Belatedly, she corrected her listening style. "When who came?"

"Shelby Verdun." Edwina pronounced the name in a way that made her dislike clear. "It upset Gordon terribly. One of his assignments was to keep the news media from finding out about—about the Saipan operation. And here was this San Francisco reporter coming to research a story about Amelia Earhart, of all things."

Laura's heart thudded. So there was a connection between Gordon and the possibility that Earhart had been in Saipan. Who would have known about that connection? Shelby Verdun? Other people in the CIA?

"Did he meet Shelby?" she asked.

"I'm sure he did. And I think he's mentioned in the book—although maybe he's just referred to as a government official. I've never read the damn thing. Gordon wouldn't have it in the house."

Laura thought eagerly of Charlotte's copy of the book safe upstairs in her hotel room. "I'll have to look," she said quietly.

"I remember him giving a talk on one of his visits," Edwina continued. "Everyone in my bridge group was going, and Gordon asked me not to go. Actually, we had quite a fight about it."

"Did Gordon go?"

"No. But I think he had someone tape the talk. I guess it counted as a big hole in the security line he tried to draw around the island. You know, it was shortly after that visit of Verdun's that the news came out about the Saipan operation."

"Yes. As I remember from Verdun's book, he felt like he had been double-crossed. He found out about it and promised to keep quiet if they let him break the story eventually—and then somebody beat him to it."

"The Guam police can't give me anything," Edwina said, suddenly switching to the present. "Not even his pocket watch. The murderer took everything." She blew her nose loudly into a frazzled tissue.

Laura decided she might as well dive into the fray. "Were you always worried when he traveled?" As soon as she said the words, she thought of Gordon's trip to San Francisco many years ago, his elaborate preparations for a dinner date with her. Was she curious as to whether Edwina worried about his fidelity or his safety?

"Of course I worried," Edwina said. "You know what kind of business he was in."

A chill went down Laura's back. Is this one spook's wife talking to another?

"I didn't know until recently," she said. "I guess the idea that he might be connected to the CIA was planted for me when I saw him once in Bangkok a couple years ago having dinner with the

station chief. But I thought he might be a source then, selling some information or something. It wasn't until after he died—no, maybe it was just before he died that I was pretty sure. Charlotte Sablán mentioned his being some sort of liaison officer up in Saipan. Before the CIA cleared out."

Edwina nodded. "That was his first job with them. So far as I know. Before that he was in the State Department. The auditor's office. As far as I know." She underlined the last words with her voice.

Laura thought that perhaps Edwina needed help sorting something out. Was there anything she could ask that would help?

"What sort of things did Captain Pérez ask you when you saw him yesterday?"

"Just what they ask on television police dramas. I felt I'd wandered into an episode of *Hill Street Blues*. Things like: Did your husband have any enemies that you know of? What was the nature of his business here in Guam?"

What had Edwina answered? Was a CIA operative's wife trained to respond to questions like that? Did the fact that Laura had never been offered such training mean that at least while she was married to him, Foster had not been an agent?

Edwina poured syrup on her banana fritters—the same thing Gordon had ordered. Laura wondered whether she and Foster had ever ordered the same thing in a restaurant.

"You know what I always wondered about the CIA operation in Saipan?" Laura asked impulsively. "Where the hell did the in-laws think their daughters and grandchildren were living?"

"Okinawa," Edwina said. "Remember, back then it was also controlled by the U.S. We didn't give it back to the Japanese until when … 1972? Long after the operation in Saipan ended. There were huge bases on Okinawa so it made perfect sense that a lot of nonmilitary government people would be stationed there. And when relatives sent presents for Christmas, they were reasonably appropriate for a tropical island. No wool sweaters or ice skates."

"But what if the in-laws wanted to visit?"

"Remember we're talking a quarter century ago. Not very many people traveled to Asia. If they wanted to, I suppose the story was that there simply weren't facilities for guests. You could meet your family in Hong Kong if they insisted on a jaunt to the Far East. I don't know what happened if someone's mother-in-law had a next-door neighbor who actually had a son stationed in Okinawa. It was never anything Gordon or I had to worry about."

"Oh?"

"My mother was in a wheelchair from the time I was fifteen. She was badly injured in the accident that killed my father. My older sister took care of her until she died … and my sister had absolutely no interest in travel. She thought Kenneth and I were very strange for leaving Ohio to go to Washington, D.C. to find jobs. You knew I was married before, didn't you?"

Laura took inventory of memories of chats with Edwina back when they both lived in Saipan. *Of course I knew that, didn't I?*

Edwina continued. "Actually, my sister thought I was a coward, running away from my share of the caretaking. Anyway, there was no danger that my relatives would want to visit us. I don't think they even wondered where we were. I don't know—maybe if we had been able to have children they would have been more interested."

"What about Gordon's family?"

"Oh, you didn't know? He's an orphan. Raised in some dreadful orphanage in St. Louis. Shorted on love as a child, I'm sure. I was always certain that was why he was so …" She seemed to search for a word.

"Flirtatious?"

Edwina smiled ruefully. "Exactly."

"It didn't bother you?"

"Not really. I figured he needed to make up for what he'd missed as a child. I'd gotten a lot of love as a kid … until the accident. I knew I was stronger emotionally than he was. And he always came home to me. He was always discreet."

Laura smiled. "You probably belong in the *Guinness Book of Records*. World's most tolerant wife."

"After all, I had my first husband to compare him to. And Gordon had gotten into this make-believe business, with all the secrets. Sometimes I thought making things up and sneaking around became a habit. I think it became a sort of practice for the life-and-death kind of pretending."

"I used to wonder if you were really as unaware as you seemed," Laura confessed.

"I modeled myself on those monkeys. Aren't they Japanese?"

"See no evil, hear no evil, speak no evil. Yes, they're carved on one of the temples at Nikko."

Edwina seemed thoughtful. "Now that I think about it, one of the really good parts of my second marriage was I didn't have to maintain diplomatic relations with a mother-in-law."

Laura thought of the friction between Foster's mother and herself when she was married. "That's a definite plus," she agreed.

"Although we did have words a couple times about the old woman he sent money to."

"Oh? Who was that?"

"Some little old lady in South Dakota. The mother of a war buddy of his. The guy saved Gordon's life and, shortly afterwards, he was mortally wounded. He died in Gordon's arms, waiting for the medics. And he made Gordon promise to look after his poor old mother. So Gordon sends her money … sent her money … every month. I used to resent it, sometimes, when there wasn't enough money to do what I wanted to do. But Gordon was adamant—a promise is a promise."

"Is she still alive?"

"Yes, just before he left for Guam, I saw him writing a check to her. Good heavens. I hadn't thought—I wonder what will happen to her now that he's gone?" Edwina was silent for a minute. "What are the ethics of this, Laura? If her son saved my husband's life forty years ago, do I still send her money after both men are dead?"

"Did you ever hear of a Chinese contract?" Laura asked. Edwina shook her head. "My mother used to say she had this guy on a Chinese contract because she'd done some major favor for him … or maybe it was his parents she'd done something for. Anyway, he would never be able to do enough for her. Of course, it was all just a joke, but I guess a Chinese contract never gets fulfilled."

"Except maybe by death?"

"That might have a bearing on it." Enough of this small talk, she thought. There's got to be some real information here. "What did you tell Captain Pérez when he asked about enemies?"

"I said none that I know of. And that's true. What I didn't tell him was I always had the sense that something more important than earning money drew Gordon back out here."

"So what was the nature of his business in Guam?"

"You saw him. What did he tell you?"

"Keeping a hand in. Looking for business opportunities. The Century of the Pacific or something like that."

Edwina nodded. "That's what he told me, too. But there was something more to it, something specifically about the islands. I think he had a sense of unfinished business out here. I used to think it had to do with his being forced out of the Trust Territory, when the new administration came into power in Washington and let it be known they didn't want a CIA connection in the TT government—too much of a hazard with all the talk of future political status … "

"How odd," Laura said.

"Why?"

"I mean the new administration that was coming in when you folks left was Republican. You'd have thought they'd want more spooks planted anywhere they could get them. It was Nixon coming in, after all."

Edwina was silent for a few seconds, just long enough for the thought to enter Laura's mind that perhaps Edwina also worked for the CIA, that she was trying to plant some disinformation on a journalist. What a cover she would have had in the old days! A lady

of leisure, learning to play mah-jongg and gossiping with all the other high muckety-muck's wives.

"It was Nixon," Edwina said, "but maybe they wanted to put their own agents out here. Or then again, what do I know? Gordon told me that's why we were leaving. But we both know how reliable his word was."

What an astonishing idea—that you could be in love with someone for—what? thirty years?—and not believe a word he said.

They had nearly finished breakfast when Edwina pulled a small, worn loose-leaf notebook from her large handbag and pushed it across the table toward Laura.

The notebook was about the size of a hard-bound book and had a dark, mottled-green cover that looked like leather, with the initials 'GH' embossed in the center, highlighted with gold that was partly worn away. Laura regarded the volume quietly. This, she was sure, was the crux of Edwina's need to talk with her.

Edwina spoke at last. "Captain Pérez asked me to bring anything with me that might help solve the murder. Papers, documents. I couldn't imagine what I could find—especially in the two hours I had to pack before I went to catch my plane. But I thought of this the minute he mentioned papers. I always believed that if there were clues to understanding Gordon Hassler, they'd be in that notebook."

Laura waited quietly.

"They're his poems," Edwina said. "Apparently he wrote poems from the time he was in high school and kept them all. I never looked inside that book. A few he wrote for me and gave me copies of, but otherwise it seemed clear to me that this was where he kept the most private pieces of his soul, so I never peeked. It took a lot of will power, but I never looked inside—until I was on the plane flying out here."

Laura stared at the leather volume. She remembered the man trying to push his way into her room at the Royal Palauan Hotel, wanting to read her his poems. And that night in her apartment in San Francisco. The same line.

It had never occurred to her to wonder if he really did write poems, and what they might be like. She fingered the notebook's cover. "So you decided not to give them to Captain Pérez?"

"I've read through them twice, Laura, and I'm mystified. I know they are full of secrets and insights—but I'm not good at reading poetry. I'm probably too literal-minded. If I thought it would help catch the killer, of course I'd give them to the police. But I can't imagine what a Guamanian detective would get out of these." She leaned across the table and stroked the cover of the book.

"When I heard you were here … well, you're a poet. I remember that about you. I remember Foster teasing you about waxing poetic in that story you wrote about the big typhoon."

Laura remembered, too. It had been one of the best stories she'd ever written, and she'd done it in the first few hours after she got the message from a friend in Honolulu that the *Star Bulletin* wanted an eyewitness account. Foster had read it out loud in a mock-portentous radio announcer voice: "The *Star Bull* asks for a news story and she gives them *The Lady of the Lake*." She shook her head at the memory. No wonder I'm not married to him anymore.

Edwina was still trying to explain what she hoped would come of Laura's reading the poems. "Maybe you'll see something I've missed and then maybe we can give it to the detectives in a … I don't know … a more straightforward fashion."

"Of course," Laura said. "I'll read them carefully. As soon as I get a story sent off to Tokyo about yesterday's Saipan jaunt."

As always when she ate out with women, Laura found herself dividing up the check with Edwina with great precision, meting out the appropriate tip to the last nickel. Edwina waited by the door to the lobby as Laura handed the cashier their pooled bills and coins.

"One other thing I wanted to mention to you," Edwina said as they walked into the lobby.

Laura was craning her neck toward the game tables, lined up along a blank wall across the large room. She spotted Teri's blonde head bent over a table, and across from her a boy with black hair

falling over his eyes. Now what do I do? Will Teri be annoyed if I go over and meet this Nashi, or will she feel neglected if I don't? Belatedly, she realized Edwina was waiting for her to respond to something.

"I'm sorry. What did you say?"

"I don't know whether to mention it to Captain Pérez or not. For all I know, he already checked in with the police here."

"Who?" Laura was completely lost. What had she missed in Edwina's hesitant conversation?

"The man we saw checking in for the flight to Guam when we were leaving Saipan last night? You saw him get out of that red car, the one we saw stopping by the trail to the hospital?"

Laura's heart thudded with excitement. Yes, the sunburned man. "You know him?" she asked quietly.

"I only caught a glimpse of him, but I'm sure it was him. I know him as Dennis Dover, although that's not necessarily his name. He came to our house a few times. I'm certain he worked with Gordon in the agency. Do you think I should mention seeing him to the police?"

"Hmmm," Laura said as they walked toward the stairs. I already told the cops about seeing him having dinner with Gordon the night before he died. Do they need to know he was in Saipan, looking over the scene of the photograph?

"Let me think about that," she said. "You don't want to give away more than necessary about Gordon's professional connections. Why don't we get together, after I've read the poems and talk about Dover then? What are your plans?"

Edwina shrugged. "I may go down and lie in the sun by the pool, but you'll be able to find me. I won't leave the hotel."

Belatedly, Laura remembered Teri. "Oh!" she said. "I've got to go over and do the mother thing, meet Teri's friend. But I'll be in touch as soon as possible. I promise."

She squeezed Edwina's hand and hurried back across the lobby toward the game tables.

– 1977 –
April

JODIE OPENED THE FAT ENVELOPE from Guam with anticipation. Good old Charlotte—once you told her you were interested in a subject, it was like having a subscription to an encyclopedia. She was certainly more supportive than the dragon lady at the reference desk at the San Francisco Public Library who was wont to send postcards with terse messages on them: "I suppose you'll want to know that the latest issue of *Aviation Week* has an article on you know who."

She unfolded several photocopied pages of a single-spaced, badly typed manuscript. Charlotte had scrawled a note in the margin of the first page:

> *JdS—I remembered that this unpublished manuscript about the Ellice Islands had some musings about AE's disappearance. The author was a Brit named Enoch Cartwright, apparently a beachcomber with delusions—he calls himself a planter in some parts of the ms. and a trader in others. Anyway, he hung on in the islands throughout the war, which was probably not enough to make the book publishable. Hope it feeds your muse. —CS*

The Ellice Islands, Jodie reflected, were south of the Gilberts and west of the Phoenix group. Both the Gilberts and the Phoenix group had been theorized as likely crash sites for Amelia Earhart. She devoured the manuscript quickly. Charlotte had sent a complete chapter, and she was several pages into it before she found the author commenting on Amelia.

> About this time—you'll know with hindsight it was July of 1937—we spotted several American planes, flying around

> in circles, looking for the lost adventuress Amelia Earhart. She was apparently meant to have passed over our part of the Pacific en route from New Guinea to her next scheduled landfall, the small island called Howland some 600 miles northeast of us. The Americans, like the bully on the playground, had appropriated the island from Great Britain, which had a far more valid claim upon it. The Yanks' only justification was to build an airfield for this stunt flier's convenience.
>
> In the years since, there has been much speculation about where Amelia Earhart disappeared to. I say why not examine first where she came from. She touched on a number of British territories and protectorates en route to New Guinea. Why was it necessary to land on an American-controlled island after leaving New Guinea? What was she now carrying which even America's closest friends couldn't see?
>
> Because most of the Pacific had no place for land-based craft to land, you may say, Howland was necessary. But why on earth (or on water for that matter) was this stunt carried out in a land-based plane? A person sets out to fly around a globe which is 70 percent water. Why does the person not fly an aircraft which can light upon the water?
>
> Therein, methinks, lies the key to the disappearance of Amelia Earhart.

The author of the memoir wandered on to other subjects for the balance of his chapter. At the end, in Charlotte's handwriting, was scrawled, "ms. was written about 1967? Received at WPRC July 10, 1972."

Indeed, why not fly a seaplane? They were probably slower and used more fuel. But as Cartwright had pointed out, seaplanes could be landed almost anywhere—at least in the Pacific. The Pan-Am Clippers, which had opened the Pacific to air travel, were flying boats. But, then, the Clippers had been crossing the Pacific for several years by the time of Amelia's flight. What challenge would there have been in using a plane with floats or an amphibious plane?

Cartwright's indignation over American "appropriation" of Howland Island was a new angle to her, but she remembered Will Hildebrandt asking ten years ago, "You thought it was logical to build an airfield in the middle of the ocean so some broad could fly around the world?"

Well, let's try this new direction. Why choose land-based aircraft? What if you had invested heavily in land-based aviation? Amelia's flight would prove your planes could go anywhere, so you might contribute generously to the costs of her expedition. Jodie had yet to find a clear explanation of how the money had been raised for the journey.

But suppose all your money were tied up in seaplanes? Then maybe you would see Amelia's flight as a threat. If a woman pilot could make it across the Pacific by land, why couldn't Pan American?

Would your fear of her success be strong enough to lead you to sabotage the flight?

She got out her copy of Shelby Verdun's book, *On the Earhart Trail,* and opened it to a certain page in the photo section. Amelia Earhart and Fred Noonan smiled at the camera in Lae, New Guinea, the caption said. They were standing with a third person, a handsome middle-aged man wearing a Stetson-style western hat. "The other man is an unidentified official of the British East Indies Company," said the caption.

"Are you the one?" Jodie asked the stranger in the photograph. "Are you really a man with investments in seaplanes?" Not that there had to have been any sabotage. As she knew so well, the Pacific was vast and the islands tiny and very far between. It was most likely that Amelia Earhart had simply gotten lost and run out of fuel.

But how intriguing to imagine another explanation.

Jodie made it a habit whenever Charlotte sent something to send a quick thank you in order to keep the information flowing her way. Now she scrawled by hand on her blue JODIE DESPAIN, PILOT

stationery, after neatly lettering in her latest San Francisco address below the crossed-out printed address.

> *Charlotte: Thanks for the Cartwright chapter. It actually started me on a new line of investigation—always a treat.*
>
> *For a long time I've been curious about a man in one of the photos in the Shelby Verdun book. It's on the first page in the second group of photos—after page 158—below the picture of the New Guinea natives greeting her on arrival in Lae. I wonder who the unidentified man is with AE and Noonan. British East Indian official? Have you seen his mug anywhere else, ever? That hat doesn't look right on a Brit. What do you think? Thanks, Jodie*

She addressed an envelope and folded the note to insert it. As often happened, her heart seemed to snag on the design on her letterhead, that exuberant scribble of Donnie's from the day of her first flying lesson. Oh, Donnie! she mourned. Will I never grow beyond you? It's been ten years since I met you—and what time have we actually spent together?

The letterhead design caught her eye again. JODIE DESPAIN, PILOT. What a joke. She worked long hours in a hospital lab in Berkeley to support herself and rented planes only often enough to keep her pilot's license current. She was meant to fly, not plod through life, commuting through tunnels under San Francisco Bay.

She decided to walk to the mailbox a couple blocks away and mail the note to Charlotte. Get out of the apartment, clear her head. Amelia Earhart had become an important part of her life, providing hours when she forgot about her own problems.

It was dusk when she returned, having stopped for a cup of coffee. A taxi had pulled up in front of her building and a tall, rangy man was leaning into it, counting out bills. A suitcase stood beside him on the sidewalk.

There was something so characteristic about the stance that she started to run even before she was sure. But she was right. He turned

from the taxi to look again at the numbers above the door and put his foot on the first step.

"Donnie!"

He turned and his face broke into that joyous grin that made everything in life seem suddenly simple.

"Blondie!" He grabbed her in a tight, enveloping hug and then covered her mouth with his. After several long, ecstatic minutes he held her back away from him. "Let's start out right this time," he said. "You living with anyone here?"

Gently she shook her head, terrified that he was just an illusion, that if she moved too suddenly he would dissolve. She focused on his close-cropped black velvet hair, now sprinkled with silver. Donnie seemed to be the only man on the planet who hadn't succumbed to shaggy sideburns and long hair. And his jeans were straight-legged—not a hint of bell-bottoms.

"Why don't you invite me in? I've got a proposition for you."

She found her key and her voice, which was suddenly low and husky. "And I've got a proposition for you."

Much later, when they seemed at last to have exhausted the possibilities of desperate bodies, he told her his idea.

"The problem was the ghosts. I've got ghosts all over in Hawaii and an ex-wife in Guam. You've got who knows how many ghosts of old boyfriends here in the Bay Area and a nagging mother somewhere in the Rocky Mountains."

"Colorado," she said softly, hearing for just an instant her mother's plaints of despair about her only daughter.

"What we need is a new place, just for us, as partners. What do you think?"

"Where?"

"Uncle Sugar and his minions finally coughed up the dough they owed me for my years in that cage in Laos so I used it to buy an airline."

"An airline?" she said in disbelief.

"Well, it's got two planes. Double the fleet I used to own in Guam. So I want you to come with me and fly one of them. We'll have to learn to land with floats."

"Where?"

"Fairbanks. Alaska. The last frontier."

— 1983 —
Sunday

IT WAS THE MOST PRODUCTIVE FEW HOURS Laura had had since she'd arrived in Guam. She'd met Nashi, who was utterly charming. She'd asked the expected polite questions about his family. She'd agreed that Teri could go down to the beach with him, provided he let his family know where he was, and provided that Teri got something to eat before they went. Then Laura went up to the room and called Will, who offered to take whatever photos she chose, along with her story, to the *Chronicle* for transmission to Tokyo. And, she supposed, the rest of the world.

She tapped out a brief story on her portable typewriter, an extended photo caption really, about Shelby Verdun's return to Saipan and his quest for Amelia Earhart. She and Will had decided the best photo showed Verdun pointing out something on the hospital wall to Jeff MacDougal, whom she identified as the island pilot who had flown Verdun to Saipan. She quoted Verdun as questioning the authenticity of the photo of Earhart in front of the hospital, and immediately felt some of her guilty anxiety lift. Was it possible that she could continue her career with the Associated Press after all?

No, she amended. The basic question was whether she could go on working as a journalist. As Foster would surely point out, the strange thing about Laura was that she had never slid into the cynicism that seemed to infect so many of her colleagues. She still looked upon the press as something approaching a sacred trust. Yet it was a trust she had betrayed sixteen years ago, and again, now.

If she reported that Verdun questioned the photo's validity, did that redeem her at all?

Of course, it would all depend upon what came out when the murder of Gordon Hassler was solved. If it were solved. If the photo became an inconsequential detail, then perhaps she could go on.

She reminded herself that it was no longer just the five pranksters who knew the photo's origins. Rudy Terlaje knew now. Certainly Charlotte had guessed. And Teri knew, of course.

Laura piled pillows from both beds against the headboard and sat on her bed to read Gordon's poems. They seemed to be arranged chronologically, with the newest one at the front of the book, although he had given them dates only occasionally. She worked her way slowly from the back to the front of the notebook. The collection began with a couple of maudlin teenager-mooning-about-love verses. There was also a rather puzzling poem called "The Faces of Mountains"—a perplexing subject for a boy raised in a city at the junction of the Missouri and the Mississippi.

And when a mountain
finally shows its face,
it comes out in masquerade.
How are we to ever know
the mountain face God made?

Had the orphan boy ever seen a mountain when he wrote that? Or was she wrong about these being chronological? Did the poem have something to do with being a spy?

Next came an oddly powerful poem called "Your Back." It seemed to be about passion and desire. But when do boys write about their lover's backs? Unless …

No, this is Gordon Hassler, the great womanizer of the Western Pacific, she reminded herself. Yet, wasn't it supposed to be true that teenage boys in boarding schools experimented with each other because there were no girls available? Was that the way it had been in Gordon's orphanage?

Another of the early poems, called "Green," managed in a few lines to make the color green seem more menacing than she'd ever imagined a color could be. Surely St. Louis wasn't tropical. How old was Gordon when he first came to the islands?

The next poem was clearly about war. Surviving an island invasion, and the guilt and wonder that went with watching friends die while he was spared. Until Edwina mentioned his war buddy this morning, Laura had never even realized that he had fought in World War II. And apparently in the Pacific. Funny how you can spend hours talking to someone through the years and never hear about their key, motivating experiences. Perhaps fighting on tropical islands explains his fear of green. How odd, though, that he ended up back in the islands once again in the sixties.

Now here was another of those adolescent-discovering-sex poems, she thought, although it was more subtle than what an adolescent would write. "Coming to Terms" it was called, and the poet seemed bent on convincing himself that roundness and softness were superior to hardness and angularity.

What can that be about, she wondered. Maybe if a man had been in love with a very lean, athletic woman—someone built like Edwina, for instance—and found himself forced to make love to a rounder woman, someone who was even fat? But he had married Edwina. What could have forced him into a relationship with "pillows of flesh, curves that balloon beneath my hands"?

Or wait. What about the back poem. What if a man were gay and found himself forced to make love to a woman?

Why would he be forced to go against his nature? Perhaps by society's expectations? Gordon had always seemed eager to keep a low profile. He was almost Japanese in his need to fit in, as though he too had been raised under the rubric that the nail that sticks out gets hammered down. Perhaps the need to conform came from being raised in an orphanage.

No, of course not. It came from working for the CIA. But could a gay person even get into the CIA? Perhaps that was what this was

about. She re-read the poem. It had a jerky, insistent rhythm. And it ended:

and I
find myself
coming to terms
coming
coming
Yes!

Nothing subtle or even very poetic here, she thought. What did Edwina make of this poem? And do I dare ask Edwina that question?

A few pages further on he had written a poem that seemed to express complete dedication to the seduction of women. "The Tune Up" he called it. In sensual detail, it recorded step-by-step making love to a woman—with a continuing analogy of working on an automobile engine.

I try not to rub my hands together
in anticipation
as I lift your sweater,
and I remember lifting the hood
of a car,
thrilled to find everything there
sweet, complete,
needing just the touch of my hand.

By the time she got to the final lines, the vivid description of how the woman's engine screamed with the touch of his finger upon the delicate throttle, and then settled into a humming purr that might just last forever, Laura felt a hot moistness between her legs that annoyed her greatly.

I suppose that's the one he wanted to read me that night at the Royal Palauan, she thought.

After closing her eyes for a moment, she then turned to the next poem, "Sleight of Hand." It seems to be about doing card tricks, but of course it has to be a metaphor—for the double life he led as a spook? She tried to remember whether she'd ever known Gordon to play cards. Edwina's life in Saipan had revolved around her bridge group and what Foster called the Mah-jongg Mafiosi. But what about Gordon?

The phone interrupted her mental scrabbling.

"'Lo," she said.

"That you, Tater-pig?"

"Foster. I was going to call you. Listen, did Gordon ever play poker? Cards of any kind?"

"That's our Laura. No time for small talk. No how are you, how's Andrea, your daughter will be on tonight's flight."

Foster's voice seemed a little blurry. She glanced at her watch. One p.m. Sunday in Guam was five o'clock Saturday afternoon in Hawaii. Hitting the bottle a little early aren't you, Foster?

"I'm sorry," she said. "It's just—I thought it might—provide some sort of clue."

"Okay." Foster made a hmmmmmmming sound for a few seconds. "Let me think … yeah. There was one time … we were on some sort of road trip out of D.C., meeting with some folks in … shit, I forget where. Gordon was pretty adamant about not wanting to join the poker game our hosts had organized—if I hadn't known better, I'd have thought he had religious scruples against gambling. But it was becoming an issue, so he gave in and agreed to play. He made me write down all the poker hierarchy—you know, three of a kind beats two pair, like that. When it came time for him to deal, he had the oddest way of shuffling cards I'd ever seen. Like he was trying very hard to make his hands look clumsy when they wanted to make those cards sing. I thought, uh, oh, we've bullied a ringer into this game. We'll be lucky to get out with our shirts. But I was wrong. He was a lousy poker player. The only person I've ever played with besides you, sweetie, who inevitably tried to fill an inside straight.

I concluded he must be a recovering gamble-holic or something. So why do you ask?"

"Edwina gave me some of his poems to read. I just came upon a rather odd one about cards."

"Gordon Hassler wrote poems?" Foster asked in apparent disbelief.

For a moment Laura couldn't believe his disbelief. You know perfectly well, she thought, and then, oh, no, of course he doesn't. She'd never told Foster about the incident at the Royal Palauan, hadn't wanted to endanger the two couples' friendship.

"Apparently so," she said.

"I'll be damned. Any other dark secrets in the man's past that have come to light?"

She considered the poems that she thought might hint at homosexuality. Did Gordon ever proposition Foster? Instead she blurted out, "He worked for the CIA."

"Zowie. Stop the presses. Brenda Starr just figured out the world's round."

"Very funny." Her voice was flat. These conversations were good for her, she decided. They reminded her why she wasn't married to him anymore. She did not ask, "So was the world round for you, too?" She really didn't want to know the answer.

"I'm sorry, babe." He sounded contrite. "So what's happening on the rock? Edwina's there? How's she holding up?"

"Yeah, she came yesterday. On the same plane as Shelby Verdun. You know, *On the Earhart* … "

" … *Trail*," Foster finished.

"Yeah. Anyway, we all flew up to Saipan yesterday to take a look at the hospital. On a plane piloted by Donnie MacDougal's son."

Foster whistled. "Whew. That must have been some outing. Oh, I meant to tell you, the photo showed up in the paper here. The same evening I talked to you. I just hadn't seen the paper yet."

"Well, there may be a follow-up in your Sunday paper. Shelby Verdun pointing out something on the hospital to a young pilot, something to support his contention that the Earhart photo is a fake."

"He thinks it's a fake? Does he have any thoughts about why and when it was taken?"

"Not that he shared with me."

"So I assume this new photo is by Will Hildebrandt?"

"Nope. He had a prior engagement. AP photo by Laura Monroe. But shot with one of Will's cameras. An old Pentax of a certain vintage."

Foster whistled again. "Curiouser and curiouser, eh, Tater-pig?" For the first time this afternoon, Laura thought to worry about a phone tap. No, Will had to be right. Who in the Guam Police Department would have time to listen to the tapes? Unless ... what about the sunburned man? Dennis Dover.

"So what's up in Lei-lei Land?" she asked.

"Oh, yeah, I did call you, didn't I? Okay, I tried to track down MacDougal. He's in the phone book and has an answering machine so I left a couple messages, but he hasn't gotten back to me yet. A guy I know here knows him, says he's always off on charter flights. Takes tourists over to Maui to look down into Haleakala or ferries people to Lanai and Molokai. When there's an eruption on the big island, he's apparently in big demand to fly folks in as close as possible to see the planet barfing its breakfast."

Good old Foster. The master of vivid, trite imagery. Did he ever write poetry? What do she really know about him?

"I can imagine that would appeal to Donnie," she said. "Must be almost as exciting as dodging antiaircraft missiles over the rice paddies of Laos."

"As for Jodie deSpain," Foster continued, "not a sign of her here in Hawaii-nei. I called a few of the flying schools and charter companies, but no one had heard of her."

"Well, since the photo seems to have been plastered all over the world, she's probably lying low, wherever she is. You know,

she wrote to Charlotte and said she was researching a book about Amelia Earhart."

"Recently?"

"No, apparently a while back. Charlotte's going to find her file for me."

"So how did you happen to talk to Charlotte about Jodie?" Was there an edge of accusation in his voice?

Laura's silence stretched out. She could think of nothing else to say. "She … uh … she thought she noticed a resemblance."

"Hmmm." At least he didn't whistle again. If Dennis Dover did have access to this conversation, it would lay everything out very clearly for him.

"So when's Teri due here?" Foster said abruptly.

"Oh, we've kept the reservation for Tuesday."

"She's doing okay?"

"I don't think I could get her to leave early, not even for you. Right now, even as we speak, she's carrying on a flirtation with Roberto Ramírez's youngest son."

"Shit," Foster said in a mild, conversational tone. "That island is a very small world, ain't it, babe."

"Feels that way to me."

"Well, keep me posted. Andrea's making broad gestures at me here, just off stage right. I think I'm supposed to be lighting the charcoal broiler."

After they said their farewells, Laura sat for a few moments, trying to remember the girl who had once been married to Foster Monroe, and what connection she had to this woman with a body that was beginning to sag a bit here and there, whose hair had shown the temerity to sprout a gray streak above one eyebrow.

She popped off the bed and went into the bathroom where she leaned into the mirror to examine her hair, strand by strand. No, the dye was holding up fine, undaunted by her binge in the sunshine on Friday.

She wasn't even sure she believed in dyeing her hair. It had just come upon her all at once, before she'd had a chance to even think about how she would deal with aging. She sat down again with Gordon's poems.

"Sleight of Hand." So he had to hide things. After all, he was a spook. It certainly wasn't significant—except perhaps the last lines:

Old habits die hard. I try
to stop the jingling dance
of coins in my own pocket.

Gordon always did that. Jingled coins. He'd done it Thursday morning, standing up from the table after he'd signed for their breakfast. Not fumbling for money for a tip—he'd added that on when he signed the bill. Just jingling coins. He'd even done it that night sixteen years ago in the public information office at Trust Territory headquarters when Will had been in the darkroom and the rest of them had been crouching under the desks.

So what was he trying to say in this poem? That once he'd done sleight of hand and now he had to hide his skill? But why?

Edwina was right. This book was full of clues to who Gordon Hassler was. It was a treasure map of his secrets. But what did they have to do with his murder?

Laura's mind wandered again. They still don't know where Donnie and Jodie were. And what about Dennis Dover? Why was he here in Guam at the same time as Gordon? Could he be responsible for bumping off Gordon? She'd better tell Will about Dover's connection to Hassler and about his going to see the Japanese hospital in Saipan—just so someone besides her knew, in case anything happened to her.

That was a chilling thought.

She moved out to a patio chair on the tiny balcony and continued reading the poems. This one was interesting. If Gordon was an orphan, how did he happen to write an after-all-you-did-for-me, I-let-you-down poem called "Mother"?

So many things to ask Edwina. Maybe she should make notes? No, she could just flip through the poems when she got together with Edwina, discuss the anomalies as they came across them.

She heard the clacking of a typewriter nearby and leaned out over the balcony railing to see if someone was typing on the lanai below her balcony. She could see Teri and Nashi down on the dining terrace. Good, she thought, at least they managed to tear themselves away from the game machines long enough to get something to eat.

The typewriter paused and she heard the sound of a sheet of paper being pulled out. Then came the whirr of another sheet rolling in and the typing resumed.

Laura leaned out far enough to see around the bit of concrete wall that separated her balcony from the one for the room next door. There, with the hotel room desk pushed halfway through the sliding glass doors sat Shelby Verdun, typing intently. Laura pulled back quickly, flattening her back against the separating wall.

Good grief, he was right next door. What might he have heard of her conversation with Foster? Or with Will when he was here earlier? Thank goodness she had the sliding doors closed to keep the air conditioning inside the room. She bet Verdun was letting the cold air spill out into the great tropical outdoors without a moment's guilt.

She sat down again, this time in the chair right beside the wall, and turned back to the poems.

"Fog."

A nice description of life in San Francisco. But when had Gordon lived in San Francisco? He'd never said anything about that—and surely he'd known she grew up there. Yes, darn it, he'd made a big thing about having her show him the city that time he came from Washington and took her to dinner. Something else to ask Edwina about. Once again, the poem's last lines caught her attention.

Fog. A good place
to hide, to transform myself,

to rediscover Dr. Jekyll
inside my own hide.

A little too cute, perhaps, but nevertheless fascinating. What transformation could he be talking about?

Then followed poems about being in Washington, "the navel of bureaucracy." Poems about seeking the truth as an accountant. That's right. Edwina had mentioned once that Gordon began his government career as an auditor.

Even so, she thought the poem showed a remarkable dedication to auditing as a calling—ferreting out some evil malefactor in "the accounts of the government." Was that the way auditors actually viewed their work? And she'd always thought it seemed like such a dull field. What a concept—an auditor who saw accounting as a sacred quest for truth just as she liked to see journalism. Was that why Gordon had always taken such an interest in her career? He saw them as colleagues in truth-searching?

Eventually the poems brought Gordon back to the islands and she felt that they lost their edge. No longer did they tell her much about the poet. They were lyrical descriptions of island sunsets and flowers and the stark cliffs of the Marianas meeting the soft, voluptuous sea. Nice, Laura thought, some even resembled ones she remembered writing, probably about the same places at approximately the same time. Now though, her attention was beginning to flag.

Until she turned the page to a poem entitled, "Shut In, Shut Out." In its last stanza, she suddenly recognized herself.

But no
you shut me out
while you shut them in,
leaned against the door,
leaned those yearning breasts
against that hard, unfeeling door,

kept that hard barrier
unrelentingly
between us.

"Awk!"

In the moment of silence that followed her indignant squawk, Laura thought it must have sounded like an angry mother crow. Surely Teri and Nashi would look up at her balcony from the terrace below. She cowered behind the railing. Surely Shelby Verdun would lean around from his balcony to see what had happened.

She retreated into her room, slammed the sliding glass door and locked it. Then she dropped onto Teri's bed and clutched the notebook to her chest and fumed.

How dare he, she raged. How dare that creep Hassler appropriate parts of my body and make them featured characters in his lecherous fantasies.

She breathed deeply, trying to calm herself. Her pulse was just settling down when the phone rang.

She rolled across the bed and picked up the receiver, pausing another moment to be sure her voice would be normal. "Hello?"

"Laura? It's Jeffrey MacDougal." The voice was deep, sounding much more mature than the boy she'd been visualizing in wispy memories that flitted through her consciousness now and then.

"Well, hello," she said, not even trying to disguise the delight she felt. Jeffrey? It does make him seem older. Perhaps that's what he has in mind.

"I ... uh ... well, we talked about maybe going out for a drink, and I wondered if you're free tonight."

"Oh." Laura felt an eagerness surge within her. Yes. Let's do it. It's meant to be. This is the sort of adventure the islands have always promised. "I don't know," she said. "You see, my daughter's here, and I'm not sure what she wants to do ... "

"How old is your daughter?"

Well, that's one way to sort us into our proper generations, young man, she thought. "She's fourteen."

"Could she come with us?" he asked, sounding doubtful.

"Yeah, maybe she could." But it's not just a drink, that's not what this is about, is it? "Uh, listen, could I call you back after I check with her?"

"Sure. I'm going out for a bit but I have an answering machine."

"Do you live ... uh ... with your family? Your mother?"

He laughed. "No, me and a buddy have our own pad. Hey, I'm a grownup. Try to remember that." His voice seemed even deeper.

"I'll try," she said, wondering exactly what they had promised each other in the past few moments. "I'll call you back and let you know what I figure out," she said.

What am I getting myself into? she wondered. Her mind raced through the possibilities. Leave Teri alone in the hotel? No way. Call the Sabláns and see whether Teri could spend the night? How on earth would I explain myself to Charlotte, who must already be scandalized by what she's guessed about the photograph.

She closed her eyes and re-created the handsome islander's profile as she had seen it in the cockpit yesterday, and heard once more that deep, flirtatious voice.

Why would such a handsome boy be interested in an older woman? Was he really interested? What kind of game could he be playing?

Her mind made a sudden leap. His sister had stolen Will's negatives. Yet neither he nor his sister had any reason to suspect she had any connection with that photo.

Perhaps she should consider Jeff MacDougal's interest in her as a small gift she'd been given by her beloved islands, something to comfort her as she navigated all the other unsettling and downright menacing events fate had strewn in her path.

Wonderful things like Jeff MacDougal were what was meant to happen in these enchanted bits of earth. She would figure out a way to be alone with him.

She sighed in pure, unfiltered longing.

Well, at least for ten or fifteen minutes, I've been spared thinking about Gordon Hassler, she thought.

Resolutely, she returned to the poems.

—1973 —

GORDON WALKED TO HIS RENTAL CAR in such a heat of fury he wasn't conscious of where he was until he found himself fumbling with the key in the door lock.

That bitch. That smug, manipulative bitch. Pretending not to find a babysitter, bringing the little girl along as a chaperone, letting me take them both to an exceedingly expensive restaurant, and then giving me a cup of coffee and a shove out the door after I lugged the sleeping kid up two flights of stairs.

"Bitch!" He tried the word out loud, then took several deep breaths to settle himself, to stop his hands from trembling.

He tried the other key and the door opened, No, it's myself I'm furious at. I've never miscalculated so badly about a woman. And this makes twice. What is it about Laura Monroe that throws my timing off?

The most humiliating thing was that he had been so confident he hadn't even booked a hotel room. He had arranged for the rental car, called Laura to confirm that he would pick her up at seven-thirty, and then whiled away a couple hours in an airport bar. So now, at—he glanced at his watch—at eleven-forty-five p.m., he had to find a hotel room.

He settled for a cheesy motel on Van Ness Avenue and lay in its too-soft bed trying to get to sleep. First his mind insisted on replaying not only the evening's discouraging denouement, but the several phone conversations he'd had with Laura before he left Washington, planning this misbegotten evening.

What did I misjudge, he asked himself. Was it just that she had such a pleasant, warm telephone voice and sounded so cordial? She

always asked about Edwina when he called—wasn't that a signal? How did he miss it?

Eventually his mind segued into another gear and he began to think about why he had come to San Francisco. After nearly thirty years of searching, he had finally found information about Tex Arnold, under the name Arnold.

Before this discovery, he had assumed for many years that Tex had used an alias in his government operations. This assumption had led Gordon to compile a list of possible pseudonyms gleaned from the documents he studied, people mentioned in connection with various projects in the 1930s. Painstakingly, over the course of several years, he had tracked down photographs to go with most of the names and thus eliminated them from his list. Or he had come across subsequent mention of those names proving their owners alive and well after 1937, and he crossed them off the list.

One recent investigative trail concerned the organization Tex had claimed to be involved with when he introduced himself to Amelia Earhart in Lae: the Consortium to Promote Land-based Aviation. There really had been such an organization—but had Tex Arnold been involved? Not under any name that survived Gordon's further investigation. All the members he tracked had identities and photographs and lives that extended well beyond 1937. Just another dead end.

Then, just six months ago, in a sudden flash of insight, it came to him. What if Tex actually had interests in an organization promoting sea planes? What if his interest in spoiling Earhart's flight had not been wanting an excuse for the U.S. government to search the Japanese Mandate, but instead had strictly economic roots—the desire to get even richer? After all, hadn't that been the first thing he learned from Tex, more than 35 years ago—that almost everything came down to money?

If there had ever been an organization dedicated to ensuring the future for seaplanes, Gordon could find no mention of it. Yet he did learn a great deal about seaplanes that surprised him.

Until 1939, the world's fastest airplanes were seaplanes, dominating many phases of aviation from racing to long-distance passenger airlines. It was only the invention of variable-pitch propellers and wing flaps, making it possible for land-based airplanes to accelerate rapidly, that signaled the decline of the seaplane.

Then what became of the companies that manufactured seaplanes, he had wondered. When he began this particular investigation, he hit the closest thing to pay dirt he had experienced in thirty years.

There was, for instance, Poseidon Industries, which still manufactured small float planes. When it was established in the 1930s, it had been located just outside New York City. And one of the major stockholders had been a man named Torrington Arnold.

Tex! He'd found him. Right there in the quiet reading room at the Library of Congress, Gordon had let out a rowdy cheer. Then, beneath the glares of his fellow library users he'd slunk away, but he was back the next day to learn everything he could about Poseidon Industries.

With America's entry into World War II, the company had outgrown its New York plant and had moved—"lock, stock and barrel" as a report in the *Wall Street Journal* had put it—to the San Francisco Bay area. Most of the need for seaplanes would be in the Pacific theater, the *Journal* informed its readers.

One of the first tacks Gordon's research had taken all those years before had been a search for an obituary or other notice of Tex's death or of his disappearance, but he had found nothing. Now he looked again. Still, nothing. Only the one mention in a 1935 column called "Nuts and Bolts of Investing" about Torrington Arnold putting a huge amount of money—garnered from his family's Texas cattle ranch—into little Poseidon Industries.

Perhaps a trip to Texas would be in order eventually. But first, Gordon had begun to look for an excuse for a business trip to San Francisco. Of course, if he had to, he would do it on his own, but it always gave him pleasure to find ways for the U.S. government to

underwrite his research into the government's involvement in the disappearance of Amelia Earhart.

Except …

Gordon sat bolt upright in his bed in the San Francisco motel.

If Tex's only concern in New Guinea had been protecting his investment in Poseidon Industries, perhaps the government had not been involved.

If that were true, where was Gordon to take the revenge he had promised himself for so long?

Or had he taken it that gory night in Lae, New Guinea?

He had to get to sleep now. He had an appointment at Poseidon Industries in Richmond tomorrow. He would be posing as an author researching a book about the history of seaplanes, but in truth he would be trying to find out whatever he could about one-time stockholder Tex Arnold.

Reluctantly, he got up and took a sleeping pill. He hated the grogginess the drug induced the next day, but sometimes he had to chance it to get any sleep at all.

Making love to Laura Monroe tonight would have solved my sleep problem. It was his last coherent thought.

Shortly before the wake-up call from the desk clerk was due, he dreamed vividly of his impending visit to Poseidon Industries across the bay in Richmond.

"Wasn't a man called Torrington Arnold once a major stockholder in this company?" he asked the vice president he was interviewing in his dream. He couldn't keep his eyes off the luxurious appointments of the office in which they sat—carpet two-inches deep, gleaming cherry wood furniture, expensive art on the walls. Edwina would know for sure, but he thought he spotted an original Picasso drawing.

"Ah, yes," the vice president said. He had a thin mustache and a face that was familiar.This is ridiculous, he thought. Clark Gable was playing the vice president of Poseidon Industries. "It's fascinating. Mr. Arnold was the majority stockholder early in this company's

history. Then back in the late thirties, he simply disappeared. He had apparently gone to Australia to do some deep-sea fishing, and he never returned."

"So what happened to his shares in the company?"

"Well, in his will he had bequeathed them to a young man—apparently his ward."

Gordon's voice trembled in his dream. "Do you know the young man's name?"

"Oh, of course, everyone in the company knows it," said Clark Gable. "The shares are still held in escrow for him, and at staff birthday parties we toast each other: May you be reincarnated as Garrett Howland."

Gordon woke up in a cold sweat, frantically trying to sort dream from reality. If Garrett Howland had been Tex's heir, he would have been a very rich young man, not a fugitive frantically scurrying from his past. No. The police would have known—they would have seen that as the prime motive for murder.

But surely there had never been any doubt as to who murdered Tex Arnold. Who had shared the hotel room with him in Lae? Who had disappeared before the body was found? Wasn't that why Garrett Howland no longer existed?

He sat up just as the phone rang. His wake-up call.

Don't be ridiculous, he told himself sternly. Tex had no more concern for Garrett Howland than he had for his fine car. Less concern. He had used the boy like a toy—like a tennis ball. And when he had lost his usefulness, his bounce, his appeal, Tex would have tossed him away.

Groggily, Gordon went to the bathroom to confront that strange face in the mirror. When was the last time he had recognized the man in the mirror? When he was a teenager, perhaps, in Spearfish, South Dakota, searching his face for enough hair to justify shaving. Ever since he had met Tex Arnold and been introduced to his particular passions, a stranger had faced him in the mirror each morning.

He plugged in his electric razor now and began work on the stranger's face. Time to slip into his persona for today. He was an author named Jim Bledsloe. He was researching a book about seaplanes. He would see what Poseidon Industries could tell him about Tex Arnold.

And on his way back from Richmond, he might look for some stores selling used books, see if any of them had that dreadful Amelia Earhart book by Shelby Verdun. Verdun was a San Franciscan, so his book might still be on the shelves of stores selling new books.

The electric razor purred gently over the contours of his face. As he watched in the mirror, it was becoming more familiar. Yes, it was his face, Gordon Hassler's.

And Gordon Hassler had never been a teenager in Spearfish, South Dakota. He'd never even been to South Dakota.

The thought came unbidden, as it sometimes did when he stood before a mirror shaving and becoming reacquainted with himself.

Someday I'll have to try using a straight-edge razor myself.

Perhaps that would be his final graduation ceremony.

— 1983 —
Sunday

THERE WAS NO ANSWER when she dialed Edwina's room, so Laura set off for the swimming pool with the book of poems tucked under her arm. She found her friend stretched out on a low lounger, apparently sound asleep.

"Edwina," she said softly.

No response.

Reluctantly, feeling as though she were invading the only peace Edwina might have known in the past few days, Laura touched her shoulder gently. "Edwina?"

Edwina's sunglasses were tinted so dark Laura couldn't see her eyes open, but suddenly she was reaching out to catch hold of Laura's hand.

"Hello. What time is it?"

Laura glanced at her watch. "Two-thirty."

"That late? Good heavens, it's a damn good thing you woke me up. I'd have burned to a crisp." She reached for a flowered silk kimono and slipped it on over her modest bathing suit. "Oh, you've got the poems."

"Yes. Like you said, they're full of … clues, I guess. But I certainly need some help figuring them out."

"Maybe we can help each other," Edwina said, getting to her feet. "Let me buy you a drink."

They retreated to the shady margin of the pool terrace and found a table. A waiter appeared as soon as they sat down and Edwina ordered a banana daiquiri while Laura asked for iced tea.

"Now, Laura, dear," Edwina said, and her tone took Laura back many years to the days when Edwina had instructed her in the finer

points of comfort in the islands. "How many chances do you get to have a banana daiquiri in Tokyo?"

"Very few," Laura said, "but if I start drinking this early I won't last 'til sunset." She was saving herself for that drink with Jeff, if she could only figure out how to manage it. "Is it okay with you if we just kind of go through these poem by poem, so I can ask you about the things that puzzled me?"

"Sounds good to me," Edwina said, taking a deep sip of the frosty concoction the waiter presented to her. She scrawled her name and room number on the bill.

Laura started at the back of the book again, flipping past the teenage love poems and then hesitating on the page with the poem "Your Back." How could she broach the idea this poem had given her about Gordon's sexual orientation? Perhaps she'd gone far enough this morning discussing the man's womanizing with his widow.

Edwina glanced at the notebook. "Ah, that one. Yes, that's one of the puzzlers. I wondered if he might have caught a glimpse of a girl's naked back when he was very young—peeping through a crack in a wall perhaps? Doesn't it seem to have a guilty tone to it? He would never talk about that orphanage he grew up in, but there must have been girls there, too."

"Maybe that is it. The first thing that occurred to me was that he might have been—that is, might have had an early, uh—experience with another boy."

Edwina's jaw dropped. "Gordon? No way. Listen, did I ever tell you about my first husband? I know from bitter experience how to tell when a man has … " She almost seemed to choke on the word. " … homosexual tendencies."

Laura nodded, disturbed by Edwina's adamant denial and by her own inclination to argue the point. Let it be, she instructed herself as she flipped to the next poem.

"This 'Green' seems to express a terror of the tropics I never saw in Gordon. I remember crashing through the brush on Saipan with you guys … "

"Yes, I found that one almost scary."

"Funny he ended up spending so much time out here."

"I know. But I assume the terror comes of his war experience. And I think he was writing about much larger, more threatening islands than the Marianas."

"Where did he fight, do you know?"

"Hmm. New Guinea? Yes, I know he'd been in New Guinea. How else could he have been there? One night years ago in Saipan he was comparing notes—you and Foster weren't there? Weren't you always there?—anyway, remember that pompous Aussie in land management, the one who had worked in New Guinea before the Trust Territory hired him?"

"Oh, what was his name? O'Reilly. Kevin O'Reilly."

"Yes, that's the one. O'Reilly. He was pontificating one night about how much better a job Australia had done in Papua-New Guinea than the U.S. was doing in Micronesia and finally Gordon couldn't stand it, I guess—he'd drunk more than usual that night, I think—and he burst out saying New Guinea hadn't looked all that great when he'd been there."

Laura remembered how irritating Kevin O'Reilly had been, how he had managed to goad her into making foolish statements more than once, and how Foster had razzed her later about letting the man get under her skin. "Who won the argument?" she asked.

"I think they finally agreed they were talking about vastly different eras of history," Edwina said.

Laura skipped past the "Coming to Terms" poem about settling for fleshiness and roundness instead of lean hardness. While Edwina was resigned to her husband's history as a womanizer, the question as to whether he had once been interested in men obviously was not open for discussion.

She came to the poem that made seduction analogous to tuning up an automobile. "I have to tell you, Edwina, this is one of the sexiest poems I've ever read."

Edwina leaned over to read a few lines. "Ah, that one." She took another long drink of her daiquiri.

"Here you are!" The words burst suddenly into their concentration on the notebook full of poems. Laura turned to find Teri with a long T-shirt pulled on over her bikini and a towel under her arm. Nashi Ramírez stood beside her. "We're off to the beach," Teri said.

"Edwina, you haven't met my daughter Teri, have you?"

"Not this trip. But we have met before. You were much younger then."

"This is Mrs. Hassler," Laura said and watched Teri's eyebrow do a startled acknowledgment. Good grief, she thought, four days on this island and she's turned into a Guamanian.

"And this is her friend, Ignacio Ramírez." Too late, Laura remembered how he felt about his name. "I'm sorry. Nashi Ramírez."

After the teenagers said polite how-do-you-dos, Teri said, "You know, there is a way to get even with her when she calls us names like Teresita and Ignacio. We can always call her Tater-pig."

Nashi laughed. "Tater-pig?"

"Yes," Edwina chuckled. "Foster used to call you that. I remember. Where on earth did it come from?"

"Yeah, how did you ever get a name like that?" Apparently Nashi had finally found something more offensive than Ignacio.

"It was on our honeymoon. We stopped in some little town in the Rocky Mountains—Montana, I guess—and there was some kind of arts festival going on in a park. These barbershop quartet guys were selling these things they called tater-pigs, in between bursting into song. They had drilled holes through baking potatoes and stuffed in little link sausages and then baked them. And Foster—Teri's father—decided … well, actually, the analogy he was making was pretty rude."

"Mother!" Teri's horror was genuine. She was blushing. So, Laura thought, was Nashi, under his brown skin.

Edwina laughed with delight. "Oh, that does sound like Foster!"

Laura was laughing, too. "And you ate them slathered with sour cream."

"And chives? All those years hearing him call you that, and missing out on that image." Edwina was beginning to sound almost hysterical. The two teenagers stared at the women in embarrassment.

Finally Edwina caught her breath. "Oh, my heavens! That's the first time I've really laughed in days. Thank you."

Still looking uncomfortable, Teri said, "I'm sorry about your husband, Mrs. Hassler."

Edwina was completely serious again. "Thank you, dear."

"Well, Mother, if you've got yourself under control again?"

"Yes, honey."

"Nashi called his family to let them know where he was. And they invited me for dinner tonight. Isn't that nice?"

"Why yes," Laura said, her unruly mind immediately conjuring up Jeff MacDougal's handsome face and sexy, deep voice.

"And then," Nashi said, "a couple of my brothers are going to a movie, and said we could go with them."

"Yes. *Revenge of the Jedi* is playing here already. We've been waiting for it to come to Tokyo for months and it's already here. So can I go, Mom?"

"We'll bring her back to the hotel safe and sound, I promise," Nashi said seriously. "Please let her come Mrs. … uh, Ms. Monroe."

Laura was touched by his sincerity. She was also alarmed by the leap of optimistic anticipation somewhere below her stomach. It's as though it were meant to be, she thought. The island love gods are clearing the way for Jeff and me.

She tried to rein herself in. There was her daughter's safety to think of. And what would a conservative Guamanian like Roberto Ramírez think about a parent who let a fourteen-year-old go out unchaperoned?

"You don't have any sisters who'll be going along?"

Teri rolled her eyes, but Nashi seemed to find it a perfectly reasonable request. "I'm sure we can get Fina to go, if I pay for her ticket. She's eighteen and her boyfriend just went off to Hawaii for a couple weeks."

"What time would you have Teri home—er, here?"

"The second show starts at eight-thirty so I'm sure we'll get her back by eleven."

"C'mon, Mom," Teri said.

"Okay," Laura said. "If you're back by eleven and if Nashi's sister goes along."

"Thanks, Mom." Teri gave her mother a kiss before she and Nashi headed off toward the beach.

"How do you survive it?" Edwina asked.

"Hmm?"

"Motherhood. The decisions. The responsibility."

"Yeah, it's a little scary sometimes. But he's such a nice boy and I know his family—I used to work with his father long ago. Of course, if I'd introduced them, Teri would want nothing to do with him, but since she found him on her own … "

Her mind shifted gears. "Edwina, I need to make a quick phone call. I'll be right back."

She hurried to a pay phone in the hotel lobby, dug Jeff's phone number out of her wallet, and dialed. The recorded strains of "Beer Barrel Polka" were followed by a loud, unfamiliar voice saying, "Hey. Roll out the barrel, this is Jason and Jeff's party pad. Bring the beer and come on over. Or leave an explanation for your absence and directions to your party." As she waited for the tone that was her cue, her heart sank. He's just a kid! It sounds like a fraternity house.

But at the tone she said, "Jeff? It's Laura. I found out Teri has plans of her own so, if you still want to have that drink, I'm game. Call me at the hotel."

She was trembling when she finished. Courage, Camille, she told herself. That wasn't Jeff who recorded the message. Surely he is more mature than his roommate.

When she returned to the pool terrace, Edwina had begun on another daiquiri and ordered Laura another glass of iced tea. We'd better speed this up, Laura thought. She'll be blotto before the afternoon is over.

"We were on that tune-up poem," Edwina said as soon as Laura sat down.

"Ah, yes. Very powerful."

"Reading it I felt … almost seduced myself," Edwina said.

"Me, too. But I find the metaphor puzzling. I never knew Gordon was mechanically inclined."

"That's what's so weird," Edwina said. "He wasn't. I never even saw him lift the hood on a car. He left everything to the mechanics. Even those years in Saipan."

"Maybe he had an auto repair course once? In high school?" Laura said.

"Or read a poetic memoir by a mechanic? What was that book a few years back? Zen and something? *Zen and the Art of Motorcycle Maintenance.*"

Or maybe it made him feel more manly to pretend familiarity with engines, Laura thought without sharing the idea with Edwina. She turned instead to the sleight-of-hand poem. "This one's interesting. I don't remember Gordon playing cards."

"No. As far as I'm concerned, that was his worst fault. I would have loved a good bridge partner."

"But he did do coin tricks? I remember him always jingling coins in his pockets."

Edwina shook her head. "Nervousness, I suppose. Gordon kept a lot of things inside that he probably should have let out. I never saw him do any tricks. He probably would have been good at it, though, with those long fingers of his."

"Here's another strange one," Laura said, pointing to a title. "Mother."

"I know. He never knew his mother. By the time I got to that one I began to wonder if I was mistaken. Maybe these weren't his

poems at all, but someone else's. Or maybe they were documents in secret code."

No. Laura thought of the one about breasts pressed against a door that was shutting him out. No, Gordon Hassler wrote these.

"Well, fancy meeting you here."

She turned to find Will Hildebrandt standing behind her chair.

"Mrs. Hassler, have you heard about the room key?"

Edwina stared at him, shaking her head.

"The hotel got the key to your husband's room back in yesterday's mail."

"In the mail?" Edwina said.

"Yeah. You know how hotels promise—have you got your room key, Laura?"

She produced it from her bag.

"See. 'Return postage guaranteed by Guam Hilton Hotel, Tamuning, Guam. So the murderer must have dropped it in a mailbox."

"Where?" Edwina asked.

Off-island somewhere, Laura wished, but rationally she knew it was too soon for the murderer to have gotten to Hawaii, say, or Manila, and for the key to travel back through the mail to Guam.

"Right here in Guam. The post office guy that opened a box up by the bowling alley found it there Friday. Only hotel key in the mail that day, apparently."

"Which bowling alley?" Laura asked.

"The old one. Chamorro Lanes."

Chamorro Lanes was on the way to the airport. The murderer could have left the island after dropping the key in the mail.

"So how did you find out about this?" Laura asked. "I didn't see a word about the investigation in this morning's *Chronicle*."

"Shelby Verdun. He's haunting the police station. Keeps bugging 'Sús Pérez with questions about the Japanese hospital and the age of the photo and whether they checked it for prints. Problem is, because it's Sunday the cop shop's just about the only place open on

the island. I suggested to Shelby that Agaña Cathedral is probably open, and he could go pray for divine revelation, but I guess for the time being Pérez is stuck with him. And vice versa."

"Good," said Edwina.

Laura nodded. "Couldn't happen to two nicer guys."

"Were there prints on the photo?" Edwina asked almost shyly.

"Only Gordon's."

"Then it wasn't planted on his body," Laura said.

"Apparently not. And to prove he's really on top of things, 'Sús also dusted the room key for prints, Shelby got quite a kick out of that."

"And were there fingerprints?" Edwina asked.

"Maybe a couple hundred different ones. It's beyond the Guam police to sort them out."

There was a pause as Laura wished Will would take the hint and leave her alone with Edwina. She needed to talk to him, to tell him about Dennis Dover's being in Saipan and his connection to Gordon, but she didn't want to do that in Edwina's presence. And Edwina certainly wouldn't discuss Gordon's poems with Will there.

"So, Laura, you've advanced to mint juleps?" Will gestured at her glass.

"Iced tea," Laura said. "I've got to keep my brain clear. Edwina and I are—uh—trying to sort something out."

"Oh." Will looked almost chagrined, as though he realized at last that he was intruding. "Well, listen, when you get done, stop by the bar. Maybe you'll let me buy you a real drink."

"Okay." Laura turned back to the poems. "This one, Fog,'" she said as Will faded back toward the bar. "I never knew Gordon lived in San Francisco."

"Oh, yes. His accounting degree was from San Francisco State College, so I think he was there at least four years."

Why was he so secretive about it? About everything. It couldn't be that he had avoided mentioning his San Francisco connection all those years in hopes that someday he would be able to ask her to

show him the city. It must just have become a habit after years in the CIA … never to reveal anything about himself.

"I was interested in these auditing poems," Laura said. "I never dreamed an auditor could be so … obsessive about tracking down the truth."

"Obsessive is a good word," Edwina said. "He was that way when I first knew him, always bringing work home, shuffling through papers for hours."

"Looking for what? Cheaters?"

"I was never sure," she said. "But I often wondered if it wasn't something separate from his regular job. There never seemed to be numbers on any of the pages I saw him poring over. They seemed to be mostly memos, letters, that sort of thing. Of course, once he switched agencies and went with the CIA, I decided it was better not to know what he was looking at, and I was careful never to look over his shoulder. You know, never take him by surprise."

She wasn't going to learn much from the dutiful spook wife about specific projects Gordon had worked on since he left Saipan. And why should she expect to? She herself had never wondered about Foster's work after he joined Gordon in Washington.

"And of course, as years went by, he spent more time working late at the office rather than at home," Edwina added. She sounds rueful. Did she suspect him of carrying on with other women when he said he was working late? Was that when he accomplished his tune-ups?

Laura massaged her brow. This was so complicated. They were attempting to find the truth in the artistic expressions of a congenital liar. And she was trying to read significance into every nuance of a woman who must still be in shock from her sudden widowhood, who had every reason to miss implications that didn't fit the way she chose to remember her husband.

And she was certainly not going to share with Edwina any of the truth she herself knew —for instance, the origin of the photo

that was the police department's best clue. It was all a giant house of mirrors.

Even so, she wished she could hold on to the poems, in case inspiration struck in the middle of the night. Reluctantly, she handed the notebook across the table. "I don't know. It just seems like we're dealing with a very complex person here."

"You don't see anything that would help the police?"

"Not on the surface. Who knows? Some of my best ideas seem to come when I'm asleep. Maybe one of us will have an insight in a few hours."

"Or a few years," Edwina said.

Laura glanced at her watch. "Wow. We've been at this almost three hours. I think I'll go take Will up on that drink. Want to come?"

Edwina shook her head. "I think I'll go have a shower and get dressed for dinner. Do you have plans?"

"Actually, I do," Laura said, wondering if Edwina could tell from her voice how tenuous her plans were.

"Thanks for everything, Laura," Edwina said, clutching the book of poems as though it were a life preserver. She walked toward the hotel lobby while Laura headed for the bar.

She found Will nursing a beer and chatting with a rather drunken-looking islander. "Okay, Hildebrandt, I've come to collect."

"Great!" he said with uncharacteristic enthusiasm. He slapped the islander on the shoulder, saying, "See you later, *paré*," and led Laura to a small table in a quiet corner.

Laura ordered a glass of wine and said, "Before I forget, let me tell you about the sunburned man. I want someone besides me to know." She quickly sketched in everything she knew about Dennis Dover—how he'd been dining with Gordon the night before he died and how he'd shown up yesterday in Saipan looking for the Japanese hospital. And how Edwina knew him as one of Gordon's CIA colleagues.

As she finished, she noticed Will staring at her in an odd way. "What?" she asked.

"Let's go for three in a row," he said.

"Three what?"

"Dinners. Have dinner with me tonight, Laura. Just the two of us. Order room service for the kid or something. Don't all kids love room service?"

Laura felt her jaw drop.

"Listen, Laura, it's been so great seeing you again—remembering old times when we were young and foolish—but in my case never quite foolish enough to say what I wanted to, to you."

She continued to stare. Now what? Will Hildebrandt was—flirting? Making a pass? Will Hildebrandt?

Will stared back, seemingly struck dumb. Then he suddenly blurted, "Laura, I was eighteen years old when the Navy plopped me on this rock. I've never made love to a white woman."

She found herself standing, staring at him in—well, it felt like horror. *Will Hildebrandt?*

"I can't believe you said that," she said.

"I can't believe I said it either," he said. "Please, sit down, finish your wine. I'll be good."

She eased back into her chair and reached for the wine glass.

"I don't know what to say," Will said. "Obviously, I don't know what to say." He sighed loudly. "Have dinner with me, anyway. You can tell me what else you've learned from Edwina. I'll behave myself."

"Oh, poor Will," Laura said. "We're all under a lot of stress. I understand. I'm afraid I already have plans for tonight. But listen, one of us has got to talk to Cory MacDougal, don't you think?"

He nodded. "Yeah. And her mother, Panda the Piranha. But I think it would be better if it were you. Cory used to work for me, the little sneak, so already that conversation will be tense. And I have such a long association with Donnie—especially in Panda's mind—I'm not sure how effective I could be with her."

Laura nodded. She felt guilty that she had expressed such horror at Will's ham-handed proposition. Perhaps because of that, she

found herself agreeing that she should be the one to talk to Cory and Panda.

"Anyway, you always were the diplomatic one in interviews. You know I usually make people mad. In fact I just demonstrated my conversational ineptness in spades."

How does this work, she asked herself. He shocks and insults me and I feel guilty so once again I end up doing the dirty work. He managed to stick me with the trip to Saipan with Shelby Verdun, too.

"Tell you what I'll do," Will said with a note of propitiation in his voice. "I'll talk to the kid, see if he knows anything about the purloined pix."

"The kid? You mean Jeff MacDougal?"

"Yeah. I doubt if he knows anything about it, but it can't hurt to have a bit of man-to-man."

Great, she thought. I hope I don't turn up as one of the subjects in your male-bonding rites.

She excused herself as soon as she finished the wine and climbed the stairs to her room. Teri had obviously been there—the two tiny parts of her damp bikini hung over the shower curtain rod. Laura wondered whether Nashi ever saw Guamanian girls in such brief swimwear—she hadn't noticed what the island girls were wearing when she and Teri were at the beach on Friday.

She sat in the balcony chair, leaving the sliding door open a bit so she would be sure to hear the phone. Her room faced away from the sunset but it was splashing colors against the northeastern sky.

Her stomach rumbled and she tried to remember when she had last eaten. Breakfast with Edwina. And now, after turning down two invitations to dine with old friends, she didn't dare leave to get a bite for fear she would miss Jeff's call. If he called.

Serve you right if you starve to death, you lecherous old lady, she thought. It's offensive when Will displays a little lust but okay for you?

She sank back into the chair, letting her mind slide into the rapidly fading colors in the sky.

— *1977* —

ON JULY 2, AS ALWAYS, Gordon spent some uncomfortable moments alone with himself.

Forty years since he saw her off to her death. Forty years since he saw to the death of Tex Arnold.

And what had he accomplished?

His life seemed a collection of very wide misses and an occasional close call. Nothing a man could sit back from and say, "There, I did that."

If he couldn't solve the mystery of who had sent Amelia Earhart to her death, could he just leave it be?

No. Because he had sent her to her death himself. Or that pathetic boy, Garrett Howland, had. Manipulated by Tex Arnold. But who had manipulated Tex?

It still wasn't clear what his motives had been. The materials they had promised to send from Poseidon Industries in California were sketchy, not much help. Yes, Torrington Arnold had been one of their major stockholders. Yes, his estate had profited nicely from the boom in seaplane construction inspired by the war in the Pacific. But shortly after the war, his survivors—a sister and a nephew—had sold the shares and that was that, as far as Poseidon Industries was concerned.

Gordon stretched and yawned. Sometimes the air got so close in this cubbyhole of a den that he longed to throw the double doors open, put a symphony on the stereo, and make the room part of the house. But he had cordoned it off so successfully, with his standoffish secrecy, he was confident Edwina had never entered the room.

He looked at the new file folder he had just filled. "Texas, '77" he had labeled it. He had made the trip two months ago, but it had been so disappointing he hadn't gotten around to making a file until today, on the anniversary. So this is all I've done this year? That lousy trip to San Antonio?

He still wished he had taken Edwina along. She would have enjoyed San Antonio—the bicultural setting, the music, the food. But he shielded her from this segment of his life even more than from his day job. Anyway, what would she have done while he pored through microfilms of newspaper pages?

Word of Tex's death seemed never to have made it back to his hometown—and that was suspicious in itself. Granted, forty years ago there hadn't been the sort of worldwide coverage of crimes one might expect today, but you would think that an American murdered in a hotel room in a distant port would get some mention in his hometown newspaper.

Or was that it? Had someone else been there in New Guinea, making sure word got out about Amelia's disappearance in order to set off the search for her, while keeping the murder of Tex Arnold under wraps?

Perhaps Garrett Howland had saved someone the trouble of getting rid of Tex. Just as Tex would have needed to dispose of the boy who did his dirty work, perhaps the person running Tex would have wanted to get rid of him after he had played his role.

There had certainly been U.S. government interest in the Earhart flight. He had found more and more evidence through the years to that effect. Many people believed she had been a volunteer spy. As far as he could determine, he was the only person who knew she had been tricked into flying into the Japanese mandate. Or had she been tricked into flying off course merely to make seaplanes seem more reliable than land-based planes? Had Tex intended to launch some sort of advertising campaign to that effect when he returned to the States?

Gordon was beginning to believe that he would never know the answer to some of his questions.

In recent years, he had become almost as concerned about the possibility of being discovered as the murderer of Tex Arnold as he was obsessed with discovering what lay behind the plot against Amelia Earhart. He would have thought the passing years would decrease his fear, but lately his wariness had grown into what he recognized as full-blown paranoia. So what? he comforted himself. Who was it who said, "Just because I'm paranoid, it doesn't mean they aren't out to get me?"

No matter how he might wish life had turned out differently, Tex Arnold and Amelia Earhart were both dead, and he must never be connected with either of them.

All these years he had assumed that it was only his connection with Tex Arnold he should worry about, but lately he had begun to think how amazing it was that nobody had ever connected the dots between the two dramatic news events that had taken place in Lae, New Guinea, on July 2, 1937. As he had become a connoisseur of books about Amelia Earhart's disappearance through the years, he'd become more and more puzzled. Why hadn't any of the authors gone to New Guinea to see the scene of Earhart's last takeoff? And once there, wouldn't it be logical to check the local newspaper files, see what else had happened that week? Wasn't that the kind of detail writers liked to add to their descriptions?

Gordon had considered cultivating some travel agents, hoping to figure out a way he could be alerted to people who booked trips to New Guinea. But how would he begin? How many travel agents would he have to befriend? He wasn't as confident of his seductive powers as he had once been.

Then he thought of making librarians his first line of defense. With inter-library loans, wouldn't a librarian in any big-city library reference section be aware of people doing lots of reading about Amelia's disappearance? And if he approached it right ...

What if he said he was a researcher himself, doing a study on the lasting fame of Amelia Earhart? He could ask the librarians to give him names of people who were especially interested in materials about Amelia, and then he could pretend he would contact them and interview them about their motivations.

But in reality, as he identified people with an unusual degree of interest in the subject, he could use his CIA contacts with the far-flung fraternity of private investigators to learn more about these folks, determine whether any of them constituted a threat to him.

He sat there in his study, turning the idea inside out and upside down. He could find nothing wrong with it.

And since the CIA was sending him to San Francisco next week, he might as well start there. After all, that first story reporting that Amelia had been spotted in Saipan had come out of San Francisco.

There was a tap at the door.

"Yes?"

Edwina peeked in. "Mail's here, honey." She stretched across the space toward his desk. "Another missive from your girlfriends."

He rose, took the letters from her and gave her a quick peck on the cheek. "I'll have lunch ready in half an hour," she said.

"Mmm." He was opening the first envelope, the newsletter from the national headquarters of Zonta International. That would be what Edwina meant by girlfriends.

He had joined Zonta as G. Hassler a few years ago after he had overheard two women talking about it at a restaurant. It was a mildly feminist organization of professional women who had made a sort of patron saint out of Amelia Earhart. Its newsletter frequently included items on the latest Earhart research. Edwina accused him—gently, just teasing—of using the organization as a way to meet women, but he had never even attended a meeting. He told her the group had somehow put him on the mailing list and just didn't remove him. He, of course, made sure they didn't remove him by sending generous contributions to their scholarship fund. And while he carefully filed all the Zonta newsletters, he never let

Edwina read them. That was how he protected her—perhaps his most chivalrous act. He never let her know he had a special interest in Amelia Earhart.

He set the newsletter aside on his reading pile. You never could tell where the next clue might turn up.

Then he glanced at the small envelope on top of a couple of bills in the mail Edwina had brought in. In tiny cramped handwriting, the return address jabbed him: R. Howland, 1214 St. Joe, Spearfish, S.D.

He tore the envelope open and smoothed out the single sheet of paper. The handwriting was so wobbly it was almost impossible to recognize, but it gave him a sense of relief. She was still alive. Redemption was still possible.

> *Dear Mr. Hassler, As always it is very generous of you to remember me and my Garrett. If it weren't for you, I would not be able to stay in my own home. The money you send makes it possible for Mrs. Quentin to stay here with me so I don't have to go to the county home. Thank you for your kindness. Yours truly, Rose Howland.*

Sighing, he blinked several times. She must be almost ninety. And still able to thank him, still able to use the payments he sent religiously, as though they were a means to buy back his soul.

Maybe we will meet again, Mother, he let his mind whisper.

But probably not.

— 1983 —
Sunday

"LAURA." The voice on the telephone was low and soft and more welcome than food or drink.

"Hello, Jeff."

"I just got your message. I'll pick you up in half an hour. Okay?"

She glanced at her watch. It was just seven. The evening was young.

"I'll be down by the main door."

"I'm driving a white Honda."

"I'll see you in thirty minutes." She suspected it was desirable from both their viewpoints that her departure with him be as inconspicuous as possible. What if Will Hildebrandt were to see her leaving with Jeff MacDougal, after their conversation earlier today? Of course, Jeff might have important information about what his sister had done with the photo but Will had assigned that investigation to himself.

She jumped into the shower and burst into song, glad that Teri wasn't there to hear her and make sarcastic remarks. She listened to the words she was belting out. "I'm getting married in the morning, ding-dong the bells are going to chime!"

Whoa! She felt just that exuberant but the words were a little extreme. She tried to think of a more appropriate song to accompany the delicious water pounding her skin.

She found a tune playing in the back of her mind and stopped to listen. "As Time Goes By." Oh, great, she thought, stepping out of the shower. Now I'm casting myself in *Casablánca*. Play it again, Sam.

Once again she stopped to consider the large block letters GH on the bath mat. They were white, like the rest of the mat, but the thick fabric was sculpted so they stood out. She wondered whether they leapt out at Edwina each time she stepped into the bathroom here at the Hilton.

She stood before the closet trying to figure out what to wear, trying to get Gordon Hassler out of her mind, trying to decide what the music playing behind this date should be.

What makes me look really gorgeous? she asked the limited selection of clothes on her side of the closet. Oh, come off it. What will make me look young? Finally she pulled on a pair of white slacks that had seemed a little tight when she'd worn them last in Tokyo. Tonight they fit nicely.

One thing about having someone I know get murdered, I've worried away some weight.

She pulled on a top she'd bought in the hotel gift shop, a batik print in bright pinks on fabric as lightweight as a handkerchief. She looked at herself in the mirror as she tied the drawstring of the blouse around her waist. The blouse had floppy sleeves like butterfly wings, and the fabric was so sheer it provided a filmy view of her bra.

Hmmm. Too provocative? She stared at the mirror. Well, she did look young. And carefree—about the way she'd felt when she first came to the islands, a married woman free to flirt just a bit with any man she met, because she and he—whomever he might be—knew she would go home where she belonged. At least everyone had understood that except Gordon Hassler.

Well, I don't have a husband to protect me tonight, she thought, but I do have a curfew. I have to get back here before Teri does.

She got out her eye makeup and tried to decide how much would be too much.

* * *

Jeff pulled up in the little white car at exactly seven-thirty. She slid into the bucket seat and half expected him to supervise the fastening of her seat belt. Wasn't that when she had first noticed this chemistry between them—as he helped her with the seatbelt in the plane? But he was just staring at her. "I'm not used to girls who are on time," he said.

Was that how he was going to deal with the issue of the differences in their ages—by calling her a girl? "I live in Japan. Everyone's on time in Japan."

"You smell great," he said. "You look great. Thanks for coming out with me."

"Thanks for asking me."

He put the car in gear and followed the hotel's curving driveway back to the street. "Close as it is, I've never been to Japan," he said. "I'd like to go. Especially if I had a friend to show me around."

Laura tried to picture herself showing Jeff MacDougal around Tokyo—making him even a temporary part of her workaday life. The image wouldn't hold. Unexpected bonuses to life like Jeff MacDougal belonged in the indolent, sweet-scented, slow-moving tropics. There wasn't time for fantasy and star-crossed romance in Tokyo.

"Have you eaten?"

"Uh, no, I haven't."

"Neither have I," he said. "You don't mind if we go to one of the other tourist hotels? It's easier … "

"Sounds fine," she said. She recalled her image of him as the Waikiki beach boy. Easier to squire a middle-aged white woman at a tourist hotel than in one of the places where he might run into folks he knows?

They ate in a Japanese restaurant in the hotel closest to Two Lovers Point. They were safely anonymous, surrounded by Japanese tourists—mostly honeymooners. He asked her to help him order, and he obviously enjoyed the food. To her very pleasant surprise, they seemed to have more to talk about than there was time to fill. While she tried to think of a way to talk about the photo and his

sister, they talked about Guam politics and moved on to events and interesting characters in all the other islands that Jeff flew to and that Laura had visited in her island days. He seemed delighted by her anecdotes about people she had known back then, and she was impressed by the good-humored balance with which he brought some of her stories up to date. There was none of Foster's sarcasm in his attitude. She remembered someone else who used to take a tolerant delight in the idiosyncrasies and variety of island cultures: Jeff's father, Donnie MacDougal.

She enjoyed the conversation so much she almost wanted to spend the whole evening there, looking across the table at that handsome face, those sparkling dark eyes, balancing the chemistry between them as a sort of future promise. But he signaled the waiter for the bill. Suddenly she worried: does he expect me to pay? But no, he was brandishing a credit card and waving away her offer to go Dutch. "Laura! I invited you."

As they strolled across the parking lot, a soft, fragrant breeze ruffled the sleeves of her blouse. She wanted to take his arm but restrained herself. The first move had to be his.

She felt her heart sag when he drove back toward the Hilton, past the other hotels lined up along Tumon Bay. Then, as he slowed by the entrance to the parking area at the public beach, it occurred to her that perhaps he was shy, not knowing how to phrase the next question.

But he found a way. "Want to sit on the beach and watch the moon rise?"

"Sounds lovely." She pretended not to notice that he reached behind him in the little car for a blanket, which he tucked under his arm. When he offered his other arm to her, she took it. When he pulled her close beside him, she was both pleased and comfortable.

They walked along the crunchy coral beach for a while, not talking, just listening to the distant sizzling sound of the surf on the reef and the closer, gentle lap as the water of the lagoon swayed gently in and out.

"C'mere," he said, pulling her back away from the beach, into a little grassy alcove nearly surrounded by thick trees and bushes. He spread the blanket out and tugged her down to sit beside him.

"I'm not sure we can see the moon rise from in here."

"Hey, it'll get up over the trees eventually," he said. And suddenly he was kissing her and she felt herself kissing him back, frantically. Oh, she sighed, when have kisses ever tasted as sweet and urgent as this?

He pulled his mouth away and gave a gasping, trembling sigh. "Oh, Laura. Wow."

They locked in another embrace, and she heard the Hollywood studio orchestra that occupied a certain sensual corner of her mind tuning up. She waited with expectation. What was the music for this scene?

When it came, it startled her so much she pulled away from him.

"I'm sorry," he said contritely, pulling his hand back from her breast.

"Oh, no," she said, feeling wanton, wanting to grab his hands, place them over both breasts, wanting him to tear the fragile fabric of her new blouse. "I love having you touch me. But a song popped into my head, a song from my high school days, and I realized you're too young to have ever heard it."

"Try me." He spoke with quiet urgency.

"Kisses Sweeter Than Wine."

His pause was too long. Perhaps he was too honest.

"Oh, Jeff, you're a handsome, charming, wonderful young man— but what are you doing here? With me?"

He sat back, gripping her shoulders. "I like you, Laura, can't you believe that? I'm very much attracted to you."

"But you could have any girl on this island. Girls your own age."

He sighed deeply. "Believe me, I've tried. I don't have trouble getting them to go out with me. But they all have marriage on their

minds, right away. And they're so boring. Even if we do—well, you know, even when there's an attraction, if I can't have a conversation with someone, I can't stay interested. Lately, my mother's been on my back, saying I'm too picky, I'm breaking too many girls' hearts. So I'm thinking, maybe that's my problem. I don't like girls. Maybe I should give women a try. And right away I met you and something clicked. For me, at least."

"Jeff, I remember you when you were a little boy, and I was already a married woman."

"But you're not married now."

Laura shook her head. "No. But I dye my hair. I have streaks of gray."

"All over your body?" He grabbed her, pushing her back on the blanket. "Can I see?" They were laughing and hugging and then once again kissing deeply. She thought, What the hell, isn't this what the islands are for? Nights of unrestrained passion?

Suddenly they heard the sound of car tires on pavement, surprisingly close to where they lay. They both sat up. Headlights sparkled through the undergrowth and then were doused. The car's engine shut down.

"Oh, no!" Jeff said. "I think I know where we are."

It suddenly seemed a familiar setting to Laura, too. "This must be where Jodie and … "

"Yes. My dad. They were here, on Liberation Day, when that policeman was shot in the parking lot."

Laura shivered. "I remember. I was living in Saipan but we read all about it in the Guam papers."

"I read it, too."

"Oh!" What a terrible shock for a child that must have been.

"Not when the trial was on. My mother wouldn't let me read about it. A few years later, I went to the library and looked up the articles. I wanted to know exactly what they were doing, how they happened to be the closest thing to eye-witnesses."

"And you found the answer in the paper?"

"Between the lines. I was fourteen by then. I had figured out that life centered on sex."

Teri's fourteen, Laura thought with some alarm. And out tonight with an island boy.

"But their description in court of where they were, what they heard—this has to be the place. Almost up against the parking lot but completely invisible." He shuddered. Has he used this private space for other rendezvous? And was his horror because of the policeman's death or because of what his father had been doing here?

"Oh, Laura, I'm sorry, I don't think ... "

"No, it's not the time nor the place. Especially not the place." She was scrambling to her feet, then pulling him up.

"I don't want to give up on women," he said.

"You mean as opposed to silly, shallow girls?"

"Yes." He sounded grateful that she understood.

"Listen," she said, playing with the fingers of his hand, "I'm putting Teri on the plane to Honolulu Tuesday night. I'll stay on here for a day or two." After all, she'd had some work assigned to her while she was here—Bosley owed her a couple more days' vacation. "Maybe we could — have another drink?"

"Yes, let's do it." He folded the blanket neatly and they walked back to the car. One other car was parked nearby. When Laura thought she saw it rocking slightly she felt cheated, then felt silly for feeling cheated.

Back at the Hilton, Jeff pulled beyond its lighted entryway, then stretched across the gearshift to give her another passionate kiss.

"I'd better go," she said at last.

"I'll call you Tuesday," he said. "We'll plan on that, okay?"

Laura walked toward the hotel entrance feeling as though she were aglow, as though anyone who saw her would assume she was in love.

Anyone who saw her. She shrank back into herself, grabbed her key at the desk, and scurried up the stairs to her room. The last thing she needed was to run into Will or Edwina.

She just had time to get settled back into her mother personality before Teri arrived back, as promised, precisely at 11 p.m.

— 1980 —
June

WEARILY JODIE CLIMBED THE STAIRS to her third-floor apartment. Why did she always end up on the third floor? No, that wasn't true. That place in the Marina had been on the second floor.

Why did she always end up with jobs that required a long commute? Of course, any rational person would find a job first and then find an apartment nearby, or at least in the same Bay Area city. But last year, when she had given up on Alaska, on Donnie, on the possibility of a future with him, she'd come straight to San Francisco and found an apartment.

She knew why. She had to be in San Francisco, be listed in the San Francisco phone book, in case he came looking for her again. She couldn't give up on him, not really. It just wasn't an option.

And yet, it was hopeless. There wasn't enough fuel in the universe for a fire that burned as hot as theirs did. Or at least, there wasn't enough fuel in Alaska.

Actually, she liked Alaska. In some ways, it took her back to her Rocky Mountain childhood. And flying over that icy wilderness was weirdly like flying over the empty sea between tiny dots of land in Micronesia—well, as similar as a negative is to its positive photographic print. But Donnie hated Alaska, hated the harsh weather, the flat light during the brief, overcast winter days that made the dark green of evergreens look black so that the entire world seemed to be painted in black and white. He seemed almost obsessed with the fear of going down in winter, being lost in the ice and snow. Yet the long days of summer also wore him down.

"I guess an island boy needs to keep regular hours," he said. "I've heard some plants can't thrive if the day length is irregular."

Yet when she suggested that he sell out and move somewhere warm, he got stubborn. "Dammit, I can make a go of it. I don't need Panda to make this thing work. I can hack it." She thought he was fighting battles with several past demons—memories of being trapped in Laos, of the trap Panda had kept him in, and now a climate trap in Alaska. She saw him flailing around frantically—and sometimes she got hit, always emotionally, never physically.

So one day she left. She left him a Dear Donnie note when he was away on his circuit of fishing camps and native villages, had an acquaintance drive her to the train station, and took the long ride down to Anchorage.

She left that way because she didn't think she could leave him in the true sense, actually walk out the door if he were there. She also couldn't stay around and watch the joy erode completely from his eyes, couldn't watch him sacrifice his soul to some challenge only he could hear.

Now in San Francisco, far away from the chilly spring of Fairbanks, Jodie shivered before the open refrigerator, hoping something inside would inspire her enough that she could make a dinner out of it and take her mind off the recent past.

Perhaps they had both been too full of guilt—his guilt over what he'd done to Panda, hers over how she'd used Reggie. The guilt turned that fiery passion into a smudge pot and it blackened both their souls.

So she had come back to San Francisco, leaving her heart in Alaska. She found a decent job at a lab halfway down the Peninsula. She tried to hang onto at least one of her dreams by flying any way she could. One day she'd seen a help-wanted ad for a small plane pilot and dialed the number. When a receptionist answered "Barton Enterprises," she hung up without saying a word. So Reggie still had a plane. But she couldn't go back to that. Renting planes was a less humiliating way to keep her license current. Mostly she worked out trades with plane owners—she typed their letters, helped keep their books—anything just so she could keep flying.

Maybe, instead of sending out for a pizza tonight, she would just have a bowl of cereal and some milk. Then she could get to work on the book.

She had started organizing all her files on Amelia Earhart and had written a couple of chapters. Trouble was, she didn't really have anything unique to say. But she liked what she had written, the narrator's voice, the style—and while she worked on it, she was free from her memories and demons.

She was pouring cornflakes into a large bowl when she heard a tap on the door. *Will I ever stop hoping it will be him?* She peered through the little peephole to see Lila, her neighbor from across the hall. She opened the door.

"Well, Jodie," Lila said, "the genius has done it again: put your mail in my box. I didn't realize it until I was in my apartment, so rather than schlep downstairs to the mailboxes I thought I'd just bring it over when you got home."

"Thanks, Lila." Jodie held out her hand but Lila held onto the envelope, staring at the return address.

"Looks like you're hearing from a TV station east of the Mississippi," she said. As far as Jodie could tell, Lila lived and breathed television. She was a secretary in the news department at one of San Francisco's largest radio-television stations, and had, in fact, arranged for Jodie to meet Shelby Verdun, the radio newsman whose book about his Amelia Earhart research was the first Jodie ever read. Verdun had not been helpful.

"WPRC," Lila said. "Where is it?" She squinted at the envelope. "Guam? That's not east of the Mississippi, is it?"

Jodie laughed. "Stands for Western Pacific Research Center. No connection to radio or television, I'm afraid."

Reluctantly, Lila handed over the letter.

Even more reluctantly, Jodie offered her neighbor a glass of wine—she longed to tear into Charlotte's envelope immediately.

"Oh, thanks," Lila said. "Wish I could, but my boyfriend's due any minute and, well, you know." She shrugged.

"Yeah," Jodie said, without enthusiasm. She had heard some fairly alarming sounds coming from Lila's apartment in the months she'd been seeing this boyfriend. Jodie thought that he was some sort of producer at the television station—maybe even married—clearly taking advantage of the woman. "A girl's gotta do what she's gotta do to get ahead in this business," Lila said, almost grimly, as she backed out of Jodie's entrance hallway.

Turning the dead bolt and fastening the door's little chain, Jodie thought for a moment about the different paths women's lives could take. Maybe her luck hadn't been so bad after all.

She took her cornflakes and the fat envelope to her best reading chair, adjusted the light, and took a deep breath full of anticipation. Then she tore into Charlotte's envelope.

A transmittal note, written on one of those squares of yellow paper with a sticky strip, was stuck on the top page.

> *JdS, I think I may have found your man in the Stetson, although it's a lousy photo. At least this fellow's from the right part of the world to wear such gear. And the dates match up. CS.*

The article was photocopied from a recent issue of a magazine called *South Pacific Monthly,* published in Australia. The article was titled, "Unsolved Murders of the South Seas."

She scanned it quickly. The article began with a brief account of the disappearance in Malaysia of the founder of Thailand's silk industry, the American Jim Thompson. Next the author recounted the disappearance of an American military officer named Earl Ellis in Palau during the Japanese occupation of the islands. Although the information was interesting it was hard to see how it had anything to do with Earhart's disappearance. And the badly reproduced oval photo of Ellis looked nothing like the man with Earhart and Noonan in the Verdun book. Still, Charlotte had said it was a dreadful photo.

As Jodie turned the page, she saw that the next segment had the subhead, "The Death of the Mysterious Texan." Her hands began to

tremble. The accompanying photo was out of focus, at least in this photocopy, but the face was familiar. Surely those pale, deep-set eyes and that slightly superior smile were the same as in the photo in the Verdun book. She dove into the text:

> Late in the afternoon of July 3, 1937, a hotel maid used a master key to open the door of a room at the Tropic Rest Hotel in Lae, New Guinea. She had a telegram from Washington, D.C., to deliver to the guest who had left a 'Do Not Disturb' sign on his door the night before. The sight she saw sent her screaming in panic from the room. A man lay in one of the room's two beds, his throat slashed, his body awash in his own blood.
>
> The hotel manager called the local constabulary who made careful notes on everything they knew about the murdered man.
>
> He had registered as 'Tex Arnold' of Alexandria, Virginia, and listed his occupation as businessman. He had been staying at the Tropic Rest with a young man listed on the hotel register only as his companion.
>
> There was no sign of the young man.'A mere boy, really,' said one British gentleman who had observed the pair in the dining room. 'I assumed they were father and son. The older man could be quite stern with the boy.'
>
> The murder weapon was obvious. A straightedge razor, apparently belonging to Mr. Arnold, had been tossed on the floor.
>
> At first, it appeared that nothing was missing from the room except the young man, so police theorized that he might have been kidnapped by the murderer. But when the hotel staff pointed out that they were short one pillowcase, the constables noted that, although the young man's suitcase had been left behind in the room, it was not packed full. The investigators then decided the boy had probably stuffed a few articles of clothing into the case before 'taking it on the lam,' as detective writers like to say.

'We are confident we know who did it,' the head constable, an expatriate from England, told the stringer from the *Port Moresby Herald*. 'We just don't know where he is.'

The constable's theory was that Mr. Arnold's companion had gone off to lose himself in the gold fields of the New Guinea highlands—and he seemed satisfied to let it go at that.

Although willing to suggest a motive ('I think that man was forcing that boy to perform repugnant acts that were foreign to his nature'), the constable never dealt with a much greater mystery: Who was Tex Arnold and why was he in New Guinea?

More to the point, why did the third-highest-ranking American diplomat in Canberra fly to Port Moresby, pick up the consular representative there, and continue on to Lae to look into the murder of Mr. Arnold? And why did the United States government pay the not inconsiderable costs to whisk the dead man's corpse halfway around the world for burial in America?

The Port Moresby newspaper reported more than a month after the murder that a Reuters reporter had unearthed one Dudley Queensbury, a charter pilot in Darwin, who recalled flying Mr. Arnold and his young companion from Darwin to Lae. Queensbury turned out to be a very methodical man. He kept a list he called his manifest of all the passengers he carried.

"In case we crash," he told the reporter, "you'll want to know ages and hometowns. Or in case the ones going into the gold fields ever make a will leaving all their worldly goods to the pilot who flew them to their fortune, I can prove it was me."

According to Mr. Queensbury's list, as reported in the *Port Moresby Herald*, he flew two passengers from Darwin to Lae on June 28, 1937: Mr. Torrington Arnold, age 53, of San Antonio, Texas, and Mr. Garrett Howland, age 19, of Spearfish, South Dakota.

> Queensbury told the Reuters reporter that he got the information for his manifest from his passengers' passports, which the Australian government required him to check before taking off for either Papua or New Guinea. He pointed out that passports list full names and birthplaces, which explained the discrepancy between the way he listed Mr. Arnold on his manifest and the way Arnold had registered at the Tropic Rest.
>
> Ah, but what explains the concern of the U.S. government with Mr. Arnold's sudden demise? Queensbury said the pair had told him that, after getting supplies in Lae, they would be heading for the highland gold fields, but "I didn't really believe them. Unless they was going up to try to cheat some blokes out of their claims. Those lads were dressed too good."
>
> The U.S. government must have thought there was more to it than lust for gold, also.
>
> So this is one murder where the relevant question is not why was a man killed, or who killed him, but why was he where death found him?"

Jodie read the last paragraph slowly, making it last. The author had neglected to make one connection. He must have been working from clippings filed away in an envelope in a newspaper morgue labeled "unsolved murders" or some such. Surely, if he'd had the entire newspaper, he would have been reminded that Torrington "Tex" Arnold died some time on the night after Amelia Earhart took off from Lae for Howland Island.

Howland. Jodie looked at the article again. Garrett Howland, Spearfish, South Dakota.

A shiver ran down her spine.

She shook it off and went in search of her stationery to write a quick thank-you to Charlotte Sablán.

— 1983 —
Monday

AS THE HOSTESS LED MOTHER AND DAUGHTER toward a breakfast table, Laura saw Shelby Verdun seated at the next table. It occurred to her that perhaps she should ask him if he remembered the liaison officer he must have dealt with during his trips to Saipan in the sixties, see whether he realized he had known Gordon Hassler as something other than a murder victim.

"Good morning," she said brightly. "May we join you?"

"Please do." He half-rose while Laura and Teri took their seats.

He actually sounds cordial. "So how are things going?" Laura asked. "Did you learn anything exciting yesterday?"

Verdun snorted. "I spent the whole day hanging out at the police station. It's pathetic. They don't have the slightest idea who killed your friend and they don't seem the least bit interested in the Amelia Earhart angle."

Perhaps it was because she was sitting at a breakfast table that she suddenly knew Verdun's voice as one of the most familiar in her life. "You did a breakfast program in San Francisco. You had breakfast with my mother every morning."

"I'm sure the pleasure was all mine," he said. "But tell me: How many years did you live out here surrounded by all these fumbling idiots?"

"You know," Laura said, "the first time I ever went to Saipan, with Teri's father years ago, we were taken out to dinner by Jose Tenorio. You know Joe Ten?"

"Anybody who ever went to Saipan knows Joe Ten," Verdun said. "Biggest businessman in the Marianas, outside Guam."

"Well, he took us to dinner, and a nephew of his went along, also named Jose Tenorio, but called Joe Eleven," Laura said.

Teri snorted. "You're kidding."

"Oh, no," Verdun said. "They're not very subtle, those Saipanese, but at least they're consistent. I met Joe Twelve and Joe Thirteen in my day."

"Well, that night, Joe Eleven just wasn't happy with the service we were getting. The waitress had forgotten one drink; when she forgot to bring bread, Joe Eleven really lit into her. We knew he felt shamed in front of us. But Joe Ten put his hand on his nephew's arm and said, very gently, 'Joe, Joe, take it easy. Remember, it's a young country.' Foster and I used that line many times through the next few years while we lived out here."

Teri was smiling as though she understood and appreciated the point Laura was trying to make. Shelby Verdun simply stared at her as though he were still waiting for the punch line.

"Well, my thought was," Laura said a little lamely, "that, in its way, Guam's a young country. Its police force doesn't have as much experience as the San Francisco police, say, when they're investigating a murder."

"Mmm. But the local newspaper might show a little more interest in prodding them. Not that they ever were very interested. I remember that the editor back in the sixties wrote some articles pooh-poohing my evidence that Earhart had been in Saipan."

Yes, thought Laura, and Rudy Terlaje caused more trouble than any of us ever guessed possible by scoffing at you. Why had the prank been perpetrated, after all, except to make the *Guam Chronicle* look silly? As Verdun returned to his assault on his pancakes, and Laura and Teri gave their orders to the waitress, Laura wished she had simply smiled at Verdun and taken that separate table. She would rather hear about Teri's dinner with the Ramírezes last night, or the movie she'd seen, than try to make conversation with Shelby Verdun. But they were here now, so she took a sip of coffee and forged ahead.

"I suppose you've read all the other books that have been published about Amelia Earhart," she said.

"Along with several that never made it into print. People send me manuscripts they've written, asking for my help getting them published. And, God help me, I read them—I suppose hoping they've come across something that I've missed. Most of them are so badly written, I fear for my own command of the English language before I finish them." He took a gulp of coffee, then continued.

"I'll tell you what's even weirder than the would-be writers. It's the lady pilots, the ones that have made Amelia Earhart their private patron saint."

"Lady pilots?" A shiver of apprehension swept down Laura's spine. Jodie had lived in San Francisco at one time.

"I guess I brought it on myself. I did radio interviews with both those gals that actually made it flying around the world solo. Back in '64, just as I was finishing up my book."

"I remember them," Laura said. "In fact, I interviewed both of them here in Guam when I was first on island. They both came through Guam because Howland Island wasn't available anymore." She turned to Teri. "It turned into a race. One woman had gotten all the publicity for her flight, retracing Amelia's route as closely as she could. Then the other one snuck in and beat her by a few days."

"That's right." Verdun seemed pleasantly surprised by Laura's grasp of the subject. "So, after I interviewed those two gals, I was besieged by requests from other lady pilots who hoped I would brush some of the Amelia magic dust on them by interviewing them about their exploits."

"So that's all they wanted? Publicity?" She began to relax. She couldn't picture Jodie as a publicity hound.

He shrugged. "Some of them. Some of them claimed to be writing books. One I remember … " he shook his head and closed his eyes for a moment. "This one gal … just a few years ago, just before

I retired … she even looked like Amelia Earhart. I almost got the impression she thought she was Amelia reincarnated."

Laura heart stopped. "And what did she want?"

"Oh, the usual. She was writing a book. Wanted to pick my brain, see what I had learned since my book came out. I had the impression she felt she was far better qualified than I to write about Amelia, being a woman and a pilot."

"So you didn't interview her on the radio?" Thank God he wasn't a television newsman, broadcasting Jodie's image to most of northern California.

"No, she wasn't looking for publicity. Just information." He speared the last bite of syrup-drenched pancake with his fork and raised it toward his lips. Then he froze, staring at something across the room.

Laura turned to see police Lieutenant Ben Guerrero walking toward the restaurant's exit with Edwina Hassler.

"Something must be up," Verdun said, washing down the quickly eaten bite of pancake with a swig from his coffee cup. "Listen, would you take care of my bill? I'll pay you back." And before Laura found time to object, he was out the door, scurrying after Ben and Edwina.

"Mom!" Teri's tone was urgent. Laura found herself giving her daughter the raised Guamanian eyebrow: Yes, what's your problem?

"Shouldn't you find out what's happened?"

"I'll give Will a call before we go out to the university to see Charlotte. He can follow through with Ben. Or with Shelby. I'm more concerned about making sure he pays for his breakfast."

"Mother!" Teri seemed shocked by her mother's priorities.

On the way out to the university in the rental car, Laura asked Teri about dinner with the Ramírezes. "Did they speak English for you?"

"Of course. Although I suppose that was Chamorro they kept talking among themselves."

"Did they talk about the murder?"

"Oh, yeah. And everyone was very impressed that I had met Mr. Hassler just the night before he was murdered. And that we introduced Nashi to the widow."

"Actually, you had met him before," Laura reminded her.

"Yeah, I told them about San Francisco, too."

"I think I'm sorry I reminded you about it."

"Don't worry. I can be discreet, you know. Nashi's father said he used to see Mr. Hassler a lot, a long time ago. He said he was always coming to the newspaper when he worked there, to talk to Mr. Terlaje."

"Oh, really." So Gordon's press liaison role while the CIA was in Saipan was known to more than just Rudy Terlaje. Hadn't 'Sús Pérez said he'd been in contact with the Guam police as well?

"What about the Amelia Earhart connection? Were the Ramirezes interested in that?"

"Not particularly. Nashi's dad says people have always been trying to connect Amelia Earhart with Saipan—he thinks it's crazy. He says he's sure she went down in the ocean thousands of miles from the Marianas."

"And the photo didn't change his mind?"

"He said he thought it might be a hospital somewhere else, somewhere he thought she might have been flying as a spy."

"Dublon," Laura said, "in the Truk atoll. There's an abandoned Japanese hospital on Dublon with the same architecture, and the Japanese had a lot of military stuff happening in Truk. I think in Shelby's book, it's his theory that Amelia flew directly over Truk to spy on the Japanese, then went down in the Marshalls, farther east, and was brought back to Saipan when the Japanese captured her. I wonder if Shelby knows about the hospital in Dublon?"

"Maybe we could suggest it to him," Teri said. "Throw him off the trail."

Laura looked at her daughter with concern. *What kind of life training am I giving this kid?*

*　　　*　　　*

Laura and Teri found Charlotte in her lair at the University of Guam library. The Western Pacific Research Center consisted of two rooms crammed floor-to-ceiling with books and file cabinets. Charlotte's desk was in the first room, but she showed mother and daughter to a small table in the back room. She had already pulled out her file on Jodie deSpain.

"You know, there's more here than I remembered. I had forgotten that I'd sent Jodie quite so much material."

Laura sat down to read the letters in the file. They were all from Jodie, beginning with an introductory letter, dated 1974. Laura stared at the address printed on the stationery under the words "Jodie deSpain, Pilot." They had been living in San Francisco at the same time, she and Jodie, with only Golden Gate Park between them.

On subsequent letters, the printed address was crossed out and other addresses typed or lettered in. She could follow Jodie's progress around the Bay Area, first to Belvedere—Had they lived there when Donnie came back from Southeast Asia with some money? Belvedere was not a low-rent area. But when had he come back? Then an address in the Marina, still pretty upscale. Then back to the Inner Richmond, a multi-ethnic, middle-class neighborhood. One letter from Alaska. Then, finally, back to San Francisco.

Most of the letters were thank-you notes, expressing appreciation for various things Charlotte had sent.

"But what did she send?" Teri whispered, reading over Laura's shoulder.

Just then, Charlotte reappeared in the back room. "How's it going?"

"I'm almost afraid to ask you this because I think I know the answer. There are no copies of your side of the correspondence."

Charlotte laughed. "Oh, my, no, I don't write letters to people like Jodie—I wouldn't have time. I just make copies of documents

or articles and scrawl a little note on the first page or on a yellow sticky and send it off." After a pause during which Laura was sure Charlotte felt drenched by Teri's deep disappointment, if not her own, Charlotte said defensively, "Well, you know, they don't provide me with a secretary. And they barely pay me enough to cover my gas driving out here every day. I can't do real letters with copies and everything."

"Of course not," Laura said. "I'm sorry. This is much more than I've known about Jodie's whereabouts, anyway. Look at this one." She pulled out a handwritten letter dated 1977. "She talks about a photograph in the Verdun book—do you have a copy here? Of course, I left your other copy at the hotel."

Charlotte hurried to a shelf and came back with the volume. Laura flipped quickly to page 158. But there was no photo of natives greeting Amelia in New Guinea, as Jodie's note had described, and no photo below it of Amelia and Fred Noonan with a man in a Stetson hat.

"Huh?" Laura started to riffle through the pages of photographs. "Do you suppose they made a mistake in binding this copy?" She turned back to page 158.

"No, look, Mom," Teri said, pointing at the innermost edge of the first photo page. "Doesn't it look like a page has been cut out?"

Laura raised the book close to her eyes. "Yes. Wow, you've got sharp eyes! Charlotte?"

Charlotte reappeared beside the little table.

"Look, someone's cut the page out of this book—the very page Jodie mentioned in her letter." As Laura spoke, it occurred to her that Charlotte might have removed the photo, needing to get a copy of it so she could find someone to identify the man in the Stetson.

But Charlotte's mind had run ahead in another direction. She clapped her hands together. "That's right! I'd completely forgotten. When that letter came, I looked in the book I had here and found the page she was talking about had been cut out. I went out into the library's general collection, and the page was missing from that

book, too. So, when I got home, I looked at the copy I had there—and it was missing there, too. That's how I happen to have that extra copy I gave you."

"How?"

"Well, of course, the next day I went to the missionary's bookstore down on Marine Drive. He tries to stock copies of books about this area, even if they are several years old and out of print. He buys used books from people who are leaving the island. He had three copies, all used, and the picture page had been cut out of each one."

"Do you realize what this means?" Laura asked. "Someone on this island keeps checking the bookstore and library for this book, and keeps cutting out that page." Someone very sick or obsessed, she thought. Someone still on this island.

"I thought that, too, but when we looked into it, every book except the copy in the Agaña public library had been bought new from the missionary—they each had the little Christian fish sticker he puts in the back cover of all the books in his store, even if they aren't religious books. I think it's his way of consecrating anything profane that might be in the secular books."

"So the phantom book mutilator only needed to hit the Agaña library and the bookstore, back when the book first came out?"

"That's my theory," Charlotte said. "Anyway, I wrote to a couple of friends in the States, asking them to keep an eye out for the Verdun book in used bookstores and send it to me if one turned up. That's how I got one extra copy. After I had almost forgotten about it, my friend Joyce in St. Louis sent me that copy I lent you."

"And did it have the page with the photo?"

"It did. But the really weird thing was that another friend who lives in Berkeley, California, sent me a copy she'd bought there—and the same page had been cut out of the book."

Jodie was in the Bay Area, Laura thought, and doing research on Amelia Earhart. And Jodie was living in Guam when the book first came out. Did she go around to bookstores cutting pages out of books? Why?

And what connection did the missing photo of Amelia Earhart have to the one that suddenly reappeared in such a gruesome setting a few days ago?

She would turn to page 158 in the book she had at the hotel with great trepidation when she got back there. What if the page was missing? Could someone slip into her room and remove the last copy of the photo that had intrigued Jodie?

Laura shook her head to clear it and went back to reading Jodie's notes and letters.

The final letter was dated June 20, 1980, and had a San Francisco address. It could only be described as effusive.

> *Dear Charlotte, Thank you, thank you, thank you! At last I think I've got something no one else has ever put together in trying to figure out what happened to Amelia Earhart. This has got to be the breakthrough. Thanks so much for remembering my quest, and for sending the article. I'll let you know what I find out as soon as I follow up on this.*

"Wow," Teri said, reading once again over Laura's shoulder. "She was excited about something."

"Charlotte!" Laura waved the letter at her friend as she returned from her desk. "Is this the last letter?"

Charlotte took the letter and reread it. "Yes. I remember at the time being very excited for her and wondering what she thought she'd found. But I never got another letter from her. If I had, it would be in the folder. Perhaps it didn't pan out after all."

"What did you send her?" Teri asked.

"Ah, there's the rub," Charlotte said. "What did I send her, indeed. I'll have to give that some thought."

"It's just three years ago," Teri said. "Almost exactly three years ago." Laura made a silent shushing motion at her.

"I know. But I handle so much material and I'm always looking out for bits and pieces for so many people—really, there are researchers all around the world who are interested in things we have here

in the center. But don't worry, dear. I'll think about it. It will come back to me."

"But I'm leaving tomorrow," Teri said. "I'll miss it!"

"I'll probably think of it in a couple of hours," Charlotte promised.

"And I'll bet you'll think better if we leave you alone," Laura said, putting all the letters from Jodie back into the folder labeled "J.deSpain" and handing it to Charlotte. "C'mon, Nancy Drew, we've got a couple of other stops to make this morning."

—1980—

GORDON WAITED FOR RUTHIE at their usual meeting place, the cozy corner banquette in a dimly lit cocktail lounge a few blocks from the San Francisco library. He noticed a strange glimmer in the smoky air above the bar and realized that there were some sort of tinsel Christmas garlands woven in and out, through the rows of liquor bottles. How strange. He must never before have been here near the holidays.

"Hello, you big handsome man," a woman's throaty, seductive voice purred right behind him, and a phrase leapt into his mind. *Alii, ruubaak.* Where the hell did that come from? He shook his head and forced a warm grin for Ruthie Firestone.

"Hello, yourself," he said, standing up as well as he could, squeezed between the table and padded bench. She slid around the corner of the banquette so that her knee brushed against his thigh. Here we go again, he thought.

At first he had feared that his idea of enlisting reference librarians as his defense perimeter was a flop. It seemed that most librarians regarded information about the reading habits of their patrons to be more sacrosanct than the National Rifle Association considered the right to bear arms. But gradually, he had located some librarians who viewed his request for information as a valid research query, and he'd begun to accumulate a list of Amelia-philes. He almost wished he had the time and freedom to actually pursue this imaginary research. Who were these people, and what was it about Amelia Earhart that held their attention after all these years? Some people were clearly just voracious readers but others seemed

especially focused, and it was those names he turned over to one or another of his detective contacts for enough surveillance to convince him that they posed no threat to him. He remembered one of the early reports from a detective in Washington, D.C.

"Mr. Smith has a very routine job selling sporting goods in a big store, while his wife has a very interesting position with the World Bank. It is my supposition that he becomes mildly fanatic about all number of subjects, one by one, so he'll have something to contribute to the dinner table conversation each evening."

Ruthie Firestone had been the first librarian he ever contacted and, at first glance, she had appeared to be the hardest nut to crack. She had laughed—loudly for a librarian—when he first approached her in the cavernous reference section of the San Francisco Public Library. She had swept her graying, straight black hair behind her ears and peered at him over her horn-rimmed glasses. "Are you out of your mind, man? Haven't you ever heard of a library user's right to privacy?"

But Gordon had seen something else in the woman's stern face, a hunger he had not noticed in years. When had he stopped looking for women to seduce? He took a chance.

"I'm sorry," he'd said in his sexiest voice. "I didn't mean to be offensive. Look, any chance I could redeem myself by taking you out for a cup of coffee or a drink? When do you get off work?"

A sly, half-smile creased one side of Ruthie's mouth. "All right," she said, "Seven p.m. I'm very fond of dry white wine."

"I'll be back," he promised. And it turned out his instincts were as good as they had been back in the days when he was choosing among the young file clerks and stenos to find one to lure into the janitor's closets at the State Department.

Ruthie Firestone was starved for male attention. "What kind of normal, heterosexual single woman settles in San Francisco?" she had asked that first evening. "I must have been out of my mind, mesmerized by the scenery and this spicy, foggy air. Every man in

this city is married, gay, or twenty years younger than I. Or all of the above."

But, in addition to being the first woman ever to proposition him, it turned out that Ruthie Firestone had her own unique take on the subject of Amelia Earhart.

There was an axe she wanted to grind: It made her furious that Amelia Earhart had been given so much attention through the years. "She was just a high-fashion, empty-headed pawn of an opportunistic, reprehensible husband," she intoned over her second glass of Chablis. Somehow she assumed that Gordon's research was based on similar indignation, so she was eager to help him prove the folly of hero worship and America's infatuation with celebrity.

That first evening, Ruthie had mentioned a woman pilot who had done a great deal of research concerning Earhart through the past several years. "I believe she's writing her book now. She's a perfectly nice woman, but really! We have enough books about Amelia Earhart already. I don't care if she does think being a pilot gives her a special insight. Why don't people put their energy into something that matters? Something that will solve world problems."

He thought back to another lifetime, remembering the vibrant woman, how he had believed he could love her, could love all women. Instead he gave Ruthie Firestone the reaction she expected. He agreed it was a mystery why people were so obsessed with Earhart, but reminded her that he intended to find out and that she could help him. He encouraged Ruthie to have another glass of wine. He turned up the level of his seductive charm. Obviously he had been right to target reference librarians.

"Your lady pilot might be the perfect interview," he said. "It's too bad you can't give me her name."

"I'll mention your project the next time she's in. See if she's willing to be interviewed." He had explained that he couldn't simply leave his card and ask people to contact him—it skewed the research to have only the folks eager to be interviewed. He needed

to balance them with people who needed a little persuasion. Ruthie understood—Amelia nuts might be particularly insistent if they had his name and phone number.

Keeping Ruthie in his stable of informants through the years turned out to require more effort than he had ever planned. She wouldn't settle for a couple of glasses of wine and a bit of thigh-against-thigh flirting under the table. Each time he showed up in San Francisco, she took him home for what she called "the full-course banquet." He wondered whether he wasn't getting too old for this sort of thing—she was the only woman with whom he had cheated on Edwina in several years. And he didn't even find her attractive—it was hard work getting inspired enough to satisfy her.

Tonight, when the waitress brought her tall glass of Chablis, Ruthie took a mouthful, rolled it around in her mouth, and threw her head back to swallow it. For a moment, Gordon thought she was going to gargle it.

"Ah!" she said. "Nothing gets the dust of the library out of my system quite like wine." She gave him a meaningful look. "Well, there is one thing that's even more effective."

"So how have you been?"

"People are so goddamn obsessive," Ruthie said. "Why do you suppose that is?"

He wondered whether she thought he was obsessed with his imaginary research project. "I don't know," he said. "Are you beginning to obsess about me?"

"No!" she snorted. "I mean your Amelia nuts. Remember the lady pilot I told you about? The one writing a book, or so she says? She was in the other day. She'd just come back from flying a small plane all the way to Texas in the name of her Amelia research. Texas!"

Gordon tried to hide his involuntary shudder. "To research Amelia? Do you know where in Texas?"

Ruthie took another mouthful of wine. "Hmm, let me think. Did she say? Dallas, maybe? No, wait, I remember. She went to see the Alamo. So it must have been … "

"San Antonio," he said, trying not to sound grim. If research on Amelia Earhart had taken someone to San Antonio, it could mean someone had finally connected Tex Arnold and Amelia Earhart.

He had always known that someday somebody would try to figure out who the man was in the cowboy hat in Shelby Verdun's book. He had carried his razor-sharp penknife into many bookstores over the past fifteen years, relieved many copies of the book of that particular page, but it was just a tiny stopgap measure. He had known that someday, someone would get curious.

"Listen, I could look up her phone number, see if she's willing for me to give you her name," Ruthie said. She was pressing her thigh against his knee. She wanted to be as helpful as possible. For the usual exchange of favors, of course.

"You know, Ruthie, this sounds like someone who may be a little outside my research. If she's gone all the way to Texas, she probably is writing a book—and she's likely to look at me as competition. Let it go for now."

"Whatever," Ruthie said. She managed to slide around on the banquette so that his knee forced her skirt up. He could feel it falling over his thigh.

He needed to rush right out and get a detective looking for a woman pilot who had flown to San Antonio recently—but he also needed to keep Ruthie on his team. He shifted closer to her and moved his hand under the table, under her skirt, caressing the taut fabric of her pantyhose.

He would have to do the full-course banquet bit, but he could afford the two hours or so that would take. He could reach his local investigator contact any time of the night. Besides, his excitement and fear about this sudden new threat should give Ruthie an especially memorable bedtime adventure.

– 1981 –
July

THIS TIME IT WOULD BE DIFFERENT.

For one thing, he had telephoned instead of just showing up on her doorstep, suitcase in hand. He'd flown in, checked into a hotel, and then called. Several times, judging from the hang-ups on her answering machine.

"I wondered if I could take you out to dinner," he said. "I'd really like to talk to you."

Needing to make sure things would be different, Jodie suggested they meet at a restaurant. It wouldn't do for him to come by the apartment and pick her up. They would end up in bed before they talked, and important things would not get said.

The things their bodies had said to each other through the years had been wonderful poetry, but she hungered for some clear prose this time, something solid enough to base any future flights of passion upon—if there were ever to be any future flights.

She had suggested a couple of moderately fancy restaurants that seemed right for a dignified reunion, but he said, "You know where I'd really like to take you, Blondie? Trader Vic's."

"Really? Isn't it kind of … phony for an authentic islander like you?"

"After Alaska, I'll take my tropical islands wherever I can find them."

And so she made her way to the tourist sector of the city, and took a deep breath of foggy San Francisco air before she entered the artificial tropical forest, perfumed with suddenly familiar aromas that almost weakened her resolve. She would fling herself into his arms, drag him home. … She caught a glimpse of herself in a mir-

ror as she passed it. She looked good: urbane, glowing with good health, surely no older than she'd looked fourteen years ago when they'd first met. She looked like a free, independent, strong woman with her own life.

She was explaining to the host that she was here to meet a tall Hawaiian gentleman when she spotted him, seated at a small table halfway across the first room of diners, keeping an eye on the entryway. He rose and grinned as the host led her toward him.

"Hello, Blondie," he said softly. "You look great."

"So do you." His hair had gone entirely silver in the eighteen months since she'd left him. He still wore it cut super short, and it still looked like velvet. Her fingertips tingled, wanting to stroke it.

"Welcome to San Francisco," she said as she gave him a quick, sisterly peck on the cheek to forestall anything deeper. She could remain cool, collected, on top of her emotions. After all, she was once admired as an actress.

But she barely noticed the waiter pulling out a chair for her, seating her across the table from him. After a few seconds she was surprised to discover that she was holding a heavy menu covered in *tapa* cloth—her eyes had been so captured by his she hadn't noticed when it was handed to her.

"God, it's great to see you again," he said.

"I'm glad to see you, too. What … what are you doing here?"

"Seeing you," he said. "The only reason for the trip."

"Oh." Don't let him disconcert you so soon, she told herself.

"I'm *pau* with Alaska," he said. "Through. *Finito*. I'm a free man again. And a warm one. Or I was until I came to Fog Central, U.S.A."

"What happened?" She wanted to cheer. He had taken some action. But she was still determined to remain detached.

"Sold the planes up there. Got a darn good price. Took my money to Honolulu and bought a sweetheart of a plane. I'll do charters, sightseeing trips to the volcanoes, or out over the little islands for bird watchers … whatever people want to pay me to do. It'll be good. There was enough left over to set up a retirement fund."

"Good for you!" She let her sincere congratulations show. He seemed so … at peace. It was wonderful to see him this way. "How long have you … "

"I've been back in Hawaii a couple months. But tell me, what have you been up to?"

Jodie remembered that, early on, when she had first known him, he had been interested in hearing about her life, amused somehow by its being so different from his. But for so long they had only seemed to worry about them, the two of them together, the goddamned star-crossed relationship, not that Donnie would ever have thought in terms of something as trendy as a "relationship."

"Well," she began slowly, "I'm working at a hospital lab down the Peninsula. Flying anything I can beg, borrow, or afford to rent."

"Good." His approval was that of a solemn guru.

"And I've been spending a lot of time on this book I'm trying to research about Amelia Earhart."

"Really? You used to talk about doing it … "

"And now I am. Donnie, I think I'm on the trail of something no one else has ever put together. I've read a lot of stuff about her in the past eighteen months, and no one else has taken the same tack as I'm on."

She had never talked to anyone else about the project—afraid she would dissipate energy that should go into the writing and research, or even that someone might steal her ideas. But talking to Donnie was like talking to her other self, so she found the story bubbling out. Somehow, they ordered food, it came, and they ate—while the kitschy island music kept playing in the background—but she went on talking about her quest, and he went on listening to her with rapt attention.

"I've been focusing on this guy Tex Arnold, who was found murdered in Lae, the day after Amelia took off for Howland Island. The New Guinea police decided it was a crime of passion because he was staying with this young guy who disappeared after the murder. The implication was that they were lovers."

Donnie made his face long in mock disapproval. "Texas faggots in New Guinea? Yechhhh!"

"I spent a lot of time trying to find out about Tex Arnold. He's in a picture with Amelia and Fred Noonan the day they arrived in Lae, but his name isn't given with the photo. I had to track it down, and that's taken years. I'm certain he had something to do with her disappearance. And he had some kind of U.S. government connections because a high muckety-muck from the American Embassy in Australia came up to Lae to claim his body."

"Wow, you have been one busy *wahine* since I last laid my sore and lonesome eyes on you." He reached across the table and patted her hand, but he was as caught up in her story as she was. "Where did they ship the corpse?"

"It's amazing the things you can find out if you're persistent. U.S. customs keeps a register of dead bodies returned to the States. Tex went to San Antonio, his hometown. I've visited his grave."

"How did you get there?"

"I do some freelance lab work for a racetrack and they let me borrow their Piper sometimes. So I flew to San Antonio, did the Alamo, drank margaritas and found a stone in a cemetery marked TORRINGTON ARNOLD, BORN 1884, DIED 1937. No days, months, or places. Someone made sure there wasn't a gravestone with a peculiar place of death lying around in plain sight."

"Maybe they didn't want to pay to carve all those extra letters into it," Donnie said.

"I don't think that was a problem for the Arnolds. They were very big in cattle and oil."

"So did you drink those margaritas all on your lonesome, Blondie? Or did you find a handsome señor to buy them for you?"

She toyed—just for a moment—with trying to make him jealous. *No,* she vowed. This is a new game, totally straight and true. "No, Donnie, I didn't. I'm not sure there are any señors in the world handsome enough for me after you."

He had the good grace to look a little embarrassed. Then once again he steered the conversation away from the personal. "So what did the Texan have to do with Amelia?"

"For quite a while I was sure he had done something at the behest of the government and, once he accomplished his assignment, they shut him up. What was it they used to say in the CIA?"

"Terminated with extreme prejudice." Donnie shuddered. "And I used to work for those folks."

"You used to fly for them. Flying is an end, and the end justifies the means."

"Ah, so that's how it works."

Whoa, girl, you're treading on fragile crust, she thought. There was an image that had stayed with her since she was seven or eight and her parents had taken her to Yellowstone—the fragile crust around the geysers and thermal pools. Her father had pointed out holes where, he said, bison must have gotten their feet trapped in the crust walking close to a geyser in winter, trying to get warm. "Probably boiled to death," he had told her. "Then, when the tourist season begins, the rangers cart the carcasses away."

Back off, she told herself. Get back on the boardwalk. She caught a glimpse of Reggie Barton's round, wistful face hanging in the air between her and Donnie.

She shook her head. "What I thought at first was that the CIA—well, their predecessors—rubbed Tex out and kidnapped his little boy-toy to make it look like a crime of passion. Then they dumped the kid's body somewhere in the Pacific."

"But why would the U.S. government want Amelia to fail?"

"They had good reason to want her to get lost, so they could search the Japanese Mandate for her. That's the usual explanation. But I started looking into Tex Arnold's business connections and found out he had major investments in the manufacture of seaplanes."

"Now we're getting somewhere." Donnie looked impressed. "I can see where that's taking you."

"Right. Amelia was about to prove you could fly across the Pacific without the escape hatch of landing on water. There go the stockholders' dividends. But then, just a month or so ago, I decided to see if I could find out what happened to the kid. What if they hadn't bumped him off? What if someone was paying him to keep quiet?"

"And you found him?"

"Not quite. But what got me started on him was a chapter I found in a very boring autobiography by an industrialist who had known a guy called Tex in the thirties. This man got to be a big deal in aviation, which is why I picked his book up in a secondhand bookstore, and why I was scanning through it. It was self-published and pretty badly written. But he had been there, investing in planes in the thirties. And suddenly I came across a passage that made my blood run cold.

"And ... " She reached into her purse and withdrew a few folded sheets of paper, "because it's so exciting, I've been carrying it around with me, re-reading it when I needed a morale boost. Are you game?"

"If you don't read it to me, I'll rip it out of your hands."

She cleared her throat and began to read.

> In its early days, aviation attracted all sorts of entrepreneurs, adventurers, even scoundrels. One I remember particularly was a rich Texan who gave elegant dinner parties in his very elegant home in the Georgetown section of Washington, D.C. It was hard to tell what 'Tex' wanted from you when he invited you but his food and liquor were so good and generous I never could resist going back, despite my discomfort with his living arrangements.
>
> 'Tex' had a young male companion. At first I took him to be a chauffeur because Tex raved about how the boy kept his car in perfect running condition. But he had him sit at table with us and Tex seemed to regard the boy with a gaze that was neither that of a proud uncle nor a satisfied employer. This was, I realized, the gaze of a lover for his beloved.

> Embarrassing though this was to those of us with more appropriate predilections, we went through several evenings in the company of this odd couple. After dessert, while the rest of us smoked cigars, Tex asked his young man to perform magic tricks for us. He was a most adept practitioner of sleight of hand—his tricks with coins were dazzling. He was very shy—embarrassed, I believe, because he guessed we understood the true nature of his relationship to his benefactor..
>
> Long after I knew him, I heard a rumor that Tex had been murdered while off on some foreign expedition and that the culprit had been the young man. Tex had managed to cheat me out of a substantial sum of money by the time he disappeared, so I must confess that I cheered that young man on, although I suppose he was hanged for his troubles, wherever they caught up with him.

Jodie folded the pages and tucked them back into her purse. Donnie was gazing at her with what she was sure was admiration.

This time it *was* different. He was seeing her as someone independent, someone to be courted, not just as an accrued benefit to be collected whenever he wanted it.

The waiter returned to their table to offer dessert. "I'll try your passion-fruit pie," Donnie said, winking at Jodie. When she asked for herbal tea, he made a face but there was a fondness about his reaction that caught at her heart. We are two separate people, she thought, but we do fit together well.

Suddenly he leapt to his feet. "Listen. They're playing our song." He had led her halfway to a tiny dance floor before she was able to tune into the music over the babble of conversing diners. It was… now, how had he engineered this? It was that song they had danced to in Guam at the Top o' the Mar, the first time he ever took her in his arms.

As she moved into his embrace, he put his lips close to her ear and sang the words softly in his mellow baritone:

For endless months and years I heard
Those dreamy tales of love.

I never found that sweet someone
Who fit me like a glove.
Now here you are before me,
The story's coming true.
I'll spend one month of forevers
In paradise with you.

When the music ended, he pressed his body tightly against hers for a moment and then pulled away, still holding both her hands. "God, Jodie, I love you."

There was a pause as she tried to figure out how to retain her sense of self while succumbing to a tidal wave of emotion. It's because he sees me enthused about something besides him, she thought. It makes me more attractive to him. Or maybe he's in love with Amelia Earhart, not me.

"C'mon, Blondie, my passion-fruit pie is calling me."

He led her back to the table, where he smacked his lips as he devoured the pie and she sipped her tea. Then suddenly he reached into the breast pocket of his aloha shirt and pulled out a small box.

"Brought you a present from Hawaii, Blondie," he said, handing it across the table to her.

Her hands trembled as she tore the white tissue paper away to reveal a small jewelry box. She held her breath and opened it. The box held a silver ring, made in the shape of a delicate bell-shaped flower whose stem and narrow leaves wound around to make the ring.

"Oh!" She finally breathed. "It's exquisite! It's that flower ... "

"Guamanians call it *ylang-ylang*," he said, his voice echoing across a gulf of years. "To the Filipinos, it's *sampaguita*. We Hawaiians call it *pi-ka-ke*. I'd like you to call it an engagement ring."

"Engagement?" Her voice cracked on the word.

"Jodie, I can't be happy without you. Will you marry me?"

"Donnie." Her reaction took her completely by surprise: she started to cry. "Donnie, I'm forty-two years old. I've never been married."

"What the hell?" He laughed. "Give it a try! I'm fifty-seven. Do you want me to get down on one knee? I'll do it."

"No, no." She was laughing and gulping back tears and waving her hands to stop him from calling any more attention to the public spectacle they must be making.

"Then say yes."

"When?"

"Right now!"

"No, I mean when do you want to get m-m-married?"

"Tomorrow? Next week? How much notice do you need to give your job? Do you have some sort of dream wedding you've always wanted to have that's going to take months to plan? Do I have to go to Colorado and meet your folks?"

She shook her head. "No. My mother wouldn't like you anyway. I'll stop on my way back and tell her about it, tell her she's not invited. Oh, Donnie, let's do it beside one of those tropical pools with a waterfall splashing into it—in Hawaii, with bare feet and flowers in our hair."

He was grinning in delight. "Perfect! The wedding I've always wanted to have. And I know the perfect pool. You don't mind if it's on Maui?"

"I love Maui," she said.

"But what do you mean, you'll see your mother on the way back? Back from where?"

"Oh, it's a trip I need to make … my racetrack friends are loaning me their plane … " It suddenly seemed as though it were the last thing she needed to do. What she needed to do was get away from this crowded restaurant and be alone with Donnie MacDougal so they could flow into each other's lives forever.

But no, she had started out determined that it would be different, and look how well it was working out for her. Jodie deSpain

still existed outside the wonderful two-backed creature they would become tonight for awhile, and Jodie deSpain still had an item or two on her agenda.

"It's my Amelia Earhart book. I told you I was trying to track the boy who was with Tex Arnold before he was killed in New Guinea?" She watched Donnie carefully. He seemed to be waiting, patiently, generously, to hear her out.

"The boy was from South Dakota. I got that much from the news reports of the murder in New Guinea. I called information in his hometown and asked if there were any families named Howland in the town. Howland—can you believe it? The kid had the same name as the island Amelia was supposed to fly to. I ended up calling one guy and he said, 'Oh, you're talking about Aunt Rose's boy. He was lost in the Pacific in the war, or maybe it just before the war.' And it turns out his Aunt Rose is still alive but very fragile and he didn't recommend trying to talk to her on the phone—he didn't think she'd understand what I was talking about. So I decided to fly up and see her, see what she knows about her son, what she thinks he was doing in New Guinea."

Donnie didn't say, "Do you really have to go?" He didn't seem to object at all. Perhaps he realized, too, that things had to be different. He just asked, "When are you planning to go?"

"What's today? Tuesday? I get the plane Saturday. I'll stop in Denver and see my mother after I do South Dakota. I'll be back Monday night." She held her breath, worried about his reaction.

She needn't have worried.

"That'll work out great," he said. "I'll start making calls to Maui, set some things up. Maybe we can fly to Honolulu the following weekend?"

She nodded happily.

"And until you flit off to South Dakota, we'll have some time to practice—what shall I call it? Pre-marital indiscretion?"

"Sounds lovely."

She took his arm and they made their way slowly out of the ersatz Polynesia toward their island future. As soon as he had paid the bill, he stopped and kissed her deeply.

"I'm out of practice, Blondie," he said. "We'd better plan on a long rehearsal tonight."

"And tomorrow, and the night after, and after I get back from Spearfish."

"Spearfish?"

"Spearfish, South Dakota. That's where the Howland kid grew up. Funny name, isn't it?"

"Spearfish, South Dakota. I've heard that somewhere before," he mused.

They stood hugging on the street, waiting for a cab.

This time it would be different.

– 1983 –
Monday

EATING LUNCH IN THE CAR—especially in Guam's torrid midday—was not what Laura had meant to do today, but Teri persuaded her to stop at the A&W drive-in at the main junction in Mangilao after they left Charlotte's research center at the university.

"C'mon, Mom, I can at least say hi to Nashi while he's working."

"It's a good thing you're leaving for Honolulu tomorrow," Laura said. "I might never get you off this island if this romance develops much further."

Teri sighed dramatically. "I thought you liked Nashi."

"I do like Nashi. It's just that you're so young." And I'm so old, she thought. Jeff MacDougal is closer to my daughter's age than to mine.

A carhop appeared at Laura's window to take their order. She was a blue-eyed blonde in a brief outfit Laura couldn't imagine a Guamanian girl wearing, at least in her own island days. Perhaps she was the daughter of one of the university professors.

Teri leaned across to say, "Will you tell Nashi Ramírez that Teri's out here?"

Laura thought the girl looked startled. Was she shocked that a "statesider" girl was asking for Nashi? Or did she have her eye on him herself?

"You're lucky they haven't progressed to the microphone order system yet," Laura told her daughter after the carhop left. "I can just hear me ordering two cheeseburgers with fries, two large root beers, and the cook called Nashi."

Nashi appeared in a few minutes bearing the tray with their order. "Here you go, Ms. Monroe," he said, fastening the tray to her side of the car. "Tracy wants to be sure to collect from you, in case you leave a tip, so don't pay me." He walked around to Teri's window. "So what are you folks up to today?"

"Oh, my mother has all these people she's got to see," Teri said with admirable discretion, Laura thought. It must be tempting to tell a little about the letters they'd read in Charlotte's back room.

"Well listen, Frank and I get off early today, and I wondered if you can go out. Frank and his girlfriend want to go bowling and invited us along."

"Mom?"

Laura tried to subdue her excitement. If Teri were to go out tonight, she might have another chance to see Jeff.

"Well, I guess that would be okay."

"Great," Nashi said. "We'll pick you up at five if that's okay."

"I'll be in the lobby," Teri promised.

When they'd finished eating and she'd paid the stern-faced carhop, Laura pulled out of the parking lot and headed back along the highway. At the intersection with the road that could take them to Agaña, she turned the other way, toward Yoña.

"Where are we going?"

"Well, I had intended to have lunch at Casa Celinda, that place we went Thursday with Charlotte."

"You're going to eat again?"

"No, I want to talk to Cory MacDougal."

"Ooh, boy!" Teri switched instantly from romance novel mode to Nancy Drew. "How much do you think we can get her to tell us?"

"I don't know. I haven't even figured out how to broach the subject. I just figure something will come to me and take us both by surprise."

"Yeah," Teri mused, "I suppose she wouldn't be surprised at all if Will asked her about the photo she stole."

But Cory MacDougal was not greeting customers today at Casa Celinda, and when Laura asked for her, she was told that Cory had called in sick, saying she would be out for two or three days.

"When did she call in?"

The hostess consulted with a waiter who said, "It must have been Friday. She wasn't scheduled to work Saturday or Sunday, but she said she didn't think she would make it back by today. She sounded awful. The flu, I guess."

"She called in sick Friday," Teri said as they trudged back across the sizzling parking lot toward their car. "The day the stolen photo shows up in the paper, she gets sick. Don't you think that sounds suspicious?"

"I do. I expect she's hiding from the wrath of Will. After all, he gave her a chance, gave her a job when she was a kid."

"Do you think he knows where she lives?"

"Maybe, but there's someone else I'd like to pop in on before I talk to Will again."

"Who?"

"Cory's mother, the Dragon Lady. Panda MacDougal."

"Why do you call her the Dragon Lady?"

"Oh, that's from an old comic strip with an elegant Oriental female villain. Actually, your father used to call women like Panda—strong, fashionably-dressed island businesswomen—Madame Nhus after the wife of the president of Vietnam."

"So today he'd probably call them Imeldas?"

Laura smiled fondly. Her kid was sharp.

* * *

Panda's travel agency was across the island in a snazzy new office building in Tamuning. Driving there, Laura tried to figure out how she would bring up the photo and therefore, Panda's blood enemy, Jodie deSpain. Laura had no script in mind as they walked into the over-air-conditioned reception room of Panda's Pacific Adventures.

The girl behind the counter showed them into Panda's private office. Panda looked exactly as Laura remembered her, small and neat, her blue-black hair carefully coifed, betraying not a speck of gray. She wore a trim little suit with long sleeves and ruffles at the throat, along with stockings and very high heels.

Laura felt like a slob in her T-shirt and culottes—which had seemed completely appropriate out at the university, especially with Charlotte bustling about in one of her brilliant muumuus.

"Please sit down, Mrs. Monroe and … "

"My daughter Teri."

"Hello, dear," Panda said brightly. "Now, what sort of trip would you like me to —" Panda stopped in mid-sentence, staring at Laura. "Wait a minute. Do I know you?"

"Yes, you did once. I lived here almost twenty years ago."

"Laura Monroe. Yes. You wrote for the newspapers. You did some stories about an airline I used to own."

More accurately, stories about a pilot you used to own, Laura thought, but she murmured assent.

"And now you're back in Guam and planning a trip … "

"Actually I'm living in Tokyo, and I have my return ticket," Laura said, feeling bad about wasting a busy woman's time. "I wanted to ask you …" She almost faltered in the face of Panda's pleasant, plastic smile. "Did you … did you know Gordon Hassler?"

"Hassler? Oh, the murder victim. Oh, of course. You're still a reporter. You're doing a story about the murder."

Laura thought, I could just hold my hands out and you would pour my excuses into them. She heard Teri whisper, "Yes!"

"I'm with the Tokyo Associated Press bureau now," Laura said. "I'm here on vacation, but my boss wanted me to look into the story."

"And because you knew I used to have an airline … " Panda continued to construct Laura's reasons for being there.

"I thought you might have known Hassler in his early days out here, when he was apparently going back and forth between Guam and Saipan regularly."

"Ah, yes. Well, of course, before 1961 when the TT administration moved up to Saipan, we wouldn't have been allowed to fly up there. All the Northern Marianas were completely sealed off."

"When did Don … uh, when did you start the airline here?"

"In 1960. And things were pretty tight. We could only fly north to Rota, or southwest to Ulithi and Yap. You needed a seaplane to land in Palau and Truk, and it was too far to go anywhere else. It wasn't really enough to keep us going except for med evacs. Sometimes, if there was a medical emergency on the other islands—except for Saipan—the government would turn to us. And those paid pretty well."

"I see."

"But yes, once we started flying to Saipan, Mr. Hassler did fly with us, quite often. And while I can't say I knew him well, it's very strange to think of him being involved in drugs. He certainly didn't seem the type."

"Drugs?" Teri asked.

Laura shot her a stern look and said, "I know that's what the police are saying, but I wonder. I mean … he did have a CIA connection once."

"Yes, he did. And with those people you never know what to expect," Panda agreed. "But wait a minute—aren't you married to one of those people?"

One of those people? What does she mean by that? Laura tried not to get flustered. "I'm divorced," she said.

"Oh?" Panda raised an eyebrow. "Welcome to the club."

Laura tried to get back on track. "What do you make of the photograph they found on his body?"

"Very strange, isn't it?" Laura watched carefully. The woman didn't flinch. "When I saw it I wondered, is Mr. Hassler another one of these people writing a book about whatever happened to Amelia Earhart? I do not understand the fascination with the subject. I mean, the Pacific's a very big ocean. Sometimes planes fall down into it. It's hard to find a little plane in a big ocean. What's the big deal?"

My God, woman, Laura thought. Your own son flies one of those little planes flying over that vast ocean. The thought reminded her of her tentative relationship with Panda's son and she nearly blushed. What would this oh-so-perfectly-put-together woman say if she knew what her son had been doing on the beach at Tumon last night?

"Suppose Mr. Hassler was writing a book and he had some new information that proved Amelia Earhart was in Saipan," Panda said. "Maybe a rival author heard about it and came to steal his evidence. I hear there is really big money in some of these best sellers."

"I'm sure there is," Laura said.

Panda broke into a sly grin. "And you know what? My son told me that one of those writers—the one who wrote the first book about Amelia Earhart being in Saipan—he's back on the island. Maybe he's the one who bumped off Mr. Hassler and cleaned out his room. Only he missed the most important piece of evidence!"

For a moment, Laura thought, yes, that is the best explanation for Gordon's death I've heard yet. And what could be more tempting than to cast Shelby Verdun as villain? But no! She shook her head. It was the photo that brought Shelby to Guam ... after Gordon's death.

"Have you ever seen that photo before?" Laura said.

"Me?" Panda shook her head. "No. I think that photo is new to everyone. Isn't it?"

"It's just that ... the woman looked a little familiar to me," Laura said lamely.

"Well, of course, Amelia Earhart looks familiar to everyone," Panda laughed. "I heard she's the most famous woman in the world, more famous even than Jackie Onassis."

"So it didn't make you think of anyone else?"

Panda shrugged. "Sorry, no."

Laura stood up. "Well, thanks for your time. My boss just thought I should talk to some people who might have known Hassler in the old days."

"Hey," Panda said, suddenly indignant. "You don't think our airline had anything to do with his drug deals?"

"Oh, no," Laura said quickly. "I agree with you. I think the police are on the wrong track looking for a drug connection."

In the car again, Laura turned the air-conditioner up full blast and sat silently for a few moments without putting the car in gear. What on earth did Panda mean about my being married to one of those people? Why would Panda even remember who I was married to? Did Foster and I ever travel together on Micronesian Pacific Airlines? Ever buy tickets together from Panda? Or has Panda seen Foster more recently?

"Wow," Teri said, "I wish I was that good a liar. It would come in handy."

Laura brought her mind back to the more immediate problem. "I don't think she's lying. I don't think she ever saw that photo before. And she doesn't see Jodie in it because she probably remembers Jodie as some kind of ogre with horns and a forked tail."

"A fat ogre," Teri said. "Abandoned wives always think their rivals are fat."

"How on earth do you know that?"

Teri shrugged. "I read it someplace. Maybe in one of Lolita's magazines when I was in Hawaii last summer."

Laura backed out of the parking place and signaled for a left turn onto bustling Marine Drive. "I hope you don't ever slip up and call your stepmother Lolita to her face."

"Don't worry," Teri said. "She wouldn't get it. She doesn't read books." She changed the subject. "But if Panda doesn't know anything about this, who does?"

"Cory. She stole the photo from Will."

"No wonder she called in sick," Teri said. "After murdering him—that would make anyone sick."

When Laura finally found a break in uncoming traffic, she dived across the two northbound lanes.

"You didn't see the 'no left turn' sign?" Teri said.

"Damn," Laura said, glancing into the rearview mirror, expecting to see Guam's finest in hot pursuit. Fortunately, they weren't.

"She must have rushed right over to the hotel after Charlotte paid the bill at the restaurant," Teri said. "Didn't they say the body was found at three-thirty?"

"But what motive would Cory have?"

"Drugs?" Teri offered. "Blackmail?"

Bumping off an old lecher, Laura thought to herself. But if Cory was involved in the murder, what about her brother? Would that explain Jeff's ... courtship? Trying to confuse me, throw me off the scent? He knew I was interested in the photo because I made that flight to Saipan with Shelby Verdun. Is he using me as a source of information, perhaps from Edwina Hassler? He would have known from that first day that Edwina and I were old friends. But last night he didn't ask me anything about Edwina. Or Gordon.

What if Jeff were trying to distract her with passion? Blind her to something obvious she should be able to figure out?

She shook her head.

"Mom." Teri sounded concerned.

"What?"

"I said, 'What next?'"

"Yes." What next, indeed. "I guess Will has to track Cory down, confront her about the photo."

"I hope he takes us with him."

"I thought you had a date tonight."

"Oh." Teri was silent for a moment, perhaps juggling her priorities. "You know what, Mom? This is the least boring vacation we've ever had."

"Well, I'm glad you appreciate it," Laura said as she pulled into a parking place at the Hilton.

The desk clerk retrieved the room key and several messages from the little cubbyhole. Laura shuffled through the messages as they headed for the stairs. Three were marked "Urgent!"

Will Hill de Brain. Mr. Foster in Honolulu. Mr. Bosley in Tokyo. And one message —apparently not urgent:

Will call again. Jeff.

Laura sat on the bed, trying to decide which call to make first. Teri disappeared into the bathroom after scooping up the Verdun book for a quick look at the photo opposite page 158.

Will answered on the first ring.

"Did you talk to Cory?" he asked.

"She called in sick at the restaurant. Do you have any idea where she lives? I checked the phone book and there's no listing."

"Damn!" Will said. "No, I don't. She's living with some guy from the air base, I think. Or the Navy. I've seen them around but I have no idea what his name is. Her mother would know."

"Or her brother?"

"That's what I called to tell you. I can't find Jeff. I was calling to see if you wanted me to talk to Panda."

"I did, just now. Will, I'm convinced she never saw the picture before and doesn't associate it with Jodie."

"Hmm. That could be true. But now you tell me Cory's disappeared, I'm really worried. The kid hasn't been seen since Saturday."

"The kid. You mean Jeff?"

"Yeah, he brought you guys back from Saipan and vamoosed. Okay, his sister knows who made that photograph. And he sees you guys up there, re-examining the scene of the indiscretion. What's it all mean, Laura?"

"I don't know, Will." She thought hard for a few milliseconds, then plunged ahead. There had to be honor among thieves from here on out. "But he didn't disappear on Saturday. I've seen him since."

"You have? When?"

Was it really less than twenty-four hours ago she had been down at the beach with Jeff? "Uh ... just last night."

"Really? Where?"

Under the circumstances, she really couldn't accuse him of invading her privacy. "Here. At the Hilton. I mean, he called me, we went out to get something to eat."

She could almost hear Will's memory clicking. Just yesterday. Yes. He had asked her to have dinner with him. She'd said … what? That she had plans. "Oh," he said in a flat voice. "I see. And did you … find out anything?"

More to the point, did Jeff find out anything. "To be completely honest, Will, I don't think I thought about Gordon Hassler or the photo the entire time I was with Jeff. It was very refreshing."

"I see."

So now you ask me if Teri went along to chaperone, she thought, but he remained silent.

Finally he spoke. "Well, I've called, left messages for him, said it was important, but he hasn't called me back. Jeez, Laura. You might have told me you were going to see him when we were dividing up the MacDougals to contact yesterday."

"I'm not sure I knew then," she said, but she had known, and he knew she had. That was when she had told him she had plans.

"I see," Will said again.

For God's sake, she thought, let's change the subject. "Did you find out where Ben Guerrero took Edwina this morning?"

"Oh, yeah. Well, Shelby's convinced 'Sús Pérez is stonewalling him. But he said there was another guy in at headquarters, and from his description, I'd guess it's your sunburned man."

"Dennis Dover."

"Or whatever his name really is. Ben Guerrero told Shelby they had been interviewing a colleague of Hassler's who had some information about what Gordon was doing here. The police asked Edwina to come in and sort out some discrepancies in the two stories. So, I guess the next move's up to you on this front, too. You're the only one Edwina Hassler will talk to, I expect. Maybe you can find out what transpired today at investigation central."

"Okay," she said. "It's my move with Edwina and where else?"

"Jeff MacDougal," he said impatiently. "Maybe he'll return a call from you. See if you can find out if he's ever seen the photo before. Tell him there's a rumor that his sister knows something about it. Maybe you can find out where his sister is."

"Uh—okay," she said. "Listen, Will, I've gotta make a call to Honolulu. Foster left an urgent message, too. As well as my boss in Tokyo."

"Well, lawzy Miss Scarlett, it looks like you're the only one around who knows anything about birthin' babies today," Will said, his voice almost icy. "Let me know if you get anything you can share."

"I will," she promised.

She hung up and took a deep breath. Teri emerged from the bathroom, freshly showered and already dressed for her bowling date. She looked so normal Laura wanted to hug her. Teri shoved the Verdun book under Laura's nose, pointing at a photo of a man in a western hat. "What do you think?"

"Well, it's not Henry R. Luce," Laura said.

"Who?"

"One of Will's suspects."

"Did you call Daddy?"

"Not yet. I just finished with Will."

"I'd better not talk to him when you do."

Laura raised a questioning eyebrow.

"I might say the wrong thing about the investigation. You know he's not going to approve … of me knowing anything."

"True," Laura said. The kid really understood her grownups.

"And anyway, what if I decide … if you decide I should stay a couple days longer. You know, to help you out?"

"To see more of Nashi?"

"Oh, I'll see Nashi again if we decide to," Teri said with a teenager's perfect confidence in an orderly world. "What is it? Three hours from here to Tokyo?"

And a few hundred dollars for a plane ticket, plus getting past his father's ethnocentric ideals for his kids' futures. "I'm sure if you and Nashi decide to meet again, you'll make it happen. Now I'll call your dad and pretend you're already out."

Teri nodded. Laura dialed the number. It was answered after a few rings by a breathless, sweet southern drawl. Lolita—no, Andrea.

"Hello, Andrea, it's Laura in Guam. I had a message that Foster called. Said it was urgent."

"Yes'm," Andrea said. Don't you dare call me ma'am, Laura thought. "'Scuse me, I ran in from the terrace to get the phone. I mean the lanai."

Sweet Andrea, trying hard to be the perfect Hawaiian wife, Laura thought. Get all the vocabulary right, like Foster expects. With Foster, form was everything, substance an afterthought. Where did Foster find Andrea, anyway?

"Foster had to go to a meeting," Andrea continued, "but he left a message for me to read to y'all."

A meeting? Laura glanced at her watch. Shortly past four in Guam made it eight in Honolulu. Eight o'clock Sunday evening. Who has meetings on Sunday evenings?

"Are y'all ready?"

"Go ahead," Laura said.

"Okay. 'Tater-pig.' I'm sorry, that's what he wrote down and he told me to read that to you, too."

"It's okay. I can handle it. Go on."

"Sounds sort of stupid to me. Okay. 'Tater-pig,' colon. That's two dots, right? Okay. Then he says, 'Still haven't located MacDougal although there have been recent sightings. I'll run him down yet. In the meantime, disturbing news about Jodie. One guy who used to know her says he's sure he heard she was killed in a plane crash a few years back. Will try to confirm this awful possibility, one way or another.' And it's just signed 'Foster.' So how's Teri?"

Laura couldn't make the quick transition in topic for a few seconds. A plane crash? Jodie? No, it couldn't be true. She had been so

vividly alive to Laura these past few days, remembering the weekend they took the silly photograph, reading her letters to Charlotte this morning. She couldn't be dead. And Foster was only repeating a rumor, after all. The island grapevine was often inaccurate.

She realized Andrea was waiting for her to speak. "Oh, she's fine. Teri's fine. Looking forward to seeing you guys. You folks." Listen to me, she thought, trying to be the perfect Hawaiian myself. I even pronounced it "foaks" like Hawaiians do.

"So you'll put her on the plane tomorrow?"

"Yeah, tomorrow evening. She'll get into Honolulu early in the morning."

"Yes. Tuesday morning. Foster has it written in big red letters on the kitchen calendar."

Tuesday morning. One of the planet's bits of true magic. Leave Guam Tuesday evening, arrive Honolulu Tuesday morning. Let both Tuesdays be good to Teri!

"Well, thanks for the message, Andrea."

"That's quite all right. I'll be looking forward to giving Teri a big hug."

Hope she doesn't knock you down, Laura thought. "Bye." She hung up and stared across the room at Teri reading the Verdun book.

"Well?" Teri asked.

Before Laura could decide whether to tell her about the rumor, the phone rang. She grabbed it and mumbled hello, still trying to place Foster's rumor into some sort of context.

"Laura? Jerry Bosley in Tokyo."

"Jerry, I just got in and was about to dial your number."

"Well, I'll make this quick. Listen, in your long-ago island days, did you ever run into a woman pilot out there? A gal named, uh, Judy … let's see … no, Jodie. Jodie deSpain?"

Part 4

—1981—
July

IT WAS ONE OF THOSE PERFECT DAYS for flying. The sky was blue from the earth to heaven, with small cumulus clouds spattered here and there like commas and quotation marks.

Even if Jodie weren't the happiest woman in the world, being here, in the air, supported by the elements, she would be happy. Even if she didn't have Donnie back, forever.

She admired the silver ring on her left hand. He'd had it custom-designed for her, that was what touched her most. He didn't just go into a jewelry store and grab something to sweep her off her feet. He'd thought about it, fished up all the details of their first night together, remembered them as vividly as she did. And that song. Of course he had to insist on dinner at Trader Vic's—where else could he find musicians who knew "Month of Forevers"?

She heard the song then, at the back of her mind at first, then swelling so it filled the cockpit.

For endless months and years I heard
Those dreamy tales of love

Silly words, actually. Kind of a silly tune, too. So simple. How could they be fraught with such powerful emotions?

I never found that sweet someone
Who fit me like a glove.

She almost heard Donnie's soft baritone beside her, thought she felt his warm breath in her ear, and found herself belting out the final chorus.

Now here you are before me,
The story's coming true.
I'll spend one month of forevers
In paradise with you.

What's wrong with simple music, she wondered. She couldn't hum Berlioz or Mahler, let alone belt it out like a Broadway star.

I should have brought him along, she thought. He would have come if I had asked him. He was just hanging out in San Francisco this weekend, making arrangements for the "big luau" as he called their forthcoming wedding, telephoning his network of buddies in Hawaii. She wondered whether Lila, her neighbor across the hall, was even aware that Donnie had been there all these days. Usually when Jodie had visitors, Lila managed to think of one pretext or another to pop over. Perhaps she was away on vacation.

She hadn't pressed Donnie to come with her. Things were working out so well this time because she had her own life, too, instead of just attaching herself to him like the tail of a high-flying kite. Checking out this lead was vital to her book. If she should find evidence that Garrett Howland was still alive—and even learn where he was—then she might want Donnie with her when she followed up on that. But interviewing a little old lady—that was surely best done woman-to-woman.

Of course the main question was whether Garrett Howland had been in on the plot against Amelia. If he had been, then he must know why she had been sent astray. But what if he wasn't? What if—as the police in New Guinea had assumed—he was simply a plaything of the true villain, Tex Arnold, and had simply snapped when pushed too far?

Or what if the boy had already run away before Tex Arnold was murdered? What if the boy had caught the eye of the government or industrial agent assigned to eliminate Arnold after he had ensured that Amelia would fail. Perhaps the boy had been warned to clear out, given a new identity.

She could imagine several scenarios that would allow Garrett Howland to survive the carnage in that hotel room in Lae. If he survived that, there was every reason he might still be alive. And able to answer questions.

Surely, the one person who would know if her son was still alive would be his mother.

A mother would lie, of course, to protect her son. But if Jodie approached it right, she might be able to get some information, some clue.

If not, she still had this incredible day of flying to add to her accumulated memories of wonderful days.

She looked down at the high plains. When you learned to fly in the middle of the Pacific Ocean where the political entities corresponded with geographic features, you expected to see maps laid out before you. Yes, there's Guam shaped like a fat Christmas stocking. And Tinian, like a giant aircraft carrier steaming toward Asia. But although she knew she was near the corner where Wyoming, Nebraska, and South Dakota met, there were no dotted lines on the land below to confirm her exact location.

Here there were two features you could navigate from: the improbable hulk of the Devil's Tower, piercing the sky in northeastern Wyoming, and on the South Dakota-Wyoming border, the Black Hills. They truly were black, from this altitude, punctuated by slashes of granite peaks.

And there, sparkling in the sun, was one particularly bright cliff. She descended for a better look.

Yes. Four faces carved into the cliff. What a strange thing to do to a mountain. And not a temporary expression of a mad artist like that character who hung curtains across valleys. Christo? Was that his name? His stuff wasn't permanent graffiti on the landscape like this.

She flew as close as she dared—there were laws about flying over national parks and monuments—and redesigned the faces in her mind. Let Amelia Earhart take the place of George Washington,

with her husband, George Palmer Putnam looming beside her in Jefferson's spot. Then Tex Arnold in his Stetson on the right, instead of Abraham Lincoln. And tucked farthest back, one more face. She left it blank for Garrett Howland. In an hour or so, she should know what he had looked like. At the very least, his mother would have photos of her son as a boy.

Maybe she would fly by again after she was finished. Complete the last face then.

— 1983 —
Monday

"JODIE DESPAIN?" Laura repeated the name slowly, as though it weren't the headline on the front page of her brain. "Yes, I knew Jodie." Take it slow. Be careful. "Why do you ask?" Maybe Foster's rumor was wrong, and Jodie had come out in the open, confessed that she was the woman in the photo.

"Well, we've got this new computer access thing they keep bugging us to use," Jerry Bosley explained. "You were here for the demonstration, right? For the mere price of an international long distance phone call, you can search the New York Times Index as well as our own AP morgue, at least as much of it as they've got plugged into the computers back in New York. And there's a rumor that the big bosses are monitoring our use of the search service, to identify any anti-technology counter-revolutionaries amongst us."

"I remember you fuming about that just before I left Tokyo."

"So I decided what the hell, I'll do a search on Amelia Earhart and see what else has been found in the past few years. And guess what comes up?"

Laura was afraid she knew what it was going to be, but she said, "I have no idea."

"One of the first items to come trickling out of the information pipeline is an AP story out of San Francisco. Headline: Earhart researcher killed in crash. And I quote:

> A woman pilot who was researching a book about Amelia Earhart's mysterious disappearance in 1937 was killed this week in the crash of her rented airplane in the Rocky

> Mountains. Jodie deSpain, 42, of San Francisco had first become interested in the lost American aviatrix when she was learning to fly in Guam in the 1960s, according to her neighbor, Lila Wayne, 28. Miss Wayne said Miss deSpain believed she was close to a breakthrough on the Earhart disappearance. However, according to Miss Wayne, Miss deSpain's Earhart files disappeared from her apartment after her death. The National Transportation Safety Board and the Federal Aviation Agency are investigating the crash. However, an FAA spokesman said, "Those are high mountains in Colorado. Sometimes planes fly into them."

Laura sat on the bed, stunned. So it was true.

"Laura? Are you there?"

"I'm here. It's just that ... Jodie was a friend back in my island days. I had no idea ... I never heard ... When was this?"

"July 21, 1981. Apparently it didn't get much coverage. I wondered why I hadn't spotted it, Amelia freak that I am, but it was the same week as the royal wedding, so it got squeezed out, at least out of what came to Tokyo."

"Or to Bangkok, I guess." Laura was trying to recalculate everything. If someone stole Jodie's files—but how did they know she didn't have them with her on the plane? How did they know they weren't destroyed in the crash?

"Listen to this, though, Laura," Jerry said. "It's another quote from the neighbor. 'Now that I think about it, Jodie even looked like Amelia Earhart.' What do you think of that?"

"I ... I guess she did," Laura said, alarmed at how easily she spoke of Jodie in the past tense. "Oh, wow, Jerry, this is awful."

"I'm sorry. Obviously this has shaken you up. Why don't you take a couple hours to absorb this and then call me back and we'll toss some ideas around. I'm going to be here pretty late. I can imagine a good feature with you remembering your friend and her quest, figure out some way to tie it to the photo in the murdered guy's pocket. I'll get to the S.F. bureau, see if they've got anything else in their files that didn't get on the wire before. Sound good?"

"Yeah, Jerry," Laura said flatly. "Just give me a little time." If you only knew how easy it could be to tie Jodie deSpain to the photo in the dead man's pocket, she thought as she hung up. She sat still, staring into space. Somehow, it was all getting connected. How much longer before Jodie is identified as the woman in the photo? What about that neighbor in San Francisco? She must have seen the photo in the newspaper there. Didn't she look at it and think, "That's not Amelia Earhart, that's Jodie deSpain."?

Once Jodie is recognized, how long before my shoulder is identified? Or Donnie's shirt. Or … She dived for the Friday morning newspaper which she had tucked into a drawer of the desk. No, you only see the ends of the fingers gripping Jodie's forearm in the photo. No rings.

"Mom?" Teri sounded concerned. "What's wrong?"

Laura could think of no way to avoid telling her. "It's Jodie. She was killed in a plane crash a couple years ago."

"Oh, no." Teri looked shocked and sad. "I was just getting to know her, reading her letters this morning."

"I know, honey." Laura crossed the room and put her arms around her daughter and gave her a hug. "I feel bad because I never tried to keep in touch with her. I just thought of her mostly as your father's friend because they'd done all those plays together. Now I realize we lived in San Francisco at the same time and … " without warning, her voice broke and she began to cry. "And Jerry Bosley wants me to write a story about her!"

"Poor Mommy," Teri said, patting Laura's back. "Do you … do you want me to stay here with you tonight?"

Laura looked at her watch. It was five minutes to five. Nashi would be here to pick Teri up. And yes, Laura did want her to stay, to remain in sight, in reach, in this world where people she knew seemed to be dying violently.

She focused on Teri's face, on the battle of emotions there. Teri wanted to help her mother, but she had so little time left with Nashi. She was a good kid.

"No, honey, you go ahead. I'll be fine. You have fun. Just ... be careful."

"Don't worry. I won't say a word about Jodie. Or anything else."

Laura gave her a quick kiss and said, "Give my best to Nashi. And get home early. Tomorrow's a busy day. You've got to get packed for Hawaii."

* * *

What to do next? Laura sat at the desk, staring again at the photograph in the lower right corner of Friday's paper. Should I call Will? Fill him in on Jodie's death—and on her research? Her mind seemed filled with fog, like the thick air of a San Francisco morning. She picked up Shelby Verdun's book and turned to page 158. She stared at the man in the cowboy hat on the opposite page, standing there between Amelia Earhart and Fred Noonan. Who was he? What had Jodie found out about him? Who had she told about her research besides Charlotte and her neighbor? Had she told Shelby Verdun? This morning he talked of meeting someone very much like her, a woman who seemed to think she was better qualified to write about Amelia than he because she was a pilot and a woman. Clearly, he had resented it.

She thought of Panda's theory that writers were competing for evidence about Amelia Earhart. How do I know for sure that Shelby didn't arrive on island until after the photo was published? Will met his plane Saturday morning. At least Will said he'd met Shelby's plane. But what if Shelby were here earlier? What if Will lied about the negatives being stolen? What if Will planted the photo on Gordon's body?

Why? To get new publicity for Amelia? Had Gordon been particularly interested in Amelia Earhart? Had he been writing a book, too?

She stared at the photo of the man in the Stetson. Well, this guy isn't Shelby Verdun, I'm sure of that.

The phone rang and she answered almost timidly. "Laura? It's Edwina. Are you free for dinner tonight? I need to talk to a friend."

That's right. I'm supposed to be finding out something from Edwina. Now what was it? "Yes. I'd love to have dinner. When?"

"Sooner rather than later. Suppose I meet you at the door to the dining room at six o'clock."

"Sounds fine."

"I've had such a day. I spent hours with the police."

That's it. I'm supposed to find out what the police wanted from Edwina and Dennis Dover.

"And then I came back to my room and passed out for hours. I don't remember if I had any lunch. I must still be suffering from jet lag."

"I'll get spruced up a bit and meet you," Laura said.

*   *   *

Laura was in the bathroom combing her hair when the phone rang again. She hesitated before answering. What if it is Will? What if he was in on Gordon's murder?"

"Hello?" she said cautiously.

"Is that you, Laura? I barely recognized your voice."

She recognized his instantly—the deep, young tones of Jeff MacDougal. Another suspect. If Will isn't lying about Cory MacDougal stealing the negative of the photo, and Jeff knows where his sister is … was I supposed to find that out from him? I can't remember.

"Well, it is me." She tried to keep her voice light and young.

"I'm just calling to see if we're still on for tomorrow. I mean, is your daughter leaving?"

"Yes, on the evening flight to Honolulu."

"And you'll stay on for a couple days, right?"

"Yeah, my boss in Tokyo's got another story idea he wants me to check out." Her mind moved rapidly. If things got too weird or scary, she could probably change her ticket again and catch the next

flight to To*kyo* after she put Teri on her flight. Explain to Bosley that she was too frightened to stay. What would that do to her career in the Associated Press? Nobody needs shrinking-violet-types in this liberated age. But it couldn't be as bad as it would be if she were exposed as one of the perpetrators of a fake news photo.

"So we can have a drink after she leaves?"

Laura was amazed at the way her body reacted to this boy's voice. She was melting.

"Yes. I'd like that."

"Why don't I meet you in the bar there at the Hilton?"

He's absolutely brilliant, she thought. If the chemistry is still there, it's just a flight of stairs to my room. "I'll see you tomorrow," she said. "I should be back from the airport by nine. Nine-thirty at the latest."

"Don't worry about it if the plane's late," he said. "I'll be waiting for you."

She hung up and hurried down to meet Edwina, trying to focus her mind on the issues of the day, instead of that handsome young islander with the disconcertingly sexy voice.

Edwina looked pale and nervous. Laura almost protested when the hostess led them to a table by a window. This was the table where Gordon Hassler had been having dinner with Dennis Dover Wednesday night, his last night alive. But she decided it would be easier on Edwina if she didn't ask for a different table. That would entail explanations, and Gordon's last dinner was surely an emotional minefield for his widow.

They scanned the large dinner menus. Laura tried to organize her thoughts. What did she need to ask Edwina? In what order? But, wait, Edwina proposed this meeting. She wants to talk.

The waiter took their orders for drinks. Once again, Laura found herself ordering gin. "I'd better get off this island before I turn into an alcoholic and my daughter marries a Guamanian."

"Teri's out with her young friend again? Well, Laura, there could be worse fates. He seems like a very nice boy."

"Oh, he is." Worse fates? Like yours, Edwina? Marrying a spy who flirts with younger women? At least the spy she herself had married—if indeed he was a spy—hadn't gotten himself murdered. At least, not by the time she'd spoken with Andrea that afternoon.

Their drinks came and they ordered dinner. Edwina took a gulp of her scotch and after a pause said, "Laura, I have been through hell today. Do you know this head detective working on Gordon's murder?"

"'Sús Pérez? I'm afraid I do. One of my oldest acquaintances on this island. But I certainly couldn't call him a friend."

Edwina shuddered. "He can really be quite brutal." She took a deep breath. "And as the icing on the cake, Gordon's colleague—you know, the man we saw up on Saipan? He was there."

"Dennis Dover?" Why worry Edwina with the news that Will Hildebrandt and Shelby Verdun already knew who she was with today.

"Apparently Dover let the cops stew for a few days even though he'd had dinner with Gordon the night before he died. He didn't bother to check in with the police until this morning. And then he tells them all sorts of things they take as being a direct contradiction to what I had already told them."

"What you had told them about what?"

"Why Gordon was here in the first place—that's your Captain Pérez's top priority. As Gordon explained it to me, he had done a little finagling to get the trip. See, he was supposed to have retired before this but we've never been terribly comfortable financially, and because I wanted to quit working he was looking for some freelance consulting he could do. So he came out here to drum up some business."

"What sort of business was he looking for?"

"He thought he could advise businesses out here on how to deal with federal regulations, that sort of thing."

Laura wondered what sort of federal regulations island businesses had to deal with. Or did Gordon have special reasons for

wanting to come back out to the islands? Some sort of unfinished business from the days when he worked in Saipan? Could there possibly be something to the drug theory 'Sús Pérez was so fond of? The Marianas would probably make a perfect transshipment point between Southeast Asia and the U.S. mainland.

"I had told the police when I first arrived on Saturday that Gordon had come out here on business for the agency and that I assumed his travel orders were classified. I didn't know enough about what sort of consulting business he was looking for to even mention that and so I didn't. Captain Pérez said the police had contacted the CIA through the Navy to see whether the agency could shed any light on the reason for his trip."

The waiter arrived with their salads. As soon as he was out of earshot, Edwina said, "And then Dennis Dover goes in there this morning and tells them that Gordon had not been authorized to make a trip out here, that he'd been turned down when he requested it and then he bought the ticket himself. He said Gordon's employers were concerned about why he'd done it, what kind of sideline—their word—he might be operating out here. Can you imagine?"

It was still difficult for Laura to imagine Gordon Hassler up to anything beyond ineffectual womanizing, but obviously something had been going on. "I think 'Sús Pérez is obsessed with drugs as an explanation for anything that goes wrong in Guam these days," she said.

"And that's exactly what Dover tried to imply. That the agency was concerned about Gordon's freelancing out here—as he called it—and that, as soon as they found out Gordon had bought a ticket to Guam, they sent Dover after him to see what he was up to. Of all the shit-eating scapegoating." Edwina spat out the last words, stared down into her salad and began to cry softly.

"Oh, Edwina, I'm so sorry!" Laura reached cautiously across the table to pat the woman's hand, afraid her sympathy might unleash another torrent of grief like the one that had overtaken Edwina Saturday on Saipan.

Edwina gulped some ice water, took a deep breath and tried to smile. "I'm okay. It's just that goddamned agency policy of deniability. If someone gets caught spying, the CIA denies they ever knew him."

"So what do you think happened?"

Edwina paused as the waiter presented their main courses. Laura tasted her chicken conquistador. It was delicious. Mexican food was the one ethnic specialty that hadn't caught on in Tokyo yet.

"I am quite certain Gordon told me the truth, that the agency sent him out here to wrap up this one last project before he retired. And either something went terribly wrong and he was murdered and Dover is trying to give the agency its precious deniability by pretending his trip was unauthorized, or perhaps the project Gordon was working on threatened somebody in the agency, or some faction in the agency, and they terminated him and tried to make it look like a robbery. Dennis Dover himself may have done it. You saw them having dinner the night before Gordon was murdered. How did they seem?"

"Actually, Teri was facing this … er, their table. I only had a glimpse. But they looked like … like business contacts, having dinner. The main thing I noticed was Dover's sunburn. It looked pretty painful."

"He blamed it on Gordon. It seems that first day he was here, the day after Gordon arrived, he was following him around supposedly trying to find out who Gordon's contacts were. And he followed him up to Windward Hills Golf Club where Gordon met someone and went out onto the course to play the full eighteen holes."

"I didn't know Gordon played golf."

"Only the past few years. Really, Laura, it's only been very recently that he's had time for any recreation. I'd started playing a few years before, and he tried it out to please me and found out he really enjoyed it. Although he always joked that we should have taken up golf when we lived in Saipan where the greens fees were so low."

"Oh, God, yes," Laura said. "What did we pay? I think we paid a dollar for nine holes at Whispering Palms in Saipan."

"Anyway, I'm sure Gordon played that day with Alex Romanov. Remember him? He was the Trust Territory liaison officer in Guam after they moved the headquarters up to Saipan. He retired and stayed in Guam and whenever Gordon was here they'd play a couple of rounds together. But of course Dover didn't know that, or so he told the cops. He figured this was some sort of double agent rendezvous or something."

"Maybe they knew Romanov's last name and thought he was a Soviet spy."

"Well, Dover decided he had to follow them all around the course. And although the pro shop could rent him clubs and arrange a caddie, there were no hats available. He was pretty furious about that." Edwina was clearly amused.

"Serves him right," Laura murmured. "I wonder what he did for shoes."

"Oh, that was part of his gripe. They had shoes in his size to loan him but not a hat to sell, loan, or give away. What kind of place is this? He kept repeating that."

"It's a young country."

Edwina looked quizzical.

"It was something I learned years ago in Saipan. Didn't you notice how much easier life was in the islands if you didn't expect everything to be up to stateside standards?"

"That's very true. I had trouble with that my first year or two in Saipan. Well, anyway, Dover blamed Gordon for his sunburn, and I'm sure the fact that he didn't see Gordon passing drugs or secrets to any mysterious figures on the golf course rankled him."

How would you play a round of golf while keeping the people ahead of you under surveillance, Laura wondered. Perhaps you didn't even use a ball. Just follow along half a hole behind, using binoculars perhaps? But then how did you explain it all to the caddy?

"So did Dover have any theory for the cops about who killed … who the culprit was?"

Edwina took a deep, slightly shuddering breath. "I'm sure he had given them all sorts of ideas before Lieutenant Guerrero came to the hotel to get me. Captain Pérez seemed to have a list of ideas he wanted to check out with me, so he could see how I reacted."

"What sort of ideas?"

"Their, quote, evidence, unquote, that Gordon had something to do with drugs was that Dover seemed convinced that Gordon was laundering money. So of course, if money needs laundering, it must have gotten dirty somewhere."

"Did they have actual evidence of this laundering?"

"Laura, this is the most infuriating part of all." Edwina seemed suddenly ravenous. She cut several bites of her prime rib and ate them quickly. "This money-laundering scheme of Gordon's involved sending small amounts of money to an address in Spearfish, South Dakota."

"To the mother of the guy in the war?"

"The man who saved his life."

"Good grief, how much was he sending her?"

"That's what I said, after I got my voice back. I was horrified that they were monitoring our personal bank account, knew where we were sending mail. I said, 'For heaven's sake, he sent the lady a couple hundred dollars a month. That's laundering drug money?' And Dennis Dover leans back in his chair and says, 'Tip of the iceberg, tip of the iceberg.' And I realized that, because they couldn't find anything bigger happening in Gordon's bank account, they were even more suspicious, thinking he had hidden things so well. It made them mad and they were determined to punish Gordon because they couldn't figure out what was going on. And all the time Dover's talking, Captain Pérez has his snaky eyes on me, seeing how I react. I'm surprised they didn't hook me up to a lie detector."

"So was this alleged money laundering Dover's only evidence against Gordon?"

Edwina sighed. "No. There was also suspicious travel."

"Suspicious why?"

"Either he traveled at his own expense—wouldn't you think that would be my business more than Dennis Dover's? Or else he, quote, manipulated a trip on behalf of the agency."

"Where were these trips? Out here?"

"No. Apparently the times he came out here before this last trip, it was their idea. No, these were piddly trips to places in the U.S. like San Francisco, for instance."

Laura's stomach bucked. After all these years, was she about to be confronted about that dreadful evening in San Francisco with Edwina's husband?

Edwina went on. "Let me see, where else? Some place in Texas. San Antonio, I think it was. And, according to Dover, South Dakota."

"Really? Maybe he finally went to meet the woman he had been helping out all those years?"

"Well, at least Dover says he went there. And I really can't think of any reason Dover could have for making that up, although I think he's trying to make me suspect there was another woman in Gordon's life so I'll turn against him and reveal something."

But you wouldn't, even if you could, Laura thought. Stalwart Edwina, loyal 'til the end of time.

"And then just before Lieutenant Guerrero brought me back to the hotel, Dover lets me have his biggest shot. 'Look, Mrs. Hassler,' he says,' I realize it's very possible that you had no idea what was going on. But even so, you'll be better off if you give us any information that can help us figure this out. Because we're looking at more than one death here. Your husband had a rendezvous in South Dakota with someone who worked with him on his sideline, whatever it may have been. A courier, perhaps. We don't know yet. Anyway there was an accident after they crossed paths, and she was killed.'"

"She?"

"This is part of his trying to get me angry at Gordon."

"When was this rendezvous supposed to have happened?"

"Oh, I'm not sure if they said. I have the feeling it was recent—maybe a couple years ago."

"I don't suppose you've got a map of South Dakota handy?"

Edwina nearly laughed. "No. Why?"

"I'm just wondering where exactly Spearfish is." A sudden chill coursed down Laura's spine. "Edwina," she said hoarsely. "Remember that poem of Gordon's about mountains hiding their faces and then putting on masks?"

"Yes, I do. I was reading his poems again this afternoon when I came back from the police station, before I fell asleep. Why?"

"Mountains with faces? South Dakota? Is Spearfish anywhere near Mount Rushmore?"

"I don't know," Edwina said helplessly. "I don't know anything. Except that poem is one of his early ones and he wasn't from South Dakota. He grew up in that orphanage in Missouri."

Or so he always said. Laura sat still for a moment. This was her big breakthrough. So he always said. Why should they believe anything Gordon said—about where he grew up, to whom he sent money, anything?

Laura walked Edwina to her room, then hurried to her own. She glanced at her watch. Eight-thirty in Guam meant seven-thirty in Tokyo. Jerry would probably still be at the office. He always worked long hours. "Too many years in Japan," she liked to tell him.

"AP. Bosley."

"Jerry, Laura. I'm—I'm working on a story idea. Do you know where was Jodie deSpain coming from when she crashed?"

"I just received the whole story, as originally filed. AP San Francisco has some kind of computer archives. Let's see ... yes, 'crashed en route to Centennial Airport outside Denver.'"

"Yes, I think her mother lived in Denver. But where had she been?"

"Let's see—yes! She had taken off an hour earlier from Clyde Ice Field at Spearfish, South Dakota, where she had apparently gone to research her Amelia Earhart project."

"Thanks, Jerry. That's what I needed. I'll get back to you soon."

Laura hung up the phone. She no longer needed a map of South Dakota. She knew where she would find Spearfish.

Mountains with false faces? What about men?

She dialed Edwina's number and asked if she could borrow the book of poems for the evening.

— 1981 —

FINISHED AT THE AIRFIELD, he drove slowly into town for the first time in forty-five years. It had changed, and yet not changed. It was familiar, the way a scene in a recurring dream would be—not like anyplace he had ever actually been. And, of course, he'd never been here. Not Gordon Hassler.

The long-ago promised tourist boom had obviously descended over the town like a bright gauze curtain. Spearfish was now home to a huge passion play. Just twelve miles down the mountain from where Wild Bill Hickock met his violent end, hundreds of people acted out the last days of Jesus Christ every year. What if there had been a passion play here when Garrett Howland was a boy? Perhaps he would have acted in it, been a Roman centurion or something. Perhaps he'd have saved his soul instead of dealing out the deadman's hand for a rich, mysterious stranger in a sleek, black Rolls Royce.

Despite the tourist glitz, the town hadn't changed as much as he expected. He found his way easily down Main Street, reading the street signs as he went—Ash, Birch, Colorado, Dakota. How it had amazed him that first week, driving east with Tex, to learn that not all towns named their streets in alphabetical order.

Jackson, Kansas, Lincoln, Michigan. Left on Nevada, then a bit of a jog to take the narrow Nash Street Bridge over the creek that still ran crystal clear, tumbling down from the canyon.

Two blocks and a right on St. Joe. The college campus loomed above, greatly expanded from his day. Across the street from it, but tinier than he remembered, the house sat, still painted white with

green trim. His heart caught unexpectedly when he saw it, tucked in behind two large honeysuckle bushes. Could they be the same bushes he had trimmed as a boy? He hoped she used some of the money he sent to hire someone to keep the yard neat and refresh the paint .

The woman pilot's rented car was parked at the curb. He continued down the wide, empty street, made a U-turn and pulled over to park by the concrete retaining wall that helped keep the college campus perched above it. He would have a perfect view of the house until she emerged—and shade, besides.

Back in his day, a man parked along a residential street in this town would have aroused neighborhood suspicion, but today the street seemed uninhabited, a modern ghost town. Perhaps all its women were at their jobs-away-from-home, the children at day care or camp. He suspected that Rose Howland was the only one who spent her weekdays on this street.

How old would she be? He calculated quickly. Ninety-three. He fingered the silky-textured gold watch in his pocket. How he wished he could see her—and tell her who he was. Return the watch to her. But that was impossible.

His investment of time, wine, and charm with Ruthie Firestone had paid off in spades, as had the retainer he paid the San Francisco detective. It had taken the detective only a week or so to identify the woman pilot who had flown to San Antonio and, after that, develop connections at several Bay Area airfields to keep tabs on any future flights she made. So it was that Gordon had received a call from San Francisco last week. "She's on the move again," the detective said. "She's lined up a plane for a weekend out of state."

"Any idea where she's headed?"

"Oh, yeah, airports are cozy little communities—no secrets. This chick's got a weird idea of travel meccas."

"How so?"

"Well, with money to blow on a private plane, you could go almost anywhere, right? Aculpulco. New Orleans. Honolulu, maybe."

"So where's she going?"

"Spearfish, South Dakota! Does that sound like a vacation paradise to you?"

And so he had come home.

*　　　　*　　　　*

He tried to read *Newsweek* while keeping an eye on the door of the little white house. What was she learning in there? What was there to learn? That Rose Howland had a son named Garrett who disappeared into the far western Pacific in 1937? If this deSpain woman had found out about Tex's death, she could probably have learned the name of his young companion who had disappeared at the same time. And Garrett's hometown was probably registered somewhere. Just because he had torn his passport into tiny bits in that Australian tub, the *Wallaby*, didn't mean someone couldn't get into whatever U.S. government records there might be of passports issued in 1937. Maybe he had even shown the passport when he registered at the hotel in Lae. Gordon Hassler had certainly been required to show his passport at any number of foreign hotels.

Having come here, what could she learn from Garrett's mother? Only that for many years she had received checks from a man whose life her son had saved in World War II.

A man who signed his checks Gordon Hassler.

How could he have done that all these years? How much trouble would it have been to set up a separate account under a false name?

He must have wanted to be caught.

But no, if he wanted to be caught, he wouldn't have just been out at Clyde Ice Field, making certain crucial adjustments in the workings of a pretty little airplane.

He admired his long, slender fingers spread out on the steering wheel of the car he had rented in Rapid City. They were fingers that had been on a detour over the past several decades, used mainly to

make many women happy. But still, after more than forty years, he hadn't lost his touch with a machine. What might he have been if Tex Arnold hadn't launched his morbid 1936 tour of famous western shoot-outs and death scenes, if Tex hadn't wandered through South Dakota that summer so long ago?

A mechanic, a simple mechanic who did clever card tricks at parties.

A happy mechanic leading a simple life.

He sat rigid behind the wheel. The door was opening. He saw the shadowy shape turned toward the room behind the screen door, saying the requisite farewells. Then she turned and stepped across the narrow porch and down the three steps to the sidewalk.

He stared. She seemed familiar. Had he seen her somewhere before? Where could he have met her? She was tall and slender, with short, dark blonde hair.

No, it wasn't Jodie deSpain he had met. He had met Amelia Earhart. This woman looked a lot like her. Funny, Ruthie Firestone hadn't mentioned that. But then Ruthie didn't approve of Amelia Earhart and she probably didn't carry around a clear image of the aviatrix.

Or was he hallucinating?

He watched Jodie deSpain get into her rented Chevy, pull away from the curb and make a U-turn that brought her right past his car. She didn't seem to see him. He waited a few seconds before starting his engine and following.

He kept at a discreet distance, all the while finding himself resenting the ease with which this interloper maneuvered through the streets of his hometown. How did she know to take Jackson Street—the easy way—across the creek and back to Main Street? Right on Main, heading for the airfield. His main concern now was that she might stop at a pay phone or a mailbox and pass on her newly acquired information, whatever it was. What would he do if she did? A mailbox would be easy to blow up. Surely he could disable a phone booth in a moment.

But she drove directly to the little airfield. From a safe distance there, screened by a clump of carAgaña bushes, he watched her put the key under the front seat of the car, pull a carry-on bag from the back seat, lock the car doors and walk out to the plane. He found himself trembling. He had already seen this happen. It was a re-enactment of Amelia Earhart heading for her doomed plane in 1937.

He watched the plane taxi to the far end of the runway. She turned the nose of the craft into the wind. And there she sat. His heart skipped. Did she sense a problem? Or was she just meticulous about her pre-take-off chores? Then the engine sound raised in pitch, and Hassler began to breathe again. All standard operating procedure. After all, an airplane is a little more complicated than a rental car.

The engine noise subsided before the plane began to move again, gathering speed, lifting off neatly. None of the will-she-make-it tension he remembered from that long-ago day in New Guinea. Jodie deSpain's plane wasn't loaded with thousands of pounds of extra fuel. It carried only one extra item—a timer that would let her fly for about an hour before it transformed her fuel tank into a bomb.

It was too bad. Now he must go back to town and find out what his mother might have told her about Garrett Howland—then figure out how to keep her from telling anyone else.

His heart pounded like that of a frightened child as he stood on the little porch, waiting for her to answer his knock. He heard footsteps, heard the inner door open, and then saw the shadowy shape standing on the other side of the green-painted screen door.

"Mrs. Howland?" Surely, this large, hearty-looking woman was not his 93-year-old mother!

"Nope, my name's Quentin. What can I do for you?"

Quentin. He had heard that name before, some place.

"I'm John Dohansky. I'm an insurance investigator and we're looking into a scam a woman is perpetrating in this town."

"An insurance scam?" Slowly she opened the door, giving him a glimpse of the tiny living room. The same overstuffed easy chair,

Dad's chair, his mother had called it, seldom allowing her son to use it all through his fatherless childhood. The same goddamned yellowish crocheted antimacassar. He felt as though time must have gotten stuck here. Perhaps the visiting lady pilot had interviewed Garrett Howland himself.

"The thing is, the suspect was seen entering this house earlier this afternoon. I need to know what she asked you, whether she tried to sell you anything."

He almost thought the woman let out a sigh of relief. "You'd better come in," she said. She motioned him over to Dad's chair. He sat down gingerly.

"She didn't say a word about insurance, did she, Rosie?" she said loudly, turning toward a large television set that sat blaring in the middle of the room. Beyond it, a tiny shell of a woman sat in a small wheelchair. Her eyes seemed glued to the TV screen.

So this was the woman whose forgiveness he had longed for all these years, who had loomed so large in his conscience. He jammed his hands into his pants pockets. His left hand clamped around the gold watch. His right hand began to play with the coins it encountered.

The faint jingle seemed to register with the ancient woman. Her head jerked away from the television and her eyes fastened on him. Saliva drooled out of her mouth.

Mrs. Quentin crossed to the other woman's side and mopped her chin. "This is exciting, isn't it Rosie? Company twice in one afternoon." Then she sat down on a small sofa, close to Gordon, and returned to his question. "No, nothing about insurance. She said she is writing a book."

"That's part of the scam," he said. "She gets as much information as she can about vulnerable elderly people. Then she uses that to develop her pitch."

"Oh, I see. Yes, she did ask about Rosie's...Mrs. Howland's son."

"Mrs. Howland has a son?" He kept his voice pleasant, neutral.

"She had a son. But he died—oh, almost forty years ago, I guess. In the war."

"I see. So the … uh … researcher who was here this afternoon was probably trying to find out what sort of …death benefits Mrs. Howland gets?"

"You mean like a military pension? Hah! Apparently the government forgot about him. All she gets is her Social Security. It's barely enough to keep her. Of course, I do what I can to help her out."

Gordon felt oddly elated. This woman was running her own insurance scam. Now he remembered the note from his mother several years ago. It said the money the kind Mr. Hassler was sending enabled Mrs. Quentin to live with her, so she could stay in her own home. Only, his mother hadn't written that note. It was this woman—and she was surely the one who made the shaky, scrabbled endorsements on his checks. She was probably ripping off Rose Howland's Social Security checks, too.

Yet he felt gratitude toward Mrs. Quentin because his mother was able to live out her years in her own home. And if Mrs. Quentin was appropriating his mother's money, there was surely no way she would have told this afternoon's visitor about the man named Gordon Hassler and the checks he sent every month.

"What sort of information did Mrs. Howland give her?"

"Rosie? Rosie hasn't been able to talk for years. I let the lady see her scrapbook. She knew the son's name. She wanted to know if Rosie knew where he'd gone after … was it New Zealand?"

Gordon shrugged. "What sort of things are in the scrapbook? If you let me see it, I may be able to anticipate what direction the scam will take."

"It's right here." Mrs. Quentin picked up an old-fashioned photo album from the cluttered coffee table and handed it to him.

He turned down Mrs. Quentin's hesitant offer of something to drink and kept his face carefully still as he opened the album and slowly turned the pages. It was his life … no … Garrett Howland's

life—starting with the first baby picture and his real birth certificate. Ah, the money he'd had to pay that scoundrel in Fiji to create a birth certificate for Gordon Hassler. As he flipped through the album, he tried to guess what Jodie deSpain might have thought of it. There were photos from the boy's childhood and his earliest report cards. A photo of him in cap and gown signified his graduation from high school. A couple of snapshots of the boy doing card tricks. One of him posing self-consciously outside the garage where he'd had his first job. Nothing here to connect this boy with Gordon Hassler.

The final pages of the album held a half-dozen picture postcards. He told Mrs. Quentin, "It's important to know what sort of information she has about her potential target." He was suddenly aware that the tiny old woman had focused all her attention on him. He felt as though he had one of those toy arrows with a suction cup on it stuck in the middle of his forehead. Her gray-blue eyes where the arrow's feather should be.

"You'd better read them cards. That lady even copied some stuff from them. Look, we thought she was writing a book. I thought it would be nice for Rosie if someone remembered her son."

Six postcards. A paltry collection for a loving son to send his mother in a year's time—but the son had been so ashamed of his situation. Gordon felt his ears reddening, even after all these years.

Four of the postcards depicted scenes in and near Washington, D.C. One showed the Empire State Building in New York and the last one bore a picture of a kangaroo and the words "Greetings from Down Under."

Gently he removed the first card from the mounting corners that held it on the album page. Surely the boy would not have written anything incriminating on a postcard!

"Dear Ma," it began in the fine penmanship he had prided himself on then.

Penmanship! Could he be identified by his handwriting? It had deteriorated through the years, but other than typing his notes when he sent one with the check to his mother, he had never thought about

anyone else comparing handwriting samples. He would have to figure out how to make these postcards disappear.

> *Mr. Arnold has a very nice house near what's in the picture and I have my own room.*

Not that the pitiful boy had been allowed to sleep in his own room very often.

> *He says I am a great deal of help to him, and I am working hard to earn my keep. Washington is beautiful, but hotter than it is at home.*

Other than confirming Garrett Howland's connection with Tex Arnold, the message seemed benign. Surely, neither Jodie deSpain nor the boy's mother derived any information from it about the real relationship between the two men.

The other cards were equally innocent. Gordon even read them with an odd sense of invading someone's privacy—perhaps that of the old woman whose attention remained fastened on him as he removed each card, turned it over, read its message, then, carefully replaced it in the album.

"It's very exciting to be in New York," the boy had written on the Empire State Building card.

> *You can't imagine how many people live in this city. I've seen everything from the top of this building to the deepest subway tunnel. What a way to travel—those trains really go! We went to a Yankee baseball game. It was exciting. More fun than listening on the radio.*

Finally he reached the card with the kangaroo.

> *Dear Ma, Well, I said I was going off to see the world, and here I am. We've seen scenery here that looks a lot like S. Dakota. You'd feel at home here—except the animals are pretty strange. Hope to see you soon. Love, Garrett.*

Nothing here for the amateur detective. Nothing the earlier visitor had read would connect Garrett Howland with Amelia Earhart

or Gordon Hassler to Spearfish, South Dakota. He almost regretted the few minutes' work he had put in on the plane at the airfield. But, then again, better safe than sorry.

The postmark on the last postcard was remarkably clear. "Darwin, WT, Australia, 6-28-37. He rubbed his thumb over the postmark to smudge it as he replaced it in the album.

A wordless noise came from the tiny woman in the wheelchair, as though in protest of his marring of her treasure. But surely she was unaware.

He closed the album and set it back on the coffee table. "Thank you very much, ladies," he said. "I think I have what I need. Now I'll write this up and send you a letter telling you what to watch for if she attempts to proceed with the scam."

He glanced at his wristwatch. Although he always carried the gold pocket watch, he never brought it out in public. In just a few minutes, Jodie deSpain would not proceed with anything, ever again. Whoever the hell the nosy bitch had been. He must remember to hate her, for his own sanity.

He stood up and spoke directly to the tiny woman in the wheelchair. "Thank you, Mrs. Howland." She was still staring at him, her mouth now moving as though she were trying to speak.

Mrs. Quentin walked to the door with him. "You may as well address the letter to me," she said, handing him a piece of paper with a name written on it. "I'm Benita Quentin."

"Thank you." He took the paper and shook her hand. Over her shoulder, he saw Rose Howland still working her mouth.

Walking to the car he thought, perhaps Rose Howland hasn't spoken for years because she had nothing to say. If she managed to get one word out now, he knew what it would be. He had seen her mouthing the two syllables clearly.

"Garrett."

His vision dimmed a bit as a tear emerged from one eye. He took the gold watch from his pocket and rubbed it slowly against his cheek before pulling away from the curb and driving off.

— 1983 —
Tuesday

AFTER BREAKFAST, LAURA AND TERI RETURNED to their room to face up to the ordeal of getting Teri packed for her flight to Honolulu that evening.

"Honey, do all these clothes need washing?" Laura said.

"Don't worry. I'll wash them when I get to Dad's."

"Oh, no, you won't!" Laura tied the laundry up awkwardly in Teri's bathrobe. Sending a child to stay with her stepmother with a suitcase full of dirty laundry seemed the height of failed custodial parenthood. "We'll go right now and find a laundromat. And, if we need to, we'll go out to Charlotte's and borrow her iron."

"Good idea," Teri said. "I don't think Lolita owns an iron."

Laura found herself contemplating the endless, mindless hours she had spent ironing Foster's white shirts during their marriage. Even here in the islands, he had insisted on crisp white shirts. Now, according to Teri's descriptions, he wore bright aloha shirts—crumpled aloha shirts, apparently.

They were just edging out the door with the bulky load of laundry when the phone rang. Teri dashed back in to grab it. "Mom! It's Charlotte." Laura thought she sounded almost as pleased as if it had it been Nashi.

Laura dragged the laundry back into the room, plopped it on her bed and picked up the phone. "Hi, Charlotte."

"Laura!" Charlotte's voice was more excited than usual. "Jodie deSpain must be on island!"

"Oh, no, Jodie's ..." she stopped herself from delivering the death sentence. Perhaps Jodie is alive, after all? Is there a way that a

fake news story can be snuck into the computer archives? Can you really trust archives of old news items that have been typed into computers years later? "Why do you say that?"

"You'd better come out to the Center and see what was in this morning's mail."

Laura started to protest that she needed to find a laundromat but decided that, whatever it was, she would never be satisfied with a description from Charlotte. She would have to go see for herself. "We'll be right out. We'll just drop some stuff off at a laundromat on the way."

"What do you think it is?" Teri asked as they hurried across the hotel parking lot to their rental car.

"I don't know. But I'm wondering if we really know Jodie's dead."

"Wasn't it in the news?"

"Not exactly. Jerry found it searching in computer files, records of old news. But he didn't remember hearing about it when it happened. So what if someone wanted us to think she was dead? What if they snuck that into the archives when someone was typing all the old stories into the computer?"

"But didn't you say Daddy also heard that she was dead?"

"Hmm. That's right. Maybe he was doing a computer search."

"Daddy? Hah! He's computer-phobic. He's proud of that."

"But I suppose the person who told him she'd been killed could also be trying to fool us for some reason." She was grasping at straws. Almost certainly Jodie is dead, no matter what Charlotte received in this morning's mail.

Laura remembered a laundromat in Barrigada Village from her earliest days on the island, nearly twenty years ago, and to her delight it was still there. "I don't think anyone has mopped this floor since then, either," Teri said. Their rubber zoris made a sticky smacking sound as they walked across the concrete floor.

"Just be sure we don't drop anything after it's clean." While Laura sorted the whites and the colors into two adjoining washing

machines, Teri borrowed a dime and went over to the pay phone. After a short conversation, she returned to her mother's side just as Laura was sliding the quarters in to activate the machines. Miraculously, they both started.

"Nashi's got the day off. He's going to come out to the university and pick me up. His sister said she would drive him."

"Oh. And then?" Laura didn't want Teri to mistake concern for her safety for disapproval of Nashi, but she wouldn't feel that Teri was really safe until she saw her settled on that plane.

"We're just going to hang out. Go to the beach. Play Galaxians."

"Where?"

"Right at the hotel. That way you don't have to worry about finding me when it's time to go to the airport."

She wished she believed the hotel was a safe place, but she made a bright smile anyway. "Okay, I'll take you both to dinner. We'd better make it early. I'll meet you at the door to the main restaurant at five-thirty."

"Thanks, Mom," Teri said, giving her a quick kiss on the cheek. It was always like this—the closer Teri got to leaving for a visit with her father, the more loving she became.

How does she do it, anyway, Laura wondered. How does she go back and forth between Foster and me and our very different worlds and remain so—so balanced? So sure of who she is.

Laura asked a young Guamanian woman who was overseeing three small children while apparently operating a half-dozen washers if she would be staying in the laundromat for awhile.

"Where else am I gonna go with this gang?"

"I just wondered if you'd keep an eye on my stuff. Make sure no one runs off with it."

"Why not? Listen, you want me to put it in a dryer when it's done? It all goes in the dryer?"

"Oh, that would be wonderful. Listen, let me pay … why don't you buy some treats for the kids?" She offered the woman a five-dollar bill. The Guamanian hesitated, then took it.

"Okay. For the kids. By the way, I'm Maria."

"I'm Laura. And this is Teresita."

"Teresita! That could be a Guamanian name. So could Laura."

Ignoring Teri's scowl, Laura said, "We feel like islanders, everyone's so nice here. Thanks, Maria. I'll be back in about an hour."

"Don't worry. I'll probably be here all morning. Folding clothes and counting kids."

"Really, Mother," Teri said when they were back in the car. "Everyone's so nice here, we feel like islanders. Oh, sure. Your friend got murdered on this nice island. How do you know she won't steal my clothes?"

"I can tell. I'm a good judge of character."

But was she really? She drove toward the university. Why did she wonder whether Will could have been involved in Gordon's murder, if she was such a good judge of character? Why did she keep questioning Jeff's motives? And what did she really ever know about her own ex-husband?

Nashi and his sister pulled into the parking lot just as Laura and Teri were walking to the library. Teri seemed torn.

"You go ahead, honey. I'll fill you in later on all the details." Laura handed the girl some money. "Be sure you buy your own lunch. That boy works too hard for his money to entertain you all the time."

Teri strolled across to the big, old Chevrolet—a classic "Guam bomb" like those Laura remembered from years past on the island. Gaping rust holes transformed the fenders to lace. She waved at Nashi, who got out to let Teri slide onto the bench seat between his sister and him. Again, it seemed so easy for Teri—moving from one world to another.

* * *

"Look at this." Charlotte handled a padded mailing envelope with reverence. Leading Laura to her back room, she laid it on the

table and stepped back, motioning Laura to sit down. "This morning's mail. Just as though we had ordered it."

Slowly, Laura slid a fat file folder out of the envelope.

"It's her Amelia Earhart file. All the stuff I sent her. And some other things, too, from other libraries, I suppose. I really haven't had time to study it. But she must have sent it to me with something in mind for it." Charlotte sounded as though she could barely contain her excitement.

Laura looked at the front of the large padded envelope. It was addressed in large, firm block printing. At first glance, it didn't look like the printing on notes from Jodie in Charlotte's file.

She looked at the smudged postmark. The package had been mailed in Agaña. Was it just yesterday? That must be it. June 26, 1983.

"That's why I said she's got to be on island," Charlotte said.

Should she tell Charlotte that Jodie had been reported dead, her Amelia file stolen? But what if Jodie had faked her death and disappeared with her own file?

Slowly Laura opened the folder and began reading through the neatly filed documents. Finally she came to the story from the *South Pacific Monthly* magazine about unsolved murders.

The tiny photo at the beginning of the third story was poor, but she recognized him … the man in the Stetson hat. She read the paragraph about Tex Arnold's young companion, whose passport linked him to Spearfish, South Dakota.

The vision of a granite mountain rose up in front of her so fast it nauseated her. Jodie's file contained the perfect tool to cut away extra stone from the mountain's face.

Bits of mountainside seemed to slide down around her as she sat and stared.

At the face of Gordon Hassler.

Before the Beginning of Time

WHEN PUNTAN—a godlike creature born of the air—was about to die, he summoned his sister Fuuna and transferred to her his magical powers. He commanded that, at his death, she was to make the sky from his breast and the earth from his back. His eyes were to become the sun and the moon, and his eyebrows the rainbows after each storm.

Every part of his body was designated to be used in creating the physical world. If you stand atop Mount Santa Rosa and look south across the length of Guam, you should be able to see the island as a giant man lying on his back.

And because Fuuna was a very wise woman, the world has survived until now.

— 1983 —
Tuesday

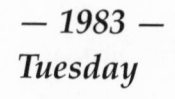

LAURA LEFT TERI AND NASHI eating dessert, and dashed up to the hotel room to try a quick call to Honolulu. She always felt better putting her daughter on a trans-Pacific flight if she had spoken to Foster just before the plane took off and confirmed that he was waiting on the other end.

After the usual long-distance clicks and pauses, Foster's recorded voice answered. "Aloha! You've reached Hacienda Monroe. Andrea and I aren't able to take your call right now, but if you leave a message at the tone, we'll get back to you as soon as possible."

"Foster, it's Laura, just calling to say I'm about to take Teri to the airport here in Guam and I hope you're all set for her arrival." She hung up, irritated at him for not being there, for having the world's most prosaic message, for not being here to suffer all the tension and uncertainty she had been going through these past few days. Whose idea had it been to take that stupid picture sixteen years ago? She honestly couldn't remember who had first suggested doing it, but she had a gut-level certainty that it had been Foster.

Damn Foster anyway. Constantly mocking my sincerity, my faith in democracy, my belief in journalism or in anything else. At least he never succeeded in molding me to match his cynicism.

And to this man I consign my daughter's well-being every summer?

Then again, to this man I consigned half my daughter's genes. And Teri is a wonderful kid.

Laura glanced at her watch. Six-thirty here makes it ten-thirty in Honolulu. He isn't really out that late.

She picked up Teri's carry-on bag and was reaching for the suitcase when the phone rang. She grabbed it on the first ring.

"Hello?"

"Laura? It's Will."

"Oh." Mentally she reproached herself for letting her voice sag with disappointment. Poor Will. I seem destined to be a drag on his self-esteem.

"You rang? At least so the lovely maiden at the answering service claims."

"You mean it actually works? I couldn't believe it when a human being answered instead of a machine."

"Yes, indeed. And they do messages in Chamorro and Japanese, as well as English. Try to get your new-fangled answering machines to do that, you young whippersnapper."

"Will, I'm in kind of a rush. Teri's flight is at eight-fifteen, and I've got to get her to the airport."

"Relax. The Hilton's ten minutes from the airport."

"I like to leave time … for flat tires, I guess. I've had too many near-misses in my life."

"But what were you calling about? Your message said important new information."

"Uh … yeah," How conflicted she had been over whether to call him. She had agonized for the ninety minutes alone with her thoughts and demons and Teri's entire clean, but wrinkled, wardrobe while slaving over the ironing board out at Charlotte's, accompanied only by the gentle slap of the ancient Carmelita's rubber zoris as she puttered around the kitchen.

She had finally decided that if Will had been involved in some plot with Shelby Verdun to murder Gordon, her new information would not make a great deal of difference—but if he wasn't, which seemed much more likely, someone besides Laura Monroe should know all this stuff. After all, Jeff might slip poison in her drink when she met him later tonight. In her current state of paranoia, anything seemed possible.

"I don't know where to begin," she sighed. "Okay, the cops had Edwina in yesterday because Dennis Dover told them Gordon was under investigation by the CIA—by which he was employed—because they suspected him of operating some sort of unauthorized sideline."

"Drugs?"

"That's everybody's first guess. They found some evidence of what they decided was money-laundering, but Edwina has a much simpler explanation, which I haven't got time to go into right now."

"Does Edwina see any connection between Gordon and Amelia Earhart? Shelby thinks he must have been working on a book."

"Edwina never knew what he was working on, I guess. She didn't know anything about a book or any other research on Amelia." How much time do I have? She glanced at her watch: 6:40.

"I've seen Jodie's files out at Charlotte Sablán's research center. Jodie found out about the guy in one of the photos. Have you got Verdun's book handy, Will?"

There was a grunting sound. "Yeah, I just unearthed it."

"Page 158. Is there a photo on the opposite page that shows Amelia and Noonan and a guy in a Stetson?"

"Yeah, I see it."

"Charlotte says someone was cutting that page out of books down at the Christian bookstore here in Guam. Where did you get your copy anyway?"

"Shelby sent me one of his author's copies as soon as it came out. I took some of the photos, remember?"

"That's right. Well, anyway, the guy in the Stetson was named Tex Arnold … are you writing this stuff down? Just in case?"

Will gave an affirmative grunt.

"Right after Amelia took off from Lae, Tex Arnold was murdered, right there in Lae."

"Wow."

"There's an article from that Australian monthly about the islands, something about unsolved murders of the South Seas. Char-

lotte sent it to Jodie because Jodie was doing a book about Amelia, and she was trying to find out who the guy in the Stetson was. In fact, I think Jodie even talked to Shelby once in San Francisco about her research. I've been afraid to mention it to him for fear he'd remember what she looked like."

"So have you located Jodie?"

"Oh, Will, that's the horrible news. Jodie's dead. She was killed in a plane crash a couple years ago."

"Oh, no."

She was certain his shock was genuine. She forged ahead. "Apparently she was doing more research on Amelia. Or on the guy in the photo who may have had something to do with Amelia's disappearance. Or on the guy who may have killed the man in the Stetson. Oh, God, Will, I haven't got time to go into this right now. But, if I'm wiped out by a truck on my way to the airport, you'll have to go out to the university and get Charlotte to show you her Jodie file. I've got to go."

"Okay, but I have one tidbit for you before you go. In exchange for all that dope."

"Okay." She tried not to fidget impatiently.

"Ben Guerrero tells me some guy on a sport fishing spree caught a key piece of evidence off Puntan dos Amantes yesterday."

"What was it?"

"A pair of painter's coveralls. At first they thought they were smeared with red-brown paint but upon investigation … "

"Blood?"

"That's right."

"Gordon Hassler's blood?"

"Human blood. The same type as Hassler's. That's as much as they know."

"Wow." It was Laura's turn. "So the murderer leaves the hotel, drives out to Marine Drive, stops off at Chamorro Lanes to drop the room key in the mailbox, then drives on out to Two Lovers' Point and throws the coveralls off. It sounds almost ritualistic!"

"Or like he wanted to leave clues. That's what Ben thinks. Like somebody's supposed to figure it out."

"God, Will, I've got chills going down my spine."

"Now you'd better hurry. Get the kid on the plane."

"Yeah."

There was something almost too vivid about those coveralls. They held her mind hostage. She picked up Teri's luggage and headed for the lobby, but her mind coursed forward on its own trail.

What if Edwina was right, and Dennis Dover had bumped Gordon off because he possessed dangerous information? Would he have dumped the coveralls into the sea? Mailed the room key back to the hotel?

Could Dennis Dover have retrieved that file of Jodie's from Gordon—assuming he'd had it—and then sent it to Charlotte? The CIA was concerned with collecting information, not disseminating it.

Or…what if Foster had been involved all these years in something with Gordon and needed to get rid of him? No! She had talked to Foster in Honolulu since the murder. But how long after the murder had it been? Wouldn't he have had time to fly back to Honolulu? No, for heaven's sake. Don't let it be Foster!

Teri and Nashi were still at the table in the restaurant, but they came out to the lobby as soon as they spotted Laura. Nashi carried the two bags to the car. "Did you want to come to the airport with us?" Laura asked.

"Yes, please," Nashi said. Laura thought Teri looked almost disappointed, although she quickly gave him a dazzling smile. But of course. With Nashi there, Teri wouldn't be able to ask what she'd learned this morning in Charlotte's office.

Just as well. The less Teri knows, the safer she might be.

"My friend Frank is going to come pick me up at the airport," Nashi said. "So you won't have to drop me anyplace."

Driving to the airport, Laura let her mind wander back to Thursday afternoon. The murderer couldn't possibly have walked through the hotel lobby smeared in blood. He must have taken off

the coveralls and stuffed them ... of course! Into Gordon's bag. That's why it was gone. And to make it look like a robbery, he took everything else—briefcase, wallet, anything else in Gordon's pockets. He put everything in the suitcase and walked out of the hotel, only missing the photo in Gordon's breast pocket. Unless ... she thought of Ben Guerrero's idea that the murderer was leaving deliberate clues.

He got in his car. What kind of car? His own car? Did he live on the island? Or was it a rental, very much like this one? He drove down this same street, past the hospital and the fancy houses along what they used to call the Gold Coast, and out to this intersection with Marine Drive.

And does the murderer have to be a man? Could a woman have done this? I should have asked about the size of the coveralls.

She pulled her foot off the accelerator so suddenly the car jerked. "What's wrong?" Teri said from the back seat.

"The bowling alley," Laura said. Was Teri with me when I heard about the room key being returned?

Apparently not. She was chortling. "Youve got a sudden urge to go bowling?"

"I had forgotten it was right at this intersection."

It would have been easy: a right turn off this street into the parking lot, drop the key into the mailbox up by the entrance to the bowling alley, then back onto this road so he would have the traffic light to help him make his left onto Marine Drive. Left to go north. Toward the airport. Or farther on, to the turnoff to Puntan Dos Amantes, Two Lovers' Point.

The murder happened sometime before three-thirty. The plane to Honolulu left at eight-fifteen. Plenty of time for a jaunt out to Two Lovers' Point. In fact, he would have to go some place isolated like that. Kill a few hours 'til plane time. She giggled and felt an edge of hysteria creeping in. Kill a few hours. Kill a few people.

In the rearview mirror she caught Teri making a screwy motion with her finger for Nashi's benefit. He sat in the front passenger seat

turned almost to face Teri. That's all right, kid. You just go on thinking I'm crazy. Years from now, when this is all solved and we're all sure we're safe, I'll explain about the bowling alley.

Laura negotiated the left turn onto Marine Drive and, after a short distance, made the right turn onto the airport access road. She should force herself to make light conversation—perhaps tell these kids what going to the airport had been like in the old days when you had to stop and get a permit from the military police to go onto the Naval Air Station.

But her mind was still fastened on the murderer. She wanted him to have mailed the key on his way to the airport, putting him safely off the island. Surely that's what a professional hit-man would have done. Get on a plane, get the bloody coveralls and all Gordon's belongings safely off the island, and then dispose of them—in the swampy dumps near Manila, perhaps, or on one of those newly dredged islands in Tokyo Bay. Why drive out to Two Lovers' Point?

Unless he were going back to Hawaii. Perhaps to be met by his sweet little wife who would unpack his gory bag.

Stop it! she ordered herself.

She dropped Nashi and Teri by the departure lobby entrance and went to park the car. She hurried back to the terminal to find the teenagers waiting for her by the escalator to the departure gates.

"All checked in," Nashi said, almost as though he were the one who was going. He had slung Teri's carry-on over his shoulder.

"Good for you."

"Well, after all, I *am* an experienced world traveler," Teri said with mock pomposity.

"I guess that's true," Laura said.

They sat in a sterile departure lounge that could have been located anywhere in the modern world except Honolulu. In the departure lounge there, people would be draping each other with lush flower leis of plumeria and vanda orchids and floral fragrance would permeate even the saddest farewells. Laura wished she had looked for a florist to make Teri a Guamanian lei. But of course that's part

of Foster's schtick. He'd greet her in the morning with a lei or two and she would go on thinking Hawaii whenever she thought of the islands. Then again, maybe not. She caught Teri gazing at Nashi's handsome bronze face.

They made the sort of inconsequential conversation people make when they have many things they want to say but there's not time to embark upon anything meaningful. I'm in Nashi's way, if he has any sweet nothings he wants to confide, she thought. But, then, he's in Teri's way if she wants to ask what was in Charlotte's mail.

Laura supposed she should be making her motherly speech again—although Teri seemed to have grown far beyond admonitions to make her bed and help with the dishes in her stepmother's house.

When the speakers boomed out the announcement of the flight, Teri turned to Laura and said, "I'm sorry to be going, Mom. You be careful." Laura wondered if the whole Gordon Hassler mess had Teri as worried as she was. Laura hugged her tight and said, "Call me as soon as you get to your Dad's place."

"I will," Teri promised. She turned to Nashi who enveloped her suddenly and awkwardly in a hug.

"*Adios*, Tering," he said and kissed her softly on the lips.

"*Sayonara*, Nashi. I'll be back," she promised.

"I'll come to Japan," he said huskily.

And then Teri was gone, following the stream of passengers into the giant tube that funneled them onto the plane.

Nashi smiled shyly at Laura. "Thanks for everything, Ms. Monroe. I'd better run. Frank's probably hanging out in the unloading zone down there, collecting parking tickets."

"Good-bye, Nashi. Thanks for helping me show Teri why I love the islands."

He loped ahead down the escalator, three steps at a time, before disappearing through the revolving doors and out to the street. Laura stood quietly riding down, coming to terms, making the transition from mother to woman on her way to meet a very charming young man for a drink.

The announcement on the public address system caught her midway down. "Laura Monroe. Please check with Hertz Rent-a-Car for a message."

She hurried across the terrazzo floor toward the rental car counters at one side of the arrival lobby. *Did I park in a restricted area?* She really didn't have a clear image of where she had parked.

Wait a minute, she thought, as she waited for the clerk behind the counter to get off the phone. *I rented from Avis.*

When she said her name, the pretty Guamanian girl said, "Oh, yes, someone left this for you."

Someone? Who knew she was at the airport? Well, Will did. And Jeff MacDougal. And of course Foster, if he was keeping track of Teri's flight time.

It was a plain white envelope with her name printed neatly on it. She tore it open. The message was short, printed in block letters.

> Tater-pig. Please meet me in the Hertz lot outside. This is urgent.

She stared at the words.

Foster. Foster is in Guam.

She dashed across the lobby to the pay phones, and started dialing—her credit card number, then Foster's number in Honolulu. Her hands shook so badly she had to start over three times.

Clicks and whirrs. Clicks and pauses. Then: "Aloha! You've reached Hacienda Monroe. Andrea and I aren't able to take your call right now, but if you leave a message at the tone, we'll get back to you as soon as possible."

Her entire body was made of ice. She looked at her watch. It was well past midnight in Honolulu. And Teri was irretrievably en route there.

Slowly, as if in a nightmare, she walked out the door and headed toward the lighted Hertz sign in the parking lot.

– 1983 –

GORDON HASSLER SAT ON THE SMALL HOTEL BALCONY, staring at the photo and the scrap of paper that had accompanied it. The envelope it had come in lay discarded at his feet.

Was this it? Was this what he had come all the way to Guam for—a photo proving Amelia Earhart had been in Saipan?

He bent over, picked up the envelope, shook it. Nothing else. Just this strange old snapshot and the curt note. He raised his eyes to the view. His room faced outward, toward the sea. The scenery seemed held in place by two bookends—on the right, the 400-foot-high cliff they called Two Lovers' Point, and on the left, the edge of the Guam Memorial Hospital peeking out from behind the hotel's other wing. And in between, the intense colors of the sea: the truest, deepest blue on earth, the turquoise lagoon, the glaring white strip of coral beach echoed a hundred yards out by the line of white foam where the surf crashed into the reef.

Everywhere else, of course, was green. Interesting— green no longer seemed a menace. He hadn't had his dream of being devoured by the jungle for several years. But that threat had receded only to be recently replaced by something more concrete: This photo and the person behind the firm block printing on the envelope and the note.

The original letter—in the same block printing—had come about six weeks ago. It, too, had been terse.

I know what happened to her plane. And why. If you meet me in Guam in June, we can figure out what happens next.

At first it had seemed absurd. Why should he pay any attention to anything as vague as this promise to solve a forty-six-year-old mystery?

Promise? Or was it a threat?

What if the person who sent the letter had some kind of evidence about the magnets he had attached to Amelia's plane?

What if someone knew what had happened in that dank hotel room the night after Amelia left New Guinea? As far as he knew, there was no statute of limitations on murder. Even in obscure, recently independent nations.

A few days after that first note came, he had checked flight schedules to Guam. Of course he wasn't going anywhere, but if he were …

Two weeks went by, and June drew closer. He found himself re-reading the note, staring at the envelope. The postmark showed only the date and a zip code, a San Francisco zip code, where that fanatic lived who wrote the original Amelia-in-Saipan book. Could he have sent this menacing note? What a coup for an author; if he could solve Amelia's disappearance, his next book would sell millions. And if he could get the culprit who had sabotaged her plane to rendezvous with him in the middle of the Pacific, what a scene that would be for his book.

The second note came from the same zip code post office.

> *I've made reservations for you at the Guam Hilton, starting the 19th of June. You'll want to be there.*

Again: A promise? Or a threat?

In the end, his curiosity, his desire to put this thing to rest at last, forced him to keep the date foisted upon him. He did a little probing about making the travel at government expense, but there just wasn't any way he could finagle a trip that would get him to a specific place at such a specific time. He'd had to charge the ticket to his Visa card.

He had tried to get information when he checked in at the Hilton. He asked the desk clerk if she knew which travel agent had booked his stay. She said she would check.

"I'm sorry, sir. Is there a problem?" A young man came to the desk from an inner office. He wore a badge that identified him as "Pedro, Assistant Manager."

"Oh, no, there's no problem. I just like to keep track of which agents handle my travel so I can keep my business with competent people."

"I see. Well, we have no record. Only a credit card number we were given to hold the room for you."

"Credit card." Gordon pulled a pen from his pocket. "What's the card number?" He had a friend in the agency who could track this down minutes after he put a call in to her. He glanced at his watch. Five p.m. Monday made it … well, something like five a.m. in Washington. He would call in four hours, after he had dinner. Then he'd call Edwina for some pillow talk.

"This is the card number we were told to use," the assistant manager said. As he slowly read the numbers, Gordon began scribbling them down. Halfway through, he recognized them. He got his Visa card out of his wallet.

The room was already charged to his own card.

Despite the heavy warm air, he shivered. Someone knew far too much about him.

And then, when Dennis Dover showed up on the golf course the next day, Gordon had really felt—well, spooked. There had been no message yet from the person who'd brought him here, but someone from the Agency showed up, seemingly shadowing him. Gordon's first thought out at Windward Hills had been that Dover must have lured him here. He and Dover went back a long way—much too far. There was the unfortunate matter of the young agency secretary Gordon had had a brief but fiery fling with … oh … ten years ago. Very satisfying until she became demanding, expecting things of him he had never promised, threatening to go to Edwina.

It was the only time he'd broken off with a woman in what he considered an ungraceful manner. He had manipulated her into a position that compromised her security clearance and her job security. She agreed to leave him alone in exchange for his silence about her peccadillo. And then she turned out to be some sort of relative of Dennis Dover—a niece-by-marriage or some such.

Dover had had it in for him ever since. But surely not enough to have tracked him all the way back to New Guinea.

Dinner last night with Dover had been strained. Dover seemed to know that something lay behind Gordon's trip to Guam, something beyond his story of getting ready for his post-retirement career as a consultant. Dover was overly interested in Gordon's financial situation, but there was no clue that he had any hint that Gordon had a particular interest in Amelia Earhart. He suspected Dover's main interest went back to the girl, Melissa.

When Gordon had spotted Laura Monroe and said, "Well, I'll be damned. I think I see an old friend over there," Dover had nodded as though he had expected this all along. After going over to chat with Laura and her daughter, Gordon had returned to find Dover standing beside the table, looking impatient.

"The years have certainly been kind to that gal," Gordon had said. "Isn't she a beauty?"

Dover had snorted. "Another one of your conquests, eh, Hassler? What have you got? A woman in every port?"

"She's an old friend from when I worked out here," Gordon said. He found his ego—always wobbly where Laura Monroe was concerned—perfectly willing to let Dover see her as a past conquest.

"It's a complete mystery to me what they see in you, Hassler." Dover had picked up the dinner check, so Gordon had invited him to the bar for a drink, something Dover seemed to agree to reluctantly and then hurried through as quickly as possible.

What was Dover's game? He was after something, trying to trip Gordon up.

But surely he hadn't sent this photo. Gordon stared at it again. It sure looked like Saipan. Although the Japanese had also built a hospital like that on Dublon, in the Truk atoll, or so he'd heard.

It was a lot more likely—given what Gordon knew about the navigational problems Earhart had faced—that she'd have gone down somewhere near Truk. And the Japanese had a huge base there—they could have picked her up, taken her to Dublon, to the hospital, for a checkup. Or maybe she had been injured when she came down. Once more, he stared at the photo. Her feet weren't shown, but she looked to be standing normally. And who was her escort? A uniformed shoulder, a hand on her forearm. A doctor? A Japanese naval officer? A policeman wearing tropical whites? Not an islander—the skin on the hand was too pale.

And who would have taken the picture? Did the Japanese realize whom they had?

After breakfast with Laura this morning, he had gone out shopping, trying to find something really special to take home to Edwina. He couldn't make up his mind. With thousands of Japanese tourists flocking to the island, the shopping opportunities had expanded dramatically since the old days. He stopped at a dark, quiet restaurant on Marine Drive in Tamuning for lunch. Maybe later he would try to contact Laura, see whether she would help him decide on a gift. She had always been fond of Edwina.

Back at the Hilton, he had stopped at the front desk to get his key and the clerk had handed him the small envelope. "Gordon Hassler" was all it said on it, but he was sure it was the same block printing as on the earlier letters. A slip of paper:

I'll stop by this afternoon. Hope you'll be in.

The photo, however, startled him so much he quickly jammed it back into the envelope.

"Do you know who brought this?" he asked the desk clerk.

She had shrugged before calling out, "Pete?" The assistant manager once again popped out of his inner office. "Did you see who dropped this off for Mr. Hassler?"

"Yes, but it wasn't anyone I know."

"A man? A woman?" Gordon asked.

"Hmm. It was just a couple hours ago," Pedro mused. "Let me think … It was a woman, I'm sure."

"Young? Old?"

"Youngish," Pedro said.

"Statesider?"

"Hmm. No, definitely an islander."

Now Gordon sat in his hotel room, still puzzling. Did he still know any island women? Of course, she could have been simply running an errand for someone else. A secretary, perhaps? Another niece-by-marriage of Dennis Dover's?

He stared at the picture of Amelia Earhart. How that face was engraved on his memory. It was as though he had just seen her last week—or only a year or two ago.

A year or two? Now, wait a minute. He took out his reading glasses to have a closer look. No. That had to be Amelia Earhart.

There was a firm knock at the door. He tucked the snapshot into his shirt pocket, folded his reading glasses and put them on the desk. He took a deep breath.

And went to answer the door.

— 1983 —
Tuesday

IT WAS VERY DARK IN THE PARKING LOT, and as Laura walked slowly between the rows of cars, she berated herself. I shouldn't have come here alone. I should have called Will. I should have …

She had just put Teri on the plane to Honolulu, and now it seemed that Foster was here. By God, he was going to give her an explanation for that.

She reached the section of the lot that was set aside for Hertz rental cars and stood under the bright "Hertz" light. Her heart was pounding loudly in her own ears and her hands were trembling. She didn't see anyone, just rows of cars. I'm a perfect target, she realized. Someone with a rifle could just pick me off. But it wouldn't do them any good. Will and Charlotte will put the pieces together if anything happens to me.

She heard a car door open and turned toward the sound. A figure was approaching, a man. She couldn't see his face in the shadows. He was tall, slender—like Foster.

"Hello, Laura. Thanks for coming."

He joined her under the lighted sign.

"Donnie MacDougal. Is that you?"

"Afraid so. Guilty on all counts."

Guilty? What did he mean by guilty? "But I thought … I mean, the note said Tater-pig."

"You were expecting to find Foster out here? I thought you might. But think about it. We all used to hear him call you that. I just hoped I spelled it right."

"Actually, I don't think Foster ever spelled it," Laura said, still stunned. "He only said it."

"C'mon, kid, let's get in out of the glare." He led her to a pickup truck parked at the edge of the lot, facing the runway. He opened the passenger door for her and she climbed in.

Donnie MacDougal! What is he doing here? And why do I feel such an inflating sense of relief, like a balloon expanding in my chest? This is all too weird. I have a date with his son right now, down at the Hilton.

Jeff. Of course. That was how Donnie knew I'd be at the airport, so he could leave the note.

Donnie slid into the driver's seat but didn't put a key in the ignition. He turned toward her. "I'm really glad you're here, Laura. I thought I was going to have to write this down and send it to Charlotte Sablán, and then I found out you were on the island."

"From Jeff? He told you?"

"He's a great kid, isn't he? I'm proud of both my kids. They're gonna be okay."

"You sent the folder with Jodie's research to Charlotte?"

"I did. I decided that was the safest place for it and I figured, sooner or later, Charlotte would write a book—tell the truth. Especially after she got my letter explaining what I did. But hell, Laura, you're a real writer. You can tell the story to the world."

Laura was sorting frantically through her mental files, trying to put things back in order.

"The story? What you did? Oh, no!" The realization came at last. Not Donnie! Not the island hero. "You killed Gordon Hassler!"

"It had to be done. I know what he did, and I spent nearly two years trying to prove it—and in the end, I decided to go back to what I heard in Sunday school when I was a little kid: An eye for an eye. That always kind of fascinated me. More than turning the other cheek."

"What did Gordon do?"

"He killed Jodie."

"You're sure?" But Laura was sure herself. He had made a trip to South Dakota, Dennis Dover had said, to rendezvous with some-

one who died afterward. And Jodie died on the way home from South Dakota.

"He did something to her plane, fixed it to blow up in mid-air. But there was nothing to prove it. They only found bits of the plane. If the explosion hadn't been seen, maybe no one would have known."

"But the news reports said it was a crash—something about tall mountains and people flying into them."

"You knew she was dead?"

"I just found out yesterday. My boss found a story in some Associated Press files."

"Yes. Well, it took a while but I have friends both in the CIA and the FAA, and we finally found out the CIA intervened, persuaded the FAA not to investigate. They were doing their own investigation of Hassler, and didn't want a scandal to break out. Now, continental geography was never a big interest of mine, but look at the map. Once you're past the Black Hills, what kind of mountains are you going to run into on the way to Denver?"

"So Jodie went to South Dakota to meet Gordon?"

"No. She went to interview the mother of a man she thought knew why Amelia Earhart disappeared. The guy had vanished about the same time as Amelia, and Jodie thought his mother would know what happened to him."

"Garrett Howland," Laura said. "I read the things in Jodie's file just this morning out at Charlotte's office."

"I'm glad Charlotte showed it to you. If I'd known you were on island, I'd have sent it to you."

"So Garrett Howland really was … " She was still trying to comprehend all this, and at the same time take in her relief that Teri really was safely on the way into her father's arms.

"Garrett Howland and Gordon Hassler were one and the same son-of-a-bitch."

"But Jodie didn't know? I wonder if she ever met Gordon when she lived in the islands? Or maybe she met him in South Dakota."

Donnie shrugged on the seat beside her. "I don't think she knew him in the islands. And he told me he hadn't talked to her in South Dakota. Just followed her out from his mother's house and watched her get on that plane that he knew was going to … "

As Donnie's voice broke, the ragged sob tore at Laura's heart. She put her hand on his right arm, and he clutched at her hand with his left hand. He drew a deep breath.

"We were going to get married. The next weekend in Maui. I stayed at her place in San Francisco, making wedding arrangements by phone, while she went off on this South Dakota jaunt she already had planned."

"Donnie, I'm so sorry. And none of your old friends heard the news when it happened. I guess it got buried under the royal wedding—Charles and Diana. You've been alone all this time."

"Never even told the kids about it. They didn't like Jodie. Well, they never knew her, but I figured after we were married would be the time to start getting closer to them. I didn't want Jodie's wedding to be spoiled by sullen stepchildren."

"So you took her Amelia Earhart file?"

"As soon as I heard about the crash. It sounded fishy from the beginning. I figured she'd gotten too close to something and they had … somebody had blown her up. I got out of that apartment with her file, and started digging."

He sat silent then, and Laura felt him tremble.

"Donnie, I … I just don't know what to say."

"She was flying into the sunset, heading southwest toward Denver when she … when it went."

Laura stroked his arm and thought how painful his grief must be to have remained so raw this long. And with nobody to help him come to terms with his loss …

She stiffened on the bench seat of the pickup as the cold realization finally hit her. Donnie MacDougal butchered Gordon Hassler. And now what? Am I his hostage so he can get away? Or am I supposed to talk him into turning himself in?

"How did you know … " she began softly.

"That it was Hassler? Something had been nagging at the back of my mind from the moment Jodie said she was going to Spearfish, South Dakota. It's a weird name, don't you think? At least if you grow up in Hawaii spearfishing all the time. The idea of a town in the middle of the continent named Spearfish strikes you funny."

"Incongruous."

"Right. Incongruous. See, you're the one to put this into words. Maybe you'll even be able to explain it to my kids. Anyway, I finally remembered, after Jodie died, where I had heard of Spearfish, South Dakota, before."

"Where?"

"Hassler was always hanging out at the airport in Saipan. I was flying a non-sched, but it was rare to land there without him being there waiting."

"That's true. He was there when you flew me to Saipan the first time."

"That's right, he was. But at least that time he was meeting you. Often he was just watching people come and go, I guess because it was his job. I didn't think that much of it then. Hell, everyone in Moen used to show up when any plane landed in Truk."

"But that airport's right on the edge of town," Laura said.

"Right. And Hassler had to drive—what? Twelve or fifteen miles from his office up on Capitol Hill to the old Saipan airfield. But he had a cover, good spook that he was."

"Which was?"

"He always had bills to pay. He liked to wait until the last minute and then he would ask me to drop his mail into the box at the Guam airport to save transit time, get his payments in on time. Remember those mailboxes? You had to sort it—mail for Guam, mail for the States, or Trust Territory and foreign. As long as you got 'em in the right box, the stateside ones went out on the next plane. Got a Honolulu postmark, I suppose."

"I do remember the mailboxes."

"So, if you're helping this guy get his mail off island on time, you read the addresses to be sure you put them in the right slot."

"And Gordon used to send letters to Spearfish."

"You knew that? Or you're guessing?"

"I just found out a couple days ago, from his wife. He told her he sent checks to the widowed mother of a guy who died in World War II saving his life."

"To Mrs. Rose Howland, 1214 St. Joe, Spearfish, S.D."

"You remember that?"

"Even the street's got an odd name. But I had someone hypnotize me. I was sure already, but I wanted to be more than sure. It's the kind of evidence that won't hold up in court, but it worked for me."

Laura covered her mouth with her hand, suddenly seeing that bloody scene in the Hilton Hotel room that Lieutenant Guerrero had described. She was sitting here in a pickup truck with a very violent man. And yet … his voice was so gentle. It reminded her of the soft voices of the Marshall Islanders who said they talked to be heard under the roar of surf.

"So you got him to come to Guam."

"Yup. A friend in the agency got me his home address, and I sent him a formal invitation."

"What did you say?"

"Something like 'I know what you did to her plane and why.'"

"Oh, Donnie, what if he came because he thought you meant Amelia Earhart's plane?"

"He did. That was clear from our conversation in his hotel room. He said something really weird, like, 'What I want to know is who was behind bringing her plane down?' I didn't think that made sense—him wondering what made him do it. But I said, 'First, I want to know how you did it.'"

Donnie snorted. "The S.O.B. was almost smug. 'Wasn't hard,' he says. 'Magnets, just enough to pull her off a few degrees so she'd miss Howland.' And there I am, completely focused on Jodie trying to fly from South Dakota to Denver. I probably yelled, 'Howland!

What are you talking about?' And now Hassler's looking really nervous. 'Bringing down Amelia,' he says. 'Your note said you knew who was behind it—who wanted me to do what I did.'"

Donnie sat silent for a moment, gripping the steering wheel. Beneath Laura's hand, his right arm felt like a steel beam.

"Finally, I say, 'Amelia Earhart? You're talking about Amelia Earhart?' And his voice sounds almost frantic. 'Who in the hell do you think we're talking about?' And I hope my voice was very scary. I'm almost whispering.'Jodie deSpain, you son of a bitch. Spearfish, South Dakota. Two years ago? You remember that?'"

Laura's voice was hushed. "He killed them both!"

Donnie's face was rock hard, impassive. "Forty-four years apart, the same man. Two of the gutsiest women I ever heard of and that one little weasel ... " Donnie shook his head sharply and whispered, "So I took out my big, sharp knife. For Jodie. For Amelia."

Laura shuddered violently. She took several deep breaths to calm herself. "You gave him that photo?"

"Yes."

"Which you got from your daughter?"

"You could have written this story without talking to me."

"Will Hildebrandt couldn't find the negatives. He remembered Cory had worked for him back then."

"She had made prints and thought at the time she could use them somehow to get even with Jodie and me—she was so angry about us. But of course, she never figured out how to use them to hurt us, and years later, when she heard Jodie and I had split up, she sent them to me. A consolation prize, I guess."

"Then after Gordon ... afterwards ... you drove out to Two Lovers' Point?"

"They found something out there?"

"The coveralls."

"Well, there's a very bloody knife and a suitcase full of clothes out there somewhere, too. All his papers are in that box under your feet. I'm bequeathing them to you."

Laura moved her feet quickly. She had been resting them on a small cardboard box the size of a ream of paper.

"I was going to leap off. But how can you jump off Two Lovers' Point when you're alone? You need a date for dat kine t'ing."

He raised his hips to reach into his jeans pocket, then pulled something out. "Here. You'd better give this to his wife."

It was an old-fashioned gold pocket watch. It felt cool in Laura's hand. Her fingers caressed the glassy face, the rougher back.

"It's engraved. Something that will probably mean something to his wife."

"I'll see she gets it." A tear squeezed out of Laura's eye and began to ooze down her cheek.

"And my kids? You'll let them know?"

"I don't know." Let them know what? When she tried to laugh, she felt an edge of hysteria creeping into her voice. "I'm not sure Jeff will be speaking to me. I'm late for a date."

"I bet he'll wait. Ask him to tell Cory where she can find her boyfriend's truck." He pressed the pickup's keys into her hand.

"Donnie, what are you going to do?"

"My plane is right out there. I island-hopped it out here. Not an easy trip, but it gave me lots of time to think. Decide I was doing the right thing. I'm going to get in it and head home toward Hawaii."

"Can you make it all the way?"

"Not without a damn sight more fuel than I'm carrying. And once I take off, I sure as hell ain't landing anywhere. Until it stops."

"Oh, Donnie."

"It's the right thing for me, Laura. No regrets."

He got out of the pickup. She started to open her door but he hurried around to open it for her and help her down. Then he picked up the cardboard box from the floor and handed it to her.

I should be protesting, talking him out of this, talking him into going to the police station, she thought frantically. She had a sudden image of him in prison. He's been there already, in Laos. He's right. This is the right thing for him.

She thought she heard a voice from long ago, a woman's voice … no, it was just a few days ago. His daughter Cory's voice. "He says a Hawaiian's meant to drown in warm water, not crawling across the ice somewhere."

She walked to the edge of the runway with him and watched as he found a place where he could pull the woven wire fence away from a steel post and slide through.

From the other side he turned to say, "Aloha, Laura Monroe."

She began to cry softly.

"Hey, kid." He started to say something else.

"Donnie MacDougal, if you say it ain't no big t'ing, I'll scream."

She watched him walk quickly into the darkness, barely glimpsed him as he climbed into the cockpit of a small plane. I should call the police. I should run into the airport building and get someone to stop him. I should call the Hilton and see if Jeff is still in the bar. This is worse than being implicated in a false news story. I am helping a murderer escape.

But she stood absolutely still. She heard the plane's engine come to life and watched it move slowly out onto the runway and turn, just as Teri's plane had done earlier in the evening.

The watch and the keys were still in her hand. She slid them into the cardboard box with Gordon's papers. 'Sús Pérez will never believe me, she thought. But Jeff will.

The high-pitched scream of laboring engines and thrashing propellers moved toward her. Then the plane zipped by, barely visible in the dark, its wheels just coming off the runway as it passed her, liberated from the pull of the world. There he went, flying east, toward the sun he would never see rise again, heading into that same wet emptiness that had absorbed Amelia Earhart nearly half a century ago.

As the drone of the plane's engines faded into the distance, she thought she heard music fading in. Honky-tonk piano and a baritone voice—that island song Donnie had sung at the Palauan bar in Saipan the night after Will developed the photos …

I don't want to leave Palau,
I like this place so,
I've fallen in love in Palau,
And that's why I've got to go.

She started toward the parking lot where she'd left her car. The voice sounded louder in her head.

If ever there was a place,
Where love had to grow,
Palau was that special place,
And that's why I've got to go.

The honky-tonk piano seemed so loud in her head she looked around to see whether other people, still trailing out of the terminal building, were hearing it, too.

For life goes on outside
This sparkling lagoon.
Life has its ups and downs,
It's not all moonlight in June.

She had reached her rental car. She slid into it, set the cardboard box on the passenger seat, brushed tears away from her eyes with one hand. Then, even after she started the car, the sound of the engine was drowned out by the song in her head.

I don't want to leave Palau,
But I've come to know.
That beauty and love grow routine,
And that's why I've got to go.

The refrain repeated and repeated in her head as she drove back to Marine Drive and headed toward the Hilton in Tamuning. Or toward the police station in Agaña.

She would have to decide soon.

IT WAS SO HOT. And she was so thirsty.

How long did she have to wait? They should have found her before now.

How can an island be this small? What is the point of having dry land at all if there's nothing worth eating growing on it, and no fresh water?

What has it all been about? Not just the flight, although that was beginning to seem very strange, hard to explain even to herself. But life itself. What did it mean? What was the point?

And yet …

And yet bits of it really had made sense. The way she felt when the air first caught under the wings and the lift began. Being born might not make much sense. But in her case, she was born to fly.

And fly she had.

7258277R00260

Made in the USA
San Bernardino, CA
28 December 2013